PEARSON

ALWAYS LEARNING

P. J. Ortmeier

Introduction to Law Enforcement and Criminal Justice

Third Custom Edition

Taken from:
Introduction to Law Enforcement and Criminal Justice,
Second Edition by P. J. Ortmeier

Cover Art: Courtesy of Larry M. Ingraham and PJ Ortmeier

Excerpts taken from:

Introduction to Law Enforcement and Criminal Justice, Second Edition
by P.J. Ortmeier
Copyright © 2006, 2002 by Pearson Education, Inc.
Published by Prentice Hall
Upper Saddle River, New Jersey 07458

Pearson Learning Solutions, 501 Boylston Street, Suite 900, Boston, MA 02116
A Pearson Education Company
www.pearsoned.com

Printed in the United States of America

1 2 3 4 5 6 7 8 9 10 V 202 16 15 14 13 12 11

000200010270784589

RR

ISBN 10: 1-256-39999-X
ISBN 13: 978-1-256-39999-5

To Jacob, Luke, Kelly,
Marcus, Yasmin, Blake, and Keira.

Brief Contents

Contents

CHAPTER
11

INVESTIGATIONS   319

Contents

CHAPTER 12

THE COURTS AND THE JUDICIAL PROCESS 352

CHAPTER 13

CORRECTIONS 382

Preface

Introduction to Law Enforcement and Criminal Justice, Third Edition, critically examines and evaluates law enforcement and the administration of justice in a post-9/11 multicultural society of the twenty-first century. The book represents a departure from other introductory texts: it is not limited to the presentation of information. Rather, its unique approach promotes a vision for law enforcement and other justice system personnel that integrates essential critical thinking, problem solving, and communications skill development with the need to deploy ethical practitioners and peacekeepers who demonstrate leadership capabilities.

The book's content is well organized, balanced, timely, and the supporting research is current. The text presents a global and detailed view of law enforcement and criminal justice philosophies, operations, tactics, strategies, and processes. It is comprehensive, yet concise and efficient, avoiding unnecessary discussion. The book's easy-to-read style promotes learning and the development of a competency base consistent with modern policing and justice system administration.

Central themes address the criminal justice system's fragmented, unsystematic approach to the administration of justice as well as practitioner professionalism, ethics, leadership, communication skill, and sensitivity to the gender, age, culture, ethnicity, lifestyle, rights, and needs of individuals living within a diverse population. Also emphasized are new laws and technologies, counterterrorism strategies, community policing, human, civil, and constitutional rights, multiculturalism, and methodologies to prevent and control crime while protecting the rights of individuals. The roles of women and minorities, as practitioners and clients in the justice system, receive special attention. Also addressed are the critical issues, problems, and challenges faced by police officers and the criminal justice system in a democratic society.

The book, published originally as *Policing the Community: A Guide for Patrol Operations* (2002), is designed specifically to meet the need for a comprehensive, up-to-date introduction to law enforcement and criminal justice text. The scope of the second edition was expanded significantly to address topics identified through extensive research and by numerous first and second edition reviewers. The text is appropriate for courses related to community policing, patrol procedures, and law enforcement field services.

In the third edition, statistics and examples have been updated and refreshed throughout. In addition, a number of case studies have been replaced or expanded to reflect current themes. In Appendix C, the police academy subjects for California, New York, and Texas have been updated.

ORGANIZATION OF THE BOOK

Each chapter begins with a set of learning objectives and a list of key terms that are highlighted in the chapter. Current, high-interest examples, case studies, websites, and additional sources of information are presented throughout the text. Each chapter ends with a summary as well as discussion questions and exercises designed to enhance learning and help develop critical thinking and problem-solving abilities.

Chapter 1 introduces the reader to law enforcement and the criminal justice system. It critiques and encourages the reader to evaluate the justice system. The history of private as well as public policing is presented to demonstrate the relationship between private and public protective services. Jurisdictional levels and the role of various law enforcement agencies are discussed. The issues, problems, and challenges facing twenty-first century law enforcement and criminal justice practitioners as well as public safety officer bills of rights are addressed.

Chapter 2 focuses on criminal law and crime control. It presents discussions on the nature and rule of law, causes of crime, prevention strategies, and general types of crime. The chapter also analyzes crime trends, distinguishes criminal from other types of law, and it highlights defenses to criminal liability. The elements of common crimes, procedures for responding to reported criminal activity, the laws and techniques for arrest and control of prisoners, use of force, and the needs of crime victims are also discussed.

Chapter 3 addresses professionalism, ethics, and leadership in law enforcement and criminal justice. Personal integrity is essential to policing and justice system administration. Adherence to a code of ethics and professional standards of conduct lays the foundation for successful and trusting partnerships with the community. Leadership development is usually limited to supervisory and command staff. In this text, however, it is addressed from the perspective of the leadership skills required of the line-level justice system worker.

The results of a national study revealed that effective verbal and written communications skills are essential for the modern law enforcement officer. Chapter 4 addresses these skills on interpersonal, team, and large group levels. Emphasis is placed on cross-cultural communication, conflict management, and communication-related alternatives to the use of force. Written communications, technology, and radio operations are also discussed.

Law enforcement is a function; peacekeeping through community action is a cause. The quality of life for all people is enhanced through effective police–community partnerships. History demonstrates that community participation is a necessary ingredient to police effectiveness. Chapter 5 discusses Robert Peel's principles of policing and it addresses the philosophy and strategy of community-oriented policing. The discussion defines and outlines the framework for community policing. Emphasis is placed on building partnerships with diverse populations.

Chapter 6 concentrates on problem solving and outlines the steps for the tactical implementation of community policing. It presents models, techniques, and examples for mobilizing a community to identify and develop solutions to community-based problems. Citizen concerns and crime problems vary among communities. Thus, the solutions must be tailored to fit problems that are unique to specific areas. Problem solving in groups, community and crime mapping, computer-driven crime statistics (Comp-Stat), Crime Prevention Through Environmental Design (CPTED), and barriers to problem solving are discussed.

Chapter 7 addresses law enforcement officer qualities and skills as well as recruitment, selection, promotion, and retention strategies. Emphasis is placed on an officer's attitude, knowledge base, and career preparation. Career considerations include the development of the proper mental orientation, training and education, and pre-service planning. The employment of women and minorities, officer survival, defensive tactics, weapons, use of force, stress management, the impact of policing on an officer's personal life, and lifetime fitness are discussed.

Chapter 8 focuses on general police operations and situations commonly encountered by the police officer. Emphasis is placed on patrol techniques as well as the proper use and maintenance of equipment, field interviews, traffic management, police-citizen contacts, vehicle stops, pursuits, administrative duties, and relationships with the news media. Traditional patrol operations are critiqued.

Chapter 9 addresses the legal aspects of policing. The U.S. Constitution and its Bill of Rights, types and presentation of evidence, search and seizure, subject identification methods, and procedures for soliciting admissions and confessions are discussed. Emphasis is placed on the protection of an individual's civil and constitutional rights.

Law enforcement involves much more than traffic management, writing citations and arresting law violators. Lost, missing, and intoxicated persons as well as elder abuse present special challenges. Medical emergencies, disputes, juvenile problems, drug abuse, and disturbances are commonplace. Environmental mishaps, fires, natural disasters, and bomb threats create hazardous situations. The potential for civil emergencies necessitates careful planning, and terrorism has emerged as a major threat to civilization. Chapter 10 addresses special circumstances, situations and operations encountered by the police officer.

Chapter 11 concentrates on investigative techniques. Emphasis is placed on interviewing, sources of information, and computerized databases as well as preliminary, collision (accident), and criminal investigations. Crime scene security, processing, and reconstruction, investigative photography, forensic science, criminal profiling, surveillance, and techniques for the collection of evidence are discussed.

The courts and the judicial process are the subject of Chapter 12. The chapter addresses court case preparation, court systems, structure, and jurisdiction as well as pre-trial, trial, and post-trial processes. Emphasis is also placed on courtroom participants, standards of proof, plea bargaining, sentencing, juvenile justice procedure, and courtroom presentation techniques.

Chapter 13 focuses on the correctional process as well as the history and philosophies (goals) of corrections. Emphasis is placed upon noninstitutional corrections, such as diversion programs, probation, and parole, and institutional corrections in the form of jails and prisons. Capital punishment and critical issues in corrections receive special attention.

Several text extras are included in the appendices. Appendix A presents the Declaration of Independence, and the Constitution of the United States is located in Appendix B. For those interested in a law enforcement career, Appendix C presents a representative sample of police academies as it correlates the text's topics with the learning domains (courses) in the basic academy curricula for the states of California, New York, and Texas.

About the Author

P. J. Ortmeier holds bachelors and masters degrees in Criminal Justice and a Ph.D. in Educational Leadership with an emphasis in Public Safety Training and Development. He is a U.S. Army veteran and a former police officer. Dr. Ortmeier has developed and implemented numerous courses and degree programs in law enforcement, corrections, security, criminal justice, and public safety.

Currently, Dr. Ortmeier is the Chair of the Administration of Justice Department at Grossmont College, located in the San Diego suburb of El Cajon, California. His current interests include homeland defense and the development of leadership skills and career education pathways for law enforcement and other public safety professionals.

Dr. Ortmeier is the author of *Public Safety and Security Administration* and *Introduction to Security: Operations and Management* as well as several articles appearing in journals such as *The Police Chief, The Law Enforcement Executive Forum, California Security, Police and Security News,* and *Security Management*. With Edwin Meese III, former Attorney General of the United States, Dr. Ortmeier co-authored *Leadership, Ethics, and Policing: Challenges for the 21st Century*. With a colleague, Tina Young, Dr. Ortmeier co-authored *Crime Scene Investigation: The Forensic Technician's Field Manual*. With Joseph J. Davis, he co-authored *Police Administration: A Leadership Approach*. Dr. Ortmeier's publications focus on law enforcement, criminal justice, professional career education, management, leadership, community policing, security administration, and competency development for public safety personnel.

Dr. Ortmeier is a member of the International Association of Chief of Police, the American Society for Criminology, the Academy of Criminal Justice Sciences, the Western Association of Criminal Justice, the International Public Safety Leadership Development Consortium, the California Association of Administration of Justice Educators, and the American Society for Industrial Security.

The author encourages and solicits comments regarding the book as well as suggestions for future editions. Additionally, the author is available to provide technical assistance to any faculty person who adopts this text for a course. The author may be contacted directly at:

P. J. Ortmeier, Ph.D.
Chair, Administration of Justice
Grossmont College
8800 Grossmont College Drive
El Cajon, CA 92020

Acknowledgments

I wish to express my appreciation to the many people who helped make the third edition of this work possible. Gratitude is extended to my many friends and supporters at Pearson Higher Education, including but not limited to Vickie Chamberlin, Tim Peyton, Eric Krassow, Adam Kloza, and Alicia Wozniak. I am deeply indebted to developmental editor Rachel Rossi, production editor David Andersen, and my editorial consultant Lauren Keller Johnson, for their professionalism and attention to detail. Thanks is also extended to Deanna Hook, retired Sgt. Larry Ingraham, San Diego County Sheriff's Department, and to retired San Diego County Deputy District Attorney Marty Martins for their assistance with manuscript preparation.

I am extremely grateful for the contributions of the manuscript reviewers: Robert Grub, Marshall University, Huntington, WV; William Kelly, Auburn University, Auburn, AL; Michael Penrod, Kirkwood Community College, Cedar Rapids, IA; Michael Kinrade, Santa Rosa Junior College, Santa Rosa, CA; Stan Malm, University of Maryland, College Park, MD; Mark Jones, Atlantic Cape Community College, Mays Landing, NJ; David Barlow, Fayetteville State University, Fayetteville, NC; and Ihekwohaba Onwudiwe, University of Maryland Eastern Shore, Princess Anne, MD; Edwin Meese, III, The Heritage Foundation and former Attorney General of the United States; James F. Albrecht, John Jay College of Criminal Justice; Angela Ondrus, Owens Community College, Ohio; Michael Palmiotto, Wichita State University; and Robert Taylor, University of North Texas. I am also deeply grateful to my family, friends, and colleagues who provided encouragement and understanding throughout the preparation of this work.

P. J. Ortmeier

Overview of Law Enforcement and Criminal Justice

LEARNING OBJECTIVES

After completing this chapter, the reader should be able to:

- describe and evaluate the criminal justice system.
- discuss the evolution of law enforcement and criminal justice.
- distinguish between federal, state, and local law enforcement in terms of jurisdiction and authority.
- describe the roles and organization of law enforcement agencies.
- evaluate critical issues and problems in law enforcement and criminal justice.
- identify police practices within the community that enhance policing.

KEY TERMS

Define, describe, or explain the importance of each of the following.

August Vollmer
Bias-based policing
Bow Street Runners
Civil rights
Code of Hammurabi
Community policing
Corruption
Crime control model
Criminal justice system
Discretionary enforcement
Due process model
Federal law enforcement jurisdiction
Field training officer (FTO)

Frankpledge system
Highway patrol
Intelligence Reform and Terrorism Prevention Act
J. Edgar Hoover
Jim Crow laws (black codes)
Kerner Commission
Law Enforcement Assistance Administration (LEAA)
Law Enforcement Education Program (LEEP)
Law enforcement officer
Magna Carta
Metropolitan Police Act of 1829

Moonlighting

Municipal police

National Advisory Commission on Criminal Justice Standards and Goals

National Commission on Terrorist Attacks Upon the United States

Omnibus Crime Control Act of 1968

Osama bin Laden

Peace officer

Peace Officer Standards and Training (POST)

Police functions and roles

Police officer

Police public image

President's Crime Commission

Private security

Psychological dynamics of policing

Racial profiling

Report on Lawlessness in Law Enforcement

Self-policing

Sheriff

Slave patrol

State law enforcement jurisdiction

State police

Team policing

Thieftaker

Under color of law

Urban decay

Watch and ward

Vigilante

Wickersham Commission

Working personality

THE CRIMINAL JUSTICE SYSTEM

The **criminal justice system** refers to the organizations, agencies, structure, and processes associated with the prevention and management of crime and disorder. The system consists of three major components: law enforcement, the courts, and corrections. The law enforcement component includes local, county, state, and federal law enforcement agencies, prosecuting attorneys, and victim and witness services. The court system includes various trial and appellate courts as well as public defenders. The corrections component of the criminal justice system includes jails and prisons as well as noninstitutional community-based programs such as probation (a function of the county or courts) and parole (a function of the state or federal prison system).

The word *system* implies that raw material is processed to create a preplanned end product. If one applies this implication to the criminal justice system, the criminal offender (raw material) enters the system and returns to society as a rehabilitated offender. However, the notion that the administration of justice operates as a system is somewhat of a myth. The interrelationships of the components and subcomponents of the system are, at best, a loose federation of relatively independent agencies that are not always effective in preventing crime or correcting criminal offenders.

However, it is the criminal justice system that is tasked with the responsibility to protect the innocent and to apprehend, prosecute, convict, and correct the behavior of criminal offenders. To accomplish its goals, the system's components are expected to collaborate to prevent and control crime while protecting the rights of individuals. These goals (crime control and adherence to due process) are often in conflict, as practitioners in the criminal justice system seek to balance the rights of society

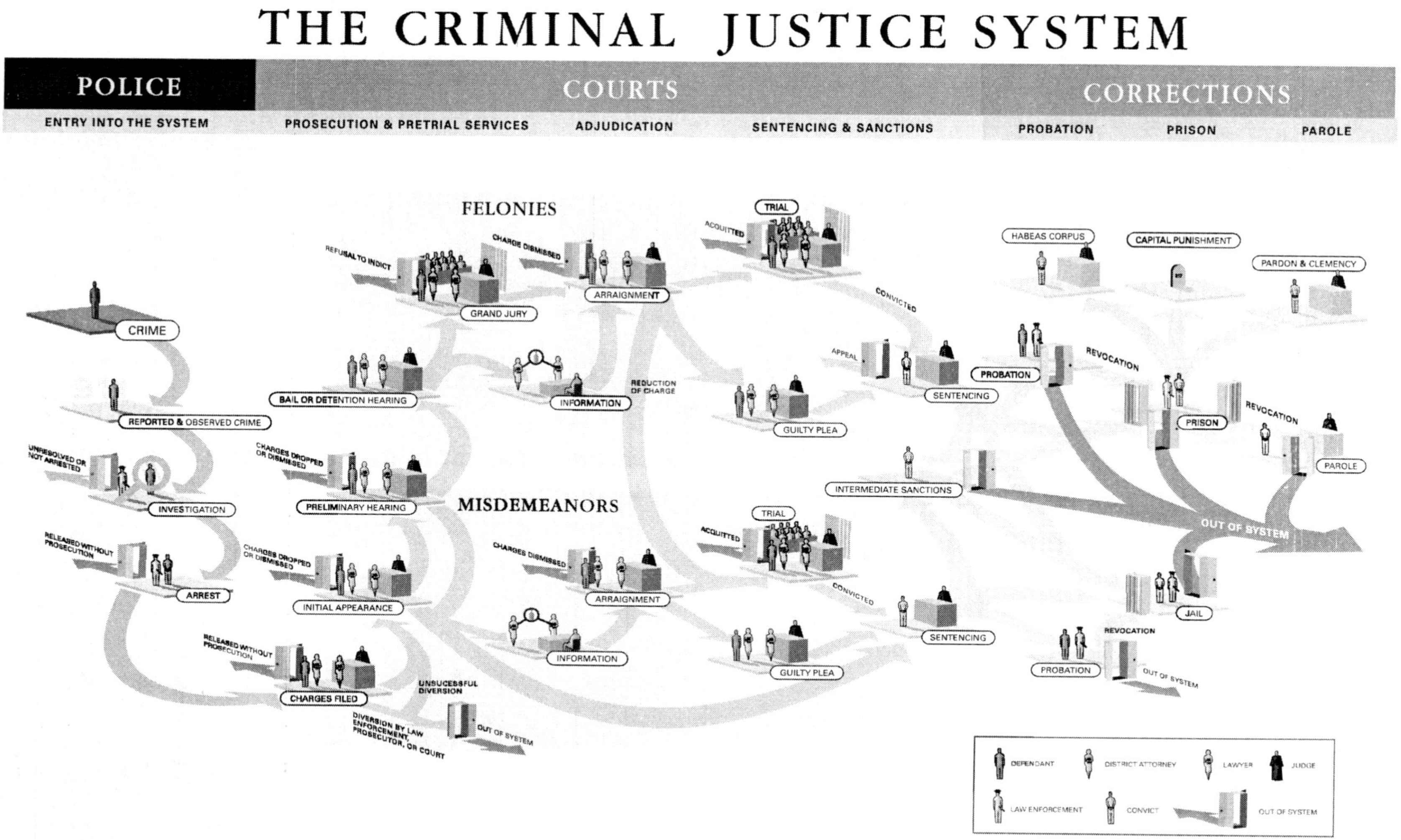

THE CRIMINAL JUSTICE SYSTEM

POLICE	COURTS			CORRECTIONS		
ENTRY INTO THE SYSTEM	PROSECUTION & PRETRIAL SERVICES	ADJUDICATION	SENTENCING & SANCTIONS	PROBATION	PRISON	PAROLE

FELONIES

MISDEMEANORS

CRIME

REPORTED & OBSERVED CRIME

UNSOLVED OR NOT ARRESTED

INVESTIGATION

RELEASED WITHOUT PROSECUTION

ARREST

RELEASED WITHOUT PROSECUTION

BAIL OR DETENTION HEARING

CHARGES DROPPED OR DISMISSED

PRELIMINARY HEARING

CHARGES DROPPED OR DISMISSED

INITIAL APPEARANCE

CHARGES FILED

DIVERSION BY LAW ENFORCEMENT, PROSECUTOR, OR COURT

UNSUCCESSFUL DIVERSION

OUT OF SYSTEM

REFUSAL TO INDICT

GRAND JURY

CHARGES DISMISSED

ARRAIGNMENT

INFORMATION

REDUCTION OF CHARGE

CHARGES DISMISSED

ARRAIGNMENT

INFORMATION

TRIAL

ACQUITTED

GUILTY PLEA

CONVICTED

TRIAL

ACQUITTED

GUILTY PLEA

CONVICTED

APPEAL

SENTENCING

PROBATION

INTERMEDIATE SANCTIONS

SENTENCING

HABEAS CORPUS

CAPITAL PUNISHMENT

PARDON & CLEMENCY

REVOCATION

PRISON

REVOCATION

PAROLE

REVOCATION

JAIL

OUT OF SYSTEM

PROBATION

OUT OF SYSTEM

DEFENDANT

LAW ENFORCEMENT

DISTRICT ATTORNEY

LAWYER

JUDGE

CONVICT

OUT OF SYSTEM

FIGURE 1.1 The Criminal Justice System *(Richard P. Seiter, Corrections: An Introduction, Pearson Education, 2005)*

3

with the rights of the individual offender. As a result, two primary models for the administration of justice emerge. The **crime control model** emphasizes the rights of society as it focuses on the efficient apprehension, conviction, and disposition of criminal offenders. The **due process model** of criminal justice focuses on individual rights. Due process is a central theme in the U.S. Constitution's Bill of Rights. The ultimate goal of the criminal justice professional is to achieve an appropriate balance between the rights of society and the preservation of individual rights under the Constitution.

In reality, most causes of crime are probably beyond the system's ability to prevent. The system, in and of itself, has had little measurable success correcting a criminal offender's behavior. The systems model for the administration of justice is simply a mechanism for explaining the actions of law enforcement, courts, and corrections practitioners as though they were systematically related. What the systems model helps to create in the human mind is a vision of a near precision-like machine in which redundancy, waste, and conflicting actions are quickly identified and their causes cured. Unfortunately, the systems model is an inappropriate metaphor for the criminal justice system. It is rife with interagency competition, organizational conflict, and political infighting with the components and subcomponents of the system often moving in different directions.

The public is generally unaware of the problems associated with the criminal justice system. Yet, people expect the system to prevent crime, react to disorder, and correct offender behavior. The public's expectations of the law enforcement community are particularly high. When people think of crime and the criminal justice system, they usually think of the police. Considered the first line of defense against crime, the police are the most visible component of the system. This visibility helps to create a situation in which the police are viewed by the public as the only line of defense against crime and disorder (Barlow, 2000; Inciandi, 2009; Reichel, 2008).

CASE STUDY—THE CRIMINAL JUSTICE SYSTEM

One of the central themes of this book focuses on the decentralized and unsystematic nature of the criminal justice system generally, and the behavior and activities of the police and other justice system workers in particular. Depending on which set of calculations one examines, there are 17,000–20,000 law enforcement agencies in the United States. Nearly 18,000 courts operate in over 55 court systems. Thousands of jails, prisons, and noninstitutional programs incapacitate and attempt to reform convicted criminal offenders. The criminal justice system, with its loose federation of over 50,000 agencies, is intended to protect the innocent, secure the rights of all individuals, and deal appropriately and effectively with those who violate society's criminal laws. Yet, the justice system is fragmented and conflicts arise between and among its various agencies and components.

Given the unsystematic nature of law enforcement and justice system administration in the United States, respond to the following.

1. Can the goals of the system be achieved?
2. Is it possible to control crime while protecting a suspected offender's rights?

A Brief History of Policing

Any serious study of law enforcement must begin with an overview of the history of law and policing. Knowledge of history assists in the creation of a perspective on the nature of law enforcement. To understand and appreciate the nature and scope of contemporary law enforcement, students of, and practitioners in, policing should be familiar with its origins, and how the role of the police has changed over time.

The history of policing is often expressed in terms of important periods or eras (Gaines & Miller, 2009; Kelling & Moore, 1991; Lasley, Hooper, & Derry, 1997; Ortmeier, 1977). These periods are described in the following sections. Since protective services have been, and continue to be, both private and public functions, the discussion will address public law enforcement as well as private policing and security.

The Pre-Public Police Period

The pre-public police era includes the historical period prior to the early 1800s. This era was characterized by **self-policing** and an assortment of activities, primitive customs, and ancient laws loosely thought of as policing. Protection of persons and property was an individual responsibility. Social control was maintained through custom, and redress of grievances was handled informally by the individual or group. As the population of the world increased, social contracts were developed to protect property and individual rights.

Beginning with the **Code of Hammurabi** in 1750 B.C. Babylonia, laws were placed in writing. King Hammurabi's code described criminal offenses and prescribed punishments for those offenses. Egypt developed a court system around 1500 B.C., with judges appointed by the Pharaoh. By 1000 B.C., public officers were performing rudimentary police functions in Egypt. Later the Romans developed a military police system. Emperor Augustus designated members of the Roman army to serve as firefighters and, later, as enforcement officers. Known as the *Vigiles* of Rome, they were responsible for keeping the peace. The latter day term *vigilante* is derived from the Roman *Vigiles*.

Around 700 A.D., the feudal **frankpledge system** was developed and implemented in France and England. This system made the entire community responsible for crime fighting. In medieval England, able-bodied male citizens were required to form teams to police 10 families in their neighborhood. Known as tithings under the frankpledge system, these teams were sworn to apprehend criminals. After the Norman Conquest of 1066, the frankpledge system was supplemented with crown-appointed or locally elected constables and reeves of the shire (county). The shire reeve (forerunner to the **sheriff**) was the principal police official of the county.

The eleventh century Norman period marked the beginning of an English court system. The courts, coupled with the common law based on custom and tradition, established a rudimentary criminal justice system. Decisions by judges became binding as precedent for future cases of a similar nature. In 1215, the **Magna Carta** under King John guaranteed basic civil rights to freeborn people. It provided for due process of law, trial by jury, and restrictions on unfair punishment. In 1285, the Statute of Winchester established a day and night watch for walled cities. Referred to as the **watch and ward** (*watch* for the night shift and *ward* for the day shift), it established continuous protection for citizens. In the mid-1600s, the monarchy in England was temporarily suspended when Oliver Cromwell imposed military rule.

In the late 1600s and early 1700s, the Industrial Revolution dramatically changed economic and social conditions. This revolution resulted in a transformation from agricultural to urban societies. Villages became cities and crime increased. In response, the central government in England passed new laws. The Highwayman Act of 1692 provided for **thieftakers,** predecessors of the bounty hunters, who were compensated for capturing thieves and recovering stolen property. The law backfired because thieftakers themselves would steal property and seek the reward for its recovery. In response to the corrupt thieftaker system, Henry Fielding, Chief Magistrate of the court on Bow Street in London in 1750 established a small group of nonuniformed homeowners to capture thieves. The unit's strategy was to get to the crime scene as quickly as possible, usually by running, to capture the criminal. Thus, the **Bow Street Runners** were created (Barlow, 2000; Bohm & Haley, 2009; Champion & Hooper, 2003; Siegel, 2004).

No formalized public police service existed prior to the 1800s. Except for the military, private policing dominated this period. In villages and towns, policing was performed by individuals through the watch and ward system. Merchants also collaborated to form private police forces to protect business districts.

The Political Period

The political era in policing extended from the early 1800s through the early 1930s. It was characterized by politics, corruption, urbanization, industrialization, migration of people, and growth in the public and private (security) police. Historians trace the rudimentary beginnings of public departments in the United States to Boston and Detroit in 1801, Cincinnati in 1803, and the first form of federal law enforcement to the U.S. Marshalls Service in 1789. However, public policing, as it is known today, is not an American invention. It began in England in 1829.

Although the French created a police organization in March 1829, London, England, is often credited with having the first full-time, paid, public police department in the world. Largely as the result of the efforts of Sir Robert (Bobbie) Peel, the British Parliament passed the London **Metropolitan Police Act** on September 9, 1829. Peel viewed the practice of self-policing as inefficient and corrupt. As communities grew, Peel believed it was necessary to have full-time, paid, professional police officers to prevent crime and apprehend criminals. Due largely to the fear of governmental interference with privacy, these new police officers were not well accepted by the public at first. In fact, the new officers were nicknamed Bobbie's boys. The London Metropolitan Police are still referred to as bobbies today. The first London police headquarters building was located behind Scotland Yard, a place where kings of Scotland were quartered when they visited London.

According to Peel, local communities were responsible for the enforcement of laws and the maintenance of order. He developed the concept of preventive patrol, the principle that conspicuous uniformed police officers (constables), patrolling the streets, deter criminal behavior. He reputedly suggested that the true measure of police efficiency is the absence of crime and disorder, not the number of arrests. Additional discussion of principles attributed to Peel is presented in Chapter 5.

In the United States, Williamsburg, Virginia, instituted one of the first municipal night patrols in 1772. Boston formed a police department in 1838, New York City in 1844, San Francisco in 1847, Los Angeles in 1853, and Dallas in 1856. The first form of state police agency, the Texas Rangers, was established in 1823 to protect settlers. In 1835, the Rangers were organized as irregular troops who fought against Mexico during the Texas revolution. The first federal law enforcement agency was formed in 1789, when President George Washington appointed eight U.S. marshals. An investigative division was formed in the U.S. Treasury Department in 1864 and the Border Patrol was created in the U.S. Justice Department in 1882.

On the American frontier, law enforcement services were provided primarily by county or city sheriffs, marshals, and constables. Lacking assistants, sheriffs and marshals were authorized to deputize citizens and form posses when necessary. In the absence of law enforcement officials, citizens formed **vigilante** groups and enforced the laws themselves. Most vigilantes were honest and sought to administer justice fairly. However, some groups enforced their own concepts of law, without regard to due process and justice.

County policing in the Southern states evolved from the eighteenth century **slave patrols.** First established in the mid-1700s, slave patrols were created to enforce slave laws and apprehend runaway slaves. The patrols were operated by slave owners, who found it difficult to control the slave population. The slave patrols evolved into structured organizations with chains of command.

Slave laws were abolished after the Civil War. However, many states continued to practice discrimination through new codes, known as **Jim Crow laws (black codes),** designed to enforce political, economic, and educational segregation and prohibit interracial marriage. These laws were abolished in the 1960s. Yet, the police–minority hostility and tension these laws created still exist in many jurisdictions.

Clearly racist in their purpose, slave patrols are considered to be the precursors of modern-style American police forces. Although policing principles attributed to Robert Peel greatly influenced the development of police departments in the United States, the role of slave patrols in the creation of American law enforcement, particularly in the South, cannot be understated. The substantial number of criminal laws supporting slavery enumerated in slave codes led to the development of slave patrols as law enforcement agencies.

Private policing (or security) flourished during this period. In 1850, Henry Wells and William Fargo established two cargo companies. One

Early American Police Officer
(*Photo courtesy of the San Diego Police Department*)

was named American Express and operated east of the Missouri River. The other, Wells Fargo, operated west of the Missouri River. In 1851, Allan Pinkerton established one of the first national private investigative and security companies in the United States. The Pinkertons provided private police services to the railroads, detective services, and, under contract, functioned as the intelligence arm of the Union Army during the Civil War. In 1858, Edwin Holmes introduced the first burglar alarms and Washington Perry Brinks introduced the first armored carriages for the transportation of money and valuables. In 1909, the Burns Security Agency was established to provide security for banks. Private police remained the dominant form of policing during this period because of the slow growth of public law enforcement.

Other significant events during this era included the formation of the Philadelphia Police in 1850, the introduction of finger printing as an identification medium in St. Louis, Missouri, in 1904, and the creation of the Bureau of Investigation (forerunner of the FBI) in the U.S. Department of Justice in 1908. The National Chiefs of Police Union, which later became the International Association of Chiefs of Police (IACP), was established in 1893 through the efforts of progressive Omaha, Nebraska, police chief Webber Seavey. With the creation of the IACP, Seavey helped to elevate the American police to higher standards. Between 1909 and 1932, **August Vollmer,** a police chief in Berkeley, California, introduced numerous innovations. He promoted the establishment of a police academy in 1923 and is believed to be the first to motorize police patrol, establish college courses for police officers, and use psychological testing for police recruits. Vollmer also created the first scientific crime laboratory in the United States.

In 1924, **John Edgar Hoover** was appointed director of the U.S. Department of Justice's Bureau of Investigation. At the time of his appointment, the bureau was characterized by inefficiency and corruption. A career federal bureaucrat employed in the Library of Congress and in the U.S. Justice Department's subversive activities unit prior to his ap-

Organized city police forces were prominent in the United States by the early 1900s (*Photo courtesy of the San Diego Police Department*)

pointment, Hoover had a law degree but no law enforcement experience prior to joining the bureau. J. Edgar Hoover moved quickly to change the image of the bureau. Hoover improved agent selection standards, maintained strict discipline, added "federal" to the bureau's name in 1935, and advertised the FBI as the preeminent law enforcement organization in the world. Hoover remained Director of the FBI until his death on May 2, 1972.

J. Edgar Hoover promoted an image of law enforcement professionalism and publicly decried police brutality and unethical conduct. He also promoted the expansion of FBI jurisdiction and the use of forensic science in the investigation of crime. In 1935, he established the National Police Academy as an advanced training school for select state, county, and local law enforcement officers.

Despite advances in police professionalism credited to Hoover, his record was not unblemished. Hoover's tenure as the FBI director was tarnished by deception and abuse of authority. He exaggerated the FBI's role in several famous criminal cases and he manipulated crime statistics to impress the public with the FBI's effectiveness. He also focused the agency's attention on small-time criminals, while largely ignoring civil rights violations, white-collar crime, and organized crime. Most serious was Hoover's violation of the constitutional rights of many individuals. He authorized illegal surveillance activities and wiretaps of political and civil rights groups, and he compiled secret files on numerous politicians and celebrities.

Although public and private police agencies proliferated during the late 1800s and early 1900s, policing remained a local function controlled at the municipal level. Consequently, the police were often adjuncts to local political machines and were highly decentralized. The police provided service to local political constituents and exercised a great deal of discretion with respect to the enforcement of the law. Police service was provided through foot patrol, call boxes, and was generally consistent with the desires of the local community. However, the politicization of policing was one of the negative consequences of the nature of early public law enforcement in the United States. This led to a great deal of political interference and opportunities for corruption at all levels of policing. (Barkan & Bryjak, 2004; Grant & Terry, 2012; Inciardi, 2009; Payton & Amaral, 2004; Wadman & Allison, 2004; Walker 1999)

The Reform Period

The reform era of policing extended from the early 1930s to the 1970s. As a reaction to public outcry regarding crime and police corruption, President Herbert Hoover appointed U.S. Attorney General George Wickersham to chair the National Commission on Law Observance and Enforcement in 1929. Referred to as the **Wickersham Commission,** its 14 reports were submitted and published in 1931. The Wickersham Commission activities represented the first national study of law enforcement and the American criminal justice system. The commission's original intent was to study crime related to Prohibition. However, it made several unintended discoveries. The commission's most shocking report, the **Report on Lawlessness in Law Enforcement,** concluded that third-degree tactics, including inflicting physical pain and mental distress to obtain confessions, were used extensively by the police (National Commission on Law Observance and Enforcement, 1931). The commission made several recommendations to improve the quality of policing in the United States. A period of police reform began.

The reform era was characterized by a trend toward professionalism, more government control of the police, and civil service protection for law enforcement officers. Police agencies became law enforcement agencies, focusing more on apprehension of offenders than on crime prevention. Other duties of the police, such as fire fighting and medical emergency response, were transferred to fire and medical emergency units. Crime control was viewed as the number one goal of the police. To reduce corruption, discretion was limited and the police became isolated from the people. Policing became impersonal as a result of this isolation.

In the 1920s and 1930s, private security declined as a result of the Great Depression. During World War II, private security increased to protect military bases and manufacturing facilities. After World War II, professionalism in law enforcement and private security increased because many returning veterans, who had acquired military police experience during and immediately after the war, selected police work or private security as an occupation (National Advisory Commission on Criminal Justice Standards and Goals, 1976).

During the reform period, police work became more specialized and police basic preservice training programs were established in many areas of the United States. California established the Commission on **Peace Officer Standards and Training (POST)** in 1959. POST responsibilities included the development, implementation, and oversight of police preservice and in-service professional training programs. In addition, the use of technology to fight crime increased during this period and preventive patrol and rapid response to victim reports and calls for service became a priority. However, the crime rate continued to increase throughout the 1960s and 1970s. Antiwar protests, campus unrest, and the Civil Rights movement also challenged the police.

In 1965, a second national commission was established to investigate the nature and extent of crime in the United States. It developed recommendations for the improvement of the criminal justice system. The President's Commission on Law Enforcement and Administration of Justice, commonly referred to as the **President's Crime Commission,** issued its reports in 1967, which called for higher police personnel standards, improved management, and increased use of science and technology to fight crime (Walker, 1999). Congress acted on many of the commission's recommendations and passed the **Omnibus Crime Control Act** in 1968. The act provided for millions of dollars to fight crime and improve the criminal justice system (U.S. Congress, 1968).

Among its provisions, the act established the **Law Enforcement Assistance Administration (LEAA)** in the U.S. Department of Justice. The LEAA was responsible for distributing federal dollars to local, county, and state governments to establish and improve police training programs and upgrade equipment and facilities. A major portion of the money was earmarked for the **Law Enforcement Education Program (LEEP).** The LEEP program provided grants and interest-free loans to preservice as well as in-service law enforcement personnel to attend college. Colleges and universities throughout the country were also eligible for federal funding. In response, institutions of higher learning established college-level education programs in law enforcement and criminal justice.

The reform period witnessed the increased role of women in law enforcement as well as tremendous growth in private policing. Although women performed a limited role in law enforcement since the early 1900s, it was not until the 1960s that women assumed patrol responsibilities traditionally performed by their male counterparts. Women first

Reforms led to professionalism, more government control, and civil service protection for the police (*Photo courtesy of the San Diego Police Department*)

worked as patrol officers in Indianapolis, Indiana, in 1968. Subsequent studies revealed that there is no appreciable difference in performance between a female officer and her male counterpart. Women also appeared to be more effective in handling domestic disputes (Bloch & Anderson, 1974; Lord & Peak, 2005; Sichel, 1978).

Private security services also continued to grow during the reform era. In fact, the number of people employed and the expenditures incurred for private security in 1970 had reached approximately the same level as that of public law enforcement (Cunningham, Strauchs, & Van Meter, 1990).

Despite the increased federal role in funding for law enforcement and improvements in the quality and quantity of police services, the crime rate increased dramatically between 1968 and the early 1970s. A third major national commission was convened in the early 1970s to investigate the scope of crime and the nature of the criminal justice system in the United States. The **National Advisory Commission on Criminal Justice Standards and Goals,** to a great extent, reinforced the recommendations of the President's Crime Commission of 1967. Both commissions recommended college degrees for police officers, additional preservice training, mandatory in-service training, better salaries, and merit-based selection processes for prosecutors, judges, and corrections personnel (Albanese, 2007).

The National Advisory Commission on Criminal Justice Standards and Goals' Task Force Report on Private Security was published in 1976. For the first time, a national commission recognized private security as an essential ingredient to public safety. The task force recommended that the private sector be encouraged to improve the nature and quality of security personnel and services to complement the law enforcement community in its efforts to fight crime. This led to an environment where private security began to assume a more responsible role in the crime fighting and prevention effort (National Advisory Commission on Criminal Justice Standards and Goals, 1976).

In the 1960s and 1970s, police–community relations emerged as a concern because of the social unrest resulting from antiwar demonstrations and urban riots. Communities experimented with the concept of team policing, which involved a reorganization of traditional police forces into integrated and versatile police teams assigned to fixed districts. **Team policing** represented a return to the 1829 concept of policing as a community-based program, attributed to Peel. It was an attempt to reconnect the police with the public to enhance police–community relationships (Ortmeier, 1999; Schmalleger, 2010).

In spite of the trend toward professionalism and experimentation, police–community relations, particularly in minority communities, were strained during the reform period. Vietnam War protests and civil rights demonstrations in the 1960s and 1970s led to police–citizen conflict throughout America. Tensions between the police and black communities erupted into a wave of disorder and riots between 1964 and 1968. Over 200 major urban disturbances were reported in 1967 alone. Subsequent to the 1967 riots, the National Advisory Commission on Civil Disorders, commonly referred to as the **Kerner Commission,** reported that deep-rooted hostility between the police and ghetto communities was the primary cause of the riots (National Advisory Commission on Civil Disorders, 1968).

The Community Policing Period

Since the early 1980s, both citizen and community participation in the policing effort have increased in many areas. This **community policing** period is characterized by a renewed emphasis on citizen participation, which is critical to solving problems within the community (Goldstein, 1990). Police strategies focus on eliminating the barriers that isolate the police from the public—the isolation that developed during the reform period.

In an effort to reconnect the police with the public, many police departments throughout the country reoriented their strategies toward community policing. Community policing involves a philosophy and a strategy that promotes community engagement, participation, and problem solving. It also involves action that leads to the discovery and implementation of solutions to community problems (Ortmeier, 1996). Community policing is based on the following assumptions: The community and the police are one entity, a community that is involved with the police in the identification of community problems and solutions to those problems is more effective, communities tend to receive the type of police service they support, and community support is vital to successful policing. Crime prevention and problem solving within the community are as important as crime fighting. Community policing also depends on the public's confidence in the integrity of the police as well as the judgment exercised by individual police officers. Thus, trust is the glue that binds the police and community together.

In 1994, Congress passed a $32 billion crime bill. Its provisions included $8.8 billion dollars in grant money for state, county, and local police agencies to hire an additional 100,000 community police officers nationwide. Although the crime rate had been declining since the early 1980s, the crime bill responded to citizen fear of crime and supported the concept of community policing. Law enforcement, in and of itself, may have little appreciable impact on crime. However, crime can be reduced significantly when the police work in partnership with, and receive support from, the community they serve (Ortmeier & Meese, 2010).

During the 1980s and 1990s, the private security industry continued to grow rapidly as a result of limited law enforcement resources. By 1991, 580,000 people were employed in public law enforcement while 1,500,000 people were employed in private security. By the year 2000, private security personnel outnumbered law enforcement personnel four to one (Cunningham, Strauchs, & Van Meter, 1990, Siegel & Senna, 2006). By 2035, it is estimated that approximately 50 percent of enforcement services currently provided by the public police will be privatized. Regulation of noncriminal conduct such as traffic management may be handled by private agencies, leaving the identification, location, and apprehension of criminal offenders to the public police (Schmalleger, 2005, Tafoya, 1991).

Since the terrorist attacks of September 11, 2001, law enforcement and homeland defense have become top priorities, with government and private organizations placing more emphasis on public safety and security. Yet, in spite of the post-9/11 emphasis on terrorism-oriented issues, the community-based problems that directly affect neighborhoods must still be addressed by the synergy of the police and the community. Regardless of the resistance from within and outside some law enforcement agencies, community policing will expand as the approach seeks to address causes of crime and social disorder and reduce fear of crime in individual communities. More agencies will shift from traditional reactive incident-driven policing (the professional model) to police leadership-centered community partnerships and problem solving as the primary means to ensure public safety and improve the quality of life for citizens (Baca, 2002; Lyman, 2010; Meese and Ortmeier, 2004).

JURISDICTION OF LAW ENFORCEMENT AGENCIES

The terms *peace officer, police officer,* and *law enforcement officer* are often used interchangeably. However, distinctions exist. A **peace officer** is designated by statute. Sworn peace officer status is applied to a wide range of public safety personnel, including police, highway patrol, probation and corrections officers, sheriff's deputies, parole agents, and fire service arson investigators. **Police officer** is a designation often applied to the sworn personnel of general-purpose law enforcement agencies, such as municipal police and sheriff's departments. **Law enforcement officer** applies to a person whose primary responsibility is public law enforcement, rather than emergency response, order maintenance, and community service. In this text, the terms *police officer* and *law enforcement officer* are used interchangeably.

Public law enforcement is a function of the executive branch of government. Federal law enforcement agents are under the authority and direction of the president of the United States. Highway patrol agencies fall under the authority of the governor of a state and city police under the direction of a mayor or city manager. Yet, law enforcement officers may be assigned to work in other branches of government. For example, sheriffs' deputies may be assigned to provide security in county courts while U.S. Deputy Marshals provide security in federal courts. However, these officers fall under the jurisdiction of the executive rather than the judicial branch of government.

Law enforcement in the United States is decentralized, with nearly 20,000 separate and distinct law enforcement jurisdictions. This includes agencies of the federal, state, county, and local governments. It includes those villages that employ at least one full-time or part-time sworn officer with general arrest powers as well as cities with large urban police departments (U.S. Department of Justice, Bureau of Justice Statistics, 2002, 2003).

Federal Law Enforcement Agencies

Federal agents have authority to operate anywhere in the United States or its territories but are limited in the types of laws they may enforce. Federal law enforcement agencies do not have general police powers because the U.S. Constitution limits the authority of the national government. Rather, their enforcement authority is limited to specific areas as defined by law.

Law enforcement agencies at the federal level fall within various departments of government. The U.S. Department of Justice contains the Federal Bureau of Investigation (FBI), the Drug Enforcement Administration (formerly the Bureau of Narcotics and Dangerous Drugs), the Bureau of Alcohol, Tobacco, Firearms, and Explosives (ATF), and the U.S. Marshals Service. The FBI has primary investigative authority over federal espionage, sabotage, and internal security laws as well as subversive activities, interstate flight to avoid prosecution, counterterrorism, and other federal laws not specific to another federal agency. The Drug Enforcement Administration has jurisdiction over federal laws relating to dangerous drugs, narcotics, and marijuana. The U.S. Marshals Service guards and transports federal prisoners, serves federal arrest warrants, and serves papers associated with lawsuits in federal courts. The Bureau of Indian Affairs oversees police departments operating on American Indian lands.

The International Criminal Police Organization (INTERPOL), although not an actual law enforcement agency, is the clearing house for information on international criminals. The U.S. National Central Bureau (USNCB) is the United States liaison to INTERPOL. It is housed in the U.S. Department of Justice. The USNCB is co-managed by the DOJ and the U.S. Department of Homeland Security (DHS). It is staffed with sworn law enforcement personnel detailed from federal, state, and local law enforcement agencies. These personnel work side-by-side with full-time DOJ employees in roles such as analysts, translators, technicians, and administrators.

There are several other federal law enforcement agencies. Some of them are located within the following departments of the United States government:

- U.S. Department of Labor
- U.S. Department of Agriculture
- U.S. Department of Defense
- U.S. Department of the Interior
- U.S. Postal Service
- U.S. Department of the Treasury
- U.S. Department of Transportation

In response to the threat of terrorism, the U.S. Department of Homeland Security was created in 2002. Representing the largest transformation of the United States government since the 1947 creation of the U.S. Department of Defense, the DHS consolidated 22 scattered domestic

Learn more about federal law enforcement career opportunities through the U.S. Office of Personnel Management at www.usajobs.opm.gov.

Learn more about the U.S. Department of Homeland Security at www.dhs.gov.

agencies with nearly 180,000 employees into one department on March 1, 2003. The DHS is organized into four major directorates. The Border and Transportation Security Directorate consolidates major security and transportation operations. It includes the U.S. Customs Service (formerly in the Treasury Department), the Border Patrol (formerly in the Justice Department), the Federal Protective Service (formerly in the General Services Administration), and the Transportation Security Administration (formerly in the Transportation Department).

The Secret Service and the Coast Guard, both previously in the Treasury Department, are now located in the DHS, remaining intact and reporting directly to the Secretary. In addition, the Immigration and Naturalization Service (INS) adjudications and benefits programs report directly to the Deputy Secretary as the Bureau of Citizenship and Immigration Services (United States Department of Homeland Security, 2003).

State, County, and Municipal Law Enforcement Agencies

Most policing in the United States is a function of the state, county, and local governments. The jurisdiction of these agencies is the opposite of federal agencies. Federal agencies have very broad territorial jurisdiction. State, county and local agencies have very narrow territorial jurisdiction; their authority is generally limited to the boundaries of the municipality, county, or state. However, these police agencies have very broad subject matter jurisdiction; that is, they enforce a wide variety of state and local laws. Thus, **state law enforcement jurisdiction** involves the exercise of broad general police powers.

State agencies include the **state police** and state **highway patrols.** Some states have one or the other while a few states have both. Although both types of agencies have full police powers within the state, the state police are typically responsible for policing state government property and providing executive protection for the governor. The primary responsibility of state highway patrol agencies is traffic law enforcement. Examples of other state agencies include fish and game, and alcohol beverage control (ABC).

The chief law enforcement officer for a county is the sheriff. The sheriff and the sheriff's deputies provide law enforcement services throughout the county and, in most jurisdictions, staff county jails. Typically, the sheriff's deputies patrol rural and unincorporated areas of the county as well as municipalities that do not possess their own police departments. They are also responsible for security in county courts not protected by county marshals or bailiffs, and they serve criminal and civil process (arrest warrants, subpoenas, and civil legal papers). In jurisdictions not served by a county medical examiner, the sheriff may also serve as the county coroner, the person responsible for determining the cause and manner of death in unnatural death cases. In a few areas of the country, county sheriff's departments have merged with city police forces to form county police departments led by county chiefs of police.

By far, most law enforcement activity takes place at the local level (Dempsey, 1992; U.S. Department of Justice, Bureau of Justice Statistics, 2003). Local, or **municipal,** police departments provide police service to villages, townships, and cities. These agencies usually confine themselves to the city or township limits and are led by a chief or commissioner who is politically appointed by the mayor, city council, city manager, or a police commission. Police officer, marshal, or constable are typical personnel titles used in municipal jurisdictions. In some areas, limited purpose police agencies exist to serve special needs. Airport, school, university, transit, housing, tribal, and port authority police are examples of limited purpose agencies (Gaines & Miller, 2009; Territo, Halsted & Bromley, 2004).

State, county, and local police agencies in the United States employ over 1,000,000 people on an equivalent full-time basis, including more than 700,000 full-time sworn officers. Of the approximately 20,000 police agencies, only about 6 percent employ 100 or more full-time sworn officers. The majority of police agencies employ less than 10 full-time sworn officers and approximately one-third employ fewer than five full-time officers. The largest local police department and largest police agency of any kind in the United States is the New York City Police Department, with over 40,000 sworn officers. The second largest is Chicago, with almost 14,000, and the third largest is Los Angeles, with approximately 10,000. The largest sheriffs' departments include Los Angeles County (near 9,000), Cook County, Illinois (near 6,000), Harris County, Texas (approximately 2,500), and Orange County (CA) (over 1,700). Six of the 10 largest sheriffs' departments are located in California. This may be a result of the large populations and the size of California counties, which tend to cover large territories (U.S. Department of Justice, Bureau of Justice Statistics, 1998, 2002, 2003).

ROLES AND ORGANIZATION OF THE POLICE

Although the police are most often viewed as being separate from the community, they are actually a part of the community and reflect the community's values. A community will receive only the type of police service it desires and supports. Ultimately, community support is absolutely essential to efficient and effective policing (Coffey, 1990; Meese & Ortmeier, 2004; Wilson, 1968).

Learn more about law enforcement agencies and career opportunities at www.officer.com.

Weaknesses in the positive link between the police and the public may be attributed to three primary causes: a general apathy and indifference displayed by the public toward the police, open hostility by some toward police, and charges of police brutality, whether true or not. Most people base their opinion of the police on what they hear and see through the mass media and police dramas, or through personal contact with a police officer as a criminal offender, traffic violator, or crime victim. Because of the nature of policing in the latter half of the twentieth century, contact between the public and the police was limited and often a depersonalizing experience. In addition, most people were led to believe that crime reduction was the sole responsibility of the police and not the entire community. Citizens were and are, therefore, reluctant to assume any responsibility for crime prevention or crime reduction.

Generally, **police functions and roles** include crime prevention, enforcement of the law, order maintenance (peacekeeping), service-related activity, and education of the public. The fundamental duties of a police officer are to serve humankind, safeguard people and property, protect the innocent, weak, and peaceful, and respect the Constitutional rights of all (California Commission on Peace Officer Standards and Training, 2012). The public's image of the police is that of crime fighters. However, the police spend most of their time keeping the peace, regulating noncriminal conduct, and responding to calls for service (Cole & Smith, 2010; Wilson, 1968). In fact, contrary to what might be depicted in fictional crime dramas, most police officers will not use their firearms during their entire career except to requalify periodically at the firearms range.

The backbone of any police agency is the uniformed patrol service. The uniformed police patrol focuses on prevention, detection, and apprehension of criminals, traffic management, emergency response, community assistance, problem solving, and service. The general types of patrol include foot, vehicular, bicycle, mounted horse, motorcycle, airborne, and marine.

The following police job functions summarize the duties performed by uniformed police officers:

- **Patrol:** This job function involves patrolling specific areas on foot, horseback, bicycle, or motorized conveyance, responding promptly to calls for assistance.
- **Evaluate:** Officers must evaluate complaint and emergency-request information to determine response requirements.
- **Monitor, note, report, and investigate:** This job function requires officers to follow up on suspicious persons and situations, safety hazards, and unusual or illegal activity in the patrol area.
- **Engage in counterterrorism activities:** Officers must participate in activities designed to prevent terrorism.
- **Prevent, detect, and investigate crimes:** This job function concerns detecting criminal activity, identifying criminals, and systematically inspecting, gathering, and controlling property and information needed to investigate and resolve crimes.

- **Document investigations, enforcement actions, and other patrol activities and contacts:** This job function involves writing clear, comprehensive, concise, accurate, and thorough reports.
- **Apprehend and arrest suspects:** This job function concerns locating, pursuing, controlling, arresting, and processing suspects.
- **Prepare for and present legal testimony:** This job function generally involves preparing for testimony at hearings or trials, giving depositions, and testifying in court.
- **Manage traffic:** This job function concerns maintaining the safe flow of traffic, citing and/or arresting vehicle code violators, and investigating traffic accidents and hazards.
- **Provide emergency assistance to the public:** This job function involves protecting or assisting people in emergency situations such as accidents, disasters, and crimes in progress.
- **Maintain order in the community:** This job function concerns monitoring activity in the community, mediating disputes, quelling disturbances, controlling crowds, and peacekeeping.
- **Advise and assist the public:** This job function involves providing information and assistance to the public in nonemergency and nonenforcement situations.
- **Work with the community to reduce crime and address community concerns:** This job function concerns the activities and programs that are intended to increase community involvement in reducing crime and addressing other community concerns.
- **Enhance police–community relations:** This job function concerns the activities and programs that are intended specifically to build public awareness, trust, and confidence in law enforcement.
- **Maintain and improve job readiness:** This job function generally involves maintaining and improving the knowledge, skills, and abilities that are necessary to effectively perform patrol officer duties (California Commission on Peace Officer Standards and Training, 1998; U.S. Department of Labor, 2004).

At the state, county, and municipal levels, large police organizations are typically organized into three broad divisions: administrative, auxiliary, and line services. Administrative services include the training unit, personnel, planning and research, legal matters, community relations, and internal affairs. Auxiliary services include emergency communications, record keeping, data processing, supply and maintenance, laboratory facilities, and temporary detention facilities. Line services include uniformed patrol, investigations, traffic management, and specialized units such as Special Weapons And Tactics (SWAT), vice control, and drug enforcement. Police organizations exist to protect life and property; assist victims of crime, accidents, and disasters and render aid to others as appropriate; arrest criminal offenders; ensure protection of rights under the Constitution; facilitate the safe movement of pedestrians and vehicular traffic; and solicit citizen and community support for crime prevention and law observance.

CRITICAL ISSUES IN POLICING

Several critical issues face the modern-day police officer. Students of policing, as well as police practitioners and those interested in law enforcement careers, should be aware of these issues and think creatively about ways to address challenges to public safety. A few of these issues are presented here.

Urban Decay

Many cities in the United States are in an advanced state of **urban decay.** Dilapidated and vacant buildings, aging infrastructures, the plight of the unemployed and homeless, as well as the flight of residents and businesses to suburban areas have left few resources for maintaining inner city areas. Crime and disorder are the end result and the police are tasked with the responsibility and often held accountable for finding solutions to these problems. Policing was never designed to correct such situations.

A strategy for attacking urban blight and decay may be extracted from the broken windows theory. First developed by James Q. Wilson and George Kelling, the broken windows theory supposes that urban decay results when a seemingly insignificant condition, such as a broken window, is left unrepaired. When the first broken window is not repaired, people who break windows will be led to believe that no one cares. These people will break more windows, which will result in the perception of decay in the neighborhood. Social disorder and crime will increase and law-abiding citizens will live in fear or flee the neighborhood. At the first sign of a broken window or graffiti, the police should act to have the window repaired and the graffiti removed; thus improving the aesthetic quality of the neighborhood, reducing fear, and enhancing the possibility that crime and disorder will not occur (Giuliani & Kurson, 2002; Wilson & Kelling, 1982).

Officer Safety and Survival

The number of police officers killed in the line of duty in the middle-to-late 1990s decreased dramatically to the lowest level since 1960, a decline that may be at least partly attributable to the major decrease in crime in many large cities in the United States. Between 1986 and 1996, the average number of officers killed per year was 166. Only seventy law enforcement officers were slain on duty in 1997, and 61 were killed in 1998 ('98 Police Fatalities . . . , 2000; Number of slain cops hits all-time low, 2000). But officer deaths in the line of duty rose to 134 in 1999 and to 151 in 2000 (Ho, 2000). There were 230 officer deaths in 2001, 72 of which occurred during the terrorist attacks on 9/11. One-hundred-forty-seven died in 2002, 132 in 2003, and 154 died in the line of duty in 2004, 69 from felonious assaults and 85 from accidents. In 2010, 160 line-of-duty deaths were recorded, 59 of them committed by gunfire. In just the first quarter of 2011, there were 44 line-of-duty deaths, almost half of them resulting from gunfire (Burch, 2011). In addition to officer deaths, nearly 60,000 line-of-duty assaults on law enforcement officers are reported each year (Law enforcement officers killed and assaulted, 2004; National Law Enforcement Officers Memorial Fund, 2004, 2011). Since 1791, a total of more than 19,000 officers have died in the line of duty. Officer fatalities and assaults have intensified interest in the use of body armor. As of March 2011, there were more than 3,100 incidents in which body armor protected officers from more serious physical injuries or death (McBride, 2011).

Increasingly, police officers face job-related dangers other than those resulting directly from violence. Officers are exposed to serious diseases, such as AIDS, capable of transmission through human blood and other body fluids. Stress and fatigue also negatively affect an officer's health, safety, performance and fitness for duty (Copes, 2005). (See Chapter 7).

The Psychological Dynamics of Police Work

The **psychological dynamics of policing** is reflected in the police sub-culture and a police officer's work. Police officers see the worst of people and people at their worst. Officers often develop a subculture that may be used as a mechanism for self-protection, and become alienated from virtually everyone in the community. The police view the criminals as the enemy along with courts and lawyers who appear to protect defendants, and citizens who complain. As job stress spills over into the officer's personal life, relationship problems with family and friends may develop. In many cases, the relationship problems may be directly attributable to the officer taking the job home. Consequently, the police divorce rate is higher than the national average (Albanese, 2007; Cole & Smith, 2010; Inciardi, 2009; Jones & Carlson, 2004).

The relationship between one's occupational environment and the way one interprets events creates a set of emotional and behavioral characteristics called a **working personality.** The police subculture produces a police working personality. The police are sworn to enforce the law and many police officers tend to interpret the law strictly. They enforce the law according to its letter rather than its spirit. The authority to use force becomes personalized, and an unruly suspect is seen by the officer as an affront to the officer's authority. Abuse of authority and excessive use of force become strong possibilities (Cole & Smith, 2010; Wilson, 1968).

Discretionary Enforcement

The organizational model for most contemporary police agencies is based on the military. Both the police and military personnel wear uniforms, have a rank structure, carry lethal weapons, and possess the authority to use force as provided by law. However, military personnel are most often submerged in a unit under direct supervision. Police officers, unlike military personnel, are rarely subject to the direct control of a supervisor.

Therefore, police officers are in a position to exercise an enormous amount of discretion with respect to the enforcement of the law (Coffey, 1990; Davis, 1975; Goldstein, 2001). An individual police officer's personal views on the law may influence officer behavior. An officer may choose to enforce a law against one person and not another. Depending on community demands, the police may select to enforce certain types of laws, for example, those relating to prostitution, because the community demands strict enforcement of prostitution statutes. Thus, **discretionary enforcement** results when some laws are enforced while others are not. Discretionary enforcement may also result in complaints of racism and abuse.

In his book *Varieties of Police Behavior,* James Q. Wilson indicated that the public itself may be responsible for police behavior and discretionary enforcement based on acceptable styles of police service. Under the watchman style, the police view themselves or are viewed as community caretakers. Under the service style, the police are expected to provide a wide range of services to the community. Under the legalistic style, the police are viewed as a militaristic force responsible for full enforcement of the law (Wilson, 1968). Currently, with zero-tolerance policing, some agencies attempt full enforcement and encourage aggressive pursuit of law violators in an effort to reduce criminal activity. Thus, discretion is limited under zero-tolerance policies. In the final analysis, a community tends to receive the type of police service it supports, desires, or tolerates. Accordingly, as government agencies, police organizations must develop public guidelines that will shape police officers' inevitable use of discretion (Kelling, 1999; Ortmeier & Meese, 2010).

Use of Excessive Force

Use of excessive force by police officers is a critical issue in contemporary American society. Incidents such as the one that occurred in Los Angeles with Rodney King portray the police as an aggressive and abusive occupying army. The media also pays very close attention to reported incidents of police abuse. Although it may appear otherwise, police authority to use force is actually dictated by the circumstances rather than the type of crime. Contrary to popular belief, the police are involved in fewer than 3,000 shooting incidents per year nationwide. Police use of deadly force occurs rarely. When used, it is usually at night, in public places, and in high-crime areas of large cities (Experts say firearms training needs to come out of the dark, 2004; U.S. Department of Justice, 1999; Ross, 2006).

Fictional television police dramas and movies depict police use of force as a common occurrence. In addition, well publicized incidents and accompanying allegations of excessive use of force, whether true or not, heighten public concern. Aggressive, zero-tolerance law enforcement policies in the 1990s may have encouraged abuse by the police. Aggressive police tactics, although designed to control crime and disorder, also aggravate tensions and conflict between the police and minority communities.

Research indicates that the police actually use force infrequently. Studies indicate that only about 1 percent of those people who have direct personal contact with the police allege that officers used or threatened force. Further, less than 25 percent of all arrest situations involve the use of any physical force. When force is used, it occurs at the lower end of the spectrum. It usually involves grabbing or shoving. Weapons are used rarely, with firearms used only two-tenths of 1 percent (.002) of the time. Most injuries resulting from police use of force are likely to be minor. The most common injury is an abrasion or bruise. These injuries occur when people are resisting arrest (Gaines & Miller, 2009; U.S. Department of Justice, 1999).

The actual number of incidents in which police use excessive force is not known. Indicators used to determine the number of excessive force incidents, such as citizen complaints and lawsuits, are seriously flawed. The types of incidents that often result in complaints are rare. Furthermore, police actions that arouse the public, such as fatal shootings and beatings by the police, occur infrequently and are not typical of most incidents in which the police use force (Territo, Halsted, & Bromley, 2004; U.S. Department of Justice, 1999). Although incidents of wrongful use of force by the police may be rare, public outrage over police brutality is not. Therefore, since public support for the police is extremely important, the police community itself must educate the public regarding police use of force. Further, the police must move quickly and decisively to counsel, discipline, terminate, or prosecute officers who use excessive force. Additional information on the use of force is presented in Chapters 2 and 7.

Police Corruption

Police officer Frank Serpico was instrumental in uncovering pervasive, organized corruption in the New York City Police Department in the 1960s. The Los Angeles Police Department was a corrupt organization in the first half of the twentieth century. Although corruption may not be pervasive today, media accounts of corruption often help to create the perception that corruption is systemic in contemporary policing. Bribery, extortion, and political favors are a constant threat in police work. Because of the nature of police business, especially when enforcing vice laws, the temptation to engage in corrupt activities and benefit financially is always present. A general definition of police corruption might be reflected in some type of official wrongdoing by the police officer as a result of the gratuity or any other gain. Accordingly, failure to perform a legal duty, failure to perform a legal act in a proper manner, or commission of an illegal act constitute **corruption** (Albanese, 2007; Walker, 1999). Additional information on police corruption is presented in Chapter 3.

Violation of Rights

Through the use of the due process clause of the Fourteenth Amendment and a doctrine of selective incorporation, the United States Supreme Court has selectively applied provisions of the U.S. Constitution's first 10 amendments (Bill of Rights) to state, county, and local law enforcement. Many of the decisions affecting law enforcement were an outgrowth of the Warren Court, during the 1950s and 1960s, when Earl Warren was chief justice of the United States Supreme Court. These decisions were precipitated by cases involving inappropriate and unconstitutional police behavior. In a democracy, one of the duties of the police officer is to protect individual rights, not abuse them. A discussion of police activity as it relates to rights under the U.S. Constitution is presented in Chapter 9.

In addition to the individual rights enumerated in the Constitution and its Bill of Rights, several federal statutes protect individual **civil rights.** The statutes are intended to protect people from abuse by law enforcement and other criminal justice personnel.

Title 42, Section 1983, of the U.S. Code permits a civil rights lawsuit for monetary damages by a person who is deprived of some legal right by government employees acting under color of law. **Under color of law** refers to an unlawful action against an individual, committed as if it were under the authority of law. A law enforcement officer may be held civilly liable if, while acting under the color of law, the officer deprives someone of a legal right (United States, 1979).

Title 18, Section 241, of the U.S. Code prescribes criminal penalties if two or more persons conspire to injure, oppress, threaten, or intimidate an individual for doing anything the individual has a legal right to do. Title 18, Section 242, of the U.S. Code provides for criminal prosecution of any person acting under the color of law, who willfully deprives an individual of any legal right, or subjects the individual to a different punishment because of the individual's color, race, or citizenship status. All law enforcement officers and other criminal justice system personnel can be criminally prosecuted for Title 18, Section 241 or 242 violations (United States, 1968).

Civil Liability

A major concern of the police and law enforcement administrators in recent years has been the development of a liability connection between the agency, individual officers, and civilian complainants. Litigation arising from several types of situations and incidents has been costly, not only in terms of dollars, but also in terms of the public image of the police. Litigation of this nature typically arises from four sources: use of excessive force, deaths and injuries resulting from high-speed pursuits, sexual harassment, and discriminatory practices. Over a period of two years ending in July 1998, one major city in the United States paid $19 million to settle lawsuits against the police. Additional millions were paid out as compensatory and punitive damages awarded by juries. In 2000, the same city paid a $15 million settlement to a single petitioner who was permanently disabled and wrongfully convicted as the result of police misconduct. In 2004, a jury verdict in a lawsuit against one of the nation's largest highway patrol agencies awarded $510,000 in compensatory damages and $4 million in punitive damages to a man whom the jury believed was maliciously ticketed over a five-year period for traffic violations (Krasnowski,1998; 2000; Krueger, 2004).

Part of the solution to the liability problem may lie in the educational level of people recruited for the police service. One study indicated that highly educated officers perform in a more satisfactory manner (Roberg, 1978). In addition, police departments with high education levels experience fewer lawsuits filed against them and their officers (Vodicka, 1994). Reducing liability payments could result in millions of dollars being made available to increase police officer salaries and attract well balanced decision makers to the police service.

Domestic Violence

Violent crime within a domestic environment is often the end result of a long history of domestic conflict. Often, in domestic homicide cases, the police have made a previous call to the home. An early study of domestic homicides conducted in Kansas City, Missouri, indicated that in 80 percent of the cases, the police had made a domestic disturbance call to the home at least once before. In 50 percent of the cases, they had been called to the residence five or more times (Wilson & Kelling, 1989).

Police responses and styles of control in domestic abuse situations generally fall into four categories: criminal, which involves arrest; compensatory, which involves persuading one person in the dispute to make restitution to the victim; therapeutic, which involves providing help to the disputants; and conciliatory, which involves seeking a settlement in the dispute. Except when the law dictates police behavior, responses depend on the situation and the discretion of the officers. Police officers find themselves in a precarious position when responding to claims of domestic violence. Police officers are not trained counselors and, in some cases, the aggressor or victim may attack the officer.

In an above-average number of cases, police officers themselves are perpetrators of the domestic violence. This phenomenon may be due, in some measure, to a failure to acknowledge that police family violence is often a symptom of a larger cultural problem. In many respects, policing is a culture that does not recognize that officers, like all human beings, can be weak and vulnerable. Further, off-duty officer behavior can become violent if officers are unable to detach themselves from the violence they experience on the job. In addition, because they do not wish to appear weak, officers are often reluctant to seek the services of mental health professionals out of fear that seeking psychological assistance may jeopardize their careers. Yet police domestic violence is preventable if one recognizes that it exists and officers as well as police agencies apply preventive and corrective action (When cops lash out, 2004).

Limited Resources

The financial resources of law enforcement agencies have become increasingly limited. Competition for tax dollars, governmental and political priorities, and the increasing cost of public police personnel and equipment, have restricted the ability of the police to keep pace with the demand for law enforcement services. In the 1990s, the Los Angeles Police Department placed the training costs of a recruit at close to $100,000

(Champion & Rush, 1997). In addition, the number of arrests and criminal court cases has risen sharply in recent years. The prison inmate population has also increased dramatically, reflecting public concern and political decisions that lead to more punitive sentencing laws (Butterfield, 2004).

Prior to 9/11, most police resources were directed toward peacekeeping, order maintenance, and traditional street crime. After 9/11, however, the police have been required to increase patrols of government buildings, landmarks, utility and nuclear facilities, and airports. Overtime costs, additional training, new equipment, and activities associated with the increased emphasis on homeland defense drain already strained agency budgets (McDonald & Thornton, 2002; Mendoza, 2011).

A few agencies have resorted to drastic measures to reduce operating costs. In April 2003 the Los Angeles County Sheriff's Department released nearly 2,600 jail inmates convicted of misdemeanors and placed them on house arrest and in supervised work details. The community-based alternatives to custody were intended to save $17 million (2,600 inmates to be released by L. A. Sheriff, 2003). L.A. County took further such steps during 2009–2010, shedding more than 3,000 inmates. This constituted a 15 percent reduction, well over the national average of about 2 percent (Faturechi, 2011).

Police agencies can conserve resources by establishing complementary relationships with private security organizations and by privatizing non-criminal public police responsibilities, such as parking enforcement. They can also leverage technology; for example, by sharing real-time investigative information with private business groups on interactive websites to help stop theft rings, locate violent crime suspects, and track fugitives. In Albuquerque, such websites contributed to an 18 percent decline in property crimes during 2010 (Johnson, 2011).

Relations with Private Security

Private security represents the largest protective resource in the United States. Many security companies possess technology and resources that surpass their local police agency counterparts. Private security personnel can also assist the police by collecting and offering information, extending protective surveillance, and providing investigative services to private companies (Cunningham, Strauchs, & Van Meter, 1990; Operation cooperation, 2001; Sniffen, 2001). Indeed; the security professional may be the one person in society who has the knowledge and technology to effectively prevent crime. Since the public police are necessarily limited in number, private security personnel can help fill the void. It is in the best interests of public police agencies to initiate cooperative efforts with the private sector and to promote improved training of security personnel to enhance the quality of crime prevention services (Ortmeier & Meese, 2010 National Advisory Commission on Criminal Justice Standards and Goals, 1976).

A source of controversy in some areas is **moonlighting,** a practice through which public police officers are employed off duty in a private se-

Learn more about security services and careers by contacting ASIS (American Society for Industrial Security) International at www.asisonline.org.

curity capacity. The off-duty officer's wage is paid by a private individual or business. Although the practice is favored by most officers, businesses, and politicians, police executives express concern regarding the possibility of the loss of an officer who is injured or killed off duty, while working in a private security capacity. Additional concerns focus on possible conflicts of interest. Police officers are sworn to enforce the law. Yet many businesses instruct police officers to arrest only when major violations, such as felonies, occur (Ortmeier, 2005; Wrobleski & Hess, 2009).

Training Methods and Content

Although the topics covered in a basic police academy do not vary widely from one academy to another, the method of training does. Many police academies still emphasize military-style stress training. However, the objectives of military operations and civilian policing are strikingly different. Granted, a small degree of stress is necessary to measure the resolve and ability of new officers to handle stressful situations and incidents encountered on the job. However, police officers most often work alone, unsupervised, and are required to exercise independent judgment and demonstrate effective decision-making ability. Therefore, training should also emphasize the development of critical thinking, problem solving, and ethical leadership abilities (Goldstein, 2001; Meese & Ortmeier, 2004; Peak & Glensor, 2008).

Obedience-oriented, military-style training may actually be detrimental to the officer on the job. It produces tough, by-the-book cops with a great deal of arrogance. It has created militaristic attitudes among many officers (Kelling, 1999). This attitude may threaten civil liberties, constitutional norms, and the overall well-being of citizens (Study Sees Cause for Alarm, 1999). Military-style marching, titles, and overemphasis on unquestioning obedience does not promote individual decision-making ability, but instead has proven to be of little value in the performance of contemporary police duties. At the very least, military-style stress training has no place in an academy classroom because stress impedes the learning process.

Police training should not be based on an outdated mid-twentieth-century basic combat training military model. Rather, training should be problem based, incorporating adult learning concepts, and it should simulate, as much as possible, the actual occupational environment of the police officer (City of Los Angeles, 2003; Goldstein, 2001).

Other training-related problems include an agency's failure to train, and negligent training. Failure to train implies a lack of appropriate skill development while negligent training involves improper training. The agency employing a police officer must ensure that the officer knows how to do the job and receives the proper equipment to do it. An officer's performance must also be evaluated to ensure compliance with training guidelines. The training must encompass the full range of possible situations a police officer may encounter. Failure to train properly may easily lead to liability accompanied by lawsuits resulting in multimillion-dollar judgments against the officer and the agency.

Post-academy field training programs must be taken seriously. **Field training officers (FTOs),** the senior officers who supervise post-academy on-the-job training of recruits, must be selected and trained carefully. The FTO has a profound impact on how a trainee views policing and how the trainee will perform in the future. If the FTO does not accept and promote ethics, leadership, and an appropriate attitude and philosophy for policing a community, it is virtually impossible for a new police officer to develop and demonstrate appropriate attitudes and behaviors (Ortmeier, 1997; Champion & Rush, 1997; Ross, 2006).

The Police Public Image

The vast majority of police officers in the United States are hardworking, conscientious, ethical, and dedicated public servants. However, as mentioned earlier, most citizens form their opinion of the police through personal contact either as a victim, witness, or suspect. These encounters often involve less than pleasant circumstances. Media and news broadcasts, movies, and television have an impact on the **police public image.**

If a law enforcement officer is identified as corrupt or is charged with using excessive force, the incident is front-page news. If more than one officer is involved, the story often appears on nationally televised newscasts. The general public may become fearful or distrustful of the police (Werner, 2000). Consequently, the police themselves must create a climate of trust and work to improve the public image through courteous, fair, and professional contact with the public.

Police recognition of common community attitudes toward law enforcement can assist officers in the development of positive relationships with the community. Many people, especially victims and witnesses, have unreasonably high expectations of the police. Citizens' attitudes are influenced by negative stereotypes of the police when officers:

- Are apathetic because of insensitive actions.
- Engage in unethical or unprofessional conduct by accepting gratuities, abusing authority, or adhering to a code of silence.
- Are prejudiced, target certain groups, and apply different standards of enforcement to different people.
- Project a poor image by inappropriate demeanor or body language.
- Are unwilling to handle service calls (California Commission on Peace Officer Standards and Training, 2012).

The image of the police can improve through the implementation of community policing and efforts to promote better relationships between the police and minority communities. Studies reveal that informal citizen contact with the police, such as speaking with officers on patrol or at community events, fosters positive opinions of police performance. Community policing promotes informal social contact between the police and the public. Further, collaborative efforts between the police and the community are more effective when the police engage in greater informal contact with citizens (Carlson, 2005; Maxson, Hennigan, & Sloane, 2003; Tyler & Wakslak, 2004).

Politics and the Police

Although history is replete with vain attempts to remove politics from law enforcement, the fact is that political influence is a reality in policing. The police often find themselves caught between the wishes of political leaders and the police mission to reduce crime and disorder. Conflicts also exist between budgetary realities and political promises. Right or wrong, law enforcement personnel become political targets when they are unable to control a public safety problem. Often the agency and its chief executive officer are blamed for situations that are beyond the ability of the police to control.

The police are ultimately responsible for and accountable to the electorate. Every community has a political process that reflects the aspirations of community political leaders. Police officials may be confronted by political leaders who wish to maintain a positive relationship with constituents even though constituents' desires are inconsistent with statutory or even constitutional mandates. A successful approach to balancing politics with the police mission often involves an emphasis on the police obligation to serve all citizens well while respecting the value system of each political leader's constituency. While no single strategy works in all communities, professional and unbiased behavior on the part of the police helps to prevent capricious and destructive politically motivated activity. When the police work with community leaders to establish a climate of trust, outcomes are generally positive. The public is unlikely to reject the wishes of a well-respected police agency.

In an effort to promote their own causes, many police unions and associations are politically active. Theoretically, budgetary constraints and political considerations should not affect policing. However, police officers who feel unappreciated and underpaid often support political causes and candidates that reflect the values of police agencies and personnel (Coffey, 1990; Champion & Rush, 1997). Thus, the police themselves may promote politics in policing.

Diversity Issues

As the United States and other societies progress through the twenty-first century, domestic and foreign populations will become wealthier, older, and more culturally diverse. Police officers must learn to work with diverse populations to better serve pluralistic communities. In some areas, the police workforce itself is becoming diverse, as evidenced by early studies of gender-related issues in policing (Bloch & Anderson, 1974; Sichel, 1978). Yet women, minorities, and other diverse groups are still underrepresented in many law enforcement agencies. The diversity of crime will also increase and the police service must keep pace with this diversity (Muraskin & Roberts, 2002; Palmiotto, 2002).

To function effectively in diverse environments, differences must be recognized rather than ignored, and people must learn to accept and appreciate the differences (Adler, 2008). A single culture contains values that are shared by members of a group. Yet, in the heterogeneous populations of the twenty-first century, crime is more likely to flourish because diverse cultures are less likely to arrive at consensus regarding societal values (Walker, Spohn, & DeLone, 2011). Cultural differences affect everyone, directly and indirectly, in personal, regional, national, and global terms. Intragroup and intergroup relations change continually, and different groups with differing values affect the whole of a society. Differences associated with race, religion, national origin, age, gender, lifestyle, sexual preference, values, perspectives, and culture pose tremendous challenges for the police. Multiculturalism, a form of diversity, will place new demands and expectations on law enforcement and the justice system (Shusta, Levine, Wong, & Harris, 2011). Similarities among groups must be recognized also, by viewing individuals as members of a single human race.

Although national surveys indicate that most Americans are satisfied with the police in their community, many citizens and police officers develop misperceptions that create tension between the police and certain groups of people. Sources of tension emanate from activites related to profiling and other police field practices. Many minority groups, for example, believe the police and other justice system personnel are biased in their treatment of minorities. Some minorities view the police as an occupying military force. Complaints associated with slow or poor police response to calls for service in inner city neighborhoods, verbal abuse, excessive questioning, discriminatory practices, under-enforcement of the law, and use of excessive force are common. Others, such as some Muslims and persons of Arab descent, sense that they are being harassed and alienated due to overzealous law enforcement efforts to combat terrorism. In particular, minority group members often suggest that the police practice of profiling, stopping or detaining subjects because they meet certain criteria favors detention of minorities (Meese & Ortmeier, 2004; Ortmeier & Davis, 2012).

A complaint received from some women and minority motorists, for example, is that they are victims of discrimination because they are stopped with greater frequency than their male or Caucasian counterparts. The complainants often blame the discrimination on the police practice of profiling, a technique that uses race, gender, age, dress, vehicle type, and other factors to identify people who the police suspect may be involved in criminal activity. The practice originated in South Florida in the early 1980s when federal and state law enforcement agencies used it as a means to identify possible drug smugglers using the highways (Carlson, 2005).

On the morning of May 8, 1992, attorney and Harvard Law School graduate Robert Wilkens was stopped for speeding on Interstate 95 in Maryland by a state police officer. After being denied permission to search the vehicle, the officer forced the Wilkens family to stand in the rain while waiting for a canine drug unit to arrive. The drug dog did not locate any drugs and Wilkens was issued a citation for the speeding violation. Wilkens subsequently sued the State of Maryland, stating that he was stopped because he is African American. Publicity surrounding the incident and the lawsuit led to a national controversy over *driving while black (DWB)* and **racial profiling** (Harris, 1997).

Complainants claim the police practice of profiling is racially biased and public opinion polls tend to support this perception. A recent study further supports this view; analysis of the study's findings shows with strong consistency that minority suspects are more likely to be arrested than white suspects (Kochel, Wilson, & Mastrofski, 2011). The police, on the other hand, believe they are unfairly accused of racial profiling. As a result of the complaints, many police agencies in the United States have instituted traffic stop data collection measures and several states have enacted laws mandating agency policies against racial profiling (McMahon, Garner, Davis, & Kraus, 2003).

However, before bias can be assumed to cause disparities in vehicle stops among different groups of people, a number of factors must be ruled out. For example, most jurisdictions that collect traffic stop data report that men are stopped more frequently than women. One possibility for this finding might be that men drive more than women. Another possibility is that men violate traffic laws more than women. Yet another possibility is that men are more likely to drive on heavily patrolled roadways. Thus, caution is urged when analyzing traffic-stop data for bias. According to researchers, most jurisdictions that collect vehicle stop data are ill equipped to analyze data properly or they are misinformed regarding what is to be accomplished through the data collection. Lack of valid data interpretation can hinder agency efforts to arrive at responsible conclusions (Police Executive Research Forum, 2004).

Racial profiling is a symptom of the larger problem of **bias-based policing**—the intentional or unintentional application or incorporation of personal, societal, or organizational biases (and/or stereotypes) as the basis (or factors considered) in decision-making, police actions, and the administration of justice (Davis, Gillis, & Foster, 2001). Many view bias-based policing as the most serious issue facing law enforcement today (McMahon, Garner, Davis, & Kraus, 2003).

The results of studies indicate that citizen judgments about whether the police engage in bias-based policing or racial profiling are associated with the level of public support for the police. Further, the findings of the studies indicate that citizens are less likely to infer that bias or racial profiling occurs if they are treated fairly, politely, and respectfully by the police (Tyler & Wakslak, 2004). The findings suggest that the police must strive to develop positive relationships with community members.

Learn more about analyzing traffic-stop data for bias through the Police Executive Research Forum (PERF) at http://www.policeforum.org.

Another diversity issue evolves from the low number of minorities and women employed in the police service. The recruitment, selection, promotion, and retention of minorities and women are necessary to ensure a police workforce reflective of the people served. Yet discrimination against minorities, women, gays, and lesbians still exists in some areas.

Employment and career advancement opportunities for minorities and women have improved in the recent past. As just one example, the United Nations Police Division wants at least 20 percent of serving officers to be female by 2014, up from almost 10 percent today. UN executives maintain that female police officers relate and communicate more effectively with women and children suffering from violence and abuse in conflict-torn countries, and that they inspire male officers to demonstrate good behavior (Orler, 2011). However, more innovative personnel recruitment and selection policies and procedures can help underrepresented populations achieve greater parity (Bayens, Birzer, & Roberson, 2005; Territo, Halsted, & Bromley, 2004).

Terrorism

In the twenty-first century, the United States, along with many other modern, industrialized, information age countries, finds itself immersed and preoccupied with the terrorist activities of weak, sometimes third world, nations. Small, yet well educated and well financed groups and radical individuals also engage in terrorism.

What is terrorism to one person may be a selfless act to another. Broadly speaking, terrorism involves the use of violence and threats to intimidate or coerce. Terrorism may be the product of an individual or a group. Within this context, terrorists include: highly organized national and international organizations; idealistic and political groups; economic opportunists; urban terrorists, such as predatory, ethnic, and economic gangs; career criminals; domestic violence perpetrators; drug cartels; and some antiabortion, pro-choice, animal rights, and environmental activists. Within a narrower context, terrorism is defined as an act of violence committed against an innocent person or noncombatant for the purpose of achieving a political end through fear and intimidation (Siegel, 2004; Maniscalco & Christen, 2002).

The most devastating terrorist attacks to occur on United States soil to date took place on September 11, 2001. Nineteen followers of **Osama bin Laden,** leader of the international terrorist organization al-Qaeda, hijacked four commercial aircraft, two of which were flown into the twin towers of the World Trade Center in New York City, one into the Pentagon, and one into the ground in rural Pennsylvania. Subsequently, the World Trade Center towers collapsed on themselves. Deaths resulting from the attacks and downed aircraft approached 3,000.

Critics argue that public pressure to combat terrorism often results in measures designed to curtail civil liberties such as rights to privacy, due process, and freedom from unreasonable searches and seizures. Similar criticisms have been leveled against the USA PATRIOT Act of 2001 and the Domestic Security Enhancement Act of 2003 (commonly referred

CASE STUDY—TERRORISM, LAW ENFORCEMENT, AND THE JUSTICE SYSTEM

On July 22, 2004, the independent **National Commission on Terrorist Attacks upon the United States** (the 9/11 Commission) issued a final report, culminating an exhaustive 20-month investigation of the 9/11 terrorist attacks. The commission cited systemic failure and charged that elected and appointed government officials in the Congress, the administrations of Presidents Bill Clinton and George W. Bush, the CIA, and the FBI failed to grasp the seriousness of terrorism as an imminent threat. Although the commission stopped short of stating that the 9/11 attacks could have been prevented, it noted many government missteps. The commission's recommendations included the following:

- The creation of a single, high-level intelligence director to supervise and oversee 15 intelligence agencies of the United States.
- The creation of a National Counterterrorism Center to coordinate data collection and analysis among intelligence-gathering agencies, including the CIA and FBI.
- A global diplomatic and public relations strategy to dismantle Osama bin Laden's terrorist network and defeat the radical fundamentalist Islamic ideology that encourages and supports terrorist groups.
- Improved homeland security, including national standards for issuing driver licenses and other identification, terrorist watch lists, and increased use of biometric identifiers to screen travelers at seaports, borders, and airports.
- Improved oversight of intelligence gathering and counterterrorism activities by the U.S. Congress, especially during transitions between presidential administrations. This recommendation supports radical changes, including a proposal for either a single, joint House–Senate intelligence oversight committee or separate House and Senate committees, with direct budget authority over the United States intelligence function (National Commission on Terrorist Attacks Upon the United States, 2004). In response to the Commission's recommendations, President Bush signed executive orders on August 27, 2004, that are designed to strengthen the CIA director's power over intelligence agencies and create a national counterterrorism center.

On December 17, 2004, the President signed the **Intelligence Reform and Terrorism Prevention Act** into law. Fashioned after recommendations of the 9/11 Commission, the law provided for the creation of a national intelligence center as well as the appointment of a national intelligence director to oversee the nation's 15 intelligence agencies. Additional changes and restructuring of the United States intelligence function are likely.

1. Is counterterrorism the responsibility of public law enforcement? If so, to what extent?
2. Who else is responsible for the prevention of terrorist acts?
3. What impact might centralization of the United States intelligence functions have on individual rights and civil liberties?

Learn more about *The 9/11 Commission Report* at www.9-11commission.gov.

to as USA PATRIOT Act II). However, if the pattern of terrorism continues, U.S. citizens may decide to sacrifice some liberties and freedoms in exchange for safety and security. Perhaps reflecting this possibility, in May 2011, Congress voted to extend three about-to-expire provisions of the USA PATRIOT Act that allow for roving wiretaps, court-ordered searches of certain business records, and tracking of "lone wolf" terrorism suspects (Urban, 2011).

The killing of bin Laden by U.S. forces in May 2011, while a major achievement in the fight against terrorism, has also raised uncertainties about al-Qaeda's effectiveness in the future. For example, bin Laden's successor, Ayman al-Zawahiri, has been described as abrasive and divisive as well as less charismatic and inspiring than bin Laden was to young militants. Experts wonder whether these flaws will weaken al-Qaeda's core (Shane, 2011). As the threat and incidents of terrorism increase, the law enforcement community must assume a leadership role as it seeks to prevent terrorist attacks and mitigate damages associated with terrorism. Community policing can play a major role in the fight against terrorism (Newton, 2002). Community policing provides a vehicle for communicating a reassuring message to a fearful citizenry and it establishes a communications link for collecting information that assists in the investigation of terrorist activities. Community policing, along with collaborative police officer ethical leadership competence, helps to create an environment in which citizens feel safer and more secure, demonstrate greater confidence and trust in the police, and are more likely to supply critical information (Nislow, 2001). (See Chapters 9 and 10.)

▲ SUMMARY

The criminal justice system comprises three primary components: law enforcement, the courts, and corrections. The history of policing can be subdivided into four periods of time: the pre-public police period, the political period, the reform period, and the community policing period. Robert Peel is credited with the establishment of the first full-time, paid police department in London in 1829. Law enforcement is a function of the executive branch of government. Federal law enforcement agencies have very broad territorial jurisdiction but very narrow subject matter jurisdiction. State, county, and municipal law enforcement agencies have narrow territorial jurisdiction but broad subject matter jurisdiction.

The roles of the police include crime prevention, law enforcement, order maintenance, service, and education of the public. Critical issues facing contemporary law enforcement include urban decay, officer safety and survival, the psychological dynamics of police work, discretionary enforcement, use of excessive force, corruption, violation of rights, civil liability, domestic violence, limited resources, relations with private security, training methods and content, public image, politics, diversity issues, and terrorism.

DISCUSSION QUESTIONS AND EXERCISES

1. What are the major components of the criminal justice system? Do the components collaborate and cooperate to function as a system?

2. Describe the history of public and private policing. Why is private policing (security) gaining the market share in the protection business?

3. How does the jurisdiction of U.S. government law enforcement personnel differ from state, county, and local police?

4. What are the primary roles of the public police?

5. How much crime and social disorder can the police prevent? Is crime reduction solely a police responsibility? Explain.

6. Several critical issues and problems in police work were presented in this chapter. Select one and discuss how this issue could be resolved.

7. How can the law enforcement community engage in counterterrorism activities while preserving and protecting civil liberties and the constitutional rights of individuals?

8. Contact and/or visit a law enforcement agency to learn of the history of the agency as well as the challenges the agency confronts currently.

Criminal Law and Crime Control

LEARNING OBJECTIVES

After completing this chapter, the reader should be able to:

- discuss the nature and rule of law.
- list and describe different types of crime.
- describe the origin of crime statistics.
- identify and describe causes of criminal behavior.
- describe the role of private individuals and groups relative to crime prevention.
- discuss issues relating to crime typologies, causation, statistics, and victimology.
- evaluate crime trends.
- evaluate preventive strategies and societal responses to criminal behavior.
- identify and describe sources of law in the United States.
- compare and contrast public with private law.
- demonstrate knowledge of the origins, types, language, and concepts of law.
- articulate a comprehensive definition of crime.
- evaluate a crime to determine the type of criminal intent involved.
- list and describe the classifications of crime.
- articulate defenses to, and justification for, criminal behavior.
- demonstrate knowledge of the elements of the most often confronted criminal code violations.
- identify the elements of the law and describe the policy with respect to a police officer's and private citizen's authority to arrest.
- distinguish public police authority from the authority of private security.
- describe guidelines for use of force.
- describe police response procedures for specific types of crime.
- explain procedures for arrest and control of prisoners.
- articulate procedures for dealing with victims of crime.

KEY TERMS

Define, describe, or explain the importance of each of the following.

Arrest
Arrest and control procedure
Career criminal
Case law
Causes of crime
Common law
Consensual encounter
Constitution of the United States
Controlled substance
Crime
Crime prevention strategies
Crime rate
Criminal intent
Criminal law
Criminal negligence
Criminology
Declaration of Independence
Defenses to criminal liability
Detention
Domestic crime
Economic crime
Equity
Felony
Hate crime
Homicide
Index Crime
Infraction
Misdemeanor
Motive
National Crime Victimization
 Survey (NCVS)

National Incident-Based Report-
 ing System (NIBRS)
Obstruction of justice
Offense against person
Offense against property
Order of authority of law
Organized crime
Party to a crime
Police officer's authority to arrest
Preliminary offense
Private law
Private person's arrest authority
Procedural criminal law
Property crime
Recidivist
Sexual Assault Response Team
 (SART)
Statute
Street crime
Substantive criminal law
Terrorism
Tort
Transferred intent
Uniform Crime Report (UCR)
Unlawful homicide
Victim assistance
Victimization
Victimless crime
Violent crime
Workplace violence

INTRODUCTION

Although crime prevention and control is the responsibility of every citizen, it is the police who are most often called upon to enforce **criminal laws.** These laws are the rules or standards of conduct that pertain to a given political order and are backed by the organized force of society. The police represent society, and the authority to enforce criminal law is relegated to the police by the people.

In this section, the discussion will focus on criminal law enforcement. The presentation addresses the nature and rule of law, causes and types of crime, and crime statistics and trends. It also includes an overview of criminal law and a brief summary of parties and basic defenses to a crime as well as categories and definitions of crimes commonly encountered by police personnel. Individual state statutes should be consulted for more detailed information regarding local crimes and their elements. Also presented are techniques for responding to many of these crimes and procedures for dealing with crime victims.

CASE STUDY—ANALYZING CRIME RATES

During 2000–2010, a decade that saw the toughest economic recession since the Great Depression, the national unemployment rate doubled from around 5% to nearly 10%. But contrary to expectations, in 2009, the nationwide robbery rate fell by 8% and the auto-theft rate dropped by 17% over 2008. Why are these crime rates falling? Considering the fact that there are multiple causes of crime, explore the following questions:

1. How might longer prison sentences affect crime rates?
2. Have potential victims adopted new behaviors that could be reducing crime? If so, what might be some examples of these behaviors?
3. What new policing practices might be helping to reduce crime?
4. How might changing demographics be affecting crime rates? (Wilson, 2011).

THE NATURE AND RULE OF LAW

Laws are created to regulate human behavior and define rights between and among individuals, organizations, and political entities. A predictable system of laws and adherence to the rule (supremacy) of law ensure a measure of stability in a society. In some measure, individual behavior is controlled by the laws of nature and societal pressure that reflects a society's values.

However, near-unanimous obedience to societal rules and values is difficult without established enforceable laws. This was evident subsequent to the American colonists' writing of the **Declaration of Independence** in 1776. Although it outlined grievances against the king of England and described the values of equality, individual liberty, and justice, the document did not create a republic or government based on law. Therefore, until the U.S. Constitution was ratified in 1789, a uniform system of fundamental laws did not exist in America.

The U.S. Constitution is the supreme law of the nation; it prescribes the workings of the democracy. It provides for a legislative branch to enact laws, an executive branch to enforce the laws, and a judicial branch to determine if violations of the laws occur. The established **order of au-**

thority of law in the United States includes the federal Constitution, federal treaties with other nation-states, acts of Congress, state constitutions and statutes, case law, and common law.

As a democratic society and its needs change, laws are enacted, repealed, and modified (amended) to accommodate the society's changing nature. The concept of **equity** (social justice) encourages such change and prescribes adherence to the principles of justice and fairness. Although law enforcement authority may be delegated to the police, the ultimate power to enforce laws is retained by the people who are citizens of the democracy (Reichel, 2008).

CAUSES OF CRIME

The scientific study of the causes and prevention of crime is known as **criminology.** Through research, the criminologist seeks to identify the causes of crime and design programs to prevent crime and treat the criminal offender. Yet it is difficult to trace a single criminal event to a specific identifiable cause. Sources of crime (poverty, slums, unemployment) are easy to identify. However, theorists do not yet fully understand how the sources cause crime. In spite of the difficulties associated with specific cause identification, **causes of crime** are generally explained through theories drawn from psychological/psychiatric, scientific, sociological, physiological/biological, economic, drug use, demographic, urbanization, cultural, and expectations perspectives (Reiman, 2010).

Psychological/psychiatric theories fall into two basic categories: the ego-state and personality disorder theories. Sigmund Freud, the father of ego-state theories, suggested that an individual's personality was divided into three parts: the id, the source of all basic drives such as hunger and sex; the ego, developed during infancy and early childhood, that provides the id with a conscious avenue to acquire satisfaction of the drives; and the superego, the conscience that inhibits immediate satisfaction of the id. According to the ego-state theory, criminal behavior results from a conflict between the id and the superego. Crime occurs because the satisfaction of the basic drives are inhibited by limited avenues for success. When the desires of the id are in conflict with societal demands, impulses of the id are repressed. If the individual is unable to repress these impulses, criminal behavior may result. One recent study found that adverse conditions such as discrimination, harsh parenting, and deviant peers promote perspectives that lead to crime—specifically, a hostile view of people, a desire for immediate rewards, and a cynical view of conventional norms (Simons & Burt, 2011).

The second category of psychological and psychiatric theories focuses on personality disorders. Examples include mental deficiency, and sociopathic and psychopathic personality disorders. A mentally deficient person is intellectually retarded. A mental deficiency promotes subnormal rather than abnormal behavior. A sociopathic personality disorder helps to create a repressed conscience. The sociopath is hostile and aggressive on occasion and usually seeks immediate satisfaction of desires.

A psychotic person loses touch with reality. The criminally insane exemplify people with psychotic personalities.

Sociological theories evaluate the impact of external forces on the individual. These theories address the ecological, cultural, and social influences that may contribute to delinquent behavior. Ecological theories focus on the environment in which one lives or works. Cultural theories address the subcultural norms of a group that contribute to crime and delinquency. Notable among cultural theories is Edwin Sutherland's theory of differential association, a theory postulating that excessive exposure to a certain set of values, whether the values are acceptable to society or not, reinforces behaviors consistent with those values. Social influences that can contribute to delinquent behavior include an abnormal family life as well as problems in school, work, or a recreational setting.

Physiological/biological theories focus on heredity, biochemicals in the human body, and anthropology. Heredity theories suggest that behavior is inherited. Biochemical theories focus on hormonal imbalances in the human body and the influences of secretions of the endocrine glands. Anthropological theories, first developed by the Italian criminologist Cesare Lombroso in the nineteenth century, correlate specific human physical features with criminal behavior. According to Lombroso, unattractiveness may produce unpleasant social experiences. The socially unattractive person can react with antisocial behavior.

Several other theoretical causes of crime have been developed and examined. Economic theories emphasize the role of unemployment and poverty. However, recent statistics from the Federal Bureau of Investigation illustrate that as the national unemployment rate doubled from 2000 to 2010, the property-crime rate actually fell significantly. Reasons may include the fact that potential victims are better protecting themselves through use of burglar alarms and locks and that the number of 14–24 year old males (those prone to committing crime) is declining (Wilson, 2011; El Nasser & Overberg, 2011). Drug culture theories focus on addiction and the enforcement of drug laws. As illegal drug prices increase, users commit secondary crime to support a drug habit. Demographic theories suggest that crime depends upon the changing composition of the population (young people tend to commit most street crime). Urbanization theories suggest that more people are concentrated in smaller areas, thus causing tension. Cultural theories focus on culture conflict within a society. Expectation-level theories address the disparity between the rich and the poor. As the gap between the poor and the affluent widens, and the ability to become affluent diminishes, frustration among the poor grows and the poor commit crime to meet their expectations (Bartol & Bartol, 2011).

In the final analysis, most crime is probably multicausal. Thus, it is difficult to isolate a single cause in an individual case and treat the cause.

Crime prevention strategies include education, treatment, diversion, rehabilitation, deterrence through law enforcement and security, and punishment through the criminal justice system. The most effective crime prevention strategies, however, involve early intervention in the delinquency cycle. When one realizes that crime is caused by a complex array of risk factors, it is not difficult to understand why single focus intervention strategies are unlikely to succeed. Crime prevention must involve comprehensive intervention approaches that address multiple risk factors. To be effective, these strategies require collaboration between and among individuals, groups, and institutions.

To date, the criminal justice system has experienced little notable success with preventing the recurrence of criminal behavior by those who have been exposed to the system. Some exposed to the system become **career criminals,** recidivists who do not react positively to crime prevention and behavior modification strategies. In response, the public tends to support tough, lengthy, and mandatory prison sentences aimed at chronic offenders (Bartol & Bartol, 2011; Ortmeier, 2005). Yet incarceration is expensive; the costs have threatened to bankrupt several state governments. Moreover, evidence has shown that increased prison sentences have a limited impact on crime levels and recidivism. For this reason, some experts propose renewed emphasis on policing for crime prevention, including allocating additional officers to heighten the perceived risk of apprehension (Bratton, 2011).

TYPES OF CRIME

Crimes are often classified into broad general categories. Generally, an **economic crime** is defined as a violation of the criminal law designed to reward an offender financially. Examples of economic crime include all forms of theft and fraud such as theft of intellectual property and proprietary information, patent and copyright infringement, industrial espionage, computer- and Internet-related crime, identity theft, bribery, political corruption, and illegal business practices. Also included in this category are forms of white collar crime, economic crimes that occur in one's occupation or otherwise legitimate financial activity. **Organized crime** refers to any relatively permanent group of individuals that systematically engages in illegal activities and provides illegal services. It is a continuous conspiratorial activity with economic gain as its primary motivation. Organized crime often infiltrates legitimate businesses and uses them as fronts for more illegal activity.

Domestic crime refers to violence perpetrated against family members or individuals involved in a past or present intimate relationship. **Street crime** focuses on those crimes that people fear most, especially the eight offenses listed in Part I of the FBI's *Uniform Crime Report.* **Victimless crime** refers to those offenses that participants engage in voluntarily. Examples include illegal gambling, prostitution, drug abuse, public drunkenness, and pornography. Broadly speaking, **terrorism** involves the use of threats or violence to intimidate or coerce. **Workplace violence** is a term applied in situations involving threats to or violence against persons in the workplace. **Hate crime** refers to offenses motivated by prejudice or hate against others because of their race, nationality, gender, or sexual orientation (Albanese, 2007; Siegel, 2004).

CRIME STATISTICS AND TRENDS

The exact nature and extent of crime is somewhat elusive. Crime rates, statistics, and trends are based on numerous variables. However, beginning in the first half of the twentieth century, attempts were made to collect reliable crime data that could be used to promote research and discover the most efficient methods for allocation of criminal justice resources.

In 1929, as the result of congressional action, the Attorney General of the United States and the FBI were authorized to develop and implement a uniform system for the collection and dissemination of crime statistics. Subsequently, the FBI's efforts led to the first publication of *Crime in the United States* (CIUS) in 1930. CIUS is a compilation of the **Uniform Crime Reports (UCRs)** submitted to the FBI by police jurisdictions throughout the United States. The system was based on the recommendations of earlier efforts by the International Association of Chiefs of Police (IACP). The system was designed to identify major crime trends by comparing seven crimes included in the Crime Index, or Part I, of the UCR. The **Index Crimes** include the offenses against persons (violent crimes) of murder and nonnegligent manslaughter, forcible rape, robbery, and aggravated assault, and the offenses against property (so-called nonviolent crimes) of burglary, larceny (theft), and motor vehicle theft that are most likely to be reported to the police. In 1979, arson was added to the property Index Crime list. Other crimes not listed in Part I are included in Part II of the UCR. The published **crime rate** refers to the number of each of the reported crimes per 100,000 population.

Crime statistics are supplied voluntarily by law enforcement agencies for inclusion in *Crime in the United States*. Initially, about 400 agencies reported crime statistics to the FBI. By 1971, approximately 8,000 of the estimated 20,000 law enforcement agencies in the United States reported such information. By 1999, nearly 18,000 police jurisdictions were submitting crime reports (Maltz, 1999). It should be noted that of the law enforcement agencies that report, they only report crime that the officers observe themselves, or crime that is reported to the police by citizens and victims.

Although most crime in the United States is not of the Index Crime variety, most fear of crime is associated with these offenses. In addition, Index Crimes are usually committed by relatively young men. The profile of the typical Index Crime–prone offender is that of a young male (approximately 14 to 24 years old), who lives in an urban area, is a **recidivist** (a repeat offender), and, in most cases, has an impoverished background and is a member of a minority group.

During the Great Depression of the 1930s, the crime rate in the United States declined somewhat. During World War II the crime rate declined dramatically. Some experts suggest that this decline was due, in part, to the fact that most young men in the crime-prone years were involved in the war effort. In the 1960s, the crime rate began to increase dramatically. Campus unrest, anti-Vietnam war protests, riots, and the coming-of-age of postwar male babies contributed to the increase in the crime rate (Albanese, 2007).

The national crime rate reached a peak around 1980 and began a slow decline in 1981. A dramatic decline began in 1991 (U.S. Department of Justice, Bureau of Justice Statistics, 1997, May). In 1997, two of the most feared crimes—murder and robbery—showed declines of 9 percent each during the first six months of the year (U.S. Department of Justice, Federal Bureau of Investigation, 1997). Overall, violent crime decreased 5 percent and **property crime** declined 4 percent. By 1999, the crime rate had dropped for the eighth year in a row to its lowest rate in 25 years (U.S. Department of Justice, Federal Bureau of Investigation, 2000). Some states' crime rates declined over 30 percent during the same period. A few areas of the United States began to experience an increase in violent crime in 2000, indicating that declining crime rates may not continue. Conflict among street gangs and changing demographics may account for the increases in crime rates (Arner, 2000; Dorning, 2000; Is LA's Crime Honeymoon Over? . . ., 2000). The nation's property crime rate held relatively steady during 2002 and 2003. Although more murders occurred in some large cities, the nation's violent crime rate declined in 2003. In 2004, many areas of the country experienced increases in crime rates (U.S. Department of Justice, Federal Bureau of Investigation, 2004). During 2010, violent crime and property crime rates fell (U.S. Department of Justice, Federal Bureau of Investigation, 2011).

A major criticism of the UCR is its inaccuracy (Siegel & Senna, 2006). It includes information relative to crime reports submitted to the FBI voluntarily by law enforcement agencies. All agencies do not report such data. Of those that submit reports, some inadvertently or deliberately underreport crime data. An audit discovered that the city of Atlanta, Georgia, in support of its bid to host the 1996 Olympics, deliberately altered or suppressed thousands of crime reports in an effort to improve its chances of being selected as the site for the games (Niesse, 2004). In addition, police agencies are only able to report crimes that officers observe or are reported to them.

In an effort to obtain more accurate information on the nature and extent of crime in the United States, the U.S. Department of Justice began to conduct national crime victimization studies, or surveys, beginning in 1972. The major purpose of the victim surveys is to uncover unreported crimes and the reasons for not reporting them. Initially, approximately 10,000 households and 2,000 businesses in several selected large cities, such as Chicago, Detroit, Los Angeles, Philadelphia, and New York, were surveyed. These early victimization surveys reported twice as much overall crime than what was reflected in the UCR's statistics, with theft-related offenses four times higher than official records. Burglary was the most commonplace crime. The reasons for not reporting crime included the victim's sense that nothing would be accomplished, that the incident was not serious enough to require police attention, and fear of reprisal. Surveys conducted in the early 1990s indicated that only about one-half of all violent crime, two-fifths of household crimes, and less than one-fourth of all theft-related crimes were reported to the police (U.S. Department of Justice, Office of Justice Programs, Bureau of Justice Statistics, 1997, May).

Learn more about the NCVS and criminal victimization through the U.S. Department of Justice, Bureau of Justice Statistics, at www.ojp.usdoj.gov/bjs.

Today, **National Crime Victimization Survey (NCVS)** data are collected by the U.S. Department of Justice's Bureau of Justice Statistics in cooperation with the U.S. Bureau of the Census. Currently, the NCVS collects data each year from a sample of approximately 50,000 households with more than 100,000 individuals age 12 or older. The NCVS does not measure murder (because of the inability to question the victim), kidnapping, or crimes against commercial establishments. Crimes such as public drunkenness, drug abuse, prostitution, illegal gambling, confidence games, and blackmail are also excluded. However, the UCR and the NCVS combined provide more extensive information about crime trends.

Although the NCVS complements the UCR by uncovering more detailed information about crime, it is not without its critics. There is, for example, the potential for false or exaggerated reports made by the victims to the interviewers with no attempt being made to validate the victims' claims. In response to the criticisms concerning the UCR and the NCVS, the FBI introduced the **National Incident-Based Reporting System (NIBRS)** in 1989, while the NCVS questionnaires were redesigned to include more detail. Each data collection system is geared toward providing more accurate information (Schmalleger, 2005; 2010).

OVERVIEW OF CRIMINAL LAW

In prehistoric times, as individuals began to live together in groups, the need arose for rules of conduct to govern behavior within a community. Gradually, people gave up certain individual rights and freedoms for the social and economic well-being of the group. In return, individuals received the benefits of group membership. Thus, unwritten social contracts developed to protect individuals as well as the rights of group members. Gradually, social contracts were formalized into written laws.

Sources of criminal law today include the **Constitution of the United States,** federal statutes, state constitutions and statutes, county and municipal ordinances, **case law** (judicial decisions), and common law (law that is based on custom or tradition). **Statutes** and ordinances are the product of a legislative activity. **Common law** originated in England and formed the foundation for early U.S. law. Common law was enforced very strictly. In other words, it was enforced according to the letter of the

Learn more about the UCR, the NIBRS, and crime trends by contacting the FBI at www.fbi.gov.

law. Today, modern constitutional and statutory language pertaining to policing encourages enforcement of the law according to its spirit, rather than its letter. Thus, interpretations of the law must be construed in terms of their relationship to other laws, the intent of the legislature, and the scope of the law's impact (California Commission on Peace Officer Standards and Training, 2012). Many jurisdictions, including California, no longer recognize any form of common law.

Types of law include those that relate to the public and those that relate to private individuals and businesses. Public law includes criminal law (both substantive and procedural), evidence, constitutional law, and regulations developed by administrative agencies. **Substantive criminal law** defines criminal behavior and prescribes a penalty for violations. Federal and state criminal statutes (codes) are a form of substantive criminal law. **Procedural criminal law** directs the process through which the substantive criminal law is to be applied. Generally, procedural criminal law outlines the administration of justice process, from arrest through disposition or sentencing of a convicted criminal offender (Zalman, 2008). **Private,** or civil, **law** refers to contracts, **torts** (civil wrongs for which the law provides a remedy), and property law.

There is no universally accepted legal definition for crime. Generally, a **crime** is defined as an offense against society. When a criminal offense is committed, the offender commits an offense against the society that designated the behavior as criminal. Therefore, if a person violates a state criminal law, the offender has harmed the citizens of that state regardless of who the specific victim is. Likewise, when one commits a violation of the federal criminal law, the offense is committed against all of the citizens of the United States.

More specifically, a crime may be defined as an intentional act (actus reus), or omission to act, in violation of the criminal law (penal code), committed without defense or justification, and sanctioned (punished) by society (government) as a felony, misdemeanor, violation, or infraction. The essential elements of the crime include a culpable mental state, guilty mind *(mens rea),* or **criminal intent** (a design, resolve, or purpose of the mind), an act, or, in some cases, omission to act, and a causal legal connection between the intent and the act itself. The body (corpus delicti) of a crime includes injury, loss, or harm and the existence of a criminal agent as its cause. In a criminal case, the prosecution is required to prove the elements as well as the corpus delicti of a crime.

Mens rea (guilty mind) is the element of a crime that focuses on the offender's intent to commit a criminal act. Generally, a person cannot be convicted of a crime unless the act or omission involved negligence, recklessness, or knowledge, or was committed intentionally or willingly (Siegel & Senna, 2006).

Types of intent fall into four basic categories: general, specific, transferred, and criminal negligence. General criminal intent may be inferred from merely doing the act. Specific criminal intent requires a specifically intended and desired result. With **transferred,** or constructive, **intent,** a person may be liable for unintended consequences. For example, if A shoots at B with intent to kill B but misses and kills C, an unintended victim, the intent to kill is "transferred" to C. **Criminal**

negligence is the failure to exercise the degree of care that a reasonable and prudent person would exercise under similar circumstances. One who operates a motor vehicle while under the influence of alcohol or drugs does so in a criminally negligent manner. Therefore, drivers may be held criminally liable for accidents or deaths caused while under the influence.

Additionally, for criminal liability to attach, one must be the actual cause (cause-in-fact) of the events leading to the result as well as the proximate (legal) cause. Essentially, to be the proximate (legal) cause of an event, the perpetrator should have foreseen the result. One is liable if an ordinary, reasonable, and prudent person could foresee (anticipate) the probable consequences of the act or omission. One is responsible for one's own actions. In some cases, such as in employer–employee relationships, the employer may be vicariously liable for the actions of the employee when the employee commits an unlawful act within the scope of employment even though the employer could not foresee the act. Furthermore, some crimes require no culpable mental state. These crimes are referred to as strict or absolute liability offenses and represent a significant exception to the rule that crimes require a proximate causal connection between the intent and the act. Strict liability offenses are crimes simply because the perpetrator does something, regardless of the perpetrator's intent. Such crimes are based on the presumption that causing harm is in itself blameworthy. In addition, corporations, as fictitious legal persons, can be held criminally liable for the acts (or omissions to act) of their employees or agents (Cheeseman, 2010).

Crimes are classified generally as felonies, misdemeanors, violations, or infractions. **Felonies** usually carry a potential penalty of a fine and more than one year in prison or death. **Misdemeanors** carry a potential penalty of a fine and/or up to one year in a municipal or county jail. Violations or **infractions** typically carry a potential penalty of a fine and are not usually punishable by imprisonment (Rutledge, 2000).

PARTIES TO A CRIME

Crimes are often committed by more than one person. Those who participate in a crime are referred to as **parties to the crime.** Under common law there were four possible classifications of parties to a crime. The principal in the first degree was the person who actually was present and consummated the crime. The principal in the second degree was the person who was constructively (theoretically) present at the crime scene. For example, the getaway car driver waiting outside during a store robbery would be constructively present in the store. The accessory before the fact was an individual who was neither actually nor constructively present during the crime but who aided (provided assistance) or abetted (encouraged) the commission of the crime before it was committed. The accessory after the fact was the person who was unaware that a crime was committed until after the event and then aided or abetted the principals or accessories before the fact.

Under many modern statutes the principals in the first and second degree as well as the accessory before the fact are treated as principals. All principals are equally liable for the crime. However, these statutes generally retain the classification of accessory after the fact for a felony because, being unaware of the crime until after it was committed, there is nothing the accessory after the fact could have done to prevent it (Hunt & Rutledge, 2010).

DEFENSES TO (JUSTIFICATION FOR) CRIME

Criminal defendants often claim they are not guilty of the criminal charges against them. These claims are called **defenses.** If a defendant asserts noninvolvement in the crime, as with an alibi, the claim is based on factual innocence. In other words, the defendant denies the allegation. In other cases, a defendant in a criminal case may be able to establish a legitimate justification or excuse for what might otherwise be classified as criminal behavior. In these cases, the defendant attempts to establish an affirmative defense, which partially or completely absolves the defendant of criminal responsibility. A partial list of these defenses and their definitions is presented as follows:

- **Capacity to commit crime**
  - **Infancy**—Those under the age of 14, absent clear proof to the contrary, are generally not held criminally liable for their actions.
  - **Diminished capacity**—Those with an IQ of 24 or less (idiots), those in an unconscious state, those who are intoxicated involuntarily, or those who are intoxicated voluntarily when the crime requires specific criminal intent may claim diminished capacity.
  - **Physical impossibility**—Those who are physically incapable of the crime charged may not be liable.
  - **Insanity**—Those who, because of a mental disease or defect, are incapable of knowing or understanding the nature or quality of their acts or distinguishing right from wrong are insane.
- **Mistake of fact**—Except for the most serious offenses, ignorance or mistake of fact may be a defense. For example, an individual charged with unlawful sexual intercourse (statutory rape) of the alleged victim (person under the age of consent) may claim mistake of fact if the victim appeared to be older and presented positive identification to verify age.
- **Mistake of law**—Generally, mistake of law is not a defense unless confusion exists regarding the law violated. For example, the finder of lost property may advertise it in the lost and found column of a local newspaper when the local law requires that the property found be turned over to the local police.
- **Duress**—Except for the most serious crimes, such as those punishable by death or imprisonment for life, duress may be a defense if

the offense was committed when, because of a threat, the perpetrator reasonably believed human life was in immediate danger.

- **Necessity**—Similar to the defense of duress, this occurs when, out of necessity, the perpetrator behaves in a way that would normally create criminal liability except the circumstances dictate the behavior. An example of this situation would be an accident victim who breaks into an unoccupied home in a remote area to use the phone to call for emergency assistance. The individual may still be monetarily liable for any damages caused.

- **Entrapment**—This occurs when a law enforcement officer or someone working in conjunction with law enforcement entices or induces a person to commit a crime the person was not otherwise predisposed to commit. Merely providing the opportunity to commit a crime, such as an undercover officer making a drug buy from a known narcotics dealer, is not entrapment.

- **Self-defense**—This defense may be claimed in situations in which one reasonably believes their own life or the life of an innocent third person is in danger of serious bodily injury or death.

- **Statute of limitations**—Based on the theory that evidence might be destroyed and witnesses' memories fade after several years have passed, these types of statutes set time limits within which prosecutorial action must commence. Under such statutes, prosecutorial action begins with the issuance of an arrest warrant. If prosecution begins after the time limit specified in the statute has expired, the defendant is entitled to a dismissal. Time limits vary in length depending on the seriousness of the offense. Statutes of limitations do not exist for theft of public money or offenses punishable by life in prison or death. Generally, the computation of time within the statutory limit is suspended when the suspect is outside the jurisdiction of the applicable state.

  With the advent of DNA technology, some jurisdictions are extending or totally eliminating statutes of limitations for rape and other violent offenses for which a DNA genetic match can help prove or disprove guilt. DNA evidence does not rely on human memory and can be used to link a victim with a perpetrator years after an offense is committed. Use of DNA technology has been used to free many defendants convicted of crimes they did not commit (Tanner, 2000).

- **Consent**—An element of several crimes, such as rape, robbery, and theft, includes lack of consent on the part of the victim. Knowing and voluntary consent on the part of the alleged victim may be a defense to such crimes.

- **Diplomatic immunity**—According to international law, diplomatic officers, their families, and aides are protected from criminal prosecution by the host country. The primary purpose of diplomatic immunity is to prevent arbitrary arrests by the host country in the event of a political disruption between two countries (Raymond & Hall, 1999; Siegel & Senna, 2006).

SPECIFIC CRIMINAL OFFENSES

The types of behavior identified as criminal as well as the name and classification assigned to each offense, rests with individual jurisdictions. The federal government and each of the states have developed separate criminal codes. Thus the names of crimes, their penal code numbers, and the elements of each crime may vary. Readers should consult their respective criminal statutes for jurisdiction-specific crimes and elements.

Preliminary (Preparatory) Offenses

In an effort to prevent more serious crimes from occurring, virtually all jurisdictions have enacted statutes that make the preparation to engage in criminal behavior a crime in and of itself. Although the intended crime is incomplete (inchoate, unfulfilled), the acts completed in preparation of the intended crime are criminal in themselves. Often referred to as **preliminary** or preparatory **offenses,** examples of these types of crime include the following:

- **Criminal attempt**—This involves an attempt to commit a crime coupled with an act completed toward the commission of the intended crime.
- **Solicitation**—This involves soliciting another to commit an intended crime. Statutes usually limit solicitation to specific types of crime, including sex and drug offenses.
- **Conspiracy**—This involves two or more persons who agree to commit any crime coupled with an overt act in furtherance of the conspiracy. Under common law, mere agreement to accomplish an unlawful act constituted conspiracy.

Offenses Against Property

Crimes that fall within the **offenses against property** category include those in which the victim is not present or is unaware of the crime being committed. The subject of these crimes is typically a material object or something of value. Examples of offenses against property include the following:

- **Theft (larceny)**—This crime involves the intentional taking (caption) and carrying away (asportation) of the personal property of another with the intent to permanently deprive the person thereof. The

Learn more about criminal laws in all 50 states through HierosGamos at www.hg.org.

distinction between misdemeanor (petty) and felony (grand) theft depends on the value specified in the statute.

- **Vehicle (auto) theft**—This crime is usually specified as grand theft regardless of the vehicle's value.
- **Fictitious check**—This offense involves writing checks without an account or willfully, with intent to defraud, writing or delivering a check knowing at the time there are insufficient funds for payment in full.
- **False pretenses**—Anyone who knowingly, by false pretense or fraud, procures money, labor, or property of another commits the offense of false pretenses.
- **Embezzlement**—This offense involves fraudulent appropriation or unauthorized disposition of property by a person to whom the property has been entrusted.
- **Breaking and entering**—This offense generally involves forcible entry into a structure intended for human occupancy without the permission of the owner or lessee, and destroying property of value in or around the structure.
- **Burglary**—This offense involves entry into a structure with the intent to commit a felony or steal property of any value. (Note: Some state burglary statutes also include a "breaking" requirement.)
- **Arson**—This offense includes those situations in which the offender willfully and maliciously sets fire to, or cause to be burned, any structure, forestland, or property.
- **Forgery**—This offense involves the false making or material alteration of any document, which, if genuine, would be of apparent legal efficacy (carry with it a legal obligation or responsibility).
- **Extortion (blackmail or theft by intimidation)**—This offense involves obtaining or withholding property of another through the threat of some future harm.
- **Trespassing**—This offense involves willfully entering or remaining on any land or in any building after receiving notice to the contrary by the person in lawful possession of the property.
- **Vandalism (malicious mischief)**—This offense involves maliciously defacing, damaging, or destroying another's personal or real property (real estate).

Other examples of offenses against property include defrauding an innkeeper, appropriation of lost property, unauthorized entry to property, alteration of property serial numbers, and receiving stolen property.

Offenses Against Persons

Offenses against persons include those crimes committed by physical contact with the victim, in the presence of the victim with the victim's knowledge, or by placing the victim in fear of an immediate harm. Crimes that commonly fall within this category include the following:

- **Assault**—This offense involves an attempted battery or placing someone in fear of an immediate battery.
- **Battery**—This offense involves willfully and unlawfully using force or violence on another person. Any harmful, offensive, and unconsented-to contact with the victim is sufficient to constitute battery. Several states do not differentiate between an assault (conveying a threat) and battery (requiring physical contact). The designated crime of battery does not exist in these states. Rather, behavior resulting in physical contact is included in assault law. Thus, the crime of battery is replaced with a more serious form (degree) of assault (Brody & Acker, 2010).
- **Criminal threat.** This offense involves a threat to harm or commit an act of violence. Examples include threatening a person with some future physical harm, and bomb threats.
- **Domestic violence**—On an adult, this offense occurs when one willfully inflicts injury on one's spouse, the father or mother of one's child, or a cohabitant in a relationship of an intimate sexual nature. On a child, it occurs when one willfully inflicts on or permits a child to suffer unjustifiable physical pain or mental suffering, or places a child in a situation in which its person or health is endangered.
- **Robbery**—This offense involves the felonious taking of property from another in the victim's presence against the victim's will by the wrongful use of force or fear.
- **False imprisonment**—This offense involves unlawfully restricting the personal liberty of another.
- **Kidnapping**—Generally, this offense involves the forcible abduction of a person to another location. However, taking a victim hostage or using a victim as a shield also constitutes kidnapping in many states.
- **Rape**—Generally, this offense involves any unconsented-to sexual penetration upon the person of another.
- **Unlawful sexual intercourse (statutory rape)**—This offense involves the act of sexual intercourse with a person under the statutory age of consent who is not the spouse of the perpetrator.
- **Homicide (unlawful)**—**Homicide** is the killing of a human being (or fetus, in some states) by another human being. All homicides are not unlawful. Excusable homicides include accidental killings. Justifiable homicides include court-ordered executions. If a homicide is not excusable or justifiable, it is **unlawful homicide.** Generally, unlawful homicide includes the following:
  - **Murder (first degree)**—This offense involves the intentional, willful, deliberate, and premeditated killing of a human being (or fetus) with malice aforethought, or a death that results during the commission of an inherently dangerous felony listed in the first-degree murder statute (the Felony Murder Rule).
  - **Murder (second degree)**—This offense involves the intentional, unlawful killing of a human being (or fetus) with malice aforethought but without premeditation.

- **Manslaughter (voluntary)**—This offense involves the intentional, unlawful killing of a human being without malice aforethought but in a sudden quarrel (fight) or in the heat of passion.
- **Manslaughter (involuntary)**—This offense involves the unlawful killing of a human being without malice aforethought in the commission of an unlawful act not amounting to a felony, or a lawful act in an unlawful or negligent manner. Motor vehicle homicide (vehicular manslaughter) is often charged as a form of involuntary manslaughter.

Other offenses against persons include mayhem (mutilation of a person), willful infliction of corporal injury on a spouse or cohabitant, carjacking, aiding or encouraging a suicide, elder or dependent adult abuse, and stalking.

Obstruction of Justice Offenses

Obstruction of justice offenses include those crimes that obstruct or hinder the administration of justice. Typical offenses in this category include the following:

- **Perjury**—This offense includes willfully lying under oath or affirmation, under the penalty of perjury.
- **Subordination of perjury**—This offense involves soliciting someone else to commit perjury.
- **Bribery**—This offense involves asking, giving, accepting, or offering anything of value to an official with specific intent to corruptly influence any act, decision, vote, opinion, or other official function or duty of such person.

Also included in this category are intimidation of witnesses, victims, or informants, violation of a court order, resisting or delaying a public officer, escape or attempted escape from a public officer, lynching, impersonating a police officer, and falsely reporting a crime or emergency.

Offenses Against the Public Peace

Offenses against the public peace are those that disturb the public peace and tranquility. Offenses in this category typically include the following:

- **Disturbing the peace**—This offense includes unlawfully fighting in a public place, challenging another person in a public place to a fight, maliciously and willfully disturbing another person by loud and unreasonable noise, or using offensive words in a public place, which are likely to produce an immediate violent reaction.
- **Unlawful assembly**—This involves two or more persons assembled with the intent to do an unlawful act or a lawful act in a violent manner.
- **Riot**—This involves two or more persons acting together without authority of law to use any force or violence in a manner calculated to induce terror.

- **Interference with judicial proceedings**—This offense involves offering false evidence, or bribery of a judicial officer, juror, or witness.
- **Interference with law enforcement**—It is a crime in many jurisdictions to resist, delay, or obstruct a public officer, peace officer, or emergency medical technician in the course of their employment.

Also included in this category are offenses related to refusal to disperse and disobedience of a dispersal order (California State, 2012b).

Offenses Against Children

Many states have enacted statutes that specifically deal with crimes against children. Examples of offenses that fall within this category include child endangerment, physical abuse, lewd acts upon a child, annoying or molesting children, possession or control of child pornography, unlawful sexual intercourse, and failure to report suspected child abuse.

Sex Offenses

In addition to the crime of rape listed in the category of offenses against persons and unlawful sexual intercourse listed in offenses against children, many states, such as California, place sex-related offenses in a special category. Crimes that fall into this category include indecent exposure, unconsented-to oral copulation and sodomy, incest, failure to register as a sex offender, assault with intent to commit rape, spousal rape, sexual battery, and unconsented-to sexual penetration with a foreign object (California Commission on Peace Officer Standards and Training, 2012).

Controlled Substance Offenses

Controlled substance offenses cover acts such as the possession, sale, transportation, manufacture, furnishing, and administering of controlled substances listed in applicable state and federal statutes. These offenses also include those that refer to the possession of drug paraphernalia and being under the influence of, or cultivating, a controlled substance. These laws focus generally on narcotics, cocaine, heroin, controlled substances, amphetamines, barbiturates, and marijuana.

A controlled substance is either controlled by law, requiring a prescription for acquisition, or is forbidden as contraband. Controlled substances are listed in Schedules I (most dangerous) to V (least dangerous) of the United States Comprehensive Drug Abuse Prevention and Control Act of 1970 (the Controlled Substance Act). Provisions of the act are incorporated into state statutes, usually in health and safety codes. Police officers must be thoroughly familiar with controlled substance laws to charge a suspect with the appropriate statutory provision.

It is illegal to manufacture, transport, possess, sell, furnish, administer, or deliver a controlled substance. Selling nonharmful placebos (fake controlled substances) as authentic is also illegal. Police response depends on the violation and the corresponding statutory provisions. In some states, possession of a small amount of marijuana for personal use is not a crime. In other states, possession of less than an ounce of marijuana is a misdemeanor that carries a fine as a potential penalty. In the latter case, an officer may issue a citation (notice to appear) similar to a traffic ticket, in lieu of arrest.

Drug paraphernalia includes all materials and equipment used to produce, distribute, sell, store, conceal, or introduce a controlled substance into a human body. Most drug paraphernalia is not illegal to possess unless the item(s) contains a controlled substance. Exceptions include opium (crack) pipes and injection devices.

Many states provide alternatives to arrest for controlled substance offenses. Except for serious cases involving the manufacture, transportation, distribution, and sale of dangerous drugs, possession of small amounts for personal use may result in diversion to a treatment program rather than arrest. In less serious cases, police response will depend on the provisions in state, county, and local laws as well as the desires of the community (California State, Department of Alcohol and Drug Programs, 2004; Ortmeier, 1999).

Liquor Law Offenses

Often referred to as alcohol and beverage control (ABC) laws, liquor law violations include selling to, or possession by, minors under a designated age, sale and consumption during statutorily restricted hours, sale to an intoxicated person, sale of liquor without a license, and other activities prohibited by a liquor licensing agency.

Driving Under the Influence Offenses

Normally written into motor vehicle codes, Driving Under the Influence (DUI) or Driving While Intoxicated (DWI) statutes refer to those cases in which an individual operates a motor vehicle while under the influence of alcohol or drugs. The statutory maximum (legal limit) for blood alcohol content is .08 percent. (Hunt, 2000).

Weapons Offenses

The possession of certain types of weapons by private persons is prohibited by law. These include specified handguns and long guns, knives, nunchakus, brass knuckles, and explosives. Many laws also address the illegal use of weapons and carrying concealed weapons. Specific offenses in this category include possession of a concealed weapon, possession of a firearm by a convicted felon or drug addict, and possession of a firearm in a gun-free school zone, playground, or youth facility. Many weapons statutes also make it unlawful to own, possess, manufacture, import, or sell short-barreled (less than 16 inches) rifles or shotguns, cane or wallet guns, zip guns, undetectable firearms, or any ammunition containing darts, explosive agents, or armor piercing bullets (California State, 2012b; California State, Department of Justice, Office of the Attorney General, 2006).

Public Safety and Morals Offenses

Public safety and morals offenses generally refer to offenses associated with pornography, obscene material, sexual exploitation of minors, contributing to the delinquency of minors, incest, indecent exposure, loitering, and prostitution.

LAWS OF ARREST

An arrest is the taking of a person into custody for the purpose of responding to a criminal charge. Effecting an arrest is risky. The arresting person risks injury, possibly death, to self, the person arrested, and others. Further, if an arrest is not justified, the person who made the illegal arrest may be charged criminally or sued civilly.

Generally, a **police officer's authority to arrest** includes effecting an arrest when the officer observes a felony being committed. The officer may also arrest for an unobserved felony if there is probable cause to believe that a felony was committed and that the arrestee committed it. Probable cause exists when the evidence present leads a reasonable person to believe that a crime has been committed. Probable cause requires more than mere suspicion, but less than absolute proof of a crime. If probable cause exists and no felony crime was committed, a police officer is protected from civil and criminal liability.

For misdemeanors, a police officer may arrest for a misdemeanor observed by the officer. In some states, if the misdemeanor is not observed by the officer, an arrest cannot be made unless an arrest warrant is on file for the arrestee, or an exception is noted in an applicable statute. The police officer is protected from criminal and civil liability for false imprisonment or false arrest if the officer effects an arrest consistent with legal guidelines and a subsequent investigation reveals that no crime was committed.

Generally, **private security person's** (or private citizen's) **arrest authority** includes effecting an arrest when the person observes a felony being committed. In the case of a felony not committed in the person's presence, an arrest can be made if the felony was, in fact, committed and the arresting person has probable cause to believe that the person arrested committed it. In some states, the person arrested must have, in fact, committed the felony. A security officer or private citizen may also arrest for a misdemeanor observed by the arresting person. However, unlike public law enforcement officers, security officers or private persons have no authority to arrest for a misdemeanor not committed in their presence. Furthermore, a private security officer or citizen is not protected from criminal or civil liability as a result of false imprisonment or false arrest.

Learn more about laws and legal concepts through resource linkages provided by the American Bar Association at www.americanbar.orglaba.html.

The person effecting the arrest must communicate three information items to the individual arrested.

- **Intent**—The arresting person must inform the individual of the arrest.
- **Cause**—The arresting person must state the reason (e.g., name of the offense, outstanding arrest warrant) for the arrest.
- **Authority**—The arresting person must communicate the authority under which the arrest is being made.

Exceptions to the arrest information conveyance requirement include situations in which the criminal suspect is in the process of committing the offense or is attempting to escape.

Although advisable, verbalizing "You are under arrest for . . ." is not necessary to create an arrest situation. Actions can communicate an arrest. Restricting a subject's freedom of movement or liberty in a significant manner has been viewed as an arrest by many courts. If the subject reasonably believes the freedom to leave has been removed, regardless of any arrest language communicated, an arrest has occurred.

USE OF FORCE

As a general rule, persons can use whatever force is reasonably necessary, including deadly force, to protect themselves or an innocent third party from serious bodily harm or death. A person may use nondeadly force in the protection of property. Nondeadly force to protect property is justifiable when the actor reasonably believes the use of such force is immediately necessary to prevent or terminate a trespass, unlawful entry, or theft of property. When effecting an arrest, or preventing escape, a police officer may use whatever force is reasonable and necessary to detain and maintain custody of the arrestee. Police officers must remember that, in many states, officers may be charged under separate felony statutes for using force without lawful necessity (California Commission on Peace Officer Standards and Training, 2012; Ortmeier, 2013).

RESPONSE TECHNIQUES

There are no specific procedures for handling every type of call for police service, only general guidelines. Ultimately, police response depends on the situation and circumstances surrounding an incident. When one considers the hundreds of different types of crimes that occur, a specific strategy for each crime would overwhelm the police. However, police responses to crime generally incorporate basic guidelines and procedures common to most, if not all, observed or reported criminal offenses. These guidelines include those associated with coordinating a response consistent with officer and citizen safety, caring for the injured, securing the crime scene, interviewing witnesses, gathering information, tracing, locating, and detaining the suspect, collecting and preserving evidence, and documenting the incident. When responding to a reported crime call, the officer's tactics depend on the answers to the following questions (Hess & Wrobleski, 2003):

- Is the crime in progress?
- What type of crime is being committed?
- How many suspects are there?
- Is the suspect armed?
- Are lives in danger?
- Are backup officers required?

These general guidelines are consistent throughout the police community. The following discussion addresses these guidelines as applied to the types of crime commonly encountered by the uniformed patrol officer. Special situational responses not addressed in this section are discussed in Chapter 10. Detailed preliminary investigation techniques for many of these offenses are contained in Chapter 11.

Disturbing the Public Peace Calls

A common police call involves a response to a report of a person or group disturbing the peace. Family arguments, loud stereos and televisions, loud parties, barking dogs, gang fights, and noisy vehicles are common complaints. What disturbs the public peace and tranquility is often subjective. What may be a disturbance to some may not be a bother to others. Consumption of alcohol may also be a factor. Intoxicated persons present a challenge to the police officer because it is difficult to reason with someone who is inebriated. Belligerent responses should be expected. A person's ego could be damaged and an inappropriate police response may result in hostility and aggressive behavior. Usually, arrest is the least appropriate option.

As a peacekeeper, the police officer's responsibility is to restore order and peace to the community. Tact and diplomacy are appropriate in most situations. The officer's attitude, posture, and tone of voice are critical to a successful resolution of the issues. The officer should not antagonize

Police response to incidents depends on the situation and the circumstances. *(Photo courtesy of the San Diego Police Department)*

the participants and escalate the situation. With noise complaints, simple notice to cease, coupled with a warning that a second police response will result in legal action, may be sufficient.

Arguments and fights require caution since the participants' ability to think rationally is diminished. A backup officer is appropriate. The disputants should be separated. Resolution of the disagreement is difficult when the disputants are in each other's presence. Once separated, tensions are often reduced and officers can assist the parties with problem identification and a solution to the dispute. Obviously, if criminal activity is involved, the officers may exercise the arrest option (Payton & Amaral, 2004).

Prowler Calls

Frantic calls from citizens often result when a resident hears strange sounds at night or notices a lone, dark human figure in the neighborhood. When responding to prowler calls, an officer must exercise caution. Although most prowlers are physically harmless, the subject could be an armed fugitive. The officer should respond quietly. Use of red lights and sirens will broadcast the officer's presence to the prowler. Complainants should be notified through the dispatcher when the officer arrives on the scene. Officers have been killed by armed complainants who mistook the police for the reported prowler. A short distance from the scene, the officer should turn the engine and lights off, reduce the radio volume, coast to a stop, and avoid use of the brakes because brake lights may be noticed by the prowler. The element of surprise is extremely important to the apprehension of an actual prowler. A search for the prowler should involve at least two officers. The search area should include the complainant's location as well as the neighborhood and vehicles within the neighborhood (Perry, 1998).

Substance Abuse Calls

Substance abuse involves the inappropriate ingestion of controlled and toxic substances into the human body. The abuse of alcohol and drugs has become increasingly common and costly, both economically and in human terms. According to the U.S. Department of Health and Human Services, drug use among 12- to 17-year-olds more than doubled between 1992 and 1995 and began to decline in 1997. Between 1997 and 1999, drug use among people 18 to 25 years of age also increased (Picture of drug use, 2000). However, illicit drug use among teenagers began to decline in 2003 (National Institute on Drug Abuse, 2003). Drug abuse in the workplace has become more common. A 1999 study revealed that 70 percent of those who use or abuse illegal drugs hold full-time jobs (Most drug abusers, 1999). This creates serious problems for society, the employer, and the individual.

A police officer should be familiar with the types of substances typically abused. A police officer must also be familiar with the behavioral symptoms of substance abuse. An awareness of the symptoms will assist

Additional information on drug abuse is available through the National Institute on Drug Abuse at www.nida.nih.gov.

the officer in the identification of persons who may be under the influence of chemicals.

In the late 1990s, law enforcement agencies reported an increasing number of arrests for the importation and illegal possession of ketamine hydrochloride. Street names for ketamine include K, Special K, Vitamin K, and Ket. Commonly used for veterinary purposes, ketamine is an anesthetic with analgesic and psychedelic properties chemically related to phencyclidine (angel dust, PCP). Ketamine is a liquid, but it can be dried into a powder. The liquid form is injected intravenously or intramuscularly. The powder can be taken orally, snorted, or formulated for smoking. The effects are similar to LSD and include hallucinations and dissociative action. The user senses that the mind is separated from the body. An overdose can cause muscle spasms, dizziness, slurred speech, respiratory depression, impaired coordination, and heart failure (Hughes, 2000).

In addition, a person exhibiting the symptoms of hallucinogen use (LSD, peyote, psilocybin) may have dilated pupils, sweat excessively, hallucinate, and have increased respiratory and heart rate. The symptoms associated with PCP use may include high pain tolerance, great physical strength, hallucinations, unpredictability, aggressive and extremely violent behavior, excessive sweating, drowsiness, nystagmus (involuntary rapid movement of the eyeball, usually from side to side), paranoia, confusion, blank stares, muscle rigidity, unusual gait or convulsions, and a possible chemical odor on the breath or body. Symptoms of stimulant use (cocaine, amphetamines, or methamphetamines) include restlessness, talkativeness, trembling, dilated pupils, sleeplessness, hyperactivity, and increased respiratory and heart rate. Finally, symptoms of depressant use (barbiturates, sedatives, tranquilizers) include slurred speech, poor coordination, unsteadiness, intoxicated behavior with no odor of alcoholic beverages, nystagmus, and decreased respiratory and heart rate.

Commonly abused substances and methods used for ingestion include the following:
- Alcohol, swallowed
- Hallucinogens, swallowed
- PCP, smoked
- Amphetamine (stimulant), swallowed
- Heroin, injected
- Cocaine hydrochloride, snorted/injected
- Cocaine base, smoked
- Methamphetamine, snorted/injected
- Barbiturates (depressants and tranquilizers), swallowed
- Cannabis (marijuana), smoked

The behavioral symptoms of substance abuse include:
- Significant change in personal appearance for the worse
- Sudden and irrational flare-ups
- Unusual degrees of activity or inactivity
- Sudden and dramatic changes in discipline and job performance
- Dilated pupils or wearing sunglasses at inappropriate times or places
- Needle marks or razor cuts, or wearing long sleeves constantly to hide such marks
- Sudden attempts to borrow money or to steal
- Frequent association with known drug abusers or pushers

The primary prevention and treatment strategies have included programs such as Drug Abuse Resistance Education (DARE), and emphasis on drug law enforcement and interdiction. DARE is a violence and drug prevention program that began in Los Angeles in 1983 and has since spread to rural and urban areas throughout the country. Police officers enter schools and use the program to educate children about the threats and consequences associated with drug activity. The curriculum focuses on building self-esteem, resisting peer pressure, assuming responsibility for one's own behavior, and making responsible decisions. Important additional benefits include the development, on the part of young people, of a more positive attitude toward and respect for law enforcement (Carter, 1995).

Because of the continuing demand for illegal drugs, the DARE Program and drug law enforcement have had little appreciable impact on reducing illicit drug use (Truth, DARE and consequences, 1998). A report issued by the Drug Policy Research Center of the Rand Corporation indicated that the impact of each dollar spent on drug treatment, when combined with drug enforcement, may be more effective in reducing the demand for illegal drugs than drug law enforcement by itself. In the long term, drug treatment appears to be more effective than interdiction (Mishra, 1998; Rand Corporation, 1999). Additionally, jail and prison sentences for determined addicts have little deterrent effect (Ainsworth, 2000a). In an experimental shift away from a punishment to a treatment approach to drug addition, California voters overwhelmingly approved Proposition 36, the Substance Abuse and Crime Prevention Act, on November 7, 2000. The measure is designed to divert many drug offenders from the justice system into treatment programs. Those convicted of illegal drug possession for the first and second time, as well as some drug-related parole violators, are eligible for treatment. The new law does not apply to drug dealers (Ainsworth, 2000b; California State, Department of Alcohol and Drug Programs, 2004).

Results of preliminary studies conducted to determine the effectiveness of California's Proposition 36 programs suggest that they have not met expectations. Study results indicate that drug offenders offered the Proposition 36 treatment alternative are more likely to be rearrested for subsequent offenses than their criminal justice–involved counterparts. To improve success rates, researchers recommend that treatment protocols

The demand for illegal drugs remains high, as evidenced by large seizures of controlled substances. *(Photo courtesy of the San Diego Sheriff's Department)*

be aligned with the ·abuser-client's addiction severity. In addition, legal pressure should be applied to clients to increase retention rates in treatment programs to maximize potential treatment benefits (Farabee, Hser, Anglin, & Huang, 2004).

Private chemical abuse reduction strategies include prevention and treatment programs sponsored by health care organizations and private rehabilitation facilities as well as employer-sponsored employee assistance programs. Appropriate employer responses to chemical abuse involve a written and communicated policy, documentation of incidents of abuse in the workplace, and employer interventions through counseling, treatment, probation, and termination. It should be noted that private employers currently have no legal right to intervene unless the chemical abuse affects job performance and safety.

Drug testing in the workplace is increasing, although the legality of such testing has yet to be firmly established. Current statutes and case law should be consulted to obtain up-to-date information regarding the legality of drug testing in public as well as private practice (Ortmeier, 2009).

Public Safety and Morals Offense Calls

Often referred to as vice laws or victimless crimes, public safety and morals offenses include pornography, prostitution, indecent exposure, and gambling. In large police agencies, these laws are enforced by specialized vice units. Public safety and morals laws are difficult to enforce because the participants usually engage in the illegal activity voluntarily and complainants are usually third parties. Vice activity can be reduced if an officer learns the beat, gathers information, and works with the community. Utilizing problem-solving skills to develop creative solutions can often eliminate the problem. The police and community working together are limited only by their ingenuity. The San Diego Police Department, in a collaborative arrangement with business owners, virtually eliminated prostitution in the Midway District of the city. The police encouraged business owners to obtain restraining orders against the prostitutes. The potential penalties for violation of the orders encouraged the prostitutes to move out of the area.

Theft Offense Calls

Numerous offenses fall into the theft category and police involvement with these cases is commonplace. Theft-related offenses include crimes such as simple larceny, shoplifting, embezzlement, fraud, bad checks, and forgery. The vast majority of theft offenses are misdemeanors in nature. With few exceptions, police officers in most states may not arrest for misdemeanors not observed by the officers. Therefore, it will be necessary for the officer(s) to collect and provide evidence and information that can be used by a prosecutor as the foundation for issuance of a criminal complaint and arrest warrant. As an alternative, a citizen-witness to a theft may make a private person's (citizen's) arrest of the suspect. In many states, the police officer must take custody of a suspect arrested by a citizen.

Vehicle Theft Calls

According to some estimates, the theft of vehicles accounts for over 30 percent of all theft losses in the United States. Many vehicle thefts are preventable. A substantial number of thefts occur because the vehicle was unlocked or the key was left in the ignition. In the 1990s, carjacking, a form of robbery, became commonplace and special carjacking statutes were enacted in several states as well as at the federal level.

The first consideration when responding to a report of a stolen vehicle is to determine if the theft actually occurred. Often the vehicle is missing because a family member took the vehicle, the vehicle was loaned to someone who did not return it, or it has been repossessed. If the vehicle has been stolen, the officer should consider juveniles in the area. Often juveniles take vehicles for joyriding purposes. Although the vehicle's use is unauthorized, a juvenile does not intend to permanently deprive the owner of the vehicle. Rather, the juvenile drives the vehicle for a short period of time and returns it to the vicinity from which it was taken.

On patrol, officers should be alert for indications that a vehicle has been stolen. Auto thieves may switch license plates or alter the characters on a stolen vehicle's plates. Suspicious actions on the part of a driver may be an indicator. Officers should also pay attention to vehicle condition. New vehicles rarely have broken windows.

Burglary Calls

Nationally, less than 2 in 10 reported burglaries are cleared by arrest (U.S. Department of Justice, Federal Bureau of Investigation, 1997, 2004). Usually the victim is not present and the burglar remains on the premises for a very short period of time. Witnesses are scarce. No wonder burglary is a commonplace crime! However, burglary calls are always potentially dangerous situations.

Procedures for handling burglary calls are similar to those for a report of a prowler except that residential burglaries often occur during daylight hours and a building search is usually necessary. A building search should never be conducted by a single officer. When approaching the building, officers should take note of vehicles in the area. Officers should also look for broken or open windows and doors, or other signs of forced entry. The officers should not stand directly in front of any door. Officers should stand to the side and reach around the door jamb to push the door open and turn interior lights on. If no building interior lighting is available, flashlights should be held away from the officers' bodies. If an armed intruder is present, the suspect is likely to attack or shoot in the direction of the light. Interior searches should be systematic. Each room, as well as closets and other hiding places within each room, must be searched.

Vandalism Calls

Most often, vandalism, or malicious mischief, is committed by juveniles. Officers responding to vandalism calls should interview people who live or work in the area. Citizens can provide valuable information regarding youths who frequent the neighborhood, gang activity, and likely suspects. Juveniles themselves are a frequent source of information. **Motive** (the perpetrator's reason) is an important consideration when adults are suspected of vandalism. Disgruntled or terminated employees, former spouses, and radical idealists who target specific types of organizations are possible adult vandalism suspects.

Assault and Battery Calls

Although the terms *assault* and *battery* are often used conjunctively, they represent distinctly separate offenses. Generally, an assault is an attempted or threatened battery while battery itself requires some harmful or offensive contact with the victim. In some states, the crimes of assault and battery have been merged into a comprehensive assault law in which assault in the first degree (formerly battery) requires contact and second-degree assault requires an attempt at harmful, unconsented-to contact with the victim. If the assault involves the use of a deadly weapon, some states provide a charge of assault with a deadly weapon (ADW). Police procedures for assault and battery calls are similar to other crimes against persons: separate the parties, arrest the violator, care for the injured, interview witnesses, and document the incident (Miller, 2000).

Domestic Violence Calls

When responding to a domestic violence call, officers must consider their safety. During 1996–2009, 106 officers were killed responding to a domestic violence call for service, most of them killed with firearms in ambushes and unprovoked attacks in their first moments on the scene (Meyer & Carroll, 2011). In addition, officers must evaluate the injury to the victim. In many states, domestic abuse is not a felony unless there is a serious visible injury. Some states, however, are increasing penalties for domestic violence. In California, for example, any visible injury, or nonvisible injury indicated by the victim's complaint, is sufficient to establish probable cause for a felony arrest. Many states have enacted laws that address stalking, and have expanded domestic violence statutes to include nonmarried domestic partners and children. Generally, the new domestic violence laws also apply in same sex relationships, violence between individuals in which a previous intimate relationship existed, and to situations in which the victim is a minor child.

If the suspect violator of a restraining order is present, a misdemeanor is being committed whether the victim consents to the suspect's presence or not. A victim cannot consent to a violation of a lawful judicial order. If the suspect is not present, a crime report should be taken. In some states, the victim of domestic abuse may be arrested for failure to identify the perpetrator.

In domestic disturbance situations in which arrest is not warranted, the law often does not prescribe the officer's actions. In these cases, officers should approach with caution, separate the disputants, use distracting techniques, identify the problem, and assist the disputants in arriving at a solution. If possible, officers should refer the disputants to community agencies such as medical, social services, welfare, child protective services, and counseling services.

However, officers should consider nonphysical symptoms of future violent acts. Many victims of domestic homicide do not experience prior physical abuse from their killers. Less overt behaviors such as stalking, enforced social isolation, and controlling behavior may be precursors of lethal domestic violence. In addition, drug and alcohol abuse, coupled with other factors, such as the desperation associated with unemployment, can help trigger a perpetrator's physically abusive actions (Domestic homicide tipoffs may be missed, 2004).

Further, batterer intervention programs are not always successful. Studies raise doubts about whether such programs positively affect a batterer's attitude or behavior. Other variables, such as home ownership, marriage to the victim, and employment, appear more influential to success (Do batterer intervention programs work? Two studies, 2003).

Robbery Calls

Robbery calls are always high risk because the suspect may be present, armed, and dangerous. Notification often originates with witnesses, victims, or the triggering of alarm systems. When responding to the scene of a reported robbery, officers should watch for getaway vehicles speeding from the scene, suspicious persons (possible lookouts) in the area, and accomplices. Unless the robbery is in progress, one (primary) unit should respond to the scene while others patrol the area's escape routes. Information gathered by the primary unit at the scene regarding the suspect and vehicles can be broadcasted to the patrolling units. If the robbery is in progress, units should establish a perimeter and wait for the suspect(s) to exit the robbery target facility. Officers should never enter the location of a reported robbery until they know what is happening inside. The suspect(s) may still be present and have hostages.

Sex Offense Cases

Sex crimes are numerous, varied, and sensitive to investigate. Sex offenses include such crimes as rape, sexual assault, child molestation, and indecent exposure (exhibitionism). Care must be exercised when responding to reported sex crimes. Not all sex crime accusations are true. In actual cases, the victim is usually traumatized. If possible, an officer of the same gender as the victim should conduct the victim interview. The victim should also be considered part of the evidence package. If a rape has been reported, the victim should be instructed not to bathe until examination and evidence collection has taken place with authorized personnel in a medical facility.

Many agencies are either establishing or adopting strategies used by **Sexual Assault Response Teams (SART).** The SART team receives specialized training on the dynamics of sexual assault, legal issues and concerns associated with sex crimes, and the nature of victimization. Adherence to SART strategies allows officers to work more effectively with sexual assault victims, medical resources, prosecutorial staff, and victim advocates.

Homicide Cases

Overall, the murder rate in the United States has been declining in recent years. This is good news since the police can do little to prevent homicides from occurring in the first place. In murder cases, the victim and the perpetrator are often acquainted and, in many situations, the victim's actions precipitate the killing.

A patrol officer's first task at a death scene is to determine if the victim is, in fact, deceased. The subject may appear dead as a result of a comatose state. Common conditions that may indicate death include lack of breathing or pulse, loss of flushing under fingernails, glazed eyeballs, and the nonresponsiveness of the pupils to light. Regardless of the victim's condition, a medical emergency unit must be dispatched to the scene. In some states, such as California, death is determined by the coroner and the deceased's body must be secured until a coroner's investigator arrives. If death has occurred, the officer must protect the scene and follow established crime scene procedures.

All murders are homicides but not all homicides are murder. Death can also occur from natural causes, accidents, or suicide. If death was caused by human action, and was not self-inflicted, the death investigation becomes a homicide investigation. All homicides are not unlawful. Some are excusable (killing by accident or in self-defense). Others are justifiable (a police officer killing an armed, inherently dangerous, felony suspect). If a homicide is not excusable or justifiable, it, by process of elimination, must be unlawful (murder or manslaughter). Evidence preservation and collection is extremely important in death investigations. The body itself will be an extremely important source of information.

CASE STUDY—DOMESTIC BATTERER INTERVENTION PROGRAMS

Domestic batterer intervention programs have proliferated in the United States in recent years. The courts offer the programs to batterers as alternatives to jail or prison. The programs usually require attendance at group therapy sessions designed to reduce the likelihood of violence and change offender attitudes toward women and battering.

Evaluations were conducted of batterer intervention programs in Broward County, Florida and Brooklyn, New York. In both programs, the underlying theory is that batterers wish to control their partners and that changing this dynamic is the key to changing offender behavior.

The Broward County evaluative study uncovered no significant difference between the treatment and control groups in attitudes toward women, whether battering should be a crime, or whether the state has a right to intervene. Victims still expected their offender partners to beat them and program attendance did not reduce the likelihood of repeat physical violence. Rather, offenders who were older, employed, married, or owned a home were less likely to reoffend.

The Brooklyn study revealed that program attendance did not change batterer attitudes toward women. However, long-term exposure to the prevention program did appear to reduce the likelihood of repeat violence (Do batterer intervention programs work? Two studies, 2003).

1. What is the solution to the problem of domestic violence?
2. In the long term, which is more appropriate for domestic violence perpetrators: punishment or treatment?

ARREST AND CONTROL OF PRISONERS

Police–citizen contacts fall within three broad categories: consensual encounter, detention, and arrest. A **consensual encounter** involves a voluntary contact between a police officer and a citizen. There is no restraint on individual liberty and the citizen must perceive that the encounter can be terminated at any time. A **detention** occurs when a police officer compels a person to stop, remain in a certain place, or perform a specific act. A detention involves a seizure of the person for a limited period of time. The officer must be able to establish reasonable, articulable suspicion that the detainee has committed, is committing, or is about to commit a crime. Reasonable suspicion justifies a detention and provides the officer with a basis for an investigation to determine if the officer's suspicions are correct. Factors that contribute to the officer's reasonable suspicion include the appearance or actions of the detainee or the location where the subject is detained.

Within the context of police work, an **arrest** involves the official taking of a person into custody for the purpose of answering to a criminal charge. An arrest can be based on an arrest warrant, made when an offense has been committed in the police officer's presence, or in the case of a felony not observed by the officer, when the officer has probable cause to believe a felony has been committed and the arrestee committed it. Police officers can arrest for misdemeanors they observe. With few exceptions, police officers in most states may not arrest for misdemeanors they do not witness unless there is a misdemeanor arrest warrant on file for the arrestee.

Effecting an arrest is one of the most dangerous tasks a police officer is ever called upon to perform. After a subject becomes a suspect and realizes that the authority of the government is being used to restrict freedom and personal liberty, the potential for violence increases significantly. Furthermore, the police officer must make every effort to

Effecting an arrest is one of the most dangerous tasks an officer is expected to perform. *(Photo courtesy of the San Diego Sheriff's Department.)*

ensure that the arrest is legal. As the first step in a criminal proceeding, an illegal arrest may taint the case and subsequently provide an avenue for the defendant to avoid prosecution and conviction. Police **arrest and control procedures** include the following:

- Announce the arrest and the offense to the suspect.
- Physically restrain the suspect as appropriate. The most common temporary restraining device is a pair of handcuffs. The handcuffs should be applied to a suspect's bare wrists and tightened snugly with both hands cuffed behind the suspect's back whenever possible. The handcuffs should be double-locked so the suspect cannot tighten the cuffs and request that they be loosened to improve blood circulation. Double-locking also reduces the likelihood that the handcuff locks can be picked or compromised. A restrained prisoner is the responsibility of the officer(s). Handcuffed prisoners should not be left unattended nor should they be handcuffed to stationary objects.
- Search the suspect and the area within the suspect's immediate reach for weapons, evidence, contraband, and means of escape. (Note: Ballpoint pens can be used as weapons and means of escape. The diameter of a ballpoint pen ink tube is about the same as a handcuff key. Arrestees have been known to manufacture handcuff keys from these ink tubes.)
- Conducting a search of a prisoner is critical to officer and public safety. Also, the potential for escape of the prisoner is always a possibility. Search techniques may vary slightly depending on the circumstances. However, the search should be systematic and include an inspection of the front waistband, upper body (chest, pockets, armpits, sleeves, and sides), back (rear waistband and buttocks area), and lower body (legs, ankles). Suspects have been known to hide weapons and means of escape in their hair, mouth, groin, small of the back, and in heels of shoes. Under ideal circumstances, two officers are available when the search is conducted. One officer controls the suspect and actually conducts the search. The second officer covers the first to ensure the safety of both officers.
- Arresting officers may search arrestees of the opposite sex if an officer of the same gender as the prisoner is not available. However, the extent of the search is limited to frisk or pat-down for weapons. Strip searches of the opposite sex are never permissible. Male officers should use the back of the hand to search female breast areas. If a weapon is detected, the male officer may reach under the blouse from behind, pull on the bottom of the bra (if any) to shake the weapon loose. When frisking the crotch area between the suspect's legs, the back of the hand should be used also.
- Inform the arrestee of the rights under the Constitution according to the *Miranda* decision if the arrestee is to be questioned regarding the incident. A discussion of *Miranda* requirements is presented in Chapter 9.

An officer must remember that the psychological impact of a handcuff being placed on the wrist of a suspect may cause the arrestee to become

Handcuffs should be applied to a suspect's bare wrists with both hands cuffed behind the suspect's back. *(Photo courtesy of the San Diego Sheriff's Department.)*

irrational and violent. The arrest and restraint should be conducted gracefully without hesitation. Career criminals can sense awkwardness on the part of the officer. Some career offenders practice counterattacks in advance and plan violent escapes from police custody. The potential for violence, officer injury, and possible escape can be minimized if the officer is firm, fair, and professional. Officers who experience the most difficulty when making arrests are those who are arrogant, abusive, and insulting.

The use of force should be limited to that which is reasonably necessary to effect an arrest. Deadly force may be used for officer self-protection, or the protection of another, against deadly force. Prisoners should be transported and booked as soon as possible. Two officers are best for handling prisoners. Nonarresting officers who take custody of a prisoner should conduct their own search of the prisoner for weapons. Officers should never assume prisoners have been thoroughly searched previously.

In addition to an arrest situation, a police officer may assume custody of an individual because of a probation or parole commitment, court-ordered commitment document, or because the subject is a prisoner en route to court or a custodial facility. When an officer takes a subject into custody, the officer's general responsibilities include:

- Caring for the subject in custody.
- Assuring that there is a lawful basis for the subject's custody.
- Protecting the statutory and constitutional rights of the subject.

- Maintaining the safety of the general public as well as other officers.
- Facilitating the processing of the subject into a detention facility, if appropriate.

As provided by law, persons in custody have the right to make telephone calls and to retain an attorney. In addition, any communication between the prisoner and the attorney is considered privileged. In many jurisdictions it is a felony to eavesdrop on or record communication between a prisoner and legal counsel. A similar communications privilege exists between the person in custody and the subject's religious advisor or licensed physician.

Certain medical conditions may require treatment prior to detention in a custodial facility. These include head injuries, diabetic shock, drug overdose, severe bleeding, chest pain, unconsciousness, or unresponsiveness. An arresting officer is also required to notify custodial personnel of any suspected medical condition or suicide risk and whether the subject requires medication. Similar notification must be made if the subject was exposed to chemical agents, tasers, or the use of a baton or carotid restraint during the arrest process.

Upon arrival at the custodial facility, the arresting officer or appropriate custodial personnel must take possession of the custodial subject's personal property. Such property may include money, wallets or purses, credit cards, documents, and various material objects. The person who takes possession of the property must immediately provide the custodial subject with a receipt for the property and enter a description of the items confiscated in the intake documents.

Prisoners who may require special treatment while in a custodial facility include those who have medical conditions, mental disorders, substance abuse problems, or persons with developmental or physical disabilities. Prisoners requiring protective custody include current and former gang members, sex offenders, escape risks, violent persons, informants, current and former police officers, celebrities, transvestites, transsexuals, gays, and lesbians. Persons being held in civil contempt for violation of a court order must be segregated from those in custody for criminal violations.

The prisoner should be searched prior to an initial appearance, or arraignment, or placement in the custodial facility population. This search should occur regardless of any previous searches of the detainee. Generally, strip or body cavity searches are not allowed unless the detainee has been arrested for a violation involving violence, weapons, or a controlled substance, and reasonable suspicion exists that the detainee may be concealing weapons or contraband. Additionally, in some jurisdictions, a strip search requires written authorization from a supervising officer.

An officer's failure to ensure the safety of a person in custody may expose the officer to serious liability. This failure could result in disciplinary action or termination from employment, civil lawsuits, or possible prosecution under applicable state penal code provisions or federal civil rights statutes.

WORKING WITH CRIME VICTIMS

To deal compassionately and effectively with crime and critical incident victims, police officers must be familiar with the psychological trauma that victims experience (Karmen, 2010). Officers should also adhere to the procedures necessary to defuse crisis situations resulting from the stress associated with victimization. Victims are not limited to individuals who are impacted directly by the negative event. Persons who witness a crime, have a close relationship with the person directly victimized, or live or work in the area where the crime or incident takes place are also victims. Police and other criminal justice professionals may be crime victims as well. In addition to being assaulted or killed, they are exposed to numerous traumatic experiences. These indirect victims may suffer economic loss and emotional trauma similar to the direct victims'.

A victim's crisis is frequently precipitated by a **violent crime,** theft, or severe accident. The victim's crisis often depends on the victim's perception of the situation. Aside from the event itself, factors that may contribute to the crisis include the victim's age and living situation, lack of a support system, special needs of the victim (i.e., language and physical disabilities), and other circumstances such as a lack of resources to assist victims. It is not unusual for a victim to respond with feelings of helplessness, anger, sadness, and fear. The victim may experience physical reactions such as nausea, hyperventilation, heart problems, or breathing difficulties in response to the crisis.

By diffusing the crisis situation, a police officer can assist victims to regain control and empower them to help themselves. Officers can effectively promote **victim assistance** by:

- Acknowledging the victim's situation.
- Listening attentively.
- Applying positive verbal and nonverbal communication techniques.
- Reassuring victims that they are safe.
- Staying calm.
- Describing and explaining the procedures and resources available.
- Assisting with the development of appropriate alternative responses to the crisis.

Police officers must exercise caution to ensure that their own personal biases do not interfere with crisis resolution and victim recovery. Officers must be aware that their own inappropriate reactions may alienate victims or impact victims' decisions in a negative way. Inappropriate behavior on the part of the police officer includes actions and reactions toward a victim that tend to blame others, disassociate, or demonstrate insensitivity or impatience. To be effective, police officers must provide meaningful information to the victims, assist them in coping with the crisis, and facilitate their participation in the legal and investigative process (California Commission on Peace Officer Standards and Training, 2012).

A victim assistance movement in the United States began in 1965 when California established a crime victim compensation program. Most other states established similar programs and all states have enacted crime victims rights laws. At the federal level, numerous laws address crime victim and witness reparations, rights, and protection. In addition, several support groups, such as Mothers Against Drunk Drivers (MADD) and the National Organization for Victim Assistance (NOVA), have been established to assist crime victims (Bohm & Haley, 2009). In addition, many states now use the Victim Information and Notification Everyday (VINE) automated system. Victims can access the system to learn where offenders are being held, as well as when parole hearings will be held and when offenders' sentences will expire. Armed with this information, victims can take steps to protect themselves from further attacks by offenders.

Victimization results from any intentional, reckless, or negligent act committed by an individual, group, or organization that produces physical or economic harm to individuals, groups, or organizations. Victimization extends beyond the impact of criminal actions to quality of life issues. Loud parties, for example, often disturb passive neighbors who are reluctant to complain to authorities. Further, by definition, the criminal offender can be classified as a victim if the offender's rights are violated or if the offender does not receive fair and impartial justice (Dempsey, 1992; Robinson, 2009).

▲ SUMMARY

Laws are created to regulate human behavior and define rights. Criminal laws are designed to punish and correct the behavior of offenders. Multiple causes and types of crime exist. Enforcement of criminal laws is a major function of the police. Although the crime rate has been declining for a number of years, the citizens' fear of crime remains high. As evidenced by the National Crime Victimization Survey (NCVS), not all crime is reported through the Uniform Crime Report (UCR). Sources of criminal law include constitutions, statutes, ordinances, case law, and common law. A crime is an offense against society and may be classified as a felony, misdemeanor, or infraction. Specific criminal offenses are included in state penal codes and federal statutes. Police officers must be familiar with laws of arrest, use of force guidelines, and response techniques to various types of offenses. Arrest and control of prisoners is critical. Safety of the officer or officers involved as well as the general public is a primary consideration. Officers also find it necessary to work compassionately and effectively with victims of crime.

DISCUSSION QUESTIONS AND EXERCISES

1. Are crime statistics accurate? Why or why not?
2. Are the police responsible for increases (or decreases) in crime rates? Explain.
3. Create a comprehensive general definition for crime.

4. Contrast corpus delicti with the elements of a crime. Are both necessary to establish criminal liability? Explain.
5. What types of crime are most often encountered by the police?
6. Compare a public police officer's arrest authority with that of a private citizen's.
7. Create guidelines for police use of lethal and less lethal force.
8. Can standardized police response techniques be developed? Why or why not?
9. Describe the procedure for arrest and control of prisoners.
10. How might the police engage a community to participate with crime reduction efforts?
11. What is victimization? How might the negative impact of victimization be mitigated?
12. Some people suggest that the causes of crime can be identified and treated, thus leading to a cure for the criminal offender. Is this possible? Can law enforcement and criminal justice system activity significantly reduce the crime rate?

Professionalism, Ethics, and Leadership

LEARNING OBJECTIVES

After completing this chapter, the reader should be able to:

- explain how professionalism, ethics, and moral standards relate to the pursuit of a career in law enforcement.
- develop and articulate a personal and professional code of ethics and the values on which it is based.
- describe the social and community norms that influence public opinion and perception of personnel in a public safety environment.
- articulate the social criteria for ethical behavior.
- identify and describe examples of unethical behavior in a profession.
- analyze situations involving human interaction and develop appropriate responses consistent with a code of ethics.
- identify symptoms, types, and patterns of police misconduct.
- describe the roles of citizen review boards, police unions, and the police subculture in relation to police behavior.
- discuss the concepts of leadership.
- articulate the history and development of leadership theory.
- distinguish between leadership qualities and competencies.
- develop a leadership competency base for a profession.
- analyze the qualities as well as the competencies of an effective leader.

KEY TERMS

Define, describe, or explain the importance of each of the following.

Actuation/implementation competencies
CALEA
Christopher Commission
Civilian review board
Citizen oversight committee
Code of conduct

Code of ethics
Communications and related interpersonal competencies
Corruption
Discrimination
Entrapment
Ethics

Integrity

International Association of
  Chiefs of Police (IACP)

Knapp Commission

Leadership

Leadership competency

Leadership quality

Leadership trait

Management

Mollen Commission

Moral standards

Motivational competencies

Planning and organizing competencies

Police subculture

Problem-solving competencies

Profession

Professionalism

Uncivil conduct

Unethical conduct

Values

Violation of Constitutional rights

Violation of rights to privacy

INTRODUCTION

Trust, honesty, and appropriate behavior are ingredients of a successful relationship. The police and the community are partners in a collaborative relationship designed to keep the peace and respond to crime and disorder. Thus, the police must act responsibly and professionally to gain and maintain the public's trust and support. Additionally, the police are in a unique leadership position that can be used to assist communities as they seek to address crime and disorder problems and improve the quality of life.

Professionalism and ethical conduct lie at the heart of morally correct and effective policing. Many experts also recognize that law enforcement officers, regardless of their rank, are ill equipped to face the challenges of modern-day policing unless they are self-contained leadership agents. Ethical leadership skills are most important for the line officer. A sound ethical foundation and leadership competence are prerequisites for the effective performance of tactical and strategic law enforcement.

This chapter addresses policing as a profession and it discusses the values, qualities, and ethical leadership skills all law enforcement officers should possess and demonstrate. The values, qualities, and skills presented are also essential for other criminal justice and public safety practitioners.

LAW ENFORCEMENT AS A PROFESSION

With the release of August Vollmer's *The Police in Modern Society* (1936), the movement to recognize law enforcement as a profession gained momentum. In 1968, a vision for police professionalism was summarized by James Q. Wilson. He stated that the characteristics of the professional police officer include the exercise of . . . "wide discretion alone and with respect to matters of the greatest importance" and that

CASE STUDY—THE DIRTY HARRY SYNDROME

During the Mollen Commission corruption hearings in 1993, several New York City police officers admitted to beating people to obtain information. In 2000, a rookie Oakland, California, police officer reported to supervisors that a group of fellow officers calling themselves The Riders planted drugs, used excessive force, and falsified police reports to make arrests and obtain convictions. The group's alleged ringleader, Officer Frank Vazquez, fled to Mexico to avoid prosecution. In 2003, three other officers were tried and acquitted on eight counts, including kidnapping and assault. The trial jury hopelessly deadlocked on 27 other charges. The three officers were retired in 2004. In May, 2002, former LAPD officer Rafael Perez, a major figure in the department's Rampart Division corruption scandal, was sentenced to two years in federal prison for shooting, and fabrication of evidence against, a gang member.

    In these cases, police officers used whatever means necessary to *put bad guys away.* The phenomenon is often referred to as the Dirty Harry Syndrome, after Clint Eastwood's character in the Dirty Harry films.

1. Do the ends (putting bad people away) justify the means (unethical, illegal, and unconstitutional behavior) used by the police?
2. Who is responsible for the prevention and correction of unethical conduct?
3. Does the police subculture help to perpetuate police misconduct? Explain.

this ability is based on a status "conferred by an organized profession" that "certifies the member has acquired by education certain information and by apprenticeship certain arts and skills that render [an officer] competent" to "handle emergency situations, to be privy to guilty information, and to make decisions involving questions of life and death or honor and dishonor." He went on to state that a professional "is willing to [be] subject to the code of ethics and sense of duty to colleagues" (Wilson, 1968, pp. 29–30).

    Attempts to achieve professional standing emerge from a variety of initiatives, not the least of which is accreditation. In 1979, the **Commission on Accreditation for Law Enforcement Agencies (CALEA)** was formed through the efforts of the International Association of Chiefs of Police (IACP), the National Sheriffs' Association (NSA), the Police Executive Research Forum (PERF), and the National Organization of Black Law Enforcement Executives (NOBLE). CALEA developed minimum professional standards for agency management and service delivery and it established and administers a voluntary five-phase agency accreditation process. CALEA standards address: agency roles and relationships; organization, management, and administration; personnel structure and processes; operations; operational support; traffic management; prisoner and court-related services; and auxiliary and technical services (About CALEA, 2004).

    Supporters of accreditation suggest that adherence to minimum standards elevates policing to professional status. Critics of accreditation

Learn more about accreditation of law enforcement agencies by contacting CALEA at www.calea.org.

contend that it is expensive, time consuming, and difficult to justify to community government. Critics also cite lack of police administration support and questionable benefits to the agency (Wrobleski & Hess, 2009). Yet adherence to accreditation standards can be beneficial. A study conducted by Crowder (1998) revealed that compliance with CALEA standards improved training programs and reduced incidents of inappropriate action and liability associated with police use of force and vehicle pursuits.

One cannot deny that law enforcement has become more professional over the past several decades (Byers, 2000). Yet, a common body of police knowledge does not exist (Goldstein, 2001) and at least one critical question must be answered: If law enforcement is a profession, have police officers acquired the wide range of skills necessary to police communities in a modern society? In a nationwide FBI study conducted for the purposes of determining law enforcement training needs, police officers themselves did not view community relations training as a high priority (Phillips, 1988).

In addition, recent trends indicate that the police are becoming more, rather than less, militarized. In many areas, attitudes and training protocols have shifted toward a singular view that the police should function as an army fighting a war on crime (Carlson, 2005; Barkan & Bryjak, 2004). However, an effective and close working relationship with the community is essential to the success of any policing strategy. To function effectively within a community, policing requires officers to acquire nontraditional police skills so they may involve the community as a coparticipant in the control of crime and maintenance of order (Goldstein, 2001; Raffel Price, 1995).

Most police activity is situational, discretionary, and agency-specific. Thus, the skills required of the police officer are "more akin to occupational attributes which are developed through the melding milieu of education, training, and police experience" (Carter, Sapp, & Stephens, 1988, p. 13). As one court observed:

> Few professionals are so peculiarly charged with individual responsibility as police officers. Officers are compelled to make instantaneous decisions, often without clear-cut guidance from the legislature or departmental policy, and mistakes of judgment could cause irreparable harm to citizens or even the community. (*Davis v. City of Dallas,* 1985, p. 215)

The term **profession** implies that its members adhere to certain ethical standards of behavior and achieve a level of competence to be employed in a particular discipline or occupation. Common characteristics of professions and **professionalism** include:

- A code of ethics and standards of conduct.
- A public service orientation.
- Common goals and principles.
- A recognized body of knowledge relative to the profession.
- A common language and unique vocabulary.
- A system for credentialing or licensing its members.
- An organization that promotes high standards and the interests of the profession.

In a quest for professional status, most members of the law enforcement community work hard to conform to the standards of a profession. Some form of preservice training is required and standards for selection and retention of police officers have improved greatly. Common goals are reflected in the police mission. Criminal justice education has emerged as a discipline and helped to create a recognizable body of knowledge. A code of conduct exists and a form of licensing has been adopted in all states.

However, unlike that which exists through the American Medical Association or American Bar Association, no national standard for law enforcement theory, practice, and discipline is adhered to in all jurisdictions. Therefore, it is left to police officers themselves to ensure adherence to high standards of professional conduct and function as leaders in their respective communities. In addition to traditional job skills learned in academies and in-service training programs, the police must expand the knowledge horizon to include subjects that will help them serve a community better. The mark of a true professional is one who demonstrates leadership and vision to help communities keep the peace rather than fight endless wars on crime (Anderson, 2000; Meese & Ortmeier, 2004).

The modern concept of police professionalism should not be based on the paramilitaristic model prevalent in policing in the 1950s and 1960s. Rather, the modern concept redefines professionalism as an approach based on corporateness, responsibility, and expertise. The modern concept incorporates ethics-based, integrity-centric community policing, competency-based training, and leadership development. The new concept of professionalism accepts the view that training the police for any conceivable event is unrealistic. However, the police must be trained to think creatively to handle any eventuality, and to react in an appropriate legal, moral, and ethical manner (City of Los Angeles, 2003).

ETHICS AND PROFESSIONAL CONDUCT

Two police officers respond to a reported robbery of a convenience store. Upon arrival at the scene, the officers determine that the suspect has fled the area. Appropriate police procedure is followed by both officers. However, while interviewing the victim-clerk, the first officer sees the second officer take a candy bar and, without paying for it, leave the store. Has an ethical standard been violated? Should the first officer intervene? If so, how should a police officer respond to another officer's unethical or inappropriate conduct? If the first officer does not intervene, is minding one's own business a valid excuse? If an appropriate intervention does not take

The movement to recognize law enforcement as a profession gained momentum in the early twentieth century.
(Photo courtesy of the San Diego Police Department.)

place, is the first officer as unworthy of the badge as the second? Police officers are sworn to uphold the law. Yet, professionalism involves more than effective law enforcement and courtesy toward the general public. Officers have a legal as well as a moral obligation to act legally, responsibly, and ethically (Ortmeier & Meese, 2010).

Ethics involves moral principles and focuses on the concept of right and wrong and standards of behavior. Unlike law or organizational policy, which is formally prescribed and enforced by a controlling authority, ethics is based on **moral standards,** whether illegal or not. These moral standards, or ethical values, are formed through the influence of others. These standards are concerned with the relationships between people and how they exist in peace and harmony.

Values are fundamental beliefs on which personal decisions and conduct are based. Societal values are based on the norms of the community. Organizational values represent the beliefs of an organization. Professional values are reflected by an occupation or discipline. Personal values are based on individual beliefs. Values may be ethical or unethical. Gang members have values but their behavior may be unethical. Behavior may be unethical, yet not illegal. Therefore, ethics assumes a special meaning and involves the systematic reflection on, and analysis of, morality. It takes on a specific form when someone assumes the roll of a professional.

Ethical standards dictate behavior when either law or precedent, which may prescribe behavior, does not exist. Whenever one possesses the power of discretional decision making, the decision should conform to what one ought to do even though law, policy, or precedent prescribing must do behaviors is not available. The ends do not always justify the means. Conducting oneself according to an acceptable ethical standard, whether the profession has a code of ethics or not, means doing the right thing at the right time.

Ethical problems in law enforcement arise from **corruption,** racial profiling, **discrimination, violation of rights to privacy, violation of constitutional rights, entrapment,** negligence, use of excessive force, **uncivil conduct,** violation of agency policies or procedure, or violations of the professional **code of ethics.** Each of these subjects should be addressed in recruit and in-service training programs.

The law enforcement community is *not* permeated with graft, criminal activity, brutality, discrimination, abuse of authority, corruption, occupational deviance, and other forms of illegal or unethical police behavior (Byers, 2000). However, one cannot deny that police misconduct is displayed by some individual officers, groups of officers, or even by a few police agencies. The law enforcement profession is tarnished every time an officer uses self-serving excuses to justify unethical behavior (Trautman, 2005).

Although unethical, even criminal, behavior on the part of the police involves a relatively small number of officers, the negative impact of this behavior on the public's image of the police can be devastating. Police officers engage in **unethical conduct** when they accept gratuities, misuse the badge of office, practice racism and discrimination, misuse privileged communications and confidential information, misappropriate property, obstruct justice, engage in inappropriate off-duty behavior, and evoke a code of silence with respect to another officer's misbehavior (California Commission on Peace Officer Standards and Training, 2012). Following are a few examples of police misconduct.

1995	A police officer, testifying during the O. J. Simpson trial, committed perjury by lying about his use of a racial slur.
1996–1999	Sixty-one officers were terminated from a large urban police department for using excessive force, lying, drug use, theft, domestic violence, and improper relationships with minors and drug dealers.
1996	Sheriff's deputies were videotaped beating illegal immigrants following a high-speed freeway chase.
1997	Two NYPD officers were charged (and convicted in 1999) of sodomizing an immigrant (Abner Louima) with a broken toilet plunger handle.
1998	A seven-year highway patrol veteran was convicted of selling drugs to an informant.
1999	Seven prosecutors and sheriff's deputies were charged with conspiring to frame an innocent man.
2000	Two federal agents were convicted of the theft of U.S. government auto parts.
2001	Two men in their late sixties were exonerated of their murder convictions after a judge determined that FBI agents withheld evidence that would have proven their innocence. One man served over 33 years in prison for his conviction and the other served 30 years before being freed.

2002   Former FBI special agent Robert Hanssen was sentenced to life in prison for spying for the Russians during and after the Cold War. Hanssen joined the FBI in 1976 and began spying for the Soviets three years later.

2003   A police officer in a major urban city organized friends, relatives, and fellow police officers into a network of thieves who stole drugs, money, and property during home invasion robberies.

2004   A decorated veteran police officer and his wife were convicted on charges of receiving stolen property. The couple grossed nearly $20,000 monthly, selling the stolen items on eBay, the popular Internet auction site.

2005   Two former police detectives were arrested for murder and other charges stemming from their activities as Mafia hit men while they were employed by the NYPD.

2009   Orange County Sheriff Michael Carona was sentenced to five and a half years in prison for witness tampering, fined $125,000, and ordered to serve two years of probation after his release (Flaccus, 2009).

2010   The Justice Department inspector general investigated whether hundreds of FBI agents cheated while taking an exam on the bureau's policies regarding the conducting of surveillance on Americans (Apuzzo & Goldman, 2010).

Numerous corruption investigations have focused on a single police department. The NYPD is the largest and one of the oldest police departments in the United States. Six investigations of corruption within the NYPD took place over a 100-year period (Chin, 1997). These investigations included the following:

1895   Lexow Committee
1913   Curran Committee
1932   Seabury Investigation
1955   Helfand Investigation
1972   Knapp Commission
1994   Mollen Commission

In 1972, Frank Serpico, a plainclothes police detective in New York City, exposed widespread corruption within the NYPD. Serpico later testified before the resulting **Knapp Commission.** The Knapp Commission recognized that the system of police accountability was inadequate. The commission recommended prosecution of corrupt officers and restructuring of the NYPD Internal Affairs Division (IAD).

After disclosure of the Knapp Commission findings, the NYPD vowed to eliminate corruption and deal harshly with officers found guilty of misconduct. In 1992, however, six NYPD officers were arrested on drug charges, prompting the formation of yet another commission, the **Mollen Commission,** to investigate police misconduct. The Mollen Commission discovered that corruption in the NYPD was still pervasive and misconduct by officers was more serious than that uncovered by the Knapp Commission in 1972. The commission suggested that a new form of police misconduct emerged in the 1980s and 1990s, one characterized by corruption as well as brutality. Corrupt officers beat drug dealers, confiscated the dealers' drugs and money, and sold the confiscated drugs to others. The Mollen Commission recommended external oversight of the NYPD, recognizing that internal oversight by the department's IAD was ineffective and corrupt.

Misconduct investigations are not limited to the NYPD. Subsequent to the Los Angeles riots of 1992, the **Christopher Commission** was formed. The Christopher Commission (1992) reported widespread racism within the LAPD and it noted that officers were rarely disciplined for the use of excessive force. Several national commissions, notably, the Wickersham Commission (1931) and the Kerner Commission (1965), also cited evidence of police misconduct, discrimination, corruption, and use of excessive force among officers throughout the United States.

The findings of commissions that investigate police misconduct are strikingly similar. The commissions cite poor officer recruiting and training standards, poor police–community relations, and inadequate or nonexistent police complaint and accountability systems as the main causes of police misconduct and brutality. The commissions also offer similar recommendations: minority recruitment, higher education, residency requirements, and improved police accountability systems, including civilian oversight (Grant & Terry, 2012).

In one of the most disturbing police misconduct scandals to hit an urban police department in decades, a corruption probe into the Los Angeles Police Department in 1999 uncovered a wide range of serious allegations. A small group of officers assigned to the Community Resources Against Street Hoodlums (CRASH) unit in the department's Rampart Division were at the center of the scandal. They were accused of beating suspects, planting evidence, fabricating testimony, and unjustifiably killing a suspect in 1996. A few officers rented an apartment for on-duty sexual liaisons with prostitutes who were also enlisted by the officers to sell drugs that the officers stole from drug dealers. Almost two dozen LAPD officers were relieved of duty, terminated, or resigned in connection with the corruption probe. The scandal may lead to the release of numerous prison inmates and probationers as they appeal convictions resulting from approximately 3,000 cases involving the corrupt officers (Krasnowski, 2000). A few of the police officers, including renegade officer Rafael Perez, were convicted on charges stemming from the corrupt activities (Officer in Rampart case pleads guilty, 2003). Due to juror misconduct, the convictions of three of the officers involved were reversed on appeal.

After the Rampart Division scandal, the U.S. Department of Justice mandated that narcotics and gang officers reveal personal financial information. The mandate's intent was to catch corrupt officers in units that frequently handle cash or drugs. Members of entire units of the

LAPD quit their assignments ahead of the March 2011 deadline for activation of the new rule. The exodus raised the question of whether gang crime would escalate during the months required to restaff the units (LAPD gang officers quit assignments amid new rules, 2011).

The LAPD has confronted additional challenges since 2000, including officer-initiated lawsuits against the department for workplace conflicts centering on issues such as accusations of sexual harassment and racial discrimination. During 2005-2010, officers sued the department over such issues more than 250 times. By mid-2011, the city had paid settlements or verdicts totaling more than $18 million. A survey revealed that LAPD officers file suit more than other large police departments across the country (Rubin, 2011).

According to Walker and Katz, "theories of police corruption fall into six different categories, depending on whether they focus on the individual officer, the social structure, the neighborhood, the nature of police work, the police organizations, or the police subculture" (Walker & Katz, 2010: 450). The most popular theory focuses on the individual officer, the so-called rotten apple in every barrel, who engages in misconduct because of some personal moral failing. Although appealing to the police as well as private citizens, the theory fails to account for the long history of widespread corruption in some agencies. Further, the theory does not explain why honest officers become corrupt.

Social structural theories suggest that police corruption is a product of the congruence of criminal law, cultural conflict, and politics. As the criminal law seeks to prohibit activities (e.g., gambling, drug use, sexual behavior) that some people view as legitimate and matters of choice, cultural conflicts arise. To reduce conflict, corruption is tolerated in some agencies because the local political environment fosters corruption.

Neighborhood theories suggest that officers are influenced by the behaviors of people in the neighborhoods the officers patrol. According to the theories, socially disorganized neighborhoods encourage or tolerate deviant behavior.

Nature of police work theories of corruption suggest that the occupational setting of the police exposes officers to corruption opportunities. Since most officers work without direct supervision, they are easily tempted to engage in corrupt activities without fear of detection. Further, the negative aspects of policing (e.g., exposure to traumatic events, bad people, and good people doing bad things) promote cynicism that can lead to misconduct.

Some police organizational cultures tolerate, even promote, officer misconduct. Police agencies that lack organizational integrity and effective leadership are prone to corrupt activities by officers. Conversely, police organizations that value integrity and organizational commitment tend to experience fewer incidents of police misconduct.

The police subculture and its code of silence contributes to an occupational climate in which officers encourage, tolerate, or fail to report corrupt actions on the part of other officers. Peer pressure, group solidarity, and loyalty to other officers restrains honest officers from exposing corruption and misconduct (Walker & Katz, 2010).

Media accounts of police misconduct as well as reports of abuse and corruption within the police service lead many citizens to stereotype all cops as bad cops. This perception is not accurate. Yet, false assumptions persist and these assumptions help to create an environment of mistrust between the public and the police. Trust and integrity are at the very core of any good and effective relationship. The police do themselves a disservice when they do not promote a **code of conduct** or demonstrate ethical behavior, which helps to establish a climate of trust.

The consequences of unethical behavior include miscarriages of justice, nonenforcement of the law, and a poor police public image. The officer and the agency may be sued and money damages can approach millions of dollars. Individual officers involved in unethical conduct may receive a reprimand, disciplinary action, termination, or may be prosecuted criminally. Public embarrassment, humiliation of family and friends, and loss of respect are also negative by-products of unethical conduct (California Commission on Peace Officer Standards and Training, 2012).

LAW ENFORCEMENT CODES OF ETHICS AND CONDUCT

Clayton Moore, as the star of television's *Lone Ranger* series in the 1940s and 1950s, crusaded against villains on his horse, Silver, accompanied by his trusty sidekick, Tonto. In his personal as well as his professional life, Clayton Moore endeavored to live up to the provisions of the Lone Ranger Creed, including respect for democracy, truth, and the importance of fighting for what is right (Germain, 1999).

Codes of ethics and conduct are common among long-established professional groups. Persons who adhere to such codes exhibit certain qualities or traits. Professionals exhibit honesty, trustworthiness, **integrity,** fairness, tolerance, empathy, respect, responsibility, loyalty, accountability, and self-control. Professionals consistently pursue excellence in carrying out their duties. Virtually every profession establishes a code of ethics and sets forth standards of behavior for its members. The **International Association of Chiefs of Police (IACP)** developed the following Code of Ethics and Code of Conduct for law enforcement officers:

Code of Ethics

As a law enforcement officer, my fundamental duty is to: serve the community; safeguard lives and property; protect the innocent against deception, the weak against oppression or intimidation and the peaceful against violence or disorder; and respect the constitutional rights of all to liberty, equality and justice.

I will keep my private life unsullied as an example to all and will behave in a manner that does not bring discredit to me or to my agency. I will maintain courageous calm in the face of danger, scorn or ridicule; develop self-restraint; and be constantly mindful of the welfare of others. Honest in thought and deed both in my personal and official life, I will be exemplary in obeying the law and the regulations of my department. Whatever I see or hear of a confidential nature or that is confided to me in my official capacity will be kept secret unless revelation is necessary in the performance of my duty.

I will never act officiously or permit personal feelings, prejudices, political beliefs, aspirations, animosities or friendships to influence my decisions. With no compromise for crime and with relentless prosecution of criminals, I will enforce the law courteously and appropriately without fear or favor, malice or ill will, never employing unnecessary force or violence and never accepting gratuities.

I recognize the badge of my office as a symbol of public faith, and I accept it as a public trust to be held so long as I am true to the ethics of police service. I will never engage in acts of corruption or bribery, nor will I condone such acts by other police officers. I will cooperate with all legally authorized agencies and their representatives in the pursuit of justice.

I know that I alone am responsible for my own standard of professional performance and will take every reasonable opportunity to enhance and improve my level of knowledge and competence.

I will constantly strive to achieve these objectives and ideals, dedicating myself before God to my chosen profession . . . law enforcement. (International Association of Chiefs of Police, 2011a)

Code of Conduct

All law enforcement officers must be fully aware of the ethical responsibilities of their position and must strive constantly to live up to the highest possible standards of professional policing.

The International Association of Chiefs of Police believes it [is] important that police officers have clear advice and counsel available to assist them in performing their duties consistent with these standards, and has adopted the following ethical mandates as guidelines to meet these ends.

Primary Responsibilities of a Police Officer

A police officer acts as an official representative of government who is required and trusted to work within the law. The officer's powers and duties are conferred by statute. The fundamental duties of a police officer include serving the community, safeguarding lives and property, protecting the innocent, keeping the peace and ensuring the rights of all to liberty, equality and justice.

Performance of the Duties of a Police Officer

A police officer shall perform all duties impartially, without favor or affection or ill will and without regard to status, sex, race, religion, political belief or aspiration. All citizens will be treated equally with courtesy, consideration and dignity.

Officers will never allow personal feelings, animosities or friendships to influence official conduct. Laws will be enforced appropriately and courteously and, in carrying out their responsibilities, officers [sic] will strive to obtain maximum cooperation from the public. They will conduct themselves in appearance and deportment in such a manner as to inspire confidence and respect for the position of public trust they hold.

Discretion

A police officer will use responsibly the discretion vested in the officer's position and exercise it within the law. The principle of reasonableness will guide the officer's determinations, and the officer will consider all surrounding circumstances in determining whether any legal action shall be taken.

Consistent and wise use of discretion, based on professional policing competence, will do much to preserve good relationships and retain the confidence of the public. There can be difficulty in choosing between conflicting courses of action. It is important to remember that a timely word of advice rather than arrest—which may be correct in appropriate circumstances—can be a more effective means of achieving a desired end.

Use of Force

A police officer will never employ unnecessary force or violence and will use only such force in the discharge of duty as is reasonable in all circumstances.

The use of force should be used only with the greatest restraint and only after discussion, negotiation and persuasion have been found to be inappropriate or ineffective. While the use of force is occasionally unavoidable, every police officer will refrain from unnecessary infliction of pain or suffering and will never engage in cruel, degrading or inhuman treatment of any person.

Confidentiality

Whatever a police officer sees, hears or learns that is of a confidential nature will be kept secret unless the performance of duty or legal provision requires otherwise.

Members of the public have a right to security and privacy, and information obtained about them must not be improperly divulged.

Integrity

A police officer will not engage in acts of corruption or bribery, nor will an officer condone such acts by other police officers.

The public demands that the integrity of police officers be above reproach. Police officers must, therefore, avoid any conduct that might compromise integrity and thus undercut the public confidence in a law enforcement agency. Officers will refuse to accept any gifts, presents, subscriptions, favors, gratuities or promises that could be interpreted as seeking to cause the officer to refrain from performing official responsibilities honestly and within the law. Police officers must not receive private or special advantage from their official status. Respect from the public cannot be bought; it can only be earned and cultivated.

Cooperation with Other Police Officers and Agencies

Police officers will cooperate with all legally authorized agencies and their representatives in the pursuit of justice.

An officer or agency may be one among many organizations that may provide law enforcement services to a jurisdiction. It is imperative that a police officer assist colleagues fully and completely with respect and consideration at all times.

Personal—Professional Capabilities

Police officers will be responsible for their own standard of professional performance and will take every reasonable opportunity to enhance and improve their level of knowledge and competence.

Through study and experience, a police officer can acquire the high level of knowledge and competence that is essential for the efficient and effective performance of duty. The acquisition of knowledge is a never-ending process of personal and professional development that should be pursued constantly.

Private Life

Police officers will behave in a manner that does not bring discredit to their agencies or themselves.

A police officer's character and conduct while off duty must always be exemplary, thus maintaining a position of respect in the community in which he or she lives and serves. The officer's personal behavior must be beyond reproach. (International Association of Chiefs of Police, 2011b).

The IACP has developed ethics training materials for law enforcement. Referred to as the *Ethics Toolkit,* the materials are available through the IACP at www.theiacp.org.

PREVENTION AND CORRECTION OF UNETHICAL CONDUCT

Unethical behavior patterns do not develop quickly. Rather, distinctive patterns of unethical behavior develop over a period of time. Typically, these patterns are exemplified by symptoms that can be identified by police management as well as the problematic officer's peers. Symptoms include involvement in an unusually high number of use of force and resisting arrest incidents, citizen complaints, and chronic performance problems. Obviously, officers who receive an abnormally high number of citizen complaints warrant closer observation. Although complaints against a hard-working police officer are not uncommon, substantial evidence suggests that in almost all police departments, a single officer or a small group of officers account for a disproportionate number of citizen complaints. Utilizing early warning symptom reporting systems to identify problem officers can lead to timely corrective interventions. Counseling, additional training, and closer supervision designed to correct officer behavior are also effective in reducing the number of police misconduct incidents (Walker, 2001, 2003; Walker, Alpert, & Kenney, 2001).

Learn more about codes of ethics through the University of British Columbia's W. Maurice Young Centre for Applied Ethics at www.ethics.ubc.ca.

Most police officers demonstrate ethical behavior, especially if they know what is expected of them. Unethical behavior can be prevented if police agencies select the right people, communicate professional values through effective training, and deal appropriately with individuals who violate codes of conduct. Adherence to a code of ethics and standards of conduct is enhanced when officers are held accountable for their actions. When unethical conduct occurs, corrective action is necessary to retain the public's trust, maintain the integrity of the agency, and prevent misconduct in the future. Ethical officers must intervene to prevent and respond to inappropriate or criminal conduct demonstrated by other officers. Police officers must clearly communicate their values in advance, intervene verbally or physically if the situation requires immediate action, and report violations once discovered. The U.S. Constitution, state constitutional and statutory provisions, and case law support such intervention. Police agencies may take corrective action through internal integrity disciplinary proceedings (California Commission on Peace Officer Standards and Training, 2012).

Adherence to a code of ethics and standards of conduct is sometimes difficult. Police practitioners confirm the existence of an officer subculture that is characterized by an unwritten informal code of ethics, which influences officer conduct. The norms of the informal code include a requirement that officers remain loyal to their peers. Disloyalty may result in unpleasant consequences (Jones & Carlson, 2004). Although solidarity and loyalty are important ingredients to survival in virtually every occupation, maintenance of the public's trust demands adherence to standards of ethical behavior.

Evidence suggests that many police agencies fail to discipline appropriately officers who are guilty of misconduct (Walker, Spohn, & DeLone, 2011). In response, some agencies are developing guidelines for disciplining of officers. However, disciplinary action must be based on legitimate infractions and balanced to render fairness and justice in individual cases. Sometimes, the strict enforcement of policies and rules designed to prevent or correct unethical conduct can produce negative side effects. Police officer morale may suffer and productivity can decline if officer behavior is unreasonably questioned and scrutinized, especially as a result of what an officer identifies as a frivolous citizen complaint.

Response to police misconduct must go beyond intervention with the officer or officers involved. Maintaining ethical standards of conduct is an organizational as well as an individual responsibility. A positive ethical culture can be established and maintained through ethical leadership by example (inspiration), unifying individuals behind ethical behavior (collaboration), ethics education and training, and ethics integration into personal and professional lives (Walker, 2001; Whisenand & Ferguson, 2009).

The issue of police accountability, an aspect of professionalism, is critically important. As the police pursue the common good, they must be ever mindful of civil rights and they must temper their actions to ensure legal and ethical practices. The nature of policing places officers in situations in which good ends can be achieved through illegal and unethical means (Crank & Caldero, 2010). Therefore, police officers must learn and demonstrate ethical leadership skills as a means to exercising effective judgment when genuine ethical dilemmas arise (Ortmeier & Davis, 2012).

Role of Citizen Oversight

In some jurisdictions, a group of citizens reviews complaints filed against police agencies and individual officers. Often referred to as **civilian review boards** or **citizen oversight committees,** the use of such groups in the United States has expanded since the 1950s. As one solution to police misconduct problems, external citizen oversight of the police is viewed as a means for "providing input into the complaint process by individuals who are not sworn [peace] officers" (Walker, 2001, p. 5).

Citizen oversight of the police remains highly controversial. Proponents of the process contend that citizen oversight is necessary because: internal police complaint procedures fail; citizen oversight is more thorough and fair; oversight sustains more complaints; more guilty officers are disciplined; discipline leads to greater deterrence; citizen oversight is perceived as independent, providing greater satisfaction to complainants, and it improves the police public image; and oversight helps to professionalize the police. Opponents of citizen oversight argue that: police misconduct is not pervasive; police officers are capable of fair and thorough internal investigations; police internal affairs units are more effective than oversight groups; internal police disciplinary procedures are more severe, have a greater deterrent effect, and provide a higher degree of satisfaction to complainants the public; and external oversight harms policing and undermines the authority of police executives (Carlson, 2005).

Role of Police Unions

Early American police were not unionized. Actually, they were anti-union and were used as strike breakers. As a result, organized labor did not view the police in a favorable light. In addition, because bribes often supplemented police salaries, officers were not interested in unionization during the years when corruption was pervasive in policing. However, as reforms suppressed corruption and officers began to view law enforcement as a career rather than a job, police unions, fraternities, and societies became more popular among officers. In 1919, the American Federation of Labor (AFL) approved a resolution to charter local police unions. During the same time period, police officers themselves began to strike, most notably in Boston and Cincinnati. Other cities, such as Los Angeles and New York City, raised officer salaries in an effort to avoid unionization and strikes by officers.

By the 1970s, police unions existed in most major cities outside the southeastern section of the United States. Angered by low salaries, punitive management, pro-individual rights, U.S. Supreme Court decisions, charges of brutality, and perceived lack of respect, rank-and-file officers around the nation formed unions. By 2004, over 4,000 police unions existed in the United States, with the strongest union activity in major cities and sheriff departments in the Northeast and on the West Coast.

In many unionized agencies, the unions contribute greatly to the welfare of officers, the agency, and the community. In other jurisdictions, the unions are a source of conflict. They function as obstructionist vehicles for departmental dissidents. Police unions can and do fulfill a vital role as they seek to improve communication and the quality of life for police practitioners. Higher salaries negotiated by unions can attract better qualified police recruits and help retain skilled veteran officers. Unions also decrease the power of police executives, thus enhancing shared governance. They are largely responsible for introducing due process into disciplinary proceedings. On the other hand, police unions rarely advocate change. They often limit their activities to fights over power sharing with management and negotiated increases in compensation and benefits relative to terms and conditions of employment (Wadman & Allison, 2004; Zhao, 2002).

Role of the Police Subculture

The single greatest obstacle to accountability for police behavior may be the **police subculture**. A subculture is an enclave within a culture that is characterized by a distinct, integrated network of attitudes, beliefs, and behaviors. Subcultures often develop as a mechanism for self-protection and as a tool for the protection of others within the subculture. In the context of a workplace, a subculture is characterized by attitudes, values, and unwritten rules, the purpose of which is to assist the worker to survive in the occupational environment. Subcultures develop in all occupations.

Early in a career, a police recruit learns to be sensitive to, and adopt the attitudes and beliefs of, peers and superiors. In many instances, a person is accepted for employment as a police officer because the person expressed or demonstrated values similar to those of senior officers who conducted the pre-employment interview of the candidate. Regardless of pre-existing values to the contrary, once the novice enters the police subculture, the new officer is confronted with a set of police occupational values and norms, and is expected to conform behavior to the requirements of the group. To survive in the group, the officer learns early that acceptance by peers does not lend itself to independent thinking about moral or ethical dilemmas encountered on the job (Champion & Rush, 1997; Crank & Caldero, 2010; Jones & Carlson, 2004).

The personal bonding that occurs in a subculture can be dangerous if it inhibits, or even prohibits, individual moral and ethical decision making. Pressure is exerted by the group, and some within the group may lose the ability to regulate their individual behavior. In a sense, individuals within a group are victimized by the group. If individuals in the group do not participate in unethical behavior, they may, at the very least, condone the behavior by failing to intervene or report inappropriate conduct. Taken to an extreme, unethical, even illegal, police conduct may be tolerated by nonparticipant officers. The result is an environment in which participant officers are not held to account for their actions.

The major distinction between subcultures in law enforcement and other types of occupational environments is often the degree to which values and beliefs are informally promulgated and supported. Occupation-related stressors probably provide the most significant distinguishing characteristics between police work and many other occupations. The presence of danger in policing and similarly dangerous occupations reinforces the subculture and fosters remarkable group solidarity. An individual officer's welfare may depend on the availability and response of other officers. Thus, mutual support, solidarity (unity of purpose), and loyalty are critical to survival. Loyalty to the group and peers often extends beyond dangerous situations. To protect others within the subculture, officers may remain loyal to other officers involved in unethical, even criminal, conduct. The police subculture is also a defense mechanism against perceived threats from criminals, the public, the courts and defense attorneys, the media, friends, family, even the agency's administration (Cohen & Feldberg, 1991; Haberfeld, 2006; Kleinig, 1996).

Positive by-products emanate from a subculture as well. The group solidarity formed in a police subculture can elevate morale and it can promote mutual responsibility among those who share danger and stress. In crisis situations, loyalty and mutual support are critical to success. Through training, teamwork, and group solidarity, the police can prevent and de-escalate conflict and violence. Subsequent to a crisis situation, the mutual support provided by members of the subculture are essential to the emotional and psychological health of the officers involved in the crisis. Especially in officer-involved death cases, whether it is the death of a criminal suspect or another officer, group support is absolutely essential to the maintenance of good mental health of the officers (Jones & Carlson, 2004).

There is no way to avoid the moral dimensions of police work (Cohen & Feldberg, 1991). At times, police officers are confronted with particularly difficult and challenging dilemmas (Crank & Caldero, 2010; Klockars, 1991). Officers may be forced to choose between group solidarity and loyalty to others and the need to prevent, intercept, or report unethical behavior. This is especially true when officers witness unprofessional conduct on the part of other officers. However, officers must strive to retain their sensitivity toward thinking and behaving in a morally and ethically correct manner regardless of the perceived personal and professional consequences (Meese & Ortmeier, 2004).

CONCEPTS OF LEADERSHIP

Effective leadership is essential in law enforcement and criminal justice and leadership development should occur at all ranks. Yet the study of leadership can be difficult because it is misunderstood. Definitions of leadership vary and the process for leadership development is often vague. As exemplified by the following discussion on leadership concepts and theories, the study of leadership is often abstract, dull, and uninteresting.

However, substantial evidence exists that leads progressive thinkers to one conclusion: Leadership skills are essential for all police officers in contemporary society.

True leadership is for the benefit of the followers, not the enrichment of the leaders (Townsend, 1970). The universal phenomenon called leadership has been the subject of a great deal of research from both the theoretical and the practical points of view. Leadership has been described variously as a trait, the focus of group process, the art of inducing compliance, an exercise of influence, a kind of behavior or act, a form of persuasion, a power relationship, an instrument in goal attainment, an effective interaction, a differentiated role, and an initiation of structure (Bass, 1990). Leadership has also been defined in terms of acts or behaviors (Carter, 1953), an act that results in others acting or responding in a shared direction (Shartle, 1956), the process of arranging a situation to achieve common goals (Bellows, 1959), and the initiation and maintenance of structure in interaction and expectation (Stogdill, 1959). It has been defined as directing and coordinating work relationships while showing consideration (Fiedler, 1967), an activity that mobilizes people to do something (Heifetz, 1994), and as a social meaning-making process that takes place as a result of activity or work in a group (Drath & Palus, 1994).

Leadership is a process through which a person influences others to achieve a common goal (Northouse, 2009). Within the context of a policing environment, leadership can be defined as the ability to influence or mobilize individual citizens, groups, businesses, and public and private agencies to act together and participate in activities designed to discover and implement solutions to community-based problems (Meese & Ortmeier, 2004; Ortmeier, 1996; Ortmeier & Davis, 2012).

Leadership is Not Management

Leadership should not be confused with management. Leadership, a concept that is broader than management, occurs anytime one attempts to motivate, influence, or mobilize an individual or group. **Management,** on the other hand, involves directing people toward organizational goals (Hersey & Blanchard, 1996). Although management and leadership may be exercised or exhibited by the same individual, both represent distinct concepts. Leadership produces change by establishing direction, aligning people, and motivating and inspiring. Management brings a measure of order and consistency to organizations by planning and budgeting, organizing and staffing, and controlling (Kotter, 1990). In other words, management follows leadership (Covey, 1998).

When considering the distinction between leadership and management, one must examine two different courses of life history: (1) leadership development through socialization, which prepares the individual to guide institutions and maintain the existing balance in social relations, and (2) development through personal mastery, which impels an individual to struggle for psychological and social change. Society produces its managerial talent through the first course of life history, while leaders emerge through the second course (Zaleznik, 1993).

Bennis (1993b, p. 214) distinguished leadership from management by stating the following:

- The manager administers; the leader innovates.
- The manager is a copy; the leader is an original.
- The manager maintains; the leader develops.
- The manager focuses on systems and structure; the leader focuses on people.
- The manager relies on control; the leader inspires trust.
- The manager has a short-range view; the leader has a long-range perspective.
- The manager asks how and when; the leader asks what and why.
- The manager has his eye on the bottom line; the leader has his eye on the horizon.
- The manager accepts the status quo; the leader challenges it.
- The manager is the classic good soldier; the leader is his own person.
- The manager does things right; the leader does the right thing.

As one author stated, the leader is the one who climbs the tallest tree, surveys the situation, and cries out, "Wrong jungle!" The manager responds with, "Shut up! We are making progress" (Covey, 1998).

Theoretical Foundation for Leadership

For many years, the most common approach to the study of leadership concentrated on leadership traits, suggesting that there were certain characteristics or superior qualities that differentiated the leader from nonleaders (Stogdill, 1948). Bernard (1926) explained leadership in terms of traits of personality and character. Thus, a **leadership trait (leadership quality)** was defined in terms of inborn characteristics unique to an individual. However, a review of the research using the trait approach to leadership has revealed few significant or consistent findings (Stogdill, 1948).

Early in the twentieth century, definitions of leadership viewed the leader as a focus for group change activity and process. According to this view, the leader is always the nucleus of the group (Cooley, 1902). Frederick Taylor (1911), a major theorist of the scientific management movement, viewed people as instruments or machines to be manipulated by their leaders. In essence, the scientific management movement emphasized the concern for output. Sigmund Freud (1922), a psychoanalytical theorist, saw the leader as a father figure, a source of love or fear, as the embodiment of the super-ego, and as the emotional outlet for followers' frustrations and destructive aggression.

In the 1920s and 1930s, the human relations movement emerged. According to human relations theorists, the organization is developed around the workers and takes human feelings and attitudes into account. The main focus, contrary to the scientific management movement, was on the needs of the individual rather than the needs of the organization (Mayo, 1945).

Cowley (1928) defined a leader as a person who has a specific program and in a definite manner is moving toward an objective with his group. Schenk (1928) suggested that leadership involves persuasion and inspiration rather than direct or implied threat of coercion. Bogardus (1929) suggested that leadership, as a social process, is a social interstimulation that causes people to set out toward an old goal with new zest or a new goal with hopeful courage. Through this view, leadership was not the cause of group action, but was an effect of it. J. F. Brown (1936) proposed five field-dynamic laws of leadership. According to Brown, leaders must have membership character in the group they are attempting to lead, represent a region of high potential in the social field, adapt themselves to the existing field structure, realize longterm trends in field structure, and recognize that leadership increases in potency at the cost of a reduction in the freedom of leadership.

Barnard (1938) declared that theories of leadership cannot be constructed for behavior in a vacuum. The theories must contain elements about persons as well as situations. In other words, leadership must focus on the interaction between the situation and the individual. The focus in the situational approach to leadership is on observed behavior, not on hypothetical inborn or acquired traits (Hemphill, 1949). For Fiedler (1967), the effectiveness of a given pattern of leader behavior is actually contingent on the demands imposed by the situation. And, according to Pfeffer (1977), understanding a leader's behavior involves exploring the leader's mind in order to determine what the leader is thinking about the situation in which leadership occurs.

Both trait theorists and situational theorists attempted to explain leadership as the impact of a single set of forces. The interactive effects of individual and situational factors were overlooked (Bass, 1981). Leadership, therefore, appeared as a manner of interaction involving behavior by and toward an individual who is lifted to a leadership role by other individuals (Jennings, 1944) and is defined in terms of the origination of interaction based on the basic variables of action, interaction, and sentiments (Homans, 1950). Each participant in this interaction is said to play a role and that one person, the leader, influences, and the other people in the group respond (Gordon, 1955).

The ability to motivate, influence, or persuade has been noted as an important element in the definition of leadership. Nash (1929) suggested that leadership implies influencing change in the conduct of people. Cleeton and Mason (1934) suggested that leadership indicates the ability to influence people and secure results through emotional appeals rather than through the exercise of authority. Tead (1935) defined leadership as the activity of influencing people to cooperate toward finding some goal that they may find desirable. Copeland (1942) maintained that leadership is the art of dealing with human nature—it is the art of influencing a body of people by persuasion or example to follow a line of action. Stogdill (1950) defined leadership as the process or act of influencing activities of an organized group in its efforts toward goal setting and goal achievement.

Tannenbaum and Schmidt (1958) believed that leaders could influence followers by either of two methods. They could tell their followers what to do and how to do it. Alternately, they could share their leadership responsibilities with their followers by involving them in the planning and the execution of the task. Blake and Mouton (1965) conceptualized leadership in terms of a managerial grid in which an individual's concerns for people were compared to concerns for production. An individual who rated high in both areas developed followers who are committed to accomplishing goals in a relationship of trust and respect. Likert (1967) suggested that leaders must take the expectations, values, and interpersonal skills of others into account. Leaders could build group cohesiveness and motivation for productivity by providing freedom for responsible decision-making and exercise of initiative.

Hersey and Blanchard (1972) synthesized Blake and Mouton's managerial grid and suggested that leader behavior is related to the maturity of the people being led. Maturity was defined in terms of the nonleaders' experience, achievement, motivation, willingness, and ability to accept responsibility. As the maturity of nonleaders increased, the leader's involvement decreased. Finally, Osborn and Hunt (1975) suggested that leadership theory must take into account and be sensitive to the larger environment in which leaders and nonleaders are embedded.

An important breakthrough in understanding the concept of leadership occurred with the publication of *Leadership* by James MacGregor Burns. Burns (1978) characterized leaders either as transactional (when one person takes the initiative, making contact with others for the purpose of the exchange of valued things) or transformational (when one or more persons engage with others in a way in which the leader and nonleader raise one another to higher levels of motivation and morality). Examples of transactional leadership through a contingent reward approach can be found in *The One Minute Manager* (Blanchard & Johnson, 1992). The function of transactional leadership is to maintain the organization's operation rather than to change it (Burns & Becker, 1988). Transformational leadership, on the other hand, focuses on the three behavior patterns of charisma, intellectual stimulation, and individualized consideration (Bass, 1985). Tichy and Ulrich (1984) presented the transformational leader as the model for future leadership excellence. They cited three identifiable activities associated with transformational leadership: creation of vision—view of a future state, mobilization of commitment—acceptance of a new mission, and institutionalization of change—new patterns of behavior must be adopted.

It is apparent that there are about as many leadership theories as there are theorists to describe the leadership phenomenon (Northouse, 2009). Yet, leadership theories help explain the concepts and dynamics of leadership. Knowledge of the concepts and dynamics assists with the creation of approaches to the development of leadership competence.

Leadership Competencies

Although the study of leadership originally focused on traits or inbred qualities that a person possessed since birth, today it is believed that leadership skills can be acquired or modified extensively through learning. These skills include competency in keeping communication channels open and functioning effectively, interacting socially, solving problems, planning, initiating action, and accepting responsibility. Such skills are not inherited, they are learned (McGregor, 1960). Also critical to the success of the leader are skills in facilitation of team interaction, effective team problem solving, and training (Miskin & Gmelch, 1985), with substantial attention being paid to the ability to communicate (K. L. Clark, 1994).

More specifically, an effective leader is likely to demonstrate excellent communications and interpersonal skills. A highly rated leader is likely to be both relations oriented and task-oriented, manage conflict successfully, and mobilize and direct individuals toward higher objectives (Bass, 1981). Bisesi (1983) suggested that successful leaders are willing to negotiate and have a high sense of organizational responsibility. Orton (1984) cited the importance of quality decision-making, commitment, implementation, and the ability to employ situational strategies. The inability to communicate and relate to other individuals may lead to conflict or incompatibility between the leader and those who are led (Smith & Peterson, 1990).

Motivational, or person-oriented, behaviors tend to promote follower satisfaction although they may not contribute to group productivity (Bass, 1981). McGregor (1966) suggested that people already possess motivation and desire full responsibility. Yukl (1971) postulated that whereas leader initiation increases subordinate task skill, leader consideration increases subordinate motivation. In turn, subordinate skill and motivation improve the subordinate's effectiveness.

Leadership competencies have also been addressed in terms of the ability to plan, organize, and set goals. Bennis (1961) suggested a revision in leadership theory to include participation in joint consultation between the leader and others to allow for integration of individual as well as organizational goals. Leaders must create clear-cut and measurable goals based on the advice from all elements of a community. Likert (1961) discovered that high-producing leaders make clear what the objectives are and give people freedom to complete the task. Argyris (1964) suggested that it is in an individual's nature to be self-directed and seek fulfillment through the exercise of initiative and responsibility. Hersey and Blanchard (1996) suggested that leadership, depending on the situation, involves goal setting, organizing, setting time lines, directing, and controlling.

Knickerbocker (1948) suggested that the functional relation called leadership exists when a leader is perceived by a group as controlling the means for the satisfaction of their needs. Group members make contributions and continue to interact because the members find social exchange mutually rewarding (Homans, 1958). Changing the expectations for rewards changes the motivation of the individual or the group (Bass, 1960). Evans (1970) suggested that the leader can determine the follower's perception of the abundance of the rewards available. Scott (1977) emphasized positive reinforcement as a means of bringing out desired behavior.

Contemporary Views on Leadership Competencies

Studies have shown that a high-priority leadership attribute is competence (Kouzes & Posner, 1993). Accordingly, contemporary authors often focus on leadership competencies. Bennis (1984, 1993a) identified four competencies of leadership.

- Management of attention—the ability to attract followers
- Management of meaning—the ability to communicate one's viewpoint or vision
- Management of trust—reliability
- Management of self—the ability to know one's skills and use them effectively

Daniel (1992) identified 13 leadership competencies. They include the following:

- Goal orientation
- Bottom-line orientation
- Communicates and enforces standards
- Initiative
- Strategic influence
- Communicates confidence
- Interpersonal sensitivity
- Develops and coaches others
- Gives performance feedback
- Collaboration and team building
- Systematic problem solving
- Image and reputation
- Self-confidence

Kotter (1993) pointed out that good leaders articulate a vision, involve people in decision-making, provide coaching, feedback, and role modeling, and finally, recognize and reward success. Drath and Palus (1994, pp. 22–23) refer to leadership as "a social meaning-making process that takes place as a result of activity or work in a group." They went on to state that leaders must be trained to participate in, rather than exercise, leadership by learning community-oriented, meaning-making capacities, such as the capacity to understand oneself as both an individual and as a socially embedded being, the capacity to understand systems in general as being mutually related, interacting, and continually changing, the capacity to take the perspective of another, and the capacity to engage in dialogue. Leaders must be flexible (Bridges, 1994) and demonstrate initiative, integrity, and the ability to empower others (Davids, 1995). They must give support, communicate, facilitate interaction, listen actively, and provide feedback (Hersey & Blanchard, 1996).

In the final analysis, there is no great divergence in central themes or philosophies regarding leadership, only differences in opinion with respect to the effectiveness of leadership approaches and the application of competencies (Wolfson, 1986). The real test of leadership lies in the performance of the groups being led (Bass, 1981) and the competencies required depending on the situation, the people involved, the action to be taken, and the desired results (Byrnbauer & Tyson, 1984). In the technologically advanced society of the future, leadership will be open to, and required of, all workers (Drucker, 1994).

LEADERSHIP IN POLICING

Introduction

Fear of crime, police responses to social unrest, and citizen perceptions of police effectiveness contribute to the rise or the decline in community support for the police. Although experts in a study conducted in 1995 indicated that police training and education programs do an excellent job of assisting police officers in the development of procedural and technical skills, these programs do little to promote the development of essential nontechnical competencies and qualities such as effective judgment, leadership, and integrity, all of which help generate community support (Ortmeier, 1996; Tyler & Wakslak, 2004). The rationale in support of leadership development for police officers may be summarized as follows:

- A community receives the type of police service it supports (Wilson, 1968).
- Community support is "absolutely vital" to successful law enforcement and this support is dependent on a positive police public image. (Coffey, 1990).
- The police public image is dependent on the public's confidence in the integrity and judgment of the police as well as the process and outcomes of human interaction between the individual police officer and the citizens.
- Police behavior is determined not only by the psychological dynamics of the nature of the work, but also by the preservice and in-service training police officers are given in police academies, college classrooms, and by fellow senior officers on the street. Simply stated, bad habits and bad attitudes are passed on from one generation of police officers to the next.
- Curricula in police academies, college-level criminal justice programs, and even on-the-job training programs, generally lack the focus necessary to develop the affective skills required for communications, human relations, critical thinking, problem solving, leadership, and integrity, which are absolutely essential to success in contemporary law enforcement.
- To secure and retain the trust of the citizenry, police officers must maintain the highest standards of personal and professional conduct by demonstrating leadership (Ortmeier, 1996; Ortmeier & Meese, 2010).

Leadership skills are among the most important competencies for a line police officer. Yet, leadership skill development is often reserved for the higher level ranks in a police agency. Many reasons for this phenomenon exist. One is the false assumption that the line officers simply follow the lead presented by the higher ranks. Nevertheless, within a policing environment, considerable attention must be given to officer competencies such as leadership that traditionally have been associated with higher ranks (Carter, Sapp, & Stephens, 1989). However, leadership of this character is not likely to develop on its own. If leadership competencies are to emerge from within the police establishment, incentives must be developed to afford police officers the opportunity to acquire a broad-based education (President's Commission on Law Enforcement and Administration of Justice, 1967). Police officers, particularly in today's policing environment, must develop leadership competencies to grasp a vision, transmit it, and help translate it into constructive action (Carlson, 2005; Meese & Ortmeier, 2004; Ortmeier, 1997, 2003; Souryal, 1981).

Although leadership is a dynamic phenomenon requiring integration of numerous attributes, qualities, and skills, it is, essentially, a means to influence, mobilize, or motivate others to accomplish common goals (California Commission on Peace Officer Standards and Training, 1990). Skolnick and Bayley (1986) reinforced the importance of leadership skills to the success of policing by stating that these skills are necessary to create a sense of purpose for the operation of a police agency. This sense of purpose emphasizes civic responsibility, self-knowledge, and a global perspective (Green, 1988). Utilizing this sense of purpose, citizens should be viewed as customers and the police should be viewed as leaders providing a community service (Haberfeld, 2006; Meese & Kurz, 1993).

With the passage of the Omnibus Crime Control Act of 1968, literally billions of dollars were spent on law enforcement training and education. As a result, the United States witnessed a proliferation of college-level education programs for preservice as well as in-service law

Leadership skills are essential for frontline officers because they have the most contact with the public. Line officers are in the best position to directly impact the lives of citizens.
(Photo courtesy of the Los Angeles Sheriff's Department.)

enforcement personnel. Through the Law Enforcement Education Program (LEEP), funded by 1968 legislation, the number of undergraduate criminal justice–related degree programs rose from 39 in 1967 to 376 in 1977 (Walker, 1999). The programs were founded on the belief that an increased level of education would produce a police officer who was more responsive and accountable to the public and an officer who could deal effectively with crime and improve the quality of life for American citizens.

However, beginning with the late 1960s, the crime rate continued to increase at a rapid pace (U.S. Department of Justice, Federal Bureau of Investigation, 1995). In addition, police alienation from the community continued to manifest itself as the result of incidents such as the riots that occurred subsequent to the Rodney King verdict in Los Angeles in April 1992.

More recently, Congress passed another multibillion-dollar crime bill (U.S. Congress, 1994). Federal dollars were again budgeted for law enforcement training and education. However, several questions persist. Aside from technical training and education, how should these dollars have been spent? Do police training and educational programs assist officers in the development of the nontechnical competencies such as leadership that are required of police officers in contemporary society? More specifically, which leadership skills are required of the police so they may restore and improve public confidence and lead communities to identify and solve problems?

Research Regarding Police Leadership

Beginning with the 1990s, several studies were conducted to identify essential police leadership competencies. Most of the studies focused on supervisory- and management-level leadership, while a few addressed leadership skills required of frontline–level officers. In 1995, Ortmeier conducted a study to identify essential front line–officer leadership competencies. The study was the first to address leadership skills at the street officer level (Ortmeier, 1996). In 1996, Anderson and King conducted two studies through the Justice Institute of British Columbia. The purposes of the Anderson and King studies were to identify necessary leadership skills for supervisors and managers in the police community and public justice and safety sectors in British Columbia (Anderson & King, 1996a, 1996b). Similar studies were subsequently conducted with the Vancouver, British Columbia, police, and the San Diego, California, Police Department.

In 1997, through a project sponsored by the International Association of Chiefs of Police (IACP), the Federal Law Enforcement Training Center (FLETC), in conjunction with the Royal Canadian Mounted Police (RCMP), developed a list of leadership competencies for all police officers. The FLETC/RCMP list includes core leadership values that were identified as the foundation for the core leadership competencies. The FLETC/RCMP core values list includes integrity, honesty, professionalism, compassion, respect, accountability, fairness, and courage. The FLETC/RCMP core leadership competencies list are categorized in eight major competency groups: change management, communication, relationship building, service orientation, critical thinking, action management, sharing power and creating opportunity, and inspiration and motivation (Anderson, 2000). In a 2001 study, Morreale (2002) discovered that leadership competence, especially as exemplified by those demonstrating a transformational leadership style, increased line officer willingness to exert extra effort, and improved officer job satisfaction.

The study conducted by Ortmeier in 1995 solicited responses to questions regarding the need for police leadership development at the operational (front line–officer) level. The study focused on the leadership competencies perceived as essential for police practitioners in an environment that emphasizes community participation, engagement, and problem solving—all of which are essential ingredients to effective policing. For purposes of the study, a competency was defined as a highly specialized knowledge or skill that relates directly to the mastery of specific capabilities of a police officer that can be measured objectively. Leadership was defined as the ability to influence or mobilize individual citizens, groups, businesses, and public and private agencies to act together and participate in activities designed to discover and implement solutions to community problems. Leadership competency was defined as the skill, or set of skills, necessary to promote community engagement, participation, and problem solving (Meese & Ortmeier, 2004; Ortmeier, 1996).

Participants in the study included Herman Goldstein, who is considered the father of problem-oriented policing, former U.S. Attorney General Edwin Meese III, police executives, and line officers throughout the United States as well as law enforcement scholars from Harvard and Stanford Universities, the John Jay College of Criminal Justice, and other institutions. Ultimately, the results of the study should be used to develop a strategy for increasing the quality of law enforcement practice through the improvement of law enforcement leadership training and education, leadership competency in individual officers, and police effectiveness. In essence, the strategy will connect the police to the community through better police leadership and public relations practices. Implementation of the strategy will promote behaviors consistent with contemporary policing requirements and will assist officers in the development of the leadership competencies necessary to effectively connect with the public and implement problem-oriented community policing.

The research design for the study was qualitative, utilizing the Delphi Technique. The benefit of qualitative research, and probably its greatest strength, is that it not only provides information to make decisions but also uncovers decisions that need to be made (Levine, 1982). The study uncovered information for curriculum decisions that need to be made in the development of a law enforcement leadership training and education strategy. Current literature demonstrates a recognition for the unique responsibilities of police personnel and the difficulty of quantifying skills for the qualitative law enforcement job tasks. The police hold a unique position with respect to public trust and responsibility. Furthermore, decision-making in police work includes the added dimension of unquantifiable judgment. Therefore, a qualitative research design and the Delphi Technique were well suited to this study.

The procedures utilized in the study included a series of three questionnaires that were consistent with those typically followed in the Delphi process. Three rounds of data were collected and analyzed. After every round the ratings for each item were tabulated and a composite rating was computed. Subsequently, the composite rating for each item was written on the next questionnaire so all panel members could view the composite rating of the group as well as their own individual ratings. At no time during the process were panelists informed as to how other individual members of the panel rated these items.

Essential Police Leadership Competencies

The leadership competencies identified as essential for line police officers in the Ortmeier study were grouped in five major categories. The **communications and related interpersonal competencies** category addresses one's ability to communicate with diverse populations. **Problem solving competencies** focus on problem identification and situation analysis. Through **motivational competencies,** a person demonstrates the ability to encourage others and build proactive relationships. **Planning and organizing competencies** are used to create a vision, prioritize, delegate, and define goals and objectives. **Actuation/implementation competencies** address the ability to implement a vision and evaluate results. The categories and competencies grouped within them are listed as follows.

Communications and Related Interpersonal Competencies. A police officer should be able to:

- Demonstrate effective verbal communication skills.
- Demonstrate effective listening skills.
- Demonstrate effective counseling skills.
- Demonstrate knowledge of different ethnic and racial cultures.
- Demonstrate empathy in a multicultural society.
- Facilitate interaction.
- Maintain group cohesiveness and member satisfaction.
- Demonstrate effective public speaking skills.
- Prepare effective, clear written communications.

Problem-Solving Competencies. A police officer should be able to:

- Analyze situations.
- Identify and evaluate constituent needs.
- Identify problems.
- Analyze problems.
- Employ situational strategies.
- Demonstrate the ability to mediate and/or negotiate.
- Provide means for goal attainment.
- Demonstrate diagnostic and hierarchical prescriptive skills.

Motivational Competencies.   A police officer should be able to:
- Encourage creativity and innovation.
- Act as a catalyst and arouse proaction.
- Engage in team building.
- Develop cooperative relationships.
- Demonstrate persistence and continuity.
- Demonstrate enthusiasm.
- Demonstrate commitment to assignment.
- Recognize and encourage responsible leaders.
- Demonstrate intellectual curiosity.

Planning and Organizing Competencies.   A police officer should be able to:
- Promote change.
- Create and maintain a vision.
- Define objectives and maintain goal direction.
- Prioritize tasks.
- Demonstrate ability to organize resources.
- Assign tasks effectively.
- Create and maintain a psychologically safe environment to encourage open communication.
- Provide for and maintain group process.
- Demonstrate effective delegation skills.

Actuation/Implementation Competencies.   A police officer should be able to:
- Translate a vision into action.
- Complete multiple projects on schedule.
- Evaluate measurable individual and group goals.
- Demonstrate capacity to represent interests and concerns of others.
- Demonstrate knowledge of, and articulate the reality of, an organization's impact.
- Demonstrate ability to learn from mistakes (Ortmeier, 1996).

Overall, the results of the study indicate that skills in effective verbal communication, listening, and demonstration of empathy or understanding in a multicultural society are essential. The ability to identify problems, make commitments, understand the reality of the police impact on crime, analyze situations, demonstrate persistence, employ situational strategies, and recognize solutions to problems are also essential competencies. Summarily, the ability to communicate, identify problems, think critically, and engage in team building and group problem solving are highly rated leadership competencies necessary for the police officer.

In essence, the underlying concepts of policing support police officer competencies that assist the community in the creation of a vision for its future. They support the creation of a process through which the community may assist itself in the identification and development of solutions to problems as well as the ability to take action in solving those problems.

CASE STUDY—A LEADERSHIP SCENARIO

Annual citizen surveys conducted in Chicago's Latino neighborhoods between 1994 and 2001 revealed that residents perceived that neighborhood conditions had deteriorated dramatically. They expressed concerns about gang violence, burglary, auto theft, drug dealing, abandoned vehicles, graffiti, and lack of order maintenance in and around the city's schools. Language appeared to play an important role in the residents' perceptions of the extent of neighborhood problems. Residents whose language preference was Spanish rated neighborhood problems as more serious than did their English-speaking Latino counterparts (Skogan, 2005; Skogan, Steiner, DuBois, Gudell, & Fagan, 2002).

1. Which leadership competencies (skills) should front line (street level) police officers use to help solve neighborhood problems perceived by the residents?
2. Do citizen perceptions affect police performance?

Some experts argue that the traditional paramilitary structure and attitudes of the police service are inconsistent with contemporary community needs (Champion & Rush, 1997). Traditionally, reporting of crime and other problems to the police has been the most frequent method by which the police have become aware that someone has been victimized or traumatized by criminal or other problematic activity. However, citizen reporting and police efficiency may be encouraged and improved through effective leadership in policing (U.S. Department of Justice, Bureau of Justice Statistics, 1992). Effective leadership may also increase the public's confidence in the integrity and judgment of the police as well as improve the process and outcomes of human interaction between the individual police officer and the citizens.

Leadership may still be viewed as a management function by some authorities. However, these skills are also required of the line police officer to improve public confidence and lead communities to identify and solve problems. Officers must be able to create and sustain community interest and activity in the law enforcement effort by fostering an environment that reinforces positive behavior and results. In essence, management follows leadership but does not supersede it. Contemporary policing requires competencies beyond those traditionally taught in police academies and college classrooms. Efforts should be made to incorporate affective competencies, such as those associated with leadership, into current curricula.

Recent initiatives demonstrate that affective competency development has become a top priority in many areas. Leadership and ethics as well as community policing concepts and skill development are being integrated with other subjects in some basic police academy training curricula (California State, Commission on Peace Officer Standards and

Training, 2003). The John Jay College of Criminal Justice in New York City launched a program designed to help rookie police officers as well as supervisors develop leadership skills (Supplying what the police academy doesn't, 2004). In addition, a leadership and ethics education program has been developed to prepare a cadre of ethical leaders to fill vacancies created as police managers and executives exit the police service. Known as the California Public Safety Leadership and Ethics Program (CP-SLEP), the four-course certificate program targets pre-service and in-service pre-supervisory professionals from all public safety disciplines, including police, fire, and corrections. The program was modeled after the Phi Theta Kappa International Honor Society Leadership Development Studies Program (Byrd, 2003/2004).

The Federal Law Enforcement Training Center has also begun offering an eight-day program designed to train law enforcement supervisors in leadership skills. The program draws on expertise from the private sector (including management of people, organizational processes, and technology). It focuses on human capital development; law enforcement mission and culture; and the application of leadership knowledge, skills, and abilities to foster accountability (Federal Law Enforcement Training Center, 2011).

Police officer leadership competency development can no longer be ignored. A review of the literature, expert opinion, and study results support the perception that leadership competencies are essential for contemporary police officers. The paramilitary automatons of the present must be replaced with self-contained human leadership agents who can guide communities safely through the twenty-first century (Meese & Ortmeier, 2004; Ortmeier, 1996, 1997, 2003; Ortmeier & Davis, 2012).

◢ SUMMARY

The new vision for police professionalism includes adherence to a code of ethics and standards of professional conduct. Unethical behavior can be prevented if police agencies select the right people, communicate professional values, train effectively, and deal appropriately with individuals who violate the code of conduct. Citizen oversight, police labor unions, and police subcultures have had a tremendous impact on police behavior. In addition to the need for professionalism and ethics in the police profession, leadership skill development is necessary for line officers and command staff, as well as other criminal justice personnel.

DISCUSSION QUESTIONS AND EXERCISES

1. How important is professionalism and ethics in law enforcement? Explain.
2. Two officers respond to the scene of a reported burglary at a residence. While interviewing the victim, the first officer sees the second officer take a watch from a table and conceal it, apparently intending to steal the watch. How should the first officer respond?

3. Should police officers be held to higher moral and ethical standards than the population they serve?

4. The law enforcement code of ethics states that officers should not act officiously and they should enforce the law courteously. What does this mean? Do all officers practice this portion of the code?

5. What types of off-duty, private behavior discredit the police profession? Should departmental policy regulate off-duty, private behavior?

6. Create a definition for leadership.

7. Distinguish leadership qualities from leadership competencies or skills. How can leadership skills be developed?

8. Is leadership development important for everyone in the police profession? Why or why not?

9. While driving a personal vehicle, an off-duty police officer (ODO) was stopped for speeding by a highway patrol officer (HPO). As the HPO approached the violator's vehicle, the ODO stated that a firearm was present. The HPO did not cite the driver when it was discovered that the traffic violator was an off-duty law enforcement officer. The violation was excused as a matter of "professional courtesy." Later, while visiting with friends, the ODO claimed to have used the same strategy to avoid traffic citations in the past. Was the off-duty officer's behavior unethical? Did the highway patrol officer's failure to cite demonstrate unethical behavior?

10. A rookie police officer assists a senior officer and a supervising sergeant with the arrest of a violent criminal suspect. After a brief struggle, the suspect is subdued, handcuffed, and incapacitated. However, the senior officer continues to punch the suspect, although the suspect offers no resistance. The sergeant observes the punching but does not intervene. Should the rookie officer assume a leadership role and intervene to stop the physical abuse of the suspect? If so, how should the rookie officer proceed?

Communications

LEARNING OBJECTIVES

After completing this chapter, the reader should be able to:

- describe the importance of effective verbal and interpersonal communications in a policing environment.
- articulate the techniques of communication in various law enforcement situations.
- demonstrate verbal communications skills appropriate to the situation.
- integrate knowledge of cross-cultural communications in one-on-one or group communication environments.
- manage communication conflict.
- demonstrate effective tactical communications skills.
- describe the importance of good notes and reports.
- discuss the purpose of notes.
- discuss the purpose of reports.
- list and describe types of reports.
- document the results of an investigation.
- list and describe parts of report.
- demonstrate effective written communications skills appropriate to law enforcement.

KEY TERMS

Define, describe, or explain the importance of each of the following.

Agency-specific report
Challenges to effective communication
Communication
Communication conflict
Contact report
Cross-cultural communication
Field notes
Incident report
Interpersonal communication
Memoranda

Note taking
Phonetic alphabet
Public speaking
Report writing
Supplemental report
Tactical communication
Task force
Teamwork
Ten (10)-code system
Traffic collision report

INTRODUCTION

Social order, harmony, and positive human discourse depend, to a great extent, on the participants' ability to communicate through a common language. This is especially true in policing because officers spend up to 70 percent of their working time in communication with others (O'Keefe, 2004; Whisenand & Ferguson, 2009). The results of a study conducted by the author revealed that the ability to communicate is one of the most important skills for a police officer. The results of the study indicate that policing experts agree that effective communications skills are critical to officer success in policing (Ortmeier, 1996). The ability to listen and communicate effectively to individuals and groups, verbally and in writing, facilitates interaction and helps maintain group cohesiveness and citizen satisfaction. Excellent communication also assists in any advisory effort, promotes harmony between and among different ethnic groups, and helps to create empathy in a multicultural society. The ability to speak and write with clarity, listen actively, negotiate, persuade, and comprehend what is read is critical to the safety and performance of the modern-day law enforcement officer (U.S. Department of Labor, 2004).

Notions about crime and justice are related to an individual's view of the world. A good communicator can facilitate understanding. Effective communication between the police and the public reduces victim distress and encourages citizen crime prevention activities. It de-escalates emotion during crisis situations, which are reflective of a high percentage of police incidents. Policing also requires that people be brought together to identify and solve common problems. Communication is the key to positive interaction and dialog, which is an important ingredient in problem-solving efforts (Schneider, 2003). Poor communication, on the other hand, can result in misunderstandings and may ultimately lead to deadly consequences.

As many as 100 definitions for communication exist. Simply stated, **communication** is a process, rather than an event, that involves the exchange of information (Wallace, Roberson, & Steckler, 2009). Through effective communication, people transmit, share, and receive ideas, facts, values, attitudes, and opinions. Communication helps to form a person's identity (self-concept), fulfills a social need, and it assists with the transmission of thought (Adler & Elmhorst, 2009; Adler & Towne, 2012; Meese & Ortmeier, 2004).

Communication takes place through a variety of media, each of which has relevancy in policing. During the intrapersonal communications process, one thinks, reasons, evaluates, and speaks with oneself. Through interpersonal communications, individuals interact with each other, learning about one another's feelings, beliefs, and desires. In group communication, a limited number of people share ideas, identify and solve problems, and often develop new ideas through the synergism of the group. Through public communication, individuals address an audience and attempt to inform or influence others to think and act in a particular manner. During the mass communications process, the media is used to persuade or entertain huge audiences. Machine-assisted communication utilizes technology and cyberspace to converse and exchange information (Gamble & Gamble, 2005).

There are many myths and false assumptions associated with the communication process (Galanes, Adams, & Brilhart, 2007).

- Many people believe they are good communicators when they are not. Most people do not reflect on their own communication deficiencies and, therefore, do little or nothing to improve.
- Another false assumption is that all human problems are communications problems. Human beings are encumbered in many ways—only one of which is poor communication. For example, citizens and officers in a policing environment may wish to improve the quality of life in a ghetto neighborhood. However, many quality of life issues and mechanisms, such as economic conditions, are beyond the control of the police.
- Good communication techniques guarantee good communication. This myth fails to account for an ingredient critical to effective communication: attitude. Communication is enhanced when one demonstrates sincerity and willingness to improve. People will forgive communication mishaps when the communicator's basic intentions are good.
- The receiver misunderstood the communication. This myth fails to account for the two-way process involved in communications. Both sender and receiver must cooperate to promote unambiguous, mutually understood messages. If a message is misunderstood, both sender and receiver must share the responsibility for the misunderstanding.
- Good communication on both sides always results in understanding. This is another myth. Perfect communication and understanding are not possible. Some communication is intended to be misleading. During an interrogation, for example, a police officer may wish to convince a suspect that a codefendant has already confessed. In other cases, the communicator may be trying to avoid hurting another's feelings. Clearly, however, when the intended outcome is mutual understanding, participants in the communications process should strive for perfection.

Communication is a complex, two-way process. The source of a message (the sender) formulates a mental image of the thought to be communicated, converts the thought to an appropriate transmission medium (verbal, physical expressions or gestures, or writing) and transmits the message to a receiver. If the message is properly formulated and transmitted, and if the receiver understands the message, the communication process is complete. Very often, however, differences in gender, age, intelligence, education, personal biases, and vocation, as well as language barriers and adverse circumstances, may inhibit the communication process. Intended meanings can be distorted through improper or inappropriate communication.

The effectiveness of communication is also determined by the circumstances in which the communication takes place. Noise distorts and interferes with the ability to send and receive messages. The context, or manner, in which the communication is presented can affect the receiver's interpretation of the message. Positive or negative feedback influences future thoughts and courses of action. Finally, as people communicate they are changed in a way that influences what follows. Communication, therefore, has an effect on the participants in the process. This effect may manifest itself emotionally, physically, or cognitively. A communication, once transmitted, is irreversible and unrepeatable. It cannot be taken back nor can it be repeated in exactly the same fashion as before. The impact of poor communication cannot be erased.

Because the consequences may be severe, police officers must be aware of the importance of a proper attitude during the communication process, and they must avoid a communication medium that may be derogatory, misleading, or illogical. According to the International Association of Chiefs of Police (1985), practitioners in the police community can avoid miscommunication if care is exercised to:

- Gather reliable and sufficient evidence.
- Distinguish fact from opinion.
- Avoid generalizations and haste.
- Avoid misleading statistics.
- Guard against illogical statements.
- Make careful comparisons.
- Guard against faulty thinking.

Police officers face extraordinary challenges during the communications process. They must ensure effective transmission of information. Yet, the officer must accomplish this feat in situations that are often charged with emotion, violence, and language barriers. Further, officers must be aware of the communicative value of nonverbal behaviors (O'Keefe, 2004).

Many of the qualities that apply to an effective message sender also apply to the message receiver. In fact, listening skills have been identified by police experts as essential for the police officer (Meese & Ortmeier, 2004; Ortmeier, 1996). According to Hess and Wrobleski (2003), the following guidelines should be used to improve listening capability.

Attitudinal

- Show interest in the person and the message. Be empathetic.
- Do not be self-centered.
- Resist any distractions.
- Do not let personal biases interfere.
- Listen with a clear mind.

Behavioral

- Be responsive with body language.
- Encourage the subject.
- Look at the subject.
- Do not interrupt.
- Make notes.

Mental

- Ask appropriate questions.
- Do not change the subject.
- Listen for ideas as well as facts. Separate facts from opinions.
- Pay attention to content, not delivery. Look for main points.
- Avoid jumping to conclusions.
- Concentrate.
- Use excess time to summarize the speaker's main ideas.
- Keep an open mind.
- Periodically clarify what has been communicated.
- Be attentive to body language.

In recent years, through efforts to reconnect the police with the community, many police and other public safety agencies have adopted the philosophy, strategy, and practices associated with community-oriented policing (COP) and problem solving. COP requires individual police officers to engage citizens and groups within a community in an effort to assist them with local problem identification and solution development. Police officers are required to speak to citizens and address community gatherings. Therefore, public speaking skills have become increasingly important in police work.

Every police contact with another human being should be viewed as an opportunity to communicate and enhance police-community relations. *(Photo courtesy of the Los Angeles Sheriff's Department.)*

In the final analysis, virtually all law enforcement and criminal justice activity involves human relations. The police are in the people business. Whether communicating with a crime suspect, attending to the injured, interviewing witnesses and victims, or speaking to a group of citizens, the ability to communicate is a critical component and necessary ingredient to effective policing. Every contact a police officer makes with another human being should be viewed as an opportunity to enhance the agency's ability to gather information and provide a foundation for the furtherance of the police mission to serve the community well.

CASE STUDY—CROSS-CULTURAL COMMUNICATION

For many Americans, the Rodney King incident will be forever etched into their memories. After a March 3, 1991, vehicle pursuit that reached speeds in excess of 100 miles per hour, Rodney King was stopped for traffic violations by CHP and LAPD officers on the Foothill Freeway in Los Angeles. During the ensuing confrontation, a citizen videotaped LAPD officers as they struck King repeatedly with their fists and batons. King, a 6 foot 3 inch, 225 pound, unemployed 25-year-old African American, was hospitalized with missing teeth, eleven skull fractures, and other injuries. In 1992, LAPD officers charged in connection with the incident were acquitted in a state court trial. The acquittals led to demonstrations in Los Angeles that quickly erupted into a riot that was more costly, both in human and economic terms, than the Los Angeles Watts riot in 1965.

A debate regarding the Rodney King incident continues. Many view the videotaped incident as an example of police use of excessive force. Others claim King sustained the injuries because he resisted arrest and appeared to be high on PCP. Still others contend that the LAPD officers' lack of respect for Rodney King as a human being as well as LAPD's failure to use appropriate communication tools contributed to the 1991 incident and subsequent riot in 1992.

1. How do one's negative perceptions promote disrespect for others?
2. How might cross-cultural communications skills be used to de-escalate and manage conflict?
3. Who is responsible for effective communication: The one who sends a message? The receiver? Both?
4. Could the use of tactical communication have prevented the physical confrontation between Rodney King and the police?

SPEECH AND INTERPERSONAL COMMUNICATION

As mentioned previously, effective **interpersonal communication** skills are essential in society generally, and in police and criminal justice activity specifically. Interpersonal communication refers to the ability to communicate with others. Experts on the subject of policing ranked effective communications skills number one of 62 competencies essential to effective leadership in policing (Ortmeier, 1996). In another survey, 1,000 personnel managers in the United States ranked effective speech communication as the number one ingredient to obtaining employment and good job performance (Hanna & Wilson, 1998). Expanding technology makes good communications skills even more critical given the nature of the overwhelming amount of information available through electronic media.

One-on-One Conversations

Face-to-face communication with individuals has many advantages. It is normally fast, easy to control, provides instantaneous feedback, and adds a personal touch to the communications process. Interviewing subjects and interrogating suspects is a large and extremely critical part of police work. Good communications skills enhance the ability to gather information and obtain admissions and confessions.

Every communication includes both task and relationship dimensions. The task dimension refers to the people, events, and phenomena that occur outside the communication. If the interviewer says, "Please describe, in your own words, what happened," the interviewee will know what task is expected. However, at the same time, the communication also involves a relationship dimension. If the parties have a strained relationship, or the message is poorly framed or misunderstood, the communication process may be ineffective. If, for example, a distrustful relationship exists, such as between a police officer and a victim who distrusts the police, the victim may not be willing to provide any information. Likewise, if the request is presented as a demand or the victim does not understand the language in which the request is made, the victim may resist or not understand what is being requested.

A key to effective communication is to overcome defensiveness on the part of the subject being communicated with. When a verbal or written message is sent in a strong or violent manner, the listener becomes defensive. On some occasions, such as when a subject (or suspect) is incorrigible and refuses to obey a lawful order from a police officer, strong language may be necessary. During most encounters with others, however, forceful language and behavior may not be appropriate. The following list notes some **challenges to effective communication.**

Behavior, whether real or imagined, that increases defensiveness in others includes (Gibb, 1961):

- Judgment (or prejudgment) of others.
- Control or manipulation.
- Neutrality (showing little or no concern).
- Superiority.
- Certainty (rigid commitment to a point of view).
- Phony sincerity.

Behavior on the part of the communicator that tends to reduce defensiveness by others includes:

- Treating others with respect.
- Cooperation and collaboration in a problem-solving effort.
- Demonstrating empathy (identifying) with another's thinking.

- Minimizing differences in status, authority, and power.
- Willingness to accept additional information that could result in a change of mind.
- Candid, straightforward expression of attitudes and beliefs.

Telephone Communications

Telephone communication is probably the most common form of technological communication used today. Proper telephone etiquette is necessary to ensure maximum productivity and to create a climate for positive police–community relations.

Every telephone call should be placed or answered with a pleasant, clear, evenly paced voice. The length of the call should be kept to a minimum. Callers should be placed on hold only when necessary and the length of the hold should also be minimized.

Most police activity is initiated as a result of citizen telephone calls placed to a 9-1-1 or similar emergency phone number, or to an agency's nonemergency phone number. An incoming call is received by an officer or dispatcher who determines the priority of the call based on the seriousness of the reported incident and the number of officers available to respond. Some agencies use telephone operators to screen and segregate incoming calls. The operator forwards the call to the appropriate department or to a dispatcher if immediate police attention is necessary.

Cell phones provide an immediate communications link between the individual citizen and a police agency. When wireless phone service providers are equipped with E9-1-1-geolocation technology, dispatchers can quickly identify the location of a cell phone caller. Thus, the technology provides an excellent communications medium and it enhances public safety personnel ability to locate a citizen in distress (Adams, 2007).

Answering Machines, Voice Mail, and Email

Answering machines and voice mail can either be useful or can be an annoyance to the caller. Outgoing messages should be short, clear, and free of background noise. The following rules apply when leaving a message on an answering machine or voice mailbox:

- Organize the message in advance.
- Speak slowly and clearly.
- Identify yourself.
- Identify the name of the person to whom the call is directed.
- Keep the message short.
- Leave a phone number for the return call.

Email messages should include a brief subject line, be as concise as possible and free of spelling and grammar errors, and avoid inflammatory content (including inappropriate humor and emotional harangues).

POLICE WEB SITES

A police department may also set up a website with which to communicate with the community it serves. Such websites enable an agency to share information with the public about police activities and events as well as gather leads from citizens that can be used to detect and prevent crime.

Meetings

One should not have a meeting just for the sake of having a meeting. A meeting is not necessary if there is no reason for it; a phone call, memo, fax or e-mail will do; key people cannot attend; time is limited; or members are not prepared.

Meetings are necessary when the participants' tasks are interdependent, more than one decision needs to be made, and misunderstandings are likely without a meeting. Good meetings have an agenda specifying the date, time, location, participants, items for discussion, and goals with the premeeting work outlined; start on time and end on time; are as short as possible; stay on track; and achieve the goal(s) of the meeting (Adler & Elmhorst, 2009).

Visual communications aids can be useful during meetings. However, presenters are cautioned not to overuse technology. For example, the use of presentation software, such as Microsoft® PowerPoint®, has been criticized because it restricts creativity and encourages presentation, not conversation. It helps illustrate a point during a presentation, yet it does little to stimulate discussion and problem solving (Keller, 2003).

Working in Teams and Task Forces

All working groups are not teams. Committees are not teams. A committee's purpose is representation of various constituencies. Teams and task forces are created to fulfill a need for interdependence and support. Effective teams are made up of highly independent individuals who work together to produce a result. Basic to the nature of teams are the assumptions that the talent necessary to achieve results is already present in the group, every member knows what needs to be accomplished, the team's potential is limited only by the self-imposed team member limitations, and teamwork can be exciting and challenging (Whisenand, 2004).

Teamwork is essential in contemporary multijurisdictional law enforcement activity as well as community policing environments in which citizens, community groups, and the police must work together to identify and develop solutions to local problems. These teams may not have designated leaders. Although informal leaders may emerge, some teams may be self-directed groups or **task forces** responsible for working together to complete a task. Effective communication among team members occurs when participants:

- Recognize team as well as personal goals.
- Promote desirable norms of behavior.
- Make sure all functional roles and expectations are fulfilled.
- Promote cohesiveness.
- Avoid excessive conformity.
- Encourage creativity.
- Positively reinforce accomplishment.

In an ideal environment, people want to participate on teams. They do not have to be forced or manipulated into serving on them. One expert suggests that two basic questions should be asked before teams are created: Who knows? Who cares? (Caroselli, 1997). In response to the first question, probable team members include those who are truly knowledgeable about the reasons for establishing the team. If the team has been created to function as a task force to solve a problem, team members should be intimately knowledgeable of the circumstances surrounding the problem. With regard to the second question, team members should be selected because they are committed to solving the problem. People who know about the reason for the team and are committed to the outcome of the team effort will communicate more effectively (What does it take to make collaboration work?, 2004; Whisenand & Ferguson, 2009).

Public Speaking

Speaking to a group of people is required in today's working world. It is common in police orientation and training sessions, briefings, and ceremonial activities. Crowds gathered at the scene of an incident and community groups also create situations in which a police officer must address an audience. **Public speaking** is used as a vehicle to inform, persuade, and rally members around a common cause. In any public-speaking situation the speaker should:

- Have a clear and realistic goal.
- Analyze the audience and the occasion.
- Organize ideas so that the presentation solicits the listeners' attention and the material is presented in a clear, brief, and orderly fashion without excluding necessary detail.
- Use supporting material and audiovisual aids when appropriate.
- Present the material with enthusiasm, sincerity, confidence, and credibility.
- Dress and act appropriately for the occasion.
- Use time effectively and efficiently (Adler & Elmhorst, 2009).

> Access Tips 'n Tricks for public speaking through Toastmasters International at www.toastmasters.com.

Special Challenges in Communications

Special challenges arise when people are non–English-speaking or are hearing- or visually impaired. When language barriers exist, bilingual officers or citizen translators can assist in the communication process. Officers can also learn the basics of non-English languages through either credit or noncredit courses offered at local colleges. Other techniques that may be used to communicate with a non–English-speaking or hearing-impaired person include the following:

- Obtain the person's attention.
- Be certain the person understands the nature of the message content.
- Keep speech slow and clear; use short sentences.
- Make eye contact with the person.
- Keep all items, such as pens, out of the mouth when speaking.
- Do not stand in front of lights.
- Use paper and pen to communicate if necessary.
- Use facial expressions and body language
- Learn basic sign language.
- Remember that the subject person may not have understood the message even if speech or body language indicates the message was understood (Gamble & Gamble, 2005).

Visually impaired people also require special attention. Initially, a police officer must be identified by the visually impaired person. An officer may place the person's hand on a badge to communicate identity. Numerous communication challenges also arise from the increased use of information technology. Although technological advancements, such as electronic mail (e-mail) and the Internet, improve communication links and provide access to a tremendous amount of information, technology's impersonal nature can have a negative impact on the interpersonal communications process and information flow.

CROSS-CULTURAL COMMUNICATION

Cross-cultural communication occurs whenever a person from one culture sends a message to, or receives a message from, a person of another culture. Misunderstanding is possible during this process since individuals from different cultures often perceive, interpret, and evaluate situations and other people differently. To communicate effectively in a culturally diverse environment, people must recognize and adapt to the differences (Adler & Elmhorst, 2009).

A person's own perceptions and biases influence assessments of and reactions to people and situations. To improve communication across cultures, law enforcement and criminal justice personnel must understand and appreciate diversity, including language differences and the cross-gender communication challenges. To do so, one must develop and effectively utilize cross-culture communication skills (Ortmeier & Davis, 2012; Shusta, Levine, Wong, & Harris, 2011).

Within a communications context, culture may be defined as a pattern of a group's behavior, including its members' beliefs, language, actions, and artifacts (Putnam & Pacanowski, 1983). Culture is not what a group has. Rather, culture involves what a group is. Cultures, whether formal or informal, ethnic or organizational, form basic assumptions about what the culture represents. Often the culture operates under the assumption that it is superior to other cultures or groups (Meese & Ortmeier, 2004; Pasquali, 1997).

Culture involves more than ethnic and racial similarities or common themes based on nationality or socioeconomic status. Organizations also tend to develop a unique culture. Organizations that develop customs and enlist new members to an institution often adopt preexisting attitudes, beliefs, and habits associated with their predecessors in the organization. During the 1990s, a major urban police department attempted to reduce the amount of racism, sexism, and bigotry in the department by actively recruiting women and minorities. The strategy did little to change the organizational culture or the ways in which its members viewed themselves. The new recruits did not change the organization; rather, the organization changed the recruits as they adapted to the organizational climate and adopted pre-existing attitudes and beliefs.

When a person moves from the comfort zone of one culture into a culture that is foreign or different, a natural anxiety emerges. The transition into an unfamiliar culture may cause fear and mistrust. When the cultural change is severe, the person making the transition may experience culture shock. This phenomenon occurs during the early stages of the transition and is accompanied by feelings of stress and anxiety. The symptoms of culture shock include irritability, loneliness, paranoia, upset stomach, and sleeplessness. Communication-based symptoms include excessive complaining, withdrawal, frustration, and defensive communication. Thus, cultural change and culture shock present challenges to effective communication in multicultural environments.

Culture shock may also occur in relatively homogeneous populations. In rural areas, for example, one might assume that members of the community tend to retain common beliefs, and think and act alike. However, even in remote areas, the degree of affluence between neighbors may be quite severe. Poor people may exist in a culture that is radically different from that of their wealthy neighbors. Religious beliefs may be quite different also and radical ideas, even violent behavior, may radiate from individuals who are isolated from mainstream society.

Adapting to new cultures and environments involves working through the culture shock first. According to Dodd (1998), the following guidelines will assist with overcoming culture shock.

- Be patient with others and do not overreact.
- Work at meeting and greeting new people.
- Explore unfamiliar culture-specific customs.
- Get enough rest and mentally reflect on the new culture.
- Think positive thoughts.
- Write about experiences.

- Observe the body language and habits of members of the new culture.
- Learn the host culture's verbal language.

Working with people in a new environment involves overcoming the stress associated with the new experience. Long-term adaptation also involves the stress-growth-acculturation dynamic. Effective communication is extremely important to the process of facilitating the adaptation. Police officers who are cognizant of cultural differences and who focus on assimilating into the host culture will be more effective and less stressed when working in a multicultural environment.

Competency in cross-cultured communications leads to positive professional job task performance. Success on the job is the result of the recognition of, and successful adaptation to, different cultures. Successful interpersonal relationships signal effective outcomes. Competence in cross-cultural communication leads to:

- High technical and professional performance.
- Resourcefulness.
- The ability to innovate.
- Effective organizational communications.
- Goal development.
- Task completion.

One might ask, so what? Is a focus on intercultural communication effectiveness simply another feel-good, politically correct strategy with no valued practical application? Not likely. There is a great deal of research that suggests that intercultural communication competence leads to successful outcomes (O'Keefe, 2004; Wulff, 2000). Since police officers are required to work with and for people from a wide cultural range, the necessity for developing competence in this area cannot be underestimated. From a police recruiting standpoint, screening for psychological barriers or mental maladjustments that may inhibit cultural adaptation and relationship building may result in fewer interpersonal problems with an officer. The screening may also reduce the likelihood of misunderstandings, use of excessive force, and indifference, which could lead to poor public image and organizational liability for an officer's actions. Psychological testing (MMPI, 16PF, Myers-Briggs, Taylor-Johnson Temperament Analysis, etc.) may be used as a screening device to eliminate candidates who are not psychologically fit to perform the duties of a contemporary police officer.

From an individual officer's point of view, cross-cultural communication competence may reduce negative job-related stress, maintain good health, eliminate barriers to effective job or task performance and promotion possibilities, and generate fewer citizen complaints. Effective intercultural communications skills are no panacea, nor are they substitutes for understanding and a sincere appreciation for differences among human beings. The development and application of these skills promote positive interpersonal relationships, an essential ingredient for effective policing in the twenty-first century.

Cross-cultural communication can occur in a variety of
situations. *(Photo courtesy of the Los Angeles Sheriff's Department.)*

Given the apparent need for intercultural communication competence, what can one do to acquire and develop the necessary skills? Dodd
(1998) suggests the following:

- Emphasize areas of similarity with others. Search for commonality
  rather than differences.
- Practice acceptance of differing opinions. Remain open and receptive
  to other points of view. Dogmatism blocks effective communication.
- Ensure that verbal messages are consistent with nonverbal messages. In the long run, a mixed message discredits the sender.
- Avoid dominating conversations. Listen and hear as well as speak.
  People who spend most of their time speaking tend to bore others
  and are less credible.
- Avoid submissiveness in conversations. Being overly submissive can
  be as harmful as domination. People respect others who have something worthwhile to contribute.
- Recognize and affirm communication from others. Avoid being overly
  critical. People appreciate understanding more than they do criticism.

Police officers are often recruited from population groups that are
different from the citizens the officers are ultimately sworn to protect
and serve. Even when recruited from the same population group, such as
an inner city area, the officers may establish residence in suburbia and
commute to work. Rarely does a police officer reside in the same area of a
community where the most serious problems associated with crime and

urban decay exist. Conflicts may result, therefore, when a police officer resides in one culture and works in another. These conflicts can be prevented. To understand the culture of a group is to understand how and why a group thinks, acts, and reacts to messages and events within its environment. Additional information on working with diverse populations is presented throughout this book.

MANAGING COMMUNICATION CONFLICT

Conflict has been variously defined as a clash, a state of disharmony, opposition, strife, and war. Conflict and the words used to define or describe it often create an image that is so powerful that people become stressed and are unable to function appropriately in conflict situations. Conflict, however, is pervasive; frequent, and inevitable. It is not a product. It is a process in human nature. It is neither good nor bad; it simply is. Conflict can serve an important interpersonal and organizational purpose. By recognizing the issues and situations that create conflict, it is possible to reduce or eliminate the problems associated with conflict (Jones-Brown & Terry, 2004). Therefore, one must learn to identify, cope with, analyze, and manage conflict to reach appropriate goals.

Inevitably, even the best efforts at establishing and maintaining open lines of communication between parties and groups can result in conflict. The notion of balanced relationships suggests that the people involved either like or dislike the same things. A relationship may become unbalanced when people like each other but do not like the same things, or when they like the same things but do not like each other. Sound like a common occurrence? It is. Each person, or group, sifts perceptions of the other through the filter of culture stereotypes. Americans tend to dislike conflict and view it as negative. However, conflict can be productive as well as destructive. Conflict is productive when participants are satisfied with the outcome. When participants think they have gained as a result of the conflict and a balance has been struck between cooperation and competition, the conflict is productive. In contrast, conflicts are destructive when participants escalate them and winning becomes more important than gaining. Winning at all costs can even be deadly.

Conflict stems from a variety of sources (Kidd & Braziel, 1999). Expressed struggle between or among people, perceived incompatible goals or scarce rewards, interdependence, and interference can cause conflicts internally and between individuals. Conflict is a natural by-product of life and can, at times, be beneficial if positive consequences result from the conflict. People cope with conflict by applying different conflict reduction styles. Through nonassertive behavior, individuals cope by

Learn more about cross-cultural communication strategies and managing communication conflict through the University of Colorado's Conflict Research Consortium at www .colorado.edu/conflict/peace/treatment.

demonstrating inability or unwillingness to express their thoughts during a conflict. They may avoid conflict altogether or accommodate by giving in to another's pressure. In contrast, some people cope through direct aggression. They attack one's character or competence. The aggressor may attack physically, ridicule, threaten, tease, or use profanity. Passive aggression occurs when a communicator expresses hostility in some obscure manner. Passive aggressive people harbor feelings of resentment, rage, and anger.

Through indirect communication, the communicator conveys a message without hostility. The indirect communicator is interested in self-protection and may suggest that someone do something rather than direct a person to do it. Assertive communication occurs when the communicator clearly expresses needs and desires without resorting to judgment or dictating to others. Assertive communicative behavior is the most direct, honest, and aggression free (Adler & Towne, 2012).

Conflict management and resolution are a major part of police work, especially when one considers cross-cultural **communication conflict.** Police officers can be very effective conflict de-escalators and managers if they understand and practice communicative leadership styles that offer solutions in conflict situations. These leadership styles often differ, depending on the situation and the context in which the situation occurs. When interviewing the victim of a serious crime, an officer may utilize a tactful, caring, and empathetic style that facilitates interaction and information flow. When searching a building for a possible armed suspect, the officer may utilize a highly structured, organized, conservative, and controlled leadership communication style. Working with a neighborhood group to identify and solve community-based problems, the officer may communicate in an open, participative, creative, resourceful, and politically aware leadership style. Finally, when effecting an arrest, the communicative leadership style may be task-oriented, decisive, assertive, and authoritarian.

TACTICAL COMMUNICATION

Major goals in police work involve soliciting information without being confrontational and generating voluntary compliance from law violators without resorting to physical force. **Tactical communication** is a message, delivered through words and actions, which can be used to accomplish these goals. Officers should always convey a professional demeanor, speak with a respectful and neutral attitude, and display mannerisms that demonstrate control of the situation. In all cases, officers should keep in mind that any encounter is potentially dangerous. For example, with angry, hostile, hysterical, or emotionally unstable individuals, officers should remain calm and determine the cause of the hostility or hysteria. Speaking in a harsh or demeaning manner is inappropriate. With very young or very old individuals, officers should be patient and calm. Young people are easily frightened and often confused. The elderly are easily upset and often misunderstand instructions.

Voluntary compliance through tactical communication may be achieved by adhering to the following:

- **Ask.** If practical to do so, give the subject the opportunity to comply voluntarily.
- **Explain the legal context.** Explain the law and/or reason for the request.
- **Present options.** Explain options to the subject, outlining possible courses of action and consequences of each.
- **Request cooperation.** Provide the subject with one final opportunity to comply.
- **Take action.** If the subject does not comply with officer requests, appropriate action must be taken that is consistent with the law and agency policy.

When confronted with noncompliant individuals, police officers are often subjected to verbal, if not physical, abuse. Officers can deflect and redirect verbal abuse by remaining calm and not becoming emotionally involved with the subject. Officers should also demonstrate respect for the subject. Disrespect promotes escalation of the conflict. When tactical communication fails, police officers must use only the force option that is reasonably necessary to gain compliance. The degree of force used must be consistent with the degree of resistance and based on the circumstances in the situation (California Commission on Peace Officer Standards and Training, 2012).

Officers must be able to justify the use of force when communication efforts fail. Fellow officers, police agencies, prosecutors, defense attorneys, the courts, the media, and the public will demand accountability for any force option used. Refer to Chapter 8 for information regarding tactical communication during vehicle stops.

Note Taking and Report Writing

Many police officers dread the thought of **note taking** and **report writing.** Since police officers tend to be people of action, they do not appreciate the slow, deliberate process demanded by good writing (Thaiss & Hess, 1999). However, a police officer's ability to document facts surrounding an incident, interview, accident, investigation, or criminal activity not only reflects on the officer's professionalism, but also on the criminal justice system's ability to process a case (California Commission

---

The words, *security, attack, flight, excessive repetition,* and *revised priorities* (SAFER) help remind officers of the situations that require more than verbal communication.

- **Security.** When people are in immediate danger or when property under the officer's control is threatened.
- **Attack.** When an officer's personal danger zone (PDZ) is violated.
- **Flight.** When a suspect unlawfully flees from an officer.
- **Excessive repetition.** When all verbal options are exhausted and voluntary compliance is not forthcoming.
- **Revised priorities.** When a higher priority requires immediate attention.

on Peace Officer Standards and Training, 2012). Poor writing ability equates to poor performance (Peat, 2004). Probably no other single activity in policing is more important than the need for effective documentation, comprehensive notes, and quality reports. Yet, police recruits tend to have poor writing skills and many fail the report-writing section of the police academy. Individual officers and some agencies place writing skills development low on the priority list. Further, many seasoned officers fail to realize that excellent written communication skills are often a prerequisite for promotion or transfer to an extremely desirable assignment (Guffey, 2005).

Police officers are required to perform writing tasks on a continuous basis. As exemplified by the following list of writing tasks developed by the California Commission on Peace Officer Standards and Training (POST), a patrol officer is required to perfrom numerous writing activities. According to POST (1998), a uniformed patrol officer should be able to correctly:

- Take notes.
- Incorporate field notes into reports.
- Summarize, in writing, statements of witnesses, complainants, etc.
- Record, in writing, formal confessions.
- Enter information on report forms consisting primarily of checkoff boxes or fill-in-the-blanks (i.e., vehicle impound reports).
- Write brief reports (one or two sentences) that serve to document an event (i.e., log entry).
- Write reports consisting of several short, descriptive phrases, sentence fragments, or very short sentences (i.e., incident reports).
- Write in-depth narrative reports containing complete sentences and paragraphs (i.e., investigative reports, supplemental/follow-up reports).
- Complete reports for other jurisdictions (i.e., weapons, vehicle parts).
- Complete state reporting forms (i.e., highway patrol report forms).
- Prepare accident statistical data for Department of Motor Vehicles, Highway Patrol, and internal records.
- Compile crime data from a number of sources (i.e., for entry onto summary sheets).
- Record number/letter series (i.e., license plate numbers, driver's license numbers, addresses, serial numbers, telephone numbers, registration numbers, social security numbers).
- Write paperwork for arrest warrants.
- Complete 5150 (mentally ill subject) petitions.
- Prepare paperwork for a process server.
- Prepare a list of known criminals and/or wanted persons (for personal or departmental use).
- Prepare wanted persons' information (for federal, state, and local law enforcement officials and agencies).
- Record bond raises, forfeitures, and reductions.
- Record disposition of civil papers.

- Enter information into activity logs, patrol logs, daily reports, or departmental records.
- Update maintenance records on patrol cars.
- Maintain inventory logs (i.e., evidence, recovered property).
- Write crime broadcasts or wanted notices.
- Write news releases.
- Write memoranda and other correspondence.
- Draft material for departmental manuals.

Although the foregoing list of writing tasks was developed by and for California police officers, the tasks listed are consistent with writing requirements for police officers nationwide.

Methods for Documentation

Documentation is often accomplished through traditional note-taking and report-writing methods. If physical, technical, and legal requirements permit, documentation may occur through the use of audiotape, videotape, stenography, or computer-assisted recording devices. If computers are used to generate notes or reports, care must be exercised to ensure that confidentiality is maintained and access is restricted to a need-to-know basis. Computer disks that have been erased still retain information that can be retrieved through technical means. Additionally, other electronic mediums such as e-mail and the Internet are often not secure from message interception by outsiders (Ortmeier, 1999; Sullivan, 2004).

Field Notes

Field notes are notations created by an officer in the field while gathering information or investigating an incident. These notes become the primary source document for any subsequent report. Field notes should be made contemporaneous to an incident. In other words, notes should be made during the course of the activity or immediately after an incident occurs. These notes are often referred to as field notes because they are recorded on the job in the field. Since memories fade and are often imperfect, notes must be written and maintained in the course of a police officer's occupation. Written communication skills are extremely important in the world of police work. Notes are personal to the note taker and may be used to refresh one's memory, as the foundation for an official report, and as supporting evidence. Although notes are generally written for the note taker's use only, caution must be exercised when writing notes because any recording may be subject to review by another person or agency.

The most effective way to document information acquired in the field is to follow a systematic process. An officer should separate the parties involved, establish rapport, listen attentively to what the subject is communicating, take notes and ask appropriate questions (what, when, where, who, how, and why), and verify the information recorded by reviewing the information given with the subject. Care must be exercised to separate facts from opinions and conclusions (California Commission on Peace Officer Standards and Training, 2012; Parr, 1999).

Reports

Reports often become part of an official record, which forms the foundation for the history of an event. Reports may be viewed by peers, supervisors, the media, social service agencies, attorneys, the courts, insurance companies, and other criminal justice and public safety agencies. They may be scrutinized in the judicial process, provide evidence for litigation against the report writer, support a petition, or provide an officer with a defense against a lawsuit or criminal charge. Reports are used to determine future courses of action and as the basis for promotion, discipline, and evaluation. They can have negative as well as positive consequences and should be taken seriously. Reports with misspelled words, poor grammar, punctuation errors, inaccuracies, or omissions are potentially costly. Defective reports also cast doubt on the professionalism of the report writer.

Reports vary in form and content, yet each report has one common purpose: to communicate information in a clear, concise, and accurate manner. Reports should always be written with the audience or potential readers in mind. Effective report writing is a matter of writing the pertinent facts concerning an issue or event in much the same way and in much the same order that a story would be told verbally.

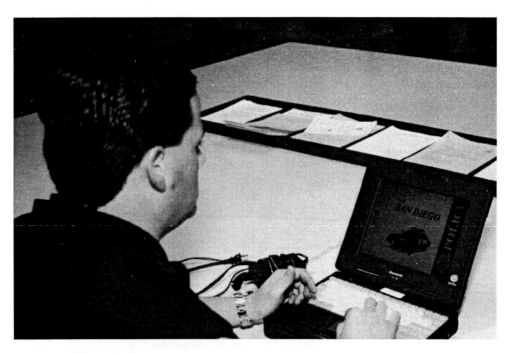

Effective documentation of facts is critical to law enforcement and the administration of justice. *(Photo courtesy of the San Diego Police Department.)*

Report Types

The following are examples of different types of reports:

- **Contact reports** are used to document information acquired during any contact with another person or persons.
- **Incident** and crime **reports** are used to document the occurrence of an event or reported criminal activity.
- Narrative and **supplemental reports** are used to narrate what happened, record witness statements, and record additional information acquired subsequent to an original report.
- Accident and **traffic collision reports** are used to record the circumstances surrounding an accident or vehicle collision.
- **Agency-specific reports** are written and completed in the normal course of business. These may include inspection and audit reports or surveys.
- **Memoranda** and letters are used for general interdepartmental and interagency communication.

The types of reports used by an agency depend on the nature of the organization's activity and its documentation requirements. Most existing police organizations have reporting forms and formats in place. New agencies seeking to develop report forms and procedures should consult with existing agencies for information. Many publishers also market report form books and form tools in computer software packages.

General Report Writing Principles

To be considered acceptable, a report must meet certain criteria. The writing must be reasonably fluent, well developed, and well organized, showing a sufficient command of the language to communicate the information. All essential information must be included in the report (who, what, where, when, how, why). The report must be free of mechanical errors (i.e., typing, grammar, punctuation, spelling, and word choice) that diminish its evidentiary value or usefulness. The time required to complete the report must be reasonable and consistent with the expectations of the job.

To write an effective report, the writer should:

- Conduct a proper inquiry into the subject material of the intended report.
- Take complete, accurate, readable notes.
- Use the proper format, depending, naturally, on for what purpose the report is intended.
- Choose the correct language.
- Write the report in the first person, using active voice and past tense, and omitting police jargon.
- Use proper sentence structure.
- Be completely accurate with all the facts.
- Not omit facts.

- Distinguish facts from hearsay, conclusions, judgments, and personal opinions.
- Strive for clarity.
- Be concise.
- Be absolutely fair.
- Be complete.
- Record the sequence of events in chronological order.
- Record the names, addresses, and, if possible, social security and/or ID numbers of all involved.
- Include an introduction, body, and conclusion in all narratives.
- Check for spelling, punctuation, and capitalization errors.
- Review the report to ensure that it adequately answers the questions who, what, when, where, how, and why.
- Proofread the report.

Occasionally, a specific report form may not be available. To ensure that the report is complete, the report writer should strive to include the following information in the report:

- **Administrative data:** Include the date of the report, file, or case number (if applicable), subjects involved, type of report, and complainant (if any)
- Name and identification of the person writing the report
- Office or agency of origin
- **Report status:** Open, pending, supplemental, or closing
- **Distribution:** Include those individuals to whom the report is to be sent
- **Synopsis:** A brief description of the case and/or investigation
- **Details of the report:** A narrative, including all facts acquired and all developed leads
- **Conclusions and recommendations:** This is the place for opinions and personal recommendations
- Undeveloped leads
- **Enclosures list:** For photographs, sketches, copies of documents, evidence receipts, and computer disks (O'Hara & O'Hara, 2003)

At a minimum, investigative reports should contain:

- Introductory information describing how the officer became involved in the situation.
- An identification of the offense, if any, and the facts necessary to establish the elements of the offense.
- The identification of all parties involved such as suspects, victims, witnesses, as well as the person(s) who reported the incident. Specific information regarding the parties includes full names, aliases, gender, ethnicity, dates of birth, residence addresses and phone numbers, work or school locations and phone numbers, and the parties' roles in the incident.

- Statements of parties involved, recorded verbatim if possible.
- Specifics relative to the scene of the incident.
- Descriptions of physical evidence as well as property damaged or stolen.
- Actions taken by the officer(s) at the scene (California Commission on Peace Officer Standards and Training, 2012).

In an attempt to sound official, police personnel often adopt a writing style and use language that is elaborate, redundant, obscure, and full of jargon and legalese. Clear, concise, simple, commonly used vocabulary is best. Word and sentence length determine readability and understanding. Long words and sentences tend to increase the need for a higher reading level. In report writing, the author of the report should present accurate information utilizing brevity and clarity as guides to readability. Writers should avoid using words of more than two syllables and sentences should not exceed 10 words. Following are examples of jargon and wordy phrases with their concise, simple English counterparts in parentheses:

- In the vicinity of (near)
- Verbal confrontation (argument)
- Inquired (asked)
- Proceeded to the location (went to _____)
- Terminate (end)
- Approximately (about)
- Initiated (began)
- Related (said)
- Party (person)
- In view of the fact that (because)
- For the purpose of (to)
- Conducted an investigation (investigated)
- Upon an individual basis (individually)
- Unit (car)
- Pursuit of alleged perpetrator (ran after suspect)
- Deceased (dead)
- Maintained visual contact (watched)
- Exited the vehicle (got out of the car)
- Executed (conducted)
- Extricate (take out of)

Learn more about effective writing through Purdue University's Online Writing Lab at http://owl.english.purdue.edu/.

In addition, when giving an interview to the media, officers often use the word *the* inappropriately. *The* with a long ē is used appropriately only when the following word begins with a vowel.

Correct spelling and word usage, as well as proper punctuation and capitalization, are also ingredients essential to good report writing. Mistakes in these areas may lead the reader to believe that the writer is undereducated, poorly trained, careless, and unprofessional. The writer should not rely on computer spell-check programs, either. The following underlined words are examples of inappropriate words that would not be identified by a spell-checker software program (Adams, 2007; Hess, 1997).

- He went to the <u>sight</u> of the accident.
- The <u>breaks</u> on the car did not work.
- She was identified as a drug <u>attic</u>.
- It was a <u>miner</u> incident.
- He injured his left <u>feet</u>.
- She did not <u>no</u> where the suspect went.
- The item was found in the car's <u>truck</u>.
- The suspect fell into a <u>whole</u>.
- He was unable to <u>here</u>.

Reports should be written to express a thought, not impress the reader. The language used in normal conversation should be the language used in the report. The vocabulary and style used should approximate what and how the writer would communicate if telling a story or explaining what happened during an incident. Active, rather than passive, voice is recommended in police report writing. For example, an officer should write, "I asked the witness for identification" rather than, "The witness was asked for identification."

Report writers should not attempt to replicate the writing style of someone else. If the author of the report is required to testify in court, the language used in the report should be the same as is presented verbally on the witness stand. First person singular pronouns are recommended for describing what the report writer did, saw, or experienced. It seems more natural to state "I" did something rather than "Officer Smith" or "this report writer" did something (Guffey, 2005; Ortmeier, 1999).

RADIO OPERATIONS

Radio communications are used by literally thousands of organizations to communicate with personnel in the field. As a result, radio airways are extremely congested. The Federal Communications Commission (FCC) is charged with the responsibility to control the airways to ensure legal and efficient use of radio frequencies. FCC regulations prohibit unnecessary transmissions, profanity, malicious interference, and unidentified transmissions.

Compared to earlier times, modern police communications equipment is very sophisticated. *(Photo courtesy of the Cobb County, GA Police Department.)*

Emergency radio communications on a frequency include officer-involved shootings, inprogress felonies, officer needs help calls, pedestrian and vehicle pursuits, and other emergency situations. Normal radio traffic includes officer status changes (out-of-service, back-in-service), normal calls for service, and all points bulletins (APBs) not related to an emergency. Before transmitting, an officer should monitor the frequency to be used to ensure the airway is clear then depress the microphone button and wait about two seconds before speaking (California Commission on Peace Officer Standards and Training, 2012).

Radio broadcasts must be accurate, brief, courteous, and clear. The microphone should be held approximately two inches from the mouth at a slight angle so the sound from the voice passes by, rather than enters directly into, the microphone. General rules for radio broadcasting include the following.

- Be courteous.
- Make no personal broadcasts.
- Avoid sarcasm.
- Do not reprimand over the radio.
- Keep transmissions brief.
- No profane language.
- Transmit essential messages only.
- Know the department's procedure and equipment.
- Broadcast correct information.
- Use radio codes when practical.

The use of a **phonetic alphabet** is encouraged when broadcasting names and vehicle registrations. Use of the phonetic alphabet helps to avoid misunderstanding and ultimately saves time because the receiver will not require the message to be repeated.

A   ADAM
B   BOY
C   CHARLES
D   DAVID
E   EDWARD
F   FRANK
G   GEORGE
H   HENRY
I   IDA
J   JOHN
K   KING
L   LINCOLN
M   MARY
N   NORA
O   OCEAN
P   PAUL
Q   QUEEN
R   ROBERT
S   SAM
T   TOM
U   UNION
V   VICTOR
W   WILLIAM
X   X-RAY
Y   YOUNG
Z   ZEBRA

To maximize efficiency and limit air time, most police agencies utilize a communications code system similar to the Associated Public-Safety Communications Officers (APCO)–recommended **10-Code System.**

10-1	Signal weak (receiving poorly)
10-2	Signal good (receiving well)
10-3	Stop transmitting
10-4	Affirmative (OK)
10-5	Relay (to)
10-6	Busy
10-7	Out of service
10-8	In service
10-9	Say again (repeat)
10-10	Negative
10-11	_____ on duty
10-12	Stand by (stop)

10-13	Existing conditions
10-14	Message/information
10-15	Message delivered
10-16	Reply to message
10-17	En route
10-18	Urgent (quickly)
10-19	(In) contact
10-20	Location
10-21	Call (_____) by phone
10-22	Disregard
10-23	Arrived at scene
10-24	Assignment completed
10-25	Report to (meet at)
10-26	Estimated arrival time
10-27	License/permit information
10-28	Ownership information
10-29	Records clerk
10-30	Danger/caution
10-31	Pick up
10-32	_____ units needed (specify)
10-33	Help quick (emergency)
10-34	Time
10-35	Reserved
10-36	Reserved
10-37	Reserved
10-38	Reserved
10-39	Reserved

If simple, clear, concise English is best for the broadcast, the 10-code should be avoided. In fact, since the number of police frequencies are not as limited as they once were, many police agencies have discontinued use of the 10-code system. Studies, such as one conducted in Lakewood, Colorado, indicate that the use of simple English creates less confusion and reduces misunderstandings in communications (Payton & Amaral, 2004). As a result, the use of plain English saves time, improves communications, and enhances public safety.

The need for cross-department communication has increased in the age of heightened attention to homeland security. However, 10-codes vary across jurisdictions. This inconsistency can confuse first responders from different agencies who are seeking to work together. Agencies that migrate from 10-codes to plain language to avoid such confusion should carefully manage the transition. Helpful practices include gathering advice on how to use plain language from officers and dispatchers (who will be most affected by the change). Agencies must also design appropriate training programs, as well as keep several agency-specific codes under-

Radio broadcasts must be accurate, brief, courteous, and clear.
(Photo courtesy of the Cobb County, GA Police Department.)

stood by officers but not the public (such as a code to alert officers to an undercover operation) (U.S. Department of Justice, Office of Justice Programs, 2010).

Dispatchers normally assign radio calls to an officer based on a priority code. A typical code system used to designate the type of call or activity includes the following.

NO CODE	Handle calls normally.
CODE 1	Normal, take this call next.
CODE 2	Urgent. Expedite, but obey traffic laws. No emergency lights or siren.
CODE 3	Emergency. Proceed immediately using emergency lights and siren.
CODE 4	No further assistance required.
CODE 4A	No further assistance required; suspect at large in area.
CODE 5	Stake out. Other units stay away.
CODE 6	Out for investigation.
CODE 7	Out of service.
CODE 8	Fire alarm activated.
CODE 9	Jail break.
CODE 10	Reserved.
CODE 11	Reserved.
CODE 12	Patrol assigned area and report disaster damage.
CODE 13	Activate disaster plan.
CODE 14	Resume normal operations.
CODE 15	Reserved.
CODE 16	Reserved.
CODE 17	Reserved.
CODE 18	Reserved.

CODE 19   Reserved.
CODE 20   Notify news media.
CODE 99   Emergency situation. The emergency button in mo-
           bile unit has been activated. No voice contact with
           unit officer.

A discussion of the types of information and databases accessible to the patrol officer is presented in Chapter 11.

CASE STUDY—POOR COMMUNICATION CAUSES DEATH

After the terrorist attack on New York's World Trade Center on 9/11, an inquiry revealed that communication failures contributed to the deaths of many on-scene police, fire, and emergency personnel. Due to poor coordination and the lack of modern communications systems, officials at the incident command center were unaware of the severity of the incident. Commanders lost track of those who entered the buildings and many responding agencies did not receive appropriate instructions.

1. How can communications within and among public safety agencies be improved?
2. Should police, fire, and emergency medical personnel use the same communications channels?

▲ SUMMARY

Effective communication skills are critical for the law enforcement officer and other criminal justice professionals. Communication is a complex, two-way process. Officers must have the proper attitude and demonstrate appropriate behavior when communicating with others. Speech and interpersonal communications strategies involve one-on-one communications, telephone communications, use of answering machines and voice mail, e-mail, meetings, working in teams and task forces, and public speaking. Police officers must also be aware of cultural differences when communicating with others, learn to manage communication conflict, and use tactical communication to de-escalate conflict.

Law enforcement professionals must document events and information and prepare comprehensive, accurate reports. Police officers must also learn to operate and communicate effectively with radio communications equipment.

DISCUSSION QUESTIONS AND EXERCISES

1. Why are communications skills important in a law enforcement environment?
2. Discuss how verbal communication and listening skills can be used to de-escalate conflict and reduce the need to use physical force.
3. What role does attitude play in the communications process?
4. Why is the knowledge of different cultures important to effective communication?
5. How should communication conflict be managed? Should approaches to conflict differ? Why or why not? Can conflict be productive? If so, when?
6. What is tactical communication? When should it be used?
7. Distinguish field notes from official reports.
8. Why is documentation vital to police work?
9. Is cross-cultural communication limited to ethnically diverse groups?
10. A patrol officer stopped a motorist for a traffic violation. While engaging the violator with a request to see the violator's driver license, vehicle registration, and proof of liability coverage, the violator is verbally abusive and refuses to produce the documents requested. How should the officer proceed?
11. Counterterrorism strategies and responses to civil emergencies require extensive and effective collaboration, cooperation, and communication among numerous law enforcement and public safety agencies. How can communication among these agencies be improved?

Community Policing: Philosophy and Strategy

LEARNING OBJECTIVES

After completing this chapter, the reader should be able to:

- define community policing.
- compare principles associated with Robert Peel to twenty-first century police behavior and activities.
- describe personal competencies necessary for a police officer in a community policing environment.
- analyze the framework for community policing.
- discuss techniques for working with diverse populations.
- discuss the roles and responsibilities of the police and the community with respect to the law enforcement function.
- describe the process for building police–community partnerships.
- identify effective police–community partnerships.

KEY TERMS

Define, describe, or explain the importance of each of the following.

Citizen–police cooperation
Community
Community mobilization
Community participation
Community policing
Community policing philosophy
Community policing strategy
Demographic change

Diversity
Philosophy
Police-community engagement
Police-community partnership
Police officer competencies
Problem solving
Strategy
Traditional policing model

INTRODUCTION

In American communities of the seventeenth and eighteenth centuries, the task of policing was carried out by citizens. To avoid central control by the government, policing in the United States was meant to be shared by community members. In the nineteenth century, as a result of the Peelian Reforms in Great Britain, law enforcement in the United States became more formalized and public police agencies were created (Cronkhite, 1995). In the early twentieth century, public police agencies became concerned primarily with crime control. As a result, throughout modern history the public as well as law enforcement's perception of police work has been thought of in terms of the enforcement of criminal law (Ortmeier & Davis, 2012).

Throughout the second half of the twentieth century policing was characterized by the crime control model. To combat police corruption, this period was also characterized by an apolitical philosophy, centralized administration, pinpointed responsibility, and strong discipline (Wilson, 1963). Many police agencies developed an organizational culture that emphasized crime control, arrest statistics, and clearance rates, insisting that aggressive enforcement, detection of major crimes, and rapid response to calls for police intervention represented the mission of the police (City of Los Angeles, 2003; Independent Commission on the Los Angeles Police Department, 1991). However, policing involves far more than the control of crime. It also involves peacekeeping, order maintenance, and numerous related responsibilities that in many instances make policing different from most occupations in America today (Coffey, 1990; Goldstein, 2001).

Policing in the twenty-first century faces many challenges. Contemporary law enforcement has become increasingly complex, yet the traditional policing model remains authoritarian and paramilitaristic. This model aspires to predictability in performance, assumes that police officers are incapable of making independent judgments, and establishes prescriptive training and highly supervised field relationships (Meese & Kurz, 1993). As Herman Goldstein noted:

> The dominant form of policing today continues to view police officers as automatons. Despite an awareness that they exercise broad discretion, they are held to strict account in their daily work—for what they do and how they do it . . . Especially in procedural matters, they are required to adhere to detailed regulations. In large police agencies, rank-and-file police officers are often treated impersonally and kept in the dark regarding policy matters. Officers quickly learn, under these conditions, that the rewards go to those who conform to expectations—that nonthinking compliance is valued. (Goldstein, 1990, p. 27)

Modern policing, particularly at the local level where the majority of police activity takes place, requires an approach that is more community and problem oriented. It must focus directly on the substance of policing—on the "problems that constitute the business of the police and on how to handle them" (Goldstein, 1990, 2001). In light of this focus on a different policing strategy, considerable attention must be given to the type of individual who joins the police service and how that person is trained and educated. It requires individual qualities such as leadership, initiative, and imagination, which have traditionally been associated with higher ranking officers. The police officer of the twenty-first century must be an information processor, community organizer, ethical leader, crime analyst, counselor, street corner politician, arresting officer, and school liaison (Meese & Ortmeier, 2004; Murphy, 1989).

Furthermore, only human beings, not technology, can fulfill the need for new strategies in police work. Thus, police agencies "must deploy the most innovative, self-disciplined, and self-motivated officers directly into the community as outreach specialists and community problem solvers" (Trojanowicz & Carter, 1990, p. 9).

Major research efforts that inquired about the nature of policing, which subsequently had a major impact on the field, were first undertaken in the 1950s. Until then, both the public and the police made certain assumptions about how the police should operate and these assumptions were often taken as descriptive of police operations even though police practices differed sharply (Goldstein, 1990). For example, the Kansas City Preventive Patrol Experiment questioned the effectiveness of preventive police patrol operations (Kelling, 1974). In addition, studies of response time undermined the premise that rapid response was effective in making arrests. Further research indicated that officers and detectives, by themselves, are limited in their ability to successfully investigate crimes (Eck & Spelman, 1987; Kelling & Bratton, 1993). The lessons drawn from these studies indicate that the police erred in investing a disproportionate amount of police resources in a limited number of practices. In the latter part of the twentieth century, Herman Goldstein, the father of problem-oriented policing, addressed the resource allocation issue. He identified five reasons why existing resources are insufficiently utilized.

- The police field is preoccupied with management and efficiency.
- The police devote most of their resources to responding to calls instead of acting on their own initiative to prevent or reduce community problems.
- The community itself is a major resource with enormous potential for problem identification and resolution.
- Rank and file officers' time and talent have not been used effectively.
- Efforts to improve policing have often failed because of the overall dynamics and complexity of the police organization. (Goldstein, 1990, pp. 10–14)

Numerous experts agree that contemporary policing requires a **philosophy** and a **strategy** that is inconsistent with the traditional model of policing. These experts suggest that a philosophy and strategy that focuses on engagement and solutions to community-based problems can improve the image, efficiency, and effectiveness of the police service (City of Los Angeles, 2003; Goldstein, 2001; Peak & Glensor, 2008; Whisenand & Ferguson, 2009). Furthermore, this new philosophy and strategy, commonly referred to as community policing, requires the officer to possess a wide variety of technical, cognitive, and affective skills. Essentially, the community policing philosophy reassesses who is responsible for public safety, redefines the roles and relationships between the community and the police, strengthens community-based efforts, and increases understanding and trust (California State Department of Justice, office of the Attorney General, 1996). The community policing strategy involves a plan of action that promotes community engagement, participation and problem solving (Meese & Ortmeier, 2004; Ortmeier, 1996; 2003).

CASE STUDY—COMMUNITY POLICING: DEAD OR ALIVE?

In 2003, Seattle Police Chief R. Gil Kerlikowske declared that "the era of community policing is over, finished, through, done." Kerlikowske qualified his statement by explaining that community policing has arrived, it is working, and people should not make the mistake of searching for yet another new policing philosophy or practice. The Chief asserted that community policing is the end result of over two decades of searching for the most appropriate policing strategy. Although continuous improvement will be necessary, community policing works because it emphasizes problem solving, line-level decision-making, and leveraging of the community in a partnership to address crime and disorder. Chief Kerlikowske stated, ". . . we should put to bed the era of community policing and engage, instead, in policing." (Community policing is dead; long live community policing. *Community Links,* August 2003, pp. 23–24.)

1. Is community policing a fad? Is it an end or a process?
2. How does community policing differ from traditional policing (the professional model)?

THE PRINCIPLES OF POLICING

To reconnect the police with the public, the traditional (professional) model of policing must be modified by a redefinition of the ways in which the police provide services to the public (Goldstein, 2001; Peak & Glensor, 2008). The basic police mission—to protect and serve—will not change. However, the culture and methodology in and through which police services are provided must change radically. Students and practitioners of policing must grasp a vision that supports an image of the police officer as, primarily, a peace officer, rather than a crime fighter. Although crime fighting is important, it does not consume a majority of a police officer's time. Most police time and effort is spent in peacekeeper and service roles.

The origins of community policing can be traced to the nine *Principles of Policing* attributed to Sir Robert Peel when he organized the London Metropolitan Police in 1829. It is perhaps ironic that while strategies, management systems, and operating mechanisms may change, the basic principles of policing remain the same. The principles *attributed to* Peel are still relevant today and have gained even greater validity as the foundation for community policing. According to these principles:

1. The basic mission for which police exist is to prevent crime and disorder as an alternative to the repression of crime and disorder by military force and severity of legal punishment.

2. The ability of the police to perform their duties is dependent upon public approval of police existence, actions, behavior, and the ability of the police to secure and maintain public respect.

3. The police must secure the willing cooperation of the public in voluntary observance of the law to be able to secure and maintain public respect.

4. The degree of cooperation of the public that can be secured diminishes, proportionately, the necessity for the use of physical force and compulsion in achieving police objectives.

5. The police seek and preserve public favor, not be catering to public opinion, but by constantly demonstrating absolutely impartial service to the law, in complete independence of policy, and without regard to the justice or injustice of the substance of individual laws; by ready offering of individual service and friendship to all members of the society without regard to their race or social standing; by ready exercise of courtesy and friendly good humor; and by ready offering of individual sacrifice in protecting and preserving life.

6. The police should use physical force to the extent necessary to secure observance of the law or to restore order only when the exercise of persuasion, advice, and warning is found to be insufficient to achieve police objectives; and police should use only the minimum degree of physical force which is necessary on any particular occasion for achieving a police objective.

7. The police at all times should maintain a relationship with the public that gives reality to the historic tradition that the police are the public and that the public are the police; the police are the only members of the public who are paid to give full-time attention to duties which are incumbent on every citizen in the interest of the community welfare.

8. The police should always direct their actions toward their functions and never appear to usurp the powers of the judiciary by avenging individuals or the state, or authoritatively judging guilt or punishing the guilty.

9. The test of police efficiency is the absence of crime and disorder, not the visible evidence of police action in dealing with them (Lee, 1901).

A review of these principles of policing, almost two centuries later, reveals that they still form the foundation of policing and modern concepts of community policing. Peel viewed the basic police mission as the *prevention* of crime and disorder. The success of police agencies, therefore, should be measured in terms of safer communities (the absence of crime and disorder), not merely the number of arrests made or traffic citations issued (the visible evidence of police action). This fundamental principle is consistent with the relationship that should exist between the police and the citizens they serve. Peel's references to the need for "public approval of police action" and for "securing the

Peel's efforts led to the passage of the Metropolitan Police Act
in 1829, creating the first recognizable police force. *(Sir Robert
Peel 1788–1850.)*

willing cooperation of the public in voluntary observance of the law" are
the basis for today's vision of successful police-community relationships.

Peel's belief in citizen responsibility for crime control and public
safety ("the historic tradition that the police are the public and that the
public are the police . . .") is the very foundation of citizen participation in
community policing. The mandate that police use force only when absolutely necessary, and in a proportionately appropriate manner, is not
only essential to Peel's themes, but is directly relevant to one of the most
serious problems faced by many law enforcement agencies today. In
short, the extent to which principles attributed to Peel are followed by
modern police departments can serve as a barometer of successful police–citizen relationships and the respect and cooperation that is received
from the public the police serve (Meese & Ortmeier, 2004).

COMMUNITY POLICING DEFINED

Over the past 200 years, the United States has changed from an agrarian society to a nation characterized by diverse social, cultural, economic, and political units. The law enforcement system, in particular, has not been able to keep pace with the changes (Earle, 1988; Meese & Ortmeier, 2004). The underlying problems associated with traditional police practices were addressed by several national commissions that studied and assessed the status of policing: the President's Commission on Law Enforcement and the Administration of Justice (1967), the National Advisory Commission on Civil Disorders (1968), the National Advisory Commission on the Causes and Prevention of Violence (1969), the President's Commission on Campus Unrest (1970), and the National Advisory Commission on Criminal Justice Standards and Goals (1976) (Goldstein, 1990). These and other studies revealed that the basic strategies of the traditional model of policing—motorized patrol, rapid response, and follow-up investigations—are, by themselves, limited in dealing with the substantive problems that face individual communities (Sheehan & Cordner, 2004). In addition, the bureaucratic and autocratic nature of most police organizations appears less likely to satisfy citizens as well as the organization's police officers (Couper & Lobitz, 1991).

As a result, several problematic realities face modern police organizations. According to Moore and Stephens (1991, pp. 112–113) these realities include the following:

- The police are having a very tough time dealing with crime by themselves.
- Effective crime control depends on an effective working partnership between the police and citizens in the communities they serve.
- The public police are losing market share in the safety and security business.
- The public police contribute to the quality of life in their communities in many ways other than by controlling crime.
- The administrative instruments now being used to ensure accountability and control of police officers cannot reliably do so.
- The police are routinely held accountable for the fairness and economy with which they use force, authority, and money.
- Rather than seek insulation from political interference, it is more appropriate for police agencies to make themselves more accountable to political institutions and citizens alike.

These realities are still relevant today.

In response to these problematic realities, a variety of police strategies have been developed (Ortmeier & Meese, 2010; U.S. Department of Justice, Bureau of Justice Statistics, 1994). The strategies include:

- Code Blue
- Community-Based Policing (CBP).
- Community-Oriented Policing (COP).
- Citizen-Oriented Police Enforcement (COPE)

- Community Patrol Officer Program (CPOP)
- Neighborhood-Oriented Policing (NOP)
- Police Area Representative (PAR)
- Problem-Oriented Policing (POP)
- Quality Policing
- Target-Oriented Policing

Regardless of the label attached to these strategies, the primary focus is on community engagement and problem solving (Community Policing Consortium, 1994). The main themes included in this approach are increased effectiveness, reliance on the creativity and expertise of line officers, and closer involvement with the public (Spelman & Eck, 1987). In a **traditional policing** environment, emphasis is placed on limiting police discretion, reducing opportunities for corruption, separation of policing from politics, and improved performance through efficiency measurements. Often referred to as the professional model of policing, this strategy promotes distance between the police and the public, resulting in less emphasis on the social function of the police.

In a **community policing** environment, emphasis is placed on decentralization, a recognition that crime control is only one function of law enforcement, and the development, through **police–community engagement,** of a more intimate relationship between the police and the public. Although the professional model of traditional policing is still valued, it is supplemented with an understanding that the police serve the community as well as enforce the law. **Problem solving** is a key ingredient in community policing. A major problem associated with the implementation of community policing is the realization that changes in policing are necessary. Both community engagement and problem solving call for behaviors that are different from those that police officers have traditionally been trained and educated to demonstrate (Meese & Kurz, 1993; Ortmeier & Davis, 2012).

In a community policing environment, emphasis is placed on police-community engagement, participation, and problem solving. *(Photo courtesy of the Cobb County, GA Police Department)*

Learn more about community policing through the Community Policing Consortium at www.communitypolicing.org.

Yet despite the apparent benefits of community policing, its implementation has been haphazard. Research indicates that many police agencies assign some officers to community policing. However, most officers are still deployed in traditional reactive patrol assignments. While community policing officers and traditional policing officers engage in overlapping responsibilities, officers assigned to community policing emphasize and engage in a broader range of tasks. Both types of officers still support traditional law enforcement practices, although community officers supplement traditional attitudes and beliefs with favorable perceptions of community policing.

The slow philosophical, strategic, and tactical shift toward community policing, in some measure, may be due to traditional police organizational reward structures. Management adherence to traditional measures of performance, which value quantitative measurements such as the number of arrests, inhibits the implementation of community policing. The use of quantitative accountability models such as CompStat tend to support traditional measurements. If recognition and promotions are based on traditional measurements, officers see little merit in the practice of community policing. As a result, implementation of community policing strategies depends on the efforts of a small number of community officers assigned to perform such duties.

However, evidence suggests that community policing officers experience a higher level of job satisfaction than do their traditional reactive counterparts. Increased job satisfaction often leads to improved morale, motivation, and higher productivity, suggesting that officers engaged in community policing are more efficient and effective (Pelfrey, 2004).

What Community Policing is Not

Community policing, as a philosophy, strategy, and practical solution to community-based problems, has been the subject of a great deal of criticism and resistance, particularly from the law enforcement profession itself. Line officers as well as police supervisors and command staff are part of the resistance movement. Each group appears to have its own reasons for not wholeheartedly adopting the community policing model. Some reasons are self-serving. Others represent sincere concerns regarding the erosion of effective police practices that have taken years to develop. In some situations, excessive enthusiasm for community policing, coupled with unrealistic expectations of what can be accomplished through implementation of the model, leads many to abandon community policing efforts. Much of the criticism may be based on misconceptions about community policing. Thus, before defining or describing what community policing is, it may be best to describe what community policing is not.

First, community policing is not radically different from what the public police mission was originally conceived to be. In 1829, Robert Peel envisioned and helped to implement a police service that worked closely with the community to identify and find solutions to community problems. This original strategy focused on crime prevention.

Second, community policing is not so radically different from traditional policing that it requires a total reorganization of a police agency. Even the most traditional police agencies engage in community policing to some extent. If some restructuring is required, it would not be the first step in the implementation of community policing. In addition, traditional police skills are still required. The new skills required of a police officer in a community policing environment are designed to supplement, not replace, traditional police techniques and practices.

Third, community policing does not increase a line officer's workload. Often, a large percentage of patrol time is uncommitted. Patrol officers in a community policing environment still respond to radio calls and engage in preventive patrol. However, in utilizing uncommitted time, police officers take the initiative to establish partnerships with the community. Eventually, the synergistic effect of the partnership tends to reduce crime and disorder, thus reducing patrol officer workload.

Fourth, community policing does not distract officers from doing real police work and thus increase the likelihood of crime. Crime is multicausal. Crime rates increase or decrease for a variety of reasons. A decrease in the crime rate may be attributable, in part, to the presence of the police. However, police presence is not the sole determining factor. In fact, the crime rate has increased in some areas where the police practice traditional aggressive crime fighting patrol techniques. In a community policing environment, patrol officers still enforce the law and cite and arrest violators. In community policing, the focus is not on what the police should do, but why and how they do it.

Fifth, community policing does not turn police officers into social workers. Even if it did, social work is important to the alleviation of pain and suffering. Social workers are, therefore, natural allies of the police. The police mission is not limited to catching bad guys. The police have a much broader role in society. The mission also involves order maintenance and service (Watson, Stone, & DeLuca, 1998).

False assumptions regarding community policing continue to inhibit its implementation. To be successful, policing philosophies must change and law enforcement institutions must challenge traditional methods of operation (Capowich, 2005).

What Community Policing Is

Until recently, the prevailing view in police management was the belief that police agencies should adopt an operational style that called on officers to be distant and unemotional. The belief was due, in part, to a commonly held view that police officers would be less corruptible. To deal with rampant police corruption in the first half of the twentieth century, organizational rules, policies, and deployment practices limited police discretion and restricted officers' activities to prescribed assignments.

Defining the resulting police behavior as "professional and objective," this philosophy often led to perceived, and sometimes real, insensitivity to the needs of the community. Contemporary wisdom, however, refutes this way of thinking. Accordingly, community policing is evolving as a way to use a sense of vision to meet the need for shared responsibility for public safety (Brann, 1999). To accommodate community needs, police agencies must change both structurally and philosophically.

Community policing requires not only a mere restructuring of some police organizations, but an orientation by the police toward an entirely different way of life (Sparrow, 1988). It goes much further than placing officers in storefronts or having them walk the beat or ride bicycles. It is a comprehensive philosophy, management style, and organizational strategy that promotes proactive problem solving and **police-community partnerships** (Goldstein, 2001; Parker, 1993). It is different from traditional policing because it causes a revolution in the way police departments interact with the public as well as in the way police agencies are organized (Trojanowicz & Bucqueroux, 1990). And, although some view as ill conceived the notion of allowing the community to be involved in the definition of the police role (Goodbody, 1995), many leaders in the police profession view community policing as a mandatory rather than an optional law enforcement strategy (Meese & Kurz, 1993; Peak & Glensor, 2008).

Although viewed by some as a soft approach to law enforcement, concrete experience in numerous police departments has shown that community policing can achieve ambitious crime control objectives, even with existing resources (Kennedy, 1993). In addition, community policing is seen as a powerful tool to increase community support for, and the public image of, the police. Both are essential ingredients to effective policing (Coffey, 1990). In a narrow sense, community policing focuses directly on the substance of policing. In its broadest context, it is a comprehensive strategy for employing resources in a way that gives high priority to addressing substantive problems and reshapes the police agency by influencing changes in personnel, organization, and procedures (Goldstein, 1990). In essence, the community problem rather than being a single incident becomes the main unit of police work (San Diego Police Department, 1993). Performance measures are not based solely on arrests, response time, and clearance rates but also on citizen involvement, reduced fear of crime, improved quality of life, and solutions to chronic community problems (Trojanowicz, 1990).

The philosophy and strategy for community policing in no way suggests that police officers should become social workers. On the contrary, those who violate the criminal law must receive whatever is due them. Offenders should not be coddled. However, a vast majority of the people with whom the police come in contact are not criminals. Even in the most crime-infested blocks of a city, 90 percent of the residents are law-abiding citizens. The responsible citizen should not be treated the same as the criminal offender. Actually, the practical application of the strategy means that the community and the police will work together to be tougher on crime.

Definitions of community policing are many and varied. One state attorney general's office defines it as "a philosophy, management style, and organizational design that promotes proactive problem-solving and police-community partnerships to address the causes of crime and fear as well as other community issues" (California State Department of Justice, Office of the Attorney General, 1996, p. 3). After extensive research on the definitions and subject matter of community policing, the author developed the following definition: "A philosophy and a strategy which promotes community engagement, participation, and problem-solving; action which leads to the discovery and implementation of solutions to community problems" (Ortmeier, 1996, p. 4).

The philosophy and strategy for community policing embody several principles that relate to different ways of thinking about, organizing, and managing police agencies. These principles were outlined very effectively by the Office of the Attorney General, California Department of Justice (1996).

- Community policing reassesses who is responsible for public safety and re-defines the roles and relationships between the police and the community to require shared ownership, shared decision making, and shared accountability. . . . The police and the community must collaborate to identify problems and develop proactive communitywide solutions. . . . The police must acknowledge that they cannot do the job of public safety alone and recognize that they have valuable resources available to them in the community. . . . Shared ownership does not mean that the community takes the law into its own hands. . . . Nor

Community policing attempts to connect the police with the citizens they serve. *(Photo courtesy of the Los Angeles Sheriff's Department.)*

does this approach diminish the role of the police who are in a unique position to facilitate problem solving.

- Community policing strengthens and empowers community-based efforts. A new view of community is emerging in society—a view that advances the importance of using an asset-based model. . . . The model recognizes that communities are naturally resilient and have the ability to identify and solve some of their own problems.

- Community policing increases understanding and trust between police and community members. Inherent in any successful partnership is a sense of equality, mutual respect and trust. Assigning officers to one beat for extended periods of time (beat integrity), and promoting on-going daily, direct and positive contact—including partnership efforts—between the police and the community, fosters understanding and trust. . . . Establishing mutual trust between the police and the community results in less fear and fewer public complaints about use of excessive force by the police.

- Community policing shifts the focus of police work from responding to individual incidents to addressing problems identified by the community as well as the police, emphasizing the use of proactive problem-solving approaches to supplement traditional law enforcement methods. . . . Shifting from an incident orientation to a problem orientation requires looking for underlying conditions, as well as patterns and relationships among incidents, that might identify common causal factors. These underlying problems, rather than individual incidents, become the main units of police work. . . . Community-oriented policing is not soft on crime. On the contrary, with increased community support and communication, good arrests often increase.

- Community policing requires a sustained commitment from the police and the community to develop long term, proactive programs and strategies that address the underlying conditions causing community problems.

- Community policing establishes new public expectations of, and measurement standards for, police effectiveness. The public and the police must have realistic expectations of what the police can and cannot do to achieve community health and well-being. Community policing is not a panacea that will correct all social problems and resolve all crime and violence. The public must be aware of the reality of police limitations and the related importance of public involvement. Police efforts are re-prioritized to focus on customer service and satisfaction. Qualitative as well as quantitative approaches are used to measure officer and agency effectiveness.

- Community policing requires the buy-in of top management of the police and other local government agencies as well as a new leadership style that makes most effective use of human resources within a community. . . . It requires vision, strategic planning, teamwork, and problem solving.

- Community policing requires constant flexibility to respond to all emerging issues. By most estimates, only 25 percent of police work actually involves enforcing the law or arresting people. Traditional law enforcement equips the police with very few tools, other than the

authority to arrest and incarcerate, to deal with the broad scope of police business. Prevention and intervention alternatives available to
police need to be greatly expanded. . . . The focus should be on developing creative, tailor-made responses to specific problems and incorporating such prevention and intervention efforts into the mainstream
of policing.

- Community policing requires knowledge of available community resources and how to access and mobilize them as well as the ability to
develop new resources within the community. . . . Being resource-
knowledgeable is a unique skill that enhances community policing
efforts.
- Community policing decentralizes and despecializes police services,
operations, and management wherever possible. It relaxes the traditional chain of command and encourages innovation and creative
problem solving by all. While specialization is necessary in some instances, such as the investigation of child abuse and gang activity, de-
specialization can often free up personnel for community beats and
improve officer communication, innovation and ownership of beat
areas.
- Community policing requires new recruitment, hiring, and promotion
practices and policies. The community policing model requires new
skills and duties for police officers. . . . Community police officers must
be able to assess situations, analyze problems and evaluate strategies.
- Community policing requires a commitment to developing additional
officer skills through training. These new skills include problem solving, networking, mediation, facilitation, conflict resolution, cultural
competency and literacy, and quality leadership skills.

The community policing model is an appropriate vehicle to restore
police–community trust. It places emphasis on service to the public and
crime prevention as the primary roles of the police in a democratic society. Rather than placing primary emphasis on arrest statistics, community policing emphasizes community-based problem solving and active
citizen involvement in those matters that are of importance to the community (Independent Commission on the Los Angeles Police Department, 1991).

In many ways, community policing is a concept in search of a definition. The concept defies a specific definition because community policing
is a philosophy and a strategy integrated into a culture based on shared
police–community values. Thus, community policing is difficult to define
in specific terms. A specific definition may not be necessary. Rather, the
elasticity associated with the concept of community policing may be its
greatest asset. Community-oriented policing efforts should be customized
to meet community needs. Therefore, community policing should be defined by the citizens and the police in a particular community.

Community policing is what policing is about and oversimplification
of the concept is often problematic. Policing is very complex. Communities and the police should not expend an inordinate amount of energy attempting to create a perfect community policing model (Goldstein, 1990,
2001). Community policing is not an outcome (end). Rather, community

Additional sources of information on community policing are available through the U.S. Department of Justice, Office of Community Oriented Policing Services at www .cops.usdoj.gov.

policing is a means (process) to achieve more efficient and effective policing (Ford, Boles, Plamondon, & White, 2000; Ortmeier & Meese, 2012).

NEW POLICE OFFICER COMPETENCIES

Police officer competencies relate to the officer knowledge and skills necessary to function in a policing environment. Officers using community policing strategies must think creatively and independently. They must be able to create a vision and develop appropriate steps for solving problems. Instead of reacting primarily to incidents, the officer is forced to analyze, plan, and take the initiative (Meese, 1993). Furthermore, recruitment, selection, training, and educational programs must be modified to develop a core of officers with the instinct and leadership competencies necessary for working with the community (Anderson, 2000; Fleissner, Fedan, & Klinger, 1992; Whisenand & Ferguson, 2009). One must remember that it is the individual patrol officer who has the greatest freedom, discretional authority, and ability to work directly with the public and who is perceived as the primary representative of the police department (Goldstein, 1990; 2001). It is this officer who has the most direct contact with the public and its problems.

In 1967, the President's Commission on Law Enforcement and the Administration of Justice observed that physical strength and aggressiveness reflected the popular image of what the police do. The commission also observed that this image was inconsistent with a careful analysis of the job requirements. It further noted that one incompetent officer could trigger a riot, permanently damage the reputation of a citizen, or alienate a community against a police department. In a community policing environment, brute strength and aggressiveness give way to a new breed of officers who are better educated, self-managed, creative, guided by values and purposes, and who are not constrained by rules and excessive supervision (Meese, 1993). Officers are team players, not subordinates, and supervisors act as facilitators (J. R. Clark, 1994). Even the day-to-day, seemingly routine, decisions officers make about their own conduct and actions have potentially far-reaching consequences and must be guided by individual introspection about values, integrity, principles, and ethics (Boehm, 1988; Lyman, 2010).

Police departments must deploy the most innovative, self-disciplined, and self-motivated officers directly into the community as outreach specialists and community problem solvers (Trojanowicz & Carter, 1990; U.S. Department of Justice, Bureau of Justice Statistics, 1992). As such, police officers must be sensitive to public perceptions and possess complex critical-thinking skills (California Community Colleges, 1992, 2003). They must be able to adapt to changing community needs (McKinnie, 1995; Wycoff & Oettmeier, 1994), and utilize a human relations approach to communicate, identify, and solve problems and look toward service to the community (California State Legislature, 1991; Coffey, 1990; Meese, 1993; Spelman & Eck, 1987). There is also a need to develop collaborative, multidisciplinary approaches to community problems by including members of civil rights groups, and health, education, social services, and child welfare agencies as well as business and industry (U.S. Department of Justice, 1993; Whisenand & Ferguson, 2009).

Skill and competency requirements for police personnel are changing to meet the challenges of the twenty-first century. Many police departments are searching for a new breed of officer—the customer-oriented cop. Police agencies from New York to San Diego, Largo, Florida, to Lawrence, Michigan, and Los Angeles to Edneyville, North Carolina, are recruiting and training police officer candidates who have the skills and commitment for community policing (Selecting a new breed, 1999). Additionally, police training and education programs that emphasize leadership, ethics, and a community orientation are being implemented (Byrd, 2003/2004; California State, Commission on Peace Officer Standards and Training, 2002, 2003; Meese & Ortmeier, 2004).

FRAMEWORK FOR COMMUNITY POLICING

Community policing is a philosophy and a strategy that governs how citizens and police work together to identify, address, and solve crime and disorder problems within a community. As such, community policing consists of two core elements: community partnership and problem solving. Both elements must be given equal consideration and emphasis. When priority is given only to the development of police–community partnerships, the result is a negligible impact on crime. When priority is given only to the problem solving half of the equation, police–community relations are strained. The community policing model is designed to supplement and complement, not necessarily replace, traditional policing models. However, change in philosophy and strategy is required because of changes in the level and nature of crime, the character and diversity in American communities, family structure, resources available to fight crime, and levels of public safety (California Commission on Peace Officer Standards and Training, 2012).

Role of the Community

The phrase community policing is derived from two words: the community and the police. In a community policing environment, the role of the community is a powerful one and community involvement is vital to success. In community policing, citizens assume two important roles. They are consumers of police services and they function as coproducers of policing itself. As community policing promotes greater **citizen–police cooperation,** it also presents an excellent opportunity to enhance police–community relations (Mastrofski, Parks, Reiss, & Worden, 1999).

The community must have equality with the police. The community needs the police and the police need the community. The community cannot be viewed as an advisory group or silent partner to the police. In fact, the essence of the police role is to reinforce and support informal crime and disorder control mechanisms of the community itself. Without committing enormous public safety resources, the police cannot be a substitute for community involvement and informal control (Kelling, 1999; Wilson & Kelling, 1982). Yet, despite the critical role of the community in the community policing effort, research and literature regarding community involvement is generally lacking. Most of the research available focuses on the role of the police officer.

One problem encountered when trying to determine the community's role involves defining what a community is. Communities are variously defined in terms of territory, like-mindedness, shared beliefs and feelings, cultural identity, lifestyle, and interaction on a continuous basis. Communities include apartment complexes, neighborhoods, cities, counties, church and business groups, government agencies, schools and colleges, Internet chatrooms, and homeless shelters. They include gangs, crack houses, and organized crime families. Communities are not always law abiding, and police interaction with each community will obviously be different.

In addition, the composition and goals of individual communities are constantly shifting. As membership and environmental changes occur, problems that need to be addressed by the police also change. Thus, from a community-oriented policing standpoint, a **community** may be defined as any collection of people who share common concerns or attitudes toward crime and disorder problems. Law-abiding residents of a neighborhood where crack houses exist share one view of the situation. Drug addicts and dealers who frequent the crack houses have a different view. Police strategies with both groups must also be different (Oliver, 2008). The police can expect law-abiding citizens to support a crack house eradication effort. The illegal drug community will resist it.

Although police strategies among groups may differ, the police should not entertain preconceived notions regarding community desires. Some law enforcement personnel may not believe people living in impoverished areas care as much about crime as do citizens from affluent neighborhoods. The belief suggests that the street culture in poor neighborhoods finds crime, disorder, and drug use acceptable. However, there is no difference in attitudes toward violence among races, ethnic groups, and social classes. A study conducted in Chicago revealed that blacks and Latinos are even less tolerant of deviance than are their white counterparts (Sampson & Bartusch, 1999).

Community policing is appropriate for suburban and rural areas as well as urban environments. Community initiatives often begin because citizens are dissatisfied with existing conditions and the criminal justice system is viewed as too formal and slow to respond to problems. In some cases, invocation of the justice system is not viewed as an appropriate and fair response. This appears to be especially true in many rural communities where carefully crafted alternatives to criminal sanctions are preferred. In truancy cases, for example, nonsystem alternatives, such as parental involvement and peer pressure, may be more effective than system-based truancy citations.

Police personnel are in a unique leadership position in rural communities to engage and encourage citizens to participate in the identification of community needs and desires. These communities are built around shared values. The police can assist the communities with the creation of opportunities and rewards based on these shared values. Law enforcement, interdiction, and negative sanctioning of law violations tend to ignore rewards for abiding by the rules. Especially in situations involving juveniles, the police and the community can collaborate to create opportunities and rewards for young people who demonstrate positive behavior.

Additionally, since many rural communities exhibit a multicultural dimension due to an influx of minorities and non–native born individuals, the police and the community can strive to honor differences while reinforcing shared community values. Participation from private as well as public organizations is often easier to muster in rural areas. As public servants serving the broader community, local police and sheriff's deputies can use their position of authority to seek assistance from state and federal agencies, private foundations, and professional associations. By adopting a problem-solving approach, law enforcement officers in rural areas can lead communities to enjoy safety and improvements in the quality of life (Dickey & McGarry, 2001; Meese & Ortmeier, 2004; Thurman & McGarrell, 2003).

To date, feedback from the public regarding community policing efforts has been favorable. Recent research reveals that the public believes community policing is beneficial to their neighborhoods. One positive side effect is the improved relationship between the public and the police. Therefore, the police should promote increased involvement of the community in the policing effort. More attention must also be given to the education of the public and inclusion of citizens in the evaluation of community policing efforts. Generally, the public has been excluded from the dialog regarding police work for the last 50 years. And, although a great deal of research has focused on officer attitudes toward community policing, more studies should include a focus on citizen attitudes and knowledge of community policing. Such studies would assist policymakers in the development of an understanding of the role of the community in policing (Webb & Katz, 1997).

The concept of government agencies working in partnership with a community is not new to the United States. Since the time of the Revolutionary War, citizen participation has been the foundation for a democratic form of government. However, as societies grow in terms of the number of citizens and economic conditions force government agencies to become more centralized, continuous participation by the populace in partnership with public officials becomes more sporadic. As a result, government agencies, including the police, become more isolated and removed from the citizens they are obligated to serve. In a community policing environment, the police must reverse the process of centralization. This process involves a return to a more democratized decision-making strategy. The role of the citizen and the community should shift away from an advisory capacity to one of more authoritative action (Oliver, 2008).

Community members, groups, businesses and institutions are responsible for voicing concerns regarding neighborhood crime and disorder, reporting crimes and other problems, providing information, helping to convict criminal offenders, employing crime prevention measures, and exercising parental authority over juveniles. Community constituents also assume responsibility for working with the police and solving some of the community problems on their own.

Role of the Police

The second part of the community policing partnership equation involves the role of the police. In a community policing environment, police officers still respond to calls, write traffic citations, and make arrests. However, patrol officers use uncommitted time more efficiently and effectively. In a community policing environment, the police also participate in community groups and activities, establish and support crime prevention programs, and prioritize and help solve community problems (Parker, 1999). Community policing acknowledges the value of the patrol function as well as the individual police officer. The patrol officer is viewed as a responsible, versatile problem solver rather than a mere automaton who responds to supervisors' orders and dispatched calls for service. Supervisors operate as facilitators rather than ranking officers with unquestioned authority.

Many police officers are skeptical, especially when someone suggests changing policing philosophy or strategy. Most people, even police officers, are resistant to change. Why should a police agency or its officers change radically from what they were originally trained to do? Will the change in philosophy and 180-degree shift in strategy benefit the agency and the individual officer? These are extremely important questions. They require practical as well as abstract answers, although most in service community policing training programs for officers focus on the abstract.

Transformational change also requires creativity, innovation, and acceptance by the most senior officials in the police agency. Senior officials in the organization, especially chiefs, sheriffs, and commissioners, can enhance partnerships with external groups, re-engineer operating systems, restructure organizational hierarchy, align human resources to fit community policing efforts, and adopt perspectives that seek continuous improvement of police services (Ford, Boles, Plamondon, & White, 2000).

Benefits to the agency and the individual officers include the possibility as well as the probability of increased productivity and improvement in the police public image. Other benefits, especially from the standpoint of the individual line police officer, include more freedom in decision-making, improved management support, better working conditions, and higher pay (Oliver, 2008). Yes, community policing may benefit officers in the form of higher pay. One major urban city converted its entire police operation to the philosophy and strategy of community policing. The change generated tremendous community support for the police.

In fact, the citizens were so pleased one year that police officers were the only city employee group to receive a pay raise even though the municipality was experiencing serious financial difficulties.

One of the greatest benefits of community policing to a police officer's career, however, may be expressed in terms of the officer's satisfaction. Community policing can improve the quality of the responses police make to community problems. The improvement is a positive change. It responds to the critical need to treat line police officers as mature individuals, demonstrate more confidence and trust in them, give officers more responsibility, make officers stakeholders in the outcomes of their efforts, and give them a greater sense of fulfillment in a job well done (Goldstein, 1990).

Community policing is implemented in different ways. One size does not fit all. Problems and priorities vary from city to city, community to community. Although every bit as applicable in small towns and rural communities as it is in urban and suburban areas, community policing must fit the community it serves (Cordner & Scarborough, 1999). The point is that the police and the community being served work together to create solutions to community-based problems and improve the quality of life for all of a community's citizens (Community Policing Consortium, 1997a; Ramsey, 2002).

WORKING WITH DIVERSITY

Tremendous **demographic changes** are taking place. Immigration to the United States and the growth in minority populations in general has dramatically changed the face of America. The United States accepts approximately 1 million new immigrants each year. Close to one-third of American children are black, Hispanic, or Asian. In addition, one-half of all marriages end in divorce and over one-quarter of the nation's households are headed by women. The population is also aging. By 2010, 25 percent of Americans were 55 or older. These groups form special interest constituencies. As the various groups are forced to compete for limited resources, the police may become involved when competition and intergroup rivalries develop (Peak, 2010).

Individuals and groups in America share a common culture based on a national heritage of democratic principles and personal freedom. Thus, Americans are expected to adhere to basic societal customs and laws built on consensus. However, America is not a homogeneous population. Rather, it is a complex mixture of diverse groups. This **diversity** affects police–community relations in numerous ways. A culture influences human behavior and the police should not ignore cultural differences. Understanding and appreciating individuals and groups within a cultural context can expand and strengthen police–community relationships and provide new opportunities for open communication, increased mutual respect, and common goal achievement.

People behave in culturally defined ways. Thus, interpersonal communications and interactions are understood in terms of the cultural context through which the interaction takes place. It is possible to have excellent communications skills, yet apply these skills in culturally inappropriate ways. It is possible to make decisions that are consistent with law and policy, yet commit acts that are inappropriate and inhumane. Misunderstanding can lead to misinterpretations of the intentions of others. Many new immigrants, for example, suffered great abuse at the hands of the police in their native countries. As a result, these law-abiding people may distrust the police and flee at the sight of a police officer.

Everyone has biases and prejudices regarding others. These preconceptions are based on past experiences and beliefs acquired within one's own culture. However, to interact fairly and objectively with others in a diverse society, police officers must be sensitive to the cultural differences of others. It is important to remember that a society is comprised of one culture as well as many subcultures. Each member of a society shares common beliefs and goals with other members. Each member of a society is also a member of a subculture within the societal culture. An appreciation of the reality of diversity can help police officers to creatively overcome communication and interaction barriers (Hunter, Barker, & Mayhall, 2011).

The philosophy and strategy of community policing are central to any discussion of police relationships with minority groups and diverse populations. The success of community policing depends, to a great extent, on strong collaborative partnerships with neighborhoods and communities. Effective partnerships promote trust, ensure a dialogue, and provide mechanisms through which the police become aware of critical issues and relevant concerns in a community. As community policing seeks inclusiveness to address crime, disorder, and quality of life concerns of all citizens, it represents a more democratic form of policing (Shusta, Levine, Wong, & Harris, 2011).

BUILDING COMMUNITY PARTNERSHIPS

Solving community-based problems requires community effort. The police cannot solve all community problems on their own. Yet citizens typically function as consumers of police services rather than contributors to the problem-solving process (City of Los Angeles, 2003). Typically, residents and businesspeople within a community are not aware of all the resources that might be at their disposal. If these citizens were aware of such resources, there might be far fewer inappropriate calls for police services.

Traditionally, the police have tried to reduce crime and disorder without a great deal of community assistance. However, various agencies and organizations within a community can be very useful resources. Government, nonprofit as well as for-profit organizations, and health and social services agencies can be very helpful. The police must also mobilize a community's grassroots population.

Communities differ in the types and number of organizations within them. Impoverished areas tend to have less community involvement than affluent areas. But the police cannot fight problems associated with crime and disorder alone. Residents and businesspersons must be organized and mobilized for the problem-solving effort. For most order maintenance and restoration issues, resources exist, if not in the immediate vicinity, then at the city, county, state, or federal levels. Although the police are not social workers, the police should know how to contact and solicit the support of social services agencies and resources when necessary.

Community mobilization starts with the identification of leaders within that community. Leaders include those affiliated with educational, religious, and business organizations. They also include public officials and officeholders. Some leaders emerge from unexpected sources. Informal and volunteer organizations typically do not appear at the forefront of a community. If the community is experiencing a problem with gang-related activity, gang leaders must also be identified. The police must create an environment in which the leadership mass within the community can work together toward a shared vision. These leaders may not, and probably will not, reach agreement on all major issues. However, they may be able to arrive at consensus on many issues and resolve most of the problems facing the community.

Leaders and other interested parties within a community can be brought together at a community meeting. The community meeting should not be viewed as simply a public relations effort. Rather, it presents opportunities to learn about citizen and community concerns and to develop strategies for problem analysis and problem solving. Leadership skills for the police officer are critically important in this effort.

There are several key points to remember when mobilizing a community and building partnerships. The police can facilitate community mobilization and help to create community organization where none exists. Alternatively, the police can limit their role when existing community organizations are accomplishing agreed-upon goals. When a crime prevention program needs to be established, the police can work with others to get it started and subsequently function as a resource to support program participants. The most effective community organizations tend to be independent of the police. These organizations also tend to be more credible if they are not seen as adjuncts to government agencies. However, communication between the police, public agencies, and community leaders is essential. The community, in collaboration with the police and other community organizations, can build an organization that can address undesirable conditions (Community Policing Consortium, 1997a).

The most effective community partnerships are initiated by three factors: a crisis that mobilizes people to action, adequate funding, and the dynamic personalities of the members. To be sustainable, a community partnership must share a common vision, develop good relationships, have adequate resources and internal operating procedures, possess leadership and commitment, generate community support, be accountable for its actions, and be adaptable to change (Phillips & Pack, 1999; What does it take to make collaboration work?, 2004).

Community partnerships must also be advertised and marketed (Chermak & Weiss, 2003). It is important to deliver the message of good works. Numerous communication channels may be utilized for this purpose. Mass media includes radio, television, newspapers, cable systems, and the Internet. Other communication media include flyers, brochures, letters, and newsletters. Direct communication involves town meetings and speakers' bureaus. Special events make excellent forums for public-speaking engagements. Public ceremonies may also be used to honor people for their personal commitment to the betterment of the community.

Beyond the obvious communication channels, numerous other opportunities to develop creative alliances exist. Partnerships must go beyond those who are within the community and the criminal justice system. These alliances may originate from nontraditional sources. The police and community members might partner with like-minded groups and individuals who share common concerns. Partnerships may also be developed with non–like-minded groups such as synagogues or churches that may sponsor seminars on crime prevention. In some cases, alliances can be established with those who may appear to be at odds with the community policing mission. If the community is experiencing a high number of incidents involving gun violence, it might appear that gun store owners would not be interested in an alliance. However, gun store owners might be encouraged to sponsor gun safety seminars and work with the community organization to prevent gun theft and violence (Campbell, 1999).

Community policing involves an outreach to the community, an outreach designed to promote partnerships with the community that reduce crime, enhance public safety, and improve the quality of life for the community's inhabitants (Stevens, 2002). Unfortunately, many community policing initiatives are limited to changes within a police agency or on community-oriented programs that have little impact on the basic functions or structure of police activity in the community. The failure of these initiatives can lead some to believe that the concept of a police-community partnership is flawed because a community is not a singly entity but a group of competing interests. Yet, partnering and collaboration with a community is of value to policing, as evidenced by successes of the past quarter century (Parshall-McDonald & Greenberg, 2002). Participants are cautioned to remember that notable success with community policing efforts can be achieved only when both the police and citizens change their attitudes and work collaboratively to identify and solve community problems (Dubois & Hartnett, 2002; Scott, 2001).

Researchers often report resistance to change and mistrust on the part of the police as well as the citizenry. Police resistance can be traced to the police subculture, numerous organizational barriers, and recalcitrant personnel who simply wish to wait until change initiatives, such as community policing, pass. Likewise, citizens and community groups often resist change and lack enthusiasm without prior positive experiences that demonstrate that change is necessary and worthwhile. Despite poll results to the contrary, many citizens also distrust the police. Police and citizen support for and participation in the community policing effort must go beyond motivation sessions and behavioral reinforcement. Implementing community policing requires substantial education and reeducation of the parties involved. Additionally, both sides must commit to a substantial amount of personal contact so trust and cooperation can develop.

Without question, community participation is essential to any community policing effort. Unfortunately, there is no magic formula for securing, and sustaining, participation by a community. Involving a community can be just as difficult as involving police officers. To secure and maintain a community's participation, the citizens of a community must be:

- convinced that participation will improve community conditions.
- organized, not randomly selected.
- trained and guided through the community policing effort.
- aware of the risk of inequitable outcomes. Those who really need community policing may be the most difficult to convince. Many residents of poor and disenfranchised neighborhoods may have been disappointed in the past. Those who generally support the police may also be skeptical. Reports of police abuse, misconduct, and corruption, true or not, can result in citizen mistrust of the police.

In many areas in which community policing strategies can have the most significant impact, the community and the police often have a history of antagonistic behavior. In these communities, the police may be viewed as arrogant and uncaring, as the enemy rather than as partners. On the community side of the equation, citizens may not support the police or may have a history of being uncooperative with police officers. Additionally, these areas often lack the organizational infrastructure conducive to community involvement. In high-crime neighborhoods, citizens often distrust and are hostile toward each other as well as the police. They may also fear retaliation from neighborhood drug dealers and gangs. In economically and ethically diverse communities, suspicion can divide citizens along class and racial lines, creating inevitable cohesiveness problems and pressure on the police to choose between competing community factions. The challenges involved in securing and maintaining community participation are significant but not insurmountable. Ethical police leadership at the line officer level can help to achieve positive results even against what appears to be insurmountable odds. Competent rank and file police personnel, skilled in the art of leadership and supported by agency command staff, can assist a community with an articulation of a vision for an improved quality of life and lead citizens in a communal effort to identify and solve community problems. The police can solicit and encourage community participation by creating meaningful roles for the community and training citizens on these roles, customizing community policing program efforts to meet the needs of various community constituency groups, and promoting active community involvement rather than simple awareness. Further, the police should focus recruitment efforts toward existing community organizations and ensure that community meetings are worthwhile (DuBois & Hartnett, 2002; Walker, Spohn & DeLone, 2011).

Learn more about the philosophy and strategy of community policing through the Police Executive Research Forum (PERF) at www.policeforum.org.

COMMUNITY POLICING IN ACTION

Examples of effective community partnerships in community policing environments are numerous and may include initiatives such as civilian review boards, citizen patrols, citizen police academies, and ride-along programs. In several communities throughout the country, Drug Abuse Resistance Education (DARE) has been introduced through collaborative efforts on the part of the police and local school districts. Officers leave patrol duties to enter schools and educate young people about the dangers of drug use. Although DARE has its critics, creative partnership initiatives are essential to meet the growing citizen demands for change, resource accountability, and improvement in the quality of life (Carter, 1995). Other programs include the following cited by the President's Crime Prevention Council (1997):

- **Allegheny County, Pennsylvania:** Juvenile Crime Prevention Throughout the County. As a response to an increase in violent juvenile crime, Allegheny County, which includes the city of Pittsburgh, launched a countywide antiviolence campaign. The campaign's first step was to form two groups. The Law Enforcement Agency Directors and the Youth Crime Prevention Council were created to develop a strategy to focus resources toward youth violence. The coalitions, through coordinated efforts, reduced juvenile violence through community driven prevention efforts.

- **Columbia, South Carolina:** Community Coordination. Columbia, South Carolina, has been involved in a multiagency crime prevention initiative since the mid-1990s. Columbia, through a massive planning and assessment effort, identified the causes of violence and criminal activity in the community and is now engaged in coordinating community services to achieve goals identified in the plan.

- **Flint, Michigan:** Funding Neighborhood Activities. In Flint, Michigan, crime prevention begins at the neighborhood level. Small neighborhood groups develop tailor-made strategies for protecting the city block by block. The Neighborhood Violence Prevention Collaborative coordinated the efforts of existing agencies and assessed the causes of violence within the community.

- **Fort Peck Indian Reservation, Montana.** The tribes on the Fort Peck Indian Reservation experienced a homicide rate 13 times higher than that of the state of Montana. Unemployment, poverty, and multijurisdictional issues aggravated the problem. Tribal Strategies Against Violence was developed by a reservation planning board to reduce crime, violence, and substance abuse. The program is bringing people and resources together for the first time.

- **Jacksonville, Florida.** The State Attorney General's Office implemented a plan to combat juvenile crime by balancing early detection, prevention, and intervention programs with aggressive violent offender prosecution. Over four years, the number of murders committed by juveniles dropped 72 percent in Jacksonville.

- **Portland, Oregon.** In 1989, Oregon developed a statewide plan to improve the quality of life for citizens of the state. After a series of gang-related murders, the Portland Bureau of Police developed a task force that included community organizations that provided gang prevention services or would benefit from reduced gang activity.

- **Salinas, California.** Between 1984 and 1994, murders committed by juveniles increased by 200 percent. Fifteen hundred documented gang members in over 20 gangs dominated this farming community. The Salinas Police Department began its Youth Firearms Violence Initiative in 1995, funded through a grant from the U.S. Department of Justice's Office of Community Oriented Policing Services. The $1 million grant funded a Violence Suppression Unit. The mission of the unit was to remove firearms from young people and gang members. The program had a positive impact and reduced youth gun violence.
- **San Antonio, Texas.** The San Antonio Crime Prevention Commission represents education, religious, business, police, media, and local government organizations. The group has been charged with the responsibility for creating and implementing a comprehensive crime prevention plan for the city. Based on the commission's recommendations, San Antonio passed several ordinances that focus on gang and crime suppression. Even the clergy became involved by presenting over 800 sermons in one week which supported the need for everyone to get involved in the crime prevention and suppression effort. The San Antonio Program consolidates and coordinates resources and, since full implementation in 1992, overall crime within the targeted areas has decreased over 30 percent.

The **community participation** and problem-solving efforts are much more comprehensive and extensive in some jurisdictions than in others. The extent to which community policing is incorporated into the fabric of a community and its policing agency depends on local circumstances and philosophical orientation. In cities such as Chicago, St. Petersburg, Florida, San Diego, Seattle, and Madison, Wisconsin, the philosophy, strategy, and problem-solving efforts permeate the community to a greater extent than in many other cities.

In Chicago, for example, new police recruits spend a great deal of time developing problem-solving skills and the entire patrol division is involved in the Chicago Alternative Policing Strategy (CAPS). Residents take an active role in solving problems and are encouraged to meet with the police regularly. The CAPS program also includes other municipal services such as the Department of Streets and Sanitation. Major changes have occurred in the way citizens view their city. Abandoned vehicle and trash complaints as well as drug and gang violence problems have declined sharply (Harnett & Skogan, 1999).

The San Diego Police Department has been involved with community policing and problem-solving strategies for a number of years. San Diego's Neighborhood Policing Program began in 1973 when the San Diego Police Foundation sponsored a Community Profile Development Project. The goal of the project was to improve patrol practices by encouraging officers to systematically analyze their patrol districts to identify and solve local problems. However, the early model lacked support. In

1988, the United States Bureau of Justice Administration selected San Diego as one of five cities for a pilot project to use community-oriented policing to address neighborhood drug problems. In 1993, San Diego implemented the Neighborhood Policing Restructuring Project. Its purpose was to realign the department to expand and strengthen the department's community policing throughout the city.

The San Diego community policing program has several components through which police officers, community groups, and the public as well as private agencies create meaningful partnerships. The components include citizen volunteer groups, nuisance and drug abatement teams, a revitalized Neighborhood Watch Program, safe streets initiatives, juvenile and domestic violence units, crime prevention through environmental design (CPTED) strategies, homeless outreach, police satellite facilities, and an analytical approach to reducing crime (California State, Office of the Attorney General, 1999, July).

San Diego's comprehensive community policing and problem-solving program has generated positive results. Overall crime declined almost 50 percent during the 1990s. Citizen surveys also give the San Diego Police Department high marks. In a survey conducted in 1999, nearly 70 percent of the community respondents rated the police department's performance as good to excellent. Only 6 percent indicated the police were doing a poor job (Nguyen, 1999).

The community policing initiatives cited in this section in no way represent all of the major community policing and problem-solving efforts throughout the United States (or elsewhere). On the contrary, commendable and progressive community policing practices are located in numerous large and small communities. Notable examples of community policing's success are located in Nashua, New Hampshire; Charleston, South Carolina; and San Jose, California (Thurman, Zhao, & Giacomazzi, 2001). Other examples of notable programs can be found in Austin, Texas; Fort Lauderdale, Florida; St. Louis, Missouri; Fresno, Hayward, and Arroyo Grande, California; Lincoln, Nebraska; Eugene and Gresham, Oregon; Grand Rapids, Michigan; Reno, Nevada; Savannah, Georgia; Spokane, Washington; Tempe, Arizona; Elmhurst, Illinois; Arlington County and Arlington, Virginia; and numerous state and federal jurisdictions (Peak & Glensor, 2008).

Utilizing funds from U.S. Department of Justice community policing grants, several agencies implemented innovative programs. The Boston Police Department modified organizational processes to establish relatively permanent beat teams. The Charlotte–Mecklenburg, North Carolina, Police Department combined greater use of technology with problem-solving. The Longmont, Colorado, Police Department reorganized its structure to improve communication with communities. The Los Angeles Sheriff's Department implemented a community policing leadership program. The Portland, Oregon, Police Bureau created an emergency information system to enhance communication with neighborhoods. The Rock Hill, South Carolina, Police Department linked community policing with a career ladder program for officers below the rank of sergeant. The San Jose, California, Police Department developed leadership models for the police and community members. The Savannah,

Georgia, Police Department explored best community policing practices. The Windsor, Connecticut, Police Department worked closely with police union officials and community members to create a community policing program (Schneider, 2003).

In the aftermath of 9/11, the role of community policing in the prevention of terrorism cannot be overstated (Newton, 2002). In fact, Marc Morial, director of the Urban League and former mayor of New Orleans, cited community policing as an indispensable tool in the fight against terrorism. He emphasized that citizen–police collaboration helps build trust and sharing of information, an absolute necessity for effective law enforcement. Collaboration based on trust and mutual respect can help balance new police counterterrorism strategies with traditional values associated with liberty and civil rights (Let freedom ring to the tune of trust, 2004).

Community partnerships must progress beyond mere lip service. They must include positive relationships, community participation, pooled resources, and shared responsibility. They must include problem solving as a process for carefully identifying crime and disorder problems and priorities, collecting and analyzing information, developing solutions (responses), and evaluating responses to determine their effectiveness. Community partnerships and problem-solving processes can help to promote meaningful community contact, sincere communication, trust, and the exchange of relevant information.

CASE STUDY—NATIONAL NIGHT OUT

The National Association of Town Watch (NATW), a non-profit organization dedicated to the development and promotion of organized, law enforcement-affiliated crime and drug prevention programs, aims to support community policing. NATW members include neighborhood watch groups; law enforcement agencies; state and regional crime prevention associations; and businesses, civic groups, and concerned individuals.

NATW sponsors an annual event—National Night Out—held on the first Tuesday each August. During NNO, areas sponsor locally tailored events such as block parties, cookouts, parades, visits from local law enforcement, contests, flashlight walks, and youth programs. NNO promotes involvement in crime and drug prevention activities, strong police-community relations, and neighborhood camaraderie as part of the fight for safer streets. Since its launch in 1984, NNO has grown to involve over 34 million people from more than 10,000 communities.

NNO has the support of many agencies and organizations, including the U.S. Congress, Justice Department, FBI, and the International Association of Chiefs of Police. http://www.nationalnightout.org/nno/about.html)

1. What advantages might the NNO program provide law enforcement agencies and the communities they serve, in addition to supporting community policing?
2. What challenges might law enforcement agencies and communities encounter in conducting NNO events?

SUMMARY

Policing in the twenty-first century faces many challenges. Although contemporary law enforcement has become increasingly complex, the model for policing remains authoritarian and paramilitaristic. A different approach, which complements the traditional policing model, is referred to as community policing. The concepts of community policing are consistent with the principles of policing articulated by Robert Peel in 1829. Community policing is a philosophy and a strategy that promotes community engagement, participation, and problem solving. It involves action that leads to the discovery and implementation of solutions to community-based problems. A community policing environment requires the introduction of new and different police officer competencies and skills. Within the framework of community policing, the community plays a major role in efforts to reduce crime and disorder. The police must learn to work with diverse populations and build partnerships with communities.

DISCUSSION QUESTIONS AND EXERCISES

1. Create a definition for community policing. Include the two core elements of community policing in the definition.
2. Do the qualities and competencies or skills required of a police officer differ between traditional and community policing environments? Why or why not?
3. Discuss the framework for community policing, describing the role of the police as well as the community.
4. Describe techniques for engaging diverse groups and the procedure for building police–community partnerships.
5. Conceptually, what is the philosophy of community policing?
6. Does community policing compete with or complement traditional policing? Is a community policing strategy designed to replace traditional policing efforts?
7. Does community policing represent a shift in the philosophy and strategy of modern law enforcement? Does community policing differ from Robert Peel's principles of policing?
8. An analysis of reported crime data reveals a dramatic increase in the number of daytime residential burglaries in a particular neighborhood. Patrol officers assigned to the neighborhood have been directed to solicit the participation of neighborhood residents to address the burglary problem. However, the residents in the affected neighborhood are reluctant to cooperate, because they tend to distrust the police. How should the officers proceed in their efforts to develop a police–community partnership?

Community Policing: Problem Solving

LEARNING OBJECTIVES

After completing this chapter, the reader should be able to:

- outline the planning and problem-solving process.
- demonstrate problem-solving techniques.
- describe the SARA problem-solving model.
- present an overview of the organization and operation of a problem-solving effort.
- develop procedures for problem solving in groups.
- conduct a community needs assessment.
- utilize community crime mapping.
- explain the need for evaluation processes.
- discuss the methods for measuring and evaluating performance.
- discuss the concept of quality assurance and common errors made in quality assurance initiatives.
- identify, critically analyze, and develop solutions to problems in management.
- analyze the effectiveness of the components of a problem-solving effort.
- evaluate major global and societal trends that affect law enforcement.
- develop strategies for improving the effectiveness of police services.
- design a crime prevention strategy utilizing crime prevention through environmental design (CPTED) techniques.
- identify barriers to effective problem solving.

KEY TERMS

Define, describe, or explain the importance of each of the following.

Analysis

Assessment

Barriers to problem solving

Community mapping

Community problem

CompStat

Consensus

Crime prevention through environmental design (CPTED)

Critical thinking

Delphi Technique
Fusion Centers
Geographic information system
  (GIS)
Group problem solving
Group think
Incident-driven policing
Intangible standard
Objective measurement
Planning
Problem analysis triangle
Problem-oriented policing

Problem solving
Qualitative analysis
Quality assurance initiative
Quantitative analysis
Response
Scanning, analysis, response,
  assessment (SARA)
  problem-solving model
Scanning
Subjective measurement
Tangible standard

INTRODUCTION

Whether they want to be or not, police officers are problem solvers. Individual citizens, business leaders, and community groups expect, and even demand, that the police solve crimes and regulate noncriminal conduct. As such, the citizenry expects the police to identify and analyze problems, employ situational strategies, evaluate constituent needs, and provide the means for attaining crime reduction and other community goals. The police are expected to mediate disputes and negotiate settlements between adversaries in noncriminal domestic arguments and landlord-tenant disputes. Problems also arise within and between police organizations. Therefore, the law enforcement professional must deal with internal as well as external problems.

Often, the police must act instinctively to diagnose problem situations and prescribe appropriate courses of action. Without critical-thinking and problem-solving abilities, which are the keys to the sound analysis of situations, problems will not be identified and creative solutions to problems will not be discovered. Problem-solving skills are important for self-management and crisis management, and they also lie at the heart of conflict de-escalation and resolution. If the ultimate goal is to solve the problem, police officers should—with time and resources permitting—strive to provide or at least assist in locating the means for problem identification and solution development. Police officers in a community policing environment must also work to mobilize the community into partnerships with others to identify and create solutions to problems (Kingsley & Pettit, 2000; Ortmeier, 1996, 2003).

Most police officers in the United States, especially those assigned to patrol duties, are rarely subjected to the direct control of a supervisor. Therefore, police officers can often exercise an enormous amount of discretion with respect to decisions that impact the lives of other people. Except for enforcement of violations of the criminal law, an individual police officer may opt to strictly enforce traffic laws while a peer on patrol in an adjoining area may not. In addition, police work often requires independent judgment in individual cases. Thus, discretion in the exercise of police authority is commonplace and often necessary if justice is to be served.

Since unsupervised, independent decision making is the method of operation for most police officers, initial and advanced training for police officers should focus on the development of independent problem-solving and decision-making skills. Accordingly, many experts agree that a great deal of police training, especially in the academies, is inconsistent with the police mission. In *Policing in the Community;* Champion and Rush (1997) state:

> Clearly, the overemphasis on lockstep obedience found in many police academies will not serve to provide new hires with a productive and independent frame of reference for performing their jobs. This is not to suggest that stress or the handling of stressful situations should not be part of law enforcement training. Clearly, police officers may well find themselves in very stressful positions while performing their duties, and it would be only prudent to evaluate their abilities to function under simulated stressful conditions. But a heavy reliance on close-order drill and other group exercises does not promote individuality and proves to be of little value in the actual performance of police duties. Moreover, stress does not belong in the classroom, as it impedes the learning process. It would be difficult to try to teach a student a concept while the student is wondering whether his or her bed has passed inspection. (p. 135).

As noted, problem solving and decision making are an integral part of police work. However, traditional police training methods may actually inhibit the development of critical-thinking and problem-solving abilities. Problem solving is emerging as a new trend in law enforcement training. This trend is depicted in police training programs in which problem solving is described variously as problem-based, scenario-based, or facilitated

---

CASE STUDY—ADDRESSING CRIME AND DISORDER

The safety and security of young people concerns everyone. Consider the following scenario and respond to the questions below.

Several students, parents, and teachers have complained to the police about major problems in and around a middle school. Specifically, their concerns include:

- Face-to-face bullying, threats, and intimidation of students by fellow students. Due to minimal supervision and a high student-to-faculty ratio, the school's hallways, cafeteria, parking lots, and student drop off/pick-up points have high incident rates.

- Cyber-bullying by fellow students, in the form of online threats and character smears posted on students' Facebook pages or delivered through text messages.

- Graffiti and vandalism of school property as well as loitering and disorderly activity by the middle school students as well as teenage students from a nearby high school.

1. Are the police responsible for solving these problems?

2. If *yes,* apply problem-solving techniques to identify the causes of the problems, determine analysis-driven responses, and establish evaluation criteria.

training. Traditional police training methods emphasize cognitive (knowledge) and psychomotor (skills) learning. Problem-based training adds a dimension that attempts to move learning to the higher level domains of analysis, synthesis, and evaluation. Cadets learn about the cognitive aspects of policing early in the training process. This is followed by skills training. Later, the cadet, working individually or in a group, is immersed in a series of scenarios in which the cadet must draw on knowledge and problem-solving skills in specific types of situations (Conser & Russell, 2000; Ortmeier & Davis, 2012). In this chapter, the reader is introduced to problem-solving techniques as well as techniques for working with groups.

PROBLEM-SOLVING TECHNIQUES

A problem involves a discrepancy between current and desired conditions. **Problem solving** is a comprehensive planning process used to move a situation from an unsatisfactory to a desirable condition. Problem solving should not be confused with decision-making. The latter refers to the act of choosing between alternatives and is part of the problem-solving process. Problem solving involves the creation and discovery of alternatives and requires numerous decisions.

All problems consist of three components: an existing condition that is unsatisfactory, goals, and the obstacles that inhibit goal achievement. Recognition of the unsatisfactory condition or situation is the incipient stage of a problem. In other words, one recognizes that a problem exists. The goal or goals include a perception of a desirable situation, one aligned with the comfort associated with a satisfactory condition. Obstacles represent anything or anyone that interferes with achievement of the goal (satisfactory condition). Examples of obstacles include lack of funding or personnel (Galanes, Adams, & Brilhart, 2007).

Problem solving is not consistent with traditional **incident-driven policing.** With incident-driven policing, the reactive posture of the police encourages superficial responses. Responding to and handling the incident quickly, filing a report, and returning to patrol duty are the cornerstones of incident-driven policing. However, in a policing environment, the **community problem,** rather than a specific incident, should be the main unit of police work. A community problem involves two or more incidents of a similar nature within a community. Problem solving is the process used to address the community problem (Goldstein, 2001). According to the California Department of Justice, Office of the Attorney General (1996), problem solving is defined as the process of identifying problems and priorities through community-coordinated community—police needs assessment, collecting and analyzing information concerning the problem in a thorough but not complicated manner, developing or facilitating responses that are innovative and tailor-made with the best potential for eliminating or reducing the problem, and evaluating and modifying the response to the problem as necessary to determine its effectiveness.

Problem solving can be used to examine crime and disorder problems, analyze underlying causes, develop a range of solutions to address these problems, select appropriate solutions, and evaluate the effectiveness of the solutions over time. Problems need to be analyzed from the standpoint of the community so that solutions can be adapted to meet community needs. The analysis may include both quantitative and qualitative data and information.

Quantitative analysis involves the use of objective measurements, while **qualitative analysis** focuses on the use of subjective measurements. Examples of **objective measurement** tools include statistical and investigative reports, surveys, and inspections. **Subjective measurements** include forecasting, the use of expert opinion, and the **Delphi Technique.** The latter is a process whereby several experts or individuals provide input on an issue or problem and ultimately arrive at a consensus on desirable alternatives, priorities, and goals. The Delphi Technique may be the most appropriate problem-solving and decision-making vehicle when emotions are high, or when a few members of the problem-solving group tend to dominate the process.

There are two general approaches to problem solving. The convergent approach solves problems systematically by utilizing a series of logical steps. These steps define the problem, generate solutions, assist with the selection of appropriate solutions, implement a course of action, and evaluate the outcome. A less structured, more creative method for problem solving involves the divergent approach. This approach calls on intuition and innovation and encourages spontaneity. Brainstorming is an example of the divergent approach.

Whether problems are solved logically or creatively, the goal is to arrive at the most appropriate solution. Both approaches may be used separately or conjunctively. When a single solution is required, the convergent approach is best. A series of burglaries committed by a single individual may require an approach that leads to the suspect's arrest and successful prosecution. When multiple solutions are necessary, as when multiple burglaries are committed by numerous individuals, a divergent approach to problem solving (with multiple solutions) may be more appropriate (Caroselli, 1997; Kingsley & Pettit, 2000).

Herman Goldstein, the father of **problem-oriented policing (POP)** spent over 40 years studying police operations. In the 1970s, Goldstein suggested that police agencies should shift their focus from an inward orientation (number of officers, staffing patterns) to an outward orientation (the agency's impact on crime and disorder). As such, Goldstein (1990, 2001) advocates moving from the traditional efficiency model of policing to an effectiveness model, placing less emphasis on statistics and number of arrests, and more emphasis on strategic initiatives to eliminate the problem. The key to problem solving in a community policing environment involves an analytical inquiry into the problem before devising solutions. Problem solving in this sense does not mean troubleshooting or guesswork. Rather, it involves **planning** as the systematic, step-by-step approach to problem resolution.

Problem-oriented policing is simple, yet complex. It incorporates a way of thinking that helps to define the police function and assist with problem solving in the community. Problem-oriented policing:

> . . . is an approach to policing in which (1) discrete pieces of police business (each consisting of a cluster of similar incidents, whether crimes

or acts of disorder, that the police are expected to handle) are subject to (2) microscopic examination (drawing on the especially honed skills of crime analysis and the accumulated experience of operating field personnel) in hopes that what is freshly learned about each problem will lead to discovering a (3) new and more effective strategy for dealing with it. POP places a high value on new responses that are (4) preventive in nature, that are (5) not dependent on the use of the criminal justice system, and that (6) engage other public agencies, the community and the private sector when their involvement has the potential for significantly contributing to the reduction of the problem. POP carries a commitment to (7) implementing the new strategy, (8) rigorously evaluating its effectiveness, and, subsequently, (9) reporting the results in ways that will benefit other police agencies and that will ultimately contribute to (10) building a body of knowledge that supports the further professionalization of the police (Goldstein, 2001).

The problem-solving process can be applied in almost any situation. It has been applied successfully to problems associated with street prostitution (Scott, 2001), false burglar alarms (Sampson, 2001), graffiti (Lamm Weisel, 2002), thefts in parking facilities (Clarke, 2002a), shoplifting (Clarke, 2002b), bullying in schools (Sampson, 2002), panhandling (Scott, 2002a), rave parties (Scott, 2002b), burglary of retail establishments (Clarke, 2002c), check and card fraud (Newman, 2003), and financial crimes against the elderly (Johnson, 2003). It can also be used as a vehicle for restorative justice, a mechanism through which the police and others seek to repair harm to victims, offenders, and communities (Nicholl, 2000).

Two Vallejo, California, police employees used problem solving to develop programs that assist needy people with noncriminal as well as crime-related problems. One program utilizes volunteers to collect donations that are used by police officers to assist needy citizens. Funds are used to pay utility bills, purchase food, and assist stranded individuals by providing short-term motel accommodations. Another program includes a registry of local Alzheimer patients. The list assists police officers seeking to find a lost Alzheimer victim's home or primary care giver and to prevest and investigate fraud and abuse cases involving the elderly (Taylor, 2002).

The problem-solving process can be used to address crime and disorder issues covering broad territories, as it has been applied in Chicago (Skogan, 2005). It can be used to target specific problems, as exemplified by a youth violence prevention program in St. Louis, Missouri (Decker, Rosenfeld, & Burruss, 2005). It also forms the foundation for crime analysis, gang intervention, and major case investigations. In 2010 alone, the Port Washington, Wisconsin, police department launched and completed a total of 14 problem-oriented policing initiatives, including programs designed to help persons with autism, improve playground safety, and mitigate domestic abuse (Port Washington Police Department, 2011).

Additional information on problem-oriented policing and successful "best practices" is available through the Center for Problem-Oriented Policing at www.popcenter.org.

THE SARA PROBLEM-SOLVING MODEL

Several "models" have emerged to assist law enforcement with community policing and problem-solving efforts. Virtually all models can trace their origin to Goldstein's problem-oriented policing model. The U.S. Department of Justice-sponsored program is Operation Weed and Seed (Simons, 2002). The Royal Canadian Mounted Police (RCMP) follow a systematic approach to proactive and reactive policing situations. The RCMP model focuses on clients, acquiring and analyzing information, partnerships, response, and assessment (CAPRA). The Florida Department of Law Enforcement developed a model that addresses safety, ethics, community, understanding, response, and evaluation (SECURE). The **Scanning, Analysis, Response, Assessment (SARA) problem-solving model** is the foundation for these models (Conser & Russell, 2000; Ortmeier & Davis, 2012). SARA is used by many police agencies throughout the United States. It integrates the convergent and divergent approaches to problem solving. The model was first developed and implemented by police officers and researchers in Newport News, Virginia, in 1984. Although several problem-solving models exist, the SARA model is presented here as an example of one approach.

Scanning

Scanning involves problem identification. It refers to the identification of patterns or persistent problems within a community. Two or more similar incidents constitute a community crime, fear, or disorder problem. Utilizing this strategy, community crime problems may be identified in ways other than through police officer observations. Community meetings, citizen surveys, one-on-one conversations with citizens, crime and community mapping, and statistical information as well as research conducted by government and private organizations may be sources of information (Community Policing Consortium, 1997b).

An additional source of information are **fusion centers**, mechanisms designed to pool multiple agencies' resources and personnel into one central location that facilitates information sharing and intelligence development regarding criminal activities. Originally set up to uncover

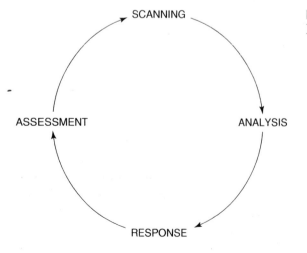

FIGURE 6.1 The SARA Problem-Solving Model

terrorist plots, fusion centers collect and distribute criminal intelligence. The intent is to foster efficient receipt, sorting, and sharing of vital information needed to uncover criminal activities before they can be carried out. Fusion centers take steps to protect citizens' privacy and civil rights, including not running names through databases unless there is reasonable suspicion to do so and preventing the misuse of government and commercial databases that contain large amounts of personal information (Dilanian, 2010).

Risk and needs assessments can be used for problem identification. Risk assessments are used to predict the likelihood of a negative outcome. A high probability of re-arrest subsequent to a solution (intervention) implementation (conviction and sentence completion) is an example of a risk. Needs assessments are instruments or processes designed to identify unmet needs. The need for treatment of chronic drug offenders and graffiti removal can be identified through needs assessments.

After a problem is identified, a working definition of the problem is created. The working definition provides the foundation for analysis and the solutions developed in subsequent stages of the SARA problem-solving model. Analysis of the situation and corrective action should focus on prevention of future occurrences.

Analysis

An **analysis** involves an intensive probe into all of the characteristics and factors contributing to a problem. It requires the acquisition of detailed information regarding the people involved (offenders, victims, others), time and location of occurrence, the environment, and the outcomes of current responses to the problem. Utilizing the information acquired, analysis leads to the development of effective responses (Baker, 2005; Goldstein, 1990).

The persistent problems and patterns of activity within a community require careful analysis. Problems develop slowly. Hasty solutions rarely eliminate the problem. The analysis must address the underlying causes rather than the symptoms of the problem. Although analysis lies at the heart of the problem-solving process, it is probably the most difficult step in the SARA model. Analytical processes are also difficult for police officers to learn and apply. It requires a look at and through the problem. Juveniles may be loitering on the street corner, for example, and police may be dispatched to disband the group. Eventually, the juveniles will return to the street corner. The reason for the loitering may be that the juveniles have no other place to congregate; thus the underlying cause of the loitering is a lack of resources for the youth in the community. Therefore, participants in the problem-solving process must carefully analyze the situation and think critically to identify the underlying causes (Glensor & Peak , 1999).

Critical thinking involves a process through which an individual or group examines information to determine if there is a logical connection between facts. Critical thinking resists emotional appeals. Conclusions are based on a logical progression of ideas that are based on available evidence rather than feelings or guesswork. According to Gamble and Gamble (2005), the characteristics that differentiate the critical from the uncritical thinker include the following.

The Critical Thinker:

- Knows what he or she does not know.
- Is open-minded and takes time to reflect on ideas.
- Pays attention to those who agree and disagree with him or her.
- Looks for good reasons to accept or reject expert opinion.
- Is concerned with unstated assumptions and what is not said, in addition to what is stated outright.
- Insists on getting the best evidence.
- Reflects on how well conclusions fit premises and vice versa.

The Uncritical Thinker:

- Thinks he or she knows everything.
- Is closed-minded and impulsive; jumps to unwarranted conclusions.
- Pays attention only to those who agree with him or her.
- Disregards evidence as to who is speaking with legitimate authority.
- Is concerned only with what is stated, not with what is implied.
- Ignores sources of evidence.
- Disregards the connection or lack of connection between evidence and conclusions.

Every individual is born with creative capacity, despite assertions to the contrary. Unfortunately, creativity is often suppressed. Over 90 percent of young children are very creative at age five. By college age, only about 2 percent of individuals tested are very creative. In American society, individuals are conditioned to respond to precreated stimuli rather than to be creative or imaginative themselves. Fortunately, creativity can be recaptured with practice. Brainstorming in groups is very effective. Emphasis should be placed on the least as well as the most likely resources that can be used to respond to and solve the problem (Caroselli, 1997).

The **problem analysis triangle** (the three factors of offender, victim, and location necessary for a crime or problem to occur) offers a simple mechanism to visualize and analyze crime and disorder problems. Because all three sides of the problem analysis triangle must be present for crime to occur, the elimination of any one of the three elements may solve the problem. If a potential victim implements measures to eliminate the opportunity for crime to occur, the crime may be prevented. Target hardening through improved locks and lighting, for example, may deter burglaries of residences and businesses.

The sides of the triangle may also be impacted positively by the presence of a capable guardian. The guardian makes the target less attractive to criminal activity. Possible guardians include the police, citizens, security personnel, abatement statutes, and signs. A noise abatement statute could be enacted for the community. No Parking signs can be posted or erected to eliminate congestion. All-night convenience store clerks can receive training on how to prevent robberies or minimize losses due to robberies (Bynum, 2001; Community Policing Consortium, 1997b).

Problems should be analyzed from multiple perspectives. Different stakeholders may view the problem and its solutions in different ways. It is often helpful to solicit the perspective of someone (or some group)

FIGURE 6.2 Problem Analysis Triangle

totally unrelated to the problem. Unrelated parties or experts from other disciplines are often more objective when analyzing a situation. Objectivity is crucial to the development of appropriate answers to the following questions that typically arise during an analysis.

- Who is affected by the problem?
- What are the possible causes?
- Are the causes considered to be problems themselves?
- What are the circumstances surrounding the causes?
- What aspects of the circumstances are not part of the problem?
- When, where, why, and how do the problems occur?

The best solutions are created when more than one person is involved in the problem-solving process. Practical applications of decision-making processes demonstrate that the synergistic effect of group problem solving helps to create better solutions.

Response

With a clear definition and analysis of the problem in mind, participants in the problem-solving process can begin to create **responses** (solutions). Crime problems may be affected by eliminating the problem altogether, reducing the harm caused by the problem, reducing the number of incidents, improving the handling of the problem, or referring the problem to another, more proper, authority (Community Policing Consortium, 1997b).

To be effective, responses (solutions) to a crime or disorder problem should affect at least two sides of the crime triangle. Police and community members must also think creatively to develop responses that are tailored to the community. Often, participants are eager to adopt a response that was developed for a similar problem in another community. Those involved in the process must remember that off-the-shelf solutions (i.e., replicas of what was done in other areas) are rarely appropriate.

More than one solution can be created to respond to a problem. Each alternative solution should be compared to the others. Effective solutions are measurable, verifiable, realistic, achievable, desirable, in accord with the values and beliefs of stakeholders, motivating, and subject to continuous monitoring and assessment (Anderson, 2000; Simons, 2002). Members of the decision-making group may arrive at consensus regarding the most appropriate solution(s) by anonymously ranking the possible alternatives presented. The rankings are tabulated and the solution(s) with the highest scores receive the most favorable consideration.

Participants in the solution development process must also consider the consequences of any action or response implemented. Will the response create a more difficult problem? Could a crackdown on gang activity result in the detention of innocent, law-abiding juveniles? How would these situations be handled? What impact might an inappropriate detention have on the juvenile detained, on media accounts of the incident, and on the public's perception of the police?

As consideration is given to the possible negative side effects of a solution, it may be determined that an alternative and less desirable course of action is more appropriate. At first glance, trained guard dogs locked in a business at night may discourage burglaries. The liability incurred, however, as the result of a would-be burglar entering the business without knowledge of the dogs' presence could create another problem. Businesses and individuals have been successfully sued for creating hazards while protecting property. A more enlightened approach might include target hardening and installation of alarm systems to deter and detect burglars.

Implementation of the response (solution) to a problem is often difficult because it produces change. Resistance to change is a problem itself. Even those who may benefit from change are often resistant to it. Therefore, the first step to response (solution) implementation is to communicate the need for change to those who might be affected. One should anticipate opposition and be prepared to explain the rationale for any change in policies and procedures. Effective persuasion includes an explanation on how the opposition will benefit. Restrictions on freedom of movement, for example, may help to create a safer environment. Metal detectors in schools can prevent weapons from endangering students, faculty, and staff (Caroselli, 1997; Kerley, 2005).

Assessment

No problem-solving process is complete without an **assessment** (evaluation) of the impact of the solutions. Assessment is an ongoing process and should be considered during the other three stages of the SARA problem-solving model. Qualitative (subjective) as well as quantitative (objective) measures may be used to assess the impact of a response (Thurman, Zhao, & Giacomazzi, 2001). The assessment measures or tools should address several fundamental evaluative questions. In addition to crime reduction or elimination, how do the participants view the success, or lack of success, of the entire operation? Are the citizens within the community, as well as the police, satisfied with the outcome? Has the outcome clearly addressed the goals initially established by the community partnership? If responses to these questions are not acceptable, the assessment can identify what does not work and create an environment where alternative solutions can be created.

Assessment has forward-looking and after-the-fact aspects. Through the forward-looking aspect, the evaluator attempts to anticipate and prevent potential sources of deviation from established standards and considers the possibility of undesirable outcomes. Crime prevention is an example of forward-looking evaluation. After-the-fact evaluation analyzes why an event or deviation from established standards has occurred and determines what corrective action is required. Determining the cause(s) of a number of reported burglaries in a particular neighborhood is an example of after-the-fact evaluation.

The first step in the assessment and control process is to measure performance based on the objectives established during the response stage of the SARA problem-solving process. These objectives, or standards, are units of measurement that serve as reference points for evaluating results. Standards can be either tangible or intangible. **Tangible standards** are quite clear, concrete, specific, identifiable, and generally measurable. These standards measure quantity and quality of the responses. They may be used to assess the impact of any corrective action taken.

Tangible standards can be categorized as numerical, monetary, physical, or time-related. Numerical standards are expressed in numbers such as crime statistics, percentage of successful calls, or number of personnel required for an operation. Monetary standards are expressed in dollars and cents. Examples of monetary standards include predetermined (planned) expenses, actual expenses, and budget analyses. Physical standards refer to quality, durability, size, weight, or other factors related to items such as equipment and supplies required for the response. Time standards refer to the speed with which the job should be completed.

Intangible standards are not expressed in terms of numbers, money, physical qualities, or time, since they relate to human characteristics that are difficult to measure. They take no physical form. Yet, they are just as important as tangible standards. Examples of intangible standards include desirable attitude, high morale, ethics, cooperation, and the organization's reputation. In policing, assessment through the use of intangible standards goes beyond traditional success measurements such as number of arrests and reductions in crime rates. Intangible standards complement tangible standards to create a better understanding of a program's impact ("Crime Statistics Don't Tell the Whole Story," 1999).

Performance may be measured through personal observation, written or oral reports of subordinates, automatic methods, and inspections, tests, or surveys. Some members of the organization may resent performance measurements. This resentment often results from the use of efficiency experts and supervisors who set unrealistic standards of performance. Managers within an organization must remember that performance standards should be based on realistic targets.

Sometimes, the most thoughtful effort fails to meet performance standards or achieve desirable results. Identification of the cause(s) of failure rather than the symptoms is extremely important if any additional corrective action is to be taken. It is important to consult with those closest to the situation to determine why the performance standards are not being met. Participation by all affected members of the organization and the community is an essential ingredient in this process (Clemmer, 1992; Schneider, 2003).

Time is also essential to the assessment process. The sooner a deviation from a standard is identified, the sooner the situation can be corrected.

Assessment, therefore, must be continuous and viewed as a thread that runs through all stages of the SARA process.

If no deviations from an established goal occur, the evaluative check has been fulfilled. However, after a careful analysis, deviations from a performance standard may be identified and additional corrective action may be necessary. Modifications, adjustments, and alterations to the original plan should not be viewed negatively. After all, objectives and standards as stated in the original plan are often based on forecasts. If the deviation from the standard is extreme or exceptional, it may be necessary to evaluate the approach used in the problem-solving process itself.

Before any corrective action is taken, the actual causes of the deviation should be analyzed carefully. Knee-jerk reactions may cause greater harm to occur. There may be many reasons why a deviation from an established standard has occurred (Haberer & Webb, 1994). It is possible that:

- The standards could not be achieved because they were based on faulty forecasts or assumptions or because an unforeseen problem arose that distorted the anticipated results.
- Failure had already occurred in some other activity that preceded the activity in question.
- The persons who performed the activity either were unqualified or were not given adequate directions or instructions.
- The persons who performed the activity were negligent or did not follow required directions or procedures.

Assessment can help assure quality or, at the very least, improve the quality of life. However, quality can be an elusive concept. It means different things to different people. In the context of assuring consumer satisfaction, quality may be defined as a phenomenon associated with products, people, services, processes, and environments that meet or exceed expectations. Quality assurance, continuous quality improvement, and total quality management (TQM) initiatives involve approaches that attempt to maximize effectiveness (or competitiveness) of an organization through the continual improvement of the quality of its people, processes, products, and environment (Goetsch & Davis, 1995). **Quality assurance initiatives** should involve all community constituencies in the process of identifying and improving aspects of community life. These initiatives should be based on:

- Decisions founded on facts rather than intuition.
- Taking personal responsibility for quality.
- Improving teamwork and commitment.
- A focus on the end user and service.

Quality assurance initiatives also involve goal setting, trust, building cohesion, developing problem-solving skills, increasing the information flow, and resolving conflict. At a minimum, a total quality assurance approach includes the following:

- Customer focus (internal and external).
- Obsession with quality.

Through quality assurance initiatives, police agencies can:
- Address the needs of internal and external customers (police personnel and citizens).
- Focus less on competitive individual officer performance measures and more on customer (officer and citizen) satisfaction. Most individual performance measures are based on organizational expectations (number of arrests, citations issued) rather than customer needs.
- Strive toward constancy of purpose and the desire for continuous improvement by all employees.
- Evaluate and measure performance on the basis of team accomplishments.
- Rely on providing the best possible service in the first instance rather than inspections to monitor services provided.

- Use of the scientific approach in decision making and problem solving.
- Long-term commitment.
- Teamwork.
- Involvement and empowerment.
- Continual improvement.
- Bottom-up education and training.
- Freedom from control.
- Unity of purpose.

Quality assurance initiatives are not a quick fix. Rather, they are an entirely new approach to administration that requires new management styles, long-term commitments, unity of purpose, and specialized training (Tos, 2000).

The police must commit to the quality as well as the quantity of service. Quality service may be addressed through appropriate quality assurance initiatives such as TQM. Although TQM should not be viewed as a cure for the vast array of police and community problems, concepts associated with TQM can be adapted to the police service. Problem-solving processes, such as the SARA model, can be accomplished through TQM strategies (Baker, 2005; Peak & Glensor, 2008; Thurman, Zhao, & Giacomazzi, 2001).

With quality assurance in mind, police officers strive, as a team, to ensure high quality customer service and satisfaction rather than focus on personal achievements within the organization (Ortmeier, 1999; 2005; Stevens, 2002).

PROBLEM SOLVING IN GROUPS

A group is a collection of people who interact with each other to achieve a common purpose. A number of people present at a specific location at the same time do not necessarily constitute a group. If these people interact with each other, establish common goals, and have a structure and a pattern of communication then a group exists. Every member of a group usually has a personal stake in the outcome of the group's effort.

In many of the situations a police officer encounters, problem solving and decision-making rests squarely on the shoulders of the individual

180   Chapter 6

officer. These situations require immediate identification of the problem, intuitive evaluation of the circumstances, the development of viable alternatives, and an instinctive reaction to resolve the problem. However, some problems develop over an extended period of time, are pervasive within a neighborhood or community, and create a situation in which hasty decisions and actions may have an unpopular and sometimes disastrous impact on the citizen stakeholders. These situations lend themselves to a group problem-solving process. When involvement of a group is appropriate, the synergistic effect of **group problem solving** often leads to better results than does problem solving by an individual.

Groups are an excellent medium for identifying and solving problems. However, working in groups can be frustrating as well as rewarding (Gamble & Gamble, 2005). It can be frustrating because group work tends to encourage laziness, and conflicts may develop between personal and group goals. A few individuals may dominate the group and stubbornness on the part of certain members may lead to dead-lock. Group work is futile if members are obstinate and refuse to be open to different points of view. Reaching a decision may also require more time in a group setting. On the positive side, group work facilitates the sharing of resources, makes errors more recognizable, and tends to increase motivation. Decisions are often better received and personal rewards much higher in group settings. Yet, conflicts can develop.

Methods for resolving conflict can take many forms. Through win–lose problem solving, one side uses power or authority (rank, physical force, intellectual ability) to overcome an opponent. In lose–lose problem solving, neither side is satisfied. As two sides attempt to win, both can suffer tremendous losses. Compromise offers an opportunity for both parties to achieve something. Partial satisfaction is better than no satisfaction at all. However, the best approach is to strive toward full satisfaction of all parties, a win–win situation. Although win–win problem solving is not appropriate in all situations, it does offer opportunity for creative solution development (Adler & Towne, 2012; Whisenand & Ferguson, 2009).

Cohesion within teams and problem-solving groups can result in negative consequences. Cohesive groups can suffer from **group think,** which is symptomatic of groups or teams that give priority to unanimous agreement over reasoned problem solving. Groups suffering from group think fail to: consider all alternatives, gather enough information, re-examine failing action plans, weigh risks, develop contingency plans, or discuss important moral issues. This type of cohesiveness can lead to overconfidence, closed-mindedness, and group pressure to conform (Johnson, 2001).

In view of the advantages and disadvantages of working in groups, when is group work most appropriate? According to Gamble and Gamble, (2005), the formation of a group to identify and solve problems is indicated when most of the following conditions exist:

- The problem is complex.
- The problem is multifaceted.
- No single person possesses all information relevant to the problem.

- A division of responsibility for the problem-solving process is necessary.
- Several alternative solutions to the problem are desirable.
- Diverse opinions are essential to solution development.
- Activities are task related.

Problem solving and decision-making in groups may be accomplished through a variety of different strategies. Taking the least offensive alternative, allowing the leader to decide, majority rule, relying on expert opinion, or total deferral of the decision are methods commonly used. The least offensive position may be politically correct and garner public support, but may not provide the best solution. In some situations, the group leader retains decision-making power and only confers with other group members. Majority rule is a common strategy in elections as well as the legislative process. However, majority rule may not effectively serve the needs of the minority. Experts often provide viable alternatives, but reliance on experts may not promote acceptance by the stakeholders. Total deferral to another authority may be appropriate under certain conditions but may not absolve the group from responsibility and accountability with respect to any outcomes. A recent trend in the political arena involves deferring problem solving and decision-making to a commission established to investigate and develop solutions to politically sensitive problems or issues. One example at the federal level is the military base closure commission, which is tasked with the identification of military facilities to be closed because they are too expensive or no longer necessary to the U.S. Department of Defense's mission. Military base closures tend to be unpopular; one reason is that local economies depend on them for survival. Therefore, elected officials are reluctant to recommend base closures in their districts. Deferral to a commission removes the officeholder from the direct decision-making process, and the voters may be left with the perception that the commission, rather than the elected official, is responsible for the base closure. This strategy does not absolve the officeholder from the responsibility for the base closure, however.

PROBLEM SOLVING THROUGH GROUP CONSENSUS

In a best-case scenario, a group will identify and confront a problem directly, assume responsibility for it, and become actively involved in the development of alternative solutions to the problem. In this best case, the most effective problem-solving and decision-making strategy is decision by **consensus.** When consensus is achieved, all members of the group formulate, support, and agree on the decision. Decisions made by a leader or expert, or through majority rule may be less time consuming, although many problem-solving situations may not lend themselves to a group consensus model. However, in most situations, the quality of decision-making is better and the satisfaction of the participants is higher when a consensus strategy is used. The consensus model, when appropriately used, facilitates interaction and permits open discussion and effective use of resources.

Building group consensus can be a formidable task for anyone, especially for police officers in situations where emotions are high and the group is heterogeneous. Opinions and goals may be extremely diverse. For group problem solving to work in real-life environments, certain guidelines must be established, understood, and adhered to (Gamble & Gamble, 2005).

- Group goals are not to be imposed by a few. Rather, group goals are cooperatively formulated and easily understood.
- All ideas and feelings are valued and all group members are encouraged to freely communicate these ideas and feelings.
- When a decision is necessary, input from all members is sought and group members seek to reach consensus.
- Equal weight is given to goal achievement and the well-being of group members. In other words, quality decisions are as important as how well members maintain themselves as a group.
- Group members are motivated to provide input, share ideas, listen to others, and engage in a team effort to develop the best solutions to the problem.
- The group's efforts are objectively evaluated to identify the strengths of the group's style as well as the flaws in the group's problem-solving process.

One excellent method for consensus building that prevents domination of the group by a few, and provides equal opportunity for input, is the Delphi Technique mentioned earlier in this chapter. The technique was developed by Olaf Helmer and several of his associates at the Rand Corporation in the 1950s in an effort to respond to urgent national defense problems. The technique is used to predict the future, assess current trends, gain expert consensus while clarifying minority opinion, and as a teaching technique. It has been applied in such diverse areas as public safety, national defense, economic forecasting, and the analysis of educational needs. It is a creative and futuristic tool that gives each participating individual equal input into the reaching of consensus, although that person may be miles from and perhaps unacquainted with the other participants (Bunning, 1979). The technique also provides documentation including the recording of dissenting opinions of group members (Rasp, 1974; Stahl, 1992).

In 1984, FBI Special Agent William Tafoya, a Ph.D. candidate at the University of Maryland, used the Delphi Technique to conduct research for his dissertation on the future of policing (Tafoya, 1986). Ortmeier, (1996) used the Delphi Technique while conducting research to identify essential leadership competencies for street-level police officers.

Basically, the Delphi Technique is a method of collecting and organizing knowledge and opinion on a subject in an effort to produce a group consensus. The convergence of group consensus is accomplished through a series of three or more questionnaires dealing with a variety of questions on a single subject (Bunning, 1979). Statements regarding the topic are formulated and the respondents, consisting of a panel of people, are asked to respond to the statements in questionnaire form according to their own perceptions (Gomez, 1985). The results of the first round of anonymous questioning are summarized and returned to the individual group members with a request that they reconsider the appropriateness of their initial responses. On each succeeding round, panel members whose responses deviated from consensus, and who wish to remain outside consensus, are requested to justify their responses (Brooks, 1979; Meese & Ortmeier, 2004).

The exact procedures of the Delphi Technique may vary depending on the type of study. The typical procedure is outlined as follows:

- The area of concern or policy is selected and defined (Stahl, 1992).

- Background information on the particular topic, problem, or policy issue is gathered and combined into a set of basic statements—each of which will become an individual item to be rated on a questionnaire (Stahl, 1992).

- If not accomplished in step two, a panel of participants is identified. No guidelines exist that describe the most appropriate number of panel members to select for the Delphi process. Various studies have employed anywhere from 15 to 20 to more than 140 well selected respondents. Panels consisting of between 17 and 29 members appear to be the most advantageous for data management purposes (Dalkey, 1969).

- An initial questionnaire, or survey instrument, is developed. The number of questions or items should be limited to as few as possible. The questionnaire should also provide space in which the participants may include additional items (Bunning, 1979).

- Designed to collect both closed- and open-ended data, the initial as well as subsequent questionnaires may utilize a combination opinion-questionnaire format. Determination of averages based on a Likert scale of 1 = not important to 7 = extremely important may be used to establish a rating for each question.

- The questionnaires are coded (to help provide a sense of anonymity) and distributed to the participants.

- After the first and each succeeding questionnaire, the ratings for each item are tabulated and a composite rating, or consensus, is computed. The composite rating for each item is written on the subsequent questionnaires so that all members of the panel can view their own ratings and the composite rating of the group.

- The second questionnaire is distributed to the participants to provide the panel with a second opportunity to rate the original statements as well as any additions. The questionnaire each person receives informs the person as to how the original statements were rated by the entire group as well as how that specific person rated all the statements included in the first round.

- The responses to the second questionnaire are tabulated and a third questionnaire is distributed to the participants to provide the panel with a final opportunity to rate the original statements as well as any additions.

- The rated responses to the third questionnaire are tabulated and the mean (average) value score of each item is calculated for presentation with the findings. The Delphi Technique formally ends with the analysis and interpretation of the results of the final round of questionnaires. Consistent with standard Delphi practice, final reports from the data usually contain a ranking of the statements by priority and a listing or summary of the minority opinions (reasons for remaining outside consensus) of the panel members (Stahl, 1992).

The extensive nature and lengthy process of the Delphi Technique make it appropriate for analyzing major problems for which the solution will have a long-standing effect (Ortmeier, & Meese, 2010).

COMMUNITY MAPPING

The problem-solving process involved in rebuilding troubled communities and improving the quality of life in others necessitates mechanisms for assessing needs and identifying assets. Needs assessment and asset identification can be accomplished through the use of comprehensive **community mapping** tools. A needs map helps to identify problem areas and deficiencies within a neighborhood. Some communities have more deficiencies than others. Impoverished neighborhoods are typically more needy than their more affluent counterparts. However, no matter how poor a neighborhood might be, it often contains valuable assets, usually in the form of law-abiding citizens, organizations, and institutional resources.

A thorough mapping of a community begins with an identification of its assets as well as its deficiencies. The asset map will include an inventory of the skills and capabilities of the community's residents. These assets are indispensable tools for creative development. They can be mobilized along with other resources to address problems, deficiencies, crime, and disorder (Bynum, 2001; Kingsley & Pettit, 2000; Kretzmann & McKnight, 1999).

One of the most sophisticated methods for anticipating, recognizing, and appraising a crime risk involves the use of computer mapping and **geographic information system (GIS) technology.** Commonly referred to as crime mapping, GIS software can be used to map and display reported crime and predict future occurrences within a community. Public agencies routinely collect and maintain data that include location information. Police databases contain addresses of reported crime and arrests. Court and corrections files contain addresses of offenders. Other agencies manage property, street, physical infrastructure, and public health data. Computer mapping and GIS technology combine these multiple databases into one display so that law enforcement agencies can isolate and treat factors contributing to crime, manage resources more efficiently, and evaluate the effectiveness of any crime prevention action taken.

GIS technology does not replace an agency's process for collecting and storing information in a database. Rather, it enhances the agency's ability to utilize the information collected. Agencies can use the geographic characteristics of crime data to identify problems and seek solutions to crime and disorder issues in a specific area. GIS technology enhances an officer's ability to utilize time more appropriately. With access to GIS technology and other data sets, such as probationer, parolee, and sex offender data, an officer can submit queries from a mobile data terminal. Such technologies thus help law enforcement officials plot criminal activity and build a database of problems and potential solutions, drawing on increasingly voluminous stored data to develop ever more effective responses to crime (Reid, 2011). Still, the creators and users of GIS data must maintain confidentiality and take necessary precautions to protect suspect and victim rights and privacy (U.S. Department of Justice, 2003).

For years, law enforcement agencies analyzed crime patterns by inserting pushpins into paper maps taped on walls. Today's computerized crime mapping allows much more detailed information to be superimposed over a map. Crime analysts can use the database to identify crime hot spots, problem areas, and resource distribution.

Through changes in organization, strategy, and management—but particularly by accepting the fact that the police department could, and should, take action to prevent and reduce crime—New York City reduced its crime rate and provided an example for police departments throughout the nation. By using computer technology to develop a multifaceted computer-driven crime statistics **(CompStat)** operations management model, local precinct commanders were held accountable for crime conditions within the boundaries of their commands (Parshall-McDonald & Greenberg, 2002). They and their officers made more flexible use of resources, were encouraged to try new initiatives, and were required to regularly explain their strategies, as well as the results they produced.

Given mapping technology advancements, one might expect to see more sophisticated police decisions, outcomes, and solutions to community-based problems. Yet this does not appear to be the case. While agencies declare that they have adopted community policing and data-based decision-making, many police managers continue to define their field operations in terms of crime control rather than problem-oriented, solution-focused terms (Bynum, 2001; Foster, 2005; O'Shea & Nicholls, 2003; Rich, 1999).

CRIME PREVENTION THROUGH ENVIRONMENTAL DESIGN

Overview

Crime and disorder prevention involves the anticipation, recognition, and appraisal of a crime or disorder risk and the initiation of action to remove the risk to an acceptable level. Police officers can anticipate crime risks by becoming intimately familiar with crime patterns and gathering information from citizens who live and work in the area. Some conditions in an area (24-hour businesses, shopping centers, automatic teller machines) may pose a higher risk than others. Police officers must be able to recognize which conditions pose the highest risk, appraise the situation, and predict where conditions are favorable for crime to occur.

Learn more about mapping and analysis for public safety through the National Institute of Justice MAPS Program website at www.ojp.usdoj.gov/nij/maps/bib.

Once high-risk areas are identified, officers can work collaboratively with businesses, residents, government agencies, and other community members to remove or reduce opportunities for potential law violators. Access control, utilization of alarm systems, directed patrol, selective enforcement, and neighborhood watch programs are examples of target-hardening mechanisms that can be recommended and used to reduce opportunities for crime (California Commission on Peace Officer Standards and Training, 2012).

An excellent mechanism for preventing crime and disorder is **Crime Prevention Through Environmental Design (CPTED).** CPTED is based on the theory that the environment can be protected and crime prevented through the proper design of buildings, neighborhoods, and communities. Emphasis is placed on architecture, building codes, and defensible space. It requires that security and safety concepts be incorporated into the planning of a facility or community. In conjunction with community policing programs, CPTED may be applied to residential and business areas to increase public safety and reduce the citizens' fear of crime.

Security planning through CPTED and the implementation of the recommendations developed as a result of such planning have been very effective in preventing and deterring crime. Conversely, poor security planning not only fails to prevent and deter but also encourages crime because the facility or neighborhood design attracts criminal activity. Failure to design residential and business environments with effective safety and security measures may also create a liability connection between victims of crime and property owners, managers, and landlords.

CPTED is not a new concept. In prehistoric times, cave dwellers cleared areas in front of their caves and stacked rocks around the perimeter to mark this space and warn intruders. In ancient Greece, temple designers used environmental concepts to affect and control behavior. The temples were built of a type of stone that contained phosphorus and reflected a golden light shortly after dawn and just before dusk. During medieval times, height was used as a defensive tactic. Sleeping quarters were high above ground level and whole communities were walled in. Louis XIV, King of France from 1643 to 1715, was the first to use outdoor lighting in the form of torches and fires to reduce crime. Napoleon III (1808–1873) authorized his chiefs of police to demolish hideouts for criminals.

Since the 1970s, the National Institute of Justice has sponsored research and promoted crime prevention strategies that focus on using CPTED and community policing to make neighborhoods safer. Research results indicate that proper design of the physical environment can and does control crime. Private individuals and businesses working in conjunction with the police have also reduced fear of crime, deterred criminals, and utilized government building codes and inspection power to discourage illicit drug use and other criminal activity.

CPTED supports the movement toward community- and problem-oriented policing. Alternately, community policing and problem solving reinforce the concepts of CPTED. Although long in coming to policing, when used in conjunction with community policing programs,

CPTED can increase public safety. Utilizing CPTED concepts, the police may actually be able to predict where crime is most likely to occur. After high risk areas are identified, the police can work closely with individuals and businesses to prevent and control crime (Kroeker, 2001; Ortmeier & Meese, 2010).

CPTED Concepts and Strategies

Assuming that criminal offenders are influenced by the vulnerability of a potential target and the possibility of being apprehended, a CPTED perspective suggests four approaches to making an environment more resistant to crime and crime-related problems:

- Appropriate housing design and block layout can make it more difficult to commit crime.
- Creating safer land use and circulation patterns in neighborhoods can reduce routine exposure to potential threats.
- Encouraging the use of territorial features and signs at the residential block level indicate that residents are vigilant and can deter would-be criminals.
- Controlling the physical deterioration of an environment may reduce criminal offender perception that an area is vulnerable and not well protected.

The conceptual thrust of CPTED is that the environment can be manipulated to produce behavioral effects that reduce the incidence and fear of crime, and improve the quality of life. The environment includes people and their physical and social surroundings. Design includes all those activities, structures, and policies that seek to positively impact human behavior as people interact with their environment. As such, CPTED focuses not only on the physical aspects of the environment but also on what social scientists, public safety and security personnel, and community organizations can do to safely meet the needs of legitimate users of a space.

CPTED utilizes traditional target-hardening techniques such as natural and artificial barrier systems, access control, and surveillance to reduce the threat from a criminal offender. It also involves strategies developed, implemented, and evaluated by security personnel, law enforcement, and the community to allow for the least-restrictive human interface with the barrier systems.

CPTED utilizes the Three-D approach to assessment of human space. The Three-D concept is based on three assumptions of how space is to be designed and used. All human space has some *designated* purpose; it has social, legal, cultural, or physical *definitions* that prescribe desired and acceptable behaviors; and it is *designed* to support and control these desired behaviors.

The three basic CPTED concepts of territorial reinforcement, access control, and surveillance are inherent in the Three-D approach. These basic concepts may be accomplished through any combination of the following:

- Provide a clear border definition of the controlled space. Public and private spaces must be clearly delineated.
- Provide for clearly marked transitional zones. The user must acknowledge movement into the controlled space.
- Relocation of gathering areas. Formally designate gathering areas in locations with good access control and natural surveillance capabilities.
- Place safe activities in unsafe locations. Safe activities serve as magnets for normal users and communicate to abnormal users that they are at greater risk of detection.
- Place unsafe activities in safe locations. Vulnerable activities should be placed within tightly controlled areas to help overcome risk and make normal users feel safer.
- Redesignate the use of space to provide natural barriers. Conflicting activities may be separated by distance and natural terrain to avoid fear-producing conflict.
- Improve the scheduling of space. The effective use of space reduces risk as well as the perception of risk for normal users.
- Redesign space to increase the perception of surveillance. Perception is more powerful than reality.
- Overcome isolation and distance. Design efficiencies and improved communication systems increase the perception of surveillance and control.

Good planning will dictate the tactical implementation of CPTED strategies. Crime analyses, demographic and land use information, and resident or user interviews should be planned with CPTED in mind. Crime prevention through environmental design is not a panacea, nor is it a substitute for a comprehensive crime prevention program. CPTED may reduce the opportunity to commit crime when implemented in the context of a crime prevention program while providing freedom from interference for legitimate users.

One of the most significant shifts in modern thinking about crime prevention is that individual action in a vacuum often increases risks to safety and security. However, the mobilization of all stakeholders in a collaborative effort to prevent crime and disorder creates an environment in which success is more likely. From a CPTED perspective, this requires effective communication and collaboration between and among business organizations, public agencies, security managers, architects, and others to engineer safe and secure environments (American Institute of Architects, 2003; Crowe, 2000; Fennelly, 2004).

Learn more about CPTED through the American Institute of Architects at www.aia.org.

CPTED Applications

CPTED concepts and strategies may be accomplished in a variety of ways. Each situation is unique. No two environmental settings are exactly the same. Some locations where CPTED should be a consideration include the following habitats:

- Commercial facilities
- Streets and highways
- Pedestrian areas
- Parking structures and lots
- Office buildings
- Industrial complexes
- Building hallways and restrooms
- Shopping malls and convenience stores
- Residential areas
- School and college campuses
- Convention centers and stadiums
- Public transit systems

This list of habitats is by no means exhaustive. On the contrary, virtually all human functions are amenable to the use of CPTED concepts and strategies. Their adaptation to produce a safe and secure environment is virtually unlimited (Crowe, 2000).

BARRIERS TO PROBLEM SOLVING

Police officers engaged in community policing and problem solving often express concern over the difficulties encountered when they attempt to translate problem-solving theory into practice. Despite the success potential associated with the problem-solving strategy as well as the financial resources available to support the effort, police officers who are able to solve problems in training sessions often experience application difficulties in the field. Problem solving is complex. It is not an easy task. This is especially true when working with groups whose membership consists of people from diverse backgrounds. Furthermore, citizens as well as police officers must realize that the police cannot prevent or eliminate every problem.

There is little the police can do to address crime and disorder problems without community support and assistance. Yet generating support and forming partnerships can be elusive. In many communities, the police must break down walls of distrust and overcome the traditional crime fighter role identification before collaborative partnerships can develop. However, appropriate police-citizen interaction, sensitivity, and awareness can engender trust and promote meaningful problem-solving efforts (Shusta, Levine, Wong, & Harris, 2011).

Barriers to effective problem solving can develop in almost any situation. As with any planned change or revision, barriers or resistance to problem solving can emerge from social, political, physical, economic, educational, legal, technological, organizational, or cultural sources. Social factors in a community associated with class, gender, or race can produce inequality that is not easily corrected. Political groups with power can promote change in favor of themselves. The physical environment can inhibit implementation of crime prevention strategies. Economically, sufficient financial resources may not be available. Community members may lack sufficient education to understand the nature of the problem and thus will be unable to assist with the creation and implementation of a solution. Legal restrictions can inhibit police ability to solve some types of problems. Technologically, more sophisticated communications and information systems may be necessary to implement the solution to a problem. Organizationally, members of a group may resist the change which will inevitably result from the implementation of a problem's solution. Finally, problem solving across cultures creates profound ethical questions that leaders must confront as they attempt to maintain integrity while making culturally appropriate decisions (Adler, 2008; Welsh & Harris, 2008).

In some jurisdictions, traditional law enforcement activities are labeled as "problem solving" when the activities are directed toward problems identified by the community. However, enforcement-based solutions to problems are likely to be short lived, because activities dominated by enforcement actions rarely advance the strategic objectives of community policing. Enforcement actions alone rarely eliminate underlying causes of crime and disorder. Neither do they attract community support for long-term solution maintenance. The growing trend toward zero-tolerance policing, for example, although based on community input, can alienate potential community partners who were unable to provide input when the zero-tolerance policies were developed (Roth & Ryan, 2000).

Many police agencies are failing or are progressing too slowly toward implementing community policing and problem-solving concepts because officers lack ethical decision-making and problem-solving skills. Failed attempts and slow progress fosters resistance and encourages many officers to regress into inefficient and obsolete traditional incident-driven policing methods. Success in the community policing effort requires competence to explore and define problems with specificity as well as assist with problem ownership.

A thorough exploration of the circumstances of a problem situation facilitates problem identification and resolution. Hunches, personal feelings, bias, emotion, and premature evaluations must be set aside in favor of a patient identification and examination of the facts and the causal connection between the symptoms and the negative consequences a problem creates. The more thoroughly a problem is explored, the more likely a high-impact solution will be developed.

Problem exploration requires a complex set of human qualities and competencies. In addition to patience and creative thinking, problem exploration requires the ability to craft and use a language that defines the problem clearly. The ability to define a problem with specificity is difficult to master. Thus, many police officers are reluctant to engage in problem-solving efforts. Supervisors may view the reluctant officer as uncooperative and malcontent. The reality is that the officer is often uncomfortable when transitioning from tradition to community policing. The transition is aggravated when officers are exposed to the concepts of community policing but do not have the benefit of proper training in the practical realties of its implementation. Community policing officers are expected to view crime and disorder problems from multiple perspectives. As a result, an officer's job can become more difficult. Rather than prescribed by a supervisor or traditional procedure, a police officer's actions in a community policing environment depend on the officer's problem-solving competence. An officer is expected to be less reactive and more proactive, preventing crime and disorder with community-based problem-solving strategies (Anderson, 2000).

CASE STUDY—CRIME ANALYSIS: STATE OF THE ART?

In 2000, the University of South Alabama conducted two national surveys and nine site visits to determine law enforcement agency progress toward the use of crime analysis operations consistent with community policing and problem solving. Researchers first surveyed all American law enforcement agencies with 100 or more sworn personnel. Sixty-five percent of agencies responded. Next, researchers surveyed a random sample of 800 agencies with fewer than 100 sworn personnel. Finally, telephone interviews with 40 crime analysts and visits to nine crime analysis units were conducted. Based on the assumption that police agencies had made great strides toward complex problem-solving activities, the study sought to produce an operations guide for the ideal crime analysis unit.

The findings revealed that nearly all crime analysts were asked by supervisors to direct their efforts toward a narrowly defined target: the apprehension of criminal offenders and possibly the identification of high-crime areas. This narrow focus suggests that police operations in the United States continue to emphasize the traditional incident-driven (professional) model of policing (catching the bad guy) rather than broadening analytic activities to identify underlying causes of crime and community problems (the community policing model) (O'Shea & Nicholls, 2003).

1. Given the remarkable advances in technology and law enforcement operations research in the past two decades, one could expect to observe correspondingly more sophisticated police tactical and strategic decision outcomes and solutions to crime and disorder problems. However, this does not appear to be the case. Why?

2. How might police administrators be encouraged to think and manage in broad problem-oriented, solution-focused terms rather than in narrowly defined crime control terms?

Additional **barriers to effective problem solving** include the following:

- **Lack of training**—problem-solving strategies represent a complete paradigm shift from traditional policing in which officers simply respond to radio calls or reported incidents. However, problem-solving skills can be learned with good, extensive, and ongoing training by qualified personnel. Short-term training sessions are not enough.

- **Lack of leadership**—police administrators often fail to support line officers in the problem-solving effort. In addition, line officers themselves have not acquired the leadership skills necessary to engage and work with community members.

- **Confusion**—police executives and line officers often confuse community policing and problem solving with community relations. Although good police–community relations are important, problem solving involves the added dimension of community participation.

- **Lack of clearly defined roles**—police officers in a community policing and problem-solving environment often experience an identity crisis. The crisis results when agencies do not clearly define the mission and values of the organization and fail to identify the roles and responsibilities of police executives, midlevel managers, front line supervisors, and field officers. Often the problem-solving activities are relegated to a few specialized community relations patrol units. The effort should permeate the entire agency.

- **Lack of technological support**—except for major crimes and arrest and conviction data, the information necessary for effective problem solving is not readily available to the officers in the field. Integrated information systems that incorporate incident data with crime mapping programs are essential to the problem-solving effort and are desperately needed.

- **The fad complex**—programs and concepts in policing come and go in agencies that view new ideas as fads or passing political fancy. To be successful, the concept of community policing and problem solving requires long-term commitment, support, and integration of the strategy into every functional area of the police organization.

- **Lack of legitimacy**—for the past half century, police strategy and tactics have focused on the identification and apprehension of criminals. As a result, police officers question the legitimacy of the police role in crime prevention.

- **Lack of effective outcome assessment**—a major criticism of community policing and problem solving is the lack of structured evaluations to assess the effectiveness of problem-solving efforts. Although anecdotal success stories are publicized, effective assessment methods and instruments have yet to be devised.

The barriers to problem solving in a community policing environment include training and information deficiencies, weak support, organizational culture, and lack of leadership and understanding. Until these issues are addressed fully, barriers to effective problem solving will continue to exist (Decker, Rosenfeld, & Burruss, 2005; Ortmeier & Meese, 2010; What does it take to make collaboration work? 2004).

SUMMARY

Police officers are problem solvers. Although problem solving is a major portion of police work, traditional police training methods may inhibit the development of problem-solving ability. In policing, the community problem rather than a specific incident should be the main unit of police work. Problem solving involves the use of quantitative as well as qualitative data and analysis.

Several problem-solving models have emerged to assist law enforcement and other public safety agencies. The model most commonly used today consists of four major components: scanning, analysis, response, and assessment (SARA). To work effectively with neighborhoods and communities to address crime and disorder problems, the police must develop the skills necessary to work with diverse groups of people. Included in a community problem-solving effort are techniques and processes for community mapping and crime prevention through environmental design (CPTED). The police must also be aware of the numerous barriers to effective problem solving.

 ## DISCUSSION QUESTIONS AND EXERCISES

1. Outline and describe the elements of the planning process.
2. Identify and describe the four components to the SARA problem-solving model.
3. How would one apply problem-solving techniques when working with a group of people?
4. Conduct a community needs assessment for a neighborhood. Review crime rates as part of the needs assessment and create a map that identifies high-crime-rate areas within the neighborhood.
5. Utilizing the SARA problem-solving model, develop an action plan to address needs identified through a community needs assessment.
6. Utilizing CPTED concepts, design a crime prevention and reduction program for a neighborhood.
7. What are the barriers to effective problem solving?
8. Discuss the role of evaluation in the planning process.
9. How can police officers and agency managers learn to think and operate in community-based, problem-solving terms?
10. Several business owners in an urban strip mall report that prostitutes are loitering and operating near their stores during business hours. The presence of the prostitutes deters customers, and sales in the mall's businesses have declined dramatically. Attempts to eliminate the problem through arrest and prosecution of the prostitutes and their solicitors (johns) have not been successful. How should the police proceed?

Career Preparation

LEARNING OBJECTIVES

After completing this chapter, the reader should be able to:

- list and describe the skills and qualities required of a law enforcement officer.
- explain the policies, procedures, and laws associated with the recruitment, selection, promotion, and retention of law enforcement and criminal justice practitioners.
- discuss the importance of a proper attitude in police work.
- describe the importance of career training and education for law enforcement officers.
- prepare for employment in law enforcement.
- explain officer survival techniques.
- evaluate the need to use force.
- identify weapons appropriate for use of force situations.
- classify lethal and nonlethal weapons.
- demonstrate knowledge of techniques to reduce stress and maintain physical fitness for duty.

KEY TERMS

Define, describe, or explain the importance of each of the following.

Attitude

Baton

Burnout

Chemical agent

Compliance continuum

Continuous professional training (CPT)

Deadly errors

De-escalation

Excessive force

Firearms safety rules

Flash-bang grenade

Higher education

Less lethal weapon

Lethal weapon

Level of resistance

Lifetime fitness

Nunchaku

Personal performance index (PPI)

Police officer skills and qualities

Police officers' bill of rights

P.R. Brooks

Pre-service training

Principle of control

PR-24

Roll call announcements

Sticky foam

Stress management

Strobe light
Stun gun
Suicide by cop
Taser®
Ten Plan

Training
Use of force options and policy
Vehicle disabler
Weaponless defense

INTRODUCTION

To be efficient and effective, every worthwhile human undertaking requires appropriate personal skills and qualities, a proper attitude, planning, and preparation. Police work is no exception. In fact, appropriate mental conditioning and preparation are absolutely essential to effectiveness and survival in law enforcement. This section presents the ingredients for preparation for a career in law enforcement. The preliminary considerations presented are by no means exhaustive. However, they represent the foundation for effective and safe performance. The career preparation and maintenance guidelines discussed are also applicable in most other criminal justice occupations.

CASE STUDY–PERISHABLE POLICE SKILLS

Most law enforcement officers are required to participate in training activities as a condition of continued employment as an officer. Often referred to as continuing professional training (CPT), in-service training, as compared to pre-service basic academy training, is used to: introduce new technology; inform officers of new laws, policies, and procedures; create awareness of new crimes and offender methodologies; and reinforce knowledge and skills already acquired.

Critical to officer safety and effective policing is the need for perishable skills training. Perishable skills are competencies that "perish" with irregular use or decline without reinforcement or refresher skill-building activities. Typically, perishable skills training programs focus on firearms use, driver training and awareness, arrest and control of prisoners, and tactical/interpersonal communications.

1. Can any other police-related skills or qualities be identified as perishable? If so, what are they?
2. What is the most appropriate method for delivering police perishable skills training?

POLICE OFFICER SKILLS AND QUALITIES

Police officers tend to be drawn from lower to middle-class backgrounds. Often the police officer recruit has a relative or friend who is already employed in law enforcement. With respect to the psychological profile of police recruits, little distinction can be made between the individual who enters police work and those from working-class backgrounds who enter other occupations. Most police recruits today still have little formal education beyond high school. They enter police work because of the relatively good income and job security, for adventure, and a desire for public service with the ability to have an impact on crime (Barlow, 2000).

One might ask, What makes a good police officer? What attributes, qualities, and competencies are required of a police officer in contemporary society? Meese and Kurz (1993) described the individual qualities for success in a contemporary policing environment:

> Among the qualities which are radically different than those required for the traditional "crime fighting" officer are: proactive problem solver, peacekeeper and developer of cooperative relationships, guided by values and goals. Other traits include personal accountability, self-reliance, self-motivation, and capability as a mediator, negotiator, and community mobilizer. . . . Finally, the police officer will be more often a professional with a college degree. (p. 296)

Police officers must think creatively and independently. They must be able to create a vision and develop appropriate steps for solving problems. Instead of reacting primarily to incidents, the officer is forced to analyze, plan, and take initiative (Meese, 1993). Therefore, recruitment, selection, training, and educational programs must be modified to develop a core of officers with the instinct and leadership competencies necessary for working with the community (California State, Commission on Peace Officer Standards and Training, 2002; Fleissner, Fedan, & Klinger, 1992; Ortmeier & Meese, 2010; Ortmeier, 1995, 1996, 1997, 2003). One must remember that it is the individual patrol officer who has the greatest freedom, discretionary authority, and ability to work directly with the public and who is perceived as the primary representative of the police department (Goldstein, 1990). It is this officer who has the most direct contact with the people and their problems.

In 1967, the President's Commission on Law Enforcement and the Administration of Justice observed that physical strength and aggressiveness reflected the popular image of what the police do, but this image was inconsistent with a careful analysis of the job requirements. It further noted that one incompetent officer could trigger a riot, permanently damage the reputation of a citizen, or alienate a community against a police department. In today's policing environment, brute strength and aggressiveness must give way to a new breed of officers who are better educated, self-managed, creative, guided by values and purposes, and who are not constrained by rules and excessive supervision. Officers should be viewed as team players, not subordinates, and supervisors should act as facilitators. Even the day-to-day, seemingly routine, decisions officers make about their own conduct and actions have potentially far-reaching consequences and must be guided by individual introspection about values, integrity, principles, and ethics (Boehm, 1988; J.R. Clark, 1994; Lyman, 2010; Meese, 1993).

Police departments must deploy the most innovative, self-disciplined, and self-motivated officers directly into the community as outreach specialists and community problem solvers (Ortmeier & Davis, 2012; Trojanowicz & Carter, 1990). As such, police officers must be sensitive to public perceptions and possess complex critical-thinking skills (California Community Colleges, 1992). They must be able to adapt to changing community needs (McKinnie, 1995; Wycoff & Oettmeier, 1994) and utilize a human relations approach to communicate, identify, and solve problems and look toward service to the community (California State Legislature, 1991; Coffey, 1990; Meese, 1993; Spelman & Eck, 1987). Officers must also develop collaborative, multidisciplinary approaches to community problems by including members of civil rights groups, and health, education, social service, and child welfare agencies as well as business and industry in the problem-solving process (U.S. Department of Justice, 1993; Whisenand & Ferguson, 2009). To function effectively in modern society, police officers must possess certain skills and qualities: These **police officer skills and qualities** include the following.

- **Proper attitude**—one of the most important qualities for the law enforcement officer involves a proper attitude. If the police officer's attitude consistently demonstrates isolationism, gestapo-like tactics, and verbally abusive language, the officer and the agency will be unable to generate the community support necessary for effective and efficient policing.
- **Leadership**—the position and status of law enforcement makes it the most visible component of the criminal justice system. The police are, therefore, in a position to assume a leadership role in the community.
- **Integrity**—probably the most important quality for a police officer is integrity. Adherence to a standard of ethics inspires trust. An essential ingredient for securing the public's trust is the public's belief that the police will act with fairness, credibility, and restraint.
- **Judgment**—police officers must be able to exercise effective judgment. Split-second decision making is required in emergency situations.
- **Communications**—oral and written (report writing) communications skills are critical. Experts agree that these skills are extremely important in law enforcement.
- **Human relations**—the ability to get along with people is essential to police work and effective police–community relations. Good relations between the police and the public equates to more and better cooperation regarding resources, reporting crime, and information supplied to the police.
- **Cognitive skills (knowledge)**—the police officer must possess knowledge of a wide range of subjects, not the least of which are the elements of law and evidence.
- **Technical**—the officer must have skills associated with defensive tactics, weapons, and procedures (Meese & Ortmeier, 2004; Ortmeier, 1999; Trautman, 2005; U.S. Department of Labor, 2004).

Possession of these skills and qualities is also appropriate for other criminal justice and public safety personnel.

RECRUITMENT, SELECTION, PROMOTION, AND RETENTION

As stated previously, police agencies must deploy innovative, self-disciplined, and self-motivated officers. In addition, citizens expect officers to demonstrate sound judgement, decisiveness, courage, and ethical leadership while keeping the peace, maintaining order, and protecting the public. Agencies are searching for, and wish to retain, individuals with the highest level of integrity as well as people who demonstrate excellent interpersonal and written communications skills and strong decision-making and problem-solving ability. Officer recruitment and selection processes must be dedicated to the appointment of those who can fulfill these roles and expectations. Yet one must remember that the best pre-employment screening process, coupled with the most effective training program, will not produce a perfect police officer. However, comprehensive recruitment, selection, and training processes can help to generate and create a professional deemed worthy of the public's trust (City of Los Angeles, 2003; O'Keefe, 2004).

At a minimum, most police agencies require an applicant to be an 18–21-year-old U.S. citizen who possesses a valid driver's license and a specified formal educational level. In addition, applicants must be free of any felony or domestic violence convictions. The pre-employment screening process normally includes elements of the following.

- **Employment application**—The written employment application requests an applicant's entire personal and professional history.
- **Aptitude test(s)**—Typically, the aptitude test is a competitive, written multiple choice test designed to measure reading comprehension, English usage, and other skills. In addition, an essay exam may be administered to assess written communications, critical thinking, and problem-solving abilities.
- **Physical abilities (agility) test**—This is a pass/fail qualifying test designed to measure physical strength, agility, endurance, coordination, and flexibility.
- **Interview**—This includes a behavior-based review of the applicant's personal history, knowledge, communicative ability, attitude and orientation, motivation, interpersonal skills, community involvement, sensitivity to diversity, and a scenario-based evaluation of the applicant's problem-solving ability.
- **Polygraph or voice stress analyzer examination**—A polygraph or voice stress analyzer exam may be administered to verify background information of the applicant.
- **Medical examination**—This exam is designed to identify medical conditions that may restrict an applicant's ability to perform police-related tasks.
- **Psychological examination**—This phase includes a written test that focuses on an applicant's personality and psychological profile. Tests designed and utilized for this purpose include the Minnesota Multiphasic Personality Inventory-2 (MMPI-2), the Myers-Briggs Type Indicator, the Strong Interest Inventory, the Watson-Glaser

Critical Thinking Appraisal, and the California Psychological Inventory (CPI). The test is evaluated by a licensed psychologist.

- **Background investigation (BI)**—The BI includes fingerprinting, photos, and a background interview of the applicant, followed by an investigation that includes a review of the personal, criminal, credit, driving, military, educational, and employment records of the applicant. Personal references are also contacted during the BI. Automatic disqualfiers include any felony or domestic violence conviction and recent illegal drug use.

- **Psychological interview**—This interview is conducted and evaluated by a licensed psychologist, using the results of written psychological examination and background investigation, to determine the applicant's ability to perform successfully in the difficult and stressful police occupation.

- **Certification and appointment**—Candidates for employment are certified to have successfully completed the pre-employment process. Appointments to the police academy are made from the certified list of candidates.

Many laws govern the relationship between employers and employees. Most of the laws apply to prospective, current, and former employee civil rights. The laws address issues such as equal employment opportunity, affirmative action, and Americans with disabilities. The following summarizes the principal legislation in this area.

- **Social Security Act of 1935**—This act established the Social Security system.

- **Fair Labor Standards Act of 1938**—This act established minimum wages to be paid to employees, the 40 hour workweek, and regulations regarding child labor.

- **The Equal Pay Act of 1963**—This law provided for equal pay for equal work for individuals of different genders working in the same job classification.

- **Title VII of the Omnibus Civil Rights Act of 1964 (amended in 1972)**—This law prohibited employers of 15 or more persons from discriminating against any individual on the basis of race, color, gender, religious preference, or national origin. None of these factors may be used in any decisions with respect to hiring, promotion, discharge, compensation, training, or any other term, condition, or privilege associated with employment. Responsibility for enforcement of the law rests with the U.S. Equal Employment Opportunity Commission (EEOC). Many state and local governments have similar legislation that parallels the federal law.

- **Executive Order 11246 of the Civil Rights Act**—This presidential order amended and added the requirement of affirmative action to Title VII of the Civil Rights Act of 1964.

- **Age Discrimination in Employment Act of 1967 (amended in 1986)**—This law prohibited employment discrimination against a person because the person is 40 years of age or older.

- **Occupational Safety and Health Act of 1970**—This law provided that employers must do everything possible to protect human resources by furnishing employees with a work environment that is free of recognizable hazards likely to cause serious injury or death. The act is administered by the Occupational Safety and Health Administration (OSHA). The act applies to every organization with at least one employee who engages in interstate commerce or an activity that affects interstate commerce. It does not apply to local, state or federal employees or workers covered by another health and safety law, such as the Federal Coal Mine Safety and Health Act or the Atomic Energy Act of 1954.

- **Equal Employment Opportunity Act of 1972**—This law amended and expanded Title VII of the Civil Rights Act of 1964 to include state and local governments.

- **Pregnancy Discrimination Act of 1978**—This law prohibited employers from discriminating against pregnant women.

- **Worker Adjustment and Retraining Notification (WARN) Act of 1988**—This law required employers to notify workers of impending layoffs.

- **Drug Free Workplace Act**—Covered employers under this law must implement certain policies to restrict employee drug use.

- **American with Disabilities Act (ADA) of 1990 (amended in 1991)**—The ADA prohibited discrimination against a disabled person with respect to employment, public accommodations and services, and services provided by private organizations. An employer may not discriminate against a disabled person because of their disability. The ADA also prohibits testing for or inquiring about a medical or physical disability until a job is offered. Pre-employment inquiries regarding substance abuse must be limited to recent and current use. The act prohibits any pre-employment, promotion or discharge test that is designed to disqualify persons with disabilities.

- **The Employee Polygraph Protection Act of 1988**—Subject to limited exceptions, this law prohibited or severely restricted the use of the polygraph or similar instruments by private employers. Under the act, private employers cannot use a polygraph for pre-employment screening. The act further prohibits employers from requiring or requesting an employee to submit to a polygraph. A private employer cannot take any action against an employee for refusing to submit to a polygraph or for the results of such a test. However, most public safety agencies, such as law enforcement organizations, are exempt from the statue.

- **Family and Medical Leave Act of 1993**—This act provided that employers must allow unpaid leave for childbirth, adoption, or illness (Cheeseman, 2010).

Public safety and law enforcement agencies must also be concerned with employee retention. Much has been written about officer recruitment, selection, training, supervision, and evaluation. Yet little attention is directed toward officer retention.

Learn more about women in policing through the Women in Policing Institute at www
.womenpolice.com.

Officer retention begins with policies and open lines of communication designed to ensure realistic expectations on the part of new and existing employees. Pre-employment interviews should be structured to describe the negative as well as the positive aspects of employment with the organization. The next step in the employee retention process involves a proper orientation to the new officer's work environment. Third, effective training of the new officer is absolutely essential, especially when skills are deficient. Although the retention of good officers cannot be guaranteed, proper orientation and training can assist with retention. Officers who demonstrate the knowledge, skills, and abilities (KSAs) necessary to do a job well are difficult and expensive to replace. Encouraging good officers to remain with an organization should be one of management's highest priorities (Robbins & Coulter, 2012). Yet many officers leave their agencies after only a few years, often to work for other agencies (Hiring and keeping police officers, 2004).

The recruitment, selection, promotion, and retention of a diverse workforce, representative of the community being served, will continue to challenge the police service. Many issues remain unresolved. In addition, the number of qualified entry-level applicants will decrease as both public and private employers compete for the best qualified people. However, employment of a group of culturally and ethnically diverse and qualified men and women can be achieved by agencies that honestly implement legitimate programs designed to develop and maintain a community-oriented workforce reflective of the public served (Orler, 2011; Shusta, Levine, Wong, & Harris, 2011).

ATTITUDE AND PERSONAL PERFORMANCE

One of the greatest enemies of the police officer is a poor **attitude.** Effective law enforcement requires a mental commitment to integrity, ethics, community service, professionalism, and the police mission (Carlson, 2005; Miller, 2000). Police work is not the most physically dangerous job in the world (Copes, 2005; Perry, 1998). Miners, construction workers, taxi drivers, firefighters, and 24-hour convenience store clerks have higher work-related death rates. However, policing is extremely taxing emotionally, mentally, and physically. Although police work can be 80 percent boredom, 20 percent can be sheer terror. Police officers must deal with dangerous people as well as uncivil behavior of normally good citizens.

Today, the public demands and expects mature behavior and judgment on the part of its police officers. Law enforcement is not the career field for immature, self-centered, overly aggressive, or abusive people. The psychological dynamics of police work also generates stress, which must be dealt with effectively (Swanson, Territo, & Taylor, 2008). The officer must not allow stress to manifest itself in uncivil conduct toward normally law-abiding citizens, use of excessive force on criminal suspects, inappropriate behavior in one's personal life, or officer suicide.

Officers who tend to experience the most difficulty with attitude are those who live, eat, and breathe police work 24 hours a day. Officers who take the job home and spend most, if not all, of their off-duty time thinking and talking about police work place their peers, the public, and themselves in jeopardy. An appropriate mental balance between an officer's personal and professional life is necessary. Successful law enforcement careers result from an everyday realization that a proper attitude is extremely important.

In addition to maintaining a proper attitude, the police officer must recognize that the public as well as the officer's agency and peers have certain expectations of a law enforcement professional. These expectations are used to evaluate an officer's performance. The public's evaluation is based on how an officer appears and behaves as well as how the officer handles crises and problem situations. The public expects an officer to know a community's perceived needs, prevent crime, maintain order, provide service, and demonstrate equal and unbiased enforcement of the law. An officer's peers expect technical competence, physical backup when appropriate, and emotional support. Finally, officers must be aware that the agency that employs them has performance expectations (California Commission on Peace Officer Standards and Training, 2012). Many departments evaluate an officer by tracking an officer with a **personal performance index (PPI)** or similar assessment tool. Entries to the PPI are based on an officer's ability to perform job tasks, complaints or lawsuits filed against the officer, conduct consistent with ethical standards, and conformance with the requirements of law and department policies.

TRAINING AND EDUCATION

The importance of proper training and educational preparation for police work cannot be overemphasized. Learning in police work is a career-long process. Basic **pre-service training** and continuing professional inservice training are an absolute necessity and should be taken seriously. **Training** assists with the acquisition, development, and maintenance of the knowledge, skills, and abilities (KSAs) necessary to perform job-related tasks. All states have some form of training requirement for police officers.

In addition to basic pre-service training, most states require field training and inservice **continuous professional training (CPT)** for police officers. Field training involves on-the-street instruction that utilizes real-life police experiences and practical problems to train entry-level police officers. Field training is conducted under the direct supervision of a field training officer (FTO) during or immediately after the basic police academy experience. Police recruits are evaluated continuously by the FTOs to document recruit performance, determine the need for remedial training, and judge the recruit's suitability for police work (Hale, 2004; Thibault, Lynch, & McBride, 2004).

Effective training of law enforcement officers is an absolute necessity. *(Photo courtesy of the San Diego Sheriff's Department.)*

CPT is used to maintain competence in the police profession and to provide supplemental training. Perishable skills such as driving, firearms, arrest and control, defensive tactics, as well as written, interpersonal, and tactical communications must be refreshed to maintain officer competence. CPT also supplements basic skills as the police encounter new types of situations and assume enforcement responsibility for new laws. In-service CPT may be accomplished in several ways. Training vehicles include roll call briefings, bulletins, and formalized workshops and seminars. Job-specific training is also offered through electronic media such as interactive virtual reality computer simulations and television programs. For example, through firearms training technology systems, officers can view videos of "shoot" and "don't shoot" situations on a computer screen, and respond using a laser-directed weapon that simulates their duty weapons (Reid, 2011). Although CPT requirements vary throughout the nation, most police agencies and states require some form of in-service training.

Higher education is also important for police officers. The need for highly educated police personnel was recognized as early as 1931 in the Wickersham Commission report. The commission conducted the first major national investigation into the nature and scope of crime and made recommendations for improving the quality of criminal justice personnel. The commission recommended a bachelor's degree as the entry-level education qualification for police officers. In 1967, the President's Commission on Law Enforcement and the Administration of Justice reaffirmed the need for four-year degrees for police officers.

The curriculum for basic police academy training includes a wide range of subjects. Although basic academy programs vary slightly, a typical curriculum may be similar to the following:
- Leadership, Professionalism, and Ethics (8 hours).
- Criminal Justice System (2 hours).
- Policing in the Community (18 hours).
- Victimology/Crisis Intervention (6 hours)
- Introduction to Criminal Law (4 hours)
- Property Crimes (6 hours).
- Crimes Against Persons/Death Investigation (6 hours)
- General Criminal Statutes (2 hours)
- Crimes Against Children (4 hours)
- Sex Crimes (4 hours)
- Juvenile Law and Procedure (3 hours)
- Controlled Substances (12 hours)
- Liquor Law Violations (2 hours)
- Laws of Arrest (12 hours)
- Search and Seizure (12 hours)
- Presentation of Evidence (6 hours)
- Investigative Report Writing (52 hours)
- Vehicle Operations (24 hours)
- Use of Force (12 hours)
- Patrol Techniques (12 hours)
- Vehicle Pullovers (14 hours)
- Crimes in Progress (20 hours)
- Handling Disputes/Crowd Control (8 hours)
- Domestic Violence (10 hours)
- Unusual Occurrences (4 hours)
- Missing Persons (4 hours)
- Traffic Enforcement (16 hours)
- Traffic Collision Investigations (12 hours)
- Crime Scenes, Evidence, and Forensics (12 hours)
- Custody (2 hours)
- Lifetime Fitness (44 hours)
- Arrest Methods/Defensive Tactics (60 hours)
- First Aid and CPR (21 hours)
- Firearms/Chemical Agents (72 hours)
- Information Systems (2 hours)
- People with Disabilities (6 hours)
- Gang Awareness (2 hours)
- Crimes Against the Justice System (4 hours)
- Weapons Violations (4 hours)
- Hazardous Materials Awareness (4 hours)
- Cultural Diversity/Discrimination (16 hours)
- Emergency Management (16 hours)
- Scenario Tests (58 hours)
- Knowledge Tests (46 hours) (California Commission on Peace Officer Standards and Training, 2012)

Training assists with the development and maintenance of skills. *(Photo courtesy of the San Diego Sheriff's Department.)*

The role of the police officer is changing ". . . from pure enforcement of the law to one of dealing with people and their problems. The police . . . are taking a more holistic approach to the community" (Scott, 1986, pp. 16–17). Higher education helps officers develop the skills necessary to deal with an entire community. College-educated officers appear to exhibit greater sensitivity to diversity, a critical skill in a multicultural society (Bohm & Haley, 2009; Carter, Sapp, & Stephens, 1989). Police work goes beyond performance of basic job skills. Police officers must be able to think as well as do (Ortmeier, 1995, 2003).

Physical conditioning is a part of basic academy training. *(Photo Courtesy of the Cobb County, GA Police Department.)*

Where do we find thinkers and how do we develop creative people for police work? How do we change human values and attitudes that are the essential prerequisites to successful changes in philosophy, organizational concepts, and strategies (Meese & Kurz, 1993; Peters, 1992)? What percentage of police academy training should focus on the vital components of critical thinking versus the technical aspects of law enforcement (Cronkhite, 1995)? Do responses to these questions lie in higher education? Studies have shown that a college education is necessary, or at least desirable, in contemporary policing (Carter, Sapp, & Stephens, 1988; Roberg, 1978). And, since the beginning of the twentieth century, some experts have professed that higher education may provide the officer with an advantage (Goldstein, 1990). It appears that more responsibility can be placed on college-educated officers. The college-educated officer sets higher professional standards and goals, which in turn command public respect and help shape public opinion. College-educated police have the potential to proactively, rather than reactively, address the problems that plague society today (Murphy, 1989). Police officers must be better educated and be self-motivated, creative, and problem-solving professionals (Meese, 1993). However, although college-level programs in law enforcement and criminal justice currently exist, many believe these programs are lacking.

Some scholars and police agency executives suggest that many college-level criminal justice programs do not help people develop many of the competencies necessary for contemporary policing. For example, some believe that the vocational approach in many programs does not fulfill desirable academic goals pursuant to the development of human relations, communications, and similar nontechnical skills. However, technique-oriented college programs can be supplemented with appropriate educational experiences that integrate vocational and academic skill development. Appropriate new learning can flow from occupational as well as traditional academic environments.

College-educated police officers tend to be more mature, possess enhanced verbal and written communications skills, exercise better judgment and critical-thinking skills, demonstrate greater empathy and tolerance for differing lifestyles, are less likely to use excessive force, and generate fewer citizen complaints and disciplinary actions. Furthermore, police agencies with highly educated officers are defendants in fewer lawsuits for inappropriate police conduct (Bohm & Haley, 2009; Vodicka, 1994). Police work often requires individual judgment in individual cases. A college education reinforces the mature and ethical decision making necessary for proper judgment (Meese & Ortmeier, 2004; Ortmeier, 1995).

About 1 percent of local police departments require a four-year degree. Most of the arguments in favor of college-educated police officers are based on the assumption that the role of the police has become increasingly complex. Some experts suggest that the paramilitary organizational structure that exists in a majority of police departments actually inhibits critical thinking skills, which a college education helps develop (Baro & Burlingame, 1999; Champion & Rush, 1997; City of Los Angeles, 2003). Yet many police administrators still oppose critical thinking among rank-and-file officers, insisting that discipline is more valuable. Therefore, a college education is still not a requirement for entry-level positions in a vast majority of police departments.

At the very least, many skills required of the police officer today are enhanced by higher education. The skills necessary to write well, speak to groups, deal with continually changing circumstances, appreciate diversity, use computer technology, and understand contemporary social issues are learned and reinforced through the college experience. Finally, even though a college degree is not an entry-level requirement, the degree might enhance promotion possibilities and selection probabilities in a competitive job market (Baro & Burlingame, 1999; Carlon, 1999; Meese & Ortmeier, 2004; Michelson & Maher, 2001).

PREPARATION FOR PATROL

Work Schedules

Police management analysis of officer activity should reveal the times and locations where police resources are required most often. The results of this analysis may be used to schedule working time for patrol officers.. Most communities maintain at least three 8-hour shifts to ensure 24-hour service. Some communities add a fourth shift for peak police activity periods. Following is an example of a basic work schedule:

A shift	2300 hours–0700 hours	(11:00 P.M.–7.00 A.M.)
B shift	0700 hours–1500 hours	(7:00 A.M.–3:00 P.M.)
C shift	1500 hours–2300 hours	(3:00 P.M.–11:00 P.M.)
D shift	1900 hours–0300 hours	(7:00 P.M.–3:00 A.M.)
(optional)		

Some police agencies utilize what is commonly referred to as the **Ten Plan:** three 10-hour shifts that overlap during peak periods. Fewer officers are scheduled for each shift but a greater number are in the field during peak periods. Ten Plans also tend to improve the morale of officers. They work four 10-hour shifts and have three days off. An example of the Ten Plan follows:

A shift	2400 hours–1000 hours	(midnight–10:00 A.M.)
B shift	0800 hours–1800 hours	(8:00 A.M.–6:00 P.M.)
C shift	1600 hours–0200 hours	(4:00 P.M.–2:00 A.M.)
D shift	1700 hours–0300 hours	(5:00 P.M.–3:00 A.M.)
(optional)		

To reduce overtime costs and sick leave abuse as well as improve morale, a few police agencies have experimented with 12.5-hour shifts. Under the plan, officers work one 4-day week and two 3-day weeks. The plan requires only two shift changes every 24 hours instead of three, reducing roll call time and resulting in more time for patrol (Hale, 2004; Payton & Amaral, 2004).

Pre-Patrol Information

Preparation for patrol includes the acquisition of knowledge necessary to function effectively. An officer should arrive ready for duty approximately 20 minutes prior to roll call. The officer should review phone, voice mail, e-mail, or written messages. The officer should read all correspondence, new wanted persons and training bulletins, hot sheets on stolen vehicles, and new agency policy statements.

During **roll call announcements,** the officer should be alert, pay attention, and record all pertinent information. Supplementary reports and information as well as current activities and events will be announced during roll call. Commendations for jobs well done may also be issued during roll call.

The officer must also be thoroughly familiar with the patrol district. The topography (natural features), geography, jurisdictional boundaries, and physical layout of the district are important considerations. The officer should be familiar with street names and numbers, problem areas, traffic patterns and routes, neighborhoods, community leaders, gang affiliations, and other characteristics peculiar to the district. The officer should remember that knowledge is power!

Personal Supplies and Equipment

A police officer's tools of the trade are many and varied. Each item has a purpose and an officer will be ineffective without it. In most police agencies, patrol activities are performed in a uniform. The uniform should be clean and free of odors and wrinkles. An extra, clean uniform should be available. Most police agencies prefer the dark navy blue uniform because the officer is less visible at night and the dark color psychologically commands greater respect for the authority of the officer. Footgear should be black, durable, practical, and comfortable. Body armor, in the form of a ballistic vest, should be worn at all times. Service belts should be functional and include the sidearm holster, handcuff case and cuffs, fresh chemical agent with, carrier, ammo pouches with fresh ammunition in speed loaders or clips, baton or **nunchaku** and baton ring or nunchaku holster, radio holder, and key carrier with ring for keys and whistle. The officer should carry at least three writing instruments (two pens and a pencil for inclement weather), extra forms, a flashlight with fresh batteries, and foul weather gear. Portable radios, helmets, shotguns, and ammunition issued by the agency should be inspected to ensure that they are functional.

Agency-approved sidearms and backup weapons must be clean and functional. Some agencies allow officers to carry a preferred caliber and type of service firearm while on duty. However, this practice is not recommended. It leads to a proliferation of weapon types with different calibers. Some officers may prefer to carry the traditional .38- or .357-caliber revolvers. Others may prefer 9 mm, .40-caliber, or .45-caliber semiautomatics. Lack of standardization can lead to disaster during a police-involved shooting. Ammunition may not be compatible. In a firefight it may be necessary for one officer to use another's weapon. Lack of familiarity with a different firearm may result in serious injury or death to the officer or some innocent third person.

Incidental supplies and equipment may be included in a kit or briefcase. Incidentals include a clipboard, report forms and citation books, extra ammunition, gloves, items for collecting evidence, chalk, code books, first-aid supplies and CPR masks, binoculars, a camera with film, matches, and a small tool kit.

Patrol vehicles must be inspected before commencing patrol. Actually, the law requires that all drivers ensure that their vehicles are in proper working order. The patrol vehicle functions as a carrier, office, and home away from home. It receives rough treatment and is driven thousands of miles. It must be inspected and treated with care. More police officers are killed or injured in traffic mishaps than die or are injured as the result of criminal action. Aircraft pilots have a pre-flight checklist. Police officers should complete a pre-drive checklist.

The following guidelines should be practiced to inventory and inspect equipment issued with the vehicle. The patrol officer should check for flares, cones, and a fire extinguisher; walk around the vehicle and note damage and condition in the vehicle log; check tires (and spare) for proper air pressure; and check the oil, coolant, transmission, and other fluids. The officer should also check the vehicle interior and trunk for any items or contraband left by prisoners, evidence left unattended, or the previous driver's personal effects that may have been left in the vehicle. When in the driver's seat, the officer should check the fuel level; adjust the seat, rearview mirrors, and seat belts; and record the odometer mileage in the vehicle log. Next, the officer should start the engine and operate (and check outside) all lights and turn signals, brakes, horn, siren, wipers, heater, air conditioner, overhead (visibar) lights, and the shotgun release. Finally, the officer should inspect the radio, computer, and video equipment, if applicable (Lyman, 2010; Perry, 1998).

OFFICER SURVIVAL

Officer survival is presented as a career planning consideration because attention should be given to this subject prior to commencing police work. Police encounters with others are always potentially dangerous. Some encounters are high-risk situations that present great risk to officer safety. Most police officers are killed or injured during four types of incidents: effecting arrests, robbery and burglary in progress calls, domestic disturbances, and vehicle stops. Police weapons themselves are hazardous to officers. Statistics imply that a police officer is just as likely to be killed accidentally by a police weapon as by an armed robbery suspect (Adams, Mc-Ternan, & Remsberg, 1980; Ho, 2000; National Law Enforcement Officers Memorial Fund, 2004).

Very often deaths and injuries to police officers can be traced to errors on the part of the police. **P. R. Brooks** (1975) outlined 10 of these deadly errors in his classic book, *Officer Down: Code Three*. The **deadly errors,** which are still relevant today, include:

- **Poor attitude**—If a police officer fails to pay attention to the job, errors will soon be made. It can cost the life of the police officer as well as of a colleague.
- **Tombstone courage**—No one doubts that officers are courageous. However, in any situation where time allows, the police officer must wait for backup. There are few instances in which, alone and unaided, a police officer should attempt to apprehend a dangerous person.
- **Not enough rest**—To function effectively, police officers must be alert. Being sleepy or asleep on the job is not only against regulations; it also places police officers and the community in danger.
- **Taking a bad position**—A police officer should never allow anyone being questioned, or a person about to be stopped, to assume a better position than the officer or the police vehicle.
- **Ignoring danger signs**—A police officer must learn to recognize danger signals. Suspicious movements, strange cars, and abnormal behavior are warnings that should alert the officer to approach with caution. The officer should be familiar with the patrol area and recognize abnormalities.
- **Failure to watch the hands of a suspect**—Is the suspect reaching for a weapon or getting ready to strike the police officer?
- **Relaxing too soon**—This involves false assumptions such as believing all burglar alarms are false or accidentally set off. A police officer should always proceed with caution and never assume any call to be routine.
- **Improper use of or no handcuffs**—After a police officer has made an arrest, the prisoner should be properly handcuffed.
- **No search or poor search**—There are so many places to hide weapons that the police officer's failure to search is a crime against fellow officers. Many criminals carry several weapons and are able and prepared to use them.
- **Dirty or inoperative weapon**—Is the police officer's weapon clean? Will it fire? What is the sense of carrying any firearm that may not function? What about the ammo? When did the officer last qualify with the weapon?

Police officer injuries and deaths result from a variety of mishaps. In addition to the criminal element, accidents, police officers mistakenly firing at fellow officers, stress, and physical exertion also take a toll.

Some injuries and deaths originate from the least-expected sources. Since 1996, officers have been killed while using slim-jim devices to enter locked vehicles equipped with side impact air bags. The prodding with the slim-jim device inside the door caused inadvertent deployment of the air bag. As a result, the slim-jim device was launched upward by the air bag with a force great enough to penetrate the chin of the officers involved and become lodged in the brain, causing almost immediate death. These disturbing incidents have caused some police agencies to issue new guidelines for unlocking vehicles. Officers must first determine if the vehicle is

Even well trained and cautious officers can become victims. A few examples are presented here.

02-28-97	Two hooded gunmen with automatic weapons robbed a Bank of America branch in North Hollywood, California. Wearing full body armor and armed with ballistically superior weapons, the bank robbers were spotted by a police unit as they attempted escape. The ensuing 44-minute gun battle with police, most of which was televised via a news helicopter, left the 2 robbers dead and 11 LAPD officers and 6 civilians wounded.
05-19-98	A Brooksville, Florida, man who was riding in a patrol car, freed himself from handcuffs and killed two police officers and a state trooper before killing himself.
09-11-01	Representing the largest number killed in a single event in United States history, 72 police officers died as the result of the terrorist attacks on the World Trade Center in New York City.
12-19-03	A motorist shot a San Bernardino County, California, sheriff's deputy during a traffic stop. Later, at a Sheriff's Department facility, the same motorist removed a .45 caliber handgun from the front of his pants and fatally shot himself in the head. He was not properly searched for weapons when he was arrested after shooting the deputy.
02-20-04	A Los Angeles police officer was fatally shot while responding to a report of a domestic disturbance.
04-21-04	A California Highway Patrol officer was shot to death outside a courthouse while he was waiting to testify in traffic cases. The officer was executed by a 16-year-old boy who was attempting to elevate his status as a gang member.
06-17-04	Three Birmingham, Alabama, officers were fatally shot while attempting to serve misdemeanor arrest warrants.
03-03-05	Four Royal Canadian Mounted Police (RCMP) officers were killed in an ambush by 46-year-old James Rozsko when they entered a building on Rozsko's farm in Alberta, Canada.
07-11-11	A Terre Haute, Indiana, officer was shot and killed in the line of duty while serving a warrant. His canine partner was also injured during the gunfight but recovered.

equipped with side impact air bags. If there is any uncertainty, the officer should not attempt to unlock the vehicle with a slim-jim device.

Officer survival is dependent upon several factors. Critical to officer safety is the need to acquire advanced protective and defensive technologies, improve procedures, and expand survival training. In addition, officers should develop and practice the types of communications skills that can assist with conflict de-escalation.

Learn more about officer fatalities and law enforcement safety through the National Law Enforcement Officers Memorial Fund at www.nlecomf.org.

WEAPONLESS DEFENSE

Weaponless defense involves the art and science of avoiding, resisting, or eliminating a suspect's ability to attack. The foundation for weaponless defense includes awareness, balance, and control by the officer. Awareness, as it relates to weaponless defense, means a police officer must be alert to any potential hazard when approaching or interacting with a suspect. Officers must be aware of objects or areas that might provide cover (protection) or concealment (place to hide) for the suspect. The environment itself may be dangerous for the officer. Uneven terrain, inclement weather, poor lighting, and water hazards may limit a police officer's response alternatives. During a confrontation with a hostile suspect, an officer must also be aware that certain parts of the body are more vulnerable to attack than others. Special consideration must be given to the protection of the head, throat, groin, heart, spine, and kidneys.

Balance refers to positioning and stance that allows the officer freedom of movement and the ability to maintain an advantage over a suspect. A balanced stance (appropriate foot position) involves positioning of the officer's body relative to the suspect in a way that prevents suspect access to the officer's sidearm. The officer must maintain an even bodyweight distribution over the balls of the feet. The officer's knees should be bent slightly (not locked) with feet approximately shoulder length apart. In a physical confrontation, a suspect could gain access to the officer's sidearm. The officer must be able to respond quickly and repel any attempt by the suspect to access the sidearm.

Control refers to acquiring and maintaining psychological and physical domination over the suspect and the situation. Psychologically, the officer must try to maintain general control of the situation, utilizing confidence and composure to influence others. Physical control implies that it may be necessary for the officer to use control holds or other techniques to obtain compliance. The primary goal of any force used is to gain compliance, not inflict pain or punishment. Some physical control techniques, such as the carotid restraint control hold, present the possibility of serious bodily injury or death to the suspect. These techniques should be used only when agency policy permits, and the suspect is violent and higher levels of force are not justified. The carotid restraint hold is a method for controlling violently resisting suspects through the use of continuing lateral compression of the carotid arteries on both sides of a suspect's neck. It should not be confused with the ill-advised bar arm choke hold applied to the front of the throat to compress the airway. Since carotid arteries supply approximately 70 percent of the oxygen to the brain, temporary compression of these arteries restricts oxygen flow, rendering the suspect unconscious within 5 to 15 seconds.

As soon as the desired effect is obtained or the suspect submits, the hold must be released. If the suspect is rendered unconscious, consciousness will be regained 20 to 30 seconds after the hold is released. The officer must take precautions to ensure the suspect's recovery. Improper application of the carotid restraint control hold may result in irreversible brain damage, fracture of the neck, or collapse of the trachea, causing suffocation. When the hold is used, the officer should test the suspect's pulse and be prepared to administer CPR and summon emergency medical personnel if necessary.

WEAPONS

Less Lethal Weapons

Chemical Agents. The first recorded use of chemical agents was in 311 B.C., when Chinese armies used stink pots of red pepper burning in oil during frontal assaults. The stink pots generated an irritating and choking smoke. Today, the three main types of **chemical agents** include CN (chloroacetophenone), CS (orthochlorobenzalmalononitrile), and OC (oleoresin capsicum). Commonly referred to as tear gas, these agents are not actually gases. Rather, they are chemicals borne on a propellant or carrier.

To varying degrees, all chemical agents cause anxiety, panic, and disorientation depending on the subject's physical condition or level of intoxication. A CN agent is the mildest of the chemical irritants. It causes irritation of the nose and throat, profuse tearing, a burning sensation on the skin, and closing of the eyes. Normally, the irritant takes effect within a few seconds of contact. About one in every one thousand persons will experience an allergic reaction. Decontamination includes exposure to fresh air and flushing the affected area with water.

CS agents are more powerful than CN agents. In addition to the physiological effects found in CN agents, CS irritants also cause heavy salivation, nasal flow, stinging of the soft body tissues, a tightness in the chest, and coughing. Decontamination for CS is the same as with CN agents. OC agents cause the most severe physiological effects. In addition to the effects caused by the CN and CS irritants, OC agents cause twitching of the eyes, respiratory inflammation, a choking sensation, exposed skin inflammation, temporary loss of upper body motion control, and temporary paralysis of the larynx. Decontamination techniques are similar to CN and CS agents.

An increasing number of public safety agencies use OC (pepper spray) to subdue and arrest dangerous, combative, violent, or uncooperative subjects. Although assumed to be safe and effective, the negative side effects of OC's use cannot be predicted with any certainty. The results of studies indicate that excessive force complaints and injuries to officers and subjects decline when OC is used and pepper spray inhalation does not appear to pose a significant health risk. However, one study indicated that pepper spray was a contributory cause of death in cases in which the subjects involved suffered from asthma. Yet, the number of in-custody deaths associated with pepper spray use appears to be very low. In most of these cases, deaths result from struggles with officers and the presence of drugs or alcohol in a person's system, rather than from the use of OC Spray (U.S. Department of Justice, Office of Justice Programs, 2003).

Although all of these agents can be delivered through fogging, pyrotechnics, plastic pellet (pepperball) guns, and blast dispersion, the most common delivery vehicle is the handheld aerosol canister carried by a police officer. In uniform, the container is probably best placed on the strong hand side of the officer's belt. This position provides concealment and restricts a suspect's access when the officer is standing in the field interview position. Although most handheld devices have a maximum effective range of 8 to 10 feet, the recommended use range is 3 to 6 feet. Officers should expect self-inflicted exposure to the chemical agent during and after use. The devices should not be stored in areas exceeding 120° F and, except for the OC irritant, the agents usually have little impact on animals (California Commission on Peace Officer Standards and Training, 2012).

Electronic Control Devices.   These include the **Taser**®, a device through which two small darts are fired, penetrating the suspect's skin. With the darts attached to the suspect, an officer can activate a 50,000 volt electric charge through small wires connecting the device to the darts. If both darts are connected to the suspect, a circuit is completed and the electric charge jolts (shocks) and temporarily immobilizes the suspect.

The Taser® is one of the most effective less lethal weapons. Many experts claim that the weapon helps to reduce the number of fatal police shootings. However, some medical experts suggest that a Taser® shock can increase the risk of heart failure, especially if a suspect is agitated, under the influence of chemicals, or suffers from underlying health problems (Garay, 2004).

The term **stun gun** is used to describe both electric shock devices and beanbag shotgun munitions. The electric stun gun has the appearance of a flat flashlight with two prongs protruding from one end. By depressing a button on the side of the device when both prongs are in contact with the suspect, an officer can transmit a high-voltage, low-amperage electric charge from a 9-volt battery. The suspect receives an electric shock that causes disorientation and muscle spasms. The beanbag stun gun utilizes a shotgun shell containing a powder charge and a leather-covered pouch containing pellets. When fired, the beanbag strikes the subject with a great deal of force, typically knocking the subject over and causing pain and disorientation (Adams, 2007).

Although some agencies are abandoning their use, 12-gauge, 37-mm, and 40-mm delivery systems have been used to fire beanbags and other flexible and nonflexible projectiles (Kester, 2002). Agencies that no longer use these less lethal weapons claim that the weapons can be dangerously inaccurate and deadlier than manufacturers indicate.

Other Technologies.   In an effort to reduce the use of lethal weapons, several other **less lethal weapons** were introduced in the latter part of the twentieth century. **Sticky foam** and people nets dispensed through a shoulder-slung apparatus can be used to immobilize a subject. **Strobe lights** and **flash-bang grenades** (impact and diversionary munitions) temporarily disorient barricaded individuals. Remote-controlled barrier strips and **vehicle disablers** may be used to limit high-speed vehicle pursuits (Conser & Russell, 2000; U.S. Department of Justice, 2004).

Lethal Weapons

Batons and Nunchakus. Designed for use as intermediate weapons to control or gain compliance from unruly suspects, batons and nunchakus are classified as **lethal weapons** in many state statutes. However, when used properly in an authorized manner, these weapons can be used to repel attack, gain compliance, or protect others. Once compliance is achieved, use of these weapons is no longer authorized. They should not be used to inflict pain or punish a suspect.

The **baton** is the most commonly used intermediate weapon. Various types of batons include straight, expandable, riot, and the police revolving 24-inch **(PR-24)** sidehandle batons. When verbal commands are ineffective, an officer may draw the baton as a show of force in an attempt to de-escalate the situation. Use of the baton on a subject always depends on the circumstances such as the size of the suspect, number of suspects, tactical riot control situations, or the suspect's exhibition of a trained fighting skill. Possible target areas for baton strikes include the legs, arms, chest, rib cage and front midsection. Body areas that should be avoided because of the possibility of serious injury or death include the head and neck, spine, kidneys, and groin (California Commission on Peace Officer Standards and Training, 2012).

Firearms. Firearms include revolvers and semiautomatic handguns, shotguns, automatic and semiautomatic rifles, and machine guns. Handguns are the most common firearms carried and used in policing. The 12-gauge shotgun utilizing 00 buckshot is also common as standard equipment in police agencies. The shotgun is an extremely effective short-range weapon and its use does not require expert shooting skills. Its presence also has a dramatic psychological impact on a suspect. Rifles are less common and typically limited to special weapons teams for use in SWAT operations. However, as more brazen criminals and gang members use fully automatic rifles, more uniformed police patrol officers may be trained and equipped with automatic and semiautomatic rifles.

During the average police career, an officer will rarely, if ever, discharge a firearm in the line of duty. It is a last resort weapon to be used only when the officer has a legal and moral justification for using it. Justification for use of firearms involves good moral judgment consistent with applicable laws and agency policy. When the use of a firearm is justified and someone dies from a police officer's bullet, the officer and the agency can expect a great deal of negative publicity and criticism (Adams, 2007).

Innovative "smart gun" technologies, including pressure-activated laser aiming devices, seek to make firearms safer (Reid, 2011).

FIREARMS SAFETY RULES

- All firearms should be handled as if they are loaded.
- When cleaning a firearm or handing it to another person, the action or cylinder should be open.
- All firearms should be stored with safety in mind. If stored loaded for self-protection, caution must be exercised to ensure that the weapons are not accessible to children.
- Duty weapons and calibers should be standardized within an agency. In a shoot-out, one officer may need to use another officer's weapon or ammunition.
- Firearms should be kept clean and maintained in good working order.
- Firearms should be carried with the finger off the trigger and out of the trigger guard.
- Warning shots are rarely, if ever, authorized except in some corrections facilities.
- Firearms should not be used on animals unless it is necessary to protect human life.
- Firearms should *never* be pointed in the direction of any person unless the person is an immediate threat to life and the officer is prepared to use deadly force.
- When discharge of a firearm in the line of duty is absolutely necessary, an officer must exercise good judgment and avoid shooting innocent third parties.

USE OF FORCE POLICY

Other than military personnel, criminal justice practitioners, especially those employed in law enforcement, are the only people authorized by law to use force, even deadly force, in the course of their occupation. Police use of force against others is a critical issue and the subject of a great deal of public debate. Police officers and their agencies have been criticized and often successfully sued for use of **excessive force.** Sheriffs' deputies in a California county were sued in 1997 for swabbing the eyes of passive protesters with pepper spray. The deputies' actions were in violation of the pepper spray manufacturer's guidelines and the California Commission on Peace Officer Standards and Training (POST) professional police standards. According to POST guidelines, pepper spray is to be used only to overcome violent resistance.

On May 27, 1998, Michael Arnold pointed an air pistol at law enforcement officers during a standoff. Arnold was shot 106 times by officers from the Hawthorne, California, Police Department, the Los Angeles County Sheriff's Department, and the California Highway Patrol. On February 4, 1999, four undercover New York City police officers investigating the shooting of a cab driver shot and killed 22-year-old Amadou Diallo, an unarmed West African immigrant. The officers fired 41 shots, hitting Diallo 19 times. The four officers involved were charged with murder and acquitted after a sensational, highly publicized trial. In August 1999, the FBI, reversing a six-year-old denial, admitted that its

Learn more about police equipment and technology through the National Law Enforcement and Corrections Technology Center at www.justnet.org.

agents may have used potentially flammable tear gas on the final day of the 1993 standoff with the Branch Davidian cult outside Waco, Texas. Although the use of the tear gas may not have caused a fire at the cult complex, which left 56 adults and 26 children dead, the use of the gas and subsequent denial resulted in a public outcry. In September, 1999, a man throwing rocks at authorities was shot multiple times by a federal agent. On February 8, 2000, a homeless man was shot and killed as he lunged at a group of San Diego police officers with a 3-foot by 3-inch sharpened tree branch. The police officers had responded to a call from a bicyclist who reported being attacked by the homeless person. Media attention resulting from incidents such as these helps to create the perception that law enforcement's use of deadly force is a common occurrence.

Although police officers are rarely criminally charged in shooting incidents, public outrage often results from police use of deadly force (Thornton, 1999, November 5). Officer-involved shootings are depicted in news accounts, on television police shows, and in the movies. Consequently, the public's perception of police use of deadly force is distorted. In reality, the police rarely use deadly force even though they often would be legally justified in doing so. Officers frequently must make split-second life or death decisions during confrontations in which the events are not nearly as clear as they are when investigated with hindsight. Yet, the public's perception is often that police officers commonly use deadly force, whether justified or not (Hughes, 1998; O'Keefe, 2004).

A disturbing trend in recent years has been characterized by a phenomenon termed **suicide by cop.** Currently, there are no reliable national statistics that clearly demonstrate the number of police-assisted suicides. However, experts estimate that approximately 10 percent of fatal shootings by the police annually are actually provoked by people seeking to end their own lives. An examination of fatal as well as nonfatal officer-involved shootings in California revealed that the rate may be higher in that state. In addition to the death of the suicide victim, an emotional toll is exacted on the victim's friends and relatives as well as the officer(s) involved. The suicide by cop trend has prompted law enforcement officials to seek nonlethal tactical alternatives to defuse such situations (Hughes, 1999; Lord, 2004).

Many police agencies have **use of force options and policies.** These policies describe use of force options based on **levels of resistance** and **principles of control.** Generally, any police officer who has reasonable cause to believe a person has committed a crime may use reasonable force to effect an arrest, prevent escape, and overcome the resistance of the arrestee. Police officers may choose the available force option that is reasonable and necessary for the circumstances. Subjects in a physical confrontation should not be allowed to gain an advantage.

Levels of resistance and principles of control follow a continuum. From the least to the most serious, levels of resistance include the following:

- Intimidation in which the subject's attitude and demeanor indicate a readiness to resist
- Verbal noncompliance represented by the subject's verbally expressed unwillingness to comply with a lawful request

- Passive resistance by refusing to respond to a lawful order
- Active resistance demonstrated by actions designed to prevent control by a police officer
- Assaultive behavior that suggests a potential for human injury
- Aggravated, active aggression that can be reasonably construed to pose a potential for serious bodily injury or death to the officer or another person

Police officers should make every attempt to **de-escalate** confrontations to avoid the use of force. When force is necessary, officers should use only that which is reasonably necessary to regain and maintain control of the situation. A **compliance continuum** provides a simple mechanism to illustrate the progressive steps used to gain compliance and control during a confrontation. From the least to the most severe, use of force options typically include:

- Police officer presence that psychologically promotes compliance by the subject
- Verbal commands to direct or redirect the subject
- Open-hand tactics or use of less lethal weapons such as chemical agents to overcome resistance if hands-on control may result in injury to the officer or the subject
- Soft hands-on control to overcome resistance, hard hands-on control utilizing powerful strikes and other techniques to control overtly aggressive subjects, or use of nonimpact weapons
- Use of intermediate impact weapons such as batons, nunchakus, or less lethal munitions to physically control or deliver strikes against the subject
- Use of lethal force in defense of human life from the threat of immediate serious bodily injury or death, or to apprehend an inherently dangerous fleeing felony suspect (one who could cause serious bodily injury or death to another if allowed to escape)

Factors that affect a police officer's choice of use of force options include the subject's ability to resist or inflict harm, the number of subjects and officers, the subject's ability to obtain weapons, and the use of force options available to the officer. Ultimately, the option chosen depends on the officer's judgment and evaluation of the situation (San Diego Sheriff's Department, 1999; Trautman, 2005).

Police officers are advised that the use of force by a peace officer under color of authority without lawful necessity is a crime in many states and is punishable as a felony. In addition, the U.S. Supreme Court, in *Tennessee v. Garner,* 471 U.S. 1 (1985), ruled that police officers have a duty to warn suspects, when feasible, before using deadly force. Further, in *Deorle v. Rutherford,* 272 F.3d 1272 (2001), the Ninth Circuit Court of Appeals held that officers must warn suspects, when feasible, before using less than lethal force, when the force used is likely to cause serious injury (Lesh, 2003).

CASE STUDY—POLICE USE OF FORCE

Police officers have several nonlethal, less lethal, and lethal weapons at their disposal. The weapons must be used consistent with a compliance continuum necessary to overcome resistance to legitimate police authority and to protect officers and other innocent persons.

The law enforcement community has been experimenting with and operating weapons labeled as nonlethal and less lethal for years, in search of the ideal weapon or weapons that will subdue violent people without causing permanent injury or death. However, several permanent injuries, even deaths, have been attributed to their use. Therefore, many police agencies are abandoning some of these weapons, such as bean-bag and electric stun guns, because they may not be as nonlethal as manufacturers claim.

1. Other than deadly force, what force options are available to the law enforcement officer?
2. Does the development of practical nonlethal and less lethal weapons technology look promising for the future, or will the choices be limited?

THE POLICE CAREER AND PERSONAL LIFE

Law enforcement organizations dedicate significant resources to the transformation of ordinary citizens into police officers. In academies and inservice training programs, officers are taught to keep the peace, enforce the law, stay safe, be assertive, take command, solve problems, and control their emotions. Yet few resources are devoted to preparing officers to transition to civilian status when their work day is completed. As a result, many officers police their families instead of loving them.

As a career, law enforcement is more a lifestyle than an occupation. An officer develops a working personality associated with law enforcement and officers often seek the comfort of the police subculture. Family members and significant others are consumed in the lifestyle also, as they experience an officer's rotating shifts, long hours, frustration, work-related trauma, and stress. Without appropriate coping skills, officers and their loved ones can be victimized if undesirable on-duty officer attitudes, anger, and behaviors surface in the officer's private life.

If thoughts and energies are not channeled appropriately, an officer's spouse, children, significant other, family members, and friends can fall victim to the officer's suspicious nature and overprotectionist attitude. An officer's inability to effectively transition from the professional to a private life can lead to alcoholism, drug abuse, misplaced anger, infidelity, and emotional indifference. Dysfunctional thinking and behavior can also lead to poor mental and physical health, officer suicide, and officer involvement as a perpetrator of domestic violence. Indirectly, discord in private life will impact negatively on the officer's career motivation, effectiveness, and on-the-job productivity.

Officers, their families, and friends can learn to cope with the law enforcement lifestyle by taking advantage of the education programs, services, and mechanisms available. In addition to counseling services, many agencies offer orientation programs for the family and friends of police recruits. The programs help to create an awareness of the expectations and demanding nature of police work. Ride-along programs provide family members with an opportunity to observe the police in their occupational setting. For police officers, a commitment to stress management and lifetime fitness is a key ingredient to good mental and physical health, and to harmony in their personal lives (O'Keefe, 2004; Trautman 2005).

STRESS MANAGEMENT

Stress is a common enemy of the police officer. Some experts identify stress as the number-one killer of officers. Stress in officers can be derived from less than obvious sources. A great deal of police stress results from poor personal relationships. Of course, police work is, by its very nature, stressful. In addition to relationship problems, stress can be caused by anger, frustration with the job or judicial system, rotating shifts, fear, conflicts with supervisors, workload pressures, high family expectations, disillusionment, off-duty employment (moonlighting), the police culture, confronting hostility on the job, and experiences, such as death scenes, that are emotionally draining. Stress leads to fatigue, eating and sleeping disorders, chemical abuse, headaches, high blood pressure, illness, disease, assaultive behavior, accidents, and even suicide.

Common themes surrounding police suicides include relationship and financial problems, job stress, alcohol abuse, ready access to firearms, frustration, slow promotions, and the unrealistic image of the police officer as a person who can handle anything. Many law enforcement agencies report suicide rates significantly higher than the national average for all suicides. As a group, police officers are ranked fourth in suicides behind dentists, doctors, and entrepreneurs. Many experts agree that the high number of police suicides may be the result of extreme stress and police officers' unrealistically high expectations of themselves. Police officers often view themselves as misunderstood warriors who fight to protect ungrateful critics from hordes of bad people. Additionally, a firearm, which is a tool of the trade for a law enforcement officer, is always readily available. Firefighters do not carry an ax home with them. Police officers often carry firearms off duty as well as on duty.

Police suicide statistics are staggering. Officers are eight times more likely to die from suicide than be the victim of a homicide (Fox, 2003). The suicide rate for police officers is 17 out of 100,000, compared to the general population's rate of 11 out of 100,000 (Badge of Life, 2011). Since 1985, at least 87 New York City police officers committed suicide, while only 36 were killed on duty. Although there were no on-duty deaths of police officers in San Diego between 1992 and 1998, five officers committed suicide. Similar situations exist in Chicago and Los Angeles as well as in some federal agencies such as the Customs Service and the FBI. While experiencing only four line-of-duty deaths between 1993 and 1998, the FBI lost 18 agents to suicide during the same period. In September, 2002, four men robbed a bank in Norfolk, Nebraska, killing five people. The next day, state trooper Mark Zach committed suicide. Zach was distraught because a week earlier he cited rather than arrested one of the soon-to-be bank robbery suspects for carrying a concealed weapon. In 2010, there was a total of 145 police suicides in the United States, a slight increase over 2009 (Badge of Life, 2011).

Many officers and agencies fear publicity associated with police suicide. They believe it tarnishes the image of the police. Police chiefs and government officials also fear lawsuits if the suicides are linked to jobrelated stress. Police officers themselves are reluctant to seek help during a crisis. The police are supposed to be tough and able to control any situation. The police culture and the public's perception of the police as crime fighters reinforce the notion that the police should not show weakness. Some believe that seeking help, such as the services of a psychologist, will hurt their career. Other officers are reluctant to report an officer who appears to be experiencing emotional difficulties. The thin blue wall of silence often prevails (By their own hands, 1999; Fox, 2003).

Apparently, one of the most common and debilitating sources of stress for the police is the officer's agency and its culture. Officers often feel torn between a distrustful and unappreciative public and a police agency that marginalizes the officers. The paramilitary structure of most police organizations actually depersonalizes and marginalizes its employees. Paramilitary decision-making structures limit input and breed cynicism among rank and file officers. In addition, some officers suffer from post traumatic stress disorder (PTSD). Although commonly associated with military combat veterans, PTSD can surface in other environments when individuals experience traumatic events or they feel dehumanized. It is not uncommon for PTSD sufferers to contemplate, attempt, or commit suicide (Copes, 2005; Fox, 2003).

Burnout is a term that is often applied to the image of people who develop negative relationships with their occupations or the overwhelming nature of the tasks to be accomplished. The scenario usually includes circumstances in which people enter into an activity or occupation with positive expectations, enthusiasm, and the motivation to achieve desirable goals. Eventually, however, circumstances change and individuals sense overwhelming exhaustion, frustration, anger, ineffectiveness, failure, cynicism, and anger. The initial flame, the fire within that existed in the beginning, has burned out. The burnout syndrome impairs personal, social, and professional functioning. As time passes, people resign their positions, retire early, or simply continue the activity or employment with minimal productivity (Maslach & Leiter, 1999).

An assumption prevails that burnout happens to overachievers (workaholics) and underachievers (incompetent or unmotivated slackers).

Learn more about police officer suicide awareness and prevention programs through the National POLICE Suicide Foundation located at www.psf.org.

That assumption supposes that there is something fundamentally wrong with the person who burns out. A more rational approach focuses on the occupation or context in which burnout takes place. Although the nature of work-related stressors (constant crises, conflict with others, the chronic nature of job demands) can lay a foundation for burnout, it is more appropriate to view burnout from the context of one's environment.

Burnout involves a sense of exhaustion, cynicism, and ineffectiveness that results from chronic stressors. Exhaustion relates to an individual's feelings of over extension and depletion of personal emotional and physical resources. The primary sources of exhaustion are overload and personal conflict. Cynicism develops as an interpersonal emotional detachment buffer. The detachment can lead to dehumanization of others. Ineffectiveness results from an individual's feelings of incompetence, lack of achievement, and low productivity. This lowered sense of self-worth is compounded by lack of resources, poor social support, or limited opportunities for professional development. Burnout involves a prolonged process of psychological and physical erosion of people that stands in contrast to energetic, involved, and engaged individuals. The erosion diminishes a burned out person's commitment, and causes personnel absenteeism, attrition, and physical illness.

Because of the stressful nature of police work and the many factors that make such work difficult, attention to burnout among officers and how to prevent it is extremely important. Understanding burnout and its implications involves knowledge of the phenomenon based on a framework that integrates the person and the environment. Addressing the person or the environment in isolation underestimates the value of the person–environment relationship. When one addresses the degree of fit (congruence) between a person and the environment, it is easier to motivate and enhance a person's adjustment to the circumstances, and seek to reduce the stress that leads to burnout (Maslach & Leiter, 1999; Meese & Ortmeier, 2004; Stojkovic, Kalinich, & Klofas, 2008).

Stress, a common condition in police work, cannot be totally eliminated. In fact, some stress is necessary to promote human growth and development. However, it can be managed and techniques for dealing with stress can be learned. Stress is unique to the individual. Therefore, **stress management** programs must be tailored to meet individual needs. Some techniques for stress management include the following:

- Leaving the job at the station house. Many officers live the life of a police officer 24 hours per day. This is mentally and physically unhealthy. If a part-time job is necessary for financial stability, one unrelated to police work is best.
- Regular exercise.
- Getting enough rest.
- Maintaining a proper diet.
- Prioritizing personal and professional activities.
- Taking vacations and engaging in hobbies.
- Meditation.
- Learning and practicing relaxation techniques.

- Discussing stressors with a friend, confessor, or counselor. Seeking professional help if necessary.

Stress among police officers intensified after the terrorist attacks of 9/11. The attacks modified many police priorities and increased police responsibilities for the protection of potential terrorism targets. The added responsibilities placed more strain on already limited state, county, and local police resources. In addition, federal law enforcement agencies, under authority granted by the USA PATRIOT Act, assumed the lead role for the investigation and surveillance of hate groups and suspected terrorists. The shift in control and inability to participate with counterterrorism efforts frustrated many line-level police officers. The phenomenon left the typical patrol officer with feelings of inadequacy and reduced self-respect. Further, it appears that few agencies have effectively addressed this new stressor (Stevens, 2005). Thus, officers themselves must take precautions and implement stress reduction techniques to avoid the negative side effects of this and other new stressors.

LIFETIME FITNESS

In addition to stress management and psychological wellness, police officers must concern themselves with maintaining a physical condition conducive to police work, a positive police public image, and the enhancement of the quality of life. Poor physical conditioning endangers the life of the officers as well as others who depend on the officer. Poor fitness lowers self-esteem, generates disrespect from peers, and may inhibit promotion possibilities. To be physically fit, police officers must be knowledgeable and engage in behaviors that promote disease prevention, body conditioning, good nutrition, and proper exercise. Physiological disablers of police officers include cardiovascular disease, lower back and gastrointestinal disorders, and chemical abuse.

The risk of coronary heart (cardiovascular) disease may be reduced through weight control, exercise, proper nutrition, stress management, and smoking cessation. Lower back disorders may be prevented by lifting properly, conditioning and strengthening lower back muscles, and job training that focuses on ergonomically correct activities. Gastrointestinal disorders may be prevented through stress management, aerobic exercise, and proper nutrition.

Substance or chemical abuse is usually associated with an inappropriate strategy for coping with stress. Alcohol, tobacco, caffeine, and legal as well as illegal drugs are substances commonly abused by police officers. While under the influence of chemicals, police officers may be physically and mentally impaired. Long-term abuse can result in psychological and physical addiction or chronic degenerative diseases.

Learn more about the impact of stress on law enforcement personnel through Heavy Badge at www.heavybadge.com.

Lifetime fitness involves a commitment to psychological and physical wellness *(Photo courtesy of the San Diego Sheriff's Department.)*

Lifetime fitness involves a commitment to a lifestyle that promotes personal psychological and physical wellness. A strategy for lifetime fitness supports the development and maintenance of a lifestyle conducive to fitness for duty as a police officer. A planned program for good health and fitness includes the following:

- An evaluation of one's current mental and physical condition
- Identification of mental and physical health risks
- Proper nutrition and exercise
- Stress management
- Commitment to a fitness program
- Development of a lifestyle conducive to fitness
- Continuing education on health-related topics

For promotion purposes, many police departments, such as the NYPD, award extra points to police officers who are physically fit and maintain a healthy lifestyle. Ultimately, psychological and physiological wellness extends beyond professional job performance into one's personal and civic life. Awareness and management of health-related risk factors can lengthen the life of a police officer and improve the quality of life for the officer as well as the officer's family, friends, and peers (California Commission on Peace Officer Standards and Training, 2012).

FBI Law Enforcement Officer Killed and Assaulted (LEOKA) statistics indicate that officer physical fitness may actually prevent assaults on police officers. According to LEOKA research, many criminal suspects admit that their decision to assault or kill an officer was based on appearance alone, citing the perception that physically fit officers can defend themselves and overcome resistance. In addition, respect of officers by the general public is enhanced because physically fit officers present images of professionalism and commitment to public service. The positive image can lead to the public's approval of increases in agency budgets and officer salaries (Blum, 2004).

PUBLIC SAFETY OFFICERS' BILL OF RIGHTS

In an effort to protect the rights of police officers, and other public safety workers some states, such as California, have enacted public safety officers' procedural bill of rights acts. Commonly referred to as a **Police Officers' Bill of Rights,** the purpose of such laws is to expressly provide public safety personnel with statutory rights protecting them from arbitrary disciplinary or punitive action. Generally, these laws provide that public safety personnel:

- Cannot be prevented from engaging in political activity, including seeking election to a school board.
- Are entitled to due process when under investigation or being interrogated.
- Cannot be subjected to punitive action or denied promotion for choosing to exercise rights under the statute.
- May not have adverse comments entered into a personnel file without notice and an opportunity to review the comments and sign the document containing the information.
- Shall have 30 days to respond to any adverse comments entered into a personnel file.
- Cannot be compelled to submit to a polygraph or similar examination nor can a refusal to submit to such an examination be used against the officer.
- Cannot be compelled to disclose information regarding personal assets or income unless such disclosure is necessary to determine suitability for assignment to a specialized enforcement activity.
- Shall not have agency owned or leased personal locker or storage space searched unless the search is conducted in the officer's presence, or with the officer's consent, or the officer is informed that a search will take place under the authority of a valid search warrant (Adams, 2007).

▲ SUMMARY

Twenty-first century policing requires special officer skills and qualities. The recruitment, selection, promotion, and retention of law enforcement officers are prescribed by numerous policies, procedures, and laws. Maintaining a proper attitude is extremely important in police work. Attitude affects personal performance, as does appropriate training and education. Police officers should prepare for patrol by reviewing work schedules, acquiring prepatrol information, and inspecting personal supplies and equipment. Officer safety and survival are critical aspects of police work. Officer injury and deaths can often be traced to mistakes made by the officers themselves. Officers should be familiar with weaponless defense, less lethal and lethal weapons, as well as the ethical and legal use of force. Officers should not allow the undesirable aspects of on-duty attitudes, behavior, and events to affect their private lives in a negative way. Stress is a common enemy of the police officer. Stress management is one of the goals of lifetime fitness. Several states have enacted police officers' bills of rights to protect officers from unsubstantiated complaints and discrimination.

DISCUSSION QUESTIONS AND EXERCISES

1. Discuss the skills and qualities required of a law enforcement officer. What should police officers know? What should they be able to do? How should they behave?
2. The police are often criticized for being discourteous and having a negative attitude toward people they contact. What is meant by a proper attitude in police work?
3. Compare and contrast training with education. Is education as important as training for contemporary police work?
4. How should an officer prepare for patrol duty?
5. What tactics and strategies should be employed to maintain officer safety?
6. Under what circumstances is the use of force by an officer justified? What role does ethics play in situations in which police use of force is necessary?
7. What techniques can an officer employ to reduce stress and maintain mental and physical fitness for duty?
8. What types of police attitudes, behaviors, and events contribute to discord in an officer's personal life? How might discord in an officer's personal life be prevented?
9. Which police-related skills are perishable? How can perishable skills be maintained at an appropriate competence (skill) level?
10. Collect, compare, and analyze use of force policies of law enforcement agencies. Are the policies uniform? Are the policies consistent with applicable laws governing use of force?

General Police Operations

LEARNING OBJECTIVES

After completing this chapter, the reader should be able to:

- list, describe, and evaluate types of patrol.
- demonstrate knowledge of patrol equipment and police communications systems.
- describe proper vehicle operations and patrol techniques.
- conduct a field interview.
- demonstrate knowledge of traffic management, radar use, driving under the influence (DUI) cases, and collision response procedure.
- discuss proper techniques and procedure for pedestrian and vehicle stops as well as pedestrian and vehicle pursuits.
- describe administrative duties associated with police work.
- demonstrate knowledge of the proper roles and relationship of the police and the news media.
- evaluate patrol operations.

KEY TERMS

Define, describe, or explain the importance of each of the following.

Administrative duty
Aggressive driving
Basic speed law
Blood-alcohol concentration (BAC)
Citation
Code Three driving
Computer-aided dispatch (CAD)
Detention
Driving Under the Influence (DUI)
Driving While Intoxicated (DWI)
Field interview (FI)
Foot patrol
Forward Looking InfraRed (FLIR) device

High-risk vehicle stop procedure
Juvenile officer
Kansas City Preventive Patrol Experiment
Low-risk vehicle stop procedure
Marine patrol
Mobile data computer (MDC)
Mobile data terminal (MDT)
Offensive intervention tactics
Patrol pattern
Peripheral vision
Planned random patrol
Police deployment considerations
Police-media relations

Preliminary alcohol screening (PAS) device

Prima facie speed limit

Preventive patrol

Radar

Traffic enforcement officer

Vehicle code violation

Vehicle pursuit policy

Vehicular patrol

Vice officer

INTRODUCTION

The largest operating unit of municipal police and highway patrol departments as well as most sheriff and state police agencies is the patrol division. In addition, most law enforcement agencies in the United States are small, employing less than 15 officers. Most of these officers are deployed in the field, working in uniform. Therefore, the backbone of the vast majority of police agencies is the uniformed patrol division (Walker, 1999).

Because resources are limited, there will never be enough police officers available to fulfill the demand for police services. To maximize service, **police deployment considerations** must address the most efficient use of human resources and equipment. Thus, police administrators must consider the following factors when deploying resources:

- Number and types of crime.
- Location(s) where crimes are committed.
- Traffic patterns and collision statistics.
- Location(s) of most police calls for service.
- Population demographics (age, gender, ethnicity).
- Geography and topography.
- Size of the agency's jurisdictional responsibility.
- Type of occupancy in neighborhood being served (business, residential, industrial).
- Citizens' attitude toward the police.
- Number and qualifications of officers available for patrol duty.
- Equipment (vehicles) and supplies available for patrol.

All factors considered, police officers are deployed in beats, precincts, or districts according to the demand for police service in the designated areas. Thus, the workload is distributed proportionately according to predictable demand. Continuous evaluation of the police deployment strategy will reveal any need for redistricting or changes in the number of officers required in a designated service area (Adams, 2007). Many agencies are utilizing statistical analysis management, such as CompStat, to assist with resource deployment decisions.

CASE STUDY—VEHICULAR FLIGHT AS A VIOLENT FELONY

In 2011, the U.S. Supreme Court ruled that vehicular flight from police counts as a violent felony under the Armed Career Criminal Act, triggering a mandatory 15-year term in federal prison if the action is a third offense. Congress had adopted the law in 1984 as an early version of a "three strikes" measure. Though the law did not define which crimes counted, it mentioned acts involving force and risk of serious injury (such as burglary, arson, and extortion).

The 2011 decision involved a third-time offender who tried to drive away in a car with no headlights when an officer flashed his emergency lights. Justices debated whether the attempt to drive away carried serious risk of physical injury to others or constituted "simple vehicular flight," and whether the law as written by Congress was too vague to answer this question (Savage, 2011).

1. In what respects could driving away from police constitute an act as aggressively violent and dangerous as burglary, arson, or extortion?

2. To what extent could the new law discourage people from fleeing police in a vehicle?

TYPES OF PATROL

Foot Patrol

Foot patrol is the oldest form of police operation. Its major disadvantage is the high cost of recruiting, training, equipping, and placing an officer in the field. In addition, urban sprawl has increased the police officer's territorial responsibility. Another disadvantage of foot patrol is the possibility that a criminal offender may escape capture if the offender has ready access to a vehicle. Major advantages to foot patrol include improved police–community relations, less fear of crime by the citizenry, and direct contact with the public. Foot patrol is also effective in highly congested pedestrian locations and areas that experience a high number of burglaries, robberies, street muggings, and purse snatchings.

Vehicular Patrol

The first official police car was deployed in Akron, Ohio, in 1910. Today, conspicuous **vehicular patrol** (i.e., marked police vehicles patrolling a designated area) is the most common form of police patrol. It is cost efficient and increases officer mobility. Most police agencies, especially on the West Coast, utilize a black-and-white color combination on the vehicles to increase visibility and promote crime prevention. In recent years, law enforcement agencies with uniformed patrol divisions have experimented with many different makes and models of automobiles.

Automobiles, as a means of patrol, were introduced in the first half of the twentieth century. *(Photo courtesy of the Cobb County, GA Police Department.)*

Rear-wheel-drive vehicles have proven to be more desirable, especially in hilly areas. Front-wheel-drive vehicles experience more mechanical problems and require frequent maintenance because of sustained and continuous use.

Vehicular patrol allows the police officer to carry additional equipment and it provides prisoner transportation capability. It also enhances communications capability as a result of increased radio range, and it provides a platform for a computer terminal. Most significantly, the officer's response time is reduced when great distances must be covered (Siegel & Senna, 2006; Wilberg, 1999).

Bicycle Patrol

Bicycle patrol is inexpensive, offers greater mobility, and is less tiring than foot patrol. Bicycles are quiet and especially effective in business districts, parking lots, and small areas experiencing numerous thefts, burglaries, and assaults. Mounted on a motor vehicle bicycle rack, the bike can be used in conjunction with a patrol car. Bicycles can a be used in areas inaccessible to a motorized patrol vehicle. Bicycle patrol helps officers maintain close contact with the public and enhances police–community relations. Offering similar advantages to bicycles are Segway Personal Transporters. These are commonly used for patrolling in places such as shopping malls and airports, and require less physical exertion than bicycles.

As a supplement to foot patrol, bicycles are inexpensive, less tiring, and they offer greater mobility. *(Photo courtesy of the Cobb County, GA Police Department.)*

Mounted Horse Patrol

Horse patrols are very effective in large remote areas where foot and vehicular patrols are impractical or impossible. Additionally, horse patrol provides the officer with greater visibility and it enhances police–community relations. Because the sheer size of the horse is intimidating to most people, it is very effective for crowd control. The major disadvantage of horse patrol is the high-maintenance costs. In some areas, reserve deputies and police officers volunteer their horses and time to provide an equestrian unit for an agency.

Motorcycle Patrol

Motorcycles, scooters, and all-terrain vehicles are very useful in dense traffic, downtown business districts, beaches, and some remote areas. When weather conditions permit, they are used in most traffic and parking law enforcement activities. Disadvantages include inclement weather limitations, greater possibility of injury or death to the officer, and maintenance costs that are equivalent to motor vehicles.

Air Patrol

The New York City Police Department began the first police air service in 1929 with a biplane. The NYPD was also the first to place helicopters in service in 1948. Since that time, helicopters and fixed-wing aircraft have proven to be very effective in traffic law enforcement and search and rescue operations. They are also very useful when tracking suspects who are on foot, and when used in vehicle pursuits and medical evacuations. Aircraft are especially helpful when large areas must be patrolled.

Helicopters are the most versatile aircraft, but are also very expensive to purchase and maintain. The initial purchase price of a helicopter

Horse patrols are very effective in remote areas where foot and vehicular patrols are impractical or impossible. *(Photo courtesy of the San Diego Police Department.)*

Motorcycle officers have patrolled in the United States for nearly 100 years. *(Photo courtesy of the San Diego Police Department.)*

is often much more than fixed-wing aircraft, and the maintenance costs for the rotary wing aircraft average $500 per flight hour. However, helicopters are the most effective observation platform for law enforcement currently available. As a complement to ground-based units, air-borne helicopter units can see what officers on the ground cannot (Alpert, 1998). At night, the helicopter can maintain surveillance by using a **Forward Looking InfraRed (FLIR) device** to detect and pursue people and vehicles. FLIR detects heat and can identify an object's heat signature at night. The warmer the heat source, such as a person or vehicle engine, the brighter the glow registered by the device on a video display in the aircraft.

Motorcycle patrol is very useful in dense traffic and business districts, on beaches, and in some remote areas. *(Photo courtesy of the Cobb County, GA Police Department.)*

Helicopters are versatile, but very expensive to purchase and maintain. *(Photo courtesy of the San Diego Sheriffs Department.)*

Marine Patrol

Watercraft have existed longer than motorized vehicles or aircraft. Thus, **marine patrol** has been used for hundreds of years to patrol the seas and waterways. Landlocked jurisdictions use boats to patrol lakes and navigate rivers and canals. In seaports, marine patrols are common. Large seaports may have a harbor police agency distinct from the local police or sheriff's department. The United States Coast Guard also has law enforcement jurisdiction in U.S. territorial coastal waters and interior waterways used in commerce.

As extensions of police officers, trained dogs are very useful. *(Photo courtesy of the Cobb County, GA Police Department.)*

K-9 Patrol

Police canine (K-9) units are used quite extensively in law enforcement. Dogs can be trained to search for humans, cadavers, narcotics, and explosives. They can search buildings for burglars and can track suspects or missing persons. Some jurisdictions, such as the San Diego Police Department, use police dogs to engage and disarm violent suspects or deranged individuals. The use of a dog to disarm a person with a weapon helps to avoid police use of firearms to subdue armed suspects and mentally ill civilians.

Although police dogs can be useful, the deployment of canine units is expensive. Most dogs used to disarm or engage a violent suspect are European-bred German shepherds and Belgian Malinois, each of which can cost several thousand dollars. Additional thousands of dollars are invested in training, and a police dog's suggested retirement age is eight years (Hughes, 2004). Yet as an alternative to the use of deadly force by an officer, the police dog may be worth the investment.

Specialized Patrol Activities

When resources permit, some agencies assign officers to specific, rather than general, patrol activities. These special activities often include traffic enforcement, vice, and juvenile operations. **Traffic enforcement officers** focus on the movement of pedestrian and vehicular traffic in the safest, most expeditious manner possible. **Vice officers** engage in law enforcement activities relative to prostitution, gambling, illegal drugs, pornography, and liquor law violations. **Juvenile officers** concern themselves with truancy, juvenile delinquency prevention, and apprehension of young offenders.

Reserve Police Officers

Some agencies appoint volunteer and compensated reserve (auxiliary) police officers and deputy sheriffs to supplement regular full-time officers. Although reserve officers are utilized in many large urban law enforcement agencies, most provide part-time assistance to smaller rural agencies. The use of volunteer reserves is controversial in some areas, especially as a result of resistance from some police labor unions. Yet, the supplemental officers can provide a valuable service to communities with underfinanced and overworked police agencies. However, the reserves should be required to complete the same pre-service screening and training requirements as regular full-time officers.

Some jurisdictions limit reserve officer duties based on the amount of training received. In California, for example, basic academy training for reserve officers is presented in three levels. Completion of Level III (the lowest level) training allows the reserve officer to perform limited law enforcement support duties such as search and rescue, traffic control, and prisoner transport. Completion of Level II training allows the reserve officer to function as a second officer or partner with a full-time regular officer on patrol. Completion of Level I (the highest level) training, along with a specified field training program, allows the reserve to work alone.

Learn more about training through the California Commission on Peace Officer Standards and Training (POST) at www.post.ca.gov.

Closed-Circuit Television and Cameras

Although not a patrol unit per se, the use of closed-circuit television (CCTV) is becoming more common. In several cities, CCTV cameras have been installed in locations that experience high-crime rates, and where traffic must be monitored or continuous surveillance is necessary. The video is transmitted to monitors located at a central station. Operators monitoring the television screens can dispatch patrol units to locations where suspicious activity is identified. Still cameras also provide additional surveillance coverage. Used primarily at busy intersections, the cameras photograph vehicles when drivers violate traffic signal laws.

PATROL EQUIPMENT

Some of the personal equipment used on patrol was discussed in Chapter 7. However, the different types of equipment that may be used by a uniformed patrol officer are quite extensive. Depending on the nature and scope of the patrol environment, a patrol officer may be required to operate over 100 different types of equipment.

In addition to weapons, vehicles, radios, and other hardware, the modern-day police officer is equipped with computers and advanced surveillance technology such as vehicle tracking systems and night vision devices. Forensic science tools are available also (Dempsey & Forst, 2012).

The acquisition of some police equipment has been criticized as inappropriate and too costly. One urban police department spent $150,000 to purchase an 11-ton military surplus tank to be used to protect officers in life-threatening situations. However, the tank proved to be too bulky and unreliable for police work.

Some agencies are installing satellite-monitored automated vehicle locator systems in patrol vehicles. Units equipped with the system can be monitored continuously by utilizing satellites. The location of the vehicle can be pinpointed to within three feet. The system enhances officer survival rates. Dispatchers monitoring a computer screen can identify the exact location of an injured officer and dispatch additional police personnel and paramedics to the scene.

COMMUNICATIONS SYSTEMS AND EQUIPMENT

History

In the past, police communications systems and equipment were extremely limited. Drums, rattles, whistles, hand signals, and church bells were used as signaling devices. The nightstick, forerunner of the police baton, was also used. Tapping of the nightstick on a masonry building or pavement could be heard for great distances and police officers often used this method to communicate with each other. With the invention of electric lights, but before the invention of the radio, signal lights connected to police stations were used to notify officers on patrol. A switch at

Two-way police radio communications systems were introduced in the 1930s. *(Photo courtesy of the San Diego Police Department.)*

the police station was used to activate a light suspended above a street corner on a police officer's beat. After observing the light, the police officer utilized a telephone call box to contact the police communications center for instructions.

In 1928, the first police radio system was placed in service in Detroit, Michigan. However, the system provided one-way communication only, with the transmitter at the police station and the receiver in a patrol car. In 1933, the Bayonne, New Jersey, Police Department introduced the first two-way police radio system. Other early police communications systems included telegraph and teletype machines, which became obsolete in the 1950s (Payton & Amaral, 2004).

Today, facsimile (fax) machines, video cameras, pagers, cellular phones, portable handheld radios, television, computers, and **mobile data terminals (MDTs)** and **mobile data computers (MDCs)** in police vehicles greatly enhance an officer's ability to communicate and access information about matters such as wanted persons, stolen property, and crime records (Reid, 2011). The Internet and electronic mail (e-mail) provide additional communication media. Specific types of computerized information systems are discussed in the section on sources of information contained in Chapter 11.

In addition to radio systems, many modern police vehicles are equipped with a mobile data terminal (MDT) or mobile data computer (MDC). *(Photo courtesy of the San Diego Police Department.)*

Dispatch Systems

Prior to the invention of police radio systems, victims and witnesses were required to locate a police officer to report an incident, or they

A Central Dispatch Center receives 9-1-1 calls. *(Photo courtesy of the Cobb County, GA Police Department.)*

called a police station where a dispatch person attempted to notify an officer through a callback light or other signaling device. Modern-day dispatch systems are much more sophisticated. Calls for police service usually originate with someone placing a call through a 9-1-1, 4-1-1, or other emergency number to a central police dispatch center. In turn, an operator at the dispatch center places a radio, cell phone, or mobile data terminal call to a police officer. The dispatch operator relays the nature of the incident or event as well as the priority assigned to the call.

Although almost 90 percent of the approximately 20,000 police agencies in the United States are small, many large metropolitan agencies are forced to handle hundreds of calls for police service each day. The workload can overwhelm a dispatch center. Consequently, many urban police departments utilize **computer-aided dispatch (CAD)** systems. Through the CAD system, the person receiving an incoming call utilizes a keyboard to enter the data into a template on a computer screen. The computer scans and transfers the information to an appropriate dispatcher for action.

VEHICLE OPERATIONS

More police officers are killed in vehicle collisions than die at the hands of law violators. A majority of these collisions are the result of human error and could have been prevented. Officer-caused collisions usually result when an officer is executing a left-hand turn, parking, following too closely, failing to yield the right-of-way, having the vehicle in reverse, or is driving at a speed that is unsafe for the road conditions. Other motorists cause the majority of officer-involved vehicle collisions. Therefore, officers must drive defensively and be aware of the actions of other operators on the roadway. Seat belts must be properly secured. Seat belts are the single most effective device for protecting vehicle occupants from serious injury or death during a collision.

Generally, police officers are authorized—after securing the right of way by displaying emergency lights and sounding a siren—to proceed through a traffic stopping device, exceed the speed limit, and disregard rules governing traffic flow. This authorization is limited to situations in which an officer is responding to an emergency call or fire alarm, is engaged in rescue operations, or is in immediate pursuit of an actual or suspected law violator. However, even though statutory provisions exist that allow police officers to violate rules of the road, officers must operate a motor vehicle in a way that is consistent with public safety and good common sense. All officers must remember that driving either aggressively or defensively necessitates proper attitude physical conditioning, knowledge, and skill. It also involves consideration of the vehicle's abilities and the road conditions.

PATROL TECHNIQUES

When an officer allows police work to become routine, the probability of an accident-injury, or death to the officer increases. In fact, the word *routine* should not be included in a police officer's vocabulary. Rather, a police officer should go about the business of police work in a systematically unsystematic manner, fully conscious of the fact that allowing the work to become routine can result in negative consequences.

The systematically unsystematic approach to patrol operations, or **planned random patrol,** cannot be overemphasized. Patrolling should not involve set patterns. Alternatively, random patrol without tactical and strategic planning wastes valuable police resources. The results of the **Kansas City Preventive Patrol Experiment** indicated that random patrol in conspicuously marked police vehicles may have little or no impact on the crime rate (Kelling, 1974). In addition, rapid response to reported crime may not dramatically increase the rate of apprehensions because most victims and witnesses wait a considerable length of time before calling the police (Petersilia, 1989). Therefore, patrol officers should not approach patrol activity on a strictly random basis. Patrol operations and techniques must involve strategic as well as tactical planning. Thus, preventive patrol should focus on the following:

- A planned variation of patrol patterns.
- Maintenance of high police visibility.
- Frequent patrol of high-crime target areas.
- A search for, and encounters with, suspicious individuals.

To patrol effectively, an officer must do more than simply walk or drive through a patrol area waiting for a radio call. A **patrol pattern** must be selected that allows the officer to cover the entire beat and observe areas requiring the most attention. The pattern must lack predictability, keeping potential criminals and law violators off balance. The pattern may be circular, unstructured, or looped. A looped pattern is suggested because it allows the officer to double back in problem areas and enhance the perception of unpredictability.

As a preventive measure, high police visibility should be maintained in areas that frequently require police attention. These areas include sites where criminal acts are a strong possibility. Shopping centers, nightclubs and bars, 24-hour businesses, special events, impoverished areas, youth gathering locations, and areas with poor lighting tend to have high crime rates. Locations with poor road conditions and other hazards to public safety also warrant frequent patrol activity. Structures, especially businesses closed at night, should be checked frequently for broken windows, property damage, unusual conditions, and suspicious people or vehicles in the area. If evidence of forced entry is observed, the officer should notify central communications, maintain surveillance of the facility, and wait for backup officers before proceeding with an investigation.

Field contacts with suspicious persons require special consideration. Officers must utilize appropriate communication and tactical skills to ensure compliance and officer safety. Officers should explain the reason for the stop and avoid inappropriate language. If appropriate, officers should conduct a wants and warrants check on individuals contacted in the field.

If the objective of the patrol activity is to apprehend an offender in the process of committing a violation, the patrol strategy selected may involve hiding from view and maintaining surveillance of the site most

Strategically and tactically planned random patrol involves variation of patrol patterns, visibility, targeting of high crime areas, and a search for suspicious persons. *(Photo courtesy of the San Diego Sheriff's Department.)*

likely to experience criminal activity. When an apprehension patrol strategy is employed, the officer should minimize activities and sounds, such as movement, lighting, and patrol vehicle noise, so the officer's presence is not revealed to the potential suspect.

On foot patrol during daylight hours, officers should walk close to the street. This approach not only makes the officer more conspicuous for crime prevention purposes, but also provides the officer with the ability to observe both sides of a street. Courteous contact with the public is critical. Citizens provide more information to officers who appear approachable. Day-shift officers should also peer into businesses, look down alleys, and glance up occasionally when patrolling districts with high-rise buildings.

Foot patrol during nighttime hours requires a modification of the daytime techniques. An officer should walk next to buildings, pausing occasionally in shadows and darkened areas to observe the street and listen for suspicious sounds such as breaking glass. Exterior doors or closed businesses should receive a security inspection. Doors left unlocked must not be neglected. Business owners should be notified. Officers should not enter unlocked businesses alone. Flashlights should be used to detect tool marks around doorknobs and locks, which may be the result of a forced entry.

On normal vehicular patrol, officers should observe traffic laws. Police units are exempt from traffic laws only during an emergency, and officers and agencies may be held civilly liable for accidents resulting from violations of the vehicle code. Safe driving also involves the use of seat belts, the avoidance of boredom and distractions, and defensive driving. When patrolling residential areas and business districts, the curb lane is especially suitable for the police vehicle. The appropriate speed for patrol is 15 to 20 miles per hour unless conditions and traffic suggest a higher speed. More is observed at slower speeds. **Peripheral** (lateral) **vision** increases and tunnel vision decreases at slower speeds. Peripheral vision is about 180° when a vehicle is stationary, but decreases to 90° at 50 miles per hour.

The best approach to vehicular patrol is to blend with other vehicles on the roadway, especially at night, since the element of surprise to actual or potential violation activity is on the side of the patrol officer. A window should be kept open to enable an officer to hear activities outside the vehicle. When patrolling a multilane street, road, or freeway, the number one lane (lane closest to the center of the roadway) is best for observing traffic. This is also a desirable lane choice because it enhances the officer's ability to move around traffic or make a U-turn to respond to urgent calls. Finally, an officer should always remove the keys when leaving the patrol vehicle.

Keen observation and perception skills are also essential for effective patrol. Cultivating the senses of sight, hearing, smell, taste, and touch are critical to the uniformed patrol officer. With time and experience on the job, an officer may develop a sixth sense, that of intuition, which will communicate an alarm to the officer when people and situations appear suspicious. A police officer is expected to be a trained observer. This means that an officer must be disciplined to observe an environment and apply training and experience to perceive what is occurring or about to occur. In police work, two plus two does not always equal four. A police officer must constantly evaluate the situation and the circumstances to recognize facts and determine if police action is warranted.

Police officers cannot realistically cover all of their assigned areas all of the time. Interruptions as a result of calls for service will force officers to prioritize patrol activity for maximum benefit. Thus, it will be necessary for officers to direct patrol operations to the enforcement activity that is highest on their list of priorities. Statistical analyses, for example, may assist officers in the patrol activity decision-making process.

FIELD INTERVIEWS

An early study conducted by the Rand Corporation of Santa Monica, California, concluded that a vast amount of information important to the police mission is discovered through uniformed patrol officers' contacts with the public (Greenwood, 1979). The gathering of information is an ingredient essential to police success in crime prevention and apprehension of criminal law offenders. During a shift, a uniformed patrol officer will encounter a wide variety of people. Homeowners, tenants, businesspeople, utility company and public works employees, mail carriers, bartenders, medical personnel, street people, and criminal suspects are all valuable sources of information. The technique used to obtain information from these people is often referred to as the **field interview (FI).**

Although an encounter with a person may lead to the arrest of that person, most police–citizen contacts on the street do not involve apprehension of criminal offenders. Most are consensual encounters with individuals who live and work within the patrol area. The purpose of the field interview is to obtain information from anyone who may possess knowledge of interest to the police. Police officers may approach any individual in a public place, identify themselves as police officers, ask for identification, and then ask a few questions while maintaining the consensual status of the encounter. The key to consent is that the individual is not detained, is free to leave at any time, and is not forced to comply with the officer's request.

A **detention,** on the other hand, involves stopping a person by exerting police authority. It is more than a consensual encounter but less than an arrest. A detention requires reasonable suspicion, whereas a consensual encounter requires no justification for the stop, and an arrest requires probable cause that a crime has been committed. When a person is detained, an officer can frisk (pat down) the subject for weapons. Officer safety justifies the frisk. The *Miranda* warning applies when probable cause to arrest has been developed.

Most agencies require officers to utilize a field interview card to document information obtained during the interview of any suspicious person. Information that should be obtained and forwarded to detective units and other appropriate personnel includes the following:
- Subject's full name, nicknames, and/or aliases
- Subject's date of birth
- Sex and physical description of subject, including scars and tattoos
- Subject's resident address and place of employment
- Social security number, driver's license, or other identification numbers
- Clothing worn
- Reason for subject contact
- Identification of the subject's companions
- Accompanying citations, if any
- Description of accompanying vehicle, if any
- The subject's criminal record
- Date, time, and location of the field interview (Miller, 2000)

TRAFFIC MANAGEMENT

The underlying philosophy of traffic management involves moving pedestrian and vehicular traffic from one point to another as quickly and safely as possible. More Americans have died in traffic collisions than in all the wars fought by Americans. Collisions, property damage, injury, and death can be prevented, or at least reduced, if traffic laws (rules of the road) are enforced, and drivers practice safety and common courtesy.

Motor vehicle laws, or codes, are enacted and enforced to promote an environment in which pedestrians and the motoring public can use streets and highways safely. Some **vehicle code violations** such as reckless driving, speed contests (drag racing), failure to obey a lawful order from a traffic officer, vehicular manslaughter, and driving under the influence (DUI) are criminal in nature. Most vehicle code violations, however, are infractions and convictions do not result in a criminal sanction.

Vehicle code violations generally fall into three broad categories: moving, equipment, and document violations. Moving violations include, but are not limited to, excessive speed, disregard for traffic signals, and failure to yield the right-of-way. Broken windshields, faulty mufflers, and malfunctioning lights are examples of equipment violations. Document violations include expired vehicle registrations and drivers' licenses and improper display of vehicle license plates.

In an effort to reduce the amount of hostile and violent behavior occurring on roadways in recent years, traffic law enforcement has increased its focus on aggressive drivers. Although traffic enforcement officers can probably do little to prevent road rage, reduce anxiety, or defuse anger between and among drivers on congested highways, officers can educate the public on good driving habits and seek out aggressive drivers. Good drivers look ahead, pay attention, share the roadway, and do not follow other vehicles too closely. Poor drivers eat, groom themselves using the rearview mirror, talk on their cell phones, or text while driving. Indeed, one recent study found that texting while steering is more dangerous than drunken driving. Recognizing such dangers, in 2008 California outlawed texting and using cell phones while driving (Schmidt, 2009). Poor drivers obstruct traffic flow by driving too slow in a high-speed lane, slowing down to look at accidents (rubber-necking), or not making room for merging traffic. Aggressive drivers tailgate, make unnecessary lane changes, drive faster (or slower) than the flow of traffic, make obscene gestures, brake suddenly to punish tailgaters, or speed up when another motorist tries to pass. A recent nationwide survey conducted by a major automobile insurer indicated that more than 10 percent of drivers admit they intentionally cut off and argued with other drivers (Farmers Insurance Group, 2004). **Aggressive driving** can be cited under various unsafe driving infractions that exist in most state vehicle codes.

Most violations are disposed of by the patrol officer through the issuance of a **citation.** Essentially, the citation includes a notice of the charge and a subpoena (notice to appear). In some police agencies, traffic management supervisors expect officers to issue a minimum number of citations for traffic violations. Other agencies do not specify a quota. In these agencies, officers are expected to write enough citations to ensure that the public is observing traffic laws and the roadways are safe. In other words, if the district is free of collisions, with no property damage, injuries or deaths, the officer deserves credit for a job well done regardless of the number of citations issued.

A great number of traffic citations are the result of speeding violations. Drivers may be cited for violation of prima facie or maximum speed limits, or basic speed laws. **Prima facie speed limits** include those that are always applicable (e.g., 25 miles per hour in residential areas) unless otherwise posted. Maximum speed limits include the highest posted speed a person can drive on a given roadway. **Basic speed laws** refer to driving at a speed higher than what is reasonable and prudent based on the road conditions, regardless of the prima facie or posted speed limit. An interstate highway or freeway, for example, may have a posted speed limit of 65 miles per hour. However, due to rain, fog, or icy conditions, the reasonable and prudent speed would be much less than the posted limit.

Operating a motor vehicle on a public roadway or off-street parking facility is a privilege, not a right. The privilege to drive may be revoked or suspended by a state's department of motor vehicles or the courts. Licenses can also be limited. For example, the California Department of Motor Vehicles is limiting the licenses of older persons with impaired vision to daytime driving or specific geographic areas. The goal is to enable people to drive as long as possible, but safely (Hawkins, 2011). The privilege to drive may be revoked even when the violator does not possess a valid motor vehicle operator's license. Generally, a person cannot legally drive

Learn more about traffic management and safety through the National Highway Traffic Safety Administration at www.nhtsa.dot.gov.

a motor vehicle without a valid driver's license or when the license has been revoked or suspended. Exceptions to the rule include situations in which the driver is seeking emergency medical assistance or is operating a vehicle in the course of employment on the employer's private property.

Radar Use

Prior to the development of radar technology, officers estimated the speed of a violator by pacing the violator's vehicle. This procedure involved following the violator and verifying the violator's speed by clocking the speed and visually noting the speed on the patrol car's speedometer. Speeding motorists are still detected visually by the officer. **Radar** is used to verify the officer's estimate of the violator's speed.

There are several types of radar devices. They include stationary and moving systems as well as vehicle mounted or handheld devices. Some use radio waves. Others, such as Vascar, use laser beams. Most traffic law enforcement vehicles are equipped with two radar guns (front and rear aimed) and a display unit, all controlled by a handheld remote control. A radar signal or beam is emitted from the patrol vehicle's radar unit. The signal reflects off of the violator's vehicle and returns to the radar unit. The radar unit then calculates the speed of the suspect vehicle relative to the speed of the patrol vehicle and displays the subject vehicle's speed on a dash-mounted monitor. To avoid contested traffic citations based on the use of radar, officers should calibrate the radar unit at the beginning and end of each shift. The calibration is accomplished through the use of a tuning fork and diagnostic test. The officer notes each calibration and test in the logbook maintained with the radar unit.

DRIVING UNDER THE INFLUENCE CASES

States vary with respect to the title or phrase attached to behavior associated with operating a motor vehicle while under the influence of drugs or intoxicating liquor. **Driving Under the Influence (DUI), Driving While Intoxicated (DWI),** or Driving Under the Influence of Liquor (DUIL) are phrases typically used in the statutes. Whatever the title, such laws have one unwritten element in common—driving under the influence is taken very seriously in contemporary American society. Nationwide, DUI is considered to be a major traffic law enforcement problem.

Statutes specify the maximum **blood-alcohol concentration (BAC)** allowable before a driver becomes legally intoxicated. The federal government and the states specify a BAC limit of .08 percent (Hunt, 2010). This concentration represents 80 milligrams of alcohol per 100 milliliters of blood. Lower BAC limits are also established for special driver categories. In some states, drivers of commercial vehicles have a BAC limit of .04 percent, while drivers under the age of 21 have a .01 percent BAC limit. Regardless of the BAC limit, however, police officers must be aware that an individual's limit is reached when the normal abilities necessary to operate a motor vehicle safely have been exceeded. There is no absolutely safe way to drive while under the influence. Even one alcoholic drink can impair driving ability.

Behavioral symptoms associated with DUI cases include excessive speed, following too close, driving without lights at night, swerving, and uncoordinated vehicle control. Suspects may slur speech, stagger, or be unable to demonstrate normal hand and eye coordination. Common field sobriety tests include the balance, finger-to-the-nose, heel-to-toe straight-line walk, and alphabet recitation. Some police units are equipped with portable breath analyzers or **preliminary alcohol screening (PAS) devices.** Chemical tests used to detect the presence of alcohol, however, will usually not detect the presence of drugs. Extensive specialized drug recognition training must be acquired by officers to become proficient in identifying persons under the influence of drugs. Some agencies also videotape suspected intoxicated drivers to corroborate officer testimony in court.

It is estimated that over one-third of all traffic fatalities each year are alcohol related. The death rate from alcohol-related fatalities is higher than the murder rate in the United States. Furthermore, the National Highway Safety Administration estimates that 40 percent of the American population will be involved in an alcohol-related accident during their lifetime. As a result, driving under the influence cases are prosecuted intensely as a means of reducing deaths and injuries.

Driving a vehicle is a privilege, not a right. Implied consent laws are based on the assumption of the privilege. Permission to drive is therefore granted by a state under the condition that the driver has consented to submit to certain tests of ability to drive, such as breath tests. Refusal to submit to such tests may result in suspension or revocation of the privilege to drive. Penalties for convicted drunk drivers vary, but they are becoming more severe in the United States. Generally, first-time conviction for DUI not resulting in personal injury or death is a misdemeanor. Subsequent convictions within seven years and DUI offenses resulting in injury or death are sanctioned as felonies. Yet some still believe the sanctions are too lenient. In England and France, convicted drunk or drug-impaired drivers may be imprisoned for one year. In Russia and Norway, one's license (or privilege) to drive may be revoked for life.

COLLISION RESPONSE

All traffic accidents are collisions, but not all collisions are accidents. Some collisions are deliberate. However, the vast majority of collision calls are the result of an accident. Damage has occurred to property and, in some cases, people have been injured or killed.

At the scene of a collision, the police officer is responsible for management of the situation. The officer must care for the injured, protect the scene, keep traffic moving, and restore normal traffic flow as soon as possible. If the collision scene is not managed properly, injuries to victims may become more serious if they do not receive proper and prompt medical attention. The injured are the officer's first priority after the scene is protected. In addition, most collisions inhibit expeditious and safe traffic flow. Additional accidents may occur if other drivers are not aware of the situation, and traffic is not diverted properly.

PEDESTRIAN STOPS AND INVESTIGATIONS

While patrolling a beat, police officers may find it necessary to initiate an encounter with pedestrians observed in the area. These encounters are often referred to as investigative stops. Factors to consider in the pedestrian stop decision include the appearance and actions of the person, time of day, location, and prior knowledge of the individual. Caution must be exercised to ensure that the person is not selected for the stop simply because of race or ethnicity (McMahon, Garner, Davis, & Kraus, 2003). A U.S. Supreme Court decision issued in January 2000 authorized police officers, within the context of the factors discussed previously, to stop a suspicious person if the subject flees at the sight of the police.

After making the decision to stop, an officer should identify a stop location that has the least number of escape routes and bystanders, notify dispatch, position the patrol vehicle (if applicable) to maximize safety to the officer, and leave the vehicle. Remaining inside a patrol vehicle places the officer at a tactical disadvantage. Approaching and encountering a subject on foot permits the officer to concentrate on the pedestrian, rather than dividing attention between driving and observation of the subject. In addition, an approach on foot provides unencumbered access to police weapons, greater visibility of the subject, better mobility, and enhanced detention and search capabilities.

As the approach is made, the officer must continuously observe the subject's hands and take notice of any suspicious movement. After the encounter is made, the officer may conduct a frisk or pat-down for weapons if the officer observes a bulge or other observations suggest the subject may be armed. In the case of consensual encounters in which the subject is free to leave at any time, the officer's communication should be courteous and respectful. The officer should always assume a field interview position at least an arm's length from the subject, with the officer's sidearm located away from the subject. Always aware of the surroundings, the officer must be prepared for unexpected activity from other persons who might be in the area.

When two officers make the approach, one officer should initiate the encounter with the pedestrian while the other officer covers the contact officer. Cover is not the same as concealment. Cover refers to objects that may stop or deflect on opponent's weapon or otherwise protect an officer. In contrast, concealment refers to anything that prevents observation of an officer. If the contact officer is the first to arrive, the backup cover officer, if any, should be briefed on arrival. If the stop is being made by a two-officer patrol unit, the officers should plan and discuss the pedestrian stop strategy prior to contact with a subject.

FOOT PURSUITS

A foot pursuit is one of the most dangerous and unpredictable situations a police officer will encounter. Foot pursuits are unplanned and often require tremendous physical exertion. As physical activity increases, the supply of oxygen to the brain decreases and the officer's reasoning ability may be impaired.

Foot pursuits should be initiated only when necessary. Flight may not be indicative of criminal activity. Some people flee only because they fear the police. Other fleeing subjects may be attempting to lure an officer into an ambush. A physical confrontation often results at the end of a pursuit. An officer must have enough physical strength and stamina remaining to control a combative subject. Uniformed patrol officers carry about 25 pounds of equipment. The extra weight challenges the officer physically. The officer must also ensure that all the equipment, especially the sidearm, is retained during the pursuit.

During a foot pursuit, an officer should exercise caution when turning blind corners, climbing over obstructions, or when losing sight of the subject. Either an unknown hazard or the subject could be lying in wait for the officer. Nightime foot pursuits present additional officer safety concerns because the officer may not be able to observe physical obstacles such as fences, clotheslines, and ground depressions. Pursuits should be terminated when the subject enters a building. This location could contain additional support for the subject, or hostages, if any, might be injured or killed. A perimeter should be established around the structure and the building searched, utilizing appropriate tactical procedures. If a foot pursuit commences during a vehicle pullover, the officer involved should not pass the subject's vehicle without checking it for additional occupants.

VEHICLE STOPS

All vehicle stops are potentially dangerous situations. Police encounters with armed suspects on the roadway are common and may occur when an officer conducts an investigative stop or a stop for what appears to be a minor traffic violation. The subject may be a fugitive. Even ordinary citizens can become violent when faced with a citation for a traffic violation.

Low-Risk Vehicle Stops

Vehicle stops for traffic infractions account for the greatest percentage of all vehicle pullovers. Although never "routine," there are no hard-and-fast rules for conducting traffic stops—only guidelines. Procedures may vary

Access links to numerous law enforcement information websites through Police Guide at www.policeguide.com.

depending on the situation and the policies of the police agency. Guidelines for nonfelony **low-risk vehicle stops** include the following:

- Control the stop and select the best-possible location to minimize exposure to traffic hazards. Pullovers should not take place in busy intersections or in the middle of the roadway.
- Position the patrol vehicle directly behind (10–15 feet) and approximately 3 feet to the left of the subject vehicle. This position will cover the officer from traffic as the officer approaches the subject vehicle on foot. Keep rear flashers and rear amber lights on.
- Before leaving the vehicle, write the vehicle license number on a notepad and notify dispatch of the location, license number, and description of the subject vehicle.
- Keep occupant(s) of the vehicle under surveillance to observe furtive (suspicious) movements such as reaching under seats or hiding to avoid detection.
- Place the gearshift in the park position, turn the front wheels to the left, turn the ignition off, and remove the ignition key.
- When leaving the vehicle, place any items being carried, such as a citation book, in the weak hand, opposite the sidearm.
- If the driver leaves the vehicle, the officer should order the driver and occupants to remain in the vehicle or order the driver to the sidewalk or shoulder of the roadway. Standing between the subject vehicle and patrol unit is not advisable. If the patrol unit is hit from the rear by another vehicle, the officer and subject could be injured if the two stopped vehicles are pressed together.
- During the approach to the subject vehicle, observe the interior for furtive movements, check the trunk lid to make sure it is secure (someone with a weapon could be hidden inside), glance into the rear seat, observe the hands of all occupants, stay close to the subject vehicle, and stop slightly behind the driver's door. Stopping in front of the driver makes the officer an easy target. If the driver has a firearm, the officer's position behind the driver would require the driver to rotate and shoot to the rear. To maintain officer safety in an area of dense highspeed traffic, such as a freeway, the approach should be made on the side of the vehicle opposite traffic flow.
- Obtain the driver's motor vehicle operator's (driver's) license, vehicle registration, and proof of financial responsibility (current insurance verification).
- Return to the patrol vehicle to check for wants and warrants and write a citation, if appropriate.
- Return to the violator vehicle with the appropriate documents, practicing the same precautions outlined previously.

Normal low-risk vehicle stops provide officers with an opportunity to improve or negatively impact the public's image of the police. The first few words spoken to a motorist by the officer during a traffic stop are critical. Derogatory comments must be avoided (Building a bridge, 1999; Tyler &

Wakslak, 2004). Consistent with the principles of officer safety and survival, a professional police officer will project a positive public image if a tactical communications process similar to the following is adhered to when conducting low-risk stops for traffic violations. The officer should:

- Begin the personal encounter with the violator with a positive, respectful greeting.
- Identify himself or herself and the officer's agency.
- Explain the reasons for the stop and provide motivation for the violator to listen.
- Ask the violator if there is any reasonable justification for that person's actions.
- Request the violator's motor vehicle operator's (driver's) license.
- Request the vehicle's registration document and proof of financial responsibility.
- Select action (warning, citation, arrest) based on the circumstances.
- Bring the encounter to closure with an appropriate comment.

High-Risk Vehicle Stops

High-risk, felony, or "hot" vehicle stops require extreme caution and a modification of the procedures used for low-risk stops. High-risk stops include those in which the officer has a reasonable belief that the occupant(s) of the vehicle could be armed or dangerous. Examples include

Vehicle stops for traffic violations provide officers with an opportunity to improve the public's image of the police. *(Photo courtesy of the San Diego Sheriff's Department.)*

situations involving felony suspects, flight to avoid arrest or hot pursuits, and possible stolen vehicles. General guidelines for **high-risk vehicle stops** include the following:

- As with low-risk stops, the officer should select a location for the stop that places the officer at the best tactical advantage and minimizes the risk of injury or death to innocent civilians. At night, the location should be well lit.

- Notify communications of location, nature of the stop, vehicle license number, and description.

- Request backup. An officer should avoid overconfidence.

- The police unit conducting the stop is considered the primary vehicle. If the primary unit contains two officers, either the driver or passenger officer will be designated the command officer depending on which side of the suspect vehicle the occupant(s) are requested to exit.

- Position the primary police vehicle to maximize protection of the officer(s). A one-officer unit should be positioned 10 to 15 feet to the rear of the suspect vehicle at a slight angle to the left. The engine compartment of the police vehicle can be used for maximum concealment and cover if the suspect fires a weapon at the officer. A two-officer unit should park 10 to 15 feet behind the suspect vehicle in a straight line. The driver officer will exit with sidearm drawn, and the backup officer (passenger) will exit with the police shotgun.

- Additional police vehicles should be positioned to maximize protection of the officers and avoid any other officer's line of fire. If civilian vehicular traffic is proceeding in the same direction and cannot be stopped immediately, a secondary police vehicle can be positioned in a straight line behind the primary unit. The secondary unit officer assumes a position to the right or left of the suspect vehicle and out of the primary officer's line of fire. If civilian traffic is not a consideration, the secondary vehicle can be positioned across the roadway from, and slightly to the rear of, the suspect vehicle. This will provide a side view of, and cross-fire position with, the suspect vehicle.

- Implement control techniques, with backup officers covering the suspect(s) with weapons on safety or double-action to avoid accidental discharge. The command officer uses the primary police unit's public address (PA) system to control the occupant(s) of the suspect vehicle. Additional backup units may be used for crowd and traffic control.

- Implement arrest procedures by utilizing the patrol vehicle's public address (PA) system. The command officer will order the suspect(s) from the vehicle. Verbal commands should be short, loud, clear, firm, and easily understood. The occupant(s) should be ordered to keep their hands in plain view by placing their hands, palms up, either on the dashboard, against the windshield, outside the windows, or on top of the seat in front of them. The driver should be ordered to remove the key from the ignition with the left hand and drop the key(s) out the driver's window. Occupants should be ordered from the vehicle one at a time, driver first, by requiring them to exit slowly with hands raised and walk backward to the front of the pri-

During a high-risk vehicle stop, the police vehicle should be positioned to maximize protection of the officer. *(Photo courtesy of the San Diego Sheriff's Department.)*

If possible, officers should not approach the suspect vehicle during a high-risk stop until the occupants are out of the vehicle and their threat level is diminished. *(Photo courtesy of the San Diego Sheriff's Department.)*

mary police vehicle. All occupants should be required to exit from the same side of the vehicle. Each occupant will be required to lie face down in a prone position or kneel facing the rear of the suspect vehicle. On a roadway, occupants may be ordered, one at a time, to exit the vehicle from the right doors and lie face down on the shoulder of the road, sidewalk, or ground.

- The suspect vehicle is searched for any occupants who may be hiding in the passenger compartment or trunk. The vehicle should be approached in a crouching position for maximum protection. At the rear of the vehicle, the officer(s) should place a hand on the vehicle to detect any movement. Extra caution must be exercised with vans, campers, and motor homes. Some of these have trapdoors, and armed suspects can fire on exposed officers. When all occupants have been removed from the vehicle, officers may approach the suspect(s), with one or two officers covering the suspect(s) with weapons while the other officers arrest, handcuff, and search the suspects. To ensure chain of custody of evidence, it is suggested that one officer be designated to handcuff and search all suspects. Handcuffed suspects are placed in separate patrol vehicles.

HIGH-SPEED DRIVING AND PURSUITS

Most police calls are not urgent. Unless the dispatcher has assigned the call as Code Three, authorizing the patrol unit as an emergency vehicle with red lights and siren, officers should obey all traffic laws. **Code Three driving** incidents include situations in which there is a danger to human life such as officer needs help calls, vehicle collisions with injuries, crimes in progress with armed suspects, and fires in habitable buildings. Even when designated as an authorized emergency vehicle, the officer should proceed in a reasonable and prudent manner consistent with traffic conditions, and exercise caution at roadway intersections.

Few events in law enforcement require a higher degree of skill and judgment than high-speed vehicle pursuit. It is more dangerous than emergency response driving. An officer must remember that pursuit driving is a perishable skill. Refresher police driver training is mandatory in many jurisdictions. Developing and maintaining excellent driving skills requires adherence to the principles of defensive driving. Safe driving habits help reduce risk and stress during vehicle operations. Safe defensive drivers operate vehicles in a manner that is consistent with environmental conditions and collision avoidance.

Approximately 100,000 police pursuits occur throughout the nation annually. Most result in successful apprehension of the fugitive with no injuries occurring. However, according to the National Highway Traffic Safety Administration, police high-speed pursuits are on the rise nationally. The number of deaths occurring as a result of these pursuits has also increased. Innocent bystanders account for 20 percent of the dead, stirring considerable debate over police pursuit policies. In urban settings, the outcome of most police pursuits is some type of collision (Greenhouse, 1998; Schmalleger, 2005; Thornton, 1999, February 27).

In addition, deaths and injuries to innocent people as well as property damage can lead to tremendous civil liability for agencies and the officers involved. As a result, jurisdictions are forced to pay millions of dollars to settle liability claims and court judgments stemming from police pursuits (Hitting the brakes, 2003).

Police pursuits in one California county over a 12-year period resulted in several injuries and deaths:

- **December 1994:** Three children were injured, two critically, when the car in which they were riding was rammed by a police car in Carlsbad, California. The officer was pursuing a motorist for a speeding violation.
- **July 1995:** Several people were injured when the car in which they were riding was hit by a vehicle being chased by police in National City, California. The chase began when the driver ran a stop sign.
- **December 1998:** Two 9-year-old girls walking along a road after school died as the result of injuries sustained when they were struck by a pickup truck previously pursued by a CHP officer in Lakeside, California. The CHP officer had terminated the pursuit prior to the collision because the pickup truck was entering a school zone.
- **February 1999:** A 32-year-old housewife was killed when a San Diego Police officer, driving Code Three in pursuit of two home invasion robbery suspects, ran a red stoplight and hit the victim's vehicle. The two suspects were eventually charged and convicted of murder for the death of the housewife.
- **June 2004:** A vacationing 18-year-old woman died and three of her companions were injured when their car was hit in the rear by a suspected drunk driver being pursued by sheriff's deputies and highway patrol officers.

Some agencies, such as those in Baltimore, Los Angeles, Minneapolis, and Columbus, Ohio, have very strict **vehicle pursuit policies** that severely limit pursuits. Most agencies, however, adhere to pursuit polices that are similar to the following:

- A police officer may pursue a vehicle if it fails to yield when the police vehicle's emergency lights and siren are activated. The officer must entertain a reasonable suspicion or have probable cause to believe that the person pursued has committed an infraction, misdemeanor, or felony, and the necessity of apprehension outweighs the risk created by the pursuit, or that the subject presents a clear and imminent threat to public safety.
- The officer must terminate the pursuit when driving conditions warrant. Traffic congestion, inclement weather, limited visibility, and road design may not support high-speed driving requirements. Air support may be utilized where available.
- No more than two units should be actively involved in a pursuit unless otherwise approved by a supervisor. The primary unit is usually the unit that initiates the pursuit. This unit notifies dispatch, the supervisor, and other field units of the pursuit, and maintains immediate field command unless relieved by the supervisor. The second-

ary pursuit unit provides support to the primary unit, follows at a safe distance, and may assume primary unit responsibilities as directed. Additional pursuit units as well as the supervisory unit normally remain uninvolved unless specifically directed by the supervisor to actively pursue the violator.

- The officer(s) must continuously evaluate the situation to determine if the seriousness of the alleged offense outweighs the pursuit's risk to public safety. Management and control of the pursuit must be maintained at all times. The safety of the pursued, the pursuers, and the general public are the most important considerations. The officers must balance the need for immediate capture of the offender against the risk of property damage, personal injury, or death. Factors that indicate a need to terminate include adverse environmental and weather conditions, the duration of the pursuit, whether the offender is known, and the nature of the offense.

- The police may not pursue across an international border and, in some jurisdictions, may not pursue across state lines unless the suspect is inherently dangerous and could cause serious bodily injury or death to an innocent person if allowed to escape. Where interjurisdictional pursuits are allowed, considerations must be given to interagency notification and communication. Most agencies retain primary responsibility for pursuits they initiate. However, initiating officers may be well advised to relinquish management and control of the pursuit to the local agency because local officers are familiar with local road and environmental conditions.

- A post-pursuit report must be filed and an analysis of the pursuit conducted. Post-pursuit analysis provides information that can be used to identify trends and training needs as well as provide data for pursuit policy development or modification.

In the excitement of a pursuit, violators frequently refuse to stop while officers feel obligated to succeed in apprehending the violator. Considering the psychological aspects of the chase, the closer the officer is to the pursued, the faster the pursued will drive, creating greater risk of injury or death. The adrenaline is flowing, and the chase may continue beyond the point at which common sense and good judgment indicate termination of the pursuit is necessary. Safety is not the concern of the person being pursued. The suspect's speed and direction of travel is based on the desire to escape.

When budgets permit, police agencies might do well to consider the increased use of helicopters in pursuit operations in areas where high-speed pursuits are frequent and necessary. Studies conducted in Baltimore, Maryland, and Miami-Dade County, Florida, indicate that helicopters can be particularly useful in police pursuits (Alpert, 1998). The helicopter aerial surveillance allows ground units to follow at a safe distance. Although not generally defined as an emergency or pursuit vehicle within the meaning of the law, the airborne unit can provide a perspective not possible on the ground. The helicopter can also assist ground units by serving as a platform from which to observe, track, and illuminate people or places on the ground.

Police officers in a pursuit driving situation must be aware of driving tactics that are inappropriate and may create tremendous risks to the officers and the public. Inappropriate tactics include driving against traffic on the opposite side of the roadway, passing other officers involved in the pursuit, caravanning or following with more than the authorized number of police vehicles, or slowing uninvolved traffic ahead of the pursuit. New laws are making drivers accountable as well. In June 2011, the U.S. Supreme Court ruled that fleeing from police in a vehicle can trigger a mandatory 15-year term in federal prison for repeat criminals (Savage, 2011).

Alternatives to lengthy high-speed pursuits include the use of **offensive intervention tactics** such as spike strips (tire deflation devices), road-blocks, ramming, and boxing in the suspect vehicle. Except for spike strips, the alternatives can be dangerous and require officers to receive specialized training. Shooting at a moving vehicle is never a good policy. Unless in a rural area, the danger to innocent people is great, and a wounded driver presents an even greater risk to public safety. Likewise, shooting out tires is a tactic best left to the movies. The centrifugal force of a rotating tire will most likely cause the bullet to ricochet, possibly resulting in injury or death to an innocent bystander. New technology may provide safer alternatives. For instance, some automobiles have built-in technology enabling an outside operator to send a signal to the vehicle, restricting its fuel flow to slow its speed (Copeland, 2008).

CASE STUDY—ERRORS CAUSE DEATH OF INNOCENT MAN

In San Jose, California, on February 17, 2004, Rodolfo Cardenas was misidentified by state Bureau of Narcotic Enforcement agents as fugitive David Gonzales. Gonzales was being sought on a parole violation stemming from illegal drug activity. In a vehicle pursuit, agents chased Cardenas, misidentified as Gonzales, after they saw him drive away from a garage where an informant told agents that fugitive Gonzales was located. During the pursuit, one of the agents shot Cardenas in the back. Subsequently, a Santa Clara County grand jury indicted the agent for shooting Cardenas.

Due to a dispatcher error during the incident, Cardenas lay bleeding and handcuffed without medical care for 12 minutes after police on the scene secured and opened the area so paramedics could treat him. According to audio recordings of the dispatcher–police communications, an officer told the dispatcher that the shooting scene was secure. However, the dispatcher, who was handling numerous calls simultaneously, failed to translate the information, which was communicated to the dispatcher in a police 10-code message, for fire department emergency medical personnel.

1. Based on the facts presented, was a vehicle pursuit justified?
2. Was the force used necessary?
3. How can similar communication difficulties be prevented?

ADMINISTRATIVE DUTIES

As has been discussed, most police work does not involve criminal law enforcement and hot pursuits. Many of a police officer's responsibilities involve **administrative duties** and public relations. The following is a partial list of such duties that a uniformed patrol officer might be expected to perform:

- Receive incoming calls from the public.
- Explain laws and procedures to the public.
- Participate in meetings with other officers (i.e., departmental staff meetings).
- Communicate information on an informal basis to other law enforcement personnel.
- Attend in-service and outside training, conferences, or seminars.
- Gather and maintain information on bonding agencies.
- Retrieve documents from records systems.
- Prepare documents for filing (e.g., label, alphabetize, place in chronological order, etc.).
- Personally file documents in records systems (i.e., fingerprint cards, correspondence, criminal reports, vehicle reports).
- Develop or revise agency forms.
- Maintain department records of warrants served.
- Maintain personal notes for future reference.
- Maintain inventory lists (i.e., departmental equipment and property).
- Maintain inventory lists (i.e., personal or departmental).
- Request equipment repair (i.e., personal or departmental).
- Photograph individuals for identification purposes (ID photos).
- Fingerprint persons for noncriminal reasons.
- Express disapproval to a fellow officer regarding the officer's misconduct.
- Take action to prevent misconduct or criminal behavior by another officer.
- Report inappropriate or illegal conduct by another officer to a supervisor (California Commission on Peace Officer Standards and Training, 1998).

THE POLICE AND THE NEWS MEDIA

The police and the news media are often viewed as two enduring adversaries. The police criticize the media for reporting police corruption and brutality as front-page news. The media criticize the police for being insensitive. The law enforcement community is well advised to accept the fact that police data and operations are news. Crime statistics, officer-involved shootings, and high-speed pursuits always make the evening news. One often hears the phrase, "If it bleeds, it leads" (*Measuring What Matters*, 1997).

The police want favorable press, that is, accounts of officer bravery and low-crime rates. However, because **police–media relations** are strained in many jurisdictions, the adversarial nature of the relationship may lead the press to report unfavorable news about the police. If police officers and agencies wish to receive more favorable press coverage, they should promote a relationship based on trust and inclusiveness. When appropriate, the media should be included in background briefings, and the police should share information that demonstrates how the law enforcement agency sets and meets goals in support of the agency's mission and the community's vision for the future. The police will never be able to control the media. On the contrary, it should not. A free and open press is absolutely vital in a democracy. However, through good relations, the police may be able to positively influence the thinking of those who report the news.

Reporters' jobs are to get and tell a story. They look for conflict, changes, and information of interest to the public. The police should develop a close working relationship with the press before a crisis occurs. Every police agency should have a designated public information officer to act as a liaison between the media and the agency. Honesty and openness is the best policy. It is better for the agency to release bad news about itself first. Officers must avoid confrontations with the media, admit problems and mistakes, and avoid police jargon, officious speech, and off-the-record statements. Responding to a reporter with "No comment" raises a red flag. Reporters generally assume the officer or agency is hiding something. It is better to respond with, "Due to its status as an open investigation, it is not appropriate to comment at this time" (Otto, 2000).

QUESTIONING TRADITIONAL PATROL OPERATIONS

Over the past 30 years, several studies have questioned the effectiveness of some police strategies and tactics. These studies focused on the effectiveness of preventive patrol, officer safety and productivity, handling domestic disturbances, the role of the uniformed officer in investigations, citizens' fear of crime, and rapid response to calls for service. The purpose of these studies was to determine if some traditional police strategies were achieving desired results.

The reader is cautioned that the studies cited here are not presented as evidence to support drastic modifications in police tactics. Rather, a discussion of the studies' findings is suggested as a means to promote a critical review of police operations and the development of appropriate new patrol strategies.

Preventive Patrol

One study focused on the effectiveness of **preventive patrol.** It was conducted by the Police Foundation in Kansas City, Missouri, from 1972 to 1973. Commonly referred to as the Kansas City Preventive Patrol Experiment, the results of the study were published in 1974. During the study, 15 beats were designated to receive one of three levels of patrol activity.

In some areas, visible patrol was increased and the district was saturated with patrol cars in a proactive attempt to maintain high visibility. In other areas, visible patrol activity was decreased and patrol cars entered the area only when there was a call for service. Patrol activity remained unchanged in some other districts.

The results of the study indicated that there is little appreciable difference in crime rates between areas that are patrolled heavily and those that are not. (Kelling, 1974; Walker, 1999). Most police activity is citizen initiated. Rarely does a police officer on patrol see a crime in progress. The results implied that considerable cost savings could be realized, without a commensurate increase in crime, if random preventive patrol was replaced with well planned, selective patrol in high-crime areas. In addition, studies conducted by M. K. Sparrow and others indicate that up to 80 percent of a patrol officer's time is uncommitted and 95 percent of dispatched calls may not require immediate response (Sparrow, Moore, & Kennedy, 1990). Therefore, random preventive patrol may be very expensive when compared to its effectiveness.

Some critics suggest that the results of the Kansas City study have been oversimplified. Indeed, the authors of the study did not intend to diminish the value of police patrol, and they cautioned readers not to conclude that the study results indicated preventive patrol has no value.

However, the experiment did have its flaws. For example, only 15 (22 percent) of the Kansas City Police Department's 69 beats and only 10 percent of its coverage areas were included in the study. In addition, the study focused solely on the preventive patrol function, leaving other police services unaffected by the study. Further, reactive-only beats shared common boundaries with proactive beats, guaranteeing available police resources to respond to calls for police service in any area (Manus, 2000).

Officer Safety and Productivity

Single-officer units may be safer and more productive than multiple-officer units. Except where immediate backup is often necessary, officers may be safer, more productive, and more cost effective if assigned to single-officer units. Officers are less careless, more attentive, and communicate more with citizens when working alone. Studies conducted in San Diego and Baltimore County, Maryland, also indicated that single-officer units receive fewer citizen complaints, are less likely to be assaulted, and experience fewer resisting-arrest situations. In the San Diego study, researchers discovered that 18 single-officer units could be placed in service for about the same amount of money as 10 multiple-officer units (Boydstun, 1977).

Learn more about studies of policing through the Police Foundation at www .policefoundation.org.

Domestic Disturbances

The results of a study indicated that arresting, rather than counseling, perpetrators of domestic violence may be more effective in reducing the likelihood of repeat offenses. The study was conducted in Minneapolis, Minnesota, from 1981 to 1982. It indicated that repeat domestic violence occurs 24 percent of the time when the offender is sent away for 24 hours, 19 percent when the offender is counseled, and only 10 percent of the time when the offender is arrested and spends a night in jail (Sherman & Berk, 1984).

Role of Uniformed Police in Follow-Up Investigations

In a study published in 1977, the Rand Corporation concluded that detective units solve only a small number of crimes by themselves. Most information used by detective units is acquired initially by uniformed officers during field interviews and communicated to the detectives. If uniformed police officers carefully gather information after the commission of a crime, communicate it to detectives, and the detectives actually use the information then detective productivity increases. Consequently, the results of the study indicated that uniform patrol officers should become more actively involved in the follow-up on criminal investigations (Greenwood, 1979).

Reducing Fear of Crime

Although the crime rate decreased dramatically throughout the 1990s, the citizens' fear of crime remained high (Maguire & Pastore, 1998). A study focusing on fear of crime determined that police methods, such as community policing, that increase the quantity and improve the quality of police–citizen interaction also reduce citizens' fear of crime. Reducing fear of crime results in more citizens on the street, which ultimately leads to prevention of additional crime (Wycoff & Skogan, 1994). A study conducted in Newark, New Jersey, in the late 1970s concluded that foot patrol may not necessarily reduce crime, but it does reduce the citizens' fear of crime and increases police officer satisfaction and morale (The Police Foundation, 1981).

Rapid Response

Police strategy throughout the latter part of the twentieth century focused on rapid response to crime reports under the theory that offenders may be apprehended more readily. However, most crimes are discovered after the fact. Furthermore, victims and witnesses often delay reporting crimes in progress (Petersilia, 1989). Therefore, rapid response may not result in an increase in the number of apprehensions. In nonemergency situations, citizens appear to be satisfied with alternatives (i.e., telephone counseling, delayed response) to rapid response (California Commission on Peace Officer Standards & Training, 2012; Hale, 2004; McEwen, 1984; Miller, 2000; Payton & Amaral, 2004).

SUMMARY

Most police officers are deployed in the field, working in uniform. Types of police patrols include foot, vehicular, bicycle, mounted horse, motorcycle, airborne, marine, K-9, and the use of closed-circuit television and cameras. The police equipment list may include more than 100 items. Officers should operate a patrol vehicle consistent with personal and public safety. Patrol activity should be random, utilizing keen observation and perception skills as well as the use of field interviews to obtain information. Traffic management involves enforcement of the motor vehicle code and response to collision scenes. While on patrol, police officers are involved in pedestrian stops, foot pursuits, high- and low-risk vehicle stops, and high-speed driving and pursuits. Officers should follow the proper procedures when involved in these activities. Administrative duties and contact with the news media are also part of a patrol officer's activities. Studies of the effectiveness of police operations can lead to improvements to patrol strategy and tactics.

DISCUSSION QUESTIONS AND EXERCISES

1. Are general patrol operations synonymous with "routine" calls for service? Explain.
2. What survival tactics should an officer use when conducting a field interview?
3. Traffic management is often a very large part of a patrol officer's workload. Identify at least three types of traffic situations that an officer may encounter and describe the procedure for handling each.
4. Outline and discuss the steps for pedestrian and vehicle stops.
5. What is the vehicle pursuit policy in your jurisdiction? Under what circumstances should a pursuit be terminated?
6. Police pursuits can lead to increased adrenaline flow, poor judgment, and errors in communication. How can police pursuit outcomes be improved?
7. Should police operations, strategies, and tactics be questioned? If so, by whom? For what purpose?
8. How can the police maintain a good relationship with the news media?
9. What community policing strategies or tactics are applicable to general police patrol operations?

Legal Aspects of Policing

LEARNING OBJECTIVES

After completing this chapter, the reader should be able to:

- explain the relevance of the Bill of Rights to law enforcement and criminal justice practices.
- list and describe types of evidence.
- list and describe rules of evidence as they pertain to search and seizure, interrogation, and custody.
- articulate the proper procedure for collecting, transporting, storing, retrieving, and presenting types of evidence.
- analyze evidentiary case situations and determine if proper procedure was followed.
- analyze case situations and determine legal courses of action.
- identify and describe the general constitutional principles relevant to public safety.
- differentiate between testimonial privileges and privileged communications.
- define hearsay and demonstrate knowledge of exceptions to the hearsay rule.
- describe methods for the identification of suspects by witnesses and victims.
- articulate conditions under which the *Miranda* rights advisory is required.

KEY TERMS

Define, describe, or explain the importance of each of the following.

Administrative search
Admission
Attenuation doctrine
Authentication
Bill of attainder
Bill of Rights
Burden of proof
Chain of custody
Circumstantial evidence
Confession

Consciousness of guilt evidence
Consent search
Contraband
Demonstrative evidence
Detention
Direct evidence
Doctrine of selective incorporation
Documentary evidence
Evidence
Exclusionary rule

Exigent circumstance

Expert witness

Ex post facto law

Frisk

Fruits of the crime

Hearsay

Hearsay evidence

Impeachment of a witness

Inference

In-field show-up

Instrumentality of a crime

Judicial notice

Miranda rule

Ordinary witness

Parole search

Photographic lineup

Physical evidence

Physical lineup

Plain-view doctrine

Presumption

Privileged communications

Probable cause

Probation search

Proof

Relevant evidence

Search

Search warrant

Seizure

Stipulation

Subpoena

Testimonial evidence

Testimonial privilege

Trier of fact

USA PATRIOT Act of 2001

Victim Bill of Rights

Voir dire examination

Warren Court

Writ of *habeas corpus*

INTRODUCTION

Evidence is any information people use to make a decision. In a judicial proceeding, evidence is used by the **trier of fact** (jury or judge, if a non-jury trial) to make decisions in a criminal or civil case. It is imperative that criminal justice practitioners be knowledgeable about the rules of evidence and search and seizure. These rules guide law enforcement personnel, attorneys, judges, and others in the collection, preservation, and transport of evidence as well as the conduct of a judicial proceeding. Criminal cases are sometimes dismissed or reversed on appeal because of violations of evidentiary and procedural rules on the part of the law enforcement community or prosecutorial staff.

Evidence consists of testimony, writings, material objects, and other items presented to a legal tribunal as proof of the existence or nonexistence of a fact. The rules of evidence govern its admissibility in judicial proceedings. **Proof** is the establishment by evidence of a requisite degree of belief concerning a fact in the minds of the judge or jurors. Proof is the desired result of evidence. The **burden of proof** is the obligation to produce evidence sufficient to prove a fact or set of facts.

Evidence is used by attorneys and is offered in court as an item of proof to establish a fact, to impeach (discredit) a witness, to rehabilitate (support) a witness, and to assist in determining an appropriate sentence (i.e., aggravating or mitigating circumstances for determinate sentences, proving no probation offense elements, and special circumstances in death penalty cases). Evidence must be relevant, competently presented, and legally obtained. The rules of evidence are often described as the rules of exclusion because their language suggests what evidence cannot be used because its use would violate a statutory or constitutional safeguard.

Sources of evidence law include state and federal evidence statutory provisions regarding witness competency, introduction of writings, privileged communications, and hearsay evidence. Sources also include criminal law provisions regarding accomplice testimony, invasion of privacy, and wiretapping; the U.S. Constitution; state constitutions; and case law regarding search and seizure, *Miranda* issues, and interpretations of evidence-related statutes.

CASE STUDY—THE USA PATRIOT ACT

In response to the 9/11 attacks, Congress amended portions of Title 18 of the United States Code by enacting the **USA PATRIOT Act of 2001.** Officially known as the Uniting and Strengthening America by Providing Appropriate Tools Required to Intercept and Obstruct Terrorism Act of 2001, the law dramatically increases the criminal investigative authority of local, county, state, and federal law enforcement agencies. The act strengthens law enforcement's ability to jail suspects, broadens search and seizure authority, enhances the power of prosecutors, promotes the sharing of intelligence, and provides for more restrictive border security. The act allows certain types of searches without prior notice or the presence of the suspect, and it increases federal authority to tap phones and monitor e-mail and Internet communications (U.S. Congress, 2001). The act's domestic terrorism provision allows surveillance of controversial activist groups. To protect uninvolved Muslim Americans and persons of Arab descent from victimization, the act also criminalizes attacks on law-abiding Muslims and those of Arab ancestry living in the United States.

In 2003, the U.S. Senate voted to retain the USA PATRIOT Act's 2005 sunset provision and passed a limited version of the act. Many lawmakers expressed concern that the 2001 law jeopardized civil liberties. The most often criticized provisions of the act are viewed as violations of the Fourth Amendment's protection against unreasonable searches and seizures. The act expands law enforcement's warrantless search authority and effectively removes judicial oversight from the search warrant application process by granting. Perhaps reflecting this possibility, in May 2011, Congress voted to extend three about-to-expire provisions of the USA PATRIOT Act that allow for roving wiretaps, court-ordered searches of certain business records, and tracking of "lone wolf" terrorism suspects (Urban, 2011) prosecutors the authority to certify (approve) search warrants.

In May 2011, Congress voted to extend three soon-to-expire provisions of the USA PATRIOT Act that allow for roving wiretaps, court-ordered searches of certain business records, and tracking of "lone wolf" terrorism suspects (Urban, 2011).

1. Does Congress have the authority to expand the investigative powers of law enforcement?

2. Is societal protection against terrorism more important than protection of individual rights and liberties?

THE BILL OF RIGHTS

In totalitarian societies, individual rights are severely limited, sometimes nonexistent. In democratic societies such as the United States, however, specified rights are viewed as necessary to protect individuals from governmental abuse. Therefore, when enforcing criminal law, the police must conform their behavior to the standards established in the Constitution. As interpreted by the U.S. Supreme Court, the rights enumerated in the Constitution are designed to restrict the scope and dimension of police power (Barkan & Bryjak, 2004).

The original U.S. Constitution was drafted at the Constitutional Convention in 1787 and it became effective in 1789. However, the Constitution expressly provided for only a few procedural safeguards: those related to *habeas corpus*, bills of attainder, *ex post facto* laws, and trial by jury. A **writ of *habeas corpus*** is a judicial order commanding a warden or jailer to bring an incarcerated person before the court to explain why the person is being held. A **bill of attainder** is a law that targets persons for punishment without the benefit of a trial. An ***ex post facto* law** operates retroactively and criminalizes behavior that took place before the law became effective. According to the U. S. Constitution, *habeas corpus* cannot be suspended and bills of attainder and *ex post facto* laws cannot be imposed.

The need for an expanded list of individual rights, expressed in writing, led the first U. S. Congress to draft the first 10 amendments (additions/changes) to the Constitution. Commonly referred to as the **Bill of Rights,** they were ratified by the states on December 15, 1791. These first 10 amendments, their limitations, and their relevance to public law enforcement are as follows.

Amendment I

> *Congress shall make no law respecting an establishment of religion, or prohibiting the free exercise thereof; or abridging the freedom of speech, or of the press; or the right of the people peaceably to assemble, and to petition the government for a redress of grievances.*

Freedom of religion refers to the right to worship as one chooses. The First Amendment also protects verbal, written, and symbolic speech. However, the U.S. Supreme Court has determined that "fighting words" and expressions that present a "clear and present danger" to public safety are not protected. Unprotected speech also includes defamatory language, obscenity, and child pornography. Reasonable restrictions, to ensure public safety, may be imposed on the freedom to peaceably assemble. Freedom of petition refers to a citizen's right to communicate with elected representatives.

Amendment II

> *A well regulated Militia, being necessary to the security of a free State, the right of the people to keep and bear Arms, shall not be infringed.*

According to the U.S. Supreme Court, an individual's right to keep and bear arms is limited to possession as it relates to a state's right to maintain a well regulated militia.

Amendment III

> *No Soldier shall, in time of peace be quartered in any house, without the consent of the Owner, nor in time of war, but in a manner to be prescribed by law.*

Amendment III severely restricts the government's ability to use private homes for military personnel lodging.

Amendment IV

> *The right of the people to be secure in their persons, houses, papers, and effects, against unreasonable searches and seizures, shall not be violated, and no Warrants shall issue, but upon probable cause, supported by Oath or affirmation, and particularly describing the place to be searched, and the persons or things to be seized.*

The Fourth Amendment protects individuals from unreasonable searches and seizures by government officials. Probable cause is required for the issuance of a search warrant. Warrantless searches are unconstitutional, subject to the limited exceptions discussed later in this chapter.

Amendment V

> *No person shall be held to answer for a capital, or otherwise infamous crime, unless on a presentment or indictment of a Grand Jury, except in cases arising in the land or naval forces, or in the Militia, when in actual service in time of War or public danger; nor shall any person be subject for the same offence to be twice put in jeopardy of life or limb; nor shall be compelled in any criminal case to be a witness against himself, nor be deprived of life, liberty, or property, without due process of law; nor shall private property be taken for public use, without just compensation.*

The Fifth Amendment guarantees due process and indictment through a grand jury, protects against double jeopardy, and contains the privilege to be free from self-incrimination.

Amendment VI

> *In all criminal prosecutions, the accused shall enjoy the right to a speedy and public trial, by an impartial jury of the State and district wherein the crime shall have been committed, which district shall have been previously ascertained by law, and to be informed of the nature and cause of the accusation; to be confronted with the witnesses against him; to have compulsory process for obtaining witnesses in his favor, and to have the Assistance of Counsel for his defence.*

The Sixth Amendment guarantees speedy, public trials, by an impartial jury, the right to confront accusers and obtain witnesses in one's favor, and the right to assistance of counsel in criminal cases.

Amendment VII

> *In suits at common law, where the value in controversy shall exceed twenty dollars, the right of trial by jury shall be preserved, and no fact tried by a jury, shall be otherwise re-examined in any court of the United States, than according to the rules of the common law.*

Traditionally, the U.S. Supreme Court has treated the Seventh Amendment as preserving the right of trial by jury in civil cases.

Amendment VIII

Excessive bail shall not be required, nor excessive fines imposed, nor cruel and unusual punishments inflicted.

The Eighth Amendment forbids excessive bail and fines as well as cruel and unusual punishments.

Amendment IX

The enumeration in the Constitution, of certain rights, shall not be construed to deny or disparage others retained by the people.

The government has no power to infringe upon the rights of people simply because the rights are not expressed in the U.S. Constitution. Thus, the right to privacy is guaranteed by the Constitution.

Amendment X

The powers not delegated to the United States by the Constitution, nor prohibited by it to the States, are reserved to the States respectively, or to the people.

Powers not granted to the national (federal) government by the Constitution are reserved to the states. Thus, general police powers reside with the states and the administration of justice is, primarily, a state function.

Most of the case law associated with the rules of evidence focuses on the application of certain amendments from the Bill of Rights and the Fourteenth Amendment to criminal procedure. The most important constitutional limitations on the administration of justice are embodied in the Bill of Rights. Before all the states ratified the Constitution, many citizens of the new country wanted some written assurances that the new central government would not infringe on the rights of individuals as did the king of England. Thus, these rights were added to the Constitution.

The rules of evidence guide law enforcement personnel. *(Photo courtesy of the San Diego Police Department.)*

Learn more about major court decisions that affect law enforcement and the administration of justice through the U.S. Supreme Court's website at www.supremecourtus.gov.

Their original intent and impact was to restrict national law enforcement activities.

The ratification of the Fourteenth Amendment in 1868 provided justification for expanding the scope of the Bill of Rights to the states. Section 1 of the amendment prohibits states from depriving "any person of life, liberty, or property, without due process of law." Subsequently, through the self-imposed **doctrine of selective incorporation** the U.S. Supreme Court used the due process clause of the Fourteenth Amendment to incorporate, on a selective basis, procedural protections of the first 10 amendments (Bill of Rights) into the restrictions placed on state criminal prosecutions. As a result, case law relative to provisions of the Fourth, Fifth, Sixth, and Eighth Amendments, in particular, has had a significant impact on the administration of justice at the state level.

Extensive use of the Court's doctrine of selective incorporation did not begin with the Fourteenth Amendment's passage in 1868. Rather, it gained prominence during the **Warren Court** years of the 1960s, when Earl Warren was Chief Justice of the U. S. Supreme Court. By the end of the 1970s, most of the protections in the Bill of Rights were applied to every governmental branch in all states (Territo, Halsted, & Bromley, 2004).

Statutory and constitutional initiatives in some states have modified judicial procedures and rules of evidence. For example, California voters' passage of a **Victim Bill of Rights** (Proposition 8) in 1982 and the Crime Victim's Justice Reform Act (Proposition 115) in 1990 greatly affected the judicial process. Proposition 8 mandated punishment and public safety, rather than rehabilitation, as the primary purposes of sentencing. Proposition 115 allows prosecutors to introduce hearsay evidence in preliminary hearings. The law also eliminated the requirement for a postindictment preliminary hearing if the defendant waives the hearing initially. Proposition 115 also forbids plea bargaining for certain crimes, requires reciprocal discovery, and places control of jury selection (voir dire proceedings) in the hands of the trial judge.

TYPES OF EVIDENCE

Evidence generally falls into four major categories: testimonial, documentary, physical (real), and demonstrative. Although all forms of evidence can be assigned to one of the four major categories, classifications of evidence are often expanded to include the following types.

- **Testimonial evidence** (Testimony)—Testimony is given by a witness, including an eyewitness to an event, a victim, or suspect who has knowledge of the issues being tried in a case.

- **Documentary evidence**—This type of evidence includes any documented or tangible form of communication offered as evidence in court. Examples of writings include notes, diaries, journals, ledgers, computer-generated data, photographs, audio tapes, and video tapes.
- **Physical evidence** (material objects)—Examples of physical evidence include fruits (proceeds) of the crime, instrumentalities (tools) of a crime, contraband (items that are illegal to possess), and other physical evidence that establishes the identity of the perpetrator.
- **Demonstrative evidence**—Examples of demonstrative evidence include objects and materials such as maps, models, charts, diagrams, displays, and computer simulations that are meant to portray or enhance the meaning of evidence presented to the judge or jury.
- **Relevant evidence**—Evidence that has any tendency to prove or disprove a disputed fact in a case is relevant evidence. Common examples of relevant evidence include motive for the crime, capacity to commit a crime, opportunity to commit the crime, prior threats or expressions of ill will by the accused, possession of writings or physical evidence linking a suspect to the crime, physical evidence linking a suspect to the crime scene, consciousness of guilt or admission by conduct evidence, evidence affecting the credibility of a witness, and modus operandi (method of operation) evidence.
- **Admissions** and **confessions**—An admission is a statement by a suspect acknowledging some fact relevant to a case. A confession is a statement by a suspect admitting liability for a crime. It is a full acknowledgment of all elements of an offense, and it negates any defenses. Both are inculpatory and tend to establish the guilt of the accused.
- **Hearsay evidence**—This type of evidence includes any out-of-court statement, presented in court by someone other than the original declarant, that is offered to prove the truth of the matter stated in court. Hearsay evidence is inadmissible subject to certain exceptions discussed later in this chapter.
- **Consciousness of guilt evidence**—This type of evidence includes conduct by the accused from which an inference of guilt or an admission can be drawn. Examples include running from the crime scene, assaulting an officer, threatening a witness, giving false information, attempting to destroy or conceal evidence, or refusing to provide personal physical evidence.

WAYS OF PRESENTING EVIDENCE

Evidence is presented in court by utilizing the following mechanisms:

- **Direct evidence**—Evidence that directly proves a fact without drawing inferences from other facts is direct evidence. If a witness testifies that the defendant actions were observed by the witness, the testimony is direct evidence of the defendant's guilt.
- **Circumstantial evidence**—Circumstantial evidence proves a fact through inference or logical association with another fact. For exam-

ple, if a defendant's latent fingerprints are recovered at a crime scene, it can be inferred that the defendant was present at the scene at some time.

- **Presumption**—A presumption is an assumption that the law requires to be made from another fact or group of facts. There are two types of presumptions: rebuttable and conclusive. A rebuttable presumption can be refuted; a conclusive presumption cannot. An example of a rebuttable presumption includes the assumption that a child between the ages of 7 and 14 is not capable of forming criminal intent unless it can be proven otherwise. Another example includes the basic assumption that a person is presumed innocent until proven guilty. A conclusive presumption cannot be refuted or rebutted. For example, a child under the age of 7 is conclusively presumed to be incapable of forming the criminal intent necessary for criminal liability.

- **Inference**—An inference is a deduction of fact that can be logically and reasonably drawn from a fact or group of facts.

- **Judicial notice**—Judicial notice involves matters of common knowledge or facts of law that are universally known, easily referenced, and not subject to debate or dispute. This information can be presented as evidence without adversarial argument. In other words, the court (judge) takes note of certain facts of common knowledge. Examples of judicial notice include courses of nature, scientific principles, meanings of words and phrases, geographic and historical facts, legal procedures, and governmental reports.

- **Stipulation**—A stipulation is an agreement between opposing parties that a fact can be offered into evidence without adversarial argument (Nemeth, 2010; Rutledge, 2000).

WITNESS TESTIMONY

Types of witnesses in a judicial proceeding include lay and expert witnesses. A lay witness is an **ordinary witness,** including most police officers, who can provide information concerning the issues being tried in a criminal case. As a general rule, a lay witness is only permitted to testify as to what the witness knows as fact (what is actually seen, heard, or otherwise perceived with the senses), and is not permitted to formulate and express an opinion or conclusion in conjunction with testimony. However, a lay witness is allowed to present an opinion in court when an event is based on the personal knowledge of the witness and the opinion would be helpful to the clear understanding of the witness's testimony. Common areas of opinion evidence by a lay witness include state of emotion; appearance and demeanor (intoxication/injuries); speed, distance, measurement, value, and other quantifiable areas; identity and physical characteristics; and physical properties of substances such as blood and narcotics.

An **expert witness** possesses some special knowledge, skill, experience, training, or education beyond that of the average juror and relevant to the matters being tried in a case. An expert witness is permitted to give a personal opinion or conclusion in conjunction with testimony. The qualifications of an expert witness are determined by the judge. Examples of expert testimony in criminal trials include that which is presented by medical, forensic, psychiatric, and police experts.

A **subpoena** (also spelled subpena) is a written order commanding the presence of a witness in court for the purpose of giving testimony. A subpoena *duces tecum* commands the witness to bring writings or material objects to court. A person can be held in contempt of court for refusing to comply with a subpoena (California State, 2012). A subpoena in a criminal case can be issued by a judge, court clerk, defense attorney, district attorney, public defender, or any of the attorneys, investigators.

WITNESS COMPETENCY AND CREDIBILITY

A competent witness is one who is properly qualified to give testimony in court. All witnesses, regardless of age, are presumed competent to testify. The burden of proof falls to the side that opposes the witness in court to prove incompetency of the opposition's witness. The question of competency is decided during a **voir dire** (to speak the truth) **examination.** A witness can be disqualified from testifying if the witness is unable to observe, perceive, recall, narrate, or understand the duty to tell the truth. Examples of potentially incompetent witnesses include young children, developmentally disabled persons, physically handicapped persons, and foreign-language-speaking persons. Credibility is the believability or weight given to a witness's testimony by the judge or jury.

Impeachment involves an attack on the credibility of a witness or lessens the weight of that witness's testimony in the mind of the trier of fact. Impeachment is a hopeful outcome of cross- or recross-examination. Common impeachment areas include physical or mental state of the witness; bias, interest, or other motive in the case; a witness's general reputation for untruthfulness or dishonesty; a prior felony conviction; or inconsistencies and manner of one's testimony. Rehabilitation of a witness tends to bolster or lend support to the credibility of a witness. Rehabilitation is a hopeful outcome of redirect examination.

DOCUMENTARY EVIDENCE

Documentary evidence is authenticated when a witness testifies to the method or mode of authorship and preparation. The best documentary evidence is an original. Secondary evidence is a copy of the writing offered in lieu of the original. In some states, a copy is admissible to the same extent as an original writing unless there is a question as to the authenticity of the duplicate, or if the admission of the duplicate would be prejudicial.

Photographs of a gruesome, bloody, shocking, or lewd nature are subject to a balancing test by the courts. The judge balances the relevancy of the photographs against their potential prejudicial effect on the defendant. If the judge rules the photographs would so inflame the jury that they would be prejudicial, the photographs will be excluded. If the judge rules the probative value (the relative weight of the evidence) of the photographs outweighs the prejudice, then the photographs are admissible.

PHYSICAL EVIDENCE

Examples of Physical Evidence

Physical (real) evidence refers to material objects offered as evidence. Examples of **physical evidence** include:

- **Fruits of the crime**—These are objects acquired as a result of criminal acts (i.e., property taken in a theft, burglary, or robbery).
- **Instrumentalities of a crime**—These are objects used by the perpetrator to commit the crime (i.e., crowbar in a burglary, gun in a murder, knife in an assault with a deadly weapon, scales and packaging materials in a narcotics sales case).
- **Contraband**—These are objects that are prohibited by law and therefore illegal to possess (i.e., narcotics, certain weapons, child pornography).
- **Other physical evidence**—This includes an entire range of trace, perishable, or personal identification evidence that has comparable individual identifying or class characteristics. Examples of this type of physical evidence include fingerprints, blood and biological fluids, bullets, hair, fibers, and other trace evidence. The defense in the highly publicized 1995 double murder trial of O. J. Simpson focused on faulty evidence collection and sloppy crime laboratory procedures. Since the Simpson trial, significant improvements have been made at forensic laboratories and accreditation standards have been developed for such facilities.

Introduction of Physical Evidence

There are several rules concerning the introduction of material objects. These rules include:

- **Authentication**—A material object is authenticated when the finder testifies to the manner or circumstances under which the evidence was discovered.
- **Chain of custody**—It is necessary to maintain a record of where evidence was stored and the persons who handled the evidence from the point of collection until the time the evidence is presented in court. The purpose is to maintain the integrity of the evidence and to counter allegations that the evidence may have been substituted or altered.

- **Legal duty to collect/preserve evidence**—There is no due process duty placed on the police to collect or preserve physical evidence for the defendant. A defendant cannot have a case dismissed solely on the grounds that authorities failed to collect or preserve possible exculpatory evidence at a crime scene. However, a defendant could attempt to impeach the quality or completeness of an investigation by showing that the police were negligent and failed to follow proper procedures. Also, the defendant could attempt to raise a reasonable doubt as to guilt by showing that if the evidence had been collected, it would have pointed to another suspect. As such, the collection and the preservation of evidence are always professional obligations and at times essential to the prosecution in proving criminal guilt.

TESTIMONIAL PRIVILEGES AND PRIVILEGED COMMUNICATIONS

Testimonial Privileges

A privilege is a constitutional or statutory provision that a witness can use to refuse to testify in court. Even though a witness may possess personal knowledge of the facts being tried in the case, if a privilege exists, the witness may refuse to testify and not be found in contempt of court. There are two types of privileges: testimonial and confidential communications. **Testimonial privileges** include:

- **Privilege against self-incrimination**—Witnesses may refuse to testify if the information provided would tend to show that they are guilty of a crime. Likewise, a criminal defendant cannot be compelled to take the witness stand and testify and can legally refuse to disclose information that may tend to self-incriminate. However, if a defendant takes the witness stand and testifies, the privilege is waived and the defendant can be cross-examined about any matter brought out during direct examination. Also, this privilege does not apply to the collection of personal identification and physical evidence during a criminal investigation because such evidence is non-testimonial (nonverbal) in nature.
- **Husband–wife testimonial privilege**—In most states, one spouse can refuse to be a witness against the other spouse during the course of a legal marriage. The testimonial privilege applies to observations, conversations, and incriminating evidence that a witness-spouse finds. Only the witness-spouse can claim this privilege. The defendant-spouse has no blocking power. The testimonial privilege is void when a crime is committed against the witness-spouse, family members, or other member of the household. If the marriage ends through divorce or annulment, the testimonial privilege ends because there is no longer a relationship to protect. The former spouse must then testify if subpoenaed. Approximately one-fifth of the states have abolished this privilege.

- **Officer–informant privilege**—Granted in a few states, this privilege provides that, unless disclosure is necessary for a defendant's fair trial, a police officer has the testimonial privilege to refuse to disclose the identity of an informant who provided official information during the course and scope of the officer's duties. However, if this informant is a material witness on the issue of innocence or guilt of the accused, the defense is entitled to the informant's name and location. If an officer still claims privilege, the officer cannot be held in contempt of court, but the defendant is entitled to case dismissal on due process grounds. The potential materiality of an informant is determined by the judge during an in camera (in chambers) hearing.
- **Journalist's privilege**—In some states, a journalist has the testimonial privilege to refuse to disclose the source of news information. This privilege does not apply to the actual witnessing of a criminal event. A news reporter or news organization has the privilege to refuse to disclose any unpublished information not released to the general public via the electronic or print media. This privilege does not apply to published information. Almost one-half of all states have adopted some form of news reporter–source privilege.

Confidential Communications Privileges

Privileged communications exist to protect certain relationships. These privileges include:

- **Husband–wife confidential communications privilege**—One spouse may refuse to disclose, and the other spouse can block the disclosure of, a confidential communication made during the course of a legal marriage. Both spouses may claim this privilege as long as the oral or written communication was made for a spouse's ears or eyes only. The confidential communications privilege is void when a crime is committed against the witness-spouse, family members, or other member of the household, or if the disclosure is made to another or in the known presence of a third party. The confidential communications privilege survives termination of the marriage.
- **Attorney–client privilege**—An attorney can refuse to disclose, or a client can block the disclosure of, a confidential communication between an attorney and the attorney's client. The privilege is meant to allow a free exchange between attorney and client without fear that these conversations will be disclosed later in court. This privilege does not apply to planning the commission of a crime in the future.
- **Clergy–penitent privilege**—A clergy member can refuse to disclose, or a penitent can block the disclosure of, a confidential penitential communication made between the two parties for the purpose of spiritual advice and absolution.
- **Physician–patient privilege**—A physician can refuse to disclose, or a patient can block the disclosure of, a confidential communication

made between the two parties for the purpose of medical diagnosis and treatment. However, the physician–patient privilege does not apply to criminal court testimony. Conversations about crime-related events void the privilege, and the physician must testify in court (California Commission on Peace Officer Standards and Training, 2012; Gardner & Anderson, 2009).

HEARSAY EVIDENCE

Hearsay is a statement made by someone other than the witness who is testifying in court, but is offered by the witness to prove the truth of the matter stated (Nemeth, 2010; Rutledge, 2000). Hearsay arises most often when a witness attempts to testify about a statement made by someone else outside of court. As a general rule, hearsay evidence is inadmissible unless the testimony falls within a recognized hearsay exception. Exceptions to the hearsay rule include:

- **Admissions and confessions**—Inculpatory (incriminating) statements by the accused are admissible when repeated by a police officer or private person as long as the statement was legally obtained. A statement that is adverse to one's own interest is presumed truthful and can be repeated by another.

- **Dying declarations**—A statement made by a dying person that relates to the cause and circumstances surrounding the person's death is admissible hearsay. The victim must be under an impending sense of death (i.e., lost hope of recovery), the statement must concern the victim's personal knowledge about the cause of death, and the victim must subsequently die. The law presumes a person nearing death would have no reason to lie and would want to expire with a clear conscience. Thus, a person would have no reason to be untruthful. If a victim survives, the statement may still be admissible under the spontaneous statement or prior statement of a witness exceptions to the hearsay rule.

- **Spontaneous statements**—A statement made under stress or excitement, close in time to a crime, and about what the declarant saw or otherwise perceived is admissible hearsay. A spontaneous statement can be offered by a police officer or private person receiving or overhearing the statement. Statements made under the stress and excitement of the event are considered trustworthy because the declarant has no time to fabricate or deliberate a falsehood. Thus, the statement reflects the declarant's true perceptions of the event. If there has been a substantial time lapse between the crime and the utterance, based on the totality of circumstances, the reliability of this statement can be challenged.

- **Business and official records**—Records and other writings kept in the normal course of business or government operations are presumed trustworthy. These records can be authenticated and interpreted by any person in the organization familiar with their preparation and content. It is not absolutely necessary to have the actual preparer of the original record testify in court. The records

Learn more about evidence-related court cases, statutes, codes, and government regulations through Westlaw's FindLaw website located at www.findlaw.com.

must be prepared in a standardized manner by a person who has personal knowledge of the event recorded, and the information must be recorded close in time to the incident or transaction recorded.

- **Prior statements of witnesses/past recollection recorded**—Once a witness testifies under oath and is subject to cross-examination, a prior statement made by that witness is admissible for the purposes of impeaching an inconsistent statement or rehabilitating an incomplete statement. Notes or recorded statements of the witness can be admitted for the same purposes.

- **Hearsay testimony at preliminary hearings**—Law enforcement officers with more than five years experience or those who have completed a related training course, are allowed to present hearsay evidence at preliminary hearings for the purpose of determining if the defendant committed a felony. The officer must have spoken personally with a victim, witness, investigator, or expert witness to offer this hearsay testimony. Subject to limited exceptions, totem pole (multiple-level) hearsay is not admissible (California Community Colleges, 2003, California Commission on Peace Officer Standards and Training, 2012).

SEARCH AND SEIZURE

Search and seizure law is very detailed and complex. The following discussion includes definitions of the various terms associated with search and seizure as well as an explanation of proper procedures for conducting legal searches.

Reasonable searches are permitted under the Fourth Amendment to the U.S. Constitution. One does not always need a search warrant to conduct a lawful search and seizure. In public law enforcement, a **search** involves a governmental intrusion into an area in which a person has a reasonable expectation of privacy. The purpose of a search is to discover evidence or contraband to be used in a criminal prosecution. A **seizure** occurs when a person's freedom of movement is restricted or when property is taken into custody by the government. A seizure involves meaningful governmental interference with a person's movement or property interest.

Probable cause involves facts that would lead a person of ordinary care and prudence to believe that there is a fair probability that evidence or contraband will be found in or at a particular location. An officer may seek a search warrant or conduct a warrantless vehicle search based on probable cause.

The *scope of a probable cause search* is limited by the circumstances under which the search is being conducted. The two elements for determining the legal scope of a search include first, what the officer is looking for (i.e., evidence, contraband, weapons, victims, or suspects), and second, where the officer is likely to find the items or people (i.e., reasonable chance for the officer to find the object or person in the area being searched). Evidence or contraband recovered outside the lawful scope of a search could be subject to suppression.

The **exclusionary rule** requires that any the evidence obtained by the government or its agents in violation of the Fourth Amendment be excluded at trial. The main purposes of the exclusionary rule are to deter misconduct by peace officers by eliminating the incentive for unconstitutional searches and prohibiting the admission of evidence that is obtained illegally, and to maintain the integrity of the judiciary by excluding tainted evidence from the trial. Not only is illegally seized evidence inadmissible in court, but any evidence that directly stems from this evidence is also inadmissible. The evidence that stems from the illegally seized evidence is excluded because it is the *fruit of the poisonous tree.*

There are several exceptions to the exclusionary rule and the fruit of the poisonous tree doctrine. If the same information is gained through a source independent of the illegal search, the information gained from the independent source may be admitted. Similarly, if the discovery of the illegally seized evidence was inevitable, in the absence of unconstitutional police conduct, the evidence is admissible. Further, through the **attenuation doctrine,** unconstitutional police conduct that taints evidence may be overcome if the tainted evidence is discovered in a manner unrelated to the police misconduct. Finally, the good faith exception allows the admission of evidence even if there is some technical defect in the process (i.e., a minor flaw in the search warrant), or if the police operated in good faith (i.e., the police had a reasonable belief that the search warrant was valid).

The **plain-view doctrine** holds that anything in plain view is not constitutionally protected. There are two elements to the plain-view doctrine. First, the officer must be in a legal position or have the authority to be where the observation is made. Second, the officer must have probable cause to believe the object or property observed constitutes evidence of a crime. A plain-view observation can serve as the basis for seizure of the evidence observed or can prompt a legal basis to search for more evidence or contraband. The plain view doctrine has been expanded to include sensory observations beyond those associated with visual recognition. Examples include plain feel (touch) and plain smell (of a distinctive odor).

A **detention** is a temporary stop of a subject for investigation and questioning to determine a person's involvement, if any, in criminal activity. Police officers are able to "seize" a person's freedom of movement based on reasonable suspicion of criminal activity, short of the reasonable cause needed for a custodial arrest. Detentions must be conducted lawfully, or any evidence or statements subsequently obtained will be inadmissible in court.

No one is permitted to detain at will. For a legal detention to occur, a police officer must have reasonable suspicion that a crime is about to take place, is taking place, or has taken place and that the person to be detained is connected with the suspected criminal activity. Reasonable suspicion is factually based on factors such as matching suspect description, matching vehicle description, subject is in the vicinity of a recent crime, known high-crime area, exhibition of symptoms of unlawful drug or alcohol consumption, method of criminal operation, flight or furtive movements, and past criminal history of the subject being detained. Police officers may not detain solely on the basis of an anonymous tip that the subject may possess a weapon. Officers may only detain a person for a period of time reasonably necessary to accomplish the purpose of the investigation.

A *consensual encounter* is any interaction between a police officer and nonsworn citizen that does not involve formal police restraint of the citizen's freedom of movement. A consensual encounter does not involve seizure of the person under the Fourth Amendment. During a consensual encounter, a person is under no obligation to cooperate with an officer or answer questions and is free to leave at any time. Actions permissible for an officer during a consensual encounter include walking up to a person or a parked vehicle and making inquiries about one's presence in an area; using a flashlight or spotlight for illumination; requesting, examining, and returning identification; and general follow-up conversation on a person's responses to the officer's questions. Actions that would convert a consensual encounter into a detention by exercising restraint over a person's freedom of movement include using a red light, directing or ordering a person to stop or remain, demanding identification, and retaining identification to conduct a warrants check. Many police officers refer to the consensual encounter as a *contact,* a reference that is erroneous. To the average juror, contact means touching. This misunderstanding could lead a juror to believe that the officer made physical contact with the subject.

A **frisk** is a cursory pat-down of a legally detained subject for the purpose of discovering deadly or dangerous weapons that could be used to assault a police officer or other person legally authorized to arrest. A frisk can be lawfully conducted when a person has been detained for a crime involving weapons, for instrumentalities that could be used as weapons, or for an offense that threatens violent conduct. The purpose of the frisk for weapons is to ensure police officer safety (*Terry v. Ohio,* 1968). A frisk may also be conducted during a contact or nonviolent detention with consent of the subject. The scope of a frisk is to find hard objects that could reasonably be defined as weapons. Hard objects can be retrieved, examined, and retained during the detention for officer safety. If the object is an instrumentality or contraband, probable cause for a police officer to arrest exists. The stop and frisk of a subject cannot be based solely on an anonymous tip that the subject may be carrying a weapon (Carelli, 2000).

A police officer may, *incidental or contemporaneous to a lawful custodial arrest,* search the person of the arrestee and the area within the arrestee's immediate control for any possible evidence, weapons, or contraband. This search includes pockets and containers in the possession of the arrestee. A private person making an arrest may conduct a similar search for weapons only.

When a person is arrested inside a residence or dwelling, a police officer may, incidental to that arrest, search the person of the arrestee and any area within the arrestee's immediate control. This would include cabinets, drawers, furniture, containers, and closets within leaping distance of the arrestee. Some general exceptions permit a police officer to extend beyond the arm's reach limitations after an arrest in a residence or dwelling. These exceptions include the plain-view, protective peek, pathway of suspect, protective sweep, and alternate search exceptions.

When a person is arrested inside or closely associated with a motor vehicle, a police officer may, search the passenger compartment of the vehicle only if it is reasonable to believe that the arrestee might access the vehicle at the time of the search or that the vehicle contains evidence of the offense for which the person was arrested (Arizona v. Gant, 2009). The passenger area is considered to be within arm's reach of the person arrested. If a police officer has probable cause to believe there is evidence or contraband in a vehicle that is mobile and accessible to the roadway, the police officer may conduct a warrantless search of that vehicle including all compartments and containers. This is referred to as the *fleeting targets exception to the search warrant requirement.*

Probable cause to search vehicles involves articulable facts that the objects of the search will be found inside the vehicle. The scope of this search is regulated by the size or nature of the evidence or contraband being sought. If probable cause exists and the scope of evidence sought is within a closed container, the container may be searched. This includes compartments, the trunk, and locked containers. As part of a police department policy, a police officer may inventory the contents of a lawfully impounded or stored vehicle prior to towing. The purpose is to protect the officer and agency from allegations of theft or damage, take an arrestee's valuables or property into custody for safekeeping, and assure that there are no hazardous objects or materials in the car that could endanger the general public. Evidence discovered fortuitously in plain view is admissible.

A **search warrant** is an order issued by a judge and directed to police officers commanding a search of a described location for described evidence or contraband. The statutory grounds for the issuance of a search warrant must be specified in the application (affidavit) for a search warrant. Search warrants are not required in some search and seizure situations (i.e., mobile vehicles with probable cause and probation or parole searches). Some search and seizure situations will almost always require acquisition of a search warrant (i.e., residential search and body intrusions). Rules regarding search warrants include:

- A search warrant requires probable cause or facts that would lead a reasonable person to believe there is strong suspicion that evidence or contraband will be found at a particular location. Probable cause can be established through a police officer's personal observations, reliable information received from citizens or other informants, and information received through official channels. Probable cause is communicated to a judge through a written or telephonic affidavit.
- Once issued, a search warrant is good for 10 days and is usually limited to service between the hours of 7:00 A.M. and 10:00 P.M., unless endorsed on good cause to be served at anytime of the day or night.
- Knock and notice rules apply to the service of search warrants. A police officer serving a search warrant must knock (or otherwise signal

to possible occupants), identify and announce purpose, demand entry, and give the person(s) inside a reasonable opportunity to open the door. A factual exigency or emergency circumstance, such as danger to officers, destruction of evidence, or escape of a suspect, may excuse knock and notice or permit a contemporaneous entry once an exigency begins. Failure to comply with knock and notice provisions can result in the suppression of evidence seized under the authority of the search warrant.

- The scope of the search under a search warrant is limited to the items and the location listed in the search warrant. Any additional evidence or contraband located in plain view or within the scope of the warrant may be legally seized as fortuitous finds. If additional evidence or contraband observed during the warrant service causes an officer to believe there is more of the same at the premises or location, a second search warrant may be necessary to legally search further for more evidence.
- Officers must maintain an inventory of evidence and contraband removed from the search location and file a return with the issuing court.

A **consent search** is one in which a person knowingly and voluntarily waives Fourth Amendment rights after having been given a request-choice by an officer. Consent allows a police officer to conduct an exploratory investigation into the area or property where the consenting party has possessory rights. The following rules apply to consent searches.

- **Knowingly and voluntarily**—Knowingly means the person giving the consent waiver has the capacity and mentality to be able to understand the choice to waive or not waive Fourth Amendment rights. Voluntarily means the consent to search was given as a result of free will and is not the product of force, coercion, inducement, promise, deceit, trick, or submission to police authority.
- **Request-choice**—When asking for consent to search, an officer must request permission to search and the request must be phrased in terms that the decision maker has the choice to refuse to consent.
- **Admonition**—An officer may advise a person verbally or in writing that the person has the right to refuse to consent to a search. The admonition will assist in upholding a showing of voluntariness.
- **Express or implied waiver**—An express waiver is one in which a person agrees to the consent search verbally or in writing. An implied waiver is one in which a person agrees to the consent search through affirmative gesture or body language. An equivocal waiver does not constitute legal consent.
- **Constitutional considerations**—A person has the right to refuse to consent to a search, limit the area of the search, and stop the search at any time after consent is given. Asserting any of these rights does not constitute consciousness of guilt or probable cause to search further.

- **Authority and no authority**—The person consenting to a search must be in an authority position. This means the person has possessory rights over the area or property to be searched. Typical situations arise when minor children, landlords, visitors, motel managers, babysitters, and household workers have no authority to consent to a search of the premises. Although these persons may be in charge of a premises or have the right to be in the area, they are not in an authority position to consent to search the area or property.

- **Husband-wife rule and exceptions**—Generally, one spouse can consent to a search of a jointly occupied house or property, even over the objection of another spouse. An exception would be areas such as dressers, cabinets, storage areas, or other containers of property that are exclusively used by the nonconsenting spouse. Consent must be sought from the spouse who actually uses these areas or another search basis must be sought.

- **Cotenant rule and exceptions**—Generally, one cotenant in authority can consent to a search of jointly occupied premises and common areas within, even over the objections of another cotenant. An exception would be areas such as a room, dressers, cabinets, storage areas, or other containers of property that are used exclusively by the nonconsenting tenant. Consent must be sought from the nonconsenting tenant for these areas or another search basis must be sought.

- **Parent–child rule and exceptions**—Generally, a parent is in an authority position to consent to police entry into a minor child's room, even if that room is solely occupied by the child. Police would get a plain-view inspection of the room. Exceptions include areas or containers of property that the child exclusively uses. Consent must be sought from the child for these areas or another search basis must be sought. Adult children living with parents fall under the cotenant rule.

An officer may conduct a warrantless entry into an area when necessary to protect life, health, or property, to prevent the imminent escape of fleeing suspects, or to prevent the imminent destruction of evidence. These warrantless entries are referred to as *exigency searches*. An **exigent circumstance** involves an emergency that requires swift and immediate action. Any evidence or contraband an officer sees in plain view while searching for victims or suspects is admissible. Specific examples of exigencies (emergencies) include the following:

- **Danger to life or limb**—These exigencies include assaults in progress, screams for help, shots fired, domestic violence calls, child endangerment or abuse, 9-1-1 calls, medical aid requests, and suicide attempts.

- **Danger of serious property damage**—These exigencies include natural disasters, accidents, explosions, clandestine drug labs, fires, burglar alarm soundings, and open doors and windows in which there is a possibility of unlawful entry.

- **Escape of suspect**—A police officer may enter a residence, building, or similar structure in the immediate (hot) pursuit of a suspect running from the scene of a reported crime. If an officer has probable cause to arrest a suspect for a felony or misdemeanor that occurred on the street or in a public place, the suspect cannot escape custody by running into a dwelling. Also, under the *investigative pursuit of a serious felon doctrine,* a police officer can conduct a warrantless entry to search for and arrest a suspect who has committed a dangerous felony involving death or serious bodily injury, even if not in immediate (hot) pursuit. Generally, this entry can be made within the first day after the crime or when it is impractical to seek an arrest warrant.

- **Destruction of evidence**—A police officer may enter and secure a crime scene pending the issuance of a search warrant when there is probable cause or when contraband is within a private area and there could be persons present who could move or destroy evidence. A protective sweep can be conducted for persons, to secure the premises, and to prevent the destruction of the evidence. Once the emergency terminates, so does the doctrine of necessity. Once victims are located, aided, or rescued, and suspects are arrested, the emergency search is over. If there is probable cause that evidence or contraband is still present, an officer must seek another Fourth Amendment basis (i.e., consent or search warrant) to search further.

A parolee is in *constructive custody* of the government after release from prison and is subject to conditions supervised by a parole officer or agent. A parolee waives Fourth Amendment rights during this parole period. In some states, a **parole search** may be conducted without a trigger or reasonable (particularized) suspicion, as long as the search is not arbitrary, capricious, or harassing. Thus, a search conducted under the auspices of a properly imposed parole search condition does not intrude on any reasonable expectation of privacy (*People v. Reyes,* 1998).

In other states, a parole search by a police officer requires a trigger or reasonable suspicion of renewed criminal activity or, a violation of a parole condition. In these situations, it is recommended that a police officer attempt contact with a parole officer for authorization to conduct a parole search. The parole officer reviews the reasonable suspicion information gathered by the police officer and makes an independent decision that the search is necessary to enforce parole conditions. If contact with a parole officer is impractical or unsuccessful, and a reasonable suspicion trigger otherwise exists, the search should be conducted. Case law supports parole searches under these circumstances.

A **probation search** is possible because of the supervised release of a probationer into the community. When a search clause or Fourth Amendment waiver is attached to probation conditions, a probation search may be conducted without a trigger or reasonable suspicion of renewed criminal activity. The purpose of a probation search is to ascertain if the probationer is complying with the terms of probation. For a police officer to conduct a probation search, prior authorization from a probation officer is not required. A probation search can be routinely conducted by any law enforcement officer as long as the search is not conducted in an arbitrary or harassing manner.

Administrative searches are based on a compelling governmental interest embodied in statutory or case law. Under these circumstances, the interests of society take precedence over the privacy interests of the individual. Administrative searches include searches associated with custodial institutions, booking searches, vehicle inventories, fish and game code enforcement, immigration and border inspections, U.S. Customs, airport and courthouse searches, and driving under the influence (DUI) sobriety checkpoints. Probation and parole searches are also forms of administrative searches.

There is no constitutional privilege to refuse to provide or to destroy evidence. With a legal seizure basis, an officer may use reasonable force to prevent the swallowing of evidence or contraband. Examples of reasonable force include verbal commands and physical restraint holds that do not involve inflicting pain, choking, or restriction of the blood supply. Unreasonable force (force that shocks the conscience of the court) is unlawful and will result in evidence suppression on due process grounds. Examples of unreasonable force include choke holds that cut off the air supply, carotid restraints that cut off the blood supply, striking the suspect, inflicting pain, and verbal threats to use unreasonable force. Force that may be reasonable to overcome resistance to arrest or prevent the escape of a perpetrator would be unreasonable to prevent the swallowing of physical evidence.

If a suspect has swallowed evidence, stomach pumping or the administration of an emetic to induce vomiting can legally take place if the suspect expressly consents to such procedures. If the ingested substance presents a clear and immediate threat to the suspect's life, as independently determined by medical personnel, recognized life-saving procedures may take place over the objection of the suspect including stomach pumping or the use of emetics. The physician may not act as an agent of the police. Evidence recovered fortuitously during this emergency procedure is admissible. Although it is legally possible to have a judge issue a search warrant for an emetic procedure, such circumstances are rare.

Taking a blood sample from a suspect involves a body intrusion. A separate search and seizure basis is required in addition to the suspect being lawfully under arrest. If a blood sample is needed as a biological control in a homicide, rape, or assault case, a police officer must obtain consent from the suspect or seek a search warrant from a judge for the seizure. This is because the suspect's blood type will not change. Therefore, there is no exigency. If a blood sample is needed as under the influence evidence in a driving while intoxicated or vehicular manslaughter case, a police officer may seize the blood sample pursuant to an exigency. This is because of the possibility of destruction of evidence. The alcohol or drug levels would metabolize in the suspect's body during the time it would take to seek a search warrant. Reasonable force may be used to take a blood sample from a resisting suspect in such cases. Police department policies differ on whether similar force is to be used in misdemeanor cases. Unreasonable force is prohibited on due process grounds and can result in evidence suppression. A blood sample can be taken from

Learn more about uniform codes of evidence through HierosGamos at www.hg.org.

an unconscious suspect if there is reasonable cause to arrest for an under the influence offense.

There is no constitutional privilege to refuse to be fingerprinted or provide exemplar evidence (i.e., handwriting, voice, photographic) incident to a lawful arrest. This evidence is nontestimonial in nature and does not violate a suspect's Fifth Amendment privilege to be free from self-incrimination. An officer may use reasonable force to obtain such evidence, although the level of resistance by the suspect may well mitigate the quality of the exemplar evidence obtained. A resistant or uncooperative suspect should be advised that the suspect has no right to refuse to provide this evidence. Any refusal or resistance can be argued later in court as evidence of consciousness of guilt.

METHODS OF IDENTIFICATION

An **in-field show-up** is a viewing of a suspect by a victim or witness in the field shortly after a crime is committed. The following are guidelines associated with infield show-ups:

- **Contemporaneous**—An in-field show-up can generally be conducted within two hours after a crime, although case law suggests that up to 24 hours may be allowed, under certain circumstances, in serious felony cases.
- **Avoiding element of suggestiveness**—A police officer bears the burden of showing that the identification transaction was controlled in a manner that prompted neutrality and avoided undue suggestiveness. Multiple victims and witnesses should be taken to the suspect and separated prior to the interview. They should also view the suspect(s) separately. No suggestive remarks or showing of material objects should take place prior to viewing. An admonition should be given beforehand telling the victim or witness that they are under no obligation to identify, they should make no inference from the fact that the suspect is in police custody or in or near a police car, it is just as important to free innocent persons from suspicion as it is to identify the guilty, and the witness should be positively sure of any identification.
- **Fifth Amendment issues**—A legally detained or arrested suspect has no right to refuse to participate in an in-field show-up. Such evidence is nontestimonial in nature. For the same reason, the suspect may be asked to repeat words or phrases uttered during the commission of a crime for voice identification purposes. There is no right to confer with counsel or have an attorney present during an infield show-up.

- **Transportation during an in-field show-up**—As a general rule, if a suspect has been detained, the suspect cannot be moved to accomplish an investigative purpose. A victim or witness must be brought to the detention scene for viewing. Exceptions to this rule include those situations in which the suspect is under arrest or consents to be moved, a victim or witness is injured or handicapped and it would be impractical for them to move, or there are other circumstances such as police officer safety, radio communication problems, or crime scene security that would justify moving the suspect.

A **photographic lineup** is an array of photographs shown to a victim or witness in an attempt to identify a suspect. It is helpful if the photographs of the persons have similar physical characteristics and background and that a victim or witness be given a cautionary admonition before viewing the lineup. A photographic lineup is generally performed long after a crime has occurred. Suspect information has been developed subsequent to the incident and an identification is part of the evidence needed to seek a criminal complaint and arrest warrant.

A **physical lineup** is a staged viewing in which a victim or witness views a number of persons in an attempt to identify a suspect. The viewing is usually conducted at the police station and the identification witness is asked to view the lineup in a controlled environment. The persons in the lineup should have similar physical characteristics and stature. If a criminal complaint has been filed against a suspect, the suspect has the right to have an attorney present during the viewing portion of the lineup because this is a critical stage in the prosecutorial process. A physical lineup is generally conducted when a suspect is in custody. The subject may be suspected in several offenses or multijurisdictional crimes, and a number of victims or witnesses are present for identification purposes.

MIRANDA AND ADMISSIONS/CONFESSIONS

The *Miranda rule* applies in the following situations:

- For an adult, when the suspect is in custody (under arrest or deprived of freedom in a significant way) and a police officer asks questions or interrogates to obtain an admission or confession to be used in a criminal prosecution.
- For a minor, when the suspect is taken into custody for a status offense, a delinquent offense, violating a court order, or escaping from a juvenile court-ordered commitment. In criminal matters, minors must be advised per *Miranda* the same as adults.

In *Miranda v. Arizona* (1966), the U.S. Supreme Court ruled that a criminal suspect must make a knowing, intelligent, and voluntary decision to waive certain constitutional rights prior to questioning. The terms *knowing* and *intelligent* mean the suspect has the mental capacity to understand the choice to speak or not speak to the police and that the suspect makes an informed choice. Voluntarily means the waiver is free from coercion, inducement, promises, or submission to police authority. If the suspect asserts the right to remain silent, no questioning regarding the incident can take place. Exceptions include those situations in which the suspect voluntarily initiates discussion on a separate and unrelated crime.

To help ensure that a criminal suspect is aware of relevant rights under the Constitution, the U.S. Supreme Court ruled that public law enforcement officers should advise the suspect of these rights. The elements of the advisory include the following:

- You have the right to remain silent.
- Anything you say may be used against you in a court of law.
- You have a right to consult with a lawyer, and to have the lawyer present during any questioning.
- If you cannot afford a lawyer, one will be appointed for you, at no charge, before questioning (*Miranda v. Arizona,* 1966).

To verify that the suspect's waiver of rights is knowing, intelligent, and voluntary, some jurisdictions require officers to ask the following questions.

- Do you understand the rights I just explained to you? A *yes* response is required.
- Do you wish to answer any questions at this time? A *yes* response is required.
- Do you wish to answer questions without a lawyer present? A *yes* response is required.

If the suspect is a juvenile, the following question is added.

- Do you wish to have a parent or guardian present during questioning? If the juvenile's response is *yes,* questioning should not begin until the juvenile's parent or guardian is present.

Officers must use extra caution when questioning juveniles without *Miranda*. If juveniles might believe they are "in custody" for questioning, *Miranda* applies (J.D.B. v. North Carolina, 2011).

If the suspect asserts the right to speak to a lawyer, no in-custody police-initiated questioning can take place about the crime. Exceptions include situations in which the suspect voluntarily reinitiates discussion regarding the incident. Statements made in violation of the *Miranda* rule are inadmissible as evidence in court. Moreover, if a defendant is held more than six hours before he or she talks, even voluntary confessions may not be used in a federal court (Corley v. United States, 2009). This is because long hours of questioning can induce people to confess to crimes they never committed.

The *Miranda* rule does *not* apply in the following situations:

- **Consensual encounters**—Everyday approaches, field interactions, or conversations with a person on the street or in a public place.
- **Traffic or municipal code infraction stops**—Because no one is in custody.
- **Detentions**—Temporary stops for investigation and questioning to determine a person's involvement, if any, in criminal activity. Even

though a person's freedom of movement is seized during a detention, the person is not in custody for the purposes of *Miranda* unless handcuffed, secured in the rear of a police car, or freedom of movement is otherwise restricted similar to an arrest. When determining if a subject's freedom of movement was restricted in a manner similar to an arrest, the courts will review the totality of the circumstances to determine if a reasonable person would believe the subject's movement was restricted. If the subject believed an arrest took place, the *Miranda* admonition by the police officer is adviseable. Though a person has the right to remain silent during a detention, the officer is under no legal obligation to inform the subject of this right.

- **Rescue doctrine and public safety exception**—The rescue doctrine is predicated on determining the health, safety, or whereabouts of a kidnap victim, stolen child, or determining the well-being of a victim during false imprisonment, hostage, or other crime victim situations. The purpose here is to rescue the victim. The public safety exception involves asking questions to solve an exigency such as the whereabouts of a gun, other dangerous instrumentalities, bomb, clandestine lab, or hazardous materials that may have been abandoned or secreted by a suspect. The purpose here is to abate a factual danger to life, limb, or property. In both instances, although a suspect may be in custody, questions may be asked absent a *Miranda* warning to resolve the exigency. If the suspect chooses to answer, responses may be used later in court.

- **General on-scene questioning**—In the field or at a subject's home when a police officer is in an investigative mode. No one is in custody.

- **Voluntary interview**—In a police station. The subject is not under arrest, is free to leave at any time, is not required to answer any questions, and is informed of these conditions. No one is in custody.

- **Phone calls**—The person being questioned over the phone is not in custody.

- When a subject (suspect) is being questioned by someone other than a police officer or agent of a police officer (Acker & Brody, 2004; California Commission on Peace Officer Standards and Training, 2012; California State Evidence Code, 2012a; Gardner & Anderson, 2009; Nemeth, 2010; Rutledge, 2000).

CASE STUDY—LEGAL RESEARCH AND WRITING

Much of the law applicable to the rules of evidence and criminal procedure is the product of judicial decisions (case law) in actual criminal cases. The ability to conduct research on case law, understand a court's reasoning for its decision, and write a synopsis (brief) of the case and the court's opinion can be helpful to students of the justice system.

Using the basic legal research and case brief writing guidelines outlined below, research and write a brief on a recent appellate court case or a case identified in this chapter.

LEGAL RESEARCH

Official and unofficial appellate court case reporters contain the court majority's opinion and the dissenting opinion (if any) in individual cases. Official reporters are published by the government and they contain the entire text of the court case opinions. Unofficial reports are published by private companies. Examples of each, along with their abbreviations, are presented below.

> United States Reports (U.S.)—Official report containing U.S. Supreme Court decisions.
> United States Supreme Court Reports—Lawyers Edition (L.Ed.). Unofficial report containing U.S. Supreme Court decisions.
> Federal Reporter (F. or F.Rep.)—Official report containing decisions of the 13 United States courts of appeals.
> California Reports (C. or Cal.)—Official report containing California Supreme Court decisions.
> American Law Reports (ALR)—Unofficial report containing selected appellate decisions across the United States.

A citation is used to locate a case in a law library.

> Example: *Miranda v. Arizona,* 384 U.S. 436 (1966).
> Case name: Miranda (appellant) *v.* Arizona (respondent)
> Reporter volume number: 384
> Report symbol: U.S. (United States Reports)
> Reporter page number: 436
> Year of decision: 1966

To locate the case in a law library, proceed to the section containing the relevant reports, select the appropriate volume (numbered on the outside binder of the text), and turn to the designated page number.

WRITING THE CASE BRIEF

Case briefs contain 400 words or less and usually follow a format similar to the following.

Case name and citation

> Type of case—A statement describing the type of case (criminal or civil) and how the case was brought on appeal to the present appellate court.
> Facts—This section contains a brief summary of the key facts of the case.
> Issue(s)—This section describes the issues or questions of law the court must decide. Example: Was the evidence seized illegally?
> Findings—This section contains the ruling (decision, holding) of the present court. The present court may affirm (agree with and let stand) the decision of the lower court or it may reverse (overturn) the lower court's decision and/or remand (send the case back) to the lower court.
> Discussion—This section contains the reasons for the present court's findings based on the facts and issues presented.

▲ SUMMARY

The U.S. Constitution's first 10 amendments, the Bill of Rights, places limitations on police practices. To be admissible in a criminal prosecution, evidence collected by the law enforcement community cannot violate restrictions enumerated in the Bill of Rights.

Evidence consists of testimony, documents, material objects, and other items presented as proof of the existence or nonexistence of a fact. Sources of evidence law include state and federal statutes, constitutions, and case law. The mechanisms used to present evidence in a court of law include the presentation of direct and circumstantial evidence, presumptions, inferences, judicial notice, and stipulations. The witness's competency and credibility may be attacked through the impeachment process. Testimonial and confidential communications privileges exist to protect one from self-incrimination and to protect relationships. Subject to certain exceptions, hearsay evidence is inadmissible. Warrantless searches are presumed to be unconstitutional except under certain circumstances. Methods of eyewitness or victim identification of a suspect include an in-field show-up, a photographic lineup, or a physical lineup. The *Miranda* rule applies whenever a suspect is in custody and subject to interrogation. Exceptions to the *Miranda* rule are outlined in applicable statutes and case law.

DISCUSSION QUESTIONS AND EXERCISES

1. List and describe the major types of evidence.
2. Describe the proper procedure for collecting, preserving, storing, and transporting evidence.
3. List and describe the types of situations in which a warrantless search may be conducted by a public law enforcement officer.
4. Compare testimonial privileges with privileged communications.
5. Under what conditions should a *Miranda* rights advisory be administered? If a criminal suspect confesses without first being advised of rights according to the *Miranda* decision, is the confession still admissible in a judicial proceeding? Explain.
6. A robbery suspect is arrested and transported to the robbery victim's location nine hours after the incident is reported. The victim positively identifies the suspect as the robber. Is the victim's identification admissible in court? Why or why not?
7. In several widely publicized criminal investigations, the police were criticized for collecting and preserving evidence improperly. How might this type of criticism be avoided?
8. Federal laws enacted after 9/11 have expanded the criminal investigative authority of law enforcement agencies. Is expansion of this authority contrary to the individual protections granted by the Bill of Rights?

9. The U.S. Supreme Court interprets the meaning and application of the U.S. Constitution. As time passes and the composition of the Court changes, the Court's decisions can differ. In some cases, the Court reverses decisions made by its justices in earlier years. Are the intent and meaning of the Constitution and its Bill of Rights unchanging, or are they fluid and open to interpretation, based on changing times?

Policing: Special Situations

LEARNING OBJECTIVES

After completing this chapter, the reader should be able to:

- list and describe noncriminal public safety concerns.
- describe the procedure for responding to calls involving special situations.
- evaluate types of emergencies and demonstrate knowledge of the appropriate response procedure.
- outline strategies for conflict resolution.
- discuss disaster management planning and response techniques.
- demonstrate knowledge of civil emergency management techniques.
- articulate procedures for handling hostage situations and barricaded subjects.
- analyze situations and evaluate the need for special weapons and tactics (SWAT) team involvement.

KEY TERMS

Define, describe, or explain the importance of each of the following.

AMBER Alert System
Animal control
Barricaded subject
Chelsea's Law
Civil disturbance
Classifications of fire
Disaster plan
Disaster response procedure
Dispute resolution
Elder abuse
Emergency command center
Environmental misfortune
Federal Aviation Administration (FAA)

Fire triangle
Hazardous material (HAZMAT)
Hostage negotiation
Incident commander
Incident control
Information officer
Intelligence and planning
Liaison officer
Logistics
Lost person
Megan's Law
Missing person

National Transportation Safety
Board (NTSB)

Natural disaster

Occupational Safety and
Health Act (OSHA)

Parens patriae

Person with mental illness

Police squad formation

Product of combustion

Rodney King

Scribe

Special weapons and tactics
(SWAT)

Sudden Infant Death Syn-
drome (SIDS)

Suicide by cop

Symptoms of suicide

Terrorism

Timothy McVeigh

Weapon of mass destruction
(WMD)

INTRODUCTION

In addition to crime prevention, investigation, and the apprehension of criminal offenders, police officers and agencies are faced with unique or unusual occurrences and circumstances that require special attention. Uniformed police officers are the primary public safety personnel in the field and are called on as first responders to the scene of domestic disputes, environmental and natural disasters, civil disturbances, bomb threats, terrorism, and other emergency situations. The police are also the primary human resource activated when a person threatens suicide, demonstrates emotional instability, or reports a child lost, missing, or dead. The police have even been drafted to perform the duties of cowboys in rounding up loose livestock. No chapter or book could address every conceivable, special situation in which police involvement may be necessary. This section is intended to provide a glimpse at a few of the special types of incidents and the appropriate corresponding police response.

CASE STUDY—TEENAGE GANGSTERS

On April 21, 2004, a 16-year-old boy fatally shot California Highway Patrol Officer Thomas J. Steiner, age 35. Steiner was wearing his uniform when he was shot three times while standing outside a Pomona, California, courthouse. The officer was waiting to testify in traffic court cases. Steiner later died at a hospital from a bullet wound in the head. The killer was motivated by a desire to elevate his status among fellow gang members.

Since the early 1970s, the United States has experienced gang problems in more jurisdictions than at any other time in its history. The increase in gang activity is attributed to the gangs' economic gain from illegal drug dealing, new immigrant groups attempting to assimilate by joining gangs, and the absence of stable male role models in many low-income households.

1. What can the police do to prevent juvenile gang activity?
2. Considering the factors that motivate juveniles to join gangs, how can gang membership be discouraged?

Uniformed police officers are the primary first responders in the field. *(Photo courtesy of Pearson Education / PH College)*

LOST AND MISSING PERSONS

A lost or **missing person** may have wandered away from a guardian or protected area. The missing person may be the victim of a kidnaping, may have run away, or simply does not wish to be found. Missing person reports should receive priority over reported property crimes.

Responding officers should verify, if possible, that the call involves a legitimate missing person situation. An accurate description and recent photograph of the missing person should be obtained. The officers should immediately determine the existence of suspicious circumstances.

Consideration must also be given to the length of time missing, the location of disappearance or last sighting, environmental factors such as the weather, any suspicious circumstances, and modes of transportation available to the person reported missing. Contact with search and rescue agencies may be necessary. All information collected should be disseminated to other appropriate public safety personnel as soon as possible.

If the missing person is a child, the officer should obtain information regarding any previous occasion when the child was reported missing. This information may provide a clue as to the child's current whereabouts. The search for the child should include the residence, immediate vicinity, and anywhere the child might be expected to go. Neighbors, friends, and relatives should be contacted. Sometimes a child is found at the home of a neighbor, and the neighbor is unaware that the child did not have permission to be away from home. The child may have run away from an abusive parent or have been the victim of a custody dispute and

Learn more about the AMBER Alert System through the National Center for Missing and Exploited Children at www.missingkids.com.

was abducted by the non-custodial parent. The news media may be a valuable resource. Print media, radio, and television news programs can broadcast descriptions of the missing child. If kidnaping is a possibility, appropriate support personnel as well as the FBI should be notified and involved in the case. A records check may reveal the location of a local convicted child molester or registered sex offender.

In 1996, Congress enacted **Megan's Law,** named after seven-year-old Megan Nicole Kanka, who was raped and murdered by a registered sex offender in 1994. Although controversial, the law authorizes public notification of the presence of convicted sex offenders who may pose a threat to public safety. In 2001, the National Center for Missing and Exploited Children launched the America's Missing: Broadcast Emergency Response (AMBER) alert system. The **AMBER Alert System** assists communities with the creation of missing children emergency alert plans and it coordinates the nationwide publication of descriptions of missing children and probable suspects. In 2010, California governor Arnold Schwarzenegger severely increased punishments for crimes against children by signing Chelsea's Law. Named after 17-year-old Chelsea King, murdered by a registered sex offender who admitted to another killing, the law reads that anyone convicted of certain sex offenses against a child in California will get life in prison without parole (Camarena, 2011).

If the person reported missing is an adult, police procedures are slightly different. Most adults are missing by choice or have a reasonable explanation for their absence. However, an officer should not assume all adults are missing by choice. The circumstances surrounding the missing person report, coupled with a thorough investigation, will dictate an appropriate course of action.

MENTALLY IMBALANCED AND INTOXICATED PERSONS

Police officers are often the first responders to the scene of a reported problem with a person with mental illness, a person who is mentally impaired, or an emotionally disturbed person. Police officers are also called upon to deal with intoxicated persons.

Dealing with the Mentally Imbalanced

A **person with mental illness** may suffer from a disease or defect of the brain that manifests itself in a personality disorder and inappropriate behavior. Individuals who are mentally impaired suffer from less than average intellectual functioning abilities. Emotionally disturbed persons may experience difficulty coping with stressors in daily living. These

disorders often manifest themselves in bizarre behavior, confusion, suicide attempts, and self-destructive or assaultive behavior.

When dealing with the mentally impaired, police officers should assess the situation, establish a perimeter, summon additional resources, if
necessary, gather as much information as possible, approach the disturbed person in a calm manner, and remove influences that upset the
subject. Officers should also utilize other resources, including family and
friends and, if necessary, place the subject in custody for the subject's
safety as well as the safety of others. Information collected before, during,
and after the incident should be reported to mental health professionals
to assist with appropriate diagnosis and treatment.

Intoxicated Persons

Intoxicated persons are also mentally impaired. The impairment is self-
induced, however, through the ingestion of excessive amounts of alcohol
or drugs. The subject may or may not suffer from the disease of chronic
alcoholism, or may be addicted to powerful mind-altering drugs. Laws
relative to intoxication often vary between and among jurisdictions. Generally, a police officer must first determine if the apparent intoxication is
the result of the voluntary ingestion of an intoxicating substance or is
caused by a form of illness or injury. Knowledge of the symptoms and
characteristics of voluntary intoxication will assist the officer in this determination.

The procedure for handling an intoxicated person depends on agency
policy and existing law. The American Medical Association and, to a certain extent, the courts recognize alcoholism and other forms of addiction
as diseases. As a result, the availability of criminal sanctions may be limited. A person may be taken into custody for a specified period of time.
This is accomplished to ensure the safety of the intoxicated person. In
some jurisdictions, detoxification centers are available and the afflicted
person may be placed in one of these centers for the purpose of protective
detention.

SUDDEN INFANT DEATH SYNDROME

One of the most emotionally devastating calls a police officer responds to
is the death of an infant. Most sudden, unexpected, and unexplained infant deaths are attributed to **Sudden Infant Death Syndrome (SIDS).**
No one should be blamed for a SIDS death. It cannot be prevented or predicted. It is not caused by suffocation, aspiration, or regurgitation. Death
occurs quietly and quickly and most often while the infant is sleeping.
Most SIDS deaths occur to apparently healthy infants within six months
of birth, with the highest SIDS mortality occurring between two and four
months of age.

In a typical SIDS case, the parent or guardian lays the infant down
to sleep. Later, the baby is found not breathing and a 9-1-1 call is placed.
Emergency medical and police personnel respond to the scene. The infant
cannot be revived and is transported to a medical facility, where the in-

fant is pronounced dead. The medical examiner or coroner performs an autopsy to determine the cause of death. SIDS is diagnosed as the cause of death by excluding all other possible causes.

When investigating a possible SIDS death, a police officer should interview family members and friends of the infant. The officer should explain to the family or parent involved that an investigation is required. Questions asked should include the following:

- Did the infant have medical problems?
- Did the infant suffer an injury recently?
- Has any other infant death occurred in the same family?
- What was the child's condition when last observed alive?
- Was the child eating, sleeping, and behaving normally?
- Was the infant given any medication?
- Who had access to the infant within the past 24 hours?

The information obtained from the interviews should be forwarded to the medical examiner or coroner. The officer should also explain the facts associated with SIDS cases and refer the parties involved to available SIDS peer support groups and public health professionals.

EMERGENCY MEDICAL RESPONSE

En route to the scene of a medical emergency, a police officer must consider other emergency vehicles that may be responding with emergency lights and siren activated. The officer must be aware of the location and direction of travel of other emergency units, and should coordinate via radio with the other units to reduce the risk of an accident. The responding officer should also consider the possibility of environmental hazards, such as a fire and gas or chemical leaks, and hazardous materials that may be located at the scene.

A police officer is usually the first public safety person to arrive at the scene of a medical emergency. As a first responder, the officer has a number of responsibilities. The officer must evaluate the situation; ensure personal, victim, and public safety; provide immediate basic medical care and request additional resources as necessary; initiate scene control; assess the victim(s) condition and set priorities for multiple victims; identify and retain, if possible, witnesses and involved parties; and preserve evidence. Additional resources such as firefighters, backup police, **hazardous material (HAZMAT)** teams, or emergency medical units may be necessary. Paramedics or emergency medical technicians (EMTs) are responsible for treatment of the victim(s) and transportation to a medical facility.

As a trained person, a police officer has a special responsibility to provide the basic medical care needed. As long as the care given is within the scope of the training and administered in good faith, the officer is protected from civil liability in a subsequent lawsuit. However, if the officer does not provide a standard of care based on abilities and training, the officer could be sued for negligence.

A conscious adult victim has the right to refuse treatment. If the victim is unconscious, consent is implied by the circumstances. Regardless of the victim's state of consciousness or consent, the officer must provide basic care if the injury or illness will degenerate to a life-threatening condition if left untreated. Once treatment is initiated, the officer must remain with the victim and continue to render aid until relieved by someone with an equal or higher level of medical training.

SUICIDES

Police officers are often called to the scene of a suspected suicide or attempted suicide. If the officer responds to an apparent suicide death scene, appropriate procedures are similar to those followed in any other death investigation. With an attempted suicide, police procedures are similar to those used with mentally imbalanced persons. The victim may be unconscious and require medical attention. Ultimately, an individual has decided to destroy (or appear to take) his or her life. Persons who attempt suicide may see no alternative to a seemingly intolerable existence. They may have contracted a terminal disease, or are in need of emotional or psychological assistance. Sometimes they simply want sympathy. It is a cry for help. Appropriate words and behavior on the part of the responding officer may prevent serious injury or death.

Virtually all potential suicide victims exhibit symptoms that indicate an attempt is likely. The **symptoms of suicide** include verbal or written statements that may communicate a death wish. Also, behavioral symptoms may demonstrate preparation for death. The suicide-prone individual may purchase additional life insurance or discard prized possessions.

In cases in which the attempted suicide victim does not require medical attention, an officer may be able to reverse the suicidal process by utilizing one or more of the following techniques:

- Talk to the person. Try to determine the motive for suicide.
- Stall for time.
- Appeal to the victim's apparent and perceived needs.
- Contact appropriate support personnel (i.e., fire, medical, psychiatric, and religious).
- Contact friends or relatives who may provide assistance.
- If possible, remove the potential victim from any life-threatening situation.

Especially troubling are situations in which a suicidal individual threatens deadly force upon the police or others in an attempt to force officers to use deadly force in self defense. Commonly referred to as **suicide by cop,** some disturbed individuals choose to end their lives through violent confrontations with the police.

On July 16, 2004, a deranged man threatened police with a knife at a Greyhound bus depot in Los Angeles. LAPD officers repeatedly shot at

Learn more about the suicide-by-cop phenomenon at www.suicidebycop.com.

the subject with a Taser® electric stun gun and a beanbag shotgun but the man shielded himself with a rubber floor mat. Finally, the subject dared the police to shoot him and he charged at the officers with the knife. Two of the five officers present opened fire with their sidearms, killing the man. On August 9, 2004, San Diego police, responding to a report of domestic violence, fatally shot a man who pointed a replica of a semiautomatic handgun at officers after asking God to take him (Adams, 2007; California Commission on Peace Officer Standards and Training, 2012)

Suicide by police officers is also common. A discussion of police suicide is presented in Chapter 7 in the stress management section.

DEALING WITH JUVENILES

Americans have become increasingly concerned about the issue of juvenile dependency and delinquency. In fact most street crimes are committed by teenagers and young adults. Youthful offenders under the age of 18 are typically referred to juvenile court. The juvenile court, acting under the principle of ***parens patriae*** and functioning as a parent on behalf of the child, has jurisdiction over dependency and delinquency. Dependency issues arise when the child has been neglected, sexually abused, or battered. Delinquency issues arise when the child commits an act that would be a crime if it were committed by an adult. Efforts by the justice system to deal with delinquency issues are often problematic because juvenile behavior is legally ambiguous. The police officer's role is equally ambiguous because of the conflict between the roles of law enforcement and crime prevention.

Juvenile Gangs

In America, membership in gangs of the early twentieth century provided a sense of identity for immigrants imbedded in an ethnically, racially, and culturally diverse population. However, today's organized gangs are typically motivated by financial gain, and many resort to criminal activity to promote their economic purposes.

Throughout the 1970s and 1980s, juvenile gangs became a major problem in urban as well as some suburban and rural areas. Although some gangs include adult members, membership consists mostly of teenagers. Specific problems associated with gangs include the use, distribution, and sale of controlled substances. In fact, it is believed that illegal drug trafficking provides the economic foundation for organized gangs today. Other problematic areas include turf conflict in which rival gangs, using public areas as private space, compete for the same area.

Finally, a major problem in dealing with gangs involves balancing law, neighborhood practices, and the image of authority without under- or overreacting to specific incidents.

Not all gang activity is criminal in nature. Some gangs are simply informal hedonistic groups that are motivated by pleasure or rebellion against authority. Other gangs are cultural or ethnic-based groups motivated by loyalty to each other and protection of the group's membership. The third category includes predatory or instrumental groups that are motivated by economic opportunity and power. Fourth, some young people are motivated to commit crime because of a gang's initiation process or a desire to elevate their status among gang members.

Each year, the U.S. Department of Justice's Office of Juvenile Justice and Delinquency Prevention (OJJDP), in conjunction with the National Youth Gang Center, conducts a youth gang survey. The latest survey indicated that approximately 28,000 gangs, with an estimated 730,000 members, are active in over 3,500 jurisdictions located throughout all 50 states. Most gang members join between the ages of 12 and 15. Most are products of impoverished and lower working class families and almost half of the gangs are multiracial or multiethnic (Miller, 2002).

Many gangs are well organized. Graffiti is a common form of communication for gangs. Gang leaders are represented by the dangerous hard-core members. Most hard-core gang members are surrounded by other initiated regular members, those who wish to become members, and youngsters who are potential gang members. Risk factors that promote gang membership include poverty, family and community disorganization, absence of male role models, academic failure, low commitment to positive peers, and a history of delinquency (Houston & Barton, 2005).

Although the prevailing view of youth gangs, with their colors, symbols, and territorial graffiti, projects an image of gangs located in large urban cities, gang activity also surfaces in rural settings. However, urban gang theories based on social disintegration and economic deprivation may not apply in rural America. Gang activity in rural areas is often reported during periods of economic growth. This phenomenon is based on an assumption that inner city families, with gang-affiliated children, relocate to rural areas in search of employment. The gang culture is transported with the families. Thus, rural gangs may be more transitory than their urban counterparts, suggesting that anti-gang policies and practices in urban settings may not be appropriate in rural environments (Weisheit & Wells, 2004). Kansas City, Missouri, tailored its antigang strategies to urban realities when it developed Aim4peace. The program sends reformed criminals into some of the city's tensest neighborhoods to calm disputes, often by explaining the unpleasant consequences of violence to feuding gang members (Gross, 2009).

In the mid-1990s, the United States increased deportations of aliens convicted of crimes, resulting in the exportation of many gang members. Potentially violent young men, experienced with weapons and the tactics for evading law enforcement, were returned to their home countries in Central America. Gangs were rare in Central America twenty years ago.

Learn more about gangs through the Institute for Intergovernmental Research's National Youth Gang Center at www.iir.com/Gangs/nygc/default.aspx

Today, gangs represent Central America's number one crime problem (Exporting a problem, 2005).

Juvenile Crime

The juvenile justice system faces unprecedented challenges. Although juvenile arrests for violent crime have declined in recent years, the current level of arrests is not acceptable. Today's juvenile does not commit more violent crime than a generation ago, but more juveniles today are violent. Juvenile arrestees are also more likely than adult arrestees to use a gun when committing a crime. Juveniles are most likely to commit violent crimes after school, and half of all high school students who carry a weapon take the weapon to school.

Juveniles are not only the perpetrators of a great deal of crime; they are victims of crime as well. Between 1985 and 1995, nearly 25,000 juveniles were murdered in the United States. The number of children identified as abused or neglected nearly doubled between 1986 and 1993. During the 1990s, the rate of violent victimization of juveniles ages 12 through 17 was nearly three times that of adults (Sickmund, Snyder, & Poe-Yamagata, 1997; Snyder, 1997). Of the 14,299 murders in 2008, 1,502 of the vicitims were under the age of 18 (Snyder, 2003; U.S. Census Bureau, 2011).

Juvenile criminal activity and victimization shall remain a major concern for all public safety personnel. Although the juvenile crime rate appears to be declining in many areas, an increase in the number of juveniles may produce an increase in juvenile crime. Since juveniles are often victims of crime perpetrated by other juveniles as well as adults, a strategy must also be developed to protect the generations of the future (Champion, 2005; Foote, 1997).

Police Procedures

Neglected or abused children require special consideration. It is estimated that 4 to 5 million children are neglected or abused in the United States every year. In addition, many youths are involved in the commission of status offenses, that is, violations of laws applying only to those in the status of being juveniles. These offenses include laws relative to underage alcohol consumption, truancy, and curfew violations.

Procedures for dealing with juveniles must be consistent with departmental policy, state and local laws, and court decisions. Generally, laws relating to police treatment of juveniles, other than serious criminal law offenders, focus on the care, protection, and positive development of the young. Officers should remember that not all juvenile gangs are involved in criminal behavior. Young people represent the future adults of

Young people represent the future adults of America. *(Photo courtesy of the Los Angeles Sheriff's Department.)*

America and the stigma of a criminal label may have a long-lasting negative impact on society (Hess & Wrobleski, 2003; Lotz, 2005).

A police officer's responsibilities with respect to juveniles is to provide protection, guidance, and rehabilitation in the absence of parental or guardian care and control. Thus, a police officer's authority to arrest or detain a juvenile is generally broader than with adults. Subject to limited exceptions or when acting under the authority of an arrest warrant, a police officer cannot arrest an adult for a misdemeanor that the police officer has not observed. In the case of juveniles, however, a police officer may detain the minor on suspicion of misdemeanor activity, although the officer did not observe the suspected criminal activity (Rutledge, 2000).

The officer shall select the least restrictive means for protection of the juvenile as well as the community. Juveniles should not be detained in a secured facility unless they present an escape risk or could do harm to themselves or others. When being detained, minors should not be allowed to come in contact with adult prisoners (California Commission on Peace Officer Standards and Training, 2012; Houston & Barton, 2005).

ELDER ABUSE

According to available statistics, elderly persons are victimized less than other age groups. However, the elderly are more likely to be victims of property crime or be physically injured than their youthful counterparts. Elderly persons are often victims of fraud by strangers. Unscrupulous

Learn more about elder abuse through the National Center on Elder Abuse at www.ncea.aoa.gov/

telephone solicitors and con artists prey on unsuspecting elderly people. In addition, the elderly are subjected to financial exploitation, mistreatment, and abuse by relatives, friends, and caregivers.

Definitions of **elder abuse** fall within three categories: domestic elder abuse, institutional elder abuse, and self-neglect or self-abuse. Domestically, elders are abused in their homes by a spouse, child, sibling, friend, or caregiver. The abuse can be physical, sexual, emotional, psychological, financial, or involve neglect or abandonment. Institutional elder abuse is similar to domestic abuse, except that it occurs in facilities such as nursing homes and care centers. Self-neglect or abuse is behavior by elderly persons that threatens their own health and safety.

Symptoms of elder abuse include bruises, bone fractures, untreated injuries, medication overdoses, elder reports of abuse, vaginal or anal bleeding, emotional upset, malnutrition, unsanitary conditions, sudden changes in financial status, and the sudden appearance of previously uninvolved friends or relatives. Almost two-thirds of abusers are family members, most often the victim's spouse or adult child. Many perpetrators have problems stemming from alcohol or drug abuse (National Center on Elder Abuse, 2004).

Police investigative response to reports of elder abuse requires knowledge of the laws and symptoms associated with elder victimization, the crimes typically committed against older persons, and likely suspects. For example, thanks to recent research into what distinguishes normal bruising in elderly people from bruising caused by abuse, police and prosecutors now have forensic markers they can use in elder abuse cases (Bulman, 2010). The appropriate adult protective services (APS) agency should be contacted. The number of elder abuse incidents requiring police attention is not likely to decline. Rather, law enforcement activity in this area will increase as the number of older persons in the population grows and APS resources become increasingly strained (Michel, 2004).

ANIMAL CONTROL

The control of animals involves encounters with dogs, cats, reptiles, cattle, horses, bats, skunks, birds, and bees. The most common **animal control** complaint involves barking dogs that are disturbing the public peace.

Officer safety and public safety are the primary considerations when determining what action to take. If the animal is suspected of having rabies, it should be quarantined. If it is necessary to destroy a rabid animal, the head of the animal should not be destroyed until tests for rabies are conducted. Animals should not be killed unless there is an immediate compelling reason (i.e., public safety) to do so.

In some jurisdictions, a private humane society may respond to animal calls. In other areas, a municipal or county animal control department will respond. In most jurisdictions, however, animal control is the responsibility of the police. Regardless of the agency responsible, complainants usually contact the nearest law enforcement agency first.

Aircraft Accidents

Aircraft crashes provide a special challenge to police personnel. Unlike motor vehicle accidents, which are confined to a small area of roadway, or railroad accidents, which are confined to railroad property, aircraft crashes may occur in residential areas and business districts. These crashes usually involve a large area. Commercial airliner crashes in particular can involve heavy loss of life for those aboard the aircraft and the high probability of injury or death to persons on the ground.

Police responsibilities at the scene of an aircraft accident are similar to those of any other accident: care for the injured, minimize property damage, and assist emergency and other disaster-related personnel as appropriate. If the accident involves a civilian aircraft, the police must also notify the **Federal Aviation Administration (FAA)** and the **National Transportation Safety Board (NTSB).** If the crash involves a military aircraft, the branch of the military to which it belongs must be notified. Maintaining a safe distance from a downed aircraft is extremely important. Special hazards associated with aircraft accidents include the possibility of explosions and fire as well as exposure to biomedical, radiological, and biochemical materials. When it is necessary to approach a downed aircraft, the approach should be made upwind of the crash site to avoid inhalation of toxic substances.

Fires

Most fires are the product of a noncriminal cause. Some, however, involve arson. An arson fire can be set by a single person to cause property damage or may be the result of a group activity.

In some cases, the loss of life, personal injury, and property damage from a fire can be tremendous. The fire at David Koresh's Branch Davidian complex in Waco, Texas, in 1993, resulted in the deaths of 72 people, including Koresh and several children. On February 20, 2003, a fire broke out during the rock band Great White's concert in The Station nightclub in West Warwick, Rhode Island. Pyrotechnics (fireworks) used during the band's performance inside the club ignited combustible interior building materials. Within minutes, flames engulfed the club. Most concert-goers were unaware that the flames were not part of the show. Subsequently, 99 people died and nearly 200 more were injured in a frantic struggle to escape the aging wood frame building. The West Warwick fire was the deadliest nightclub fire in the United States since the Beverly Hills Supper Club fire in Southgate, Kentucky, killed 165 in 1977 (Zuckerman, 2003).

In late October, 2003, three major fires in the California county of San Diego killed 16 people, including a firefighter, and destroyed nearly 2,500 homes and businesses. One of the fires, designated the Cedar Fire, was the largest in California history. It consumed almost 300,000 acres in under three days. The Cedar Fire's origin was traced to a lost hunter who lit fires to alert rescuers of his location (*End in Sight*, 2003). Failures with evacuation protocols as well as communication failures and lack of coordination among fire and other public safety agencies were cited as the major causes of the incredible devastation resulting from the fire. In addition, policies that limited the use of fire-fighting aircraft restricted air support for ground units (Gross, 2004). In June 2011, Arizona experienced the largest wildfire in its history. Likely caused by a campfire, the wildfire, driven by wind, had consumed 773 square miles by mid-June (Montoya Bryan, 2011).

Approaches to fire safety include strategies for fire prevention as well as protection. Fire prevention applies to policies that focus on preventing a fire from occurring. Fire protection involves minimizing personal injury and damage to property once the fire has started. The nature of fire and its prevention and suppression can be explained simply by addressing the three major components of the classic **fire triangle:** heat, fuel, and oxygen. All three must be present in appropriate amounts and under appropriate conditions for a fire to occur. **Products of combustion** include flame, heat, smoke, and invisible toxic gases. From a life safety standpoint, limiting exposure to all products of combustion is extremely critical. Exposure to flame and heat may cause serious injury and death within a very short period of time. Smoke obscures vision 0and exit routes. Toxic gases displace life-sustaining oxygen. Most fire deaths result from the inhalation of toxic gases. **Classifications of fire** include:

Class A—ordinary combustibles such as paper and wood
Class B—flammable liquids such as gasoline
Class C—electrical
Class D—combustible metals

Fire prevention involves controlling the fire triangle. It involves strategies and tactics designed to prevent a fire from occurring in the first place. It also involves training and education of individuals as well as organizations as to the nature, extent, and realities of fire and its prevention. Once a fire has started, protection strategies are used to minimize the damage and spread of fire. Typically, these strategies include the use of personnel and fire protection and suppression equipment such as alarms, extinguishers, sprinkler systems, and fire fighting equipment. Strategies also include the use of fire escapes, exits, evacuation routes, and fire doors to help contain the fire.

In the early days of public policing, officers were often responsible for fire fighting. As crime rates rose and the police service focused on crime fighting, volunteer as well as paid firefighters assumed the role of fire prevention and protection specialists. At a fire scene, the fire company captain or commander is responsible and assumes command and control authority. Police involvement with fire suppression is usually limited because of the lack of specialized equipment and training. Police responsibility involves crowd control, diversion of traffic, protection of firefighters and equipment, and access and exit control, for firefighters and emergency medical personnel. In other words, the role of the police at fire scenes is to assist fire fighting and other emergency personnel.

If, as initial responders to a fire scene, the police are confronted with a situation in which victims may be trapped, the officer(s) must first determine the level of danger to the victims and the estimated arrival time of fire fighting personnel. If the situation demands immediate entry into the fire scene and firefighters are not available, the officer must consider personal safety first. If entry is permissible, the officer should determine the safest route, stay low to minimize exposure, and proceed with extreme caution.

Environmental Misfortune

Environmental misfortune includes accidents, exposure to hazardous materials, conventional and nuclear power failures, and gas line or water main breaks. Often referred to as technological or human-caused disasters, environmental misfortune also results from the use of nuclear, biological, chemical, and radiological weapons (Haddow & Bullock, 2003). Responding officers should assume initial command and isolate the hazard at the scene, maintain a safe distance, direct assisting emergency units, limit access, and ensure that proper notifications are made. In addition to the possibility of personal injury or death, direct costs associated with these events include increased public safety expenditures as well as expenses to private individuals and business. Indirect costs include lost productivity.

To assist in the creation of a safer work environment, Congress passed the **Occupational Safety and Health Act (OSHA)** in 1970. This law outlined specific requirements for employers. Although police officers do not enforce OSHA regulations, knowledge of the law may help officers to provide suggestions to those who are in violation. According to the law, employers must:

- Know and comply with OSHA regulations and standards.
- Eliminate hazards and provide a safe and healthy work environment.
- Establish a record-keeping and reporting system covering all work-related injuries, deaths, and illnesses.
- Conduct periodic safety and health inspections and correct any hazards found.
- Allow OSHA to inspect the company's facilities.
- Provide protective equipment.
- Keep workers informed about their rights, the company's safety record, and safety standards.
- Develop and enforce safety and health standards.
- Provide safety training for employees.

A majority of accidents result from carelessness, failure to have or follow safety rules, and horseplay. Hazardous materials emergencies require extreme care as a result of the volatile nature of toxic gases, chemicals, liquids, and corrosive materials. Public utility failures may also be life-threatening and backup systems and procedures should be preplanned. As with fire scenes, the responsibility of the police at scenes where an environmental mishap has occurred is to assist hazardous materials specialists and other emergency personnel.

Environmental disasters are caused by the impact of human action on the natural environment. These events become more common as the human population increases. Currently, the world's population exceeds 6 billion, and approximately 100 million people are added to the population each year.

Many local, county, state and federal statutes are designed to protect the environment. In some cases, statutes provide for criminal prosecution as well as compensation under civil law. Under these laws, civil and criminal liability may be incurred for conduct resulting in air and water pollution, improper pesticide distribution and use, excessive noise, and possession or emission of regulated chemicals. Corporations as well as individuals may be held civilly and criminally liable for violations. The laws hold corporate officers and other employees liable if they know or should know environmental laws are being violated. Specific intent to commit a crime is not required. Simply stated, an environmental crime is any human activity that violates an environmental criminal statute.

NATURAL DISASTERS

A **natural disaster** is any sudden, extraordinary misfortune in nature. Types of natural disasters include earthquakes, tornadoes, hurricanes, tsunamis, forest fires, floods, and storms. Any natural disaster can result in injuries, property loss, and deaths. Some disasters are more deadly than others. Floods, for example, contribute to a greater loss of life in the United States than any other type of natural disaster. Contingency plans should be developed in advance of any natural disaster. These plans involve an assessment of the potential risk, prioritization of tasks necessary to prevent or reduce losses, preparation for various disaster scenarios, and a plan to recover from the disaster.

Some disasters result when adequate precautions have not been taken to minimize the damage caused by natural occurrences. During the summer of 1999, a massive heat wave engulfed most of the Midwest and eastern regions of the United States. Over 200 deaths were attributed to heat-related factors. Many of the deaths could have been prevented if the victims had received advanced warning, and if proper air conditioning had been installed to reduce the impact of the heat.

In early 2004, winter storms in the Midwest and Northeast halted transportation, closed businesses and schools, and shut down electric power to 250,000 customers. Nearly 80 deaths were blamed on the storms. During August and September 2004, hurricanes Charley, Frances, Ivan, and Jeanne were responsible for the deaths of nearly 120 people and an estimated $26 billion in property damage in the southeastern portion of the United States. In June 2011, a massive tornado in Joplin, Missouri, killed almost 160 people.

Some natural disasters can be predicted, others cannot. An earthquake is a natural disaster that cannot be predicted with any certainty. However, areas that are prone to earthquakes must have established emergency preparedness plans to deal with transportation problems, injuries, deaths, utility outages, fires, and explosions. One of the greatest problems associated with earthquakes is poor, or no, communications. Landline communications systems as well as airwave communications relay towers are often destroyed.

On December 26, 2004, a magnitude 9.0 earthquake, the most powerful in forty years, erupted under water off the island of Sumatra. The earthquake caused tsunamis that crashed into the coastal areas of Thailand, Sri Lanka, India, Indonesia, the Maldives, Malasia, and Somalia. Almost 300,000 people were killed or reported missing (Ortmeier, 2005; Waldman, 2004).

In March 2011, a magnitude 9.0 earthquake and tsunami hit northern Japan, resulting in more than 28,000 people dead, missing, or injured, and damaging nuclear reactors that began leaking radiation.

DISPUTE RESOLUTION

A large percentage of police calls involve some type of dispute. Although these calls are potentially dangerous, most **dispute resolution** involves restoring order and keeping the peace rather than law enforcement. From an officer safety standpoint, the most critical time is when the officer approaches and enters the location of the dispute. The police rarely retain the element of surprise in dispute situations. Therefore, dispute calls should be handled by more than one officer.

Responding officers should not park the patrol vehicle in front of the dispute location. Officers should avoid sidewalks, remain separated, keep hands free, and keep the location, including any doors or windows, under surveillance. If the dispute is taking place inside a residence, officers should stand to the side of the door and listen to the dispute for a few seconds before announcing police presence. Listening to the dispute may provide clues regarding the nature of the argument. Officers must remember that dispute situations are charged with emotion. The disputants may be armed and temporarily out of control. Officers must be concerned with the safety of the responding officers as well as the disputants and others present at the location.

At the scene, officers must first determine if a crime was committed and take action as appropriate. Police action may include a warning, citation, or arrest. In most dispute situations, no crime has been committed. Therefore, officers should enter with the consent of one or more of the parties unless uninvited entry is warranted to protect the parties. Officers should stay calm, gain control of the situation, separate the disputants if possible, and determine the nature of the dispute. Separating the disputants keeps them from attacking each other and allows the officers to interview and verify the parties' statements independently. When the situation has been calmed, officers should use reasoning and mediation to resolve the dispute.

Sometimes disputes arise when an automobile or other property is being repossessed or when confrontations occur between landlords and tenants. In most jurisdictions, a seller has the right to repossess property being sold under an installment contract. These contracts typically contain a clause that gives the seller the right to repossess over the objection of the buyer. When such clauses do not exist, the seller must resort to the judicial process if the buyer has possession of the property and refuses to relinquish it. The seller may retain the property only if repossession takes place prior to the buyer's objection.

Landlord–tenant disputes typically arise from nonpayment of rent. In most jurisdictions, landlords cannot deny a tenant access unless an eviction order has been issued by a competent court. In repossession and landlord–tenant disputes, officers should avoid arrest. Officers should mediate and help the disputants to achieve a resolution. Under no circumstances should officers provide legal advice. Most of these disputes are civil, not criminal, in nature. The parties should be advised to seek legal counsel and reach a final settlement through the judicial process.

CIVIL DISTURBANCES

A **civil disturbance,** or disorder, may be defined as any group activity that disrupts the normal peace and tranquility of a neighborhood or community. These activities can be legal or illegal. According to a U.S. Supreme Court interpretation of the First Amendment to the Constitution, all citizens have the right to assemble. Legal assemblies include strikes and labor disputes, legal demonstrations, and special events (sporting, concerts, parades). Illegal assemblies include riots and other unlawful gatherings.

Pre-Incident Considerations

Any nonviolent group may become violent if conditions conducive to violence exist. The potential for property loss, injuries, and death is tremendous. The riot in Los Angeles that commenced on April 29, 1992, subsequent to the acquittal of police officers involved in the **Rodney King** incident, resulted in over $1 billion in losses, 10,000 businesses destroyed, at least 1,300 injuries, and 44 deaths. The damage and casualties were greater than the Los Angeles (Watts) riot in 1965 and the Detroit riots of 1967 (Path of destruction, 1992). In late November and early December 1999, civil protests during the World Trade Organization conference in Seattle, Washington, developed into a riot. Downtown Seattle was placed under curfew and the National Guard was activated to quell the disturbance. The opening of the conference was postponed and it was terminated early as a result of the civil unrest.

As with natural disasters, contingency plans should be developed to deal with civil disturbances and minimize property loss and casualties. Police involvement with and responsibilities for action before, during, and after a civil disturbance depends on the nature of the event. In those situations in which unlawful activity is predicted or actually takes place, the role of the police is quite clear. The objectives of the police in the event of any unlawful assembly include crime prevention, containment, dispersal, prevention of reentry, and arrest and detention of violators. The police must restore normal operations through the establishment of priorities.

In some cases, it may be possible to predict an unlawful assembly or riot of any magnitude. Preincident signs help the police to forecast the possibility of a major incident. Danger signs include the following:

- Gang warfare and intergang rivalry
- Numerous threats or attacks on private property
- Obvious disrespect for authority
- An increase in incidents of violence
- Pervasiveness of a rumor regarding police misuse of authority or reports of police abuse
- An increase in the number of disturbances at public or private events

Psychological factors influence the psyche of the participants in an unlawful assembly. Except for identifiable leaders, the members of the group often possess a sense of anonymity, thus a feeling that they will not be identified because they are members of a large group. Activities within a large group also tend to be contagious. Unlawful activity that is instigated by a few people may spread rapidly to other members of the group.

Civil Disorder Management

Violent mobs usually form in three stages. In Stage 1, a crowd forms but the crowd is simply a mixture of individuals. In Stage 2, the members of the crowd start to lose their individuality and begin to function as a unified whole as leaders emerge. In Stage 3, the mob functions as a single unit and the leaders are in control. Police reasoning with the mob is not a likely solution because the members have temporarily lost the ability to think rationally. Police action at Stage 3 must be decisive and firm. The police must assess the situation, muster sufficient resources, give a dispersal order, and physically disperse the crowd if necessary. Dispersal fragments the mob into smaller, more controllable groups. In addition, dispersal helps to reduce the feeling of anonymity on the part of the participants, thus encouraging the noncriminal element to leave the area.

Containment and dispersal of riotous crowds are essential to the activity's termination. The police must respond rapidly and in sufficient numbers to establish a perimeter, control the situation, prevent the riot from spreading, minimize damage to property and personal injury, and systematically disperse the crowd. The appearance of a professional, organized, properly trained, competent, and disciplined group of police officers can restore order to a riotous situation. Teamwork is essential.

During civil disturbances, such as riots, teamwork is essential and police squad formation may be necessary. *(Photo courtesy of the San Diego Sheriff's Department.)*

Police squad formations may be necessary. The skirmish line formation can be used to contain or move a crowd in a specific direction. Wedge formations can penetrate and split a crowd. Diagonal formations are used to move a crowd away from an area or building. Column formations are used to divide a crowd or deploy officers from one area to another. Ultimately, crowd and mob control depends on the situation. Consideration must be given to the size of the crowd as well as its activities, attitude, and demeanor. Consideration must also be given to tactical withdrawal of the police for safety purposes (Adams, 2007; California Commission on Peace Officer Standards and Training, 2012; Nichols, 2003).

BOMBS, BOMB THREATS, TERRORISM, AND WEAPONS OF MASS DESTRUCTION

Bombs and other **weapons of mass destruction** have been used by individuals, drug traffickers, organized crime, and terrorist groups to kill a single person or a great number of people. Relatively inexpensive to produce, these devices and agents are commonly used by perpetrators who wish to be far from the scene when the detonation takes place. The Unabomber sent pipe bombs through the mail to specific targets. The deaths resulting from the bombing of the World Trade Center in New York City in 1993 and the Alfred P. Murrah federal office building in Oklahoma City in 1995 demonstrate the catastrophic nature of explosives assembled for mass

murder in a single event. The Tokyo subway saran nerve gas attack in
1995 enlightened the world on the devastation that can be created through
the use of biological and chemical weapons. Terrorists used commercial aircraft as explosive devices during their suicide bombings on 9/11.

Bombs and Bomb Threats

Police responding to the scene of a bombing should focus on disaster recovery and crime scene investigative techniques. Although the majority of
bomb threats are hoaxes, they should be treated seriously. In most jurisdictions, the threat itself is a crime. In the event a person has reported a suspicious package, it should be treated as an actual explosive device. Upon
arriving at the scene where a suspicious package is reported, the initial responding officer should contact the person who reported the package so the
reporting person can direct emergency personnel to the correct location. A
safe distance around the package should be established. Patrol
officers should not handle, touch, smell, or attempt to dismantle any suspected or known explosive device. Bomb disposal experts or explosive technicians should be summoned. Officers should use landline telephones
rather than cellular phones or radios for communication because of the
possibility of a radio-activated device. Electric and gas utilities should be
disconnected, a no smoking policy must be enforced, and any flammable
combustibles in the vicinity of the device should be removed.

If a bomb threat call was received and no suspicious package has
been located, a search for the device must be conducted. Contrary to early
practice, the best people to conduct the initial search for a suspicious
package are not the police but the people who live or work in the area.
These people are familiar with the area and are more likely to observe
something that is out of place or does not belong to an occupant. Guidelines for a bomb search can be obtained from the U.S. Bureau of Alcohol,
Tobacco, Firearms, and Explosives (ATF) at www.atf./gov (U.S. Department of Justice, Bureau of Alcohol, Tobacco, Firearms, and Explosives,
2000). If a suspicious package is located, an evacuation is necessary.

It is also important to interview the person who received the bomb
threat. If the threat was received via telephone, the interview should
focus on what the caller said, the sound of the caller's voice, and any
background noises apparent to the listener. If an explosive incident has
occurred, the patrol officer(s) should treat the affected area as a crime
scene unless determined otherwise.

Terrorism and Weapons of Mass Destruction

Terrorist acts originate from domestic or international sources. On April
19, 1995, **Timothy McVeigh** bombed the Alfred P. Murrah federal office
building in Oklahoma City. One-hundred-sixty-eight men, women, and
children died as a result of the bombing. Hundreds more were injured.
McVeigh was subsequently convicted in U.S. District Court in Denver
and executed for the killing of eight federal law enforcement agents who
were present in the building at the time of the bombing. McVeigh's ac-

complice, Terry Nichols, was convicted in federal court in 1998 and received life sentences for killing the agents. In 2004, Nichols was convicted in Oklahoma state court of 161 counts of first degree murder and he received a sentence of life without parole on each count. A bombing at the Olympic Games in Atlanta in 1996 killed one person and injured over 100. In May 1998, the Unabomber, Theodore Kaczynski, received four life sentences plus 30 years for deaths and injuries resulting from bombs he sent through the U.S. mail between 1978 and 1995.

Numerous terrorist incidents initiated by international terrorists have occurred over the past several years. Osama bin Laden, an exiled Saudi Arabian financier, was the leader of a worldwide **terrorism** network and was killed by U.S. Forces in Pakistan on May 2, 2011. In addition to the 9/11 terrorist attacks, Bin Laden and his Al Qaeda organization were responsible for the 1993 bombing of the World Trade Center in New York City, the 1998 bombings of the U.S. embassies in Tanzania and Kenya, and the attack on the U.S.S. "Cole" on October 12, 2000. The Cole, a U.S. Navy ship, was refueling in Aden, Yemen. The bombing of the Cole left 17 sailors dead.

A year after the 1995 Oklahoma City bombing, Congress enacted the Anti-Terrorism and Effective Death Penalty Act of 1996. The law:

- Allows victims to sue countries that sponsor terrorism.
- Established a special removal court to oversee the deportation of aliens suspected of terrorists activities.
- Provides immigration officials with more authority to deport aliens convicted of any crime.
- Forbids fund-raising activities in the United States by any foreign group identified by the U.S. government as engaged in terrorist activities.

Although not included in the law, the Clinton administration wished to expand the power of federal authorities to increase their ability to surreptitiously monitor suspected terrorists through the use of electronic surveillance equipment.

Emerging technology and expanding economic growth promote new and different threats. Computer technology allows hackers to penetrate American businesses and vital public safety infrastructure databases without an accompanying physical intrusion. A foreign or domestic hacker, utilizing a computer, can manipulate and destroy vital and top secret information, create havoc with air traffic control systems, deactivate public utilities, and slow emergency communications systems.

New-age terrorism requires government and military capabilities characterized by stealth, speed, accuracy, mobility, and intelligence that are different from the counterterrorism mechanisms used in the past. Private, nonmilitary counterterrorism strategies are also required.

Few experts suggest that the threat of terrorism is not increasing. However, a lack of preparedness to prevent terrorism or mitigate the damage from acts of terrorism exists in many areas. Some fail to recognize that weapons are plentiful and prevention strategies are often inadequate.

The weapons of terrorism range from traditional low technology firearms and improvised explosive devices (IEDs) to information warfare and weapons of mass destruction (WMDs), sometimes referred to as weapons of mass effect (WMEs). The threat from WMDs is particularly frightening. Many nationstates as well as nonstate organizations either possess or have access to nuclear, biological, or chemical (NBC), even radiological, devices that have the potential to cause loss of life and property destruction on a scale never before experienced (Maniscalco & Christen, 2002; Nason, 2000).

Due to limited resources and inadequate intelligence gathering capabilities, law enforcement agencies and security organizations have not been able to prevent some terrorist attacks. However, the terrorist attack of 9/11 provided the catalyst to develop more proactive counterterrorism strategies. The 9/11 attack represented the most destructive criminal event perpetrated on United States soil to date. Experts suggest that the United States and its foreign interests will continue to be a preferred target for international terrorists (Martin, 2003). Reaction from the United States is likely to be swift and certain.

Federal government initiatives to combat terrorism include the enactment of various laws designed to reinforce security in the United States and elsewhere. Chief among these initiatives are the Aviation and Transportation Security Act of 2001, the USA PATRIOT Act of 2001, the Homeland Security Act of 2002, the Domestic Security Enhancement Act of 2003, and the Intelligence Reform and Terrorism Prevention Act of 2004.

Of the federal legislative initiatives, the USA PATRIOT Act is the most controversial. The act centralizes federal law enforcement authority in the U.S. Department of Justice and expands the CIA's domestic intelligence gathering capabilities. In particular, the USA PATRIOT Act impacts criminal procedure and due process in significant ways. The act broadens law enforcement search authority, permits longer incarceration for certain suspects arrested without an arrest warrant, and it expands the power of prosecutors. The act also expands law enforcement's authority to monitor telecommunications, track a subject's Internet usage, and share information (U.S. Congress, 2001; Urban, 2011).

Balancing individual rights and liberty with collective security and crime prevention will challenge everyone as government counterterrorism activities continue. Public pressure to combat terrorism may result in measures designed to curtail civil liberties, such as the right to privacy, due process, and freedom from unreasonable searches and seizures. However, if terrorism patterns continue, U.S. citizens may wish to sacrifice some liberties in exchange for safety and security.

Counterterrorism initiatives and the maintenance of homeland security will continue to challenge police agencies. Officers must prevent terrorist attacks within diverse communities while avoiding stereotypes and bias based on race, culture, religion, and nationality. Officers must sustain community policing activities, especially in multicultural and diverse communities, to establish trust and secure the cooperation of citizens in the homeland security effort.

DISASTER PLANNING AND RESPONSE

Disaster Planning

Predisaster planning is absolutely essential to prevent or minimize property damage, injuries, and death. A disaster may affect a neighborhood, an entire community, or a region. The following outline illustrates the detail and comprehensiveness associated with a major **disaster plan.**

- Authority—from the chief executive to designated emergency coordinator
- Purpose—clearly stated transition from normal to emergency operation
- Types of emergencies covered
- Execution instructions
- Supporting information
    - Maps
    - Procedure charts
    - Telephone lists
    - Local resource list
    - Mutual-aid agreements
    - Liaison with Federal Emergency Management Agency (FEMA) or Department of Homeland Security
    - Glossary
- Emergency control center/emergency operations center
    - Location
    - Communications
    - In-house communications
- Protection of vital records
    - Agency or corporate records
    - Data files
    - Personnel and client lists
    - Financial records
- Emergency shutdown procedures
- Protection of personnel
- Evacuation and movement to shelter
- Education and training—emergency plan manual
- Testing the plan
- Role of supervisors

There may be several versions of a disaster plan depending on the type of disaster. At the very least, disaster contingency plans should include the emergencies that may be anticipated, who will be involved, the roles and responsibilities of the disaster recovery participants, and how the response procedures will be analyzed to improve response to subsequent catastrophic events.

Disaster Response

The law enforcement mission at the scene of a disaster or any other major unusual occurrence is to establish and maintain order, and enforce emergency rules and applicable laws. This may involve crowd control, provision of emergency services, care and custody of prisoners, crime and looting prevention, and assistance with rescue operations. An established **disaster response procedure** should be followed by the responding officer to a disaster scene. This should include responsibility for officer safety, assessment of the situation, assumption of initial command, establishing a perimeter, notification of necessary personnel, determining safe routes for responding units, providing updated information, locating responsible parties, identification of potential problems, and determining the location of an initial **emergency command center.**

Major **incident control** involves five functional areas or sections. The command section includes the **incident commander, information officer, liaison officer** (point of contact with the media as well as assisting mutual-aid agencies), and a **scribe** responsible for documenting events and actions taken. The **intelligence and planning** section gathers information and formulates strategic plans to deal with the incident. The operations section implements the strategic plan by utilizing tactics. The **logistics** section is responsible for obtaining necessary personnel, equipment, and supplies. When financial accountability is required (typically on large-scale operations), the finance section analyzes the costs associated with the incident.

As first responders to disaster scenes, law enforcement officers are confronted with tremendous challenges and risk to their personal safety. They are tasked with enormous responsibility. Officers must accurately and efficiently assess the incident, determine the severity of the danger, isolate hazards, and control the situation. They must use whatever resources are available to maintain public safety and restore normalcy. In doing so, knowledge of the affected community's culture and practices will assist officers to establish security and attend to victims (Shusta, Levine, Wong, & Harris, 2011).

HOSTAGE SITUATIONS

Hostage situations arise from a variety of circumstances. They may arise from terrorist activity, at the scene of prison riots, when a crime is in progress, or when the police respond to a domestic disturbance. Hostage takers may be mentally unstable individuals, criminals who use a bystander as a shield, riotous demonstrators, political extremists, or religious zealots.

Police response and styles of control in hostage situations typically fall into three broad categories: do nothing and wait out the hostage-taker, attack or assault the hostage-taker's position, or negotiate with the hostage-taker. To do nothing invites injury to the hostage and generates negative publicity for the law enforcement agency. Assaults on hostage-taker positions are rarely successful. A majority of the attacks on hostage-takers result in death to hostages. The most desirable and successful option in a hostage situation is to negotiate. **Hostage negotiations** benefit the situation because stalling for time allows the initial state of high emotion to subside and the scene can be isolated and contained. As time passes, the lives of the hostages become more secure as the hostage-taker realizes the value associated with human life and the hostages' continued safety. The hostage-taker might even develop affection for the hostages.

Many large police organizations have trained hostage negotiators. Since most police agencies are small, the patrol officer or a dispatcher may be required to assume the responsibilities of a negotiator. Regardless of the personnel used, the incident commander and the negotiator should not be the same person. The commander must devote full attention to the entire situation. Furthermore, if the hostage-taker realizes that the negotiator is in charge, the hostage-taker knows the negotiator does not need to seek another's approval to grant requests. Additionally, the following guidelines apply in hostage negotiation situations:

- Weapons are not negotiable items.
- Negotiators should never substitute for hostages.
- Negotiators should be truthful whenever possible.
- Deadlines should be avoided.
- Relatives and friends should not be allowed to negotiate.
- Negotiators should not converse with hostages because this increases the hostages' value to the hostage-taker.
- Intelligence should be gathered concerning the hostage-taker.
- Face-to-face negotiations are best, but telephones, radios, and bullhorns are safer (Lyman, 2010; Maher, 1989).

Hostage negotiations often cover an extended period of time. Negotiators should be patient, talkative, and able to suspend judgment of the hostage-taker. Virtually all police officers are potential hostage negotiators. Therefore, basic training in hostage negotiations for most police officers may be beneficial.

BARRICADED SUBJECTS

The guidelines and techniques used in hostage situations are also appropriate when confronted with **barricaded subjects.** These subjects may not be a threat to others. They may be suicidal. However, unlike hostage situations, if no threat to human life exists, it may be best to wait out a barricaded subject.

If the subject is barricaded because of a suicide attempt or crisis situation, police officers should do the following:

- Demonstrate an empathetic attitude.
- Secure the scene.
- Safeguard people and property.
- Establish rapport with the subject.
- Reassure the subject.

- Determine the reason for the crisis.
- Comply with requests, if possible.
- Follow procedures for mental evaluation, if appropriate, when the crisis is over (Ortmeier & Davis, 2012; Russell & Beigel, 1990).

When responding to a hostage or barricaded subject incident, an officer's primary responsibility is to protect lives. The responding officer(s) should approach the scene quietly, identify and verify the location of the subject, request additional resources, if necessary, and establish a perimeter and a command post. In addition, response personnel should remove all uninvolved individuals from the area, establish and maintain communication with the subject, and develop contingency plans for alternative resolutions of the situation.

CASE STUDY—THE MILITARIZATION OF LAW ENFORCEMENT

In February, 1997, two heavily armed men wearing full body armor were caught in the act of robbing a bank in North Hollywood, California. Rather than give up or flee when LAPD officers arrived, the robbers opened fire with fully automatic AK-47 rifles, firing armor-piercing bullets from clip magazines containing 100 rounds each. The ensuing firefight lasted nearly 30 minutes, leaving both suspects dead and 18 civilians and police officers wounded. Initially, the encounter favored the suspects because they were wearing body armor and their weapons were ballistically superior to the firearms carried by the responding uniformed patrol officers. However, the patrol officers succeeded in preventing the robbers' escape until SWAT officers arrived.

In 1992, federal agents attempted to arrest white separatist Randy Weaver on a weapons charge at his rural compound near Ruby Ridge, Idaho. During the encounter, Weaver's wife and son were killed by the agents. Later, a Senate subcommittee report faulted the agents for using military-style rules of engagement. In 1993, four ATF agents and 72 Davidians died during a confrontation between David Koresh's Branch Davidian followers and federal agents near Waco, Texas. The agents were killed during the initial military-style assault on the compound. The 72 men, women, and children died in a fire during a subsequent military-style assault on the Koresh compound.

In 2000, the media covered the successful removal of young Elian Gonzalez from a Miami, Florida home. The boy was returned to his custodial parent in Cuba. However, the televised image of federal agents in combat gear, armed with military-style assault rifles, was heavily criticized.

1. Is the North Hollywood incident typical in police work?
2. Is militarization of civilian law enforcement necessary?

SWAT OPERATIONS

Some types of police operations require specialized tactics and weapons not commonly used by the uniformed patrol officer. Hostage and barricaded suspect situations may require the use of **special weapons and**

tactics (SWAT) teams . . ., sometimes referred to as mobile response teams (MRTs) or emergency service units (ESUs). Team members receive intensive training to deal with high-risk incidents requiring paramilitary tactics. SWAT teams are also equipped with the types of hardware necessary to control and contain dangerous situations. When used appropriately, SWAT teams have been very effective and have minimized loss of life to citizens, police officers, and suspects.

The first SWAT team was formed by the LAPD in the early 1960s. Since then, the number of SWAT teams has grown. The 1990s experienced the largest proliferation of SWAT teams in the history of the United States. By 1996 almost 65 percent of police agencies in the United States had special weapons teams. Many experts argue that SWAT teams are expensive and, contrary to television and movie accounts of police work, are rarely required in the police service. Small-town SWAT teams are particularly problematic because the team may become extremely bored. Officers are trained in paramilitary operations and are armed with sophisticated weapons and equipment. Since few, if any, incidents in small towns require a SWAT team, they are often used in situations such as executing search warrants in which they are really not needed ("SWAT Team May Prove Costly," 1999).

The results can be devastating when SWAT teams make mistakes or are used inappropriately. In Fresno, California, in 1999, a federal jury awarded $12.5 million to the family and estate of a Dinuba man who was shot 15 times (and subsequently died) during a 1997 police raid on his home. Using information from a confidential informant (information the informant subsequently recanted) the police and the department's SWAT team executed a search warrant on the deceased's home. The officers, wearing camouflage uniforms, hoods, and masks, entered the home around 7:00 A.M. The family members thought the SWAT team members were burglars and resisted. The jury award in this case was one of the largest ever against a California law enforcement agency. The city of Los Angeles's $3.8 million settlement with Rodney King was almost 75 percent less ($12.5 million awarded, 1999).

Although SWAT teams are, and will continue to be, important to officer survival and to some civilian police agency missions, many view the proliferation of such teams as unnecessary militarization of the police. The symbols law enforcement agencies use to define themselves are also important, particularly from the standpoint of police–community relations. The primary mission of a police agency is peacekeeping. It is not military in nature. Therefore, the agency and its personnel should not attempt to be, or function as, an occupying army (Carlson, 2005).

◢ SUMMARY

During the course of a police officer's career, the officer may encounter several types of special situations. These special situations include locating lost and missing persons, dealing with mentally imbalanced and intoxicated persons, responding to calls related to Sudden Infant Death

Syndrome, medical emergencies, suicides, juvenile disturbances, gangs, animal problems, aircraft accidents, fires, environmental misfortune, and natural disasters. The officer will respond to domestic disputes and altercations between other individuals as well as civil disturbances. Less common, but nevertheless life-threatening, are the incidents involving bombs, bomb threats, terrorism, weapons of mass destruction, hostage situations, and barricaded subjects. Occasionally, these special situations require the use of special weapons and tactics (SWAT) teams.

DISCUSSION QUESTIONS AND EXERCISES

1. Discuss the procedure for responding to patrol calls involving environmental threats and hazardous materials.
2. Identify four different types of emergencies and describe appropriate patrol officer responses for each.
3. Create a civil emergency or disaster management plan outline for your jurisdiction.
4. Describe the procedure for handling hostage and barricaded subject situations. Is the response procedure identical for both? Why or why not?
5. SWAT teams have proliferated in the United States in recent years. Are all of these teams necessary? Why or why not? How can the inappropriate use of SWAT teams be prevented?
6. A SWAT team responded to the scene of a barricaded subject who was holding hostages. A police sniper shot and killed the subject. Later, a local newspaper criticized the police for use of excessive force and failure to utilize a hostage negotiator. How should the police respond to this criticism?
7. While on patrol in a marked police vehicle, an officer is dispatched to the scene of an explosion at a chemical plant. The plant is located near an elementary school where classes are in session. The dispatcher indicates that the explosion could be the result of terrorist activity. As a first responder, how should the officer proceed?
8. At 2:00 P.M. on a Wednesday, a 50-year-old woman, armed with a knife, a hammer, and what appeared to be a handgun, barricaded herself in an unoccupied office on the seventh floor of a 10-story office building. From the office, she placed a 9-1-1 call to the police, threatening to kill her husband who was not in the building at the time. How should the police proceed?
9. Are certain types of incidents beyond law enforcement's ability to prevent and control? If so, who is responsible?

Investigations

LEARNING OBJECTIVES

After completing this chapter, the reader should be able to:

- list and describe the common elements of the investigative process.
- locate and develop sources of information.
- describe crime reporting systems and computerized databases including the UCR, NCVS, and NIBRS.
- evaluate information gathered from public and private sources.
- demonstrate appropriate interviewing and interrogation techniques.
- conduct a preliminary investigation.
- conduct a basic collision investigation.
- conduct a basic criminal investigation.
- describe procedures for processing a crime scene.
- analyze evidence gathered in a criminal investigation.
- explain the roles of forensic science and profiling in criminal investigations.
- describe the qualities of the investigator as a witness.
- discuss the procedure for investigating specific types of incidents.

KEY TERMS

Define, describe, or explain the importance of each of the following.

Auto Theft Bureau (ATB)

Automated electronic vehicle locator (AVL)

Automated Fingerprint Identification System (AFIS)

Automated Property System (APS)

Baseline sketch

Chain of custody

Collision investigation

Compass point sketch

Computer crime

Crime scene reconstruction

Criminal profiling

Criminalist

Criminalistics

Cybercrime

Cross-projection sketch

DNA

Drugfire

Economic crime

Forensic science

Forensic specialist

Geographic Information System
(GIS)

Grid search pattern

Identity theft

Interrogation

Interview

Instrumentation

Integrated Ballistic Identification System (IBIS)

Investigation

National Crime Information Center (NCIC)

NCIC 2000

National Incident-Based Reporting System (NIBRS)

Preliminary investigation

Rectangular coordinate sketch

Sources of information

Spiral search pattern

Stolen Vehicle System (SVS)

Strip search pattern

Surveillance

Triangulation sketch

Zone search pattern

INTRODUCTION

An **investigation** may be defined as any systematic inquiry to determine the facts surrounding an event or situation. It involves the patient, step-by-step process of observation, search, and examination. The term *investigate* is derived from a Latin word, *vestigare,* meaning to track or trace. This derivative is especially appropriate in police work in which most investigations involve tracking or tracing a law violator. Investigations are warranted when an accident or unexplained loss occurs, or when alleged individual misconduct or criminal activity is reported. Well documented investigations are critical to the success of any law enforcement agency.

Investigation is an art as well as a science. The competencies and attributes of good investigators include integrity and honesty; open-mindedness; excellent verbal and written communications skills; excellent human relations skills; knowledge of civil as well as criminal law; knowledge of the judicial process; research, analytical, and critical-thinking skills; and problem-solving ability.

The purpose of an investigation is to determine who, what, where, when, how, and why an event or incident happened. Several elements are common to any investigation. These elements include identification of the problem, issue, or situation; identification of the essential facts that must be acquired or proved; identification of potential sources and location of information; selection of an efficient investigative method; location and preservation of information or evidence; and reevaluation and reinvestigation, if necessary.

Investigative methods include interviewing, interrogation, instrumentation, and surveillance. Any or all of these methods may be utilized during the course of a single investigation. Verbal (testimonial) information is derived from victims, witnesses, and suspects during an investigation. Victims, witnesses, and subjects are interviewed. Suspects to a crime are interrogated. **Interviews** should be conducted in an environment that makes the interviewee feel comfortable. This reduces nervousness and encourages a free flow of information. **Interrogations,** on the other hand, should be conducted in an environment that is foreign to the suspect. A rights advisory, according to the *Miranda* decision of 1966, is required when a suspect is in custody, being interrogated, and the public law enforcement officer conducting the interrogation intends to use information gained in a prosecution.

Instrumentation refers to the application of the physical sciences to the investigative process. These sciences include physics, chemistry, biology, anatomy, and physiology. **Surveillance** involves the observation of persons, places, or things. Observation methods include spot checks, stationary plants, and moving surveillance. (Berg & Horgan, 1998; Gilbert, 2008; Ortmeier, 1999; Osterburg & Ward, 2010).

CASE STUDY—LAW ENFORCEMENT DATABASES

Marco Carrillo had posed as a United States citizen for nearly 15 years when he attempted to enter the states at the San Ysidro, California, international border crossing with Mexico. He was carrying a United States passport and claimed the State of Indiana as his birthplace. Curious immigration inspectors scanned his passport through the Interagency Border Inspection System (IBIS), which alerted authorities that Carrillo deserved closer scrutiny. However, because the IBIS capabilities were limited, it took 90 days and searches of numerous other databases, including a nongovernment Internet site, to learn Carrillo's real identity: Ismael Lizama, a convicted Mexican drug smuggler.

Law enforcement databases are not infallible. Despite mandates to integrate and streamline the information systems, data entry and user errors, complexity, lack of coordination, and information overload lead to mistakes and missed opportunities. In some cases, innocent persons are mistakenly incarcerated.

1. Should all federal and state law enforcement databases be integrated into a single system?
2. How can individuals be protected from the misuse of personal information contained in law enforcement databases?

SOURCES OF INFORMATION

Common **sources of information** for an investigation include physical evidence, specialized databases, victims, witnesses, suspects, records, informants, and the Internet. Records include local, state, and federal law enforcement and other government data. Private individual and business records as well as various publications may also be valuable sources of information. Access to records may be gained through permission, the legal process, the information's status as a public record, and through computerized databases.

Informants are also an important source of information. Informants are indispensable in many criminal investigations. When informants are utilized, care should be exercised to evaluate their motives, as well as the

Sources of information include numerous types of records.
(Photo courtesy of the Cobb County, GA Police Department.)

information provided, to ensure reliability. In a criminal prosecution, the reliability of informant information is critical. Failure to test the reliability of informant-supplied information could result in the suppression of evidence derived from the informant's information.

The Internet is an excellent vehicle for gathering information. Search engines (tables of content for the World Wide Web) provide useful windows to view websites throughout the world. All search engines operate in a similar fashion. They run computer software programs that search the content of websites. They create an index in a large database consisting of key words from website pages they examine. When a user enters key words, the search engines compare the key words entered with the website pages in the database and deliver the results to the user in the form of links. The key words or phrase entered should be specific to narrow the search parameters and to allow the search engine to identify websites relevant to the purpose of the search.

Government agencies maintain websites that contain considerable resources and Internet links of interest to the law enforcement professional. In addition, the text of government regulations and laws can often be accessed through government agency websites.

Each state government also maintains a website. Typically, an individual state's website can be located at www.state.us. ("state" is replaced with the two-letter abbreviation for the state sought).

Popular search engines include the following:
- www.altavista.com
- www.askjeeves.com
- www.dogpile.com
- www.excite.com
- www.google.com
- www.hotbot.com
- www.infoseek.com
- www.lycos.com
- www.multicrawl.com
- www.webcrawler.com
- www.wisdomdog.com
- www.yahoo.com

Noteworthy government websites include the following:
- www.fbi.gov. This is the FBI's website and it contains information about FBI programs and services.
- www.fedworld.gov. This website is a clearinghouse for government information.
- www.loc.gov. This is the Library of Congress website that contains valuable and timely information about pending legislation and statutes.
- www.nacic.gov. This is the website for the National Counterintelligence Center (NACIC) that provides information about trends in foreign and domestic espionage against American businesses.
- www.secretservice.gov. This U.S. Secret Service website provides information about financial crimes such as counterfeiting and electronic fraud.

Information on new computer viruses may be obtained by accessing the websites of the major anti-virus software producers. These include:
- www.f-secure.com
- www.networkassociates.com
- www.norman.com (Norman Data Defense Systems)
- www.sophos.com
- www.symantec.com

Additional law enforcement and criminal justice information resources are available through the National Criminal Justice Reference Service at www.ncjrs.org.

VICTIM AND WITNESS INTERVIEWS

Police officers and investigators should be aware that the perceptive faculties and observations of victims and witnesses depend on external as well as internal factors. External factors that may distort an object or observation include distance from or proximity to the object or event, lighting, weather, noise, and other environmental conditions. Other external factors that may distract victims and witnesses include the size of an object, movement, odors, and similarities between the observer and a subject. If a victim or witness observes a characteristic on a subject that is similar to a characteristic of the observer such as both wearing mustaches, the observer is likely to recall the mustache as the most outstanding characteristic.

Internal factors that may affect a victim's or witness's observations include personal characteristics of the observer such as physical condition, eyesight, hearing, and other perceptive capabilities. In addition, an individual's ability to observe and recall another human being, object, or event accurately depends on internal factors other than sensory capabilities. Emotional and psychological problems, experience and educational level, personal prejudices and bias, moods affected by color, and memory capacity affect observation and recognition faculties.

Standard formats are generally used to describe persons. Adherence to a standard enhances uniformity of practice and helps to ensure completeness in reporting. Victims and witnesses should first be asked to describe something unique about the subject or recall any similarities between the subject and the observer. After the victim or witness provides unsolicited information, the officer or investigator should ask for additional descriptive data based on the following protocol (Adams, 2007; O'Hara & O'Hara, 2003):

- Name, if known
- Gender
- Race and nationality, if known
- Age (estimated or exact, if known)
- Height (approximate)
- Weight (approximate)
- Hair (color, style, length, baldness)
- Eyes (color, shape)
- Complexion (color, acne, freckles, birthmarks)
- Other physical features (scars, tattoos, sideburns)
- Eyeglasses
- Cap or hat
- Shirt and tie (color, style)
- Coat or jacket (color, style)
- Trousers, shorts, or dress (color, style, fabric)
- Shoes or boots
- Jewelry

COMPUTERIZED DATABASES

A wealth of information is available to the contemporary law enforcement officer through computerized databases. Many of these databases are accessible through the dispatch center or in police vehicles equipped with mobile data terminals (MDTs) or mobile data computers (MDCs). Major databases include the following:

- **National Crime Information Center (NCIC).** Established in 1967, this system is maintained by the FBI and services all 50 states, federal law enforcement agencies, Puerto Rico, the U.S. Virgin Islands, the District of Columbia, and Canada. Organized into 17 databases, it contains a great deal of information including data on missing and wanted persons; stolen vehicles, aircraft, and vessels; and stolen vehicle license plates. It also provides criminal history information and serves as a link to many other computerized information systems. Connections are available to other countries through the International Police Organization (INTERPOL).

- **NCIC 2000.** This enhanced NCIC system utilizes optical scanners to read fingerprint patterns. Officers may identify a missing person or fugitive by placing the subject's fingers on a scanner port. The image is transmitted to the FBI's NCIC computer, which replies to the officer if the subject's fingerprints are on file. It also searches all derivatives of names and contains mug shots and data on sexual offenders, probationers, parolees, and persons incarcerated in federal prisons. In addition, the system enables electronic access to federal prison and Canadian criminal justice records. It includes data relating to wanted and unidentified persons, stolen property, criminal histories, gangs, and information compiled during investigations. It also allows insurance agencies access to stolen vehicle information (Reid, 2011).
- **Automated Property System (APS).** The NCIC's APS article file lets officers process identification numbers and descriptions of suspected stolen objects if the numbers are registered in the system.
- **National Incident-Based Reporting System (NIBRS).** This system is a function of the FBI's Uniform Crime Report (UCR) system. The NIBRS replaces the UCR Part I and Part II offenses with Group A and B offenses. The new categories are much more comprehensive and up to date. For example, while the existing Part I crimes focus on street crimes, the new Group A widens criminological interest to other offenses including white-collar crime. The NIBRS and the UCR contain information regarding offenses reported to the police and subsequently reported to the FBI. However, the NIBRS provides more detailed information about the nature and scope of reported crimes.

The FBI introduced the NIBRS in January 1989. The traditional UCR system presented the total number of reported occurrences of Part I offenses as well as arrest data for Part I and Part II offenses. As an alternative to summary reporting, the new enhanced UCR (or NIBRS) was developed to deal with the volume, diversity, and complexity of crime. The NIBRS requires more detailed reports. Agencies collect data regarding individual crime incidents and arrests and submit them in reports detailing each incident. This incident-based reporting provides much more complete information about crimes than do the summary statistics of the traditional UCR system.

Detailed information is provided for each of these crimes. Included among the 52 data elements collected is information detailing the crime circumstances, offender characteristics, arrestee data, victim information, and offense and property data (U.S. Department of Justice, 1988). Less detailed information is required for the 11 Group B offenses.

Other features of the NIBRS include the following:

- New offense definitions. Rape, for example, in addition to cases involving force, now includes cases in which consent was not given because of temporary or permanent mental or physical incapacity.
- New UCR codes.

Group A offenses include the following:
1. Arson
2. Assault offenses
3. Bribery
4. Burglary/breaking and entering
5. Counterfeiting/forgery
6. Destruction/damage/vandalism of property
7. Drug/narcotic offenses
8. Embezzlement
9. Extortion/blackmail
10. Fraud offenses
11. Gambling offenses
12. Homicide offenses
13. Kidnaping/abduction
14. Larceny/theft offenses
15. Motor vehicle theft
16. Pornography/obscene material
17. Prostitution offenses
18. Robbery
19. Sex offenses, forcible
20. Sex offenses, nonforcible
21. Stolen property offenses
22. Weapons law violations

- Elimination of the hierarchy rule. All crimes occurring during the same incident are recorded.
- Introduction of a new category called crimes against society. This provides an additional category to complement the existing crimes against property and crimes against person and includes crimes such as gambling, prostitution, drug sales, and use.

The Group B offenses include the following:
1. Bad checks
2. Curfew/loitering/vagrancy violations
3. Disorderly conduct
4. Driving under the influence
5. Drunkenness
6. Family offenses/nonviolent
7. Liquor law violations
8. Peeping tom offenses
9. Runaway offenses
10. Trespass of real property
11. All other offenses

- Mechanisms for distinguishing between attempted and completed crimes.
- Expanded data on the victim–offender relationship.

NIBRS was intended to be fully operational by 1999. However, the cost of implementing necessary changes to the reporting system, concerns regarding the impact of the NIBRS on agency reported crime rates, and lack of understanding on how the information is to be used, has delayed implementation. To date, less than one-third of state crime reporting systems have been certified for NIBRS participation.

Additional major databases include the following:

- **Automated Fingerprint Identification System (AFIS)**—This system utilizes optical scanners to record and electronically transmit fingerprints to a state or FBI fingerprinting identification (ID) database. It is designed to replace manual fingerprinting ID systems currently used by most agencies.
- **National Law Enforcement Telecommunications System (NLETS)** —This system links all states, Puerto Rico, the District of Columbia, and most federal law enforcement agencies for the purpose of exchanging information.
- **California Law Enforcement Telecommunications System (CLETS)** —Similar to the NLETS, the CLETS is a high-speed California state-based computer network that allows the agency user to access information directly from numerous federal and state computerized information files.
- **Criminal History System (CHS)** —This database contains criminal history information and is available to agencies on a right-to-know and need-to-know basis. The database includes the Master Name Index (MNI), a human subject identification index maintained by criminal history repositories. The MNI includes names and other identifiers for each person about whom a record is held in the systems.
- **Criminal Offender Record Information (CORI)** —Information stored in CORI summarizes a criminal offender's personal identifiers such as the offender's gender, name, date of birth, physical description, fingerprints, photographs, and justice system proceedings.
- **Department of Motor Vehicles (DMV)** —DMV databases include information associated with drivers' licenses, state identification cards, vehicle and vessel registration, and motor vehicle law violations.
- **Stolen Vehicle System (SVS)**—Stolen vehicle identification numbers (VINs) and stolen vehicle components with identification numbers are recorded and retrievable within this system.
- **Criminal Justice Information System (CJIS)** —This is a state-based system that provides a wide range of information on wanted persons, guns, and stolen property. Many CJIS databases provide information on the progress of criminal cases from arrest through conviction and final disposition. Officers may access CJIS for follow-up information.

- **Automated Statewide Auto Theft Inquiry Service (AUTO STATIS)**—This state-based system operates in conjunction with the NCIC and specializes in information regarding stolen, impounded, and repossessed vehicles.
- **Domestic Violence Restraining Order System (DVROS)**—This California state-based system tracks restraining orders issued against individuals as a result of domestic violence or family court orders (Payton & Amaral, 2004; Foster, 2005; Schmalleger, 2005; Siegel & Senna, 2006).

In addition to the previously described computerized data, some law enforcement agencies are taking advantage of new computerized crime mapping technology. **Geographic Information System (GIS)** technology enables law enforcement agencies to analyze and correlate various data sources to create a detailed view of crime incidents and related factors within a specific geographic area. The crime-related data are plotted against a digitized map of a community, city, or region. Crime incident data is geocoded (assigning x and y coordinates to an address so information can be coded to a map) by using either street centerlines or parcels of land to identify a geographic location. Crime mapping analysis can be used for geocoding offense (arrest and incident) data, calls for service, and vehicle recovery information. Police agencies that utilize crime mapping report improvements in information dissemination, evaluation, and administration. Specifically, crime mapping data are useful to:

- Inform police personnel of crime incident locations.
- Make resource allocation decisions.
- Evaluate intervention strategies.
- Inform citizens about crime activity.
- Identify hot spots and locations with repeat calls for service.

Although a majority of police departments engage in some form of crime analysis, usually compiling statistical reports to fulfill UCR requirements, only about 15 percent of police departments surveyed utilize any computerized crime mapping. Larger departments with dedicated crime analysis staff primarily responsible for performing computerized inquiries are more likely to utilize the latest technology. Significant financial resources, time, and training are necessary to establish a computerized crime mapping operation. Because most police departments in the United States are small, few police patrol officers currently use computerized crime mapping. However, use is likely to increase over time, since mapping has been shown to be a valuable tool for law enforcement (Bennett & Hess, 2004; Mamalian & La Vigne, 1999).

Computerized databases make the process of collecting, storing, analyzing, and retrieving vast amounts of data much simpler and faster.

For links to justice information technology resources, contact the National Consortium for Justice Information and Statistics at www.search.org.

However, any system is only as strong as its weakest link. Since the data is contained in an electronic medium, unauthorized access, system collapse, and inadequate linkages between databases often create obstacles to effective information retrieval and exchange. The United States Immigration and Naturalization Service's IDENT system, for example, failed to identify Raphael Resendez-Ramirez as a suspected serial killer on the FBI's Ten Most Wanted List. Resendez-Ramirez was accused of eight murders, four of which occurred after the United States Border Patrol released him to return to Mexico on June 2, 1999. IDENT is an electronic system designed to store fingerprints and photographs of people who are apprehended after entering the United States illegally. Apparently, however, the IDENT system was self-contained and did not have appropriate linkages to other databases that would have allowed the Border Patrol to discover Resendez-Ramirez's wanted status (Stern, 1999).

PRELIMINARY INVESTIGATIONS

Most often the uniformed patrol officer is the first police representative to arrive at the scene of an accident, death, or crime. As the initial responder, the patrol officer is in the best position to conduct a **preliminary investigation** at the scene. Essential steps to preliminary investigations include the following:

- The officer should proceed safely to the scene. Public safety and the safety of the responding officer(s) are the most important considerations.
- Upon arriving at the scene, the officer should establish control. Citizens already at the scene may be excited, confused, or hysterical. The first responder should have a plan and set priorities for assuming leadership to process the scene.
- Inquiries should be made to determine if anyone is injured. Priority should be given to medical emergencies. If a body is located at the scene, the responding officer should check the victim to ensure that the person is, in fact, dead. In some states, determination of death at the scene is the responsibility of the coroner. If the victim is deceased, the body should not be moved.
- The officer should determine if a crime has been committed. An incident, which may appear noncriminal initially, may have a criminal agent as its cause.
- The officer should arrest the suspect(s) to the crime, if present.
- The officer should notify dispatch as soon as possible regarding any follow-up information. If a crime has been committed and the perpetrator is not present, the broadcast should include a description of the suspect, the suspect's mode of travel and direction of flight, type of offense, location, time, weapons used, and property stolen.
- The officer should secure and protect the scene.
- The officer should locate and retain for questioning any witnesses to the incident.

- The officer should interview witnesses as appropriate and provide dispatch with any follow-up information.
- The officer should secure, collect, and preserve physical evidence.
- The officer should take appropriate notes and prepare an official report.

In a few large police departments, as well as most small departments, the uniformed officer also conducts follow-up investigations. Allowing uniformed officers to conduct follow-up investigations improves morale, provides the uniformed officer with the opportunity to process an entire case, and gives detective-specialists the ability to concentrate on cases that require extensive, detailed investigation.

COLLISION INVESTIGATIONS

Most accidents involve collisions, but not all collisions are accidents. Some collisions are intentional and are staged or faked for insurance purposes. Accidents result when the consequences of one's actions are not deliberate. In large police departments, vehicle collisions or accidents are usually investigated by an officer who has been trained in the techniques of **collision investigation** and reconstruction. However, since most police departments in the United States are small, accident investigation becomes the responsibility of the highway patrol or one of the officers responding to the scene.

A patrol officer responding to the scene of a collision should proceed according to agency response policy. Consideration must always be given to the traffic congestion in the area, which may have resulted from the collision. While approaching the scene, the patrol officer should watch for hit-and-run vehicles and note any spilled materials or situations, such as downed power lines, which may create hazardous conditions. The officer should be prepared to handle unique safety requirements for positioning the police vehicle, traffic and spectator control, emergency medical care, tow trucks, removal of the affected vehicles from the roadway, and resumption of normal traffic flow.

After injured parties have received necessary emergency medical treatment and the collision scene is under control, an officer may proceed with the investigation. Witnesses and victims must be separated and interviewed. Officers should not ask leading questions, that is, questions that suggest answers. Rather, officers should ask victims what happened and ask witnesses about what they observed. Drivers and passengers of vehicles involved may be biased. Anger and fear of economic loss or criminal prosecution, loss of driving privileges, and civil liability may lead involved parties to distort the facts. Statements from witnesses not involved in the collision may be used to corroborate involved persons' statements and other evidence available at the scene.

Subsequent to victim and witness interviews, the investigating officer should conduct an examination of the vehicle and the scene. Specific measurements should be recorded, and detailed drawings made when an accident involves personal injury or may lead to a civil lawsuit or criminal prosecution. The officer should record the point of impact, the length

Officers use special techniques to investigate collisions. *(Photo courtesy of the Cobb County, GA Police Department.)*

and location of skid marks, the final position of the vehicle(s), and roadway and other physical features at the scene. Photographs and a detailed written narrative should accompany the collision scene sketch. Notations should also be made of the roadway and weather conditions, the environment, and odometer reading in the vehicle(s) involved. Persons involved in the collision should exchange identification and insurance information. The investigating officer should provide information regarding the parties' rights and responsibilities. Accident reconstruction, because of its potential legal consequences, should be conducted by someone with specialized training and experience in the science of traffic accident analysis. A surveyor's total station system can support collision investigations. This equipment electronically takes measures to record distances between different elements of a collision scene. The information can then be stored in memory and later downloaded onto a computer, to be used in vehicle homicide cases (Reid, 2011).

When a collision involves a motor vehicle and a pedestrian, a thorough investigation must be conducted, and a detailed report should be written.

The results of a collision investigation may be used as supporting evidence in a civil lawsuit or criminal prosecution. Traffic engineers may also use data from reports to improve roadway conditions, traffic control devices, and traffic flow.

CRIMINAL INVESTIGATIONS

The purposes of a criminal investigation are to determine if a crime was, in fact, committed; identify the suspect; locate the suspect; and recognize, collect, and preserve evidence that may establish guilt (or innocence) of the accused in a judicial proceeding. A criminal investigation may be considered successful if all available physical evidence is collected and preserved properly, witnesses have been intelligently interviewed, the suspect, if willing, has been effectively interrogated, all leads are properly developed, and the investigation is reported properly.

The first step in a criminal investigation is to determine if a crime was committed and, if so, what type of crime. Criminal, or penal, codes specifically describe what behavior is criminal. Each element of an offense must be established in the incident under investigation for a crime to have occurred. Furthermore, a police officer's powers to arrest differ depending on whether the crime was a felony or misdemeanor. Thus, failure to know the law may result in civil and possibly criminal liability for false arrest or false imprisonment.

The identification of a suspected perpetrator may be accomplished in one of several ways. First, the suspect may be apprehended at the scene and provide the investigator with an admission or confession. Second, eyewitnesses to the crime may be available. Third, circumstantial evidence in the form of motive, opportunity to commit the crime, or trace evidence that can associate or place the suspect with the crime scene may be available. If the suspect is not present at the crime scene, it will be necessary to trace and locate the suspect. Usually, crime suspects are not in hiding. Their location is simply unknown. However, locating and apprehending a suspect may require persistence. A systematic procedure will enhance the possibility of apprehending a suspect.

Before launching a search for a fugitive, the investigator should be certain that the legal requirements for a possible arrest have been satisfied and all pertinent background information and identification data on the suspect have been gathered. The investigator should collect as much information as possible regarding the suspect's history. Criminal records, if available, provide information regarding aliases used, location of previous arrests and convictions, arresting agencies, the nature of previous offenses, and fingerprints. Other forms of trace data include telephone, city, and criss-cross directories, credit bureaus, motor vehicle records, identification data from the U.S. Immigration Service, passport or military records, informants, county assessors' and recorders' offices, past and present friends and acquaintances, union halls, blood banks, and lodging establishments.

CRIME SCENE PROCESSING

In addition to the elements of interviewing witnesses and interrogation of suspects, criminal investigations often involve the processing of a crime scene to collect physical evidence. Adherence to strict procedure used in the identification, collection, and preservation of physical evidence at a crime scene is critical.

The scene itself should be secured to prevent tampering until appropriate personnel arrive to process the scene. If detectives or evidence technicians are not available to process the scene, uniformed police officers must process the crime scene. If a crime scene search is warranted, the search should be organized and conducted carefully. Physical evidence located at a crime scene should be photographed before it is collected, drawn into the crime scene sketch, and collected and preserved to maintain its legal integrity. The latter involves careful marking or labeling of the evidence for future identification, protection of the evidence from contamination, and maintenance of the chain of custody of the evidence.

Crime Scene Reconstruction

The purpose of **crime scene reconstruction** is to determine what event, series of events, or sequence of events occurred during the commission of a crime. The reconstruction is accomplished through a careful analysis and interpretation of the physical evidence available at the crime scene. Inferences are drawn from the analysis and interpretation that can lead an investigator to test various theories regarding the events that occurred.

During the crime scene reconstruction process, the investigator identifies possible evidence and notes its location in relationship to its known former position. Attention focuses on objects that appear foreign to the environment. The reconstruction process is systematic, meticulous, and complex (Gilbert, 2008; Ogle, 2004).

The Crime Scene Search

As the first public safety responder to virtually all crime scenes, the patrol officer's primary responsibilities are to care for the injured, arrest a suspect, if present, retain witnesses, and secure the scene. After the primary responsibilities have been discharged, it may be necessary to conduct a search. In large agencies, the search and other detailed aspects of crime scene processing may be conducted by evidence or forensic technicians, criminalists, or others specifically trained in the techniques of evidence identification, collection, preservation, and analysis. However, in most police agencies the crime scene search and relevant crime scene processing are the primary duties of the uniformed patrol officer.

The search must be organized and conducted in a manner that adheres to constitutional safeguards. Care must be taken to ensure that relevant evidence is not overlooked or destroyed. If two or more officers are available, one officer should be designated the search leader. The leader determines the number of personnel needed as well as the search technique. Search techniques, or patterns, are determined by the circumstances. Exterior searches covering vast areas require search patterns

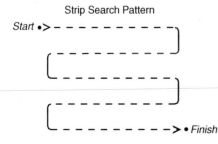

FIGURE 11.1 Strip search pattern.
(Illustration by Robert Myers.)

that are distinct from interior searches covering small areas. Regardless of the search pattern selected, the search must be thorough and systematic.

Common crime scene search techniques include the strip, spiral, grid, and zone patterns. The **strip search pattern** may be used in large or small search areas by a single officer or several persons. The area is divided into a series of imaginary lanes and searchers move up and down each lane until the area is searched.

The **spiral search pattern** is typically used outdoors by a single search person. The searcher starts at an outer corner and proceeds in a spiral pattern toward the center of the search area.

The **grid search pattern** is similar to the strip search except that the entire search area is covered twice. After completing the first search of each lane, the searchers double back at right angles to search the same area a second time.

When utilizing the **zone search pattern,** searchers divide the entire search area into zones, each of which can be searched using a pattern described previously. This technique is useful when covering very large areas.

Regardless of the search pattern used, it is best that the area be searched twice, utilizing different personnel to search the same area. The

Spiral Search Pattern

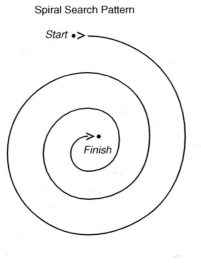

Start

Finish

FIGURE 11.2 Spiral search pattern. *(Illustration by Robert Myers.)*

Grid Search Pattern

Start

Finish

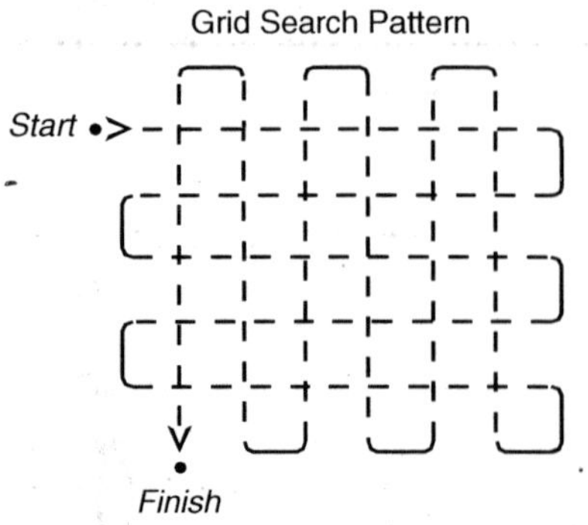

FIGURE 11.3 Grid search pattern. *(Illustration by Robert Myers.)*

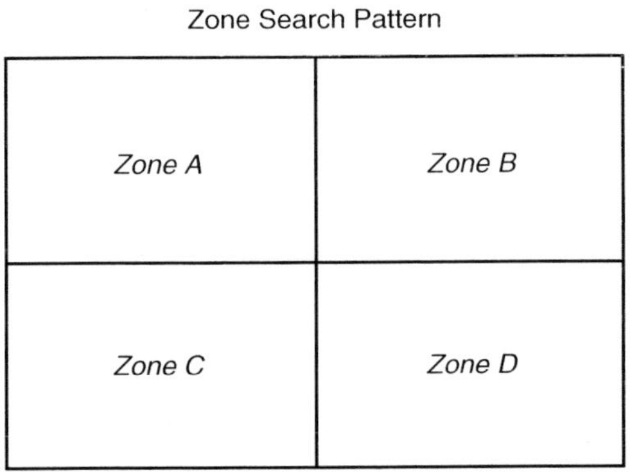

Zone Search Pattern

Zone A	Zone B
Zone C	Zone D

FIGURE 11.4 Zone search pattern. *(Illustration by Robert Myers.)*

second searcher may discover something that was overlooked by the first person in the original search.

Investigative Photography

Investigative photography can be used during a surveillance or laboratory analysis, in lineups, for photographs of persons arrested, and to document evidence discovered at a crime scene. Photographs are particularly useful in assisting the investigative, prosecutorial, and judicial processes because they provide an objective visual representation of a scene. Photographs of a crime scene should be taken before anything is disturbed. They should be taken in an organized sequence, showing the location of all relevant objects and items of evidence. The photographer should take as many photographs as necessary, beginning with general overall views of the area and ending with close-up photos of specific items. Long-range photos should be taken of the general area. Medium-range photos should focus on the immediate crime scene, and close-ups should be taken of specific items such as fingerprints, blood stains, weapons, and spent ammunition and shell casings. For close-ups it may be necessary to place some measuring device (usually a ruler) next to the item to give the viewer of the photo a proper perspective on the item's size. Since the ruler is an object that is foreign to the crime scene, one photo should be taken without the ruler and another photo should be taken of the item with the ruler.

Investigative photographs must be marked for identification by the photographer, filed, and continuously secured to maintain the **chain of custody** for courtroom presentation. The photographs should be marked on the back, not the front, with the date, sequence, case number, type of crime, and subject of the photograph. Other identifying information that should be included on the photograph and accompanying field notes includes the photographer's name, weather conditions, distance from the object photographed, and camera-specific information such as shutter and film speed, lens type, and lighting required.

Recent advances in investigative photography include the use of videotape and digital imaging technology. Videotape is an excellent supplement to, but not a replacement for, conventional still photographs. Once videotaping begins it should continue uninterrupted. Continuous videotaping eliminates the possibility of questionable gaps in the recording. The first few seconds of the tape should include the same type of identifying information included on still photographs. The same general principles used in conventional photography should be applied when videotaping. The tape should include views of the entire scene and immediate surrounding area. Long shots and close-up views should be videotaped in a slow and systematic manner. It is also recommended that the events and scenes being video-taped include a narrative as taping occurs.

With the advent of computer technology, the use of digital imaging has become more common. When utilizing this technology, an image is converted into a digital file composed of numerous square electronic dots called pixels. Digitally stored in a computer, an image can be adjusted using computer software. The adjustments enhance the image so that characteristics of the image are more distinguishable. Photographs and images can be placed into the digital imaging system through the use of scanners, digital cameras, or video cameras. The images can also be transmitted via the Internet (Saferstein, 2011).

Crime Scene Sketches

While photographs provide a pictorial view of a crime scene, sketches present accurate and detailed information regarding the location of objects at the scene and the relationship between these objects. Sketches are drawn while or after photographs of the scene are taken. Sketches are an excellent supplement to photographs, can be used to refresh the investigator's memory, and provide other criminal justice personnel as well as juries with an exact replica of the scene.

There are two types of crime scene sketches. Rough sketches are drawn in the field at the scene of the incident. Finished sketches are completed using the rough sketch as a guide. Finished sketches are drawn to scale. The finished scale drawing is completed at the police station by utilizing graph paper or computer-aided design (CAD) software.

There are at least five basic crime scene sketch methods. The method selected depends on the size and location of the scene as well as the number of objects to be included in the sketch. The **rectangular co-**

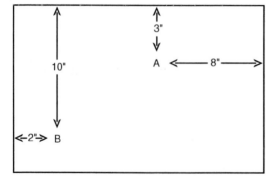

FIGURE 11.5   Rectangular coordinate sketch method. *(Illustration by Robert Myers.)*

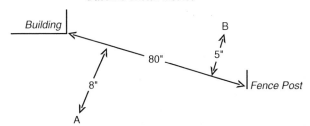

FIGURE 11.6 Baseline sketch method. *(Illustration by Robert Myers.)*

ordinate sketch method utilizes measurements at right angles from two fixed lines, such as adjoining walls of a room. Distances to objects from the walls are measured at right angles (perpendicular) to the walls.

The **baseline sketch** method requires measurements along and at right angles from a fixed reference line or baseline. This method may be used in large outdoor areas.

The **triangulation sketch** method utilizes straight-line measurements from fixed objects to the item to be included in the sketch. It can be used indoors or outdoors. Unlike the baseline sketch method in which the distance to an item is measured at right angles (90°) to a reference line, in the triangulation sketch the angles need not be at 90°.

The **compass point sketch** method utilizes a protractor or surveying equipment to measure angles between a baseline and an imaginary line to the evidentiary item. Some point, such as the corner of a room, is used as the point of origin from which angles can be measured.

The **cross-projection** (exploded view) **sketch** method is used to depict the floor, walls, and ceiling of a room. It resembles a cardboard box with the top, bottom, and sides laid flat. This method may be used when items of evidence, such as bullet holes, are located in the walls or ceilings.

Equipment required for the crime scene sketch includes a ruler, steel tape measure, graph paper, clipboard, indelible marker, pencils, compass, string, protractor, chalk and chalk-line string, and templates. The sketch must include as much information as is necessary to visually recreate the scene. Items of evidence should be marked with letters. These letters and corresponding item descriptions should be included in a legend on the sketch. Identifying information such as case number, date, sketch artist, time, scale, and north arrow pointing toward the top of the sketch, must also be included. All measurements should be verified by a second person.

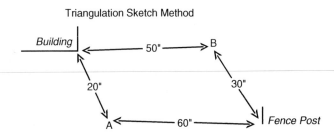

FIGURE 11.7 Triangulation sketch method. *(Illustration by Robert Myers.)*

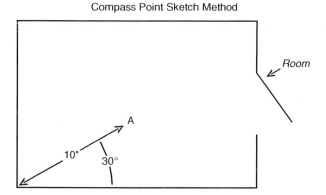

FIGURE 11.8   Compass point sketch method.
(Illustration by Robert Myers.)

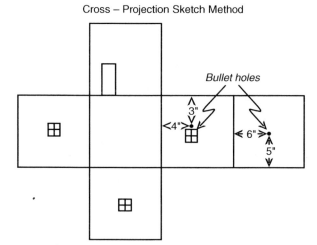

FIGURE 11.9   Cross-projection sketch method.
(Illustration by Robert Myers.)

Collection and Preservation of Evidence

Evidence collected at a crime scene must meet certain legal tests to maintain its evidentiary value. The courts will examine the chain of custody of the evidence and will want to know who, where, and when the evidence was located and how it was preserved for analysis and presentation in court. Therefore, evidence must be carefully collected, marked, and preserved.

Investigators should wear latex gloves when collecting evidence to avoid possible contamination. Without destroying the integrity of the evidence, small as well as large items should be permanently marked for identification wherever possible. Large caliber spent bullets, for example, can be marked with a stylus, scribe, or sharp object at the base of the bullet with the date and initials of the investigator. The base of a bullet will not be subject to ballistics tests. Small-caliber bullets should be placed in a container, and the container should be marked for identification.

All items should be placed in appropriate containers, and the containers should be marked with the same identifying information that was written on the back of the crime scene photographs and on the crime scene sketch. Liquids should be placed in bottles, and small, delicate items should be wrapped in cotton and placed in an envelope, bottle, or box. The investigating officer who found the evidence should place an identifying mark or initials on the evidence as it is collected. All containers should be sealed and identified with the appropriate evidence or property tag. Each item should be logged in the field notes and official report.

Some types of evidence such as fingerprints, blood, hair, soil, and fibers require a standard for comparison. In other words, the evidence found at the scene must be subsequently compared with an item of known origin. For example, a latent fingerprint lifted at the crime scene must be compared later with the fingerprints taken from the crime suspect. Therefore, great care must be exercised when collecting evidence that may be subject to comparison. This type of evidence must also be collected in sufficient quantity to make the comparison possible.

To maintain the chain of custody of evidence, items must be secured and transported with an accompanying officer. Shipping evidence to a crime lab may be accomplished through registered mail, air express, or via private transport that provides proof of delivery. Signatures for receipt of the evidence are required (Gilbert, 2008).

ROLE OF FORENSIC SCIENCE

Traditionally, the term *instrumentation* has been applied to laboratory analysis of physical evidence found at the crime scene. Instrumentation evolved into the fields of criminalistics and forensic science. These terms are often used interchangeably.

Criminalistics is defined as the science and profession that deals with the recognition, collection, identification, individualization, and interpretation of physical evidence, and the application of the natural sciences to law-science matters (U.S. Department of Justice, Office of Justice Programs, 2004).

Forensic science involves the application of the physical as well as some social sciences to the investigation of crime. Sophisticated laboratory procedures and analyses are currently available, with more being developed. Psychological profiling, anthropology, spectrographic analysis, biology, chemistry, DNA analysis, and new ballistics testing technologies are used in contemporary criminal investigations. Thus, forensic science may be defined as the application of science to the enforcement of law and has become extremely important to policing in the twenty-first century.

One of the most significant advances in forensic science in the latter half of the twentieth century was the development of **DNA** (deoxyribonucleic acid) profiling technology. Contained within a gene, DNA is a molecule that is present in all forms of life. It is unique to the life-form, determines the organism's traits, and assists with the development of a genetic fingerprint specific to the organism from which the molecules are taken. Blood, semen, and body tissues are good sources of human molecular cells containing DNA. Human biological samples collected at crime scenes can be used to develop a DNA profile. Comparison samples taken from victims and suspects can be profiled and analyzed to determine if both samples have a common origin. For example, the DNA profile developed from a semen sample taken from a rape victim can be compared with the DNA profile of blood taken from the rape suspect.

In 1985, Alec Jeffreys and several of his colleagues at Leicester University in England discovered that elements of the DNA structure of certain human genes are as unique to an individual as are fingerprints. Jeffreys and his colleagues referred to the process of isolating and documenting these DNA elements as "DNA fingerprinting." The terms DNA typing and DNA profiling are also used to describe this technology.

DNA technology has helped condemn the guilty and free the innocent. Since 1989, more than 250 people have been exonerated nationwide, thanks to DNA testing (Debruin, 2011). However, the use of DNA technology is not without its critics. Privacy advocates argue that it endangers individual liberty. Unlike fingerprints, which do not contain intimate information, DNA contains information on up to 4,000 diseases. Currently, all 50 states collect DNA from at least some convicted offenders, and many states are enacting statutes requiring DNA collections from arrestees. Critics argue that forcible collection of DNA violates the Fourth Amendment's protection against unreasonable search and seizure. Although a DNA profile obtained for identification purposes does not reveal information about diseases or other traits, the sample from which the profile is created contains an individual's entire genetic blueprint. The U.S. Department of Justice's National Commission on the Future of DNA Evidence maintains that profiling arrestees is constitutional (National Commission on the Future of DNA Evidence, 2000; Saferstein, 2011; Siegel & Senna, 2006).

In February, 2005, DNA evidence was credited with helping to solve the 31-year-old BTK (bind, torture, kill) strangler case in Wichita, Kansas. Beginning in 1974, Dennis Rader, 59, the self-proclaimed BTK strangler, killed at least ten people in the Wichita area. Semen collected at the early crime scenes was stored and examined later when DNA analysis became available. The DNA profile of the semen was matched to the profile of a DNA sample voluntarily supplied by Rader's adult daughter.

The FBI's **Drugfire** and ATF's **Integrated Ballistic Identification System (IBIS)** automated firearms search systems are additional advancements. For many years, the police community has used manual techniques to compare a suspect bullet with the weapon that fired it by matching grooves on the bullet with the firearm's barrel rifling. However, if the bullet is deformed, conventional ballistic examination techniques do not work. Therefore, a shell casing found at the crime scene may be the only firearms evidence of any value.

In utilizing Drugfire or IBIS, the problems associated with poor firearm identification evidence are solved. Drugfire focuses primarily on the markings located on expended cartridge casings, although bullet markings (striations) can also be examined with this system. The subject cartridge or bullet is examined through a microscope that is attached to a video camera. The image is digitized and stored in a database. The database has search capabilities, enabling forensic scientists to compare fired bullets and casings and

Learn more about forensic science concepts and employment opportunities through the American Academy of Forensic Sciences (AAFS) at www.aafs.org.

to determine whether an in-custody firearm was used in other shootings (Reid, 2011). IBIS processes digitized images on expended bullets and cartridge casings utilizing the Bulletproof and Brasscatcher software programs. In addition, by using computerized imaging technology, firearms identification laboratories can be networked. This allows the sharing of information between laboratories in different agencies.

Forensic science professionals engaged in the identification, collection, documentation, preservation, examination, analysis, and evaluation of physical evidence fall into two broad categories: forensic specialists (evidence technicians and identification technicians) and criminalists. **Forensic specialists** process crime scenes and perform specific tasks, such as fingerprint searches and comparisons. They identify, collect, document, and preserve physical evidence for subsequent examination and analysis. Technical skills required of the forensic specialist typically include the ability to properly gather physical evidence, identify and collect fingerprints, photograph crime scenes and evidentiary items, and document activities. Specialized training or an associate degree in forensic technology are often required of forensic specialist candidates.

Criminalists examine, analyze, evaluate, and perform scientific tests on physical evidence collected by forensic specialists. They analyze drug, DNA, trace, and toxicological evidence in forensic science laboratories. Criminalists must have an extensive background in the natural sciences. Usually, criminalists are required to possess a bachelors degree or higher in chemistry, biology, or biochemistry.

Other knowledge, skills, and abilities (KSAs) are important to all forensic science practitioners. These include competencies associated with critical thinking (quantitative reasoning and problem solving), decision-making, computer literacy, laboratory use, public speaking, oral and written communications, observation, and safety. Practitioners are also expected to maintain high ethical and professional standards of behavior (Saferstein, 2011; U.S. Department of Justice, Office of Justice Programs, 2004).

SURVEILLANCE AND UNDERCOVER ASSIGNMENTS

Surveillance and undercover operations are used to gather information when conventional investigative methods fail to produce desired results. The investigator conducting a surveillance is referred to as the surveillant, while the person observed is identified as the subject. Surveillance is time-consuming, expensive, and requires tremendous patience, alertness, and resourcefulness on the part of the investigator. Surveillance is most successful when the surveillant's appearance and activities do not attract attention from the subject or the public.

The type of surveillance conducted depends on the nature of the investigation and the circumstances. Stationary or fixed surveillance, the stakeout, is used when the subject either frequents or is suspected of criminal activity at a specific location. Observations may be made from a vehicle, natural hiding places, or buildings in the area. A moving surveillance (tail) is used to maintain observation of a moving subject. A close (tight) tail is used when continuous observation of the subject is necessary. Rough (loose) tails are used when continuous observation is unnecessary.

When tailing on foot, surveillants must have numerous plans for alternative activities that will allow them to remain undetected. When using vehicles, the surveillant's vehicle should be inconspicuous and changed frequently. Descriptions of all vehicles used by the subject should be obtained. In some cases, it may be possible to mark or place an electronic monitoring device on the subject's vehicle in advance.

Audio monitoring is also a very common surveillance method. This usually involves a wiretap or electronic monitoring of conversations. However, since wiretaps and similar activities are considered searches, the exclusionary rule requires court authorization through a search warrant. The courts are reluctant to issue warrants for electronic surveillance unless there is a demonstrated need and all other investigative procedures are exhausted.

Undercover assignments involve a surveillance in which the surveillant makes personal contact with the subject using a fictitious assumed identity or cover. Undercover surveillance is warranted when criminal activity is suspected, but no hard evidence of a crime exists. The surveillant gains the confidence of the subject in the hope of obtaining incriminating evidence. Undercover assignments are often dangerous; surveillants must exercise great care to avoid detection. Criminals tend to be paranoid and are suspicious of people around them. Subjects of a surveillance may themselves be on the lookout for police undercover activity. Criminals watch for unusual activity and movements. Anticipation and planning to avoid detection may prevent the subject's countersurveillance from being successful.

CRIMINAL PROFILING

Profiling is the practice of identifying, viewing, and analyzing characteristics and descriptors of individuals and situations in an effort to predict human behavior. **Criminal profiling,** also known as criminal investigative analysis, focuses on characteristics or descriptors that are indicative of criminal behavior or the person most likely to be involved in criminal activity.

The Border Patrol, the Customs Service, and the Drug Enforcement Administration utilize profiling techniques to identify individuals who are most likely to be involved with smuggling people, illegal drugs, and other contraband. The Transportation Security Administration uses profiling techniques to decide which airline passengers, luggage, or cargo require closer inspection.

Based on the experience of the law enforcement agency and its personnel, personal indicators and characteristics are used to form a profile of the person most likely to be involved in a criminal enterprise. Factors such as gender, age, nationality, country of origin, behaviors, vehicle used, travel plans, type and quality of personal identification, language spoken, and response to questions are used as predictors.

In another context, criminal profiling is used to develop a nonphysical portrait of a criminal offender. This type of profiling is often used when the identity of the suspect is unknown and physical descriptors are not available. Personality traits, psychological characteristics, and methods of operation and expression are used to describe the type of person most likely to be involved with the criminal activity under investigation. In this context, the profiler draws upon specialized investigative experience and training in the forensic and behavioral sciences.

Criminal profiling should not be confused with racially biased profiling. Criminal profiling, properly used, has a legitimate purpose. Alternatively, racially biased profiling, as discussed elsewhere in this book, targets a disproportionate number of racial and ethnic minorities, simply because of their race or ethnic heritage. Studies indicate that the majority of law enforcement officers do not practice or tolerate racially biased profiling.

INVESTIGATION OF SPECIFIC OFFENSES

As first responders to a crime scene, patrol officers should follow the steps outlined for any preliminary investigation. Once the preliminary steps have been completed, it may be necessary for the patrol officer to proceed with the initial phases of the follow-up investigation. The different types of criminal offenses that a patrol officer encounters often have unique characteristics requiring special consideration. A few of these crimes and their unique investigative needs are discussed here.

Burglary Investigation

Points of entry and exit must be determined in a burglary investigation. The patrol officer should search for broken windows, damaged doors, and tool or pry marks adjacent to windows and doors. The marks should be removed or photographed for subsequent comparison to any burglary tools found in the possession of a suspect. The investigation should also include a search for shoe prints, tire tracks, and latent fingerprints left at the scene. Neighbors or persons who frequent the area may also be excellent sources of information.

Assault Investigation

At the scene of an assault or battery, the officer should determine if medical treatment is necessary. If the offense is a sex crime, contact should be made with sexual assault crisis services. It is best if the investigating officer and the victim are of the same gender. A forensic medical examination may be required in cases in which penetration is alleged. Evidentiary items include clothing, bedding, foreign objects, and restraints used during the commission of the act.

Crimes Against Children

Because of their unique vulnerabilities, children require protection by the law more than any other group. In addition to physical and sexual abuse, molestation, pornography, incest, and kidnaping, children are often victims of abandonment, neglect, exploitation, and emotional abuse. Child abuse can result in serious permanent damage to the young.

The investigation of crimes against children presents special problems. Often, it is necessary to protect the child from further harm. The child's parent or guardian may be responsible for the offenses against the child. The child must be removed from the threatening environment. Other public safety agencies, such as child protective services, may require notification and become involved in the investigation. In addition, children provide unique challenges for the patrol officer during an interview. Although children tend to tell the truth to the best of their ability, young people often fabricate information, distort the facts, experience imaginary happenings, and are vulnerable to suggestion. A child's perception of an incident, to a great extent, determines responses given to questions regarding the event. Care must be exercised to ensure that additional emotional damage is not inflicted on the child as the result of police involvement in the child's situation.

Prior to the interview of a child victim, the investigating officer should gather as much information about the event as possible. The person or persons who reported the offense, friends, neighbors, relatives, child protection agency personnel, and school officials are possible sources of information. The child's age and ability to understand the nature of the questioning are important preinterview considerations. The interview of the child should take place in a setting which is comfortable to the child. Young children are more likely to provide information if the environment is familiar and free of distractions, provides the opportunity to play, enhances mobility, and generates emotional support from a significant other. Rapport must be established with the interviewee. A climate of trust will help establish a bond between the officer and the child, which can lead to an effective interview.

Homicide Investigation

Upon arrival at a death scene, the patrol officer should first determine if the victim is dead. Breathing, pupillary reaction to light, or a pulse are signs of life. Obvious signs of death include decomposition of the body, decapitation, postmortem lividity (dark discoloration of the body at lower extremities), or rigor mortis (stiffening of muscles after death). The body should not be disturbed. In some states, the death scene falls under the jurisdiction of the coroner or medical examiner. Evidence necessary to conduct a homicide investigation must be released to the police by the coroner's office.

Based on witness interviews, the condition of the body, and the environment, an approximate time of death can be established. This information will assist in the development of a list of suspects who do not have alibis for the approximate time of death. Determining the exact time and cause of death is obviously beyond the jurisdiction of the police. These determinations are made by the coroner's office from the results of an autopsy. However, based on the patrol officer's experience, training, and examination of the scene, a preliminary cause of death may be identified. Classifications of death include accident, suicide, natural, homicide, or undetermined.

Vehicle Theft Investigation

Sources of information for a vehicle theft investigation include witnesses, the victim, the last driver, and the financial institution holding a loan on the vehicle. The patrol officer must establish if a crime has been committed. Appropriate questions to ask during a vehicle theft investigation include the following:

- Does anyone else have keys to the vehicle?
- Was the vehicle misplaced?
- Was the vehicle repossessed for failure to make payments? (California Commission on Peace Officer Standards and Training, 2012).

The **Auto Theft Bureau (ATB)** reports that more than 1 million Americans are victims of auto theft each year. Additionally, almost 3 million people have either the contents or parts stolen from vehicles each year. To prevent theft and enhance stolen vehicle recovery capabilities, many vehicles are equipped with alarms and **automated electronic vehicle locators (AVLs).** Vehicles equipped with the high-tech AVLs can be tracked by law enforcement personnel using computers and satellites to trace vehicles emitting a signal from a small transmitter located within the vehicle.

Economic Crime Investigation

Generally, an **economic crime** may be defined as any act that violates the criminal law and is designed to bring financial gain to the offender (Siegel, 2004). Specifically, the term economic crime is often used to describe activities traditionally referred to as white-collar crime (Coleman, 1994). Virtually any business and all sorts of information are potential targets. Intellectual property in the form of trade secrets, client lists, financial information, and technical and strategic plans may be of interest to business competitors and foreign governments. Information can be stolen electronically through computers and the Internet or through reverse engineering of a product, surveillance, undercover work, hiring an employee away from a company, phony contract negotiations, and bribery. From a national security perspective, one of the greatest concerns is the threat of cyberattack in which a hacker or foreign government could penetrate top secret databases using the Internet (Global crime cartels are tech-savvy, U.S. says, 2000; Raum, 1999).

Large-scale economic crime schemes often cross state boundaries as well as international borders. Theft of copyrighted materials through the Internet has led to multistate copyright infringement cases (Balint, 2000). Internationally, counterfeiting and product piracy are used to replicate legitimately produced brand products (China's piracy plague, 2000). On January 9, 1997, Volkswagen (VW), Europe's largest auto-maker, agreed to pay General Motors (GM) $100 million to settle a lawsuit stemming from a four-year-old allegation that VW stole trade secrets from GM. Volkswagon also agreed to purchase more than $1 billion worth of parts from GM over a seven-year period. The settlement is one of the largest in corporate espionage history. Without admitting wrongdoing, VW acknowledged the possibility that GM proprietary information may have been transferred when several GM executives defected to VW (Meredith, 1997).

Other types of economic crime include various forms of fraud perpetrated against organizations as well as individuals. Warranty fraud takes place when merchants fraudulently claim a product is under warranty and obtain replacement parts under a warranty exchange program. Investment fraud occurs when bogus stocks are sold. Telemarketing fraud, which involves telephone sales of high-priced, low-value items, targets older people and many businesses. Internet fraud and computer system hacking of all types are growing rapidly. As much as 10 percent of every health care dollar spent can be attributed to fraud. Fraudulent checks, credit card scams, and fraudulent loans threaten financial institutions. Occupational fraud is a form of embezzlement. Padding expense accounts and lost production time also result in financial losses to businesses and cause a drain on the U.S. economy. Occupational fraud alone may account for more than $400 billion in losses to American companies annually.

Organized crime ("the mob") is involved in economic crime as well. An example of the mob's influence came to light in November 1997, with the arrest of 18 people alleged to have been involved with a stock price-fixing scheme. Members of the Genovese and Bonanno crime families collaborated with HealthTech International, Inc., a Mesa, Arizona, health and fitness center company, to artificially inflate the company's assets and stock prices. Through the scheme stockbrokers convinced unwitting buyers that the company's assets were eight times their actual value. As a result, the company's stock trading value increased more than 250 percent and participants in the scheme stood to gain enormous profits through the sale of the inflated stocks (Ortmeier, 1998, 2003).

Mob activity can reach enormous proportions. For example, in January 2011, federal agents arrested about 125 people from seven crime clans based in several New England states. The criminal allegations included murder, racketeering, extortion, loan-sharking, money, laundering, and gambling (Rashbaum, 2011).

A form of economic crime that is becoming more prevalent is **identity theft.** The crime is committed when an imposter fraudulently uses another's personal identification information to obtain credit, merchandise, or services in the name of the victim. The personal identification information often stolen and used by criminals includes drivers license

Additional information regarding identity theft, its prevention or reporting, can be accessed on the Federal Trade Commission's website at www.consumer.gov/idtheft or on the Social Security Administration's identity theft website at www.ssa.gov/pubs/idtheft.htm.

and social security numbers, addresses, phone numbers, and dates of birth. In some cases, the perpetrator obtains the personal information through the Internet or by accessing an organizations client account information. Other methods include theft of personal mail, eavesdropping, searching a persons trash for personal information, or simply observing the victim entering personal data on a form or at an automatic teller machine (ATM). In most cases, victims of identify theft are unaware that they are being victimized until they receive bills and invoices for goods and services they did not purchase themselves.

Although sophisticated forms of economic crime do not represent the types of crime typically encountered by the patrol officer, it is the most costly (and potentially the most common) type of crime. Patrol officers may be the first to respond to reported incidents. Preliminary and follow-up investigations of economic crime are challenging and often require special skills as well as interjurisdictional co-operation (Global crime cartels are tech-savvy, U.S. says, 2000). The perpetrator is rarely, if ever, present. Stealth translates to wealth for the economic crime offender because the victim may not discover the crime until long after its occurrence.

Computer Crime Investigation

Since the early 1970s, computer technology has dramatically changed the way information is acquired, analyzed, stored, and retrieved. It has changed the working world, and it is part of almost everyone's daily life. Computerized cash registers exist at virtually every retail checkout counter. Onboard computers are used to detect problems in late-model motor vehicles.

The increased use of computers has been accompanied by a commensurate increase in computer-related crime. No longer limited to a few high-tech hackers, crimes involving computers have become increasingly common. Computer crime is limited only by the ingenuity of the criminal and the offender's knowledge of computer technology. With computers, funds can be stolen from financial institutions without physically entering a bank. Business trade secrets and classified government information can be obtained without physically penetrating a business or country.

Computer crime is defined generally as any crime committed with computer technology. It may involve the actual destruction of computer hardware and software, or it may be used as a tool in a criminal enterprise. More commonly, it involves unauthorized access (or exceeding authorization) to the computer's database. Computers are used to commit acts involving fraud, theft, burglary, embezzlement, espionage, sabotage, and even murder. Computers are also used in crimes related to child pornography, prostitution, gambling, illegal drugs, and organized crime. Misuse of computers in the workplace, such as computer game playing and personal communications, diverts employee production time and is a form of internal theft. Internet access capabilities increase the risk of theft to many forms of intellectual property (Boni & Kovacich, 2000; Foster, 2005; Hess & Wrobleski, 2003).

Currently, the total indirect and direct costs associated with computer crime could approach $200 billion annually. Losses can be devastating and the threat often originates with unknown sources. On March 2, 1998, the night before Microsoft Chairman Bill Gates was scheduled to testify at a congressional committee hearing, a computer hacker launched a massive attack against computers using Microsoft network software. The hacker targeted computers in government and universities running Windows NT software. On May 19, 1998, a group of seven hackers testified before a U.S. Senate Government Affairs Committee that they could destroy the foundation of the Internet within 30 minutes by interfering with the links between long-distance carriers. According to the hackers, poor computer security can be blamed on the multitude of Internet networks, inadequate security measures in software programs, and lack of government regulation. According to the congressional Government Accountability Office, U.S. State Department computers, the Federal Reserve System, individual credit and medical records, utilities, and stock exchanges are also at risk.

Nearly 75 percent of all businesses report at least one incident of detected cybercrime (Rantala, 2004). **Cybercrime** involves the use of computer technology and the Internet to commit offenses such as embezzlement, fraud, theft of proprietary information, denial of service, vandalism, sabotage, and terrorism. Common cybercrimes against persons include the transmission of obscene and pornographic material, stalking, and harassment. Common cybercrimes against property include hacking and the insertion of computer viruses. Cybercrime is virtually unpredictable and the damage it can cause is incalculable.

CASE STUDY—PREVENTING CYBERCRIME

In an effort to mitigate the damage from cybercrime, the U.S. Department of Homeland Security unveiled a new cyber-alert system in 2004. The system is designed to transmit Internet threat warnings. To receive the warnings, computer users can subscribe to free cyber-alerts and advice by enrolling in the service at www.us-cert.gov.

Critics contend that the cyber-alert system is inadequate because it issues warnings after most attacks are underway. The critics also predict that hackers will falsify alerts to trick legitimate computer users.

1. What can individuals and organizations do to prevent cybercrime?
2. How should law enforcement and the criminal justice system respond to cybercrime incidents?

The personal computer is linked through cyberspace by the Internet, which eliminates the need for an actual physical intrusion into a business, government agency, or personal residence. Advances in technology have created a virtual world with no physical boundaries or barriers. Virtual organizations, which exist mostly in cyberspace, have been created. These organizations exist but are not represented in a physical form. This phenomenon presents new challenges for the law enforcement community.

Although the average individual personal computer user has little to worry about, hackers pose one of the greatest threats to computer systems. The case of Kevin Mitnick, captured in 1995 after a nationwide hunt aided by Tsutomu Shimomura, a researcher at the University of California, San Diego, Supercomputer Center, highlighted the damage a single hacker can cause. Mitnick stole computer passwords, damaged the computers at the University of Southern California, and allegedly pilfered software valued in the millions of dollars from high-tech companies.

In a dramatic demonstration of the Internet's vulnerabilities, computer hackers disrupted some of the Web's largest and most popular e-commerce sites in early February 2000. Internet sites victimized by the unprecedented attack included Yahoo!, eBay, Buy.com, Amazon.com, and the Cable News Network (CNN). Hackers broke into less secure high-speed computer servers at the University of California at Santa Barbara and Stanford University and installed stealth programs designed to flood targeted websites with bogus requests for information. The targeted sites became jammed and shut down as a result of an overwhelming number of calls.

As recently as January 28, 2011, two men were arrested and charged with being involved in a security breach targeting AT&T and Apple iPad users. According to prosecutors, the men created a computer script called the "iPad 3G Account Slurper" and used it to attack AT&T's servers. They designed the script to imitate the behavior of an iPad 3G so it would trick AT&T's servers into thinking that they were communicating with an actual iPad. In addition, the script was designed to randomly guess the unique identifier for each iPad, which resulted in the iPad's email address being displayed on AT&T's Web site. The attack allegedly allowed the men to obtain email addresses and personal information of roughly 120,000 iPad users (Bray, 2011).

The security of computer databases is probably the greatest single challenge facing business and government in the twenty-first century. During testimony before the U.S. Congress in 1997, FBI Director Louis

Learn more about computer crime from the following sources:

The Federal Computer Incident Response Center (Fed CIRC) www.us-cert.gov/federal/
The National Infrastructure Protection Plan. www.dhs.gov/nip,
The National White Collar Crime Center at www.cybercrime.gov

Freeh intimated that the greatest threat facing U.S. national security was economic crime, most of which could occur through the illegal use of computer technology.

Security for computer systems must include strategies to protect the equipment, software, and information stored in the database. Physical security may be utilized to prevent fire or access to computer terminals. Administrative controls can be implemented to maintain accountability for those who have legitimate access to the system and database. Logical controls may be used to restrict access to information stored in the database. Passwords and data encryption are examples of logical controls. Finally, backup duplicate files should be maintained to prevent total loss of data as a result of criminal activity, accident, or natural disaster.

Investigation of computer crime is extremely difficult because traditional criminal investigative methods are inappropriate. Most law enforcement agency expertise focuses on street crime, not computer crime. Cyberspace investigations require different skills. The computer nerds of today will be the sophisticated information technology hackers of tomorrow. Computer crime investigators must know as much about computer technology as cyberspace criminals do (Bennett & Hess, 2004; Coleman, 1994; Ortmeier, 1998, 2005; Osterburg & Ward, 2010; O'Hara & O'Hara, 2003; Young & Ortmeier, 2011; Schmalleger, 2005; Sniffen, 2001).

▲ SUMMARY .

The process of investigation is an art as well as a science. It involves a systematic inquiry to determine the facts surrounding an event or situation. Numerous sources of information exist to assist with an investigation. They include people, documents, and computerized databases. Since the uniform patrol officer is often the first police representative to arrive at an incident scene, the officer is responsible for conducting a preliminary investigation. Follow-up detailed investigations may be required if the incident involves a vehicle collision or a crime. Processing of a crime scene includes a systematic search, photographs, a crime scene sketch, and the involvement of forensic science. On occasion, police officers may be required to conduct a surveillance or undercover activity as part of an investigation. Criminal profiling may be used to help identify a crime suspect. Different types of criminal offenses often require unique investigative techniques.

DISCUSSION QUESTIONS AND EXERCISES

1. List and describe the common elements of the investigative process.
2. What types of information sources are most commonly used by law enforcement personnel?

3. When and how should information be gathered? How should information be evaluated?

4. Compare collision investigations with criminal investigations.

5. How should evidence gathered in an investigation be evaluated and analyzed?

6. Technology available today allows almost everyone, including the police, to gather a vast amount of information on individuals. What strategies might the police employ to ensure that information gathering for law enforcement purposes does not violate a subject's right to privacy?

7. Describe how communication barriers can be overcome and information solicited from citizens to assist with an investigation.

8. Test your observation, recollection, and documentation skills. Arrange for someone, preferably a stranger, to appear before you for 1 or 2 minutes and recite personal information, such as name and occupation. After the person leaves the area, document descriptive information about the person. Compare your description with your subject. How accurate are you?

9. Select five websites identified in this chapter. Access the websites through the Internet and examine the contents of each site.

10. Do many television crime dramas, such as *CSI,* accurately portray the application of forensic science to criminal investigations?

11. How can science and technology be best used in support of the investigations process?

The Courts and the Judicial Process

LEARNING OBJECTIVES

After completing this chapter, the reader should be able to:

- articulate the proper procedure for criminal case preparation.
- describe the history and nature of the courts in the United States.
- outline the court system at the state and federal levels.
- list and describe the major roles and responsibilities of courtroom participants.
- discuss standards (degrees) of proof.
- outline pretrial, trial, and posttrial processes in criminal cases.
- articulate the reasons for court delay in the United States.
- evaluate the impact court decisions have on public safety and law enforcement.
- describe juvenile justice procedure.
- demonstrate proper attitude, appearance, demeanor, and testimonial techniques for courtroom presentations.

KEY TERMS

Define, describe, or explain the importance of each of the following.

Appellate court
Arraignment
Booking
Case preparation
Challenge for cause
Challenge to the array
Community courts
Concurrent sentences
Consecutive sentences
Coroner's jury
Court case preparation
Court of general jurisdiction
Court of last resort

Court of limited jurisdiction
Courtroom demeanor
Criminal complaint
Cross-examination
Defense attorney
Determinate sentence
Direct examination
Drug courts
Expert witness
First appearance
Grand jury
Homeless court
Impeachment

Indeterminate sentence
Indictment
Information
Judge
Jury panel
Jury pool (venire)
Juvenile courts
Juvenile delinquency
Juvenile dependency
Juvenile petition
Mandatory sentence
Military tribunal
Original jurisdiction
Peremptory challenge
Plea bargaining

Preliminary hearing
Prosecutor
Supreme Court of the United States
Teen court
Three-strikes law
Transcript
Trial court
Trial jury
Tribal courts
Truth in sentencing
U.S. courts of appeals
U.S. district courts
U.S. magistrate courts
Victim impact statements

INTRODUCTION

The courts are the pivot on which the justice system turns. Probably no other single component of the criminal justice system affects the other components or society in a more significant way. The courts determine guilt or innocence, adjudicate civil disputes, and render decisions that dictate the process through which criminal and civil cases must pass.

A police officer's responsibility does not terminate with the resolution of a dispute, solution to a community problem, issuance of a citation, or formal arrest of a criminal suspect. The officer is often required to function as a witness in court. Knowledge of court operations as well as proper case preparation, attitude, appearance, and demeanor in court are essential.

CASE PREPARATION

The ultimate success with respect to enforcement of the law is reduced to the answer to one simple question: Has justice been served through the effective presentation of evidence and conviction of the guilty in a court of law? Alternatively, have the innocent been freed? Regrettably, many officers tend to believe their responsibility ends when their report on an incident or arrest is filed. Actually, the police officer's role in any prosecution does not terminate until there has been a final disposition in the case.

Police officers and other justice system personnel are often called as witnesses to testify in a criminal or civil proceeding or to provide a deposition to be used in the judicial process. It is extremely important to prepare for such testimony. Notes, reports, and evidence should be reviewed to refresh one's memory. Consulting with the attorney for whom one will testify is also a must. The attorney may discover weak points in the preparation for court.

CASE STUDY—IS JUSTICE BLIND?

In 1995, former National Football League star and wealthy celebrity, O. J. Simpson, was acquitted of the 1994 double murder of his former wife, Nicole, and her friend, Ronald Goldman. Simpson hired a group of expensive lawyers, referred to as the *dream team*. His sensational trial was televised and it received national attention, leading many to believe that Simpson, because of his wealth, was able to retain one of the best legal teams and virtually purchase a not guilty verdict.

The high-profile criminal proceedings against Martha Stewart, Kobe Bryant, Robert Blake and Michael Jackson further illustrated that wealth may purchase some of the best legal talent available. These and similar cases have led many to conclude that justice is not blind or unbiased when one considers the financial means available to a wealthy defendant.

Bias cited in the justice system is also associated with other characteristics such as a defendant's race, ancestry, religion, gender, and lifestyle as well as the type of offense committed. Some people suggest that the courts and other components of the criminal justice system are biased against those who are poor, disenfranchised, and different from people who are in the majority. The results of a study released by the American Bar Association in 2005 indicated that thousands of people may be wrongly convicted each year because they are represented by incompetent attorneys or pressured to enter guilty pleas for crimes they did not commit (Bad convictions of poor blamed on lawyers, plea pressure, 2005).

1. Is justice blind?
2. How can the scales of justice be balanced to ensure equality under the law?

Police officers should prepare to defend their actions in court. Many cases are lost because the officers did not follow proper police and legal procedures. Others are lost because the officer did not prepare adequately to make an effective courtroom presentation. Sloppy case preparation or a poor appearance may be used to discredit an officer in court. The finder of fact, the jury (or judge in a nonjury trial), may be led to favor a defendant if the police officer is an embarrassment to the prosecution.

The amount of preparation necessary depends on the nature of the case. If the case involves a traffic citation, the officer should, at a minimum, review the citation as well as the circumstances and location involved with its issuance. If the defendant is on trial for murder, a considerable amount of time involving weeks or months may be necessary to prepare adequately.

Case preparation involves the careful and detailed collection, preservation, transportation, analysis, and review of all evidence in a case. It also involves a forecast of defense strategy and the anticipation, recognition, and appraisal of defense tactics. Defense attorneys are often skilled at intimidation and attacking the credibility and integrity of prosecution witnesses. To counter defense attorney attacks, a comprehensive approach to case preparation is necessary as follows:

- **Refresh memory**—Field notes and official police reports must be reviewed to recall details surrounding the case. A trial may occur months or even years after the occurrence and initial investigation of an incident. Memories fade and the officer may have been involved with hundreds of similar cases during the intervening time period. The officer should also review the **transcripts** of any previously recorded statements. Officers are often required to give depositions or provide testimony at preliminary hearings. Testimony presented during the trial that is inconsistent with previously recorded statements will open the door to defense impeachment (attack on the credibility of the officer). Finally, the officer should review statements of witnesses, documentary and physical evidence, and the crime scene itself to refresh memory regarding details in the case.

- **Consult with the prosecuting attorney**—There is nothing unconstitutional or unlawful about discussing the facts and evidence in a case with the prosecuting attorney before, during, or after a trial. It is essential to the effective and efficient presentation of the government's (people's) case-in-chief. If time permits, a rehearsal of the officer's testimony is also appropriate. The prosecutor can assume the role of the defense attorney and subject the officer to the questions and demeanor of the defense which are anticipated during cross-examination.

- **Take necessary documents and evidence to court**—An officer should possess a copy of the official police report. To refresh memory while on the witness stand, the officer may refer to the report. Also, the testifying officer is often responsible for ensuring that physical evidence in the case is available in court. In small departments, the officer must retrieve evidence from the police property room or vault. In large departments, requests for delivery of the evidence may be filed with the property room clerk in advance to ensure it is available for retrieval. The officer must examine the evidence to determine that it is the same as that collected during the investigation. The officer is responsible for maintenance of the chain of custody of the evidence transported to and from court.

- **Write notations in personal calendars with the exact date, time, and location of an anticipated court appearance**—An officer should also contact the prosecutor's office at least one day prior to the scheduled appearance to confirm this information (Miller, 2000).

THE COURTS

An Adversarial System

The judicial process in the United States is adversarial. The government, through state and federal prosecutors, must establish guilt beyond a reasonable doubt. Defendants and their defense attorneys work to refute the government's case. The adversarial process requires an impartial person (or persons) to function as a referee to ensure that the parties follow the rules and justice is served. The courts, through judges and juries, function as the referees in the criminal justice system (Reichel, 2008).

Each of the American colonies had its own court system. The Massachusetts Bay Colony formed a combined legislature/court in 1629 to make laws, conduct trials, and impose sentences. By 1639, county courts were created and the original court that was formed in 1629 served primarily to hear appeals. By 1776 all American colonies had established court systems. After the American Revolution, the colonial courts provided the basis for the development of state court systems. By the late nineteenth century, the growing population, the settlement of the West, and the movement toward urbanization led to an increase in civil lawsuits and criminal arrests. To service this increase, legislatures passed laws that created numerous courts and a variety of court structures. Federal courts were established by the U.S. Constitution, the Federal Judiciary Acts of 1789 and 1925, and the U.S. Magistrate's Act of 1968 (Law Enforcement Assistance Administration, 1976). State constitutions and statutes established court systems in the states. Since the early 1900s, court systems in the United States have become more uniform and streamlined. The federal court system is three-tiered, while state court systems include three to five levels of courts.

Court Systems and Structure

The judiciary in the United States operates as a dual system consisting of state and federal courts. State courts address violations of law and other legal matters pertaining to the laws of the particular state. Federal courts address violations of law as defined by the U.S. Congress. State

The courts affect the criminal justice system and society in a significant way. *(Photo courtesy of the San Diego Sheriff's Department.)*

and federal court systems operate autonomously. In some cases, both systems have concurrent jurisdiction over the same criminal activity. Robbery, for example, is a criminal law violation in every state. If the robbery is committed against a federally insured financial institution, such as a bank, the criminal activity (the robbery) is also a violation of federal law. Thus, the state government as well as the federal government have concurrent jurisdiction over the same case. Under such circumstances, a defendant could be tried, convicted, and sentenced in both systems without violating the Fifth Amendment's double jeopardy provision because the perpetrator committed two separate offenses. The bank robbery represents an offense against the citizens of the United States as well as an offense against the citizens of the state in which the robbery is committed.

The U.S. Constitution specifically provides for only one court, the Supreme Court of the United States. Article III, Section 1 of the Constitution reads that the judicial power of the United States shall be vested in one Supreme Court, and in such inferior courts as the Congress may from time to time ordain and establish. It was the Judiciary Act of 1789 that established other federal courts, namely the U.S. District Courts and the U.S. Circuit Courts of Appeals.

There are at least 56 separate and distinct court systems in the United States and its territories. They include the federal system, 50 state systems, and one system each in the District of Columbia, Guam, Puerto Rico, the U.S. Virgin Islands, and the Northern Mariana Islands. The total number of separate courts operating within these systems exceeds 10,000.

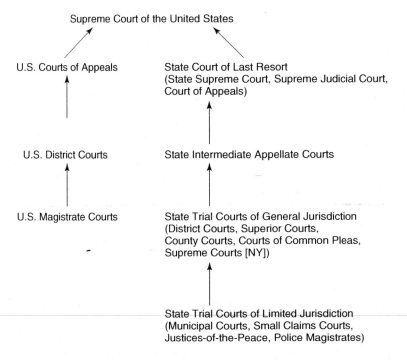

FIGURE 12.1   Court Systems

There are two basic types of courts: trial courts and appellate courts. **Trial courts** are courts in which trials, whether criminal or civil, take place. Trial courts have **original jurisdiction** in these cases. **Appellate courts,** on the other hand, rarely try (originate) cases. Rather, they review appeals brought before them from the trial or lower appellate courts. Appellate courts review the written record (transcript) of the trial court proceedings as well as written briefs submitted by both sides. The appellate court may also entertain short oral arguments from the petitioner and respondent or their representatives. Appeals from trial courts proceed through either a state or federal appellate review process and culminate at the U.S. Supreme Court.

The Federal Courts

Basically, the federal court system consists of the U.S. Supreme Court, 13 U.S. courts of appeals circuits, 94 U.S. district courts, and the U.S. magistrate courts. The federal court system does not supercede a state court system. Rather, the federal courts have jurisdiction over violations of federal (national) law, while state court systems address violations of their respective state laws.

The **Supreme Court of the United States** functions as an appellate court. It reviews constitutional challenges to federal and state statutes as well as appeals from criminal and civil trial court cases brought before it through state appellate courts and the U.S. courts of appeals. The U.S. Supreme Court's ability to choose cases it will review is known as *certiorari*. In these cases, the Supreme Court will issue a writ of certiorari, ordering the lower court to forward the case record to the Supreme Court. Occasionally, the Supreme Court will respond to a question of law certified to it by a U.S. Court of Appeals.

In most cases, the U.S. Supreme Court reviews appeals from the lower state and federal courts. However, the Court does not review all appeals brought before it. The Court receives over 8,000 appeals annually; it may review fewer than 100. The right of review of lower federal court rulings by the U.S. Supreme Court are enumerated in Article III, Section 1 of the U.S. Constitution. With respect to state court judgments, an appeal from a state's court of last resort or a U.S. court of appeals is a matter of right when the validity of a federal statute is questioned in a state court or when a state statute is challenged as violating the U.S. Constitution.

The U.S. Supreme Court has no authority to make a final determination in a state case. The Court may affirm (agree with) the decision of the lower court or reverse (disagree with) the decision and remand (return) the case to the lower court for a decision not inconsistent with the U.S. Supreme Court's opinion. If the constitutionality of the entire state court proceeding is at issue, the charge against a defendant in a criminal case must be dismissed. If only certain evidence is declared inadmissible, the state court may order a new trial based on the admissible evidence remaining. Trying the defendant a second time does not violate the Fifth Amendment double jeopardy clause because there has not been a final judgment in the case. The second trial is considered *de novo* (a new), as if the original trial never occurred.

Located in Washington, D.C., the U.S. Supreme Court is the highest court in the United States. Eight associate justices and one chief justice make up the Court. As are all federal judges, the justices are appointed by the President, confirmed by the U.S. Senate, and they have lifetime tenure. An appeal is reviewed by the Court when at least four justices vote in favor of review.

According to federal statute, a term of the U.S. Supreme Court begins on the first Monday of October, and it ends in July. Each term is divided into *sittings* in which the court can review up to two dozen appealed cases approved for review. During the review of a case, the Court may allot each side (appellant and respondent) five minutes for oral arguments before the Court. Decisions of the Court are rendered by majority vote in order of seniority, with the most junior justice voting first. The chief justice votes last and is responsible for breaking a tie vote. The judgment of the Court is presented in a majority opinion written by one of the justices on behalf of the Court. Justices in the majority who agree with the Court's judgment, but for different reasons, may write concurring opinions. Justices in the minority may write dissenting opinions.

The intermediate appellate courts in the federal system are the **U.S. courts of appeals.** Known as circuit courts of appeals until 1948, the decisions of these courts are usually final except through the certiorari process to the U.S. Supreme Court. They have appellate jurisdiction over all U.S. district court decisions except:

- When a three-judge district court has enjoined (stopped) enforcement of a federal or state statute on grounds of unconstitutionality; it then goes to the Supreme Court.
- When a U.S. district court declares a federal statute unconstitutional and the United States is a party to the action.
- On a showing that a case requires immediate settlement because of imperative public importance.

The U.S. courts of appeals includes 12 regional circuit courts of appeals and one U.S. court of appeals for the federal circuit. The circuit courts of appeals review cases appealed from U.S. district courts, the U.S. Tax Court, U. S. territorial courts, and administrative agencies of the federal government. The U.S. Court of Appeals for the federal circuit reviews appeals from the U.S. Court of Veterans Appeals, the U.S. Court of International Trade, which addresses international trade and customs issues, and the U.S. Court of Federal Claims, which tries financial lawsuits against the United States.

Authorized by the U.S. Judiciary Act of 1789, the **U.S. district courts** are the trial courts of general jurisdiction in the federal system. They have original (or trial) jurisdiction over civil actions on copyrights, patents, postal matters, civil rights, and almost all other civil as well as criminal cases arising under the laws and treaties of the United States and the U.S. Constitution. They have concurrent jurisdiction with the

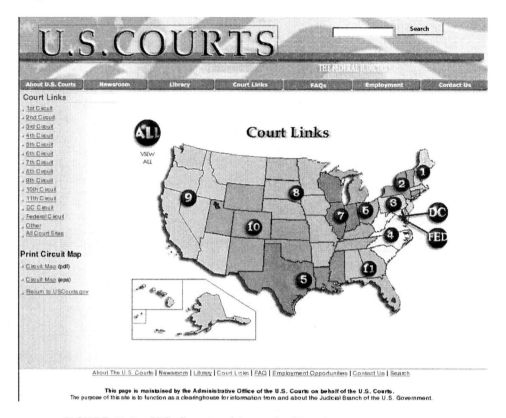

FIGURE 12.2   U.S. Courts of Appeals Circuits

states with respect to criminal cases in which a criminal act violates federal as well as state law. They have jurisdiction over civil cases in which the dollar amount in dispute meet's a statutory minimum, and the parties to the action are residents of different states. Each U.S. district court contains, as one of its units, a U.S. bankruptcy court.

The **U.S. magistrate courts** have authority to issue federal warrants, set bail, hold preliminary hearings in federal cases, and conduct summary trials for minor federal crimes in which the defendant waives the right to a trial in the U.S. district court. Specialized federal courts outside the U.S. district court and U.S. circuit courts of appeals arena include military trial courts and the U.S. Court of Military Appeals.

State and Local Courts

State and local courts are created by state legislatures and state constitutions. They adjudicate criminal and civil cases arising from incidents occurring within the state that involve violations of state and local laws. Each state has a **court of last resort** to review cases that were tried and appealed from lower state courts. In some states, the court of last resort is referred to as the state supreme court. In others, the state court of last resort may be entitled the *court of criminal appeals, supreme court of*

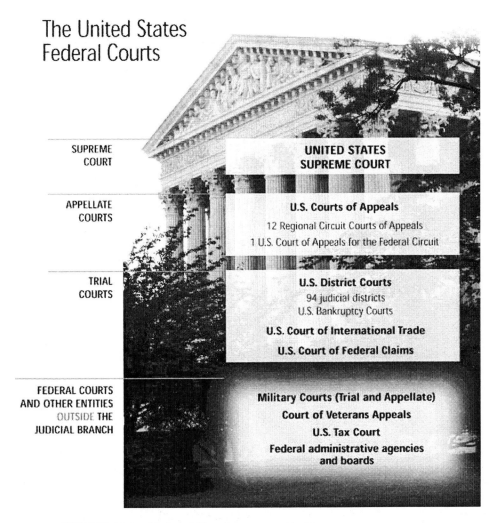

The United States Federal Courts

SUPREME COURT	**UNITED STATES SUPREME COURT**
APPELLATE COURTS	**U.S. Courts of Appeals** 12 Regional Circuit Courts of Appeals 1 U.S. Court of Appeals for the Federal Circuit
TRIAL COURTS	**U.S. District Courts** 94 judicial districts U.S. Bankruptcy Courts **U.S. Court of International Trade** **U.S. Court of Federal Claims**
FEDERAL COURTS AND OTHER ENTITIES OUTSIDE THE JUDICIAL BRANCH	**Military Courts (Trial and Appellate)** **Court of Veterans Appeals** **U.S. Tax Court** **Federal administrative agencies and boards**

FIGURE 12.3   Federal Courts

appeals, or the *supreme judicial court.* Appeals from state courts of last resort are taken directly to the U.S. Supreme Court.

All states have some form of intermediate appellate court. They serve a similar function in a state court system as the U.S. courts of appeals do in the federal system. They review appeals from trial courts. However, much like the state court of last resort, state intermediate appellate courts have original jurisdiction only in cases involving *habeas corpus* review. A writ of *habeas corpus* (Latin for "you have the body") is a court order that directs a person, typically a jailer or warden, who is detaining another to bring the prisoner before the court to determine the lawfulness

Learn more about the federal courts through the Federal Judiciary home page located at www.uscourts.gov/about.

> Learn more about state court systems and structure through the National Center for State Courts at www.ncsconline.org.

of the detention. Like other state courts, state intermediate appellate court titles vary. District court of appeals, appellate court, and circuit court of appeals are typical of state intermediate appellate court titles.

State trial courts are divided into two categories: courts of general and limited (or special) jurisdiction. **Courts of general jurisdiction** may try any state criminal or civil case brought before it. Depending on the state, they may be referred to as district courts, superior courts, supreme courts, state courts, county courts, circuit courts, or courts of common pleas. State courts of general jurisdiction are typically limited to one per county, although the court may have several branches or satellite locations. These courts are often referred to as courts of record because the proceedings are recorded (transcribed) and archived for future reference. The activities of general jurisdiction courts are usually subdivided into divisions or dockets, each responsible for civil, criminal, probate, domestic relations, or juvenile matters (Cheeseman, 2010). **Courts of limited** or special **jurisdiction** are restricted in their authority. These courts typically try misdemeanor cases, specialize in specific areas of law, or they may conduct preliminary hearings in felony cases. If, as the result of a preliminary hearing, the court determines that probable cause exists to hold the defendant on the felony charge, the defendant is bound over to the court of general jurisdiction for arraignment and trial. Examples of courts of limited or special jurisdiction include municipal, juvenile, traffic, justice-of-the-peace, family, drug and small claims courts. Some states have merged the courts of limited jurisdiction with the courts of general jurisdiction to save costs. The courts of general jurisdiction assign cases to criminal, civil, juvenile, probate and other specialized dockets, departments, or divisions (Cole & Rutledge, 2000; Smith, 2010; Siegel & Senna, 2006; Worrall, 2004).

Specialty Courts

Numerous courts are created to address specific issues and unique types of cases. Notable examples follow:

Juvenile courts focus on the special needs of children. These special needs were first recognized formally when the State of Massachusetts enacted legislation in 1870 requiring that juvenile proceedings be separate from adult courts. Juvenile courts address issues associated with a child's delinquency, dependency, neglect, abuse, and lack of discipline.

Drug courts address the special needs of those involved with, or addicted to, drugs and alcohol. They provide an alternative to a criminal justice sanction. Drug courts use nonadversarial approaches that emphasize treatment, rehabilitation, and monitoring of abstinence programs through alcohol and drug testing (Pearlman, 2011).

Community courts are neighborhood-based courts that address problems that plague local areas. Community courts work closely with neighborhood organizations, public agencies, and civic leaders to identify and solve localized problems. They seek to improve the quality of life in business districts and residential neighborhoods.

Tribal courts are located on Native American reservations. Designated by Congress as foreign nations, Native American tribes are unique. Although reservations are located within the United States, tribes are allowed to form reservation-based governments and sign boundary treaties. Thus, Native American tribes have the authority to create public safety entities, such as tribal courts, designed to address legal issues on reservations.

Homeless courts are a relatively recent development. Founded in San Diego in the late 1980s and adopted in several other cities, homeless court programs are designed to assist people who encounter legal problems associated with chronic drug addiction, alcoholism, and homelessness. Through the collaborative efforts of the courts, prosecutors, defense attorneys, and public service agencies, infractions, citations, and misdemeanor warrants pending against homeless persons are dismissed or deferred for those willing to invest time and energy in self-improvement and rehabilitation initiatives.

Military tribunals are used by the United States during times of national crisis. The tribunals function outside the traditional United States civilian court systems as they try enemy combatants charged with war crimes. In the aftermath of the terrorist attacks of 9/11, military tribunals have been promoted by some as a means to try suspected terrorists (Territo, Halsted, & Bromley, 2004; Wrobleski & Hess, 2009).

Veterans courts are on the rise nationally and are used for veterans convicted of misdemeanors or felonies that allow probation. To qualify for these courts, a veteran must have a service-related mental health problem or be the victim of sexual abuse that occurred in the military. Veterans convicted of violent felonies are not eligible (Steele, 2011).

Juries

There are several types of juries. Notable among them are the coroner's jury, grand jury, and the trial jury. A **coroner's jury** conducts an inquest to investigate and determine a cause and manner of death. In many U.S. counties, the coroner is an elected official, or the role may be assigned to the county sheriff. In other counties, the coroner is a medical doctor, trained as a pathologist. In some jurisdictions, the coroner's jury has been replaced and its functions are performed by a county medical examiner/pathologist.

The **grand jury** dates to twelfth-century England, when King Henry II declared that a specific number of law-abiding males in a village must identify villagers suspected of committing crimes. Today, a grand jury consists of 12–23 people, and is tasked with the responsibility to investigate criminal activity and, if a criminal perpetrator is identified, issue an indictment (true bill) formally charging the criminal offender. If evidence is insufficient, the grand jury renders a *no bill* decision. Grand juries also investigate complaints from citizens and they often provide civilian oversight of government officials and agencies.

Grand jury proceedings are not public. Typically, during criminal investigations, only the grand jury members, the prosecutor, and the witness testifying are present. Grand juries have tremendous power. They can issue subpoenas (legal orders calling witnesses to present testimony), they can grant immunity from prosecution in exchange for testimony, and they can cite a witness for contempt for refusal to testify after immunity is granted. A contempt citation can lead to incarceration of the witness.

A **trial jury** (petit or common jury) is always the trier (finder) of fact in a trial. Its purposes are to determine the facts and to render a verdict.

Courtroom Participants

Numerous individuals participate in the judicial process. Some are judicial professionals who engage in the process on a full- or part-time basis. These professionals include the judge, prosecutor, defense attorney, bailiff, court reporter, court clerk, judicial assistant, law clerk, court administrator, and expert witnesses. Nonjudicial participants include the defendant, jurors, lay witnesses, victims, and media representatives.

The **judge** is the central figure in the courtroom whose primary responsibility is to ensure justice. The trial (or appellate) court judge functions as the interpreter of the law. In nonjury trials, the judge also fulfills the jury's role and functions as the finder of fact.

Judges are selected through a variety of methods. Federal judges are appointed by the President, confirmed by the U.S. Senate, and serve for life. State court judges are elected or they may be appointed, usually by

The judge ensures justice, interprets the law, and functions as the fact-finder in non-jury trials. *(Photo courtesy of the San Diego Sheriff's Department.)*

the governor. Some states utilize the Missouri Plan, a judicial selection and retention scheme that integrates election and appointment processes. Under the plan, judicial nominees are screened by a nonpartisan state judicial selection committee. The committee's approved list of nominees is forwarded to the governor, who appoints a nominee to fill a judicial vacancy. After appointment and a specified term in office, the judge is required to answer to the electorate by running unopposed in an election. Thus, the citizens have an opportunity to vote the originally appointed judge out of office. Almost all states require judicial nominees to be licensed attorneys who are members in good standing with the state's bar association.

The **prosecutor** represents and serves the government (people) in a variety of ways. Ultimately, like the judge, the prosecutor's role is to ensure justice. However, the prosecutor also advises the police, approves applications for arrest and search warrants, writes legal opinions, files criminal complaints, and represents the people in grand jury, pretrial, trial, posttrial, and appellate proceedings. Often referred to as the most powerful person in the criminal justice system because of the tremendous discretionary authority associated with the position, the prosecutor initiates formal criminal charges, takes an active role in plea bargaining, participates in bail decisions, and may discontinue a prosecution at any time by drafting and filing a no prosecute (*nolle prosequi*) document.

The public or private **defense attorney** develops a defense strategy and represents the defendant in all judicial proceedings. Right to counsel is a fundamental right guaranteed by the Sixth Amendment. Although ill advised, defendants may waive the right and defend themselves. If right to counsel is asserted, a defendant may retain (employ) a private attorney or, if indigent (poor), accept a government-compensated defense attorney appointed by the court. In large jurisdictions, the court-appointed defense attorney may be employed full- or part-time in a government public defender's office or with a private organization under contract to the government. In small jurisdictions, especially those in rural areas, the court (judge) may appoint a local attorney to act as the criminal defense attorney in the case. In such cases, the quality of the legal defense may be lacking. Most private local attorneys do not practice, nor are they experts in, criminal defense law. Some also believe criminal defense work is distasteful. Occasionally, an attorney will provide defense services *pro bono* (without compensation).

Numerous other professionals are engaged in the judicial process. The bailiff, usually an armed court officer, county marshal, or deputy sheriff, provides security and ensures order in the courtroom, announces the judge's entry, calls witnesses to testify, controls access, guards the defendant, and monitors sequestered juries. Deputy United States marshals

---

Learn more about prosecutors through the National District Attorneys Association at www.ndaa.org.

Learn more about defense attorneys through the National Association of Criminal Defense Lawyers at www.nacdl.org.

function as bailiffs in the federal courts. Court reporters record verbatim and process a transcript (written record) of all that is said in the courtroom. The court clerk maintains the records of the court and processes court-related documents. The judicial assistant functions as the judge's secretary. The law clerk is typically a law school student or recent graduate who assists the judge with legal research. The court administrator manages the nonjudicial activities of the court, assuming administrative duties historically handled by judges and clerks of the court. The court administrator formulates plans, schedules cases, analyzes case flow, manages the court's budget, and supervises its human resources. Expert witnesses (as compared to lay witnesses) are recognized experts in a particular field and are allowed, while testifying, to express opinions based on their area of expertise. Fingerprint and firearms specialists, psychiatrists, pathologists, and document examiners represent examples of expert witnesses.

Standards of Proof

In an adversarial legal system, opposing parties in a dispute operate under varying burdens or standards of proof (degrees of certainty). In criminal cases, a defendant is presumed innocent until proven guilty. The prosecution has the burden to proceed first with a criminal complaint and the burden of establishing guilt beyond a reasonable doubt. This is the highest standard of proof. It does not imply a mere possible doubt nor does it mean that guilt must be established beyond any doubt. Rather, guilt must be established in the mind of the finder of fact in a way that the fact finder is morally certain that the defendant committed a criminal act.

Unlike criminal prosecutions, through which convictions may result in imprisonment or execution, lower standards of proof are required for proceedings in which one is not subject to culpability for a criminal act. Lower standards of proof include clear and convincing evidence, proof by a preponderance of the evidence, *prima facie* proof (probable cause), sufficient evidence, reasonable suspicion, and mere suspicion. The clear and convincing standard of proof is used to establish a probability that the evidence presented is based on fact. This standard is used, for example, to deny bail or to determine if a juvenile under a designated age appreciated the wrongfulness of an act.

A preponderance of the evidence standard of proof is met if the evidence demonstrates a probability—over 50 percent likelihood—that the facts in issue are true. This standard is used in civil lawsuits. *Prima facie* (on its face) proof is the standard used to establish, through probable cause, that the circumstances in a particular situation are as they appear.

Probable cause is defined as a set of facts or circumstances that would lead an ordinary, reasonable, and prudent person to entertain a certain belief. Probable cause allows the fact finder to draw a certain conclusion, if no contradictory evidence is present. *Prima facie* proof is the standard required in a preliminary hearing. It also satisfies the proof standard necessary to make an arrest or issue a search warrant.

Lower standards of certainty are associated with terms such as *sufficient evidence, reasonable suspicion,* and *mere suspicion.* Sufficient evidence is applied in appellate courts when a review indicates adequate evidence exists to reverse a lower court's decision. Reasonable suspicion (less than probable cause) surfaces through a rational and reasonably entertained belief that facts warrant further investigation. This standard of certainty is necessary to stop and frisk a suspicious-acting person. Mere suspicion, the lowest degree of certainty, warrants prudent police actions to ensure personal safety. Mere suspicion is based on an intuitive guess or hunch. It is not a legally recognized standard of certainty (Osterburg & Ward, 2010).

The Pretrial Process

Pretrial processes in criminal cases typically proceed through the following steps:

- **Arrest or citation**—The initiation of the pretrial process in a criminal case is made through a physical arrest or through the issuance of an arrest warrant. A criminal citation, which includes a notice of the charge and an order (summons) to appear in court, is issued in lieu of arrest for minor offenses.
- **Booking**—Once arrested, the arrestee is booked. **Booking** involves the official recording of the arrest in the records of the arresting law enforcement agency. The arrestee is usually fingerprinted and photographed.
- **Initial incarceration**—If the arrestee cannot be released on recognizance (ROR) without a bail hearing, and if a magistrate or judge is not immediately available, the arrestee may be detained in a jail or lockup for a reasonable time (about two court working days) until a first appearance.
- **First (initial) appearance**—A **first appearance** takes place in the presence of a judge or magistrate. The accused is informed of the charge(s), advised of rights under the Constitution, and bail is set if possible. Bail is a security deposit left with the court to ensure the defendant's appearance at future proceedings. In most states, the accused can secure the bond through a contract with a bail bond agent. The agent insures the full bond amount in return for a nonrefundable fee (usually 5–20 percent of the full value of the bond) paid by the accused. Generally, the law favors the least restrictive means to ensure that the accused will return for future judicial proceedings.

Bail is not a matter of right. Rather, the Eighth Amendment provides that bail, when provided, shall not be excessive. Further, bail may be denied or revoked if the accused is a danger to self or others, or is likely to flee the jurisdiction of the court.

In addition to ROR, alternatives to the traditional private bail bond system include property bonds used as substitutes for cash, conditional release, third-party custody, unsecured bonds that require the accused to pay the full bond amount for failure to appear, and court-administered deposit bail. Deposit bail replaces the private bail bond agent with the court and the accused pays the percentage fee directly to the court. In most cases, the fee, minus a small administrative charge, is returned to the accused if court appearance dates are met. In minor cases, the accused may be allowed to waive a trial and plead guilty at this stage. In some jurisdictions, the first appearance is a nonadversarial proceeding entitled the arraignment on the complaint, which should not be confused with a post-information or post-indictment proceeding called an arraignment.

- **Indictment, information, or complaint**—In federal felony cases, the formal charge against the accused must be issued by a federal grand jury in the form of an **indictment.** In state cases, the prosecuting attorney (states attorney, district attorney) may present the case before a county grand jury for possible indictment or, in felony cases, the prosecuting attorney at the state level may file an **information,** which is a formal charge issued from the prosecuting attorney's office subsequent to a preliminary hearing. The formal charge for a misdemeanor is usually called a **criminal complaint.**

- **Preliminary hearing**—Many states do not normally use a grand jury. In lieu of a grand jury proceeding, these states utilize an adversarial preliminary hearing. The accused may waive the right to a **preliminary hearing** and plead guilty. If not waived, the accused is again informed of the charge(s) and rights under the Constitution. The hearing is conducted to determine if probable cause exists to hold the accused on the charge and bind the defendant over for trial. During this hearing the prosecution must establish a prima facie case, this is, on the face of the evidence presented by the prosecution, probable cause must exist that a crime occurred and the defendant committed the offense in question.

- **Arraignment**—A number of significant events occur at the **arraignment.** The court advises the defendant of constitutional and statutory rights, formally appoints retained or government-provided counsel, entertains a waiver of counsel, inquires into the defendant's mental competence to stand trial, and requires the defendant to respond to the accusatory pleading (government complaint). The defendant has two choices: to demur or enter a plea. A demurrer is an attack on the legal sufficiency of the pleading because of a factual or technical defect in the accusatory pleading. In most cases, the defendant enters a plea. Except for minor offenses, the arraignment usually provides the first opportunity for a person to answer to a criminal charge. Pleas available include:

Guilty—Most often, the defendant pleads guilty either to the original charge or to an amended charge arrived at through a plea bargain.

Not guilty—A date and time for the trial is set.

Not guilty by reason of insanity (NGI)—Through a NGI plea, the defendant claims that, although an act was committed, a mental defect or disease renders the defendant incapable of forming the criminal intent that is an element of all true crimes.

No contest (*nolo contendere*)—This plea is not an admission of guilt, but the defendant will not contest a declaration of guilt by the court (judge). Since it is not an admission of guilt, this plea cannot be used against this in a subsequent civil proceeding.

Stand mute—In American criminal jurisprudence, a defendant cannot be forced to say anything. Therefore, if a defendant stands mute, a not guilty plea will be entered by the court on the defendant's behalf and a trial date is set.

Several technologies are available to support the arraignment process, including satellite-based videoconferencing and remote two-way television to foster communication between jails and the court building (Reid, 2011)

- **Pretrial motions**—If the defendant is proceeding to trial, the defense attorney may file pretrial motions (oral or written requests) to have the charges dismissed, suppress prosecution evidence as inadmissible, discover what evidence the prosecution has, or delay the trial. Dilatory (delaying) tactics may benefit the defense because evidence may be misplaced and witnesses' memories may fade. Motions may also be filed to change the venue (location) of the trial, consolidate charges arising from a single criminal transaction, sever multiple counts or defendants, and disclose the identity and location of an informant (Acker & Brody, 2004; Cole & Smith, 2010; Germann, Day, & Gallati, 1988; Rutledge, 2000; Stuckey, Roberson, & Wallace, 2010).

The rules of discovery outline procedures for the disclosure of evidence to an opposing party. A prosecutor must voluntarily supply or disclose exculpatory evidence (evidence that indicates innocence) to the defense without request or demand. Examples of exculpatory evidence include a confession to the crime made by a person not the defendant in the present case, alibi witnesses, and other evidence that tends to exclude the defendant as the perpetrator. If the defense wishes to view or examine inculpatory evidence (evidence that indicates guilt), the defense must file a discovery motion with the court (judge). The motion cannot contain a blanket request for all inculpatory evidence in the prosecutor's possession. Rather, the defense must specifically request the list of witnesses and the physical evidence, photographs, documents, and testing results the prosecutor intends to use at trial. Attorney work product, such as personal notes and the strategies to be used by the prosecution or defense, are not subject to discovery by the opposition.

At any time during the pretrial and trial process, the accused, the defense attorney, and the prosecutor may participate in negotiations known as **plea bargaining.** Through plea bargaining, the defense offers a plea of guilty in exchange for a reduction in the original criminal charge(s), a dismissal of some of the charges pending in the case, or a sentencing recommendation by the prosecutor.

The Trial Process

The following is a brief explanation of the steps in a criminal trial:

- **Jury selection**—According to the U.S. Supreme Court, the Sixth Amendment guarantee to a jury trial applies to the federal government and in state cases in which the potential penalty for the crime charged exceeds six months in jail or prison or could result in a fine of more than $500. Since states can grant greater protections to a defendant than is afforded by U.S. Supreme Court interpretations of the U.S. Constitution, some states extend the right of trial by jury to all misdemeanors, regardless of the potential penalty. Thus, in some states, a defendant may request a jury trial in a misdemeanor case for which the potential penalty is only a fine. However, states do not extend the right to a jury trial to cases involving infractions (violations less severe than misdemeanors).

  The jury always functions as the finder (trier) of fact. Although the U.S. Constitution does not prescribe a specific number of jurors, 12 people traditionally make up a trial jury. If the prosecution and defense agree, a case may be tried with fewer than 12 jurors unless it is a capital case. Some states allow a six-person jury for minor offenses and civil cases.

  The initial list of potential jurors is selected from a list of registered voters, vehicle registration or property tax records, or from the department of motor vehicle's list of those who hold drivers' licenses. From the initial list, a **jury pool (venire)** of several hundred people is randomly selected. The jury pool reports to the criminal courts building. From the jury pool, a **jury panel** of approximately 30 people is randomly selected and referred to the court for jury selection. At the trial court, members of the jury panel are interviewed by the judge, prosecution, and defense during a voir dire (to speak the truth) examination to determine their suitability for serving on the trial jury.

  Potential jurors may be challenged from the jury panel for cause or may be excused because of a peremptory challenge. **Challenges for cause** are unlimited. However, **peremptory** (no cause need be given) **challenges** are limited in number. If the appropriate number of jurors and alternates cannot be selected from the 30 jury panel members, the bailiff or clerk of the court will return to the jury pool for additional candidates for the jury.

A third type of challenge, a **challenge to the array,** seeks to excuse an entire pool of potential jurors. Generally limited in its use to the defense, the challenge is based on a belief that the entire pool is bias or prejudiced, or that the pool is not representative of the population from which the pool is drawn.

After the trial jury is selected, the jury is sworn in (impaneled) and the actual trial begins. To avoid being influenced by outside publicity, the jury may be sequestered. While sequestered, jury members are not allowed to communicate with others regarding the trial.

- Opening statement by prosecution—The prosecutor briefs the trier of fact on the evidence to be presented as proof of the allegations (unproven statements) in the complaint, indictment, or information.
- Opening statement by defense—The defendant or the defendant's attorney provides an overview of the evidence to be presented to deny the allegations made by the prosecutor. The defense may waive the opening statement and reserve the right to make the statement when the prosecution has completed its case presentation (when the prosecution rests its case).
- Presentation of evidence and **direct examination** of witnesses for the prosecutor—Each witness for the prosecution is questioned. Other evidence such as documents or physical evidence in favor of the prosecution is also presented.
- **Cross examination** of witnesses by the defense—The defense has the opportunity to question each witness. Questioning is designed to attack the credibility of (impeach) the witness in the minds of the jury members.
- Redirect examination by prosecution and re–cross examination by defense of prosecution witnesses.
- The prosecution rests its case. After the government has presented its entire case, the focus of the trial shifts to the defense.
- Motions for dismissal or directed verdict—If the prosecution's basic case has not been established from the evidence introduced, the judge can end the case by granting the defendant's motion to dismiss or by entering a directed verdict of not guilty. If the defense motions are not granted, the case for the defense proceeds.
- Presentation of evidence and direct examination of witnesses for the defense—Each defense witness is questioned.
- Cross-examination of the witnesses by the prosecution—The prosecution has an opportunity to cross-examine each defense witness.
- Redirect examination by the defense and recross-examination by prosecution of defense witnesses.
- The defense rests its case.
- Rebuttal and surrebuttal—The prosecutor may offer rebuttal evidence to respond to the defendant's proof. If the prosecutor offers rebuttal evidence, the defendant may offer a surrebuttal to refute the prosecutor's rebuttal evidence.
- Opening argument (summation) by the prosecution—The prosecutor summarizes all the evidence presented (noting uncontradicted facts),

Learn more about the judicial process through resource linkages provided by the American Bar Association at www.abanet.org.

states how the evidence has satisfied the elements of the charge, and asks for a finding of guilty.

- Argument (summation) by the defense—This is similar to the opening argument by the prosecution except the defense asks for a finding of not guilty. The defense is entitled to only one argument at the end of the trial.
- Closing argument (rebuttal) by the prosecution—The prosecutor has the right to reply to statements in the argument made by the defense. Jurisdictions vary regarding the number and order of final arguments (summations) at the end of a trial. Some states allow only two arguments at the end of a trial: one closing argument each for the defense and the prosecution.
- Instructions and charge to the jury—The judge instructs the jury (if any) regarding the points of law that apply in the case. The judge also charges the jury with the responsibility of deliberating honestly and rendering a fair and just verdict.
- Jury deliberations—These deliberations are not public and the jury may be sequestered.
- Verdict—In most states, a unanimous verdict is required. If the jury cannot reach a unanimous decision, it is said to be a hung jury and the case may be tried again. In other states and in civil cases, a substantial majority verdict is sufficient (Stuckey, Roberson, & Wallace, 2010).

Posttrial Processes

If a jury's verdict is not guilty, the defendant is released. Not guilty verdicts cannot be overturned or reversed. If the defendant is found guilty, the judge will typically order a presentence investigation to be conducted by the probation department. The results of the investigation will assist the judge in determining the most appropriate sentence.

Prior to sentencing, victims of the defendant's criminal actions or the victim's survivors may be allowed to present verbal or written **victim impact statements.** Judges are encouraged and expected to consider such statements when determining the most appropriate sentence for the offender.

Postconviction remedies for the defendant include appeal and *habeas corpus* review. Most convictions are affirmed on appeal. Yet, convictions have been reversed when an appellate court determines that a material (critical) error was made during the trial. Examples of material error include the admission of unconstitutionally seized evidence, impropriety on the part of trial court participants, misinterpretations of the law, and inappropriate instructions presented to the jury by the trial court judge.

If the death penalty is imposed by a jury, the sentence alone is automatically appealed in many jurisdictions. On appeal, appellate justices must determine if the sentence of death was appropriate. When a convicted and incarcerated person has exhausted all appeal procedures, the person may file an application for a writ (court order) of *habeas corpus*. If granted, the writ commands the person who is holding the imprisoned person to show cause why continued confinement is necessary (Inciardi, 2009).

Sentencing

In *Apprendi v. New Jersey* (2000), the U.S. Supreme Court ruled that any fact, other than the fact of a prior conviction, that increases the penalty for a crime beyond the prescribed statutory maximum must be submitted to a jury and proved beyond a reasonable doubt (*Apprendi v. New Jersey*, 2000). In *Blakely v. Washington* (2004), the U.S. Supreme Court reaffirmed its ruling in *Apprendi,* holding that facts supporting a convicted person's sentence enhancement in state courts must be admitted by the defendant or determined by a jury beyond a reasonable doubt (*Blakely v. Washington,* 2004). The Court reasoned that a crime's aggravating circumstances are elements of the offense that must be submitted to the jury.

On January 12, 2005, the Court ruled that sentencing guidelines for federal courts, as prescribed in the 1984 Sentencing Reform Act, were contrary to the Court's decision in *Blakely.* In effect, the court reversed nearly twenty years of federal sentencing practice by ruling that federal judges need not follow the complex mandatory sentencing guidelines established by Congress in the 1984 legislation. Again, the court reaffirmed its position in *Blakely,* stating that the Sixth Amendment requires juries, not judges, to determine facts that are used to enhance sentences (*U.S. v Booker,* 2005; *U.S. v Fanfan,* 2005).

The *Apprendi* and *Blakely* decisions severely restrict a judge's ability to enhance a sentence unilaterally. Still, judges have a variety of sentencing options at their disposal. The options include probation, a fine, community service, restitution, house arrest, electronic monitoring, or commitment to a community corrections center, jail, or prison.

If incarceration is warranted, sentences may be determinate (fixed, definite) or indeterminate (variable). A **determinate sentence** specifies a fixed period of time and a reasonably definite release date. A variation of the determinate sentence, the **mandatory sentence,** removes discretionary authority from the sentencing judge. If the law prescribes a mandatory sentence, a judge must impose the required sanction. Three-strikes laws, for example, impose mandatory minimum prison terms.

Alternatively, indeterminate sentencing laws grant judges wide sentencing discretion. An **indeterminate sentence** is variable, providing a range of time (e.g., 3–6 years) to be served. In some jurisdictions, a person serving an indeterminate sentence may earn *good time* through good behavior and self-help rehabilitation efforts. The good time is exchanged for time subtracted from the maximum term of years and early conditional release from prison (parole) is possible.

If a defendant is convicted of several offenses in a single trial, multiple prison sentences may be imposed. The judge may direct that the sentences be served concurrently or consecutively. **Concurrent sentences** are served at the same time (simultaneously). **Consecutive sentences** are served individually, one after another.

The federal government virtually eliminated good time credit and parole in 1984 with the passage of the Comprehensive Crime Control Act. The act prescribed **truth in sentencing,** a concept that limits the discretion of federal judges and emphasizes serving the actual time specified in the prison sentence without a sentence reduction for good time. The act also established a nine-member U.S. Sentencing Commission, tasked with the responsibility for developing definite federal sentencing guidelines. The guidelines, which became effective in 1989, specified a sentencing range for each federal criminal offense. Federal judges could depart from the guidelines only if mitigating or aggravating circumstances existed (U.S. Sentencing Commission, 1987). However, as discussed earlier, the U.S. Supreme Court rulings in the 2005 *Booker* and *Fanfan* decisions support federal sentences that deviate from the statutory guidelines.

The public's fear of crime and the belief that many offenders are released too early led lawmakers in many states and at the federal level to pass legislation that prescribes severe penalties for those who are convicted repeatedly of serious offenses. Several jurisdictions enacted **three-strikes laws** designed to incarcerate recidivists (repeat offenders) for long periods of time, in many cases for life. Between 1993 and 1996, 25 states and the federal government enacted three-strikes laws. Since the mid-1990s, many other states have enacted similar mandatory sentencing laws. Several jurisdictions also severely curtailed or totally eliminated release on parole.

Washington and California were the first states to enact three-strikes laws. In Washington, all three strikes must be for felonies specifically listed in the statute. Under California law, only the first two strikes need be from the state's list of strikeable offenses. Any subsequent felony counts as a third strike. California's law also contains a two-strikes provision through which a person convicted of any felony who has one prior conviction for a strikeable offense may be sentenced to double the prison term the person would otherwise receive. In 1996, the California State Supreme Court ruled that judges have the discretion to eliminate strikes when sentencing defendants.

The long range impact of three-strikes legislation is still uncertain. A few preliminary studies indicate it may reduce the crime rate slightly. However, the results of these studies are not definitive because other studies have reached different conclusions. A recent study indicates that cities in three-strike states experienced no significant reduction in crime rates (Kovandzic, Sloan, & Vieraitis, 2004). In fact, jurisdictions that frequently impose three-strikes sentences often experience higher crime rates than jurisdictions that impose similar sentences less often. Three-strikes and other mandatory sentences can lead to prison overcrowding. The number of prisoners serving life sentences increased over 80 percent in recent years. The average time served on a life sentence (as compared to life without parole) also increased, from 21 to nearly 30 years (Clark, Austin, & Henry, 1997; Grant & Terry, 2012; Moran, 2004).

CASE STUDY—"THREE STRIKES AND YOU ARE OUT!"

In October, 1993, 12-year-old Polly Klaas was abducted by Richard Allen Davis during a girls' slumber party at the Klaas home in Petaluma, California. The kidnapping led to a nationally publicized search for Polly. After Polly's body was discovered, Davis, a repeat violent offender, was convicted for her kidnapping and murder. Subsequently, Polly's father, Marc Klaas, collaborated with Mike Reynolds to promote the passage of California's three-strikes law. Reynolds' daughter, Kimber, was fatally shot in the head nearly 18 months prior to Polly's murder. California voters overwhelming approved the three-strikes proposition (the Polly Klaas Memorial Habitual Offender Act) in November, 1994.

Unlike similar laws in other states, California's law does not require that the third strikeable offense be a violent or serious felony. Grand (felony) theft qualifies as a strike. Thus, a thief may be exposed to a mandatory 25-years-to-life sentence, compared to someone who receives a 15-to-life sentence for second-degree murder.

1. Are three-strikes sentences effective deterrents to crime?
2. Is a three-strikes law that mandates a harsh sentence for *any* felony in violation of the Eighth Amendment to the U.S. Constitution?

JUVENILE JUSTICE PROCEDURE

Juvenile justice procedure differs from the adult criminal court. Juvenile courts accept petitions of delinquency rather than criminal charges, adjudicate rather than convict delinquents, and they impose dispositions rather than sentences in delinquency cases. The goal of juvenile justice is rehabilitation rather than punishment. The juvenile courts must also balance the need for public safety with the best interests of the minor child.

Generally, the juvenile court system has jurisdiction over cases involving individuals under a statutory maximum age. Most states place the maximum age of juvenile court jurisdiction at 18. Some states are lower, with a few setting the maximum at age 16. Public perceptions that violent crime committed by teenagers had reached epidemic proportions led some states to statutorily mandate the transfer of violent juvenile offenders to adult court. New laws also reduce the confidentiality of juvenile court proceedings and limit the use of probation when young offenders are allowed to remain in the juvenile justice system. Juvenile courts address **juvenile dependency** issues (minor at risk of physical or emotional harm), status (predelinquency) offenses such as truancy, civil disobedience, and **juvenile delinquency** (criminal acts). In many states, a minor as young as 14 may be tried as an adult if the juvenile court determines the juvenile is not a good candidate for rehabilitation in the juvenile justice system.

In juvenile proceedings, the minor has no right to bail or a jury trial. Yet juveniles have other constitutional rights, including the right of notice of the charge(s) against them, the right to an attorney, the privilege to be free from self-incrimination, and the right to confront and cross-examine witnesses against them (*In re Gault,* 1967). As in adult proceedings, proof of guilt must be established beyond a reasonable doubt (*In re Winship,* 1970). The Miranda rights advisory is also extended to juveniles and they can waive their rights if they understand the consequences of their waiver (*Fare v. Michael C.,* 1979). However, to be admissible, a juvenile's self-incriminating statement must be made in the presence of a parent or other "concerned adult" (*Illinois v. Montanez,* 1996).

Young people enter the juvenile justice process when taken into custody by the police or through a **juvenile petition** filed by the child's parent, guardian, or other person who has contact with the juvenile. If detained and confined, a detention hearing is conducted by a judge, juvenile probation officer, or other intake person, to determine if the juvenile presents an immediate threat to self or others. If continued confinement is not warranted, the juvenile may be released to a parent, guardian, foster parent, or group home.

If the juvenile is charged with a violation of law, a preliminary hearing is conducted to determine if probable cause exists that the juvenile committed the offense. Often conducted in conjunction with the detention hearing, the results of the preliminary hearing can lead to informal probation or referral to an adjudication hearing if probable cause is established. Similar to a nonjury adult trial, the adjudication hearing is a fact-finding process to determine if the juvenile petition is sustainable. If the allegations in the petition are sustained, and the juvenile is adjudicated to be delinquent, a disposition hearing is conducted to determine the most appropriate course of action. An adjudicated delinquent may be confined in a youth authority facility, or committed to some form of non-confinement disposition alternative, such as probation.

Some jurisdictions have established **teen court** programs designed to provide an early intervention alternative to the juvenile court. Also referred to as youth or peer courts, teen courts utilize young volunteers who encourage first-time, nonviolent juvenile misdemeanants to behave responsibly (Lotz, 2005; Houston & Barton, 2005).

THE COURTS' IMPACT ON LAW ENFORCEMENT

The courts represent complex social agencies with many interrelated subsystems. The police, prosecutors, defense attorneys, judges, probation officers, and many others have a role in court operations. Decisions from the courts have a tremendous impact on law enforcement. Some decisions are viewed as positive, while others appear to impact negatively on the ability of police personnel to accomplish admirable goals. Reversed convictions and the development of procedural law and rules of evidence are often viewed negatively by those who have been tasked with the protection of persons and property. Over an extended period of time, however, it would appear that common good may be achieved through adherence to the constitutional principles that established the United States as a republic.

COURTROOM PRESENTATION

Attitude

The police and other justice system officers are ultimately responsible for criminal investigations that include the identification, location, apprehension, and interrogation of criminal suspects. As a result, officers may, because of their background and nature of their jobs, view criminal suspects negatively. Many suspects end up in court as criminal defendants. Since the officer-witness is an advocate for the prosecution, the officer may be antagonistic toward the defendant and defense counsel. However, in a court of law the professional officer must avoid favoritism. The officer should focus on an outcome that best serves the people's interest in justice. To enhance credibility, the officer must act and speak with impartiality, dedicated to an unbiased presentation of the evidence collected in the case. Conclusions (guilt or innocence) drawn from the evidence are the responsibility of the finder of fact, not the justice system officer.

Appearance

One never gets a second chance to make a first impression. This is especially true in a courtroom situation. To a great extent, the appearance of an officer in court may be more critical to the outcome of the case than what the officer says during testimony. Regardless of the facts in a case, juries are often influenced more by appearance than the presentation of the facts. Defense attorneys are also well aware of the importance of appearance. The suspect may look like an unkempt person when arrested but will be neat, clean, and well dressed for court appearances.

When dressing for success in the courtroom, an officer should appear in professional attire. Depending on agency policy, this means appearing in uniform or business attire. Some jurors are repulsed by the uniform. Previous encounters with officers may have been negative experiences or the jurors may reject authority. Officers should avoid casual or faddish clothes. Conservative dress is more appropriate. Clothes should also be color coordinated and reflect the conservative color scheme (black, grey, or dark navy blue) appreciated by most jurors. Shoes should be black and highly polished. Jewelry should be kept to a minimum and sunglasses should not be worn. If not in uniform, an officer should not display a badge, firearm, or other weapons. Visible weapons may have a negative impact on jurors who view firearms as abusive and militaristic. This may also lead some jurors to believe that the defendant was coerced or intimidated by the officer.

The courtroom is a formal environment. Therefore, law enforcement officers and other criminal justice personnel should present themselves as professionals. *(Photo courtesy of the San Diego Sheriff's Department.)*

(Photo courtesy of the San Diego Sheriff's Department.)

Demeanor

Justice system officers should act in a professional manner at all times when in or around a courthouse. Prosecutors, police officers, witnesses, defendants, defense attorneys, and jurors often utilize the same hallways, elevators, and restroom facilities. Officers should not tell jokes, discuss system business, chew gum, smoke, or behave in an obnoxious or offensive manner.

When called to testify, an officer-witness should walk and sit erect, avoid casual posture, and crossing of legs. Both feet should be placed firmly on the floor. Hands should be placed with palms down on legs or clasped together on the lap. Arms should not be folded. Body language communicates as much or more than the spoken word. When reciting the oath administered by the clerk or bailiff, the officer should raise the right hand, upper arm parallel to the floor, fingers together, with the palm of the hand flat and facing the person administering the oath. Nervous habits must be avoided.

Testimonial Technique

Police officers are expected to be apprehensive about testifying in court. Even seasoned actors experience stage fright and nervousness in front of a camera or audience. Unlike acting, however, the participants in a real-life courtroom are involved in an adversarial proceeding. The process as well as the opposing party can be very intimidating. Experienced officers still get nervous on the witness stand.

In a judicial proceeding, it is the responsibility of the officer to serve as a witness and communicate facts to the jury and the court. In so doing, the officer should act as natural as possible in the unnatural environment of the courtroom. Sarcasm, inappropriate or profane language, speaking out of turn or in excess, and expressing an opinion (unless as a qualified **expert witness**) must be avoided. If the officer is asked to repeat a vulgar statement made by the defendant, the officer should first apologize to the court for what is about to be said. The officer should listen to all that is said, and answer questions clearly, concisely, and deliberately in a voice and language that is easily heard and understood. Responses to questions should be addressed to the jury or the court in nonjury trials. Officers should avoid the use of jargon or legalese. Responses should be based on the question asked. Information beyond what is called for in the response should not be volunteered. If the officer-witness does not hear or understand a question, the officer should request that the question be repeated or clarified.

Defense attorneys will often ask tricky questions and solicit responses that are designed to reduce the credibility of the officer-witness. This process, called **impeachment,** is designed to make the officer appear less believable in the mind(s) of the trier or finder of fact (judge or jury). Consider the credibility of the prosecution witness in the minds of jury members after the following exchange:

Defense Attorney: "Did you advise the defendant of constitutional rights before you interrogated?"

Police Officer: "Yes."

Defense Attorney: "Did you advise the defendant of constitutional rights as outlined in all of the amendments to the U.S. Constitution?"

Police Officer: "No."

Defense Attorney: "Well then, you did not advise the defendant of all of the constitutional rights. You advised the defendant only of certain rights under the Constitution. Is that correct?"

Police Officer: "Yes."

During this exchange, the jurors become uneasy and the police officer less credible. Jurors could erroneously conclude that if this small part of the officer's testimony was incorrect, then other parts of the testimony relative to guilt or innocence could also be incorrect.

Before responding to any question, the officer-witness should hesitate slightly, mentally formulate an appropriate and correct response, and truthfully reply to the question without becoming emotional. Hasty answers set the stage for mistakes. Officers often, and naturally, possess strong feelings toward a particular case or defendant. Defense attorneys are aware of this and will deliberately antagonize the officer-witness. If an officer is caught in an innocent mistake, the officer should apologize, admit to the mistake, and correct the error. Respect for the truth will impress the trier (finder) of fact. If the prosecutor or defense attorney objects to a question or moves to strike a witness response, the officer-witness should stop speaking, remain silent, and wait for the ruling and instructions from the judge.

Occasionally an officer-witness will be asked to demonstrate a procedure or diagram a scene to illustrate a point. Care should be exercised to ensure that the demonstration does not inflame the jury, and that diagrams are clear and large enough to be viewed easily by jury members. The use of visual aids enhances presentations. However, if possible, visual aids should be preapproved by the prosecutor to avoid misrepresentation and surprises during the trial.

When excused, the officer-witness should quietly leave the courtroom unless instructed to do otherwise. Remaining in the courtroom could have a negative impact on the jury (Cole & Smith, 2010; Guffey, 2005; Miller, 2000).

▲ SUMMARY

Police officers and other justice system professionals must prepare to defend their actions in court. Officers should review the case file to refresh their memory, consult with the prosecuting attorney, and ensure that necessary documents and evidence are available in court. The courts are the pivot on which the criminal justice system turns and their decisions have a tremendous impact on law enforcement, the justice system, and society.

Courts systems and structures in the United States vary. Generally, there are two types of courts: trial and appellate. In addition, numerous specialized courts exist to adjudicate special issues. Standards (degrees) of proof range from proof of guilt beyond a reasonable doubt (the highest standard) to mere suspicion (a hunch). Criminal procedure progresses through an elaborate pretrial, trial, and posttrial process. Juvenile justice procedure differs from adult criminal justice procedure. During a courtroom appearance, the justice system practitioner-witness must maintain a proper attitude and demeanor, wear appropriate attire, and demonstrate an effective testimonial technique.

DISCUSSION QUESTIONS AND EXERCISES

1. Describe criminal court case preparation and presentation processes. Include a discussion of the importance of proper attitude, appearance, and demeanor in the courtroom.
2. Outline the federal and state court systems and describe the jurisdiction of each level of court.
3. List and describe the stages or steps in the pretrial, trial, and posttrial processes. Which stages are most critical from a criminal defendant's perspective?
4. Contrast adult criminal justice procedure with juvenile justice procedure.
5. Discuss the role of specialty courts.
6. List and describe standards of proof (degrees of certainty).
7. Visit a criminal court and observe the courtroom proceedings. Document the experience. Are the rights of the accused as well as society protected?
8. How can the concept of social justice (equality and fairness under the law) be preserved? In other words, how can society ensure that justice is blind?
9. Are mandatory three-strikes sentences appropriate punishment for crimes committed? Do three-strikes sentences function as a deterrent?

Corrections

LEARNING OBJECTIVES

After completing this chapter, the reader should be able to:

- discuss and analyze the correctional process.
- outline and discuss the history of corrections.
- compare and contrast philosophies in corrections.
- evaluate common beliefs regarding the role of punishment in contemporary society.
- list and describe mechanisms in noninstitutional and institutional corrections.
- evaluate the effectiveness of capital punishment.
- determine the extent to which justification for punishment is compatible with corrections.
- collect and analyze statistical data to evaluate the effectiveness of correctional treatment.
- compare and contrast the mechanisms used in adult and juvenile corrections, including but not necessarily limited to jails, prisons, fines, capital punishment, probation, parole, diversion, and community service.
- identify and discuss issues in corrections.

KEY TERMS

Define, describe, or explain the importance of each of the following.

Accreditation
Capital punishment
Community-based corrections
Deterrence
Diversion program
Incapacitation
Intermediate sanctions
Jail
Juvenile Justice and Delinquency Prevention Act of 1974
Parole
Prison

Prisonization
Privatization of corrections
Probation
Recidivism
Rehabilitation
Reintegration
Restoration
Restorative justice
Retribution
Special housing unit (SHU)
Status offenses

INTRODUCTION

Students and practitioners of criminal justice should be familiar with the corrections component of the system. Police officers often encounter probationers, parolees, and other convicted criminal offenders. Decisions regarding the correctional client are made at various points in the criminal justice process by specialists from vastly different organizations. The specialists include the police, prosecutors, defense attorneys, judges, probation officers, jail and prison personnel, and parole officers.

CASE STUDY—WHAT WORKS?

The number of individuals under the jurisdiction of the corrections component of the criminal justice system in the United States is at an all-time high. Jail and prison populations as well as the number of convicted offenders on probation and parole have increased. Part of the increase may be attributed to the growth in the general population. However, the growth in the correctional population has occurred during a period when the crime rate in the United States has declined or remained relatively stable. Well over two million people are in jail or prison, and the majority of those incarcerated are members of minority groups. Some experts suggest that the most likely reason for the increase is the cumulative effect of tough mandatory prison sentences and an emphasis on public safety and punishment rather than rehabilitation.

1. Can the United States punish its way to lower crime rates?
2. What accounts for the incarceration of a disproportionately high number of minority group members?
3. Is there a viable alternative to mandatory prison sentences?

THE CORRECTIONAL PROCESS

The pretrial period is the port of entry into the correctional process. The port of entry is staffed by the police. This period is crucial to prevention of future offenses because the likelihood of repeat offenses increases the longer the offender remains in the system. In addition, the consequences of any detention may have a negative impact on the offender's family, job, and social relationships. Families may become dependent on public assistance. Thus, the total cost of incarceration may increase dramatically.

During the trial period, the offender may be led to believe that the system can be manipulated through negotiations and plea bargaining. In addition, defense attorneys, prosecutors, judges, and juries make decisions that have long-term consequences. If the defendant is found guilty, the posttrial period will involve any combination of fines, jail, probation, prison, and in some cases, the death penalty. The offender is now labeled or marked for life as a convicted offender. The label often negatively affects the offender's self-concept, which can lead to repeat offenses.

During the postincarceration period, an offender is expected to reintegrate into society. However, incarceration and exposure to the system enhance the problems associated with reintegration. The offender is released as a different person because of personal problems and personality shifts that were developed during extended stays in a security-conscious setting. Upon release, the offender is expected to be self-sufficient and responsible in the community rather than passive and obedient. However, self-sufficiency and responsibility are not the hallmarks of a multitude of ex-offenders. On the contrary, many correctional clients will contact the system again.

HISTORY OF CORRECTIONS

Early Punishments

The recorded history of corrections can be traced to ancient Greece, Israel, Rome, and Egypt. Punishments in early Greece included confiscation of property, fines, imprisonment, and death. Punishments inflicted by the Hebrews of ancient Israel included banishment, branding, mutilation, scourging with thorns, and numerous forms of death by execution, including crucifixion. Ancient Roman penalties ranged from the payment of compensation to exile or death. The pharaohs of Egypt ordered mutilation of offenders. Although numerous nonlethal forms of corporal (physical) punishment were used, the most common punishments involved some form of instant (merciful) or lingering (torturously painful) death, including flaying (skinning alive) and dismembering of the body while the condemned person was alive.

Although confinement by chaining, jailing, and other means were used in ancient times, incarceration as punishment began to replace corporal punishment by the 1500s. Penal bondage was imposed on criminals, debtors, vagrants, and other social misfits. They were forced to work on public projects and fight in military engagements. Workhouses (houses of correction) were created in England and elsewhere in Europe to deal with the massive number of vagrants resulting from the breakdown of the feudal system and the societal shift from agricultural-based to industrial-based economies. The first workhouse in England, called Bridgewell, opened at St. Bridget's Well. Although originally used as industrial training facilities where misfits and petty criminals could develop responsible behaviors and learn a trade, workhouses soon became facilities for confinement rather than reform.

With the dawn of the Age of Enlightenment (Age of Reason) in the late 1600s, prisons emerged to replace workhouses, as new laws limited confinement to criminals, and reformers criticized the use of corporal punishment. The reformers provided the catalyst for a philosophical shift away from punishment of the body toward redemption of the human spirit (soul). Frenchman Charles de Montesquieu (1689–1755), a believer in individual rights, sought humane conditions for prisoners and punishments that fit crimes. Another Frenchman, Francois-Marie Votaire (1694–1778) was appalled at the lack of equal protection under the law. William Penn (1644–1718), the founder of Pennsylvania, and his Quakers abolished corporal punishment and restricted the death penalty to premeditated murder. Englishman John Howard (1726–1790) promoted corrections as a mechanism for reformation, rather than punishment. Another Englishman, Jeremy Bentham (1748–1832), advocated the concept of utilitarianism (the greatest good for the greatest number of people) and applied the concept to public policy. He promoted law as a means to achieve good by making undesirable social behavior less pleasurable.

One of the most influential thinkers and writers during the Enlightenment was Italian Cesare Beccaria (1738–1794). He is considered the father of the classical school of criminology. In his classic work, *An Essay on Crimes and Punishments,* Beccaria wrote that crime prevention is better than punishment, laws should serve the needs of society, an accused should be presumed innocent until proven guilty, punishment should fit the crime, and that punishment should be swift and certain. Beccaria's ideas formed the foundation for many approaches to corrections that still exist (Reichel, 2008; Seiter, 2011).

American Approaches

Approaches to American colonial corrections were patterned after English methods. However, differences did exist. For example, England continued to use capital punishment for a wide range of crimes, while the American colonists preferred corporal punishment, fines, and confinement. After the American Revolutionary War and well into the nineteenth century, large-scale penitentiaries (places where one could do penance and reform one's soul) replaced many other forms of punishment. Penitentiaries were viewed as places where a criminal could reflect, repent, and reform. However, as the demand for inexpensive labor increased, many prison populations were exploited and used as secured and forced slave labor. As alternatives to incarceration, the community-based supervision programs of probation and parole were established in the early 1800s.

The National Prison Association, forerunner of the American Prison Association and, later, the American Correctional Association, was founded in 1870. The association's mission is to provide training and technical assistance, establish a national correctional philosophy, and set correctional standards. Yet corrections professionals today still struggle with the roles and functions of corrections in American (Champion, 2005). Whether noninstitutional, community-based, institutional, or deadly, corrections professionals, policy makers, and citizens still debate the effectiveness of the various correctional philosophies and mechanisms.

PHILOSOPHIES IN CORRECTIONS

Throughout history several philosophies have developed in corrections. These philosophies include retribution, deterrence, incapacitation, rehabilitation, reintegration, and restoration. Each involves a set of assumptions and a rationale for corrections.

Retribution is based on the concepts of revenge and vengeance. Atonement, suffering, and punishment are central themes. In theory, the offender should associate pain with wrongdoing and seek to avoid pain by demonstrating legally acceptable behavior.

Deterrence operates under a theory that punishment, in and of itself, may operate to deter future criminal activity. Through the concept of general deterrence, it is assumed that punishing the offender will deter others from committing similar offenses. Through specific deterrence, it is assumed that punishment will deter the individual offender from committing another offense. Yet deterrence as a correctional strategy has not been effective in many areas. In spite of the threat of punishment, people still commit crime. Even murderers are not deterred by the threat of long-term incarceration or death.

Incapacitation involves rendering the offender incapable of repeat offenses. Isolation of the offender through institutionalization in a jail or prison removes the offender from society, thus incapacitating the offender from victimizing members of an open community. Other forms of incapacitation include female sterilization, male chemical castration, or total isolation in a maximum security facility.

Using a medical analogy, **rehabilitation** implies that there are identifiable causes of crime and these causes may be treated and cured. The philosophy also implies that the offender is capable of rehabilitation even though the correctional client may not have had the ability to conform behavior to the requirements of the law in the first place. Rehabilitation (reformation) remains a dominant philosophy in corrections.

Reintegration as a corrections goal is based on programming that helps an inmate adjust to life outside an institution. Most individuals who enter the correctional system will, at some future date, be discharged and released from custody. Hopefully, through exposure to the correctional process, the correctional client will return to society and not reoffend. The true measure of success in corrections may lie in reintegration without **recidivism** (repeat offenses).

The most recent correctional philosophy to emerge is that of **restoration.** Strategies associated with this philosophy are designed to restore, as much as possible, all those affected by a crime to their condition prior to the commission of the offense. Commonly referred to as **restorative justice,** restoration strategies focus on problem solving, restitution, damage repair, victim rights, offender responsibilities, and, possibly, offender repentance and forgiveness by the victim. Thus, it emphasizes healing for victims, offenders, and society as it promotes an inclusive approach to harm identification and repair.

NONINSTITUTIONAL CORRECTIONS

A majority of all convicted offenders are exposed to some form of noninstitutional community-based correctional program. Generally, noninstitutional corrections programs include diversion, probation, parole, and numerous other supervised and unsupervised community-based corrections programs. Noninstitutional corrections programs are intended to facilitate offender rehabilitation, accountability, and reintegration, promote restorative justice, and provide an array of alternative punishments. Noninstitutional, community-based corrections programs help to relieve jail and prison overcrowding. In addition, the programs provide mechanisms through which offenders may learn to act responsibly in the communities in which they live.

Diversion Programs

Diversion programs provide early intervention for first-time minor offenders. The offender may not acquire a criminal conviction record if the client successfully completes the diversion program. Types of diversion programs include detoxification, youth activities, and civil commitment to public or private treatment facilities. In other cases, the offender may be sentenced to complete a community service activity, such as roadway litter removal or other public works. These types of programs produce the additional benefit of reducing operating costs for the correctional component of the criminal justice system.

Probation

Probation is usually a function of the courts. Probation involves a sentence of conditional release to the community without jail or prison time. Exceptions include shock probation programs through which first-time offenders are incarcerated briefly to expose them to institutional life. Properly administered probation programs with recommended probation officer caseloads of 30 to 40 clients claim low recidivism rates. However, actual caseloads often exceed 100 clients. Over four million people are on probation at any given moment (U.S. Department of Justice, Bureau of Justice Statistics, 2005).

The likelihood of receiving probation depends on the pre-sentence investigation and recommendation made by the probation officer. Probationers who violate a condition of probation may be returned to the sentencing court for reevaluation. Violations include additional criminal activity. However, a significant number of probation violators do not commit new offenses. Rather, their probation status is revoked because they violate a noncriminal condition of probation.

Formal probation is supervised by a probation officer for a specified period of time with rules and conditions established by the sentencing judge and a probation officer. Summary, or informal, probation is unsupervised and the conditions of probation are established by the sentencing judge. The probation period for a misdemeanor usually does not exceed three years. Felony probation usually does not exceed the maximum prison term indicated for the offense.

In the case of adult probation, typically administered by the county, terms and conditions commonly imposed are no alcohol or illegal drug use, no association with undesirables, no weapons possession, regular contact with a probation officer or check-in through a kiosk that uses biometric technology to recognize the invidual (Reid, 2011), and waiver of Fourth Amendment rights relative to search and seizure. Juvenile probation is governed by the juvenile court, typically a division of the county's court of general jurisdiction. Juveniles on probation are commonly ordered to mind their parents or guardians, obey all laws, attend school, meet with a juvenile probation officer, and comply with the other conditions of probation.

Parole

Most prison inmates will be released from prison eventually, either after completion of their full sentence or on parole. **Parole** is a function of the prison system and involves a form of conditional release from a prison facility. The conditional release results from a parole board decision or is based on a mandatory conditional release provision. As with probation, parole officers typically encounter heavy caseloads and effective supervision of the parolee is difficult. Most sentencing statutes provide for early release from prison if the inmate follows a prescribed course of treatment and is not involved in misconduct while incarcerated. Commonly referred to as good time laws, these statutes allow for a 15 to 50 percent reduction to a prison sentence.

The origins of parole in the United States can be traced to the early nineteenth century. Problems associated with overcrowding, discipline, security, and the effectiveness of rehabilitation led to the use of parole as a means of encouraging positive behavior within prison populations. The first notable effort to provide some flexibility in prison sentences was the New York State good time law enacted in 1817. In 1837, Massachusetts passed the first comprehensive parole law in the United States.

Eligibility for parole depends on the type of sentence imposed by the trial court judge, statutory requirements, and the recommendation of the parole board. The primary purposes of parole are to reintegrate the offender into society and to protect the public from any future criminal activity of the parolee. Parole is often subject to several conditions. The parolee must obey all laws and not possess weapons except work tools and cooking and eating utensils. The parolee must maintain contact with a parole agent or officer as directed, and must notify the parole officer of changes in places of residence or employment. The parolee is also subject to warrantless search by an agent of the state department of corrections, a police officer authorized by a parole officer to search the parolee, or when a police officer has reasonable suspicion that the parolee is involved in criminal activity.

In an effort to get tough on criminals, several states and the federal government abolished or severely restricted the use of parole. Many argue that indeterminate sentencing and early conditional release from prison does not enhance rehabilitation. In addition, parole boards are often criticized for utilizing a closed, subjective decision-making process. Thus, many believe that parole decisions are not based on an objective standard.

Neither probation nor parole is a right. Rather, probation sentences rendered by judges and the granting of parole by parole boards is discretionary. However, once placed on probation or parole, offenders may not have their noninstitutional status revoked for violations or the commission of new crimes unless they are afforded due process rights. These rights include written notice of the charge, access to a lawyer, disclosure of incriminating evidence, and a hearing and judgement before an objective, neutral person. In addition, probationers and parolees have the right to confront and cross-examine witnesses, and the right to a written statement of the reasons for probation or parole revocation.

Other Noninstitutional Programs

Community-based corrections is a term that is often used to refer to noninstitutional correctional programs, including diversion, probation, and parole. However, in its broadest context, community-based corrections involves a wide variety of community resources that may be utilized to assist and treat an offender. These resources include social and health services, work and study release programs, counseling, and chemical abuse programs.

Noninstitutional corrections also includes various forms of **intermediate sanctions.** These sanctions are more restrictive than probation but less restrictive than jail or prison. Intermediate sanctions include fines, day fines (based on an offender's daily income), forfeiture (seizure of property), restitution, community service, use of drug courts, intensive supervision programs, day reporting, remote monitoring with electronic devices or global positioning systems (GPS), and house arrest. In addition, they include residential centers, halfway houses (used to reintegrate previously incarcerated offenders into the community), and military-style boot camps (a form of short-term shock incarceration) (Schmalleger & Smykla, 2008; Seiter, 2011).

INSTITUTIONAL CORRECTIONS

At any given time, less than half of all correctional clients are institutionalized. Typically, these institutions include jails and prisons. By 2009, over one and a half million people were institutionalized (Sabol & West, 2010). Many inmates are drug offenders. In the federal system, nearly 60 percent are incarcerated for drug violations. In state and local facilities, almost 25 percent are drug offenders.

Jails

Municipal or county **jails** are facilities that are usually under the control of the local chief of police or county sheriff. In some areas of the country the jails have been separated from the jurisdiction of the sheriff, and the county maintains a separate department of corrections. The federal government operates several jail (detention) facilities, usually located in large metropolitan areas. Many are operated by private corrections contractors. In rural areas, federal prisoners serving short-term sentences are housed in local or county jails.

Nearly 13 million people are admitted to jails in the United States each year. Jails incarcerate people who have been arrested, are awaiting trial, or are serving short sentences of one year or less. Because of the short length of stay, effective vocational education or counseling programs are practically nonexistent. In addition, overcrowding in urban jails is a major problem. Many convicted felons also serve time in the county jail, usually as a condition of felony probation (Michelson, 1999).

Jails were first established in England in 1166 A.D. by King Henry II. Referred to as *gaols,* these early institutions held vagrants, paupers, drunkards, thieves, and murderers. Men, women, and children were often housed in common rooms. The jails were operated by shire-reeves (forerunner of the modern-day sheriff) and were locally controlled. Shire-reeves received a daily fee for each inmate held.

Jails were commonplace in the early American colonies. The first American jail opened on Walnut Street in Philadelphia in 1776. The Walnut Street Jail and other jail facilities quickly deteriorated into deplorable environments. In 1787, several Pennsylvania Quakers formed the Philadelphia Society for Alleviating the Miseries of Public Prisons (the Society). Society members visited jails and sought to improve conditions for inmates. In 1790, through the efforts of the Society, the Pennsylvania legislature designated a section of the Walnut Street Jail to be renovated and transformed into a penitentiary. Prisoners were segregated and isolated, with frequent visits from Quakers, who provided religious instruction. The Quakers believed the penitentiary should be a place where offenders would repent for their unlawful deeds and reform and rehabilitate themselves.

Overcrowding in urban jails is a major problem. *(Photo courtesy of the San Diego Sheriff's Department.)*

Prisons

Prisons, both at the state and federal levels, incarcerate convicted offenders who are serving long-term sentences. Some historians credit a facility established in Simsbury, Connecticut, in 1773, as the first prison. Referred to as the Newgate Prison, the punishment-centered facility was actually a converted underground copper mine. Most historians, however, cite Philadelphia's Walnut Street Jail as the first American prison established for reformation and rehabilitation. Often referred to as a Pennsylvania-style system, it promoted segregation and isolation of prisoners. In 1823, a prison was opened in Auburn, New York. The Auburn penitentiary buildings were constructed with several levels (tiers), a design made common as more prisons were established. The Auburn model promoted congregate labor and communal eating facilities with little segregation. Most prisons in the United States were constructed using the Auburn model (Champion, 2005; Inciardi, 2009).

According to Schmalleger and Smykla (2008), prisons in the United States progressed through nine stages of development. Each stage emphasized a different correctional philosophy.

Penitentiary Era (1790–1825). This first period in United States prison history witnessed the creation of 30 state prisons modeled after the penitentiary constructed in Auburn, New York. The model promoted congregate labor, rehabilitation, and deterrence.

Mass Prison Era (1825–1876). With an emphasis on punishment, incapacitation, and deterrence, 35 additional Auburn-style prisons were constructed, most notably, New York State's Sing-Sing in 1825 and California's San Quentin in 1852. Pennsylvania's Eastern State penitentiary, opened in 1829 and modeled after Quaker principles, was converted to an Auburn-style prison during this era.

Reformatory Era (1876–1890). Enforcing indeterminate (variable) sentences to promote education, training, and rehabilitation, the first young men's reformatory opened in Elmira, New York in 1876. Twenty other men's reformatories were established throughout the United States. The first reformatory for women opened in Indianapolis, Indiana, and the first women's prison was established in Ossining, New York.

Industrial Era (1890–1935). Based on the philosophy of incapacitation, inmates during this era worked in prison industries, on public works projects, and were leased to private businesses. Eventually, labor unions viewed unpaid or poorly paid prison labor as unfair competition. The unions pressured Congress to pass laws restricting the interstate shipment of goods produced with prison labor.

Punitive Era (1935–1945). During this period, the emphasis was placed on retribution, custody, and strict punishment. The super-secure federal prison opened on Alcataz Island in San Francisco Bay in 1934 was characteristic of prisons of this era. Alcatraz was closed in the early 1960s, judged an expensive failure.

Treatment Era (1945–1967). Poor prison conditions led to riots that generated public support for treatment and rehabilitation of inmates.

Community-Based Era (1967–1980). Based on an assumption that the community was the source of most offender problems, the reintegration of offenders focused on the use of community resources. Probation programs, work release centers, community corrections centers, and halfway houses proliferated. However, the community-based approach did not reduce prison populations or lower crime rates.

Warehousing Era (1980–1995). Promoting incapacitation rather than rehabilitation, indeterminate sentences were replaced with determinate (fixed) sentences and the discretion of parole boards was restricted. Overcrowding flourished and access to rehabilitation programs was limited.

Just-Deserts Era (1995–present). This era focuses on retribution and punishment and supports the practice of warehousing prisoners. Just-desserts proponents are not concerned with rehabilitation, although opportunities exist for inmate self-improvement. The emphasis is on determinate and mandatory sentences, three-strikes laws, and the death penalty.

Prisons are classified as minimum, medium, maximum (close/high), or super maximum (supermax) security facilities, and inmates are assigned to each depending on their level of dangerousness and escape risk. Various security levels may also exist within a single institution. In addition, some prisons contain a **special housing unit (SHU).** An SHU is a designated temporary housing assignment for inmates who violate prison rules, pose a threat, or are in need of protection from other inmates. Inmates who commit serious violations are placed in the SHU for disciplinary segregation. Others are placed in the SHU on administrative detention status. Securing prisoners is a primary function of prisons. Following a relatively recent trend, supermax facilities are "no frills" prisons that warehouse violent and escape-prone inmates who cannot conform their behavior to acceptable standards in general prison populations. Supermax prisoners are segregated and housed in solitary confinement. Additionally, the goals of a prison system are to provide academic and vocational education as well as treatment, administer parole services, improve correctional strategies, and educate the public regarding the role of correctional programming (California Commission on Peace Officer Standards and Training, 2012).

Similar to public law enforcement, prison administration and services are a function of the executive branch of government. At the state level, a governor typically appoints a state director of corrections. In turn, the director appoints wardens to manage prison facilities. State prison organizations vary in size, depending on the population of the state and the resources devoted to corrections. Prison facilities are expensive to build and operate. Approximately 90 percent of a prison's annual operating budget is consumed through expenditures for staff salaries and bene-

Modern prison facilities do not resemble prisons of an earlier time. *(Photo courtesy of the San Diego Sheriff's Department.)*

fits. Nationally, the average annual cost of incarcerating one offender in a state prison is approximately $30,000.

At the federal level, prisons are also a function of the executive branch of government, located within the U.S. Department of Justice. In 1891, Congress authorized the establishment of the first federal prisons in Atlanta, Georgia, Leavenworth, Kansas, and McNeil Island, Washington. Previously, those convicted of federal offenses were confined, under federal contract, in state prisons and local jails. In 1930, the Federal Bureau of Prisons (BOP) was established to provide more humane and progressive care for federal offenders, to professionalize federal prison services, and to ensure centralized and consistent administration of the eleven existing prison facilities. Today, the BOP operates over 100 prisons and detention centers, two staff training centers, and nearly 30 community corrections offices that monitor federal community corrections centers and home confinement programs (U.S. Department of Justice, Bureau of Prisons, 2004).

Many prisons offer special programs. These programs include treatment and counseling for physical, psychological, and chemical abuse problems; work-related activities, such as prison industries and work-release programs; vocational training; educational programs, such as high school and college; and religious programs. Inmates, or residents, within a prison are classified according to their custodial (security) requirements, violent tendencies, program needs, and type of offense. In some states, inmates are also classified according to their level of maturity.

Problems with Prisons

The problems associated with prisons are many and varied. Often the need to secure the inmate population conflicts with the desire for effective treatment. Control and supervision of residents to prevent escapes, disorder, and the introduction of contraband are the primary factors of prison security and custody. Problems associated with sexual behavior also develop. Nonconsensual homosexuality increases in prisons. To prevent such behavior, a few institutions permit conjugal visits between inmates and their spouses.

Prisons also develop subcultures and inmate social systems. Institutionalization, or **prisonization,** develops as inmates internalize the values and norms of the inmate population. In many cases, inmates become more criminal in their behavior. The impact of long-term incarceration in prisons appears to have little effect on the recidivism rate, since approximately two-thirds of all inmates released from prison will repeat offenses and return to prison.

Disorder in prisons as a result of conflict and disturbances is commonplace. Extreme disorder may manifest itself in riots and deaths to inmates as well as staff. One of the most notable prison riots occurred in 1971 at the Attica Correctional Facility located in upstate New York. Rioting inmates seized the facility. State police and correctional officers subsequently assaulted the prison to regain control, killing 29 prisoners and 10 officer-hostages in the process. Constructed in 1931, Attica was the scene of poor inmate living conditions, violations of inmate rights, and racism on the part of correctional staff. Most of the inmates were members of minority groups from New York City. One hundred percent of the correctional staff were white officers recruited from the rural labor pool in and around Attica, New York. As inmate gangs developed at Attica, the institutional climate was ripe for the riot that erupted on September 9, 1971.

One report estimates that U.S. correctional institutions experienced more than 1,300 riots during the twentieth century (James, 2009). Although early prison riots led to numerous reforms, it appears that rioting and other disturbances in prisons are increasing. Many of the problems and cultural conflicts the inmates experienced while living outside the prison are magnified once they are incarcerated. The presence of ethnic, cultural, and economically based prison gangs and overcrowding

The presence of gangs and overcrowding in prisons lead to tension that can explode into a riot. *(Photo courtesy of the San Diego Sheriff's Department.)*

Learn more about prisons through linkages provided at www.justice.gov/prisoninfo.htm.

leads to tension that can easily explode into a riot or other major distur-bance.

Prison gangs are a major problem in many prison facilities. Gangs form for self-protection, to intimidate prison staff and other inmates, to control illegal drugs and other prison-based criminal activity, and to gain power or influence. Many are extensions of noninstitutional street gangs. Prison gang members typically have extensive criminal backgrounds. They participate in fewer programs, and they are more likely to abuse chemicals than their nongang counterparts.

To control prison gangs, correctional staff employ strategies to iden-tify gang members, detect and investigate gang activity, and deny display of gang colors and symbols. Hard-core gang members are often trans-ferred to maximum-security facilities. Staff also recruit and use inform-ants, conduct gang surveillance and intelligence-gathering activities, and limit gang-member access to cash and other forms of currency to restrict the development of an underground economy (Seiter, 2011).

Overcrowding is a major problem and is predicted to get worse (Champion, 2005; Gilliard & Beck, 1996; Stephan, 1997). In 1987, Califor-nia's adult prisons housed almost 67,000 inmates. By 2009, the state's prison population grew to over 168,000. (California Department of Correc-tions and Rehabilitation, 2009). To address the crowding problem, some prisons are considering moving inmates to county jails (Faturechi, 2011).

Offender reentry is another challenge. As former inmates transition out of prison, they need to build skills and gain access to services as well as disability benefits—all of which can help reduce the risk of recidivism.

The rehabilitative effect of long-term incarceration appears to be negligible. Most imprisoned individuals will be released at some point and will reoffend. If the purposes of long-term imprisonment are punish-ment and incapacitation, society's goals have been met. However, harsh prison sentences may only postpone the inevitable: more crime commit-ted by parolees and others subsequent to their prison experience.

CAPITAL PUNISHMENT

Capital punishment (the death penalty) is the subject of a great deal of debate. Most people have opinions regarding the death penalty but few people actually know much about it. Only a small percentage of first-degree murder convictions result in the imposition of a death sentence. And, although executions are actually rare in the United States, capital punishment generates an enormous amount of discussion, media cover-age, and anger. Does the death penalty operate as a deterrent to crime?

Do the benefits of execution outweigh the costs? An execution is a specific deterrent because the offender who is put to death will not reoffend. However, does the possibility of execution operate as a general deterrent to deter others and prevent murders from occurring in the first place? Evidence suggests that few individuals reflect on the possibility of execution before killing another human being (Nelson & Foster, 2001).

The second major question associated with the death penalty involves the cost. The average cost of incarcerating an individual for 50 years is approximately $1 million. However, the cost of an execution, if the taxpayer expenses associated with appeals and an average stay of ten years on death row are included, can approach six times the cost of life imprisonment. Apparently, considerable taxpayer dollars could be saved if incarceration for life without parole replaced the death penalty (Albanese, 2007; Bruce & Severance, 2005). Concerns about costs have promoted lawmakers in some states, including Maryland, Colorado, Kansas, Nebraska, and New Hampshire, to argue for abolishing the death penalty (Urbina, 2009).

Between 1930 and 1967, there were 3,859 executions in the United States, 60 percent of which were in 17 southern states. Thirty-three were federal executions. Executions began to decline in the 1950s. The last federal execution during this period occurred in 1963. Between 1967 and 1977, there were no executions in the United States.

In *Furman v. Georgia* (1972), the U.S. Supreme Court suspended death penalty statutes. Since a disproportionate number of minorities were being executed, the court held that the death penalty was cruel and unusual and, therefore, in violation of the Eighth Amendment because it was being applied in a discriminatory manner. In *Furman,* the Court ruled that the Georgia death penalty statute, as written, allowed juries to determine issues of guilt while simultaneously considering sentencing options. Under these circumstances, the Court reasoned that juries could use their unguided discretion to apply the death penalty arbitrarily and conpriciously. Several other states had death penalty statutes similar to Georgia's.

The Supreme Court's ruling led states to develop a two-stage process for capital cases. In the first stage, guilt is decided. In the second stage (the penalty phase), the sentence (death or an alternative prison sentence) is determined. During the penalty phase, juries may consider aggravating and mitigating circumstances as well as evidence not admitted during the trial. States that wished to retain the death penalty were required to rewrite their death penalty statutes to conform to the Supreme Court's new guidelines.

In *Gregg v. Georgia* (1976), the U.S. Supreme Court approved the two-stage process and held that capital punishment itself was not cruel and unusual punishment. On January 7, 1977, executions returned to the corrections scene with the execution of Gary Gilmore by firing squad in Utah. Between 1977 and 1997, 432 people were executed in the United States: two by firing squad, three by hanging, nine by gas, 134 by electrocution, and 284 by lethal injection. In 1995, 3,054 prisoners were under the sentence of death, and 56 executions occurred in 16 of the 38 states that had death penalty statutes (Barlow, 2000; Snell, 1996).

In 2002, 37 states and the federal government held 3,557 prisoners under the sentence of death. Sixty-five inmates were executed in 2003, six fewer than in 2002. Most executions were administered through lethal injection. All those executed had committed murder (U.S. Department of Justice, Bureau of Justice Statistics, 2004). In 2010, there were 46 executions (Death penalty information center, 2011).

On June 11, 2001, Timothy McVeigh, convicted of killing federal law enforcement agents during his bombing of the federal building in Oklahoma City in 1995, was executed. McVeigh's death represented the first federal execution in 38 years.

Considerable time elapses between the imposition of the death penalty and the actual execution. On average, an execution occurs approximately 10 years after the sentence of death is imposed. The delay is attributed to the numerous appeals filed by those under the sentence of death.

Methods of execution include lethal injection, electrocution, lethal gas, hanging, and the firing squad. Most jurisdictions use lethal injection and several states offer the condemned person a choice of lethal injection or one of the other approved execution methods.

In 2002, the U.S. Supreme Court ruled that execution of the mentally challenged (those with extremely low IQ test scores) violates the Eighth Amendment (*Atkins v Virginia*, 2002). Further, the Court has ruled that executions are unconstitutional unless the convicted offender was at least 18 years old at the time of the crime for which the death sentence is imposed (*Roper v Simmons*, 2005).

ISSUES IN CORRECTIONS

Many problems associated with crime are beyond the control of corrections and other criminal justice professionals. Yet corrections personnel still struggle to identify and implement appropriate correctional strategies. As a result, several critical issues confront the twenty-first century corrections person. The following presents a discussion of a few of these issues. The list of issues presented here is by no means exhaustive. However, they provide a foundation for additional research and a means to stimulate further discussion.

Accreditation of Corrections Programs

Through **accreditation** the status and performance of corrections facilities, programs, and personnel are measured against nationally adopted minimum standards. In the United States, the American Correctional Association (ACA) and its Commission on Accreditation for Corrections (CAC) develops and revises standards and accredits correctional services, programs, and operations. Founded in 1870 as the National Prison Association, the ACA is the oldest correctional association. It administers the only recognized accreditation program for all aspects of noninstitutional and institutional juvenile and adult corrections. ACA standards are used by the courts to determine if the management of correctional facilities meets Eighth Amendment constitutional requirements.

Learn more about accreditation standards by contacting the American Correctional Association at www.aca.org.

Mandatory and nonmandatory ACA standards apply to a correctional program's administration, fiscal process, personnel selection and training, physical facilities, policies and procedures, sanitation, food service, and correctional client rules and discipline. To receive a three-year accreditation, the program must be 100 percent compliant with mandatory standards and 90 percent compliant with nonmandatory standards.

Although some resist accreditation initiatives, they can be extremely beneficial. Accreditation and its processes can improve staff training and professional growth, assess program strengths and weaknesses, provide a defense against liability lawsuits, and they establish measurable criteria for improvement. Accreditation can also help improve the morale of personnel and clients, promote a safer environment for staff and clients, and reduce liability insurance premiums. It offers proactive, cost-effective, performance-based standards to measure goal achievement (American Correctional Association, 2004).

Correctional Officer Selection and Training

As minimum entrance qualifications, most jurisdictions require that candidates for correctional officer positions be 21 years old, have no felony or domestic violence convictions, possess a high school diploma or equivalent, be of good moral character, and be in good physical health. Additional requirements include successful completion of a written examination and an interview. Some jurisdictions also require pre-employment drug testing and psychological screening. After employment, correctional officers complete a classroom and on-the-job training program. Probationary periods average nine months.

Correctional officers experience job-related stressors similar to those experienced by law enforcement personnel and many other public safety employees. Stress is a nonspecific response to perceived threats. Although a moderate amount of stress enhances learning and creative abilities, high stress levels can lead to officer burnout and high attrition (labor turnover) rates. Correctional officer stress stems from several sources, including job dissatisfaction, role conflict and ambiguity, high risks and liabilities, and lack of participation in decision-making processes.

To reduce burnout and attrition, correctional officer selection procedures and training protocols should simulate, as closely as possible, the

Learn more about corrections job openings and other announcements at www.corrections.com.

types of activities and situations an officer is likely to encounter on the job. Selection and training should be based on job task analyses and expose officer candidates to situations that will limit unrealistic expectations and measure their tolerance for uncertainty. In addition, correctional administrators should involve line personnel in decision-making processes and in-service training should emphasize perishable skills associated with problem solving, communications, motivation, and maintaining good interpersonal relationships. Training in sex-offender supervision, motivational interviewing, officer safety in the community, family dynamics and domestic violence, and individual and group cognitive-behavioral approaches is also valuable (Community Corrections e-Learning Collaborative, 2011).

Juvenile Corrections

Issues surrounding juvenile corrections focus on the institutionalization of status offenders, the treatment of juvenile offenders as adults, and the application of the death penalty.

Status offenses are infractions committed by young people in their status as juveniles. Examples include juvenile curfew violations, truancy, underage smoking and consumption of alcohol, and running away from home. Affected juveniles can be labeled delinquent and stigmatized for life. In an effort to encourage states to deinstitutionalize juvenile status offenders and offer treatment alternatives, Congress passed the **Juvenile Justice and Delinquency Prevention Act of 1974.** The act provides for federal financial assistance to states in support of juvenile treatment and diversion programs.

Few juvenile delinquents are transferred to adult criminal courts. However, a disproportionate number of young nonviolent property crime and drug offenders are referred to adult court. The referrals are viewed as a means to prevent the juveniles from progressing to violent crimes against persons. Yet the available evidence does not support the contention that escalation from nonviolent to violent crime occurs. Viable alternatives to adult criminal court and corrections mechanisms should be pursued. Outdoor experience and wilderness programs, for example, can improve a delinquent's self-concept, pride, and trust in others, personality traits generally lacking among juvenile offenders. In recent years, more resources have also been devoted to juvenile delinquency prevention.

Public opinion appears divided on how best to deal with violent juvenile offenders. The age at which juvenile offenders are tried as adults varies among jurisdictions. Three states try juveniles aged 16 and above as adults. Nine states refer juveniles to adult court at age 17, while 38 states and the District of Columbia try all juveniles as adults at age 18.

Although many are transferred to adult court to face harsh penalties, the impact of severe punishment on the juvenile recidivism rates is the subject of great debate. Access to firearms and illegal drug use are closely associated with violence committed by and against juveniles. Restricting access to firearms and decreasing illicit drug use among juveniles may do more to reduce juvenile violence than the threat of harsh punishments.

The Death Penalty

Probably no other issue in corrections is more controversial than the death penalty. Proponents cite the need for retribution and deterrence. Those in opposition are concerned with the perceived immorality of taking another human life, executions of the mentally ill, international opposition, the expense associated with death penalty cases, and the possibility of executing an innocent person. Opponents also suggest that the death penalty is not an effective deterrent, that its application is arbitrary, and that it continues to discriminate against ethnic and racial minorities. The opinions of proponents and abolitionists may be ill informed, however, because such opinions are often based on personal views, emotions, and political appeal.

Although proponents suggest that the death penalty is applied consistently, factual evidence reveals that the likelihood of receiving a death sentence depends on where the capital offense is committed as well as the perpetrator's gender, age, social class, race, and mental capacity. Other determinative factors include plea bargaining, trial court participant error, prosecutorial discretion, and U.S. Supreme Court decisions. Death penalty abolitionists, on the other hand, reject retribution as a justification for execution, contending that it appeals only to the emotions of the public and a victim's family.

Regardless of one's view of the death penalty, any worthwhile debate over capital punishment should be accompanied by facts that can be used to dispel false assumptions. For example, studies reveal that only a small percentage (less than 2 percent) of those sentenced to death in the United States are actually executed. A disproportionate number of minorities are sentenced to death, yet over 50 percent of those executed within the last 25 years were white males. It has also been demonstrated that executing an offender is more expensive than incarceration of the offender for life. Finally, there is clear evidence to suggest that innocent people may have been executed. Through DNA testing, a few jurisdictions discovered that some persons on death row did not commit the crimes for which they are awaiting execution. Improving the quality of defense counsel and mandatory DNA testing in capital murder cases may help prevent the execution of innocent people (Bruce & Severance, 2005; Death Penalty Information Center, 2004).

A lengthy discussion of the pros and cons of the death penalty is beyond the scope of this book. It is suggested that proponents as well as opponents of capital punishment examine the facts and participate in a fact-based dialogue designed to address the practicality and goals of the death penalty. Ultimately, retention or abolition of the death penalty in the United States may be more dependent on public opinion than on fact or concepts of morality.

Learn more about the death penalty through the Death Penalty Information Center at www.deathpenaltyinfo.org.

The Incarceration of Women

The number of women incarcerated in correctional facilities has increased dramatically, both in terms of absolute numbers, and as a percentage of the total number of men and women entering institutions. Incarcerated women tend to be young, poor, unskilled, undereducated, single, heads of households who are members of a minority group and have children under the age of 18. Nearly one-third are incarcerated for drug violations and most were involved with the commission of economic crimes. Less than 20 percent committed a violent crime. A majority of adult female offenders have been physically abused. Almost one-third have been sexually abused. Some may be pregnant as they enter a correctional facility.

As political and cultural beliefs in the latter part of the twentieth century led to many crime control initiatives such as three-strikes laws and mandatory prison sentences, more nonviolent women were incarcerated. Due to the special needs of many of these women, the public's economic costs associated with the incarceration increased also, especially the expenses for health services, child care, and other special needs (Fein, 2005). Considerable public resources could be saved if viable alternatives to the incarceration of many nonviolent women are developed and utilized.

Prisoner Rights

Prior to the 1960s, it was believed that prisoners forfeited personal rights except for those basic rights afforded all human beings under the law. However, the cultural revolution of the 1960s led many Americans to acknowledge social injustices. Vocal Americans changed public opinion as they clamored for reform. Many oppressed groups, including prison inmates, discovered that judges were more sympathetic and receptive to their complaints. Prisoner lawsuits proliferated as inmates sought access to the courts and redress of grievances associated with prison conditions, brutality, solitary confinement, the quantity and quality of food and medical care, religious freedom, and censorship. Judges intervened in the management of institutions and corrections administrators responded with changes.

Prisoner rights were, and are, derived from the U.S. Constitution, particularly the First, Fourth, Fifth, Sixth, Eighth, and Fourteenth Amendments, as well as section 1983 of the Civil Rights Act of 1871. In addition, rights are derived from state constitutions as well as federal and state statutes. Although not absolute, the rights are interpreted within the context of due process of law. The 1970s witnessed a decline in the prisoner rights movement. Several justices appointed to the U.S. Supreme Court after the 1960s held views reflective of public sentiment that shifted toward a crime control model of criminal justice. By the late 1980s, judges were reluctant to interfere in prison operations if a legitimate government interest existed to justify the operations, and the nature of the confinement was not unconstitutional. Further, judges refused to consider numerous prisoner lawsuits that had no foundation in fact.

Currently, the prevailing view of the U.S. Supreme Court supports basic prisoner rights as specified in the Constitution. However, the judiciary is reluctant to address prisoner rights petitions that do not focus on the limited constitutional rights already afforded inmates. Although great progress was made during the prisoner rights movement, several problems have not been addressed. Notable among these problems are overcrowding and the increasing need for medical care as inmate populations age or inmates become infected with HIV/AIDS (King, 2005).

Privatization of Corrections

The **privatization of corrections** involves the use of private sector contractors to provide correctional services. The services range from the assessment, testing, treatment, and monitoring of low risk community-based offenders to the construction, staffing, and management of prison facilities. The privatization of some aspects of corrections is controversial, especially as it relates to the staffing and administration of detention centers, city, county, and federal jails, transfer centers, juvenile facilities, and prisons. However, many jurisdictions realized considerable cost savings through the use of private contractors such as the Corrections Corporation of America, the Management and Training Corporation, the Wackenhut Corrections Corporation, the Geo Group, the Correctional Services Corporation, and Alternative Programs, Incorporated.

The privatization of corrections is not new. Historically, inmate labor was placed under contract to private enterprises. Today, many organizations contract with corrections facilities to provide goods and services through inmate work programs. Manufacturing, training services, computer programming, and drafting are a few examples of work performed by correctional clients.

Privatization of corrections reflects two points of view. Advocates contend that private administration of correctional facilities can provide the same or higher level of quality service in a more efficient, economical, and less political manner. Opponents cite moral, legal, and ethical issues. Opponents argue that the power of the people (government) to punish cannot be relegated to a private entity. Further, opponents suggest that private enterprise is less accountable than government, that prison labor may be exploited by private interests, and that private correctional personnel lack the professionalism of their public sector counterparts. Currently, there is little evidence in support of either point of view.

Corrections: What Works?

Burgeoning prison populations, budget constraints, and high recidivism rates have led many policy makers, corrections professionals, and citizen groups to re-examine correctional mechanisms. If punishment and incapacitation of offenders are the purposes of the criminal justice system, the corrections component of the system is probably well on its way toward meeting its goals. However, if first priority is given to correcting offender behavior, it is apparent that many corrections programs fail to achieve the intended result. If correcting behavior, rehabilitation, and restorative justice are the most desirable outcomes, attention should focus on what works.

CASE STUDY—DNA FREES THE INNOCENT?

In 2000, the results of DNA tests revealed that 13 condemned prisoners on Illinois' death row did not commit the crimes for which they were sentenced to death. The discovery led the state's governor, George Ryan, to declare a moratorium on the application of Illinois' death sentences. Although he originally favored the death penalty, Ryan subsequently commuted the death sentences of all 167 Illinois death row inmates to life in prison without the possibility of parole.

In 2001, Kenneth Waters was released from prison after serving 20 years for a murder he did not commit. Exculpatory DNA evidence was discovered by his sister, Betty Ann Waters, a high school dropout who earned bachelor's, master's, and law degrees in a quest to free her brother. After receiving her law degree in 1998, she sought assistance from the Innocence Project, a group that uses DNA evidence to free those wrongly convicted. The DNA discovery led two prosecution witnesses to recant testimony presented during Kenneth Waters' murder trial 20 years earlier

Since 1989, more than 250 people have been exonerated nationwide, thanks to DNA testing (Debruin, 2011).

1. Should DNA tests be conducted on evidence presented in all capital cases?
2. Should wrongfully convicted persons be compensated? If so, how and by whom?

Correctional administration is influenced by many factors external to the correctional programs themselves. Whether based on reality or false assumptions, public support for punishment and crime control often translates into a harsh political response. Elected officials respond to public opinion with long mandatory prison sentences and restricted use of noninstitutional corrections programs (Vandiver, 2005).

Spending for corrections has increased more than 50 percent due to mandatory sentences, tough drug laws, an aging inmate population, mentally ill offenders, and an expansion of the number of prisons. Yet history demonstrates that it is difficult for a society to punish its way to lower crime rates. Although the death penalty and correctional institutions serve the purposes of punishment and incapacitation, it is unlikely that the interests of reform, restoration, and justice are served by executions and the incarceration of large numbers of offenders (Grant & Terry, 2012; Muraskin, 2005; Nicholl, 2000). The reader is challenged to visualize an appropriate balance among the seemingly contradictory philosophies and goals of corrections.

▲ SUMMARY

The correctional process begins during the pretrial period, when an offender encounters the police. It progresses through the courts and corrections to release or death of the criminal offender. The history of corrections can be traced to ancient times. The philosophies in corrections include retribution, deterrence, incapacitation, rehabilitation, reintegration, and restoration.

Noninstitutional corrections includes diversion programs, probation, parole, and numerous other community-based programs. Institutional corrections includes jails and prisons. The ultimate criminal sanction is the death penalty.

Issues in corrections include accreditation of corrections programs, correctional officer selection and training, juvenile corrections, the death penalty, the incarceration of women, and prisoner rights. Issues also include the privatization of corrections and the effectiveness of correctional programs.

DISCUSSION QUESTIONS AND EXERCISES

1. Describe the correctional process, from the port of entry to a convicted offender's release from the jurisdiction of the criminal justice system.
2. Outline and discuss the history of corrections.
3. Evaluate correctional philosophies. Which philosophy is most prominent today?
4. Define and discuss the purposes of restorative justice.
5. List and describe institutional and noninstitutional mechanisms in corrections. Which appears to be more effective in preventing recidivism? Explain.
6. Is the death penalty an effective deterrent to capital crimes? Explain.
7. In a community policing environment, officers engage communities and solicit citizen participation with crime and disorder prevention efforts. How could the police collaborate with corrections personnel to prevent or reduce crime?
8. Identify, discuss, and develop solutions for the major issues and problems in corrections.
9. Arrange to visit and tour a correctional facility. If possible, interview a correctional client and a corrections employee. Document the experience. Does incarceration help to correct behavior?
10. What should the primary goal of the corrections process be?
11. If successful outcomes in corrections are measured by a reduction in the number of repeat offenders, how might recidivism rates be improved?

Appendix A

Declaration
of Independence

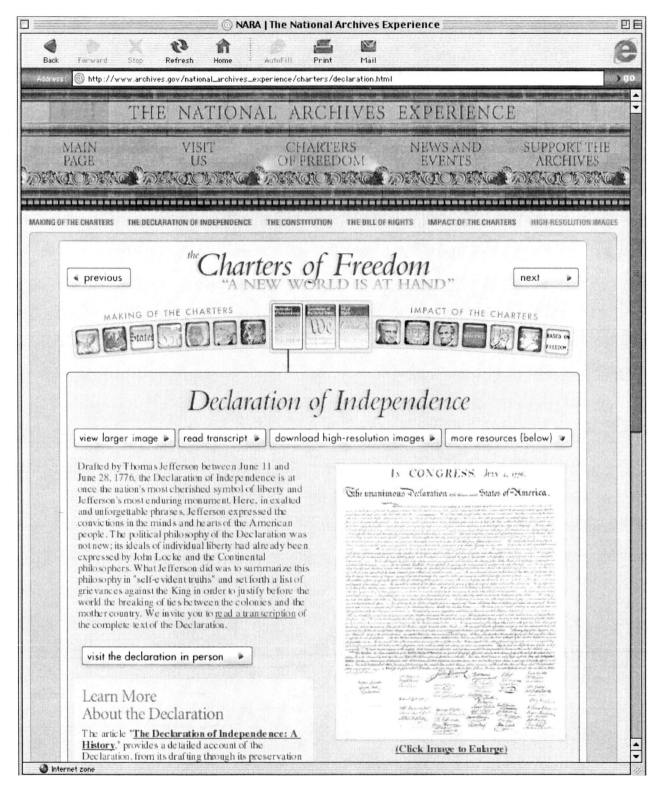

To view this entire document access this book's companion web site at: http://www.archives.gov/
national_archives_experience/charters/declaration.html.

Appendix B

Constitution of the United States

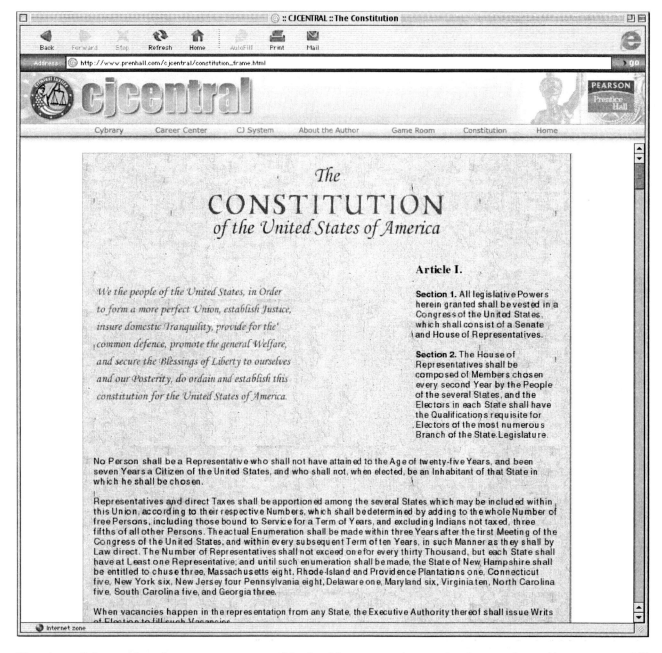

To view this entire document access this book's companion web site at: http://www.prenahll .com/cjcentral/constitution_frame.html.

Appendix C

Correlation of California, New York, and Texas Basic Police Academy Subjects with *Introduction to Law Enforcement and Criminal Justice*, Third Edition

CALIFORNIA COMMISSION ON PEACE OFFICER STANDARDS AND TRAINING (POST) REGULAR BASIC COURSE LEARNING DOMAINS

POST Learning Domain (LD)	Relevant Text Chapters
LD1 Leadership Professionalism, and Ethics	1, 3
LD2 Criminal Justice System	1, 12, 13
LD3 Policing in the Community	1–8
LD4 Victimology/Crisis Intervention	2, 6
LD5 Introduction to Criminal Law	2
LD6 Property Crimes	2
LD7 Crimes Against Persons/Death Investigation	2, 11
LD8 General Criminal Statutes	2
LD9 Crimes Against Children	2
LD10 Sex Crimes	2
LD11 Juvenile Law and Procedure	2, 12, 13

NEW YORK STATE BASIC COURSE FOR POLICE OFFICERS
1/2009
Division of Criminal Justice Services

Excerpted from: http://criminaljustice.state.ny.us/ops/docs/training/pubs/basicpolice/
bcpooutline.pdf. Accessed 09/29/2011.

Topic		Required	Relevant Text Chapters
Administration of Justice – Part I			
Introduction to Criminal Justice	Part 1-A	1	1, 12, 13
Jurisdictions and Responsibilities of Law Enforcement	Part1-B	1	1
Adjudicatory Process and Court Structure Civil & Criminal	Part1-C	2	12
Total of Part 1		**4**	
Introduction to Law Enforcement – Part 2			
Constitutional Law	Part 2-A	2	2, 7, 9
Discretionary Powers	Part 2-B	2	1, 3
Ethical Awareness	Part 2-C	12	3
Physical Fitness and Wellness	Part 2-D	65	7
Laws of New York State – Part 3			
New York State Penal Law Offenses	Part 3-A	16	2
Justification—Use of Physical Force & Deadly Physical Force	Part 3-B	7	8
New York State Criminal Procedure Law	Part 3-C	21	9, 12
New York State Juvenile Law and Procedure	Part 3-D	5	2, 8, 12, 13
Civil Liability and Risk Management	Part 3-E	2	1
Ancillary New York State Statutes	Part 3-F	2	n/a
New York State Vehicle and Traffic Law	Part 3-G	5	8
Law Enforcement Skills – Part4			
Field Note-Taking	Part 4-A	2	4
Report Writing	Part 4-B	7	4
Communications	Part 4-C	4	4
Observation and Patrol	Part 4-D	4	7, 8
Case Preparation and Demeanor in Official Proceedings	Part 4-E	7	12
Mental Illness	Part 4-F	14	10
Crimes in Progress	Part 4-G	4	2

Topic		Required	Relevant Text Chapters
Arrest Processing	Part 4-H	5	2, 9, 12
Professional Traffic Stops	Part 4-I	5	8
Interpersonal Skills—Arrest Techniques	Part 4-J	40	4
Emergency Medical Services	Part 4-K	40	10
Emergency Vehicle Operation and Control	Part 4-L	21	8
Firearms Training	Part 4-M	40	7
Supervised Field Training Review and Orientation	Part 4-N	160	7
Traffic Direction and Control	Part 4-O	2	8
Traffic Enforcement	Part 4-P	4	8
DWI Detection and Standardized Filed Sobriety Testing	Part 4-Q	21	8
Physical Evidence	Part 4-R	12	9
Off-Duty and Plain Clothes Encounters	Part 4-S	2	3
Community Interaction - Part 5			
Intoxication	Part 5-A	2	10
Community Resources—Victim/ Witness Services	Part 5-B	3	2
Crime Prevention and Crime Against the Elderly	Part 5-C	4	10
Cultural Diversity/Bias Related Incidents and Sexual Harassment	Part 5-D	5	1, 3, 4, 5
Persons with Disabilites	Part 5-E	2	10
Community Oriented Policing and Problem Solving—Media Relations	Part 5-F	2	5, 6, 8
Mass Casualties and Major Events – Part 6			
Standardized Response Plans for Unusual Events	Part 6-A	8	10
Counter Terrorism	Part 6-B	8	10
The Nature and Control of Civil Disorder	Part 6-C	2	10
Investigation – Part 7			
Domestic Violence	Part 7-A	14	1, 10
Organized Crime Familiarization/ Enterprise Corruption	Part 7-B	2	11
Preliminary Investigation and Information Development	Part 7-C	2	11
Interviewing Techniques	Part 7-D	5	11
Common Criminal Investigation Techniques	Part 7-E	10	11

Topic		Required	Relevant Text Chapters
Basic Crash Management and Reporting	Part 7-F	14	8, 4
Injury and Death Cases	Part 7-G	3	2, 11
Sex Crimes	Part 7-H	2	2, 11
Narcotics and Dangerous Drugs	Part 7-I	3	2, 11
Missing and Abducted Children—Missing Adult Cases	Part 7-J	3	10, 11
Animal Abuse Cases	Part 7-K	2	10
Contemporary Police Problems	Part 7-L	4	1
Human Trafficking	Part 7-M	2	2

Grand Total		**639**	

Texas Commission on Law Enforcement Officer Standards and Education 618-hour Basic Course

Available From: http://www.swtjc.net/programs/workforce-training/law-enforcement-academy.asp.

Course	Section	Relevant Text Chapters
1.	Fitness and Wellness and Stress Management	7
2.	Professional Policing	1, 3
3.	Professionalism and Ethics	3
4.	Constitution and Criminal Justice System	1, 9
5.	Multiculturalism and Human Relations	1, 3, 4, 6
6.	Code of Criminal Procedure	9, 12
7.	Arrest—Search—Seizure	9
8.	Penal Code	2
9.	Traffic Law	8
10.	Intoxicated Driver & Standard Field Sobriety Testing	8
11.	Civil Process and Liability	1
12.	Texas Alcoholic Beverage Code	2
13.	Health & Safety Code—Controlled Substance	2
14.	Juvenile Issues—Texas Family Code	2, 8, 12, 13

15.	Written and Verbal Communications	4
16.	Spanish	n/a
17.	Force Options	2, 8
18.	Strategies of Defense—Mechanics of Arrest	8
19.	Strategies of Defense—Firearms	8
20.	Emergency Medical Assistance	10
21.	Emergency Communications	4, 10
22.	Professional Police Driving	8
23.	Problem Solving	6
24.	Patrol	8
25.	Victims of Crime	2
26.	Family Violence & Related Offenses	2
27.	Crisis Intervention	10
28.	Hazardous Materials Awareness	10
29.	Criminal Investigations	11

References

About CALEA. (2004). *CALEA online*. [On line]. Available: www.calea.org.

Acker, J. R., & Brody, D. C. (2004). *Criminal procedure: a contemporary perspective* (2nd *ed.*). Sudbury, MA: Jones and Bartlett Publishers.

Adams, R. J., McTernan, T. M., & Remsberg, C. (1980). *Street survival: Tactics for armed encounters*. Northbrook, IL: Calibre Press.

Adams, T. F. (2007). *Police field operations* (7th ed.). Upper Saddle River, NJ: Pearson Prentice Hall.

Adler, N. J. (2008). *International dimensions of organizational behavior* (5th ed.). Cincinnati: South-Western/Thomson Learning.

Adler, R. B., & Elmhorst, J. M. (2009). *Communicating at work* (10th ed.). New York: McGraw-Hill.

Adler R. B., and Towne, N. (2012). *Looking out/looking in* (13th ed.). Fort Worth, TX: Harcourt College Publishers.

Ainsworth, B. (2000a, August 6). Prison is no deterrent for determined addict. *San Diego Union-Tribune,* p. A19.

Ainsworth, B. (2000b, December 19). Drug measure a challenge to carry out. *San Diego Union-Tribune,* pp. A3, A8.

Albanese, J. S. (2007). *Criminal justice* (4th ed.) Boston, MA: Allyn & Bacon.

Allen, H. E., Simonsen, C.E., & Latessa, E. J. (2010). *Corrections in America: An introduction* (12th ed.). Upper Saddle River, NJ: Pearson Prentice Hall.

Alpert, G. P. (1998). *Helicopters in pursuit operations*. Washington, DC: National Institute of Justice.

American Correctional Association. (2004). *Accreditation and standards*. [On line]. Available: www.aca.org.

American Institute of Architects. (2003). *Building security through design*. [On line]. Available: www.aia.org/security.

Anderson, T. D. (Ed.). (2000). *Every officer is a leader: Transforming leadership for police, justice, and public safety*. New York: St. Lucie Press.

Anderson, T. D., & King, D. (1996a). *Managerial leadership training needs assessment in justice and public safety*. New Westminster, BC, Canada: Justice Institute of British Columbia.

Anderson, T. D., & King, D. (1996b). *Police supervisory leadership training needs assessment.* New Westminster, BC, Canada: Justice Institute of British Columbia.

Apprendi v. New Jersey, 530 U.S. 466 (2000).

Apuzzo, M., & Goldman, A. (2010, July 29). "Extent of FBI exam cheating unclear." *San Diego Union Tribune,* p. A3.

Argyris, C. (1964). *Integrating the individual and the organization.* New York: Wiley.

Arizona v. Gant. (2009, April 21). 556 U.S. ____; slip opinion No. 07-542.

Arner, M. (2000, October 16). Crime rate falling in this county and in U.S.—for now. *San Diego Union-Tribune,* pp. A1, A15.

Atkins v. Virginia, 122 S.Ct. 2242 (2002).

Baca, L. D. (2002, April 7). Address. Speech presented at Academy of Criminal Justice Services (ACJS) annual meeting, Anaheim, CA.

Bad convictions of poor blamed on lawyers, plea pressure. (2005, February 11). *San Diego Union Tribune,* p. A10.

Badge of Life (2011). Badge of Life announces 2010 police suicide figures. [Online]. http://www.policesuicideprevention.com/id48.html.

Baker, T. E. (2005). *Introductory criminal analysis: Crime prevention and intervention strategies.* Upper Saddle River, NJ: Pearson Prentice Hall.

Balint, K. (2000, September 8). Copyrights take a licking on Net frontier. *San Diego Union-Tribune,* pp. A1, A23.

Barkan, S. E., & Bryjak, G. J. (2004). *Fundamentals of criminal justice.* Boston: Pearson Allyn and Bacon.

Barlow, H. D. (2000). *Criminal justice in America.* Upper Saddle River, NJ: Prentice Hall.

Barnard, C. I. (1938). *The functions of the executive.* Cambridge, MA: Harvard University Press.

Baro, A. L., & Burlingame, D. (1999, Spring). Law enforcement and higher education: Is there an impasse? *Journal of Criminal Justice Education, 10* (1)57–73.

Bartol, C. R., & Bartol, A. M. (2011). *Criminal behavior: A psychosocial approach* (9th ed.). Upper Saddle River, NJ: Pearson Prentice Hall.

Bass, B. M. (1960). *Leadership, psychology and organizational behavior.* New York: Harper.

Bass, B. M. (1981). *Stogdill's handbook of leadership: A survey of theory and research.* New York: The Free Press.

Bass, B. M. (1985). *Leadership and performance beyond expectations.* New York: The Free Press.

Bass, B. M. (1990). *Handbook of leadership.* New York: The Free Press.

Bayens, G. J., Birzer, J. L., & Roberson, C. (2005). *Police management and leadership in the 21st century.* Belmont, CA: Wadsworth/Thomson Learning.

Bellows, R. M. (1959). *Creative leadership.* Englewood Cliffs, NJ: Prentice Hall.

Bennett, W. W., & Hess, K. M. (2004). *Criminal investigation* (7th ed.). Belmont, CA: Wadsworth/Thomson Learning.

Bennis, W. G. (1961, January). Revisionist theory of leadership. *Harvard Business Review, 38*(1) 26–36, 146–150.

Bennis, W. G. (1984, September). The four competencies of leadership. *Training and Development Journal, 38*(9) 14–19.

Bennis, W. G. (1993a). *An invented life: Reflections on leadership and change.* Reading, MA: Addison-Wesley.

Bennis, W. G. (1993b). Managing the dream: Leadership in the 21st century. In W. E. Rosenbach & R. L. Taylor (Eds.), *Contemporary issues in leadership* (3rd ed., 213–218). Boulder, CO: Westview Press.

Berg, B. L., & Horgan, J. J. (1998). *Criminal investigation* (3rd ed.). Westerville, OH: Glencoe/McGraw-Hill.

Bernard, L. L. (1926). *An introduction to social psychology.* New York: Holt.

Bisesi, M. (1983, Fall). Strategies for successful leadership in changing times. *Sloan Management Review, 25*(1) 61–64.

Blake, R. R., & Mouton, J. S. (1965). A 9.9 approach for increasing organizational productivity. In E. H. Schein & W. G. Bennis (Eds.), *Personal and organizational change through group methods.* (169–183). New York: Wiley.

Blakely v. Washington, 124 S.Ct. 2531 (2004).

Blanchard, K., & Johnson, S. (1992). *The one minute manager.* New York: Morrow.

Bloch, P. B., & Anderson, D. (1974). *Policewomen on patrol: Final report.* Washington, DC: The Police Foundation.

Blum, J. (2004, January/February). Image is not everything—but it helps. *The Law Enforcement Trainer,* 19 (1), 18–22.

Boehm, N. C. (1988). *P.O.S.T. career ethics/integrity training guide.* Sacramento, CA: Commission on Peace Officer Standards and Training.

Bogardus, E. S. (1929). Leadership and attitudes. *Sociological Society, 13,* 377–387.

Bohm, R. M., & Haley, K. N. (2009). *Introduction to Criminal Justice* (6th ed.). New York: McGraw-Hill.

Boni, W., & Kovacich, G. (2000). *Netspionage: The global threat to information.* Woburn, MA: Butterworth-Heinemann.

Boydstun, J. E. (1977). *Police staffing in San Diego: One- or two-officer units.* Washington, DC: The Police Foundation.

Brann, J. E. (1999, July). Where we've been . . . where we're going: The evolution of community policing. In California State, Office of the Attorney General, *Community oriented policing and problem solving: Now and beyond* (11–20). Sacramento, CA: Office of the Attorney General.

Bratton, W. J. (2011, February). "Reducing crime through prevention not incarceration." *Criminology & Public Police.* 10 (1), 63–68.

Bray, C. Two arrested in iPad security breach. (2011, January 19). *Wall Street Journal,* 1.

Bridges, W. (1994, September 19). The end of the job. *Fortune, 130,* 62–64.

Brody, D. C., & Acker, J. R. (2010) Criminal law (2nd ed.). Sudbury, MA: Jones and Bartlett Publishers.

Brooks, K. W. (1979). Delphi technique: Expanding applications. *North Central Association Quarterly, 53*(3) 377–385.

Brooks, P. R. (1975). *Officer down: Code three.* Schiller Park, IL: Motorola Teleprograms.

Brown, J. F. (1936). *Psychology and the social order.* New York: McGraw-Hill.

Bruce, A. S., & Severance, T. A. (2005). The death penalty. In R. Muraskin (Ed.), *Key correctional issues.* Upper Saddle River, NJ: Pearson Prentice Hall.

Building a bridge to the community can begin with a better handled traffic stop. (1999, September 15). *Law Enforcement News, 25* (517) 1, 9.

Bulman, P. (2010, April). "Elder abuse emerges from the shadows of public consciousness." *National Institute of Justice Journal.* Issue No. 265, 4–9.

Bunning, R. L. (1979). The Delphi technique: A projection tool for serious inquiry. In *The 1979 annual handbook for group facilitators,* (174–181) San Diego, CA: University Associates.

Burch, J. H., II. (2011, May). "Promoting Officer Safety: A priority focus of the U.S. Department of Justice." *The Police Chief.* 78 (5) 34, 36.

Burns, J. M. (1978). *Leadership.* New York: Harper & Row.

Burns, L. R., & Becker, S. W. (1988). Leadership and decision making. In S. M. Shortell & A. D. Kaluzny (Eds.), *Health care management: A text in organization theory and behavior* (2nd ed., 142–186). New York: Wiley.

Butterfield, F. (2004, May 3). Cost of fighting crime zooms in U.S. *San Diego Union Tribune,* p. A8.

By their own hands: PDs grope for answers to cop suicide. (1999, June 30). *Law Enforcement News, 25,* (514) 5.

Byers, B. (2000, September/October). Ethics and criminal justice: Some observations on police misconduct. *ACJS (Academy of Criminal Justice Services) Today,* 21 (3), 1, 4–7.

Bynum, T. S. (2001). *Using analysis for problem-solving: A guidebook for law enforcement.* Washington, DC: U.S. Department of Justice, Office of Community Oriented Policing Services.

Byrd, M. (2003, December/2004, January). Leadership and ethics in career development. *Community College Journal,* 74 (3), 27–29.

Byrnbauer, H., & Tyson, L. A. (1984, September). Flexing the muscles of technical leadership. *Training and Development Journal, 38*(9) 48–52.

California Community Colleges. (1992). *Public safety curriculum project: Expanded executive summary:* Sacramento, CA: Chancellor's Office of the California Community College System.

California Community Colleges. (2003). *Public safety curriculum and professional development project: Law enforcement curriculum.* Sacramento, CA: Chancellor's Office of the California Community College System.

California Department of Corrections and Rehabilitation. (2009).

California State. (2012a). *Evidence Code.* Sections 1–1605.

California State. (2012b). *Penal Code.* Sections 1–15003.

California State. Commission on Peace Officer Standards and Training. (1990, November). *Syllabus: Supervisory Leadership Institute.* Sacramento, CA: POST Center for Leadership Development.

California State. Commission on Peace Officer Standards and Training. (1998). *Entry-level uniformed patrol officer job analysis.* Sacramento, CA: Commission on Peace Officer Standards and Training.

California State. Commission on Peace Officer Standards and Training. (2002, April 10). *Proceedings of the April 10, 2002, POST Commission meeting.* Culver City, CA: California Commission on Peace Officer Standards and Training.

California State. Commission on Peace Officer Standards and Training. (2003). *Supplemental guide: Integration of leadership, ethics, and community policing into the regular basic course* (Draft). Sacramento, CA: Commission on Police Officer Standards and Training.

California State. Commission on Peace Officer Standards and Training. (2012). *Regular peace officer basic course.* Sacramento, CA: Commission on Peace Officer Standards and Training.

California State. Department of Alcohol and Drug Programs. (2004). *Alcohol and drug programs.* [On line]. Available: www.adp.ca.gov/SACPA/prop36shtml.

California State. Department of Justice, Office of the Attorney General. (1996). *Community oriented policing and problem solving: Definitions and principles.* Sacramento, CA: Office of the Attorney General.

California State. Department of Justice, Office of the Attorney General. (2006). *California firearms laws.* Sacramento, CA: Office of the Attorney General.

California State. Department of Justice, Office of the Attorney General. (1999, July). *Community oriented policing and problem solving: Now and beyond.* Sacramento, CA: Office of the Attorney General.

California State. Legislature. (1991, January). *California law enforcement training in the 1990's: A vision of excellence.* Sacramento, CA: Assembly Concurrent Resolution 58 Study Committee.

Camarena, E. (2011, April 29). Address. Speech presented at the annual conference of the California Association of Administration of Justice Educators. San Diego, California.

Campbell, J. (1999, May/June). Community oriented justice: Marketing your partnerships. *ACJS (Academy of Criminal Justice Sciences) Today, 17*(6) 1, 3–5.

Capowich, G. E. (2005). A case study of community policing implementation: Contrasting success and failure. In K. R. Kerley (Ed.), *Policing and program evaluation* (138–153). Upper Saddle River, NJ: Pearson Prentice Hall.

Carelli, R. (2000, March 29). High court curbs stop-search based on an anonymous tip. *San Diego Union-Tribune,* p. A5.

Carlon, P. E. (1999, Spring). Occupational outcomes of criminal justice graduates: Is the master's degree a wise investment? *Journal of Criminal Justice Education, 10*(1) 39–55.

Carlson, D. P. (2005). *When cultures clash: Strategies for strengthening police–community relations* (2nd ed.). Upper Saddle River, NJ: Pearson Prentice Hall.

Caroselli, M. (1997). *That's no problem: A problem-free approach to problem solving.* West Des Moines, IA: American Media Publishing.

Carter, D. L. (1995, June). *Community policing and D.A.R.E.: A practitioner's perspective.* Washington, DC: U.S. Department of Justice, Bureau of Justice Assistance.

Carter, D. L., Sapp, A. D., & Stephens, D. W. (1988). Higher education as a bona fide occupational qualification (BFOQ) for police: A blueprint. *American Journal of Police, 7*(2)1–27.

Carter, D. L., Sapp, A. D., & Stephens, D. W. (1989). *The state of police education: Policy direction for the 21st century.* Washington, DC: Police Executive Research Forum.

Carter, L. F. (1953). Leadership and small group behavior. In M. Sherif & M. O. Wilson (Eds.), *Group relations at the crossroads* (312–322). New York: Harper.

Champion, D. H., Sr, & Hooper, M. K. (2003). *Introduction to American policing.* New York: Glencoe McGraw-Hill.

Champion, D. J. (2005). *Corrections in the United States: A contemporary perspective* (4th ed.). Upper Saddle River, NJ: Pearson Prentice Hall.

Champion, D. J., & Rush, G. E. (1997). *Policing in the community:* Upper Saddle River, NJ: Prentice Hall.

Cheeseman, H. R. (2010). *Business law* (7th ed.). Upper Saddle River, NJ: Pearson Prentice Hall.

Chermak, S., & Weiss, A. (2003). *Marketing community policing in the news: A missed opportunity?* Washington, DC: U.S. Department of Justice, Office of Justice Programs.

Chin, G. J. (Ed.). (1997). *New York City police corruption investigation commissions 1894–1994* (Vols. 1–6). Buffalo, NY: William S. Hein.

China's piracy plague. (2000, June 5). *Business Week,* pp. 44–46.

City of Los Angeles. (2003). *Training the 21st century police officer.* Santa Monica, CA: RAND Public Safety and Justice.

Clark, J. R. (1994, April 15). Does community policing add up? *Law Enforcement News, 20*(399), 8.

Clark, J., Austin, J., & Henry, D. A. (1997, September). *Three strikes and you're out: A review of state legislation.* Washington, DC: U.S. Department of Justice, Office of Justice Programs.

Clark, K. L. (1994). *Retrofitting the bridge between academics and business: Here is how it is done.* Paper presented to the Second Annual Conference on Global Business, Sun Valley, Idaho.

Clarke, R.V. (2002a). *Thefts of and from cars in parking facilities: Problem-oriented guides for police series no. 10.* Washington, DC: U.S. Department of Justice, Office of Community Oriented Policing Services.

Clarke, R. V. (2002b). *Shoplifting: Problem-oriented guides for police series no. 11.* Washington, DC: U.S. Department of Justice, Office of Community Oriented Policing Services.

Clarke, R. V. (2002c). *Burglary of retail establishments: Problem-oriented guides for police series no. 15.* Washington, DC: U.S. Department of Justice, Office of Community Oriented Policing Services.

Cleeton, G. U., & Mason, C. W. (1934). *Executive ability—its discovery and development.* Yellow Springs, OH: Antioch Press.

Clemmer, J. (1992, April). 5 common errors companies make starting quality initiatives. *Total Quality, 3,* 7.

Coffey, A. (1990). *Law enforcement: A human relations approach.* Englewood Cliffs, NJ: Prentice Hall.

Cohen, H. S., & Feldberg, M. (1991). *Power and restraint: The moral restraint of police work.* New York: Praeger.

Cole, G. F., & Smith, C. E. (2010). *The American system of criminal justice* (12th ed.). Belmont, CA: Wadsworth/Thomson Learning.

Coleman, J. W. (1994). *The criminal elite: The sociology of white collar crime.* New York: St. Martin's Press.

Community Corrections e-Learning Collaborative (2011). Online course summer schedule.

Community Policing Consortium. (1994). *Understanding community policing: A framework for action.* Washington, DC: Community Policing Consortium.

Community Policing Consortium. (1997a). *Module two: Mobilizing the community for collaborative partnerships.* Washington, DC: Community Policing Consortium.

Community Policing Consortium. (1997b). *Module three: Community policing problem solving: Taking a problem solving approach to tackling crime, fear and disorder.* Washington, DC: Community Policing Consortium.

Community policing is dead; long live community policing. (2003, August). *Community Links,* 23–24.

Conser, J. A., & Russell, G. D. (2000). *Law enforcement in the United States.* Gaithersburg, MD: Aspen Publishers.

Cooley, C. H. (1902). *Human nature and the social order.* New York: Scribners.

Copeland, N. (1942). *Psychology and the soldier.* Harrisburg, PA: Military Service Publishing.

Copeland, L. (2008, December 11). "Technology may halt hot pursuit." *USA TODAY*, p. 1A.

Copes, H. (2005). *Policing and stress.* Upper Saddle River, NJ: Pearson Prentice Hall.

Cordner, G. W., & Scarborough, K. E. (1999, July). Operationalizing community policing in rural America: Sense and nonsense. In California State, Office of the Attorney General, *Community oriented policing and problem solving: Now and beyond* (118–125). Sacramento, CA: Office of the Attorney General.

Corley v. United States. (2009, April 6). 556 U.S. ___; slip opinion No. 07-10441.

Couper, D. C., & Lobitz, S. H. (1991). *Quality policing: The Madison experience.* Washington, DC: Police Executive Research Forum.

Covey, S. R. (1998). *The seven habits of highly effective people.* New York: Simon & Schuster.

Cowley, W. H. (1928). Three distinctions in the study of leaders. *Journal of Abnormal Social Psychology, 23,* 144–157.

Craighead, G. (2009). *High-rise security and fire life safety* (3rd ed.). Boston: Butterworth-Heinemann.

Crank, J. P., & Caldero, M. A. (2010). *Police ethics: The corruption of noble cause* (3rd ed.) Cincinnati: Anderson Publishing.

Crime statistics don't tell the whole story. (1999, November/December). *Community Policing Exchange, 7*(29), 1–2.

Cronkhite, C. (1995, October–November). An eclectic approach to policing: Applying past principles to community policing. *CJ (Criminal Justice) in the Americas, 8*(5)9–11.

Crowder, W. S. (1998). *Law enforcement accreditation: Has it professionalized American law enforcement?* Ann Arbor, MI: University Microfilms International (Bell & Howell Information and Learning) Dissertation Services.

Crowe, T. D. (2000). *Crime prevention through environmental design* (2nd ed.). Woburn, MA: Butterworth-Heinemann.

Cunningham, W., Strauchs, J. J., & Van Meter, C. W. (1990). *Private security trends 1970 to 2000: The Hallcrest Report II.* Boston: Butterworth-Heinemann.

Dalkey, N. (1969). *The Delphi method: An experimental study of group opinion.* Santa Monica, CA: The Rand Corporation.

Daniel, T. (1992, March). Identifying critical leadership competencies of manufacturing supervisors in a major electronics corporation. *Group and Organizational Management: An International Journal, 17*(1) 57–71.

Davids, M. (1995, January–February). Where style meets substance. *Journal of Business Strategy, 16*(1) 48–55, 57–60.

Davis v. City of Dallas, 777 F.2d 205 (1985).

Davis, K. C. (1975). *Police discretion.* St. Paul, MN: West.

Davis, R. L., Gillis, I., & Foster, M. (2001). *A NOBLE perspective: Racial profiling— a symptom of bias-based policing (Next steps—creating blindfolds of justice).* Alexandria, VA: National Organization of Black Law Enforcement Executives.

Death Penalty Information Center. (2004). *Age requirements for the death penalty in the U.S.* [On line]. Available: www.deathpenaltyinfo.org.

Death Penalty Information Center (2011). *Facts about the death penalty.* [Online]. Available: http://www.deathpenaltyinfo.org/documents/FactSheet.pdf. Retrieved: June 27, 2011.

Debruin, L. (2011, May 8). "Exoneration makes a mother happy." *The San Diego Union Tribune*, p. A10.

Decker, S. H., Rosenfeld, R., & Burruss, G. W., Jr. (2005). Evaluating elusive policing programs: The case of the St. Louis consent-to-search program. In K. R. Kerley (Ed.), *Policing and program evaluation* (42–58). Upper Saddle River, NJ: Pearson Prentice Hall.

Dempsey, J. S., & Forst, L. S. (2012). An introduction to policing (6th ed.). Belmont, CA: Wadsworth/Thomson Learning.

Dempsey, T. (1992). *Contemporary patrol tactics: A practical guide for patrol officers.* Englewood Cliffs, NJ: Prentice Hall.

Dickey, W. J., & McGarry, P. (2001, February). *Community justice in rural America: Four examples and four futures.* Washington, DC: U.S. Department of Justice, Office of Justice Programs, Bureau of Justice Assistance.

Dilanian, K. (2010, November 15). "Fusion centers" gather terrorism intelligence—and much more. *Los Angeles Times*.

Do batterer intervention programs work? Two studies (2003). U.S. Department of Justice, National Institute of Justice.

Dodd, C. H. (1998). *Dynamics of intercultural communications* (5th ed.). Boston: McGraw-Hill.

Domestic homicide tipoffs may be missed. (2004, February). *Law Enforcement News,* 30 (614), 9.

Dorning, M. (2000, August 28). U.S. violent crime rate dropped again last year. *San Diego Union Tribune,* p. A2.

Drath, W. H., & Palus, C. J. (1994). *Making common sense: Leadership as meaning-making in a community of practice.* Greensboro, NC: Center for Creative Leadership.

Drucker, P. F. (1994, November). The age of social transformation. *The Atlantic Monthly,* 53–80.

Dubois, J., & Hartnett, S. M. (2002). Making the community side of community policing work: What needs to be done. In D. J. Stevens (Ed.), *Policing and Community Partnerships* (pp. 1–15). Upper Saddle River, NJ: Prentice Hall.

Earle, J. H. (1988, April). Law enforcement administration: Yesterday, today, and tomorrow. *FBI Law Enforcement Bulletin.* 57(4), 2–7.

Eck, J. E., & Spelman, W. (1987, January–February). Newport News tests problem-oriented policing. *National Institute of Justice Reports,* 2–8.

El Nasser, H., & Overberg, P. (2011, June 3). "In many neighborhoods, kids are only a memory." *USA TODAY*, pp. 1A, 6A.

End in sight. (2003, November 2). *San Diego Union Tribune,* pp. A1, A10.

Engel, R. S. (2003). *How police supervisory styles influence patrol officer behavior.* Washington, DC: U.S. Department of Justice, Office of Justice Programs, National Institute of Justice.

Evans, M. G. (1970). The effects of supervisory behavior on the path–goal relationship. *Organization Behavior and Human Performance, 5,* 277–298.

Experts say firearms training needs to come out of the dark. (2004, Fall). *Law Enforcement News,* 30 (625), 3.

Exporting a problem. (2005, January 16). *San Diego Union Tribune,* pp. A1, A16.

Farabee, D., Hser, Y., Anglin, M. D., & Huang, D. (2004, November). Recidivism among an early cohort of California's Proposition 36 offenders. *Criminology & Public Policy,* 3 (4), 563–584.

Fare v. Michael C., 442 U.S. 707 (1979).

Farmers Insurance Group. (2004). *Drivers admit to experiencing road rage.* [On line]. Available: www.farmers.com/FarmComm/content/RoadRage.jsp.

Faturechi, R. (2011, May 22). "Crowded? This jail is anything but." *Los Angeles Times*, pp. A1, A15.

Federal Law Enforcement Training Center. (2011). *Law Enforcement Supervisor Leadership Training Program (LESLTP).* [Online]. Available: http://www.fletc.gov/training/programs/law-enforcement-leadership-institute/. Retrieved: June 8, 2011.

Fein, K. (2005). Women prisoners. In R. Muraskin (Ed.), *Key correctional issues.* Upper Saddle River, NJ: Pearson Prentice Hall.

Fennelly, L. J. (2004) *Handbook of loss prevention and crime prevention* (4th ed.). Boston: Butterworth-Heinemann.

Fiedler, F. E. (1967). *A theory of leadership effectiveness.* New York: McGraw-Hill.

Flaccus, G. (2009, April 38). "Ex-Calif. sheriff gets 5 1/2 years for witness tampering." *San Diego Union Tribune,* p. A4.

Fleissner, D., Fedan, N., & Klinger, D. (1992, August). Community policing in Seattle: A model partnership between citizens and police. *National Institute of Justice Journal,* 9–18.

Foote, J. (1997). *Expert panel issues report on serious and violent juvenile offenders.* Washington, DC: U.S. Department of Justice, Office of Juvenile Justice and Delinquency Prevention.

Ford, J. K., Boles, J. G., Plamondon, K. E., & White, J. P. (2000). Transformational leadership and community policing: A road map for change. In T. J. Fitzgerald (Ed.), *Police in society* (pp. 156–172)). New York: H. W. Wilson.

Foster, R. E. (2005). *Police technology.* Upper Saddle River, NJ: Pearson Prentice Hall.

Fox, R. A. (2003, May 15/31). The blue plague of American policing. *Law Enforcement News,* 29 (599–600), 9.

Freud, S. (1922). *Group psychology and the analysis of ego.* London: International Psychoanalytical Press.

Furman v. Georgia, 408 U.S. 238 (1972).

Gaines, L. K., & Miller, R. L. (2009). *Criminal justice in action* (6th ed.). Belmont, CA: Wadsworth/Thomson Learning.

Gaines, L. K., & Miller, R. L. (2010). *Criminal justice in action: The core* (5th ed.). Belmont, CA: Wadsworth/Thomson Learning.

Galanes, G. J., Adams, K., & Brilhart, J. K. (2007). *Effective group discussion* (12th ed.). Boston: McGraw-Hill.

Gamble, T. K., & Gamble, M. (2005). *Communication works* (8th ed.). Boston: McGraw-Hill.

Garay, A. (2004, November 30). Popularity of Tasers rises, as do concerns. *San Diego Union Tribune,* pp. A4, A5.

Gardner, T. J., & Anderson, T. M. (2009). *Criminal evidence: Principles and cases* (7th ed.). Belmont, CA: Wadsworth/Thomson Learning.

Germain, D. (1999, December 29). Clayton Moore, TV's Lone Ranger dies at 85. *San Diego Union Tribune,* p. A3.

Germann, A. C., Day, F. D., & Gallati, R. R. J. (1988). *Introduction to law enforcement and criminal justice.* Springfield, IL: Charles C Thomas.

Gibb, J. R. (1961, September). Defensive communication. *Journal of Communication, 2,* 141.

Gilbert, J. N. (2008). *Criminal investigation* (8th ed.). Upper Saddle River, NJ: Pearson Prentice Hall.

Gilliard, D. K., & Beck, A. J. (1996, August). *Prison and Jail Inmates, 1995.* Washington, DC: U.S. Department of Justice, Bureau of Justice Statistics, Office of Justice Programs.

Giuliani, R. W., & Kurson, K. (2002). *Leadership.* New York: Hyperion.

Glensor, R. W., & Peak, K. J. (1999, July). Complexities of the problem solving process: Barriers and challenges to daily practice. In California State, Office of the Attorney General, *Community oriented policing and problem solving: Now and beyond* (76–82). Sacramento, CA: Office of the Attorney General.

Global crime cartels are tech-savvy, U.S. says. (2000, December 16). *San Diego Union Tribune,* p. A12.

Goetsch, D. L., & Davis, S. (1995). *Implementing total quality:* Englewood Cliffs, NJ: Prentice Hall.

Goldstein, H. (1990). *Problem-oriented policing.* New York: McGraw-Hill.

Goldstein, H. (2001, December 7). Address. Speech presented at the annual International Problem-Oriented Policing Conference, San Diego, CA.

Gomez, C. C. (1985). *Emerging curricula for computer science.* Unpublished dissertation, Arizona State University, Tempe.

Goodbody, W. L. (1995, April 30). What do we expect new-age cops to do? *Law Enforcement News, 21* (422) 14, 18.

Goodman, D. J. (2008). *Enforcing ethics* (3rd ed.). Upper Saddle River, NJ: Pearson Prentice Hall.

Gordon, T. (1955). *Group-centered leadership—a way of releasing the creative power of groups.* Boston: Houghton Mifflin.

Grant, H., & Terry, K. J. (2012). *Law enforcement in the 21st century* (3rd ed.) Upper Saddle River, NJ: Prentice Hall.

Green, M. F. (1988). *Leaders for a new era.* New York: American Council on Education/Macmillan.

Greenhouse, L. (1998, May 27). Supreme Court eases liability of police in chases. *San Diego Union Tribune,* p. A1.

Greenwood, P. W. (1979, July). *The Rand criminal investigation study: Its findings and impacts to date.* Santa Monica, CA: The Rand Corporation.

Gregg v. Georgia, 428 U.S. 153 (1976).

Gross, G. A. (2004, March 4). Lapses in fighting blazes cited. *San Diego Union Tribune,* pp. A1, A10.

Gross, A. (2009, July 12). "Ex-cons now help defuse gang violence." *San Diego Union Tribune*, p. A2.

Guffey, J. E. (2005). *Report writing fundamentals for police and correctional officers.* Upper Saddle River, NJ: Pearson Prentice Hall.

Haberer, J. B., & Webb, M. L. W. (1994). *TQM: 50 ways to make it work for you.* Menlo Park, CA: Crisp Publications.

Haberfeld, M. R. (2006). *Police leadership.* Upper Saddle River, NJ: Pearson Prentice Hall.

Haddow, G. D., & Bullock, J. A. (2003). *Introduction to emergency management.* Boston: Butterworth-Heinemann.

Hale, C. D. (2004). *Police patrol operations and management* (3rd ed.). Upper Saddle River, NJ: Pearson Prentice Hall.

Hanna, M. S., & Wilson, G. L. (1998). *Communicating in business and professional settings* (4th ed.). New York: McGraw-Hill.

Harnett, S. M., & Skogan, W. G. (1999, April). Community policing: Chicago's experience. *National Institute of Justice Journal,* 2–11.

Harris, D. (1997). "Driving while black" and all other traffic offenses: The Supreme Court and pretexual traffic stops. *Journal of Criminal Law and Criminology,* 87 (2), 563–564.

Hawkins, R. J. (2011, January 19). "CHP program seeks to improve assessment of elderly drivers." *San Diego Union Tribune,* pp. A1, A8.

Heifetz, R. A. (1994). *Leadership without easy answers.* Cambridge: The Belknap Press of Harvard University Press.

Hemphill, J. K. (1949). *Situational factors in leadership.* Columbus, OH: Ohio State University, Bureau of Education Research.

Hersey, P., & Blanchard, K. H., (1972). The management of change: Change and the use of power. *Training and Development Journal, 26*(1) 6–10.

Hersey, P., Blanchard, K. H. & Johnson, D. E. (1996). *Management of organizational behavior: Utilizing human resources* (7th ed.) Englewood Cliffs, NJ: Prentice Hall.

Hess, K. M. (1997, December). The ABCs of report writing. *Security Management, 41*(12) 123–124.

Hess, K. M., & Wrobleski, H. M. (2003). *Police operations: Theory and practice* (3rd ed.). Belmont, CA: Wadsworth.

Hiring and keeping police officers. (2004, July). Washington, DC: U.S. Department of Justice, National Institute of Justice.

Hitting the brakes. (2003, January 15/31). *Law Enforcement News, 29* (591, 592), 1.

Ho, D. (2000, December 29). 151 police officers killed this year, up 11% from 1999. *San Diego Union Tribune,* p. A15.

Homans, G. C. (1950). *The human group.* New York: Harcourt Brace.

Homans, G. C. (1958). Social behavior as exchange. *American Journal of Sociology, 63,* 597–606.

Houston, J., & Barton, S. M. (2005). *Juvenile justice: Theory, systems, and organization.* Upper Saddle River, NJ: Pearson Prentice Hall.

Howard, R. D., & Sawyer, R. L. (2004). *Defeating terrorism: Shaping the new security environment.* Guilford, CT: McGraw-Hill/Dushkin.

Hughes, J. (1998, July 18). Police shootings—a question of perception vs. reality. *San Diego Union Tribune,* p. B3.

Hughes, J. (1999, December 8). Suicide by cop may be trend. *San Diego Union Tribune,* p. A1.

Hughes, J. (2000, January 21). Ketamine-related drug arrests on the rise at border. *San Diego Union Tribune,* pp. B1, B3.

Hughes, J. (2004, March 13). Cops' K-9 unit hit by budget bite. *San Diego Union Tribune,* pp. B1, B7.

Hunt, D. D., & Rutledge, D. (2010). *California criminal law concepts* (11th ed.). Upper Saddle River, NJ: Pearson Custom Publishing.

Hunt, T. (2000, October 24). U.S. sets .08% line for drunk driving. *San Diego Union Tribune,* p. A2.

Hunter, R. D., Barker, T., & Mayhall, P. D. (2011). *Police community relations and the administration of justice.* (8th ed.). Upper Saddle River, NJ: Pearson Prentice Hall.

Illinois v. Montanez, No. 95-1429 (1996), *certiorari* denied.

In re Gault, 387 U.S. 1 (1967).

In re Winship, 397 U.S. 358 (1970).

Inciardi, J. A. (2009). *Criminal justice* (9th ed.). New York: McGraw-Hill.

Independent Commission on the Los Angeles Police Department (Christopher Commission). (1991). *Commission report.* Los Angeles: Los Angeles Police Department.

International Association of Chiefs of Police. (1985). *Police supervision.* Arlington, VA: International Association of Chiefs of Police.

International Association of Chiefs of Police. (2011a). *Law enforcement code of ethics.* [On line]. Available: www.theiacp.org.

International Association of Chiefs of Police. (2011b). *Law enforcement code of conduct.* [On line]. Available www.theiacp.org.

Is LA's crime honeymoon over? Gangs blamed for surge in violent crime rate. (2000, July/August). *Law Enforcement News, 26* (537–538), 8.

J.D.B. v North Carolina. (2011, June 16). ___564 U.S. ___; 2011 U.S. LEXIS 4577; slip opinion No. 09-11121.

James, R. (2009, August 11). "Prison Riots." *Time.* Available online: http://www.time.com/time/magazine/article/0,9171,1916301,00.html.

Jennings, H. H. (1944). Leadership—a dynamic re-definition. *Journal of Educational Sociology, 17,* 431–433.

Johnson, C. E. (2001). *Meeting the ethical challenges of leadership: Casting light or shadow.* Thousand Oaks, CA: Sage Publications.

Johnson, K. D. (2003). *Financial crimes against the elderly.* Washington, DC: U.S. Department of Justice, Office of Community Oriented Policing Services.

Johnson, K. (2011, April 25). "Police tap technology 'to appear bigger'." *USA TODAY*, p. 2A.

Jones, J. R., & Carlson, D. P. (2004). *Reputable conduct: Ethical issues in policing and corrections* (2nd ed.). Upper Saddle River, NJ: Pearson Prentice Hall.

Jones-Brown, D. D., & Terry, K. J. (2004). *Policing and minority communities: Bridging the gap.* Upper Saddle River, NJ: Pearson Prentice Hall.

Karmen, A. (2010). *Crime victims: An introduction to victimology* (7th ed.): Belmont, CA: Wadsworth/Thomson Learning.

Keller, J. (2003, February 24). Presentation software has become a national crutch. *San Diego Union Tribune,* pp. E1, E7.

Kelling, G. L. (1974). *The Kansas City preventive patrol experiment: A summary report.* Washington, DC: The Police Foundation.

Kelling, G. L. (1999, October). *"Broken windows" and police discretion.* Washington, DC: National Institute of Justice.

Kelling, G. L., & Bratton, W. J. (1993, July). *Implementing community policing: The administrative problem.* Washington, DC: National Institute of Justice and Harvard University.

Kelling, G. L., & Moore, M. H. (1991). From political reform to community: The evolving strategy of police. In J. R. Green & S. D. Mastrofski (Eds.), *Community policing: Rhetoric or reality* (14–15, 22–23). New York: Praeger.

Kennedy, D. (1993, January). The strategic management of police resources. In *Perspectives on policing* (4–5). Washington, DC: U.S. Department of Justice, Office of Justice Programs, National Institute of Justice and Program in Criminal Justice Policy and Management of the J. F. K. School of Government, Harvard University.

Kerley, K. R. (2005). Evaluation research in policing: Learning from the past and looking toward the future. In K. R. Kerley (Ed.), *Policing & program evaluation* (pp. 14–26). Upper Saddle River, NJ: Pearson Prentice Hall.

Kester, D. (2002, March/April). Less lethal technology expands. *The Law Enforcement Trainer, 17* (2), 12–13.

Kidd, V., & Braziel, R. (1999). *Community oriented policing cop talk: Essential communication skills for community policing.* San Francisco: Acada Books.

King, K. (2005). Prisoners' constitutional rights. In R. Muraskin (Ed.), *Key correctional issues* (pp. 149–160). Upper Saddle River, NJ: Pearson Prentice Hall.

Kingsley, G. T., & Pettit, K. L. S. (2000, October). Getting to know neighborhoods. *National Institute of Justice Journal,* pp. 10–17.

Kleinig, J. (1996). *The ethics of policing.* New York: Cambridge University Press.

Klockars, C. B. (1991). The Dirty Harry Problem. In C. B. Klockars & S. D. Mastrofski (Eds.), *Thinking about police: Contemporary readings* (2nd ed.) (pp. 413–423). New York: McGraw-Hill.

Knickerbocker, I. (1948). Leadership: A conception and some complications. *Journal of Sociology Issues, 4,* 23–40.

Kochel, T. R., Wilson, D. B., & Mastrofski, S. D. (2011, April-June). "Effect of suspect race on officers' arrest decisions." *Criminology,* 49 (2) 473–512.

Kotter, J. P. (1990). *A force for change.* New York: The Free Press.

Kotter, J. P. (1993). What leaders really do. In W. E. Rosenbach & R. L. Taylor (Eds.), *Contemporary issues in leadership* (3rd ed., 26–35). Boulder, CO: Westview Press.

Kouzes, J. M., & Posner, B. Z. (1993). The credibility factor: What people expect of leaders. In W. E. Rosenbach & R. L. Taylor (Eds.), *Contemporary issues in leadership* (3rd ed., 57–61). Boulder, CO: Westview Press.

Kovandzic, T. V., Sloan, J. J., & Vieraitis, L. M. (2004, June). "Striking out" as crime reduction policy: The impact of "three strikes" laws on crime rates in U.S. cities. *Justice Quarterly,* 21 (2), 207–239.

Krasnowski, M. (1998, June 1). Lawsuits against cops continue to add up to millions for LA. *San Diego Union Tribune,* p. A4.

Krasnowski, M. (2000, January 26). Corruption prompts reversal of 10 verdicts. *San Diego Union Tribune,* p. A3.

Krasnowski, M. (2000, November 22). Rampart case victim gets $15 million. *San Diego Union Tribune,* p. A-3.

Kretzmann, J. P., & McKnight, J. L. (1999, July). Community mapping. In California State, Office of the Attorney General, *Community oriented policing and problem solving: Now and beyond* (97–105). Sacramento, CA: Office of the Attorney General.

Kroeker, M. A. (2001, September). Proper design helps stem crime. *Community Links,* 7 (3), 15–16.

Krueger, A. (2004, April 27). $4.5 million verdict in CHP suit. *San Diego Union Tribune,* pp. A1, A7.

Lamm Weisel, D. (2002). *Graffiti: Problem-oriented guides for police series no. 9.* Washington, DC: U.S. Department of Justice, Office of Community Oriented Policing Services.

"LAPD gang officers quit assignments amid new rules." (2011, February 3). *San Diego Union Tribune*, p. A2.

Lasley, J. R., Hooper, M. H., & Derry, G. M., Ill. (1997). *The California criminal justice system.* Upper Saddle River, NJ: Prentice Hall.

Law Enforcement Assistance Administration. (1976). *Two hundred years of American criminal justice.* Washington, DC: U.S. Government Printing Office.

Law enforcement officers killed and assaulted. (2004). [On line]. Available: www.fbi.gov.

Lee, W. L. M. (1901). *A history of police in England.* London: Methuen (Oxford University Press).

Lesh, D. N. (2003, March/April). The duty to warn. *The Law Enforcement Trainee,* 18 (2), 16–18.

Let freedom ring to the tune of trust. (2004, August). *Community Links,* i.

Levine, A. (1982). Qualitative research in academic decision making. In E. Kuhns & S. V. Martorana (Eds.), *Qualitative methods for institutional research.* (78–92). San Francisco: Jossey-Bass.

Likert, R. (1961). *New patterns of management.* New York: McGraw-Hill.

Likert, R. (1967). *The human organization.* New York: McGraw-Hill.

Lord, V. B. (2004). *Suicide by cop.* New York: Looseleaf Law Publications.

Lord, V. B., & Peak, K. J. (2005). *Women in law enforcement careers: A guide for preparing and succeeding.* Upper Saddle River, NJ: Pearson Prentice Hall.

Lotz, R. (2005). *Youth crime in America: A modern synthesis.* Upper Saddle River, NJ: Pearson Prentice Hall.

Lyman, M. D. (2010). *The police: An introduction* (4th ed.). Upper Saddle River, NJ: Pearson Prentice Hall.

Maguire, K., & Pastore, A. L. (1998). *Sourcebook of criminal justice statistics* (p. 100). Washington, DC: U.S. Department of Justice.

Maher, G. F. (1989). Hostage negotiations. In W. G. Bailey (Ed.), *Encyclopedia of police science* (274–277). New York: Garland Publishing.

Maltz, M. D. (1999, July). *Bridging gaps in police crime data.* Washington, DC: U.S. Department of Justice, Office of Justice Programs, Bureau of Justice Statistics.

Mamalian, C. A., & La Vigne, N. G., (1999, January). *The use of computerized mapping by law enforcement: Survey results.* Washington, DC: National Institute of Justice.

Maniscalco, P. M., & Christen, H. T. (2002). *Understanding terrorism and managing the consequences.* Upper Saddle River, NJ: Prentice Hall.

Manus, R. P. (2000, November 30). Random thoughts on the KC patrol study. *Law Enforcement News,* 26 (544), 8–10.

Martin, G. (2003). *Understanding terrorism: Challenges, perspectives and issues.* Thousand Oaks, CA: Sage Publications.

Maslach, C., & Leiter, M. P. (1999). Burnout and engagement in the workplace: A contextual analysis. In T. C. Urban (Ed.), *The role of context: Advances in motivation and achievement* (pp. 275–302). Stamford, CT: JAI Press, Inc.

Mastrofski, S. D., Parks, R. B., Reiss, A. J., Jr., & Worden, R. E. (1999, July). *Policing neighborhoods: A report from St. Petersburg.* Washington, DC: U.S. Department of Justice, National Institute of Justice.

Maxson, C., Hennigan, K., & Sloane, D. C. (2003). *Factors that influence public opinion of the police.* Washington, DC: U.S. Department of Justice, Office of Justice Programs.

Mayo, E. (1945). *The social problems of art industrialized civilization.* Boston: Harvard Business School.

McBride, R. (2011, May). "Officer Safety: A multidimensional challenge." *The Police Chief.* 78 (5) 28–33.

McDonald, J., & Thornton, K. (2002, May 27). 9/11 aftermath drains cops: New duties overtax budgets, add worries. *San Diego Union Tribune,* pp. A1, A16.

McEwen, J. T. (1984, September). Handling calls for service: Alternatives to traditional policing. *NIJ (National Institute of Justice) Reports,* 4–8.

McGregor, D. (1960). *The human side of enterprise.* New York: McGraw-Hill.

McGregor, D. (1966). *Leadership and motivation.* Cambridge: MIT (Massachusetts Institute of Technology) Press.

McKinnie, R. L. (1995, July 6). Cops take a partner: The people-community policing aids rapport, crime control. *San Diego Union Tribune,* pp. B1–B2.

McMahon, J., Garner, J., Davis, R., & Kraus, A. (2003). *How to correctly collect and analyze racial profiling data: Your reputation depends on it!* Washington, DC: U.S. Department of Justice, Office of Community Oriented Policing Services.

Measuring what matters—part two: Developing measures of what the police do. (1997, November). Washington, DC: U.S. Department of Justice, Office of Justice Programs.

Meese, E., III. (1993, January). *Community policing and the police officer.* Washington, DC: National Institute of Justice.

Meese, E., & Ortmeier, P. J. (2004). *Leadership, ethics, and policing: Challenges for the 21st century.* Upper Saddle River, NJ: Pearson Prentice Hall.

Meese, E., III, & Kurz, A. T., Jr. (1993, December). Community policing and the investigator. *Journal of Contemporary Criminal Justice, 9,* 289–302.

Mendoza, M. (2011, June 26). "Border security costs: $90 billion over 10 years." *San Diego Union Tribune*, p. A13.

Meredith, Robyn. (1997), January 9). VW will pay $100 million to GM, settle spying suit. *San Diego Union Tribune,* p. C1.

Meyer, S., & Carroll, R. H. (2011, May). "When officers die: Understanding deadly domestic violence calls for service." *The Police Chief.* 78 (5) 24–27.

Michel, M. (2004, June). Elder abuse. *The Informant,* 24 (5), 8.

Michelson, R. (1999). *The California criminal justice system to accompany introduction to criminal justice.* New York: Glencoe/McGraw-Hill.

Michelson, R., & Maher, P. T. (2001). *Preparing for promotion: A guide to law enforcement assessment centers* (2nd ed.). San Clemente, CA: Law Tech Publishing.

Miller, M. (2000). *Police patrol operations* (2nd ed.) Incline Village, NV: Copperhouse Publishing.

Miller, W. (2002). *The growth of youth gang problems in the United States: 1970–98.* Washington, DC: U. S. Department of Justice, Office of Juvenile Justice and Delinquency Prevention.

Miranda v. Arizona, 384 U. S. 436 (1966).

Mishra, R. (1998, March 18). Drug addicts need treatment, not punishment, doctors say. *San Diego Union Tribune,* pp. A1, A21.

Miskin, V., & Gmelch, W. (1985, May). Quality leadership for quality teams. *Training and Development Journal, 39*(5) 122–129.

Montoya Bryan, S. (2011, June 18). "Wind-driven wildfires prompt more evacuations, test fire lines." *San Diego Union Tribune*, p. A5.

Moore, M., & Stephens, D. (1991). *Beyond command and control: The strategic management of police departments.* Washington, DC: Police Executive Research Forum.

Moran, G. (2004, March 7). 10 years later, "3 strikes" is still in dispute. *San Diego Union Tribune,* pp. A1, A14.

Morreale, S.A. (2002). *Analysis of perceived leader behaviors in law enforcement agencies.* D. P. A. dissertation: Nova Southeastern University.

Most drug abusers have steady jobs. (1999, September 9). *San Diego Union Tribune,* p. A6.

Muraskin, R. (2005). Conclusions. In R. Muraskin (Ed.), *Key correctional issues* (pp. 359–364). Upper Saddle River, NJ: Pearson Prentice Hall.

Muraskin, R., & Roberts, A. R. (Eds.). (2002). *Visions for change: Crime and justice in the twenty-first century* (3rd ed.). Upper Saddle River, NJ: Prentice Hall.

Murphy, P. (1989). Foreword in *The state of police education: Policy direction for the 21st century* by D. L. Carter, et al. Washington, DC: Police Executive Research Forum.

Nash, J. B. (1929). Leadership. *Phi Delta Kappan, 12,* 24–25.

Nason, R. R. (2000, October). Threats for the new millenium. *Security Technology & Design, 10*(10), 12–14, 16, 18.

National Advisory Commission on Civil Disorders. (1968). *Report.* New York: Bantam Books.

National Advisory Commission on Criminal Justice Standards and Goals. (1976). *Report of the task force on private security.* Washington, DC: U.S. Government Printing Office.

National Center on Elder Abuse. (2004). The basics: Major types of elder abuse. [On line]. Available: www.elderabusecenter.org.

National Commission on the Causes and Prevention of Violence. (1969). *Violence in the United States.* Washington, DC: U.S. Government Printing Office.

National Commission on Law Observance and Enforcement. (1931). *Report on lawlessness in law enforcement.* Washington, DC: U.S. Government Printing Office.

National Commission on Terrorist Attacks Upon the United States, (2004). *The 9/11 Commission Report.* [On line]. Available: www.9-11commission.gov.

National Commission on the Future of DNA Evidence. (2000, November). *The future of forensic DNA testing: Predictions of the research and development working group.* Washington, DC: National Institute of Justice.

National Institute on Drug Abuse. (2003). *Teen drug abuse declines across wide front.* [On line]. Available: www.nida.nih.gov.

National Law Enforcement Officers Memorial Fund. (2011). *Law enforcement fatalities.* [On line]. Available: www.nleomf.com.

National Night Out (2011). http://www.nationalnightout.org/nno/

Nelson, L., & Foster, B. (2001). *Death watch: A death penalty anthology.* Upper Saddle River, NJ: Prentice Hall.

Nemeth, C. P. (2010). *Law and evidence: A primer for criminal justice, criminology, law, and legal studies* (2nd ed.). Upper Saddle River, NJ: Prentice Hall.

Nemeth, C. P. (2004). *Criminal law.* Upper Saddle River, NJ: Prentice Hall.

Newman, G. R. (2003). *Check and card fraud.* Washington, DC: U.S. Department of Justice, Office of Community Oriented Policing Services.

Newton, S. J. (2002, March). The community becomes the first line of defense. *Community Links,* 1–3.

Nguyen, D.-P. (1999, December 20). 67% give SDPD high marks, poll finds. *San Diego Union Tribune,* p. A1.

Nicholl, C. G. (2000). *Toolbox for implementing restorative justice and advancing community policing.* Washington, DC: U.S. Department of Justice, Office of Community Oriented Policing Services.

Nichols, L. D. (2003). *Law enforcement patrol operations: Police systems and practices* (6th ed.). Berkeley, CA: McCutchan Publishing.

Niessa, M. (2004, February 21). Audit says Atlanta diluted crime reports. *San Diego Union Tribune,* p. A3.

'98 police fatalities down 13% from '97. (2000, January 28). *San Diego Union Tribune*, p. A3.

Nislow, J. (2001, October 15). Secret weapon against terrorism? Chiefs say community policing is an ace in the hole. *Law Enforcement News,* 27 (563), 1, 10.

Northouse, P. G. (2009). *Leadership: Theory and practice* (5th ed.). Thousand Oaks, CA: Sage Publications.

Number of slain cops hits all-time low. (2000, May 15/31). *Law Enforcement News, 26* (533–534), 7.

O'Hara, C. E., & O'Hara, G. L. (2003). *Fundamentals of criminal investigation* (7th ed.). Springfield IL: Charles C Thomas.

O'Keefe, J. (2004). *Protecting the republic: The education and training of American police officers.* Upper Saddle River, NJ: Pearson Prentice Hall.

O'Shea, T. C., & Nicholls, K. (2003). *Crime analysis in America: Findings and recommendations.* Washington, DC: U.S. Department of Justice, Office of Community Oriented Policing Services.

Officer in Rampart case pleads guilty. (2003, February 19). *San Diego Union Tribune,* p. A4.

Ogle, R. R., Jr. (2004). *Crime scene investigation and reconstruction.* Upper Saddle River, NJ: Pearson Prentice Hall.

Oliver, W. M. (2008). *Community oriented policing: A systematic approach to policing* (4th ed.). Upper Saddle River, NJ: Pearson Prentice Hall.

Operation cooperation. (2001, January/February). *ASIS (American Society for Industrial Security) Dynamics* (157), 1, 4.

Orler, A-M. (2011, June). "Recruiting women, qualified officers to the United Nations Police Division." *The Police Chief,* 78 (6) 22, 24, 26–27.

Ortmeier, P. J. (1977). Lectures presented at University of Nebraska and Metropolitan Community College.

Ortmeier, P. J. (1995, July–August). Educating law enforcement officers for community policing. *Police and Security News, 11*(4) 46–47.

Ortmeier, P. J. (1996). *Community policing leadership: A Delphi study to identify essential competencies.* Ann Arbor, MI: University Microfilms International (Bell & Howell Information and Learning) Dissertation Services.

Ortmeier, P. J. (1997, October). Leadership for community policing: Identifying essential officer competencies. *Police Chief,* 64 (10), 88–91, 93, 95.

Ortmeier, P. J. (1998). *Security management: A brief introduction.* San Diego: Star Source International.

Ortmeier, P. J. (1999). *Public safety and security administration.* Boston: Butter-worth-Heinemann.

Ortmeier, P. J. (2003, February). Ethical leadership: Every officer's responsibility. *Law Enforcement Executive Forum, 3* (1), 1–9.

Ortmeier, P. J. (2004, March 11). Speech presented at the annual meeting of the Academy of Criminal Justice Sciences, Las Vegas, NV.

Ortmeier P. J. (2005) *Security Management: An introduction* (2nd ed.). Upper Saddle River, NJ: Pearson Prentice Hall.

Ortmeier, P. J. (2013). *Introduction to security: Operations and management* (4th ed.). Upper Saddle River, NJ: Pearson Prentice Hall.

Ortmeier, P. J., & Davis, J. J. (2012). *Police administration: A leadership approach.* New York: McGraw-Hill.

Ortmeier, P. J., & Meese, E. III. (2010) *Leadership, ethics, and policing: Challenges for the 21st Century* (2nd ed.). Upper Saddle River, NJ: Pearson Prentice Hall.

Orton, A. (1984). Leadership: New thoughts on an old problem. *Training, 21*(28) 31–33.

Osborn, R. N., & Hunt, J. G. (1975). Relations between leadership, size, and subordinate satisfaction in a voluntary organization. *Journal of Applied Psychology, 69,* 730–735.

Osterburg, J. W., & Ward, R. H. (2010). *Criminal investigation: A method for reconstructing the past* (6th ed.). Cincinnati: Anderson.

Otto, P. (2000, January/February). The importance of building strong media relations: They will tell the story with or without you. *ACJS (Academy of Criminal Justice Sciences) Today, 19*(1), 8–9.

Palmiotto, M. J. (2002). The influence of community in community policing in the twenty-first century. In R. Muraskin & A. R. Roberts, (Eds.), *Visions for change: Crime and justice in the twenty-first century* (3rd ed.) (pp. 124–136). Upper Saddle River, NJ: Prentice Hall.

Parker, P. A. (1993, April). Reorganize and reprioritize. *Police,* 26.

Parker, T. (1999, July). Community responsibilities in neighborhood policing. In California State, Office of the Attorney General, *Community oriented policing and problem solving: Now and beyond* (110–117). Sacramento, CA: Office of the Attorney General.

Parr, L. A. (1999). *Police report writing essentials.* Placerville, CA: Custom Publishing.

Parshall-McDonald, P., & Greenberg, S. F. (2002). *Managing police operations: Implementing the New York crime control model—CompStat.* Belmont, CA: Wadsworth/Thomson Learning.

Pasquali, A. (1997). The moral dimension of communicating. In C. Christians & M. Traber (Eds.), *Communication ethics and universal values* (24–45). Thousand Oaks, CA: Sage Publications.

Path of destruction. (1992, May 10). *Los Angeles Times,* A31.

Patton, M. Q. (2002). *Qualitative evaluations and research methods* (3rd ed.). Newbury Park, CA: Sage Publications.

Payton, G. T., & Amaral, M. (2004). *Patrol operations and enforcement tactics* (11th ed.). San Jose, CA: Criminal Justice Services.

Peak, K. J. (2010). *Justice administration: Police, courts and corrections management* (6th ed.) Upper Saddle River, NJ: Pearson Prentice Hall.

Peak, K. J., & Glensor, R. W. (2008). *Community policing and problem solving: Strategies and practices* (5th ed.). Upper Saddle River, NJ: Prentice Hall.

Pearlman, K. (2011, June 23). "Drug users learn the way out of addiction." *San Diego Union Tribune*, p. PG3.

Peat, B. (2004). *From college to career: A guide for criminal justice majors.* Upper Saddle River, NJ: Prentice Hall.

Pelfrey, W. V., Jr. (2004, September). The inchoate nature of community policing: Differences between community policing and traditional police officers. *Justice Quarterly,* 21 (3), 579–601.

People v. Reyes, 968 P.2d 445, 19 Cal.4th 743 (1998).

Perry, T. (1998). *Basic patrol procedures* (2nd ed.). Salem, WI: Sheffield Publishing.

Peters, T. J. (1992). *Liberation management.* New York: Alfred A. Knopf.

Petersilia, J. (1989). The influence of research on policing. In R. G. Dunham & G. P. Alpert (Eds.), *Critical issues in policing: Contemporary readings* (223). Prospect Heights, IL: Waveland Press.

Pfeffer, J. (1977). The ambiguity of leadership. *Academic Management Review, 2,* 104–112.

Phillips, R. G., Jr. (1988, August). Training priorities in state and local law enforcement. *FBI Law Enforcement Bulletin, 57*(8) 10–16.

Phillips, R., & Pack, C. (1999, Spring). Sustaining community partnerships: A road map for the long haul. *Community Links, 6*(2), 2–3. Washington, DC: National Sheriffs' Association.

Picture of drug use by young mixed. (2000, September 1). *San Diego Union Tribune,* p. A6.

Police Executive Research Forum. (2004). *By the numbers: A guide for analyzing race data from vehicle stops.* [On line]. Available: http://policeforum.mn-8.net.

Port Washington Police Department (2011). Available online: http://pwpd.org/reports_statistics_problem.html.

President's Commission on Campus Unrest. (1970). Campus unrest. Washington, DC: U.S. Government Printing Office.

President's Commission on Law Enforcement and Administration of Justice. (1967). *Task force report: Police.* Washington, DC: U.S. Government Printing Office.

President's Crime Prevention Council. (1997). *Helping communities fight crime: Comprehensive planning techniques, models, programs and resources.* Washington, DC: U.S. Government Printing Office.

Putnam, L., & Pacanowski, M. (Eds.). (1983). *Communication and organizations: An interpretive approach.* Beverly Hills, CA: Sage Publications.

Raffel Price, B. (1995, June 15). Police and the quest for professionalism. *Law Enforcement News, 21*(425) 8.

Ramsey, C. H. (2002). Preparing the community for community policing. In D. J. Stevens (Ed.), *Policing and community partnerships* (pp. 29–44). Upper Saddle River, NJ: Prentice Hall.

Rand Corporation. (1999). *The benefits and costs of drug use prevention: Clarifying a cloudy issue.* Santa Monica, CA: Rand Corporation, Drug Policy Research Center.

Rantala, R. R. (2004). *Cybercrime against businesses.* Washington, DC: U.S. Department of Justice, Office of Justice Programs.

Rashbaum, W. K. (2011, January 21). "FBI's 'largest mob roundup' targets crime families." *San Diego Union Tribune*, p. A4.

Rasp, A., Jr. (1974). A new tool for administrators: Delphi and decision making. *North Central Association Quarterly, 48*(3) 320–325.

Raum, T. (1999, February 5). U.S. found vulnerable to bombing attacks. *San Diego Union Tribune,* p. A11.

Raymond, W. P., Jr., & Hall, D. E. (1999). *California criminal law and procedure.* Albany, NY: West Legal Studies.

Reichel, P. L. (2008). *Comparative criminal justice systems* (5th ed.). Upper Saddle River, NJ: Pearson Prentice Hall.

Reid, M. R. (2011). *Technology in criminal justice.* Lectures presented at Los Angeles Harbor College, Wilmington, CA, Spring 2011.

Reiman, J. (2010). *The rich get richer and the poor get prison: Ideology, class, and criminal justice* (9th ed.). Upper Saddle River, NJ: Prentice Hall.

Rich, T. (1999, October). Mapping the path to problem solving. *National Institute of Justice Journal,* 2–9.

Robbins, S. P., & Coulter, M. (2012). *Management* (11th ed.). Upper Saddle River, NJ: Prentice Hall.

Roberg, R. R. (1978, September). An analysis of the relationship among higher education, belief systems, and job performance of patrol officers. *Journal of Police Science and Administration, 6,* 336–344.

Robinson, M. B. (2009). *Justice blind? Ideals and realities of American criminal justice* (3rd ed.). Upper Saddle River, NJ: Pearson Prentice Hall.

Roper v. Simmons, No. 03-633. Argued 10/31/04, Decided 03/01/05.

Ross, D. L. (2006). *Civil liability in criminal justice* (4th ed.). Cincinnati: Anderson.

Roth, J. A., & Ryan, J. F. (2000, August). *The COPS program after 4 years— National evaluation.* Washington, DC: National Institute of Justice, Office of Justice Programs.

Rubin, J. (2011, May 8). "LAPD officers' lawsuits costing city millions." *Los Angeles Times,* pp. A1, A16.

Russell, H. E., & Beigel, A. (1990). *Understanding human behavior for effective police work* (3rd ed.). New York: Basic Books.

Rutledge, D. (2000). *California criminal procedure* (4th ed.). Incline Village, NV: Copperhouse Publishing.

Sabol, W., & West, H. (2010). "Prisoners in 2009." Available online: http://bjs.ojp.usdoj.gov/index.cfm?ty=pbdetail&iid=2232.

Saferstein, R. (2011). *Criminalistics: An introduction to forensic science* (10th ed.). Upper Saddle River, NJ: Pearson Prentice Hall.

Sampson, R. (2001). *False burglar alarms: Problem-oriented guides for police series no. 5.* Washington, DC: U.S. Department of Justice, Office of Community Oriented Policing Services.

Sampson, R. (2002). *Bullying in schools: Problem-oriented guides for police series no. 12.* Washington, DC: U.S. Department of Justice, Office of Community Oriented Policing Services.

Sampson, R. J., & Bartusch, D. J. (1999, June). *Attitudes toward crime, police, and the law: Individual and neighborhood differences.* Washington, DC: National Institute of Justice.

San Diego Police Department. (1993, February). *Neighborhood policing: A guide for building a police/community partnership.* San Diego, CA: San Diego Police Department.

San Diego Sheriff's Department. (1999). *Use of force guidelines.* San Diego, CA: San Diego County Sheriff's Department.

Savage, D. G. (2011, June 10). "Supreme Court rules car chases are violent felonies." Los *Angeles Times*, p. A9.

Schenk, C. (1928). Leadership. *Infantry Journal, 33,* 111–122.

Schmalleger, F. (2005). *Criminal justice today* (8th ed.). Upper Saddle River, NJ: Pearson Prentice Hall.

Schmalleger, F. (2010). *Criminal justice: A brief introduction* (9th ed.). Upper Saddle River, NJ: Prentice Hall.

Schmalleger, F., & Smykla, J. O. (2008). *Corrections in the 21st century* (4th ed.). Boston: McGraw Hill.

Schmidt, S. (2009, June 28). "More and more drivers ignoring law requiring hands-free cell phone use." *San Diego Union Tribune*, pp. A1, A7.

Schneider, A. (2003). *Community policing in action: A practitioner's eye view of organizational change.* Washington, DC: U.S. Department of Justice, Office of Community Oriented Policing Services.

Scott, M. S. (2001). *Street prostitution: Problem-oriented guides for police series no. 2.* Washington, DC: U.S. Department of Justice, Office of Community Oriented Policing Services.

Scott, M. S. (2002a). *Panhandling: Problem-oriented guides for police series no. 13.* Washington, DC: U.S. Department of Justice, Office of Community Oriented Policing Services.

Scott, M. S. (2002b). *Rave parties: Problem-oriented guides for police series no. 14.* Washington, DC: U.S. Department of Justice, Office of Community Oriented Policing Services.

Scott, W. E. (1977). Leadership: A functional analysis. In J. G. Hunt & L. L. Larson (Eds.), *Leadership, the cutting edge.* Carbondale, IL: Southern Illinois University Press.

Scott, W. R. (1986). College education requirements for police entry level and promotion: A study. *Journal of Police and Criminal Psychology, 2*(1) 16–17.

Seiter, R. P. (2011). *Corrections: An introduction* (3rd ed.). Upper Saddle River, NJ: Pearson Prentice Hall.

Selecting a new breed of officer: The customer-oriented cop. (1999, March/April). *Community Policing Exchange, 6*(25), 4.

Shane, S. (2011, June 17). "New Al Qaeda chief called flawed figure." *San Diego Union Tribune*, p. A4.

Shartle, C. L. (1956). *Executive performance and leadership.* Englewood Cliffs, NJ: Prentice Hall.

Sheehan, R., & Cordner, G. W. (2004). *Police administration* (5th ed.). Cincinnati, OH: Anderson.

Sherman, L. W., & Berk, R. (1984). The specific deterrent effects of arrest for domestic assault. *American Sociological Review, 49*(2) 261–272.

Shusta, R. M., Levine, D. R., Wong, H. Z., Harris, P. R., & Olson, A. T. (2011). *Multicultural law enforcement: Strategies for peacekeeping in a diverse society* (5th ed.). Upper Saddle River, NJ: Pearson Prentice Hall.

Sichel, J. (1978). *Women on patrol: A pilot study of police performance in New York City.* Washington, DC: U.S. Department of Justice.

Sickmund, M., Snyder, H. N., & Poe-Yamagata, E. (1997, August). *Juvenile offenders and victims: 1997 update on violence.* Washington, DC: U.S. Department of Justice, Office of Juvenile Justice and Delinquency Prevention.

Siegel, L. J. (2004). *Criminology: Theories, patterns, and typologies* (8th ed.). Belmont, CA: Wadsworth/Thomson Learning.

Siegel, L. J., & Senna, J. J. (2006). *Essentials of criminal justice* (5th ed.). Belmont, CA: Wadsworth/Thomson Learning.

Simons, C. F. (2002). The evolution of crime prevention. In D. Mitchell Robinson (Ed.), *Policing and crime prevention* (pp. 1–18). Upper Saddle River, NJ: Prentice Hall.

Simons, R. L., & Harbin Burt, C. (2011, April-June). "Learning to be bad: Adverse social conditions, social schemes, and crime." *Criminology*, 49 (2), 553–598.

Skogan, W. G. (2005). Evaluating community policing in Chicago. In K. R. Kerley (Ed.), *Policing and program evaluation* (pp. 27–41). Upper Saddle River, NJ: Pearson Prentice Hall.

Skogan, W. G., Steiner, L., DuBois, J., Gudell, J. E., & Fagan, A. (2002). *Community policing and "the new immigrants": Latinos in Chicago.* Washington, DC: U.S. Department of Justice, Office of Justice Programs.

Skolnick, J. H., & Bayley, D. H. (1986). *The new blue line: Police innovation in six American cities.* New York: The Free Press.

Smith, P. B., & Peterson, M. F. (1990, August). Leadership, organizations, and culture. *Education Administration Quarterly, 26*(3) 235–259.

Snell, T. L. (1996). *Capital punishment 1995.* Washington, DC: U.S. Department of Justice, Bureau of Justice Statistics.

Sniffen, M. J. (2001, January 6). Companies cooperate with FBI in fighting computer crime. *San Diego Union Tribune,* p. A11.

Snyder, H. N. (1997, February). *Juvenile arrests 1995.* Washington, DC: U.S. Department of Justice, Office of Justice Programs, Office of Juvenile Justice and Delinquency Prevention.

Snyder, H. N. (2003, December). *Juvenile arrests 2001.* Washington, DC: U.S. Department of Justice, Office of Justice Programs, Office of Juvenile Justice and Delinquency Prevention.

Souryal, S. S. (1981). *Police organization and administration.* New York: Harcourt Brace Jovanovich.

Sparrow, M. K. (1988, November). *Implementing community policing.* Washington, DC: National Institute of Justice and Harvard University.

Sparrow, M. K., Moore, M. H., & Kennedy, M. (1990). *Beyond 911.* New York: Harper.

Spelman, W., & Eck, J. E. (1987, January). Problem-oriented policing. *National Institute of Justice: Research in Brief,* 2–3.

Stahl, N. (1992). Providing a data base for considering policy options: Applications of the Delphi technique using an illustrative case study. In N. L. Haggerson & A. C. Bowman (Eds.), *Informing educational policy and practice through interpretive inquiry* (83–109). Lancaster, PA: Technomic.

Steele, J. (2011, February 7). "War-scarred veterans can get help from special court." *San Diego Union Tribune*, pp. B1, B6.

Stephan, J. J. (1997, August). *Census of state and federal correctional facilities, 1995.* Washington, DC: U.S. Department of Justice, Office of Justice Programs.

Stern, M. (1999, July 3). INS computer system in spotlight following release of wanted man. *San Diego Union Tribune,* p. A1.

Stevens, D. J. (2002). Community policing and police leadership. In D. J. Stevens (Ed.), *Policing and community partnerships* (pp. 163–176). Upper Saddle River, NJ: Prentice Hall.

Stevens, D. J. (2005). Police officer stress and occupational stressors: Before and after 9/11. In H. Copes (Ed.), *Policing and stress* (pp. 1–24). Upper Saddle River, NJ: Pearson Prentice Hall.

Stogdill, R. M. (1948). Personal factors associated with leadership: A survey of the literature. *Journal of Psychology, 25,* 35–71.

Stogdill, R. M. (1950). Leadership, membership and organization. *Psychology Bulletin, 47,* 1–14.

Stogdill, R. M. (1959). *Individual behavior and group achievement.* New York: Oxford University Press.

Stojkovic, S., Kalinich, D., & Klofas, J. (2008). *Criminal justice organizations: Administration and management* (4th ed.). Belmont, CA: Wadsworth/Thomson Learning.

Stuckey, G. B., Roberson, C., & Wallace, H. (2010). *Procedures in the justice system* (9th ed.). Upper Saddle River, NJ: Pearson Prentice Hall.

Study sees cause for alarm as police adopt a more paramilitary posture. (1999, October 15). *Law Enforcement News, 25*(519) 1–9.

Sullivan, A. (2004, January 26). Net fraud, ID theft on the rise, FTC says. *San Diego Union Tribune,* pp. C1, C3.

Supplying what the police academy doesn't. (2004, Fall). *Law Enforcement News,* 30 (625), 6.

Swanson, C. R., Territo, L., & Taylor, R. W. (2008). *Police administration: Structure, processes and behavior* (7th ed.). Upper Saddle River, NJ: Prentice Hall.

SWAT team may prove costly for small farm town. (1999, April 6). *San Diego Union Tribune,* p. A3.

Tafoya, W. L. (1986). *A Delphi forecast of the future of law enforcement.* Ph.D. dissertation: University of Maryland.

Tafoya, W. L. (1991, May/June). The future of law enforcement? A chronology of events. *Criminal Justice International,* p. 4.

Tannenbaum, R., & Schmidt, W. H. (1958, March–April). How to choose a leadership pattern. *Harvard Business Review, 36*(2) 95–101.

Tanner, R. (2000, March 18). DNA brings shift in statute of limitations. *San Diego Union Tribune,* p. A10.

Taylor, F. W. (1911). *The principles of scientific management.* New York: Harper & Brothers.

Taylor, G. (2002, Spring). Untraditional police programs. *California Police Recorder, 22* (2), 26.

Tead, O. (1935). *The art of leadership.* New York: McGraw-Hill.

Territo, L., Halsted, J. B., & Bromley, M. L. (2004). *Crime and justice in America: A human perspective* (6th ed.). Upper Saddle River, NJ: Pearson Prentice Hall.

Terry v. Ohio, 392 U.S. 1 (1968).

Thaiss, C., & Hess, J. E. (1999). *Writing for law enforcement.* Boston: Allyn & Bacon.

The Police Foundation. (1981). *The Newark foot patrol experiment.* Washington, DC: The Police Foundation.

Thibault, E. A., Lynch, L. M., & McBride, R. B. (2004). *Proactive police management* (6th ed.). Upper Saddle River, NJ: Pearson Prentice Hall.

Thornton, K. (1999, February 27). Tragedy stirs debate over police pursuits. *San Diego Union Tribune,* p. A1.

Thornton, K. (1999, November 5). Cops rarely charged in shootings, experts say. *San Diego Union Tribune,* p. A1.

Thurman, Q. C., & McGarrell, E. F. (2003). *Community policing in a rural setting* (2nd ed.). Cincinnati: Anderson Publishing.

Thurman, Q. C., Zhao, J., & Giacomazzi, A. L. (2001). *Community policing in a community era: An introduction and exploration.* Los Angeles: Roxbury Publishing.

Tichy, N., & Ulrich, D. (1984). The leadership challenge—a call for the transformational leader. SMR Forum, *Sloan Management Review, 26*(1) 59–68.

Tos, D. (2000, January/February). A fortune 500 police department. *Community Policing Exchange, 1*(30), 5.

Townsend, R. (1970). *Up the organization.* New York: Alfred A. Knopf.

Trautman, N. E. (2005). *Police work: A career survival guide* (2nd ed). Upper Saddle River, NJ: Pearson Prentice Hall.

Trojanowicz, R. C. (1990, October). Community policing is not police–community relations. *FBI Law Enforcement Bulletin, 59*(10) 6–11.

Trojanowicz, R. C., & Bucqueroux, B. (1990). *Community policing.* Cincinnati: Anderson.

Trojanowicz, R. C., & Carter, D. L. (1990, January). The changing face of America. *FBI Law Enforcement Bulletin, 59*(1) 9.

Truth, DARE and consequences: What impact is anti-drug effort having? (1998, April 15). *Law Enforcement News, 24*(487), 1, 10.

$12.5 million awarded in police-raid shooting death. (1999, March 16). *San Diego Union Tribune,* p. A3.

2,600 inmates to be released by L.A. Sheriff. (2003, March 20). *San Diego Union Tribune,* p.A11.

Tyler, T. R., & Wakslak, C. J. (2004, May). Profiling and police legitimacy: Procedural justice, attributions of motive, and acceptance of police authority. *Criminology, 42*(2), 253–281.

U.S. Census Bureau (2011). *The 2011 Statistical Abstract*, Table 307.

U.S. Congress. (1968). *Omnibus Crime Control and Safe Streets Act.* Washington, DC: U.S. Government Printing Office.

U.S. Congress. (1994). *Violent Crime Control and Law Enforcement Act of 1994.* Washington, DC: U.S. Government Printing Office.

U.S. Congress. (2001). *USA PATRIOT Act of 2001 (Public Law 107–56).* Washington, DC: U.S. Government Printing Office.

U.S. Department of Homeland Security (2003). DHS organization. [On line]. Available: www.dhs.org.

U.S. Department of Justice. (1988). *Uniform crime reporting: National incident-based reporting system, Vol. 1. Data collection guidelines.* Washington, DC: U.S. Government Printing Office.

U.S. Department of Justice. (1993, November). *NIJ outreach confirms support for multidisciplinary collaborative approach.* Washington, DC: Office of Justice Programs.

U.S. Department of Justice. (1999, October). *Use of force by police: Overview of national and local data.* Washington, DC: Office of Justice Programs.

U.S. Department of Justice. (2003). *Crime mapping: How GIS is used in law enforcement.* [On line]. Available: www.ojp.usdoj.gov/ovc/publications/infores/geoinfosys2003/cm3b.html.

U.S. Department of Justice. (2004, October). *Impact munitions use: Types, targets, effects.* Washington, DC: U.S. Department of Justice, National Institute of Justice.

U.S. Department of Justice, Bureau of Alcohol, Tobacco, Firearms, and Explosives. (2000). *Bomb threats and physical security planning guide.* [On line]. Available: http://www.atf./gov.

U.S. Department of Justice, Bureau of Justice Statistics. (1992). *Criminal victimization in the United States, 1991.* Washington, DC: U.S. Department of Justice.

U.S. Department of Justice, Bureau of Justice Statistics. (1992, December). *Drugs, crime and the justice system.* Washington, DC: U.S. Government Printing Office.

U.S. Department of Justice, Bureau of Justice Statistics. (1994). *Neighborhood-oriented policing in rural communities: A program planning guide.* Washington, DC: U.S. Government Printing Office.

U.S. Department of Justice, Bureau of Justice Statistics. (1998). *Census of state and local law enforcement agencies.* Washington, DC: U.S. Department of Justice.

U.S. Department of Justice, Bureau of Justice Statistics. (2002). *Census of state and local law enforcement agencies.* Washington, DC: U.S. Department of Justice.

U.S. Department of Justice, Bureau of Justice Statistics. (2003). *Federal law enforcement officers.* Washington, DC: U.S. Department of Justice.

U.S. Department of Justice, Bureau of Justice Statistics. (2004). *Corrections statistics.* [On line]. Available: www.ojp.usdoj.gov/bjs/correct.htm.

U.S. Department of Justice, Bureau of Justice Statistics. (2005). *Corrections statistics.* [On line]. Available: www.ojp.usdoj.gov/bjs/correct.htm.

U.S. Department of Justice, Bureau of Prisons. (2004). *The bureau in brief.* [On line]. Available: www.bop.gov/ipapg/ipabib.html.

U.S. Department of Justice, Federal Bureau of Investigation. (1995, November 19). *Crime in the United States.* Washington, DC: U.S. Government Printing Office.

U.S. Department of Justice, Federal Bureau of Investigation. (1997). *Uniform crime report.* Washington, DC: U.S. Government Printing Office.

U.S. Department of Justice, Federal Bureau of Investigation. (2000). *Uniform crime report.* Washington, DC: U.S. Government Printing Office.

U.S. Department of Justice, Federal Bureau of Investigation (2004). *Uniform crime report.* Washington, DC: Federal Bureau of Investigation.

U.S. Department of Justice, Federal Bureau of Investigation. (2011). *Uniform crime report 2010.* [Online]. Available: http://www.fbi.gov/stats-services/crimestats. Retrieved: June 29, 2011.

U.S. Department of Justice, Office of Justice Programs, Bureau of Justice Statistics. (1997, May). *Criminal Victimization in the United States 1994.* Washington, DC: National Criminal Justice Reference Service.

U.S. Department of Justice, Office of Justice Programs. (2003). *The safety and effectiveness of pepper spray.* Washington, DC: National Institute of Justice.

U.S. Department of Justice. Office of Justice Programs. (2004). *Education and training in forensic science: A guide for forensic science laboratories, educational institutions, and students.* Washington, DC: National Institute of Justice.

U.S.. Department of Justice. Office of Justice Programs. National Institute of Justice. (2010, October). *10-4 no more? Law enforcement agencies are phasing out old radio codes.* Washington, DC: U.S. Department of Justice.

U.S. Department of Labor. (2004). *Occupation information network: O-net online.* [On line]. Available: online.onetcenter.org.

U.S. Sentencing Commission. (1987). *Federal sentencing guidelines manual.* Washington, DC: U.S. Government Printing Office.

U.S. v. Booker, 543 U.S.—(2005). (No. 04-104, Argued 10/04/04, Decided 01/12/05)

U.S. v. Fanfan, 543 U.S.—(2005). (No. 04-105, Argued 10/04/04, Decided 01/12/05)

United States. (1968). *U.S. Code.* Title 18, sections 241–242.

United States. (1979). *U.S. Code.* Title 42, section 1983.

Urban, P. (2011, May 29). "Congress extends expiring Patriot Act tools." *Las Vegas Review Journal*, p. 14A.

Urbina, I. (2009, February 25). "Citing costs, states mull abolishing death penalty." *San Diego Union Tribune*, pp. A1, A8.

Vandiver, D. M. (2005). California, Texas and Florida: The big three in corrections. In R. Muraskin (Ed.), *Key correctional issues* (pp. 227–247). Upper Saddle River, NJ: Pearson Prentice Hall.

Vodicka, A. T. (1994, March). Educational requirements for police recruits: Higher education benefits officers, agency. *Law and Order, 42*(3), 91–94.

Vollmer, A. (1936). *The police in modern society.* Los Angeles: University of California Press.

Wadman, R. C., & Allison, W. T. (2004). *To protect and to serve: A history of police in America.* Upper Saddle River, NJ: Pearson Prentice Hall.

Waldman, A. (2004, December 27). Disaster in Asia. *San Diego Union Tribune*, pp. A1, A17.

Walker, S. (1999). *The police in America: An introduction* (3rd ed.). New York: McGraw-Hill.

Walker, S. (2001). *Police accountability: The role of citizen oversight.* Belmont, CA: Wadsworth/Thomson Learning.

Walker, S. (2003). *Early intervention systems for law enforcement agencies: A planning and management guide.* Washington, DC: U.S. Department of Justice, Office of Community Oriented Policing Services.

Walker, S., Alpert, G. P., & Kenney, D. J. (2001, July). *Early warning systems: Responding to the problem police officer.* Washington, DC: U.S. Department of Justice, National Institute of Justice.

Walker, S., & Katz, C. M. (2010). *The police in America: An introduction* (7th ed.). New York: McGraw-Hill.

Walker, S., Spohn, C., & DeLone, M. (2011). *The color of justice: Race, ethnicity, and crime in America* (5th ed.). Belmont, CA: Wadsworth/Thomson Learning.

Wallace, H., Roberson, C., & Steckler, C. (2009). *Written and interpersonal communication methods for law enforcement* (4th ed.). Upper Saddle River, NJ: Prentice Hall.

Watson, E. M., Stone, A. R., & DeLuca, S. M. (1998). *Strategies for community policing.* Upper Saddle River, NJ: Prentice Hall.

Webb, V. J., & Katz, C. M. (1997). Citizen ratings of the importance of community policing activities. *Policing: An International Journal of Police Strategies and Management. 20*(1) 7–23.

Weisheit, R. A., & Wells, L. E. (2004, July). Youth gangs in rural America. *National Institute of Justice Journal,* (251), 2–6.

Welsh, W. N., & Harris, P. W. (2008). *Criminal justice planning & policy* (3rd ed.). Cincinnati, OH: Anderson.

Werner, E. (2000, February 27). Dishonest cops? It's no surprise. *San Diego Union Tribune,* p. A3.

What does it take to make collaboration work? (2004, July). *National Institute of Justice Journal,* (251), 8–13.

When cops lash out. (2004, January). *Law Enforcement News,* 29 (613), 1, 9–12.

Whisenand, P. M. (2004). *Supervising police personnel: The fifteen responsibilities* (5th ed.). Upper Saddle River, NJ: Pearson Prentice Hall.

Whisenand, P. M., & Ferguson, R. F. (2009). *The managing of police organizations* (7th ed.). Upper Saddle River, NJ: Prentice Hall.

Wilberg, E. (1999, September 5). CHP goes suburban as it road-tests Volvo sedan as possible police car. *San Diego Union Tribune,* pp. A1, A16.

Wilson, J. Q. (1968). *Varieties of police behavior: The management of law and order in eight communities.* Cambridge, MA: Harvard University Press.

Wilson, J.Q. (2011, May 28–29). "Hard times, fewer crimes." *The Wall Street Journal,* pp. C1–C2.

Wilson, J. Q., & Kelling, G. L. (1982, March). Broken windows: The police and neighborhood safety. *The Atlantic Monthly,* 29–38.

Wilson, J. Q., & Kelling, G. L. (1989, February). Making neighborhoods safe. *The Atlantic Monthly,* 46–52.

Wilson, O. W. (1963). *Police administration.* New York: McGraw-Hill.

Wolfson, P. G. (1986). *The perceptions of corporate executives and member company general managers concerning the competencies essential for agribusiness leaders.* Carbondale, IL: Southern Illinois University.

Worrall, J. L. (2004). *Criminal procedure from first contact to appeal.* Boston: Pearson Allyn and Bacon.

Wrobleski, H. M., & Hess, K. M. (2009). *Introduction to law enforcement and criminal justice* (9th ed.) Belmont, CA: Wadsworth/Thomson Learning.

Wulff, D. (2000, January/February). Winning strategies offered for working with different cultures. *Community Policing Exchange,* 7(30) 1–2.

Wycoff, M. A., & Oettmeier, T. N. (1994). *Evaluating patrol officer performance under community policing: The Houston experience.* Washington, DC: The National Institute of Justice.

Wycoff, M. A., & Skogan, W. G. (1994). Community policing in Madison: An analysis of implementation and impact. In D. P. Rosenham (Ed.), *The challenge of community policing.* Newbury Park, CA: Sage Publications.

Young, T., & Ortmeier, P. J. (2011). *Crime scene investigation: The forensic technician's field manual.* Upper Saddle River, NJ: Pearson Prentice Hall.

Yukl, G. A. (1971). Toward a behavioral theory of leadership. *Organization Behavior and Human Performance, 6,* 414–440.

Zaleznik, A. (1993). Managers and leaders: Are they different? In W. E. Rosenbach & R. L. Taylor (Eds.), *Contemporary issues in leadership* (36–56). Boulder, CO: Westview Press.

Zalman, M. (2008). *Criminal procedure: Constitution and society* (5th ed.). Upper Saddle River, NJ: Pearson Prentice Hall.

Zhao, J. (2002). The future of policing in a community era. In W. Palacios, J. Cromwell, & R. Dunham (Eds.). *Crime & justice in America: Present reality and future prospects* (2nd ed) (pp. 191–204). Upper Saddle River, NJ: Prentice Hall.

Zuckerman, E. (2003, February 22). Nobody had a chance. *San Diego Union Tribune,* pp. A1, A16.

Index

Index